W9-APB-680

Macrosociology

Macrosociology

AN INTRODUCTION TO HUMAN SOCIETIES

Second Edition

STEPHEN K. SANDERSON
Indiana University of Pennsylvania

HarperCollins*Publishers*

Sponsoring Editor: Alan McClare
Project Editor: Susan Goldfarb
Art Direction: Heather A. Ziegler
Cover Coordinator: Heather A. Ziegler
Cover Design: Circa 86, Inc.
Photo Research: Mira Schachne
Director of Production: Jeanie Berke
Production Assistant: Linda Murray
Compositor: Circle Graphics
Printer and Binder: R. R. Donnelley & Sons Company
Cover Printer: New England Book Components

Text and illustration credits begin on page 541.

Macrosociology: An Introduction to Human Societies, Second Edition

Library of Congress Cataloging-in-Publication Data

Sanderson, Stephen K.
Macrosociology : an introduction to human societies / Stephen K. Sanderson. —2nd ed.
p. cm.
Includes bibliographical references.
ISBN 0-06-045714-7
1. Macrosociology. I. Title.
HM51.S26 1991
301—dc20 90-35676
CIP

90 91 92 94 9 8 7 6 5 4 3 2 1

For Ruth, Derek, and Sarah

No description can even begin to lead to a valid explanation
if it does not effectively encompass the whole world.—*Fernand Braudel*

Contents

Preface

This second edition of *Macrosociology* continues to be guided by the comparative, evolutionary, and materialist perspective of the first edition. The warm reception accorded that edition suggests that many sociologists see that there are numerous advantages to a macrosociological approach. These include greater scientific rigor; a heightened ability to combat ethnocentrism; a focus on the all-important issue of social change; and a unique capacity for preparing students for life in the global social order in which we all now live.

In this edition I have improved the book's accessibility to a wider student audience by adding several pedagogic aids. There are now many more tables summarizing theoretical discussions and societal comparisons. I have also added maps depicting the expansion and evolution of the capitalist world-economy from the sixteenth century to the present. Other changes include keeping the Special Topic sections at the end of each chapter fresh and up-to-date, adding six new ones: "The Microfoundations of Macrosociology" (Chapter 1); "*Perestroika* and Its Sociological Significance" (Chapter 8); "East Asia and Theories of Underdevelopment" (Chapter 9); "The Puzzle of Nationalism" (Chapter 12); "The Question of Black Progress" (Chapter 13); and "An Evolutionary View of Scientific Change" (Chapter 19).

Throughout, I have updated important statistical data wherever desirable and possible; I have also updated the annotated bibliographies at the end of each chapter. The most extensive changes occur in the chapters on economic underdevelopment, racial and ethnic stratification, education, religion, and the future. These changes and other important chapter-by-chapter changes are detailed below:

- *Chapter 1:* Improved definition of an evolutionary theory.
- *Chapter 2:* New section on socialization; discussion of recent developments in evolutionary biology; updating of section on human evolution; clarification of the role of symbols in the creation of culture; updating of Special Topic on sociobiology.
- *Chapter 3:* Improved definition of sociocultural evolution; expanded discussion of the concept of adaptation; new section comparing biological and sociocultural evolution.
- *Chapter 4:* Updated discussion of hunter-gatherers as the "original affluent society"; response to critics of population-pressure models of technological evolution.
- *Chapter 5:* Qualification of role of markets in precapitalist societies.
- *Chapter 7:* Revised and expanded discussion of theories about the transition from feudalism to capitalism.
- *Chapter 8:* Discussion of major evolutionary trends within capitalism; clarification of

the relationship between capitalist evolution and the Industrial Revolution; revised interpretation of the relationship of state socialist societies to the capitalist world-economy.

- *Chapter 9:* A more critical discussion of dependency theory, along with a new section on the world-system approach to underdevelopment; improved discussion of the "widening gap thesis."
- *Chapter 10:* Consideration of recent alterations of Wright's Marxian class model; updating of Special Topic on social democracy.
- *Chapter 11:* Updating of Carneiro's circumscription theory; reorganization of assessment of theories about state origins.
- *Chapter 12:* Updating of discussion of semiperipheral and peripheral states; new section on the interstate system; revised explanation of state socialist totalitarianism; new material on *glasnost*.
- *Chapter 13:* New chapter formed by condensing old Chapter 13 and combining it with old Chapter 14; revised discussion of race relations in South Africa; new section on race relations in contemporary Britain, replacing section on Brazil.
- *Chapter 15:* Revised discussion of polygyny.
- *Chapter 16:* New data and expanded discussion of household patterns in early capitalist Europe; updating of section on female-headed black families.
- *Chapter 17:* More critical discussion of Bowles and Gintis; new section on educational expansion as a nation-building process; reorganization of assessment of theories about education and educational change; elimination of section on educational reform.
- *Chapter 18:* New sections on the Reformation and on secularization theory.
- *Chapter 20:* New sections on war in the history of capitalism, the possibility of predicting the next major war, and the prospect of a future world state; elimination of the section on Stavrianos's optimistic assessment of the future.

To accommodate all of the new discussions, I have eliminated some discussions no longer essential and condensed others. The result, I believe, is a significantly improved book that is only slightly longer than the earlier edition.

I am grateful to various colleagues in my own university and elsewhere who have made suggestions for this edition, especially Thomas Conelly, Thomas Hall, Harvey Holtz, Jonathan Lewis, Lawrence Mencotti, Jack Sattel, James Sheehy, and Pierre van den Berghe. Reviewers selected by HarperCollins to make recommendations for this revision or to critically evaluate the end result (or both) were Christopher Chase-Dunn of Johns Hopkins University, David Maume of the University of Wyoming, and Robert K. Miller of the University of North Carolina at Wilmington. I thank these people for their ideas, many of which have been incorporated into the text. I am also grateful to the Institute of Social Studies in The Hague, Netherlands, for allowing me to spend a sabbatical semester there during early 1988. This helped enormously with the revision of Chapter 9.

As always, I have found the editorial staff of HarperCollins to be first-rate professionals as well as wonderfully pleasant people to work with. I am delighted to acknowledge Alan McClare for his overall editorial guidance and good judgment; Susan Goldfarb for skillfully seeing the book through the production process; and Mira Schachne for her acute skills at tracking down the illustrations.

I am extremely fortunate to have a wonderful wife and two delightful children who, both cheerfully and amusedly, put up with all my foibles when I was conceptualizing and writing. They contributed to the end product far more than they know. And so it is again to them—Ruth, Derek, and Sarah—that I dedicate this book.

STEPHEN K. SANDERSON

Macrosociology

CHAPTER 1

Sociology and the Scientific Study of Human Societies

The degree of diversity in human social life is quite remarkable. Some societies are small and simple in organization; others are large and extremely complex. Some societies depend for their livelihood on the hunting of wild animals and the collecting of wild plants, others depend upon agriculture, and still others depend upon modern industry. Among those dependent upon industry, some have capitalist economies while others have established socialism. Democratic governments prevail in many modern societies, totalitarian governments in a number of others. Many societies of the past had no formal governments at all, a situation that persists in even some present-day societies. Warfare has been a chronic feature of a large number of societies, yet among some groups it is virtually unknown. Men in most of the world's cultures have preferred to take more than one wife, yet in modern industrial societies this practice is prohibited by law. People in some societies value individual ambition and competition, while the members of other groups emphasize instead intensive forms of cooperation and sharing. Women in many cultures are regarded as inferior and treated as such by men, while numerous other cultures regard women as more or less the equals of men and treat them accordingly. The list could go on almost endlessly.

Despite the great range of variation in human thought and action, however, there are a number of characteristics common to all or most societies. All societies have economic systems, modes of marriage and family life, means of maintaining law and order, and forms of religious belief and ritual. All societies prohibit or discourage incest. No society is governed by women, nor does any society give women primary responsibility for the conduct of war. In short, human societies have common as well as variable features, similarities as well as differences.

Another noteworthy feature of human social life is the degree to which societies change. Contemporary Americans, for instance, live in a society that has changed enormously over the past 200 years and is currently undergoing substantial social change. The changes that have occurred have been not only deep but rapid as well, and the speed of change is constantly increasing. Yet some societies change very little, even over very long periods of time. One can find even today a few groups still dependent upon the hunting of wild animals and the collection of wild plants. These groups perpetuate a lifestyle that differs little from that carried on by their ancestors thousands of years ago.

What accounts for these phenomena? Why

are societies similar in certain broad respects? Why do they differ from one another in important ways? Why do some change with great magnitude and speed while others change so little and so slowly? These questions and others are the central focus of this book, which is an introduction to that science of social life known as **sociology.**

THE NATURE OF SOCIOLOGY

Microsociology Versus Macrosociology

Sociology is the scientific study of human social life. Sociologists inquire into the nature and causes of regularized and repeatable *patterns* of human thought and conduct. Unlike psychologists, who focus on the thoughts and actions characteristic of distinctive individuals, sociologists are interested only in those thoughts and actions that are shared by persons as members of groups or societies. Yet sociology is a broad and diverse discipline, and there are different kinds of sociologists who study different things with different aims in mind.

It is conventional to distinguish between two major types of sociology, known as microsociology and macrosociology. **Microsociology** investigates the patterns of thought and behavior that occur in relatively small-scale social groups. Persons identifying themselves as microsociologists are interested in such things as styles of verbal and nonverbal communication in face-to-face social relationships, the process of decision making by juries, the formation and disintegration of friendship groups, and the influence of individuals' group memberships on their outlook on the world.

Macrosociology, by contrast, devotes itself to the study of large-scale social patterns. It focuses on total societies and their major elements, such as the economy, the political system, the mode of family life, and the nature of the religious system. It also has an abiding concern with world networks of interacting societies. Many macrosociologists limit themselves to the study of a single society in a single historical period. Macrosociologists in the United States, for example, frequently restrict their research to the broad social patterns characteristic of contemporary American society. Other macrosociologists have somewhat broader fields of inquiry; they expand their interests to include the comparative study of many different contemporary societies. Some macrosociologists go much further still and focus on the comparative study of the entire range of human societies, both past and present.

This book is exclusively concerned with macrosociology, and it is macrosociological in the broadest sense (but see the Special Topic at the end of the chapter). It is devoted to the systematic examination of the major similarities and differences among societies, and it is concerned as well with the nature of the changes that societies undergo.

The version of macrosociology presented in this book is one that overlaps extensively with and draws heavily upon the concepts, theories, and findings of two other social sciences: anthropology and history.

Anthropology is a very broad field devoted to the study of humankind. It is actually a composite discipline consisting of four separate yet closely related subfields. **Cultural anthropology** aims at understanding the patterns of organized social life among preindustrial or primitive peoples. A major concern of cultural anthropologists is the construction of **ethnographies,** or detailed descriptive accounts of the ways of life of contemporary primitive peoples. Cultural anthropologists are, however, concerned with more than just descriptions of different cultures. Many of them spend much of their time attempting to build coherent theories about why different cultural patterns exist. Therefore, cultural anthropologists engage in explanatory as well as descriptive endeavors.

Physical anthropology is principally devoted to understanding the course of human biological evolution through a detailed examination of the record of the fossilized remains of earlier human beings. **Anthropological linguistics** studies the nature and formation of human languages and the relationship between these languages and patterns of social life. **Archaeology** is that branch of anthropology that is concerned with the remains of ancient societies. By studying the remains of earlier societies, archaeologists hope to learn about their patterns of social life, as well as about some of the major social changes that occurred in the past. These subfields of anthropology are intimately related to each other, and the practitioners of one subfield frequently draw upon the findings of one or more of the other subfields.

History is a large and varied field of study concerned with describing and explaining what happened in the past, and a large number of historians study various aspects of social life characteristic of societies of earlier times.

Many of the findings and theories of history and anthropology (particularly cultural anthropology and archaeology) form an important part of this book. These findings and theories are connected with those produced by sociologists on the nature of contemporary industrial societies. The result is a very broad-based comparative and historical macrosociology. It is only through this sort of broad-based approach that the nature and causes of human social life can be properly understood. And that, indeed, is the primary aim of sociological investigation.

The Role of Science in the Study of Social Life

As indicated earlier, sociology is the **scientific** study of human social life. The most distinctive characteristic of science is its **empirical** approach. Scientists require that all claims to truth be submitted to rigorous scrutiny and tested against the facts derived from observation of the world. A claim to truth is valid in the scientific sense not because it has an intuitive plausibility or because a person or group with prestige or authority proclaims it. It is valid only to the extent to which it is in agreement with known facts.*

Many scientists spend much of their time doing basic descriptive work: identifying, characterizing, and classifying the phenomena they are concerned with. However, description alone is not the aim of science, and it is in fact only a preliminary stage of scientific investigation. The ultimate aim of science is *explanation:* the identification of the basic causes of the phenomena under investigation. Scientific explanation in sociology proceeds through the construction of **theoretical strategies** and **theories.** Theoretical strategies are highly global sets of basic assumptions, concepts, and orienting principles (cf. Harris, 1979). They are designed to apply to social phenomena in the broadest possible sense. Their purpose is to generate specific theories and initiate lines of research to test those theories. A theory is a specific statement or interrelated set of statements designed to explain some particular phenomenon. A theory is thus much narrower and more specific than a theoretical strategy. A theoretical strategy applies broadly to a great range of phenomena and is composed of a great many interrelated theories. While these interrelated theories apply to different phenomena, they have much in common, for they all proceed from the same global set of assumptions, concepts, and principles.

Sociologists engage in the empirical testing of both theoretical strategies and theories. A theoretical strategy is a good one only to the

*This is a substantial oversimplification of the nature of science. However, this is not the place for a detailed discussion of the many interpretations that have been advanced concerning just what science is, how it is to be distinguished from nonscience, and how it changes or progresses. Such a discussion will be found in Chapter 19.

extent that it generates specific theories that hold up under empirical scrutiny. We can have great confidence in a theoretical strategy that has generated and continues to generate many well-supported theories. By contrast, a theoretical strategy that contains few well-supported theories and many theories known to be false is judged to be inadequate. It inspires little confidence and is a poor guide to further theorizing and research.

It is important to note that all theoretical strategies contain at least some theories that must be rejected as false. But the rejection of any particular theory is not a sufficient basis for the rejection of an entire theoretical strategy. So long as a theoretical strategy contains many well-supported theories, continued reliance on it is justified, regardless of the fact that some of its theories are unacceptable.

A number of diverse theoretical strategies currently exist within contemporary macrosociology. All of these strategies have, of course, their proponents and their detractors. Following is a discussion of the general nature of these strategies and an indication of the ones that provide the orienting framework for this book.

THE MAJOR THEORETICAL STRATEGIES IN CONTEMPORARY MACROSOCIOLOGY

Materialist Versus Idealist Theoretical Strategies

The Idealist Strategy Sociologists have long debated the relative merits of **idealist** versus **materialist** approaches to the study of human social life. Idealist approaches—and there are several varieties of these—attempt to explain the basic features of social life by reference to the creative capacity of the human mind. Idealists believe that human uniqueness lies in the fact that humans attach symbolic meanings to their actions. Humans create elaborate networks of ideas and ideals and use these mental constructs to guide their patterns of behavior. Different behavior patterns characteristic of different societies are seen as the result of different sets of ideas and ideals. However, idealists usually give little attention to the problem of how different sets of ideas and ideals originate in the first place, a serious weakness in their theories.

One of the best-known contemporary versions of idealism is found in the work of the French anthropologist Claude Lévi-Strauss (1963). Lévi-Strauss advocates an approach to the study of societies known as **structuralism.** The major idea behind this approach is that humans everywhere have a fundamental tendency to think in terms of **binary oppositions,** or sharply contrasting pairs of concepts. This tendency to think in terms of binary contrasts is believed to be deeply imbedded in the human mind. Basic binary oppositions include pairs such as male/female, nature/culture, earth/sky, raw/cooked, land/water, and so on. The basic organization of society is said to follow from the nature of the binary oppositions that are most important within a given culture or society.

The anthropologist Sherry Ortner (1974) has applied structuralist theorizing to explaining sex roles in the world's cultures. In particular, she attempts to explain why women are universally the subordinate sex—why in every known society women and their activities are devalued and judged to be inferior. The reason for this, she asserts, involves the binary opposition "nature/culture," an opposition that is fundamental in all societies. In human thinking, women are associated with "nature," men with "culture." Women are viewed as being closer to nature in terms of both their bodily processes and their social activities. Women menstruate, become pregnant, give birth, lactate, and have a close association with children, and such facts make women seem closer to nature than men. By contrast, men are seen as closer to culture since they tend to be associated with those activities—such as politics and religion—whereby humankind transcends nature. Since humans universally elevate culture above nature, women come to be universally devalued.

A similar theory has been developed by Marshall Sahlins (1976a), another anthropologist. Sahlins has developed an explanation of American dietary habits that is provocative but, if the pun may be excused, difficult to swallow. He notes that beef is the most highly valued meat in contemporary American society. He believes that this dietary preference is linked to the ancient Indo-European association of cattle with virility, an association that has been preserved for thousands of years and continues to guide our thinking about "a proper meal." Sahlins also wonders why Americans do not eat dogs, especially since a number of other cultures have done so (such as some North American Indian societies and the Chinese). We do not eat dogs, he says, because "they remind us of people" (Harris and Ross, 1978:88). Since we keep dogs as household pets and develop close relationships with them, we are repelled at the thought of having them for dinner.

Another version of idealism is found in the writings of the late contemporary American sociologist Talcott Parsons (1937, 1966). Parsons holds that the core of every society is a network of socially shared meanings, beliefs, and values. The beliefs and values that the members of a society are able to create structure the basic ways in which they organize their social life. For instance, Parsons sees modern Western societies as strongly organized around fundamental values associated with Christianity and liberal democracy. He believes that because Westerners have developed these systems of religious and political values they have been able to solve certain societal problems that still plague other societies, whose members live according to very different beliefs and values.

The Materialist Strategy Materialists strongly reject the kinds of theories just mentioned. Rather than giving ideas and ideals causal priority, they attempt to explain the basic features of social life in terms of the practical, material conditions of human existence. These conditions involve such things as the nature of the physical environment, the level of technology, and the organization of the economic system. Materialists see these factors as constituting the basic prerequisites of human existence. The first concern of human life is adaptation to the natural environment, and this must be done by constructing a technological and economic system. Once certain technologies and economies are created, they constrain the nature of the other social patterns that humans will create. Different kinds of technologies and economies give rise to different kinds of social patterns. Furthermore, materialists generally see human ideas and ideals as arising from previously created social patterns. Like idealists, they recognize the creative capacity of the human mind. Unlike idealists, however, materialists hold that ideas and ideals are not self-generating, but arise as responses to the material and social conditions already established.

The materialist approach to social life began with the work of the famous nineteenth-century German social theorists Karl Marx (1818–1883) and Friedrich Engels (1820–1895). Marx and Engels (1970; orig. 1846) developed what they referred to as the "materialist conception of history," and what has since come to be known as **historical materialism** (also frequently called **dialectical materialism**). This was a theoretical approach to social life developed in direct opposition to the current of idealism that prevailed at that time in German philosophy. Although historical materialism was constructed primarily as a means of understanding modern capitalist societies, Marx and Engels understood it to be applicable as well to the whole range of human societies in both the past and the present.

Marx and Engels divided human societies into two major components. One of these they referred to as the *infrastructure*, sometimes also called the **mode of production.** The infra-

Karl Marx (1818–1883). Marx was born in Germany, lived for brief periods in Paris and Brussels, and resided in London for the second half of his life. It was there that he produced his great work, *Capital*. Long held in low esteem by most sociologists, in recent decades Marxism has been revived and has come to hold an influential position in Western sociology.

structure was in turn divided into two categories: the *forces of production* and the *relations of production*. The forces of production consisted of the raw materials necessary for a society to engage in economic production: the available level of technology and the specific nature of natural resources, such as the quality of the land. The relations of production referred to the ownership of the forces of production. Marx and Engels noted that in some societies the forces of production were owned communally by the entire group, but in other societies private ownership of the productive forces had emerged. The group that acquired ownership of the productive forces was able to compel other groups to work for it. Marx and Engels noted that several different forms of private relations of production existed in different societies.

The other major component of human societies identified by Marx and Engels was the *superstructure*. This component consisted of all those aspects of a society not included in the infrastructure, such as politics, law, family life, religion, and ideas and ideals.

Marx and Engels held that a society's infrastructure and its superstructure were directly related. Although they noted that the superstructure could occasionally influence the infrastructure, they argued that the primary direction of causation ran from the infrastructure to the superstructure. They believed, in other words, that the patterns of human thought and action found within a society's superstructure were largely shaped by the features of the society's infrastructure. They also thought that social changes within the superstructure were brought about mainly by changes that had already occurred within the infrastructure. This was the essence of their materialism.

The materialism of Marx and Engels was long rejected by most sociologists as an inadequate strategy for studying social life. In recent years, however, it has been significantly revived, and many contemporary sociologists adhere to the basic principle of materialistic causation that Marx and Engels advocated. However, many other contemporary sociologists continue to reject this principle, either in whole or in part. Contemporary idealists generally reject it entirely, preferring instead to reverse the direction of causation specified in the Marxian strategy. Yet others reject it only in part, claiming that it has some validity but that by itself it greatly oversimplifies the nature of social reality. Such sociologists frequently advocate combining materialist and idealist strategies. They argue that social life is the joint product of both material conditions and ideas and ideals.

This book takes an explicitly materialist approach to the study of social life. It accepts as fundamentally valid the basic principle of causation put forth by Marx and Engels. However, the materialist approach of this book is a modernized version of classical historical materialism.

Functionalism

The theoretical strategy known as **functionalism** came to be a part of sociological analysis during the 1940s. It reached its peak level of influence during the 1950s; during this time, functionalism became the standard theoretical strategy of the majority of sociologists, and it received little theoretical opposition. Beginning in the 1960s, however, functionalism's theoretical dominance came to be severely challenged, and its adequacy was called increasingly into question. It entered a period of rapid decline. Nonetheless, even though a majority of sociologists today do not seem to advocate a functionalist approach to the study of social life, functionalism is still seriously endorsed by a significant sociological minority. In fact, since the early 1980s a notable functionalist revival has occurred (J. C. Alexander, 1982, 1984, 1985).

Functionalism's main principles are essentially as follows: (1) Societies are complex systems of interrelated and interdependent parts, and each part of a society significantly influences the others. (2) Each part of a society exists because it has a vital function to perform in maintaining the existence or stability of the society as a whole; the existence of any part of a society is therefore explained when its function for the whole society is identified. (3) All societies have mechanisms that integrate them, that is, allow them to hold together; one of the most important of these mechanisms is the commitment of a society's members to a common set of beliefs and values. (4) Societies tend toward a state of equilibrium or homeostasis, and disturbances in any part of a society tend to bring about adjustments elsewhere in the society in order to restore the state of harmony or stability. (5) Social change is an uncommon occurrence in societies, but when it does occur it generally leads to beneficial consequences for the society as a whole.

Functionalists have shown interest in the debate between materialists and idealists, yet few of them have explicitly chosen one side or the other in this debate. Although a few functionalists have leaned strongly toward the idealist side, most have opted for a middle-ground position, arguing that both material factors and ideas and ideals are crucial influences on the nature of social patterns. This position is consistent with the typical functionalist claim that societies are systems of interdependent parts in which each one vitally affects the others.

As indicated earlier, functionalism came under severe criticism during the 1960s. The major criticisms that were leveled against the functionalists may be summarized as follows (Dahrendorf, 1958; P. Cohen, 1968; Zeitlin, 1973): (1) Functionalists tend to overemphasize the degree to which human societies are harmonious, stable, and well-integrated systems. (2) Because of this overemphasis on harmony and stability, functionalists tend to neglect or underemphasize the degree to which social conflict is a basic feature of most societies. (3) With their exaggeration of social harmony and underemphasis of social conflict, functionalists tend to encourage a conservative bias in the study of social life; that is, they appear to argue for the necessity of preserving whatever social arrangements exist in a society. (4) Functionalists generally limit themselves to the study of a society at only a single point in time (the present), and thus apply a remarkably ahistorical approach to the study of social life. (5) Since functionalists ignore the historical dimension to social life, they have considerable difficulty in accounting for social change.

An important distinction must be made between functionalism and **functional analysis** (G. A. Cohen, 1978). Functionalism involves the basic substantive principles set forth earlier. Functional analysis, however, is distinctively different. Rather than being based on a set of substantive principles, it represents the basic methodological tactic of assuming that certain phenomena should be analyzed and understood from the point of view of their adaptive significance, that is, from the vantage point of their usefulness in fulfilling some aim or objective. Functional analysis is widely used in the social sciences apart from the functionalist principles just mentioned. In fact, social theorists who disagree strongly with functionalism often use forms of functional analysis in developing their theories. Karl Marx, for instance, would have been severely repelled by modern functionalism, but he frequently engaged in a type of functional analysis. When he argued that a society's ideas and ideals should be understood in terms of the purposes they serve for powerful social groups, he was undoubtedly engaging in functional analysis. For another example, a number of modern social theorists have attempted to explain why the ancient Israelites placed a taboo on the eating of pork, a taboo that is still respected by Orthodox Jews. Some of these theorists have approached this problem by attempting to discern the ways in which this taboo may have been useful for the ancient Israelites—how it may have assisted them in solving certain basic problems of living they confronted (Harris, 1974, 1977). This kind of approach is a classic instance of what is meant by functional analysis.

Another way of thinking about the distinction between functionalism and functional analysis is to deal with the level of analysis at which each operates. A major feature of functionalism is the idea of **societal needs.** Functionalists believe that societies are much like biological organisms in that they have fundamental needs that must be met for the society to continue to exist or at least to function smoothly. The basic features of social life—the structures of society—emerge in order to fulfill these societal needs. Although the notion of societal needs may appear at first sight to be entirely reasonable, on closer inspection it is revealed to be troublesome if not downright mystical. Careful thought will show that societies cannot have needs in any meaningful sense; only individual persons can. While it is true that people develop particular needs as a result of living together, these are still the needs of concrete, flesh-and-blood persons rather than of some abstraction called "society." Functional analysis recognizes this crucial distinction and makes it basic to its mode of inquiry. Those who engage in functional analysis (but not functionalism) propose that the aims or objectives fulfilled by specific social phenomena are always the aims or objectives of concrete persons or social groups. Functional analysts recognize that what we call "society" does not exist as an entity in and of itself; rather, it is simply a word that we use for a collectivity of people who interact in certain ways in order to satisfy their needs and desires.

The major criticisms of functionalism are more or less valid; however, these criticisms do not apply to functional analysis. Although this book does not advocate or make use of functionalist principles, it does make frequent use of functional analysis. It does so, however, largely in the context of a materialist perspective and, moreover, in conjunction with what is often referred to as a conflict approach.

The Conflict Theoretical Strategy

What is usually called **conflict theory** began to emerge in American sociology during the 1960s. Actually, the emergence of conflict theory was really the revival of many of the ideas set forth much earlier by Karl Marx and another famous early German sociologist by the name of Max Weber (1864–1920). Although both Marx and Weber were conflict theorists, and thus agreed with each other in important ways, they nonetheless developed rather different versions of conflict theory. Modern conflict theory is therefore split into two main types: neo-Marxian and neo-Weberian conflict theory. The neo-Marxian version is the better known and more influential of the two.

What all conflict theories have in common, and thus what Marx and Weber were agreed on, is the rejection of the idea that societies tend toward some basic consensus or harmony in which the features of society work for everyone's good. Conflict theorists see **conflict** and struggle—the opposing interests and concerns of different individuals and groups—as the prime determinants of the organization of social life. In other words, the basic structure of society is mainly determined by the efforts made by individuals and groups to acquire scarce resources that will satisfy their needs and wants. Since these resources are always, to one degree or another, in short supply, conflict over access to them is always occurring. Marx and Weber applied this general notion to their sociological theories from different vantage points.

Marx held that structured forms of conflict between individuals and groups arose primarily through the establishment of private relations of production. At a certain point in the evolution of human social life, private relations of production began to supplant communal ownership of the forces of production. Societies were thus split into groups that owned and groups that did not own the productive forces—into social classes. In any given class-divided society, the social class that owned the productive forces was able to subordinate other social classes and to compel them to work to satisfy its particular interests. The dominant class was therefore related to subordinate classes through a process of economic exploitation. Naturally enough, subordinate classes came to resent being exploited and threatened to rebel against the dominant class and to take away its privileges. But the dominant class, sensing the possibility of rebellion from below, created a powerful political apparatus—the state—capable of suppressing any such rebellion by force.

Marx therefore saw the existence of private relations of production and social classes as the key elements in a great many societies. He believed that social class relationships played a crucial role in shaping the other social patterns of a society, such as the political and religious systems. He also thought that the struggle between dominant and subordinate classes played a central role in producing major forms of social change. Indeed, as he once announced, "the history of all hitherto existing society is the history of class struggle."

The modern Marxian conflict strategy is mainly a formalization and elaboration of the ideas just discussed. The major principles of this strategy are as follows: (1) Social life is primarily an arena of conflict or struggle between and among opposing groups. (2) Economic resources and social power are the primary things over which groups struggle with each other. (3) The typical outcome of the struggle among groups is the division of a society into economically dominant and subordinate groups. (4) The basic social patterns of a society are heavily determined by the social influence of economically dominant groups. (5) Social conflict and struggle within and between societies constitute powerful forces for social change. (6) Since conflict and struggle are basic features of social life, social change is common and frequent.

It should be obvious that the Marxian conflict strategy is essentially a materialist rather than an idealist one. This is not surprising in view of the fact that Marx was the originator of both materialist and conflict theoretical ideas. Marxian conflict theorists see social conflict as primarily arising over access to the material conditions that sustain life, and they see both of these phenomena as crucial determinants of the basic social patterns characteristic of a society.

Where Max Weber disagreed with Marx was mainly in regard to the latter's materialism. Weber believed that conflict occurred in a much broader way than simply in regard to basic material conditions (R. Collins, 1985a). Weber recognized that conflict over economic resources was a basic feature of social life, but he thought that many other types of conflict occurred as well. Of these types, Weber tended to emphasize two. He regarded conflicts in the political arena as very fundamental. For him,

Max Weber (1864–1920). This historical sociologist has been highly regarded for many years by scholars in several of the social sciences. Weber was both respectful and critical of Marx, and many of his ideas today provide a useful complement to Marxism.

social life was to a large extent a struggle for power and domination of some individuals and groups over others, and he did not regard this struggle for power as simply motivated by the desire for economic gain. On the contrary, he saw it to a large extent as an end in itself. Weber thought that the struggle for power was not confined to formal political organizations, but occurred within all types of groups, such as religious or educational organizations.

A second type of conflict Weber frequently emphasized was conflict in regard to ideas and ideals. He thought that people often struggled to gain dominance for their own view of the world, whether it be a type of religious doctrine, a social philosophy, or a conception of the best sort of cultural lifestyle. Furthermore, not only were ideas and ideals things that people struggled over, but these ideas and ideals could be used as weapons or tools in other kinds of struggles, such as political struggles. That is, people could fight for power while at the same time trying to convince one another that it wasn't really power that they were after, but the victory of the right ethical or philosophical principles.

It is clear that Weber was neither a materialist nor an idealist. In fact, he is usually referred to by modern sociologists as a major example of a thinker who combined both materialist and idealist modes of explanation within his general sociological approach. Thus Weber thought that ideas were not mere results of underlying material conditions, but that they frequently had causal significance in their own right.

One other way in which Marx and Weber disagreed was in regard to the possibility of resolving basic conflict in a future society. Marx thought that since conflict mainly arose over access to the forces of production, once these forces were returned to the control of the entire society, basic conflicts would be eliminated. That is, once socialism replaced capitalism, classes would be abolished and class struggle would cease. Weber took a much more pessimistic view. He believed that struggle was one of the great, ineradicable principles of social life. In any type of future society, whether socialist, capitalist, or something else, people would always struggle over some types of resources. Weber therefore expected social divisions or cleavages to be a permanent feature of all complex societies, although of course the particular forms these might take, as well as their degree of severity, could vary substantially.

Although both Marxian and Weberian conflict approaches have been embraced by many modern sociologists, these approaches have by no means achieved universal endorsement.

However, this book argues for the great usefulness of the conflict ideas set forth by Marx and by Weber and thus makes extensive use of many of them, especially those of Marx.

Evolutionary Theoretical Strategies

An **evolutionary** theoretical strategy is one that attempts to describe and explain sequences of long-term social change. Evolutionists generally argue that many societies have undergone broadly similar changes from earliest times to the present, and they are concerned with identifying the nature of these changes and explaining why they have occurred.

Erik Olin Wright (1983) has given us a more precise conception of an evolutionary theory. He suggests that all evolutionary theories share the following characteristics: (1) They organize history into a typology of stages. (2) They assume that this stage ordering represents a direction along which societies tend to evolve. (3) They postulate that the probability of movement to a later (or "higher") stage exceeds the probability of movement back to an earlier (or "lower") stage. (4) They identify a mechanism or set of mechanisms that is said to explain the movement from one stage to another. As Wright is at pains to point out, evolutionary theories need not assume that the sequence of stages through which societies move is a rigid one that is the same for all societies, or that social evolution is some sort of automatic process of unfolding of latent tendencies or potentialities inherent in the nature of societies. They do not even need to assume that forward movement always occurs. Regression is acknowledged as a possible (and sometimes actual) occurrence, and it is fully recognized that for many societies and at many times in history long-term steady states (rather than social transformation) may be the normal order of things. It is important that these points be established and well understood, because there are still many misconceptions concerning the nature of evolutionary theories.

Evolutionary approaches to social life were extremely popular among both sociologists and anthropologists in the latter half of the nineteenth century. In fact, evolutionary theorizing dominated these two disciplines at that time. One of the most famous of the nineteenth-century evolutionists was the English philosopher and sociologist Herbert Spencer (1820–1903), who developed a theory of social evolution that was broadly similar to Darwin's theory of biological evolution. Spencer attempted to understand the operation of all things in the universe by reducing them to a single universal principle that he called the "Law of Evolution." According to this law, all things in the universe have a tendency to "evolve from a state of indefinite, incoherent, homogeneity to a state of definite, coherent, heterogeneity." What Spencer meant was that all things tend to develop from simple and unspecialized forms into more complex and specialized forms. Spencer saw this universal tendency as the master key to unlocking all the great riddles of the universe. He considered the evolution of human societies as but a special instance of a great cosmological tendency inherent in the nature of the universe itself.

Another well-known nineteenth-century evolutionist was the American lawyer and amateur anthropologist Lewis Henry Morgan (1818–1881). Morgan was much concerned with the evolution of technology. He divided human history into three great stages, each of which was associated with a different level of technological development: Savagery, Barbarism, and Civilization. The stage of Savagery was characteristic of peoples who subsisted primarily by hunting wild animals and gathering wild plants. The transition to Barbarism was marked by the domestication of plants and animals and the development of additional improvements in overall technology. The emergence of Civilization marked the transition from "primitive soci-

Herbert Spencer (1820–1903). This English philosopher and social theorist developed a grandiose evolutionary scheme that is not acceptable by modern scholarly standards, but some of his more specific ideas about social evolution provide important insights.

ety" (what Morgan called *societas*) to "civil society" (what Morgan called *civitas*). Morgan saw the development of the phonetic alphabet and writing as a major characteristic of this stage.

Although the ideas of these and other early evolutionists were provocative, they contained a number of serious flaws. One of these was the tendency to pass off mere descriptions of evolutionary transformations as explanations for those transformations. This tendency was especially characteristic of the work of Spencer. Spencer held that social evolution was inherent in the very nature of things, and he seemed to regard this observation as sufficient to explain why social evolution occurred. But merely to note that evolution tends to occur says nothing about why it comes about. Another flaw in the thinking of the nineteenth-century evolutionists was their **ethnocentrism.** They viewed their own society (Western civilization) as superior to all others, holding that societies at earlier evolutionary stages represented various gradations of inferiority to their own. They therefore claimed that social evolution was indicative of **progress,** of a general improvement in human rationality, happiness, and morality. They tended to see Western civilization as the end point of social evolution, as the culmination of millennia of human progress. These are views that are sharply rejected today by many modern sociologists and anthropologists, as Chapter 3 will show more thoroughly.

Because of these and other flaws, evolutionary thinking came under severe criticism beginning near the end of the nineteenth century. As the criticisms mounted against it, evolutionism was ultimately abandoned by most social scientists. Throughout the first several decades of the twentieth century, social scientists turned their attention to questions and problems other than those dealing with long-term social change. But evolutionism was not dead; it was only dormant. Beginning in the 1940s, it staged a significant revival, and the whole problem of long-term evolutionary change began once again to preoccupy the minds of many social scientists. Today evolutionary approaches to the study of social life are embraced by many sociologists and anthropologists.

However, there is currently no single evolutionary strategy for the study of human societies. Many different evolutionary theories exist, most of which can be placed in one of two distinct evolutionary strategies: a **functionalist evolutionary** strategy and a **materialist evolutionary** strategy. Although these two strategies are both evolutionary in the sense identified earlier, they are actually more different than similar. The assumptions they make about which evolutionary events are most important, and the way in which they explain these events, differ markedly.

The functionalist evolutionary strategy involves the application of a functionalist approach to the study of social evolution (A. D.

Smith, 1973). In this strategy, social evolution is viewed primarily as a process of **social differentiation,** of increasing societal complexity. As societies evolve, they develop an increasing diversity of parts, and these parts come to be related to each other in complicated ways. Increasing differentiation is held to lead to greater adaptive capacity: By developing increasing internal diversity, societies become more and more capable of making successful adaptations to their environments. The implication is clearly that more complex societies are "superior" to less complex ones.

Functionalist evolutionary thinkers generally see social evolution as resulting from the functional needs of societies as whole systems. Evolutionary changes are presumed, therefore, to lead to beneficial consequences for entire societies. This notion is a very prominent feature of the work of Talcott Parsons (1966), the best known of all the functionalist evolutionary theorists. Parsons claims, for example, that the evolution of social stratification—of inequalities in wealth and power—was a major achievement in social evolution, having beneficial consequences for the members of society in general. He believes that the unequal rewarding of the members of a society is a means of motivating some individuals to assume important positions of responsibility and authority. Privileged individuals and groups will use their positions of authority to undertake activities that will benefit the other members of society. Parsons therefore sees the emergence of social stratification as an important evolutionary "breakthrough."

The functionalist evolutionary approach is scarcely an improvement on the leading ideas of the nineteenth-century evolutionary theorists, and it tends to share the same flaws. For example, the functionalist evolutionary strategy tends to view contemporary Western society as the most highly adapted of all societies, and it generally holds that small-scale, simple societies have low adaptive capacity. This view is ethnocentric in the extreme. Furthermore, the functionalist evolutionary approach is obviously subject to the same criticisms as functionalism in general, since it merely represents the application of functionalism to the study of evolutionary processes. Like other functionalists, functionalist evolutionists overemphasize societal harmony, underemphasize the degree and importance of social conflict, and argue that the features of any society exist out of functional necessity. Inasmuch as functionalism represents an inadequate approach to societies in general, functionalist evolutionism represents an inadequate approach to the study of long-term social change.

The materialist evolutionary strategy is strikingly different. This approach involves the application of a general materialist strategy to an understanding of social evolution. It assumes that social changes are most likely to begin in the material conditions that sustain life. These changes, once they occur, set off corresponding changes in a society's social patterns and in its ideas and ideals. Unlike functionalist evolutionists, materialist evolutionists make no assumption that evolutionary changes lead to improved forms of societal adaptation. They do not assume that evolutionary changes lead to increasing benefits for entire societies. On the contrary, they emphasize that such changes are just as likely, if not more likely, to lead to a deterioration in the quality of life for a great many members of societies. Materialist evolutionists hold that conflict and struggle are crucially important elements in human social life, and they believe that these phenomena are closely related to processes of evolutionary change. They argue that conflict and struggle are both causes and consequences of social evolution. There is thus a strong affinity between the materialist evolutionary strategy and the Marxian conflict strategy.

This book adopts a materialist evolutionary strategy as its major approach.

Eclecticism

Many social scientists are committed to one or the other of the theoretical strategies we have been discussing. They use the strategy they prefer as a more or less exclusive means of orienting their thinking and guiding their research efforts. However, a significant number of social scientists believe that it is intellectually inappropriate to commit oneself to any one approach. Such social scientists claim that it is far preferable to acknowledge the usefulness of all approaches. Such a view is known as **eclecticism.** Eclectics believe that each theoretical approach provides a partially valid understanding of reality, and that when all approaches are used in combination a more complete understanding of reality is achieved. One version of eclecticism holds that different issues must be explained through different theoretical approaches. Other eclectics go further than this and claim that even a single issue must be explained by the use of multiple approaches. Some eclectics are even more extreme. They hold that there is no such thing as scientific "truth" and therefore that there is no "correct" explanation for any given phenomenon. Different theoretical approaches simply constitute different, and more or less equally valid, ways of looking at that phenomenon.

Eclectics like to think that their stance is preferable because it is open-minded and that the refusal to maintain eclecticism is an indication of dogmatism and rigidity. What eclectics generally fail to recognize is that they are no more open-minded than those they criticize for dogmatism. Eclectics themselves are committed; ironically, they are committed to the view that it is inappropriate for one to have commitments. The question of open-mindedness versus dogmatism is therefore a false issue.

This book takes the position that eclecticism is an unacceptable scientific stance. The main problem with it is that it leads to severe theoretical confusion (Harris, 1979; Sanderson, 1987). Since different theoretical strategies employ not only different but often contradictory assumptions and principles, to accept all of them as valid is to engage in self-contradiction. For example, one cannot be a functionalist and a conflict theorist at the same time, for these strategies offer opposing interpretations of social reality. The problem of self-contradiction and inconsistency is only made worse when more than two approaches are embraced simultaneously.

The major goal of science (and hence of sociology) is to achieve a coherent and unified understanding of all relevant phenomena (cf. Maxwell, 1974a,b). Coherent and unified explanations are achieved (or approached) when the explanation of one phenomenon is closely tied to the explanation of other phenomena. The fewer the number of principles used, and the greater the number and variety of phenomena these principles explain, the better.* Eclecticism leads directly away from this goal and is therefore an unsound strategy for the conduct of science. The goal can only be reached when scientists commit themselves to a particular strategy and attempt to explain as much as they can with it. Of course, no strategy is capable of explaining everything. From time to time other strategies have to be drawn upon to explain certain phenomena. But to do this is not to practice eclecticism; it is simply to recognize the great complexity and diversity of the phenomena that scientists study.

THE THEORETICAL STRATEGY OF THIS BOOK

As mentioned earlier, this book is committed to a materialist evolutionary view of human social life. This view is evolutionary in the sense that it

*This is a statement of what is often referred to as the **principle of parsimony.** This principle is widely respected by natural scientists of all sorts, and its regular employment as a fundamental aim of their research and theoretical efforts is heavily responsible for the intellectual progress so characteristic of their fields (cf. Sanderson, 1987).

Table 1.1 MACROSOCIOLOGICAL THEORETICAL STRATEGIES

Theoretical strategy	Major characteristics	Role in this book
Materialism	Assumes that the material conditions of human existence—such things as the level of technology, the mode of economic life, and the features of the natural environment—are the leading causes of the organization of human societies and the major changes that occur within them.	This book is consistently materialist throughout.
Idealism	Argues for the significance of the human mind and its creations—thoughts, ideas, symbolic codes, language, and so on—in determining social organization and social change.	Idealist theories are consistently criticized and rejected throughout.
Functionalism	Attempts to explain the basic features of human social life as responses to the needs and demands of societies as ongoing social systems. Assumes that existing social traits contribute in important ways to the survival and well-being of whole societies or their major subsystems.	Numerous functionalist theories are discussed throughout, but are consistently criticized as wrong or strongly overstated.
Conflict strategies	View societies as arenas in which individuals and groups struggle for and against each other for the satisfaction of their needs and desires. Conflict and struggle lead to domination and subordination, and dominant groups use their power to structure society for their own benefit. Marxian conflict theories are materialist and emphasize class struggle, whereas Weberian conflict theories are broader and stress the multidimensional nature of conflict and domination.	This book consistently employs a conflict perspective that makes use of the insights of both Marx and Weber (but that gives the edge to Marx).
Evolutionary strategies	Focus on describing and explaining long-term social transformations, which are assumed to exhibit an overall directionality. Functionalist evolutionary theories concentrate on growing societal complexity, which is taken to indicate increased functional efficiency and social progress. Materialist evolutionary theories stress that social evolution is a response to changing material conditions, and are skeptical of equating evolution and progress.	This book employs a materialist (and conflict-oriented) version of evolutionism as a unifying perspective throughout.
Eclecticism	Advocates tolerance toward all points of view, which in practice means using bits and pieces of every strategy to explain the many features of social life. Claims that some things are to be explained by one approach, other things by different approaches.	Although all scholars must maintain the right to express their views, all views cannot be considered equal. Eclecticism is rejected in this book because of its tendency to produce confusing, contradictory, and unparsimonious explanations.

focuses on patterns of long-term social change. Attention is given to how and why the major similarities and differences among human societies originate, persist, and change. It is materialist in the sense that it holds that the material conditions of human existence are the principal causes of social similarities and differences. Inasmuch as materialist evolutionists share many of the principles of the conflict theoretical strategy, these principles also play a very significant role in the book. Although the conflict and materialist evolutionary strategies are not identical, they overlap extensively, and their similarities greatly outweigh their differences. Since these approaches are highly compatible rather than contradictory, to employ major elements of both is not a disguised version of eclecticism.

The materialist evolutionary and conflict strategy of this book stands sharply opposed to both functionalism and idealism. The main difficulties with functionalism have already been discussed. The major difficulty with an idealist approach is that it consistently leaves unanswered a crucial set of questions: Where do different ideas and ideals come from, and how and why do they change? An answer to such questions is imperative when it is claimed that ideas and ideals are the leading causes of social life. Thus, failure to answer these questions all but invalidates the idealist approach. (As later chapters will show, materialists *can* answer questions concerning where different sets of material conditions come from and how and why they change.)

The materialist evolutionary strategy is discussed in much greater detail in Chapter 3. There its main principles are formally stated, and a justification for the claim that it is a superior theoretical approach is provided.

SUMMARY

1. Sociology is the scientific study of human societies. Microsociologists specialize in the study of social behavior in relatively small groups and social settings. Macrosociology, by contrast, focuses on large-scale social patterns, such as total societies and the larger global networks within which societies are placed. Macrosociologists commonly emphasize a comparative and historical perspective.

2. Sociological investigation requires theoretical strategies and theories. Theoretical strategies are highly abstract sets of concepts and principles, whereas theories represent the application of these concepts and principles to specific phenomena. Theoretical strategies consist of networks of mutually interpenetrating theories.

3. Modern sociology, macrosociology included, is a highly divided discipline characterized by great theoretical diversity and disagreement. Thus, numerous theoretical strategies compete for the allegiance of contemporary macrosociologists. These include materialism, idealism, functionalism, neo-Marxian and neo-Weberian conflict strategies, functionalist and materialist versions of social evolutionism, and eclecticism. Summaries of the basic features of these strategies, and of the role they play in *Macrosociology,* are to be found in Table 1.1 (page 15).

SPECIAL TOPIC: THE MICROFOUNDATIONS OF MACROSOCIOLOGY

The relationship between microsociology and macrosociology has recently garnered increasing attention from a wide variety of sociologists. To understand their concerns, a further clarification of the distinction between these two forms of sociology is essential.

Not everyone agrees on exactly how microsociology and macrosociology should be distinguished, and it must be admitted that the boundary between the two is sometimes rather fuzzy. To my mind, the most useful way of conceptualizing these forms of sociological analysis is that of Randall Collins (1988a). Collins suggests that there are three basic factors that are fundamental to sociology: time, space, and number. At one extreme, sociologists can study the social behavior of small numbers of persons concentrated within small spaces and persisting over very short periods of time. This is what microsociologists do. They normally study the interactions among a handful of individuals (say between two and a dozen), and these individuals may be interacting within a space no larger than a few dozen or a few hundred square feet and over a time period of minutes, hours, or days. Macrosociologists, by contrast, study social behavior in which time, space, and number are, so to speak, "stretched out." They study the interaction of thousands, millions, or hundreds of millions of people as it occurs over vast territorial expanses (hundreds, thousands, or millions of square miles) and extremely long periods of time (decades, centuries, or even millennia).

This way of thinking quickly disabuses us of the faulty notion that micro- and macrosociology somehow pertain to different phenomena, as many sociologists used to think. No, that is not the right way of thinking about the distinction. Micro- and macrosociology are in fact concerned with fundamentally the same thing: the patterned interactions of individuals. It is just that they are analyzing these interactions from different temporal, spatial, and numerical vantage points. The difference between microsociology and macrosociology, then, is simply one of perspective, not of subject matter.

If we accept this argument, then it follows that there should not be two completely different sets of sociological theories, one for microsociologists and one for macrosociologists. In fact, though, this is largely the case, and the reason is that we have only belatedly come to recognize the artificiality of the distinction between the two forms of sociology (many sociologists still do not recognize, or at least acknowledge, it; cf. Collins, 1988a: Chapter 11). For many decades micro- and macrosociologists have operated with entirely different bodies of theory, and only recently have some sociologists sought to see whether these theories can be brought together into simpler and more comprehensive models. My own position is that this kind of theoretical integration can, and should, be done. This position can be stated by claiming that *macrosociology should have microfoundations.* By this it is not meant that microsociological theories are sufficient to explain the behavior in which macrosociologists are interested. Macrosociologists will always have, to some extent at least, theoretical principles of their own that are not reducible to microsociological principles. Rather, what is meant is that the behavior that goes on in total societies and world networks of societies cannot be theoretically detached from the behavior of handfuls of individuals over hours or days. Social action on the large scale has to be interpretable in terms of the motives and interests of persons as they exist in everyday life. Following Collins (1981a, 1981b, 1988a), we might call this *the microtranslation of macrosociology.*

What kinds of theoretical strategies are available to allow us to engage in microtranslation? At present, the most important microsociological theories are symbolic interactionism, ethnomethodology, and rational choice theory. The first two are quite similar to each other. **Symbolic interactionism** originated as an American sociological approach in the early part of this century and has continued to be an influential perspective. It emphasizes the capacity of individuals to interact through the use of symbols and to impose their own subjective definitions of reality onto social situations that they confront. An early symbolic interactionist, William Isaac Thomas, coined the term *definition of the situation,* which he explained by the phrase "If men define situations as real they are real in their consequences." Thomas was stressing that people's subjective definitions of reality can be so powerful that they bring about objective consequences that conform to those subjective definitions regardless of whether the definitions were originally objectively true. Two contemporary symbolic interactionists are Herbert Blumer and Howard Becker. Blumer (1969) took a rather extreme position that emphasized the almost limitless ability of individuals to define situations in their own way and to act accordingly. Becker took a less extreme position, but he also made the social definition of reality the linchpin of his theoretical position. For example, he wrote a famous essay (1963) in which he claimed that the experience of smoking marijuana was due at least as much to the social definitions surrounding the drug's effects as to their actual physiological consequences for the body. To experience marijuana smoking as a pleasurable experience, he argued, one had to be a part of a group that defined it as pleasurable. Otherwise, the effects could be very different.

Ethnomethodology is a recent strategy that carries symbolic interactionism's emphasis on the subjective definition of reality to a greater extreme. The key phrase in this perspective is "the social construction of reality" (Berger and Luckmann, 1966). In its most extreme form, this means that society or social life does not exist in an objective form—that is, in actuality. Rather, it exists only in people's minds as a set of perceptions, definitions, and ways of talking. Ethnomethodology's "founding father" was Harold Garfinkel (1967). Garfinkel and the many students he has influenced have been interested in the same problem that has preoccupied the functionalists: the problem of social order, or social continuity and stability through time. However, whereas the functionalists have seen this order as an objective (and macro) one, the ethnomethodologists have viewed it as a distinctively subjective (and micro) one. For the latter, social order is merely definitional, and it persists the way it does because of people's attachments to their subjective definitions. Ethnomethodologists claim to be most interested in finding out just how it is that people construct reality, and how and why they come to be so attached to the particular definitions that they develop.

Both symbolic interactionism and ethnomethodology are extreme versions of idealism. They give far too much emphasis to the power of people to construct reality in their own way free from any larger social constraints (R. Collins, 1988a). Much of what these theories are suggesting is, in a very important sense, quite true. People do engage in subjective definitions of reality that play a crucial role in shaping social life. However, these definitions are not arbitrary and do not occur in a vacuum. People do indeed construct reality, but they do not do so in simply any old fashion. They do so in the context of powerful sets of constraints, and it is these constraints that determine the way in which the definition of reality will go. As Marx said long ago in another context (1978:595; orig. 1852): "Men make their own history, but they do not make it just as they please; they do not make it under circumstances chosen by themselves, but under circumstances directly found, given and transmitted from the past. The tradition of all the dead generations weighs like a nightmare on the brain of the living."

A more suitable approach for microtranslation, in the opinion of this author at least, is **rational choice theory** (Homans, 1961; Coleman, 1986, 1987; Hechter, 1983; Friedman and Hechter, 1988). Long spurned by sociologists, this old approach has been making a significant comeback since the early 1980s. It emphasizes that humans are self-interested organisms who calculate courses of action that allow them to maximize their benefits and minimize their costs. Individuals are thusly motivated at the micro level, and the features of societies and world networks over long periods of time are the aggregate result of these micro-level interactions. The social constructions of reality that characterize particular societies at particular times are therefore the ones that maximize the self-interest of individuals acting within particular social and historical circumstances.

It can be quickly seen that rational choice theory is highly compatible with materialist and conflict theoretical strategies at the macro level. In fact, the particular versions of materialist and conflict theory consistently embraced in this book are explicitly predicated on rational choice micro-level assumptions. Of course, rational choice theory is hardly a perfect strategy for microtranslation. People are not as cold-blooded or as rationally calculative as the approach often seems to make them out to be. Moreover, people follow motives other than those of self-interest. By and large, though, this micro-level theoretical strategy seems to be the most promising one currently available for examining the microfoundations of macrosociology.

FOR FURTHER READING

Collins, Randall. *Theoretical Sociology.* San Diego: Harcourt Brace Jovanovich, 1988. Easily the best textbook on contemporary sociological theory. Well written and loaded with insightful analyses by one of the leading sociological theorists in the United States.

Collins, Randall. *Three Sociological Traditions.* New York: Oxford University Press, 1985. Chapter 1 provides a very informative summary of the conflict approach in classical and contemporary sociology, including both its Marxian and Weberian versions. Chapter 2 develops a number of insights regarding the functionalist tradition and shows what is of greatest value in that tradition.

Harris, Marvin. *The Rise of Anthropological Theory.* New York: Harper & Row, 1968. An excellent and highly comprehensive treatment of the development of competing theoretical strategies within cultural anthropology. Much of the discussion is organized around the opposition between materialist and idealist approaches.

Harris, Marvin. *Cultural Materialism: The Struggle for a Science of Culture.* New York: Random House, 1979. Sets forth the major elements of the theoretical strategy that Harris calls *cultural materialism*, an approach that is broadly the same as the materialist evolutionary strategy of the present book. Also discusses and severely criticizes a range of alternative theoretical strategies currently advocated by different groups of cultural anthropologists and sociologists.

Ritzer, George. *Sociological Theory.* Second edition. New York: Knopf, 1988. Probably the best textbook available that covers the entire range of social theory from the classical thinkers to contemporary currents.

Sanderson, Stephen K. *Social Evolutionism: A Critical History.* Oxford: Blackwell, 1990. Compares, contrasts, and evaluates evolutionary theories in the social sciences from the middle of the nineteenth century to the present. Also includes a systematic comparison of social and biological evolutionism.

Sociological Theory. A leading journal devoted to the latest contributions, debates, and controversies in social theory. Appears twice annually. Available in many libraries.

Theory and Society. Another leading journal devoted to issues in modern social theory. Appears six times a year. Also available in many libraries.

Tucker, Robert C. (ed.). *The Marx-Engels Reader.* Second edition. New York: Norton, 1978. A collection of excerpts from the major writings of Marx and Engels. Provides a good introduction to the leading ideas propounded by these two great thinkers.

Zeitlin, Irving M. *Rethinking Sociology: A Critique of Contemporary Theory.* Englewood Cliffs, N.J.: Prentice-Hall, 1973. A critical discussion of several of the leading theoretical strategies in contemporary sociology. Provides an excellent critique of functionalism and functionalist evolutionism.

CHAPTER 2

Human Evolution and the Emergence of Human Society and Culture

The human animal is a very special kind of creature. Like all other organisms, humans have a biological structure that has evolved over a very long period of time. This biological structure helps to determine how human beings act and think. It opens up a vast range of possibilities for variation in human thought and action, but it also sets definite limits to how humans are likely to think and act. Like many other creatures, humans are social animals. They live in groups and societies and depend upon each other for survival and satisfaction in life. But unlike all other creatures, humans are cultural animals. They and they alone create and transmit learned and shared traditions of thought and behavior that are remarkably free from genetic control. Only humans manufacture complex tools, devise monetary systems, appoint or elect political leaders, marry one another, engage in religious ritual, or attach specific symbolic values and beliefs to any of these activities. In short, humans are a lot like other creatures, but they are also unique.

This chapter explores the nature of the human animal as a biological, social, and cultural creature. It examines the general process of biological evolution and shows how humans evolved from an apelike ancestor several million years ago. It discusses the implications of calling humans unique, culture-bearing animals, and it delineates those physical traits that have allowed humans to invent, transmit, and modify culture.

THE BASIC PRINCIPLES OF BIOLOGICAL EVOLUTION

The Development of Evolutionary Biology

The idea of **evolution**—the notion that life forms have arisen from one another in an unbroken chain of transformation and modification—was not, as is often assumed, first expressed by Charles Darwin. Indeed, some rough notion that life forms have arisen from one another was anticipated as far back as the ancient Greeks, and a number of thinkers since that time have postulated something approximating an evolutionary understanding of the origin of life. Many of Darwin's immediate forerunners, including his own grandfather, accounted for the variety and diversity of life by the hypothesis of evolutionary modification. Darwin was therefore hardly alone in his belief in evolution. The distinctiveness of Darwin's contribution to evolu-

Charles Darwin (1809–1882). Although not the first to propose the idea of biological evolution, Darwin did identify the specific mechanism responsible for the occurrence of evolutionary changes.

tionary thinking lay in the mechanism that he held to be responsible for evolution. This mechanism he called **natural selection.** The idea of evolution by natural selection is the leading idea in his great book *Origin of Species*, and this theoretical principle is now accepted by virtually all modern biologists and physical anthropologists as the key to explaining evolutionary processes.

Darwin achieved a coherent (though incomplete) understanding of evolution despite his unfamiliarity with the processes of heredity. In fact, when he published *Origin of Species* in 1859 the science of genetics did not yet exist. It remained for Gregor Mendel to establish the principles governing the inheritance of characters. He did this in a series of experiments on garden peas, publishing his findings in 1865. The results of his work passed without any real notice, however, and Darwin and those scholars who championed his case were forced to defend the theory of natural selection against its hostile critics without an adequate knowledge of the processes of heredity. This left the theory in a vulnerable position throughout the remainder of the nineteenth century and prevented it from gaining widespread intellectual support.

Yet all this was soon to change. At the turn of the twentieth century, the principles of heredity established by Mendel were rediscovered and applied toward gaining a more definitive understanding of how natural selection actually worked. By the early 1930s the science of genetics had been extended to the study of the nature of heredity in whole populations of animals, and the science now known as population genetics was formed. This gave a tremendous boost to the theory of natural selection, and Darwin's great idea could now be defended and elaborated in a much more definitive way. Evolutionary biology and population genetics came to be blended into the "modern synthesis," or the so-called modern synthetic theory of evolution (cf. Dobzhansky, 1962; Huxley, 1942; Simpson, 1949, 1953).

The modern synthetic theory, or neo-Darwinism as it is sometimes called, remains the leading intellectual framework from which contemporary evolutionary biologists understand the process of biological evolution. However, from the early 1970s some evolutionists began to challenge some of this framework's assumptions. For example, Niles Eldredge and Stephen Jay Gould (1972; Gould and Eldredge, 1977) have challenged the neo-Darwinist assumption that evolutionary modifications are slow and gradual. They have proposed instead a perspective they call the *theory of punctuated equilibrium*. This perspective holds that biological evolution occurs as rapid and sudden modifications of otherwise unchanging organisms.

This challenge to the modern synthetic theory, though, as well as others like it, is still highly controversial and has not won acceptance by the majority of evolutionary biologists (cf. Stebbins and Ayala, 1981; Futuyma, 1986). For this reason, and because your author is not persuaded by most of the arguments of the challengers to neo-Darwinism, the account of biological evolution given here is a modern synthetic one.

Heredity and Genetic Variability

Knowledge of a few principles of genetics is essential for a proper understanding of how evolution by natural selection occurs.

The basic unit of heredity is the *gene*, a unit of biochemical information. Genes are composed of the fundamental building block of all life, deoxyribonucleic acid, or, for short, DNA. DNA has the unique capacity of making a perfect replica of itself. Since genes consist of DNA, they are capable of making exact replicas of themselves from one generation to the next and thus of perpetuating themselves indefinitely.

Most of the time, genes replicate themselves perfectly in succeeding generations. Occasionally, however, something goes wrong with the replicating mechanism, and a gene fails to copy itself exactly. This occurrence is known as a *gene mutation*. In any population of animals, such mutations are always arising; at least a few occur in each new generation. Because of the constant production of mutant genes, new genetic variability is always arising in animal populations. The overwhelming majority of these mutant genes are harmful to the organisms in which they arise. From time to time, however, a mutant gene may confer some benefit on the organism that contains it.

These mutations are operated on by a selective force that systematically eliminates those that are harmful and preserves and perpetuates those few that are beneficial. This selective force is called **natural selection.**

Adaptation, Natural Selection, and Survival of the Fit

Natural selection is that process whereby nature selects those particular genetic materials that allow an animal to adjust to the environment in which it lives. By allowing an animal to survive and prosper in a particular environment, natural selection is an **adaptive** process. If a species is highly adapted to its habitat, and if that habitat is largely stable or unchanging, we may presume that no further evolution (of any substantial sort) is being undergone by the species.

If major changes in the environment begin to take place, however, the species may no longer be well suited for survival. In order to readapt to the changed conditions, the species will have to undergo some degree of evolutionary modification or else be threatened with extinction. Whether or not it will be able to change depends on many factors. In a hypothetical case, an animal species confronted with a changing environment may produce a number of mutant genes in its next generation of offspring. Since most of these will be harmful to the organisms that contain them, most are likely to be eliminated by the next generation (or at least within a few generations), because the organisms containing them are not well designed to survive and prosper and thus to reproduce and leave their genes in future generations. Natural selection has therefore operated selectively to weed out and minimize these harmful mutants.

But if a mutant gene that arises confers some benefit on the organism and assists it in adapting to the changing environment, the organism is likely to prosper and grow to reproductive age. It will then reproduce itself by leaving copies of its genes—including the beneficial mutant gene—in the next generation. The mutant gene will now be contained in several organisms, and these organisms in turn will have a slight adaptive edge over those without the beneficial mutant. These organisms with the beneficial gene in turn prosper, reproduce, and leave yet more copies of the once-mutant gene. The original mutant gene will begin to spread throughout the total gene pool of the species, and it may eventually characterize the species as a whole. If so, then a small bit of evolutionary modification has occurred in this species of animal.

Of course, other beneficial mutants may also arise in this species in due time; if so, they are

In nature, those genetic traits that assist organisms in adapting to specific environmental conditions prevail over those that do not. During the Industrial Revolution black moths gained a selective advantage over white ones because the soot deposited on trees helped to camouflage the black moths against predators.

likely to be preserved and to spread throughout the species by natural selection. Over a considerable period of time, such genetic modifications may accumulate to a point at which the species will have a substantially different genetic structure. It may even come to be so different from what it once was that it constitutes a new species.

The process of genetic mutation is vitally important to evolution. It provides the new genetic variability on which natural selection can operate, and without which major evolutionary modifications could not occur (Dobzhansky, 1962). Evolution is therefore the result of the interaction between natural selection and genetic mutation.

In the scenario given above, the species confronting environmental change was successful in adapting to the new environment through evolutionary modification. This evolutionary process led to the "survival of the fit"; fit genes were preserved and proliferated, and unfit genes were gradually eliminated. Fit genes are simply those that confer adaptive advantage on an organism in a particular environment; likewise, unfit genes are those that are maladaptive with respect to the environment. The fitness of a gene is entirely relative, and it is the environment that determines whether or not a gene is fit. The fitness of an organism must be defined in terms of *differential reproductive success.* An organism that is able to leave more offspring in future generations than another organism has superior fitness.

It must be emphasized that evolution is a "blind" and "accidental" process, proceeding without regard to any preordained purpose and without regard to reaching any goal. This must be so since the raw material on which natural selection operates—genetic mutation—arises entirely by accident. Were it not for the mistakes occasionally arising in the replication of DNA, no significant evolutionary modification could ever occur. This process has been responsible for the existence of all the diverse varieties of life that have appeared on the earth over the past three billion years, including, of course, all species of human being.

HUMAN EVOLUTION

In the phylogenetic scale of life, humans belong to the taxonomic order known as *Primata*, the primates. Other members of this order include the members of the family *Cebidae* (the New World monkeys) and the family *Cercopithecidae* (the Old World monkeys), primates to which humans are rather distantly related. They also include the members of the family *Hylobatidae* (the gibbons and siamangs) as well as the members of the family *Pongidae* (the great apes: chimpanzees, gorillas, and orangutans). To these primates, especially the great apes, humans are very closely related. Humans, however, belong to their own family within the primate order, the *Hominidae*, and they are the only living members of this taxonomic category. Furthermore, all contemporary human beings are representatives of only one genus and species, *Homo sapiens*, and all of them likewise belong to their own separate subspecies, known as *sapiens*. The correct taxonomic classification for all modern human beings is thus *Homo sapiens sapiens*.

Since humans are closely related to the contemporary great apes, it is often assumed that they evolved from them. This assumption is incorrect. In actuality, both human beings and contemporary apes evolved from a common ancestor. The apes split off from this ancestor and evolved along one line, while human beings split off and evolved along a different line.

The Australopithecines

While many details remain to be filled in, the broad outlines of the process of human evolution are now fairly well known. It is generally agreed among students of human evolution that the first hominid (that is, the first significantly human creature, or the first member of the family *Hominidae*) was a creature belonging to the genus *Australopithecus*. The creatures making up this genus are known collectively as the *australopithecines*. The first fossil evidence of *Australopithecus* was an infant skull discovered by Raymond Dart in Taung, South Africa, in 1924. Since that time, much additional fossil evidence of the australopithecines has been found. Australopithecine fossils have now been discovered dating back as far as three or four million years, and a variety of such fossil remains span the period 4–1 million B.P. ("B.P." stands for "before the present"). These creatures are usually regarded as "ape-men" rather than as true human beings; the latter term is generally reserved for members of the genus *Homo*. Nevertheless, the australopithecines definitely appear to be much more like humans than like apes, and there is very strong evidence for thinking of them as hominids.

In terms of size, the australopithecines were quite small compared to modern human beings, standing perhaps no more than four or five feet in height, and weighing on the average probably no more than 50 pounds. They had achieved an almost fully upright posture and a bipedal (or "two-footed") means of locomotion. These latter qualities clearly set them apart from apes, who have a pronograde (or "hunched over") posture and an essentially quadrupedal (or "four-footed") mode of locomotion. The upright stance and bipedalism of the australopithecines are distinctively human traits and constitute strong evidence for considering them hominids.

Another reason for placing the australopithecines in the hominid line is their dental pattern. The shape of the dental arcade is much like that of contemporary humans, and it differs appreciably from the dental patterns found among the great apes. The canine teeth have been significantly reduced in size and are quite similar to modern human canines. The more recent australopithecines also have extremely large molars, much larger in fact than those found in modern humans. Since molars are grinding teeth, this has been interpreted to mean that the australopithecines were primarily vegetarians and that these large molars were adaptations to a diet of tough, fibrous, gritty vegetation found in the australopithecine savanna habitat. While *Australopithecus* was probably also a meat eater, the dental pattern clearly suggests the primacy of a vegetarian diet.

Estimates of australopithecine cranial capacity suggest a brain averaging around 450–550 cubic centimeters in size. This is much smaller than the average brain size of modern humans (about 1400 cubic centimeters). The implication is clearly that the australopithecines were substantially inferior to modern human beings in intelligence. There is some evidence, however, to suggest that the australopithecines were making and using tools and thus had begun to form the rudiments of culture.

The study of the australopithecines is somewhat complicated by the fact that several species have been identified. For a long time physical anthropologists talked simply of two species, *Australopithecus africanus* (often known as the gracile australopithecines) and *Australopithecus robustus* (frequently known as the robust australopithecines). *A. africanus* was smaller and slighter of build than *A. robustus*. Both species had massive molars, and thus both were probably adapted to a vegetarian diet. No doubt both species lived contemporaneously, at least for a while, although it is not known whether they ever came into contact with each other.

In recent years a third australopithecine species has been added, *Australopithecus afarensis*. The fossilized remains of this species have been discovered in eastern, rather than southern, Africa. These remains suggest a more primitive hominid, especially in terms of dentition. The canine teeth, for instance, are large and pointed (Nelson and Jurmain, 1985). There is evidence to suggest that *A. afarensis* may also have been more primitive in terms of cranial capacity, although a definitive establishment of cranial size is not yet possible (Nelson and Jurmain, 1985).

How are these three species of australopithecines related? We cannot say for certain, but the most likely scenario is one in which *A. afarensis* gave rise to *A. africanus*, which in turn led to *A. robustus*. *A. africanus* and *A. robustus* may have been "side branches" off the direct line of continuing human evolution (Johanson and White, 1979; cf. Nelson and Jurmain, 1985). If so, this would make *A. afarensis* the australopithecine hominid that remained in the direct line of human evolution leading to modern hominids. Whatever the situation, by about a million years ago all of these australopithecine species had become extinct, and bigger and brainier hominids had emerged on the scene.

Homo habilis and *Homo erectus*

The transition from the australopithecines to *Homo habilis* and *Homo erectus* marks the emergence of what many scholars consider the first "true" human beings—those belonging to the genus *Homo*, the same genus to which modern humans belong. Let us discuss *H. erectus* first because the fossilized remains of this hominid are much better understood and were discovered much earlier than those of *H. habilis*.

H. erectus fossils can be dated to about 1.6 million years ago. By about 1 million B.P. these hominids had completely replaced the australopithecines. *H. erectus* differed from the australopithecines in several important ways. For one thing, they were bigger and more rugged. In fact, they had an essentially modern postcranial skeleton (that is, the skeleton exclusive of the skull and face), and in this regard they closely resembled modern humans in basic anatomy. In addition, the cranial volume of *H. erectus* is estimated to have averaged around 800–1000 cubic centimeters, indicating that they had a brain nearly twice the size of the australopithecines. Compared to modern humans, however, *H. erectus* had a number of sharply distinguishing anatomical features. They had thicker skull bones, a more sloping forehead, and a large brow ridge over the eyes. Most important, they had a smaller cranial volume than modern human beings have, and therefore they were clearly not as intelligent as we are today.

As noted earlier, although the australopithecines engaged in meat eating, they were principally vegetarians. *H. erectus*, on the other hand, made meat a more prominent part of their diet. They probably hunted on a fairly large scale, and there is good evidence that their social life was strongly oriented around the hunting of big game animals. The transition to *H. erectus* therefore meant that human beings had moved from an economy based mainly on gathering to one based on both gathering and large-scale hunting. Assisting greatly in the hunting adaptation of *H. erectus* was the development of better and more efficient tools, and there was probably strong selective pressure on *H. erectus* populations to develop more efficient tools and hunting capabilities (Harris, 1975). *H. erectus* was clearly a hominid who had developed culture, and they had gone substantially further in this regard than had the australopithecines. Because of their superior adaptive capacity, *H. erectus* was able to adjust to a wider variety of environments. The geographical range of *H. erectus* populations was much larger than that of the australopithecines. The latter were limited to Africa; but *H. erectus* fossil remains have been found not only throughout several parts of Africa, but also in Java, China, and apparently in the Middle East and Europe.

Students of human evolution used to think of a direct transition from the australopithecines to *H. erectus*, but in the early 1960s some discoveries led them to alter this interpretation. At this time the famous physical anthropologist Louis Leakey uncovered fossil remains in eastern Africa (at Olduvai Gorge) that he dubbed *Homo habilis* ("handy man"). The Olduvai fossils were dated to between 1.85 and 1.6 million years ago. The skulls among these fossils were estimated to have an average cranial size of 646 cubic centimeters (Nelson and Jurmain, 1985). More recent discoveries from the Lake Turkana region of eastern Africa, dated to about 2 million B.P., include a skull with a cranial capacity of 775 cubic centimeters (Nelson and Jurmain, 1985). Thus *H. habilis* appears to be a species intermediate between *Australopithecus* and *H. erectus* in cranial capacity, and this appears to be the only major difference between these two species. A reasonable inference is that *H. habilis* was the first species of the genus *Homo*, and that it eventually gave rise to *H. erectus* (Nelson and Jurmain, 1985). Of course, this is only a hypothesis, and by no means is there a consensus among physical anthropologists.

The Neandertals and Modern Human Beings

The next major stage in human evolution is represented by those human beings known as the *Neandertals*. These hominids represent an early form of the genus and species *H. sapiens*, but they are assigned to their own subspecies, *Neandertalensis*. It is estimated that they evolved from *H. erectus* sometime around 110,000 B.P. and survived until the advent of modern humans around 35,000 B.P.

With the emergence of the Neandertals, human evolution was largely completed. The Neandertals had achieved an average cranial capacity of about 1350 cubic centimeters, approximately the average capacity of modern humans. There is thus every reason to believe that they acquired a degree of intellectual capability equivalent to that of modern humans. The Neandertals differed from us primarily in the structure of their cranial and postcranial skeletons. They were particularly rugged hominids, with massive faces and large brow ridges over the eyes. The bones of the postcranial skeleton were also rugged. It is generally thought that this ruggedness was a specialized adaptation to the extremely cold climate in which the Neandertals lived. Despite the distinctive ruggedness of their physical structure, however, in most essential respects they had achieved modern human status.

The Neandertals were not only more biologically advanced than *H. erectus;* they were more culturally advanced as well. They developed a more sophisticated and efficient tool kit and were more capable hunters who exploited a wider range of resources. They also began to wear clothing, and even developed the rudiments of religious and ritual life.

By 35,000 B.P. fully modern human beings had emerged on the scene, and the Neandertals rapidly became extinct. The major biological changes characterizing the transition to *H. sapiens sapiens* mainly involved alterations in the ruggedness of the physique. The ruggedness so characteristic of the Neandertals was replaced by the modern human anatomy. The other major changes that took place occurred largely in the realm of culture, not biology. By now human beings were sophisticated hunters and gatherers who had developed a sizable cultural apparatus with which to adapt to their various environments. All significant changes that have occurred in the realm of human life since the first modern humans to the present have been cultural.

The Major Developments in Human Evolution

A crucial development in human evolution was the transition to an upright posture and bipedalism. Indeed, these are major characteristics that we associate with being human. The development of upright posture and bipedalism was of great importance because these characteristics freed the hands, which would otherwise have been needed for locomotion. The hands, being freed, became available for other ends, the most important of which was tool use. Other primates besides humans have been known to make and use very crude tools, but only in humans has tool use been extensive. Without the development of upright, bipedal locomotion, it is doubtful that tool use could ever have emerged in any significant way, and it is doubtful that culture-creating hominids would ever have evolved.

The great advantage of tools is that they allow for a highly advantageous exploitation of the environment. The emergence of tool use among humans allowed them eventually to develop complex technologies that in turn allowed for the increasing development of culture. But other factors were also important for the development of culture. Chief among these was the gradual increase in the size and complexity of the brain. This increase gave human beings a tremendous capacity for learning. Humans began to gain an enormous flexibility in their capacity to adapt to nature in ways other than that simply dictated by their genes; and as they began to do so, they began to live successfully in wider and more various environments.

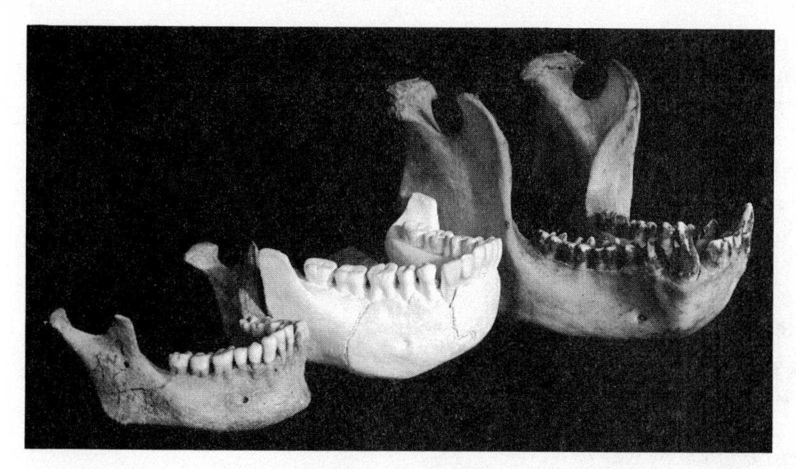

From left to right, the lower jaws of (1) a modern human, (2) *Meganthropus* (*Homo erectus*), and (3) a gorilla. Note that the modern human dental arch is much less elongated than the other two and that the canine teeth of *Meganthropus* and the modern human have diminished in size in comparison with those of the gorilla jaw.

THE EVOLUTIONARY UNIQUENESS OF HUMANS

The most important development in hominid evolution was the development of culture, the existence of which sets humans apart from all other animals. The emergence of culture clearly had a great deal to do with the evolution of the brain and the expansion of learning capacity. More specifically, however, culture was made possible by the development of a unique mode of human communication: *symbolic communication*. While all animals communicate—that is, transmit behaviorally relevant information—only humans do so through the use of **symbols.**

Symbolic Communication and Human Language

Nonhuman communication systems take a wide variety of forms involving a range of sensory organs. Like human communication, much animal communication contains both vocal and nonvocal elements. At the nonvocal level, communication can take place through the use of the senses of smell, touch, and sight. Honeybees communicate information about a new food source by performing a "waggle dance" resembling a figure eight (E. O. Wilson, 1975). A variety of primates and other mammals indicate their own territorial space by marking it with urine to discourage would-be transgressors. Chimpanzees pat each others' hands and faces and kiss in affection (Jolly, 1972). At the vocal level, the primates and many other mammals produce a variety of sounds, each of which transmits some bit of information.

Although enormously variable, all nonhuman communication systems share one fundamental feature: All are based on the use of *signs* or *signals*. The distinctive quality of a sign is that the relationship between it and the meaning it is intended to convey is genetically fixed. The honeybee's "dance," the chimpanzee's grunt, and the hyena's cry are all genetically programmed acts of communication in which there is a strictly limited, one-to-one relationship between the act and its meaning. Signs are thus *closed*, or *nonproductive*, mechanisms of communication; their meaning is rigidly predetermined, and there is no possibility of new meanings being added.

Human communication is distinctive in that it is based on symbols. Symbols differ from signs in that *their meanings are arbitrary.* The meaning of a symbol is determined by those who make use of it in a certain way, and thus symbols lack the rigidity or restrictiveness of signs. In contrast to signs, symbols are *open,* or *productive:* They are capable of attaining new or different meanings (or even several different meanings simultaneously) depending on the use to which their users put them. Both signs and symbols transmit information, but because of their open, or productive, quality, symbols can do so in an enormously more efficient way. Symbols not only make communication more efficient; they are capable of communicating information of much greater quantity and complexity than is possible with signs.

Individual symbols provide the building blocks for that distinctive human accomplishment, *language.* Language may in fact be defined as a complex arrangement of symbols. With the development of language, humans crossed a kind of evolutionary threshold.

Hockett and Ascher (1964) have specified four primary characteristics of true language. First, language has the quality of *openness.* The symbols out of which language is built can take on new and varied meanings, as opposed to the predetermination of meaning characteristic of sign systems. In addition, speakers can emit new utterances that have never been heard or said before. This makes language *productive* in that it is capable of producing new utterances, new meanings, and new combinations of utterance and meaning. Second, language is characterized by the feature known as *displacement.* Displacement refers to the ability to speak of things that are out of sight, of things that are in the past or in the future, or for that matter of things that are even nonexistent. By contrast, signs are confined to those situations in which their expression is relevant. Hockett and Ascher note, for instance, that gibbons do not emit their food call unless they have found food. Third, *duality of patterning* is a distinctive characteristic of language. Language has, on the one hand, a patterning of a basic set of elementary sound units, themselves meaningless in isolation, and, on the other hand, a patterning that combines these individual sound units into prescribed sequences that render them meaningful. Sign systems lack such duality, and each vocalization carries a single, predetermined meaning. Finally, language is *transmitted by learning.* This transmission contrasts sharply with the genetic transmission of sign systems.

The Origin of Language

Exactly when and how language first arose is still very imperfectly understood. Linguists are in sharp disagreement as to how old language may actually be. Some see it as a relatively recent evolutionary development, perhaps no more than 100,000 years old, while others believe that it may have evolved as long as a million years ago.

One well-known attempt to understand the origin of language is that of Hockett and Ascher (1964). These scholars attempt to describe the step-by-step process by which the *closed call systems* of our prehuman ancestors evolved into true languages. They begin by describing the basic features contained in a call system. Such a system consists of a small number of distinct signals, each of which is relevant to a recurrent and biologically important situation. Such situations involve, among other things, the discovery of food, the detection of danger, the desire for companionship, the indication of one's whereabouts, the desire for sex, and the occurrence of pain. As our prehuman ancestors came out of the trees and began to assume a terrestrial existence, the hands, previously necessary for climbing and swinging in an arboreal existence, came to be freed for other uses. They came to be used for such purposes as the fashioning and carrying of crude weapons and tools and the transportation of scavenged food. This, in turn, left the mouth, previously used for such carrying purposes, free for other things. Hockett and Ascher argue that the new use to which the mouth was put was chattering.

It is at this point in our evolutionary history that Hockett and Ascher see the first real beginnings of language. They view language as emerging from the "opening" of the call system. It is possible, for example, to imagine a situation in which a sequence of letters, say ABCD, represented a call meaning "food here," while a sequence EFGH meant "danger coming." It is conceivable that in a situation in which there was both food and danger, an early hominid might have emitted a new call, ABGH, meaning "food and danger." Hockett and Ascher suggest that this must have been very much like the first step necessary in the opening of the call system and thus the first step toward true language.

Of course, the new utterance, ABGH, is itself only a new call and not a symbol (it might be called a composite call). However, the new call is one of greater complexity: It transmits more information in a more efficient manner. Eventually, Hockett and Ascher argue, entire systems of such composite calls must have evolved; in addition, such systems must have come to be transmitted to new generations by strong reliance on teaching and learning. Such systems, which Hockett and Ascher refer to as prelanguages, must have served as an intermediate link between the earlier closed call systems and true languages.

These prelanguages, while representing a type of "open call system," lacked one essential ingredient of true languages: duality of patterning. Eventually, with the further development of the call system in terms of the quantity and complexity of calls, this too evolved. The basic features of sound came to represent a fundamental set of elementary phonological components that could be combined and recombined into prescribed sequences carrying arbitrarily assigned meanings. Hockett and Ascher see the essentials of this process as having been achieved by about one million years ago. Having evolved a system of true language, humankind crossed what can only be regarded as a critical evolutionary threshold.

The Functional Significance of Language

The evolution of language was of crucial significance for humankind because it paved the way for the emergence of *culture,* that complex system of tools, thoughts, and actions that has provided humans with their uniquely effective means of adaptation. As Leslie White puts it (1949:33):

> All culture (civilization) depends upon the symbol. It was the exercise of the symbolic faculty that brought culture into existence and it is the use of symbols that makes the perpetuation of culture possible. Without the symbol there would be no culture, and man would be merely an animal, not a human being.

Culture requires symbolization capacity because it intimately depends upon a means for storing and transmitting vast quantities of socially learned information. Only a complex symbol system—that is, language—provides such a means.

Some scholars have suggested that this emphasis on symbols as the basis of culture reflects a hidden form of idealism (Sahlins, 1976a; Fluehr-Lobban, 1986). Carolyn Fluehr-Lobban (1986), for instance, has counterposed White's emphasis on symbols to Friedrich Engels's (1940; orig. 1876; cf. Woolfson, 1982) argument for the role of human labor—manipulation of the natural environment through the use of tools—in the creation of culture. She argues that Engels's theory is a materialist one that is superior to White's idealist position. This is a dubious argument. There is nothing idealist about White's theory. The idealist position is that it is the *specific content* of human symbolic constructions—the particular form they take in a particular time and place—that shape culture. White's position, though, is that it is the *general human capacity* to symbolize that makes culture possible. It is the capacity to store and transmit information that allows for culture to emerge and be accumulated over time. This position is perfectly consistent with Engels's stress on the role of human labor and tool making. In fact, as we have already argued, it was human tool making that set in motion a chain of events in human evolution that ultimately led to the emergence of the capacity to symbolize.

Is Symbolic Communication Uniquely Human?

The results of recent attempts to teach apes the rudiments of language have cast doubt on the uniqueness of human symbolization capacity. Many scholars have concluded from these results that symbolic communication is not a human monopoly, and therefore that the gulf between humans and other animals is less wide than once believed.

David Premack (1970) taught a young chimpanzee named Sarah a kind of symbol system. Sarah was required to place a variety of plastic chips on a magnetized board, with each chip representing a word, and a sequence of chips representing a phrase. Sarah apparently acquired the use of about 130 "words." Furthermore, in a famous long-term experiment in language teaching, Gardner and Gardner (1969) attempted to teach the chimp Washoe a more complex and elaborate system. Washoe was taught the use of American Sign Language for the Deaf (Ameslan). She was taught this language by a system of rewards and through direct guidance, and she also acquired a number of words through direct observation. She was ultimately able to attain a vocabulary of well over 100 words; in addition, she strung many of these words together into a number of short sentences. More recent experiments have involved teaching rudimentary language skills to gorillas. Psychologist Francine Patterson of Stanford University has been highly successful in teaching Koko, a young female gorilla, Ameslan. At last report, Koko had acquired a vocabulary of approximately 300 words and was able to combine these words into a wide variety of sentences (cf. J. H. Hill, 1978).

The results of these experiments appear to contradict the argument that symbolization, and hence language, is uniquely human. All the great apes are clearly capable of using, in a limited way, the essentials of a symbolic communication system. Yet it seems unwise to rush toward hasty and dramatic conclusions based on such findings. It must be borne in mind that these apes were taught symbol use by human beings, not by other apes. While apes have learned the use of a few symbols, they did not create those symbols. So far as we know, humans have been the only animals to have *invented* symbols.

SOCIETY, CULTURE, AND HUMAN ADAPTATION

The Societal Mode of Organization

A species of animals is social when its members live together, interact, and depend upon one another for their survival. Human beings are social animals because they live together in organized groups that we call *societies*. Yet this scarcely makes humans unique, for a great many animal species live in societies, and the societal mode of organization is not even confined to the so-called higher species. Many insects live in rather elaborate and complex social groups, the individual members of which intimately depend upon one another for survival. In short, social life is a widespread phenomenon in the animal world.

Nevertheless, social life is not randomly distributed among animal species. The evolutionary status of a species bears a direct relationship to the prevalence of the societal mode of organization. The higher a species stands on the phylogenetic scale of life, the greater the likelihood of its exhibiting organized social life. Thus, while only some insects live in societies, most mammals are social and all primates carry on their lives within a societal framework.

It would be a serious error, however, to assume that the respective societies of bees, chimpanzees, and human beings are fundamentally similar. The specific nature of and basis for societal existence are strikingly different in each instance. The social life of bees, ants, and wasps is complex and elaborate, but the social behavior of such species is wholly regulated by instinctual mechanisms. The social insects come preprogrammed with a ready-made set of behavioral responses. Learning plays virtually no part in their actions.

Such a description of the basis for social behavior does not apply to nonhuman primates. For instance, while much of chimpanzee social life is genetically determined, recent research now makes it clear that learning plays a significant role in their social behavior. The role of learning in this case is one illustration of the general principle that the greater the evolutionary complexity of an organism, the greater the influence of learning (van den Berghe, 1978).

This principle is helpful in understanding the basis for human social life, for it is in the human species that the role of learning far exceeds the part played by biological factors in the

Chimpanzees greeting each other. Sociality is universal among the primates, extremely widespread among the mammals, and in general a common feature of animal species.

shaping of social behavior. But it is not sufficient merely to claim that human social behavior is highly subject to learning. It is essential to point out that human behavior is learned through culture, and thus that human societies, as opposed to all other animal societies, are *culturally ordered* or *culturally regulated* systems.

Culture and Human Adaptation

The concept of culture is indispensable for the study of human behavior and human societies. Unfortunately, there is no universal agreement as to the meaning of this concept. Some social scientists use it to refer solely to the symbolic meanings that individuals attach to their behavior, thereby excluding behavior itself from consideration as a part of culture (cf. Goodenough, 1969; D. M. Schneider, 1968). This book takes the position that such a conceptualization of culture is much too narrow, since it is limited to only one of many relevant aspects of human social life. Accordingly, we shall define culture in a much broader way as *the total lifeways characteristic of the members of a society, including tools, knowledge, and patterned ways of thinking and acting, that are learned and shared and are not the direct product of biological inheritance.* This definition of culture stresses that it is a complex totality consisting of three interrelated sets of phenomena: the tools and techniques—in short, the technologies—that humans have invented to adapt to their environments; the patterns of behavior that individuals engage in as members of society; and the shared beliefs, values, and rules that humans create as a means of defining their relationships to one another and to their natural environments.

There are four primary characteristics of culture. First, culture *rests on symbols*. Symbols are essential to culture in that they are the mechanisms necessary for the storage and transmission of the large quantities of information that constitute culture. Second, culture is *learned* and does not depend upon biological inheritance for its transmission. Third, culture is a system that is *shared* by the members of a society; that is, it is representative of the members of a society considered collectively rather than individually. While there are differences in the degree to which various individuals accept or conform to the patterns of their culture, a culture by definition is representative of the members of a society considered collectively. Finally, culture tends to be *integrated*. The various parts or components of culture tend to fit together in such a way that they are consistent with one another, despite the conflicts, frictions, or contradictions that are also present.

Considerable attention has been given by both sociologists and anthropologists to distinguishing between the concept of society and that of culture. Society is generally used to refer to the "patterned relationships obtaining between people," while culture is often regarded as "the products of such patterned relationships" (i.e., the technology, beliefs, values, and rules that both serve as guides to, and result from, such patterned relationships). While this distinction may be a useful one for various analytical purposes, it is highly artificial and is rather sharply divorced from the concrete reality of the lives of human beings. The distinction therefore has little to commend it, and it has probably done more harm than good. Accordingly, to avoid this distinction it is useful to follow those who have used the hybrid term *sociocultural system* (Harris, 1985b; Lenski and Lenski, 1987). The real advantage of this term is that it brings into relief the full range of factors constituting the "systems" in which individuals conduct their lives. The nature of sociocultural systems, and the way in which they may be appropriately compartmentalized, is the subject of Chapter 3.

The real significance of culture is its adaptive nature. Culture has created for human beings a new means of adaptation to the conditions of their existence, and this mode of adaptation is one that has been vastly superior to biological adaptation. At a lower phylogenetic level, societies themselves were adaptive mechanisms developing out of a long process of biological evolution. As societies evolved to higher levels of complexity, and as the conditions were developed for the emergence of symbol systems out of call systems, culture itself came about as an evolutionary product. As all of this happened, the stage was set for the development of sociocultural systems in which culture rivaled, and eventually replaced, biology as the prime basis for human adaptation.

Is Culture Uniquely Human?

The recent discovery that some nonhuman primates frequently engage in rudimentary forms of tool use has led a number of observers to challenge the conventional wisdom that culture is uniquely human. Chimpanzees, for example, have been shown to use blades of grass as crude tools for withdrawing termites from their holes. Furthermore, the chimps actually shape or fashion these tools before using them (Jolly, 1972). It has been discovered that groups of Japanese macaque monkeys have developed the practice of washing sweet potatoes and wheat before eating them. These practices are learned by other members of the group, although by observation and not by direct teaching (Jolly, 1972). Baboons have used stones as weapons, and chimpanzees actually seem to aim at targets and club with objects (Jolly, 1972).

These crude forms of tool use clearly must be regarded as a rudimentary form of culture.* They vary from one group of the same species to another, and therefore they are learned and shared behavior patterns that cannot be accounted for in terms of biological inheritance. Nevertheless, it is inappropriate to draw dramatic conclusions about nonhuman "culture." While nonhuman primates have a few rudimentary elements of culture, and thus while the distinction between humans and other primates must be regarded as quantitative, this quantitative difference is so large that it seems feasible to argue that culture is a uniquely human product for all practical purposes. In a technical sense humans are not the only creatures with culture, but they are certainly extraordinarily better at creating it than any other animal. No investigator has ever discovered a group of chimpanzees who worshiped gods, transferred bride payments, or painted murals on the walls of caves.

*Some social scientists now use the term *protoculture* to refer to this sort of crude infrahuman tool use, reserving the term *culture* for human achievements alone.

The Transmission of Culture: The Concept of Socialization

Because of the exceptional capacity of humans for learning, most sociologists and anthropologists place great emphasis on the process of **socialization.** This is the process whereby humans come to absorb the content of the culture into which they are born. Many of these social scientists believe that it is this process, whereby senior generations teach and junior generations learn, that accounts for the stability or continuity of culture over time.

It is impossible to deny that humans have an extraordinary capacity to acquire the content of their culture, that senior generations spend an inordinate amount of time attempting to transmit this culture to junior generations, and that junior generations usually bear the enormous imprint of these instructional efforts. It is therefore hard to deny that the socialization process is a crucial aspect of the human experience everywhere, and thus that the concept of socialization is a sociologically important one. However, to recognize all of this is not equivalent to agreeing that the concept has important theoretical value, at least for macrosociologists. In other words, although socialization is a fundamental part of the lives of humans everywhere, to invoke the existence of this process does not really get us very far in explaining why cultural systems persist over time. And it certainly gets us nowhere in explaining how and why cultures change, or, indeed, how they come to be the way they are in the first place.

This tricky and rather subtle point needs some elaboration. A particularly delightful way of approaching this problem is that of George Homans (1984). As Homans points out, many sociologists explain human behavior as being what it is "because of the culture." They contend that people act and think the way they do because they have been socialized into a particular culture that they accept for themselves as right, proper, and normal. But to the extent that this explanation is true, it is certainly trivial. Homans calls social scientists who rely on such an explanation of human behavior "culture vultures." His objection to the "culture vultures" is at once profound and obvious. As he points out, what this explanation leaves out is what we really want to explain in the first place: why the culture came originally to be the way it is. In other words, it does little good to point out that people absorb the content of their culture, when what cries out for explanation is how there came to be a culture of a particular type that people would become emotionally attached to and have a powerful interest in transmitting.

Homans's objections to the "culture vultures" seem especially well taken when we realize that one of the most fundamental things that sociologists want to explain—and in fact, a central focus of this book—is how and why cultures change. How could we get anywhere by invoking the process of socialization? After all, change is really the absence of socialization: it is the modification, rather than the preservation, of the content of a particular culture. How can we explain change by using a concept explicitly designed to explain the absence of change?

But even when we are dealing with continuity and stability rather than change it will be seen that the concept of socialization is unhelpful. As Homans and various other sociologists and anthropologists have claimed, what really explains the continuity of culture from one generation to the next is not the socialization process, but the fact that the junior members of a society are responding and adapting to the same set of historical circumstances as did the senior members of that society. When those historical circumstances change, then people will alter the way in which they respond and adapt, even in the face of strong pressures from the senior generation to maintain the old patterns of response.

In effect, socialization is a given, a universal part of the human experience. By using the socialization concept, we can learn something about the powerful desires of senior generations to transmit the content of their culture to their offspring. At the microsociological level of everyday life and the subtleties of the interactions among individuals, the concept may have great value. But, for macrosociologists, it has no theoretical or explanatory merits. It cannot explain anything about the macrostructure of society and the transformations in that macrostructure over time.

Ethnocentrism and Cultural Relativism

A basic feature of human life that quickly comes to be realized by any aspiring anthropologist or sociologist is the extraordinary degree of diversity in sociocultural systems. Social scientists frequently find themselves confronted by cultures that differ dramatically from their own. The sense of horror and shock that is often experienced by anthropological field-workers when first confronting a vastly different culture is vividly described by Napoleon Chagnon upon his first meeting with the Yanomamo Indians of South America (Chagnon, 1983:10–11):

> I looked up and gasped when I saw a dozen burly, naked, sweaty, hideous men staring at us down the shafts of their drawn arrows! Immense

> wads of green tobacco were stuck between their lower teeth and lips making them look even more hideous, and strands of dark-green slime dripped or hung from their nostrils—strands so long that they clung to their pectoral muscles or drizzled down their chins. We arrived at the village while the men were blowing a hallucinogenic drug up their noses. One of the side effects of the drug is a runny nose. The mucus is always saturated with the green powder and they usually let it run freely from their nostrils. . . . My next discovery was that there were a dozen or so vicious, underfed dogs snapping at my legs, circling me as if I were to be their next meal. I just stood there holding my notebook, helpless and pathetic. Then the stench of the decaying vegetation and filth hit me and I almost got sick. I was horrified. What kind of welcome was this for the person who came here to live with you and learn your way of life, to become friends with you? . . .
>
> As we walked down the path to the boat, I pondered the wisdom of having decided to spend a year and a half with this tribe before I had even seen what they were like. I am not ashamed to admit that had there been a diplomatic way out, I would have ended my fieldwork then and there.

The extreme culture shock experienced by Chagnon is not limited to professional social scientists. It can be, and has been, experienced by virtually all persons suddenly encountering a way of life remarkably different from their own. This reaction results from the phenomenon known as ethnocentrism: the tendency for individuals to view their own way of life as superior to all others. Thus, Chagnon was horrified by what he saw since Western industrial culture had hardly prepared him for such phenomena as drawn bows, nakedness, green slime dripping from the nose, and filthiness when he approached the tribe as a visitor. To a very substantial degree, we are products of our own culture, and virtually all of us are conditioned to think of our own way of life as the most desirable and other cultures as representing various gradations of less desirable lifestyles. Ethnocentrism is a universal human phenomenon. The Yanomamo themselves are no exception to this rule. Chagnon reports that, since he was a non-Yanomamo, they tended to regard him as less than human. The Yanomamo are one of the world's most hostile and warlike societies, yet when Chagnon described to them the conduct of Americans in the Vietnam War they were morally repelled and regarded such behavior as savage and inhumane!

Ethnocentrism creates a special problem for research in other cultures since, if powerful enough, it represents a severe barrier to any sort of objective (and hence accurate) study. Had Chagnon been unable to overcome his ethnocentrism, he could never have carried out even a remotely successful research project. Anthropologists and sociologists have combated this problem through the development of a counter doctrine known as **cultural relativism.** Cultural relativism is the doctrine that no culture is inherently superior or inferior to others, but that, since every culture represents an adaptive solution to fundamental human prob-

"His blood ran cold as he saw the sinister round blue eyes and pink face of Johnny Jones staring at him over the window sill."

Ethnocentrism is a universal phenomenon.

lems, all cultures are "equally valid." Cultural relativists believe that the standards of one culture cannot be used to evaluate another, and therefore that the standards for the evaluation of a culture can only be those of that culture itself. If we were to apply this doctrine in judging the propriety of female infanticide (the selective killing of female infants) among the Yanomamo, all we could really say would be something like "while it's wrong for us, it's right for them, and cannot be categorically condemned." And we would say this through recognition of the fact that infanticide "iş right" for the Yanomamo since it represents an adaptive solution to a problem of human existence.

As a moral or ethical perspective, cultural relativism has been subjected to severe criticism, and it does not constitute a satisfactory system of ethics (Kohlberg, 1971; Patterson, 1977). The problems with it are fairly well known. For one thing, it can quickly collapse into "the disease of which it is the cure" (Kohlberg, 1971). That is, "it leads to the approval of practices that are patently inhumane" (Hatch, 1983:81). For example, a strict cultural relativist perspective would have us endorse such practices as the Nazi effort to exterminate the Jews, Soviet forced labor camps, Roman slavery or black slavery in the New World, Yanomamo gang rape of women, and countless other cultural phenomena that seem morally repulsive by most reasonable standards—all in the name of tolerance toward other ways of life. In addition, cultural relativism seems to perpetuate a kind of "tyranny of custom" by leaving little or no room for the autonomy of the individual (Hatch, 1983).

In fact, the limitations of cultural relativism have appeared obvious even to many of the cultural relativists themselves, some of whom have actually violated their own principles in practice despite formally enunciating them. For instance, Ruth Benedict, one of the major architects of cultural relativism in the early decades of this century, has consistently undermined her own relativist stance when she has discussed cultural differences (Hatch, 1983). In her well-known book *Patterns of Culture* (1934), Benedict clearly shows a preference for certain cultural traits over others, displaying, for example, a particular dislike for cultures in which force plays a major role.

Elvin Hatch (1983) has suggested a way around cultural relativism that overcomes its basic deficiencies while at the same time retaining what seems to be of value in it: its general plea for tolerance. Hatch proposes what he calls a "humanistic principle" as a means of judging other cultures. This principle holds that cultures can be evaluated in terms of whether or not they harm persons by such means as torture, sacrifice, war, political repression, exploitation, and so on. It also judges them in terms of how well they provide for the material existence of their members: the extent to which people are free from poverty, malnutrition, disease, and the like. Beyond this consideration, cultures cannot really be meaningfully evaluated (Hatch, 1983:138):

> Relativism prevails in relation to the institutions that fall outside the orbit of the humanistic principle, for here a genuine diversity of values is found and there are no suitable cross-cultural standards for evaluating them. The finest reasoning that we or anyone else can achieve will not point decisively to the superiority of Western marriage patterns, eating habits, legal institutions, and the like. We ought to show tolerance with respect to these institutions in other societies on the grounds that people ought to be free to live as they choose.

While Hatch's proposal does seem to improve considerably on cultural relativism, such complex ethical questions unfortunately cannot be settled quite so easily. It is highly doubtful that even Hatch's strongly modified version of cultural relativism can be taken as a truly acceptable ethical philosophy. Yet despite our objections to either of these versions of relativism, we must recognize that cultural relativism is useful and necessary as a sort of practical guiding premise in exploring the nature of sociocultural systems. It therefore has *methodological,* if not ethical, value. It has methodological value because it compels the examination of cultural patterns in terms of their adaptive character. Without cultural relativism as a methodological tool, we would confront other cultures wearing a set of cultural blinders, the result of which would undoubtedly be the perpetuation of ignorance rather than the illumination of the basic workings of sociocultural systems.

Culture, Subculture, and Counterculture

The term *culture* is usually applied to the total way of life of a society considered as a whole. However, in sociocultural systems of great complexity, such as Western industrial societies, it is essential to recognize the nature of diverse cultural patternings that exist within such societies. For this reason sociologists have developed the concepts of **subculture** and **counterculture.**

A subculture is a smaller culture existing within the framework of a larger culture. The members of a subculture share specific cultural patterns that are in some way different from those that prevail in the larger culture, while at the same time generally accepting and sharing in the patterns of the larger culture. American college students, for example, constitute a subculture in the sense that they act and think in ways that are in some respects distinct from American culture as a whole. Diverse ethnic groups in complex industrial societies—groups that are distinguished on the basis of cultural or national origin—display rather distinctive subcultural patterns in that they carry on ways of thinking and acting that are in some way unique. College professors, doctors, coal miners, and professional athletes also embody certain subcultural differences, the differences in these cases arising from distinctive occupations. Many other subcultures exist in complex societies, of course, with such factors as race, religion, regionalism, and social class serving as important criteria for subcultural distinctions.

Like subcultures, countercultures contain distinctive cultural patterns existing within some larger culture. Unlike subcultures, however, the members of countercultures generally do not share in the dominant cultural patterns. Instead, countercultures tend to be based on hostility to, and rejection of, such dominant patterns. Some countercultures are genuinely revolutionary in that they are predicated upon an attempt to make a fundamental alteration in the dominant culture. Most countercultures, however, are not imbued with such revolutionary intentions; instead, they are generally organized around a withdrawal from the mainstream of cultural life. In this category would fall such groups as the "beatniks" of the 1950s and the "hippies" of the 1960s. One of the most recent countercultures to appear in Western society is that of the "punkers" of the 1980s.

SUMMARY

1. Biological evolution is a process whereby organisms acquire those genetic materials that allow them to be highly adapted to particular environments. Evolution occurs through the selective effect of the environment on gene mutations. Most mutations are negative in their effect on the organism and are selectively eliminated through the death or sterility of the organisms containing them. Beneficial mutations, though, are selectively preserved because the organisms containing them are differentially favored for survival. The unequal survival of favored and unfavored organisms is a process known as natural selection.

2. The earliest humans were known as the australopithecines. They evolved more than three million years ago in southern and eastern Africa. *Homo erectus* was the next major human species. This creature was bigger and more rugged than the australopithecines, had a greater cranial capacity (and hence greater intelligence), and was found in a wider range of environments. Around 110,000 years ago the Neandertals evolved. These hominids had achieved an intelligence level essentially equivalent to that of modern humans, and had developed much in the way of tools and culture. Modern humans—*Homo sapiens sapiens*—emerged some 35,000 years ago.

3. The most important developments in human evolution have been the transition to an upright posture and bipedal means of locomotion, the acquisition of tool use, and the enormous increase in the size and complexity of the brain.

4. Another great achievement in human evolution was the development of symbolic communication and language. Whereas all other animals communicate through the use of signs, humans communicate by using symbols, or sounds and gestures that are arbitrary, learned, and shared. Complex systems of symbols constitute languages. Numerous social scientists have speculated about the origins of language in human evolution, but there is still wide disagreement as to just when and how it may have evolved from earlier sign systems.

5. The great significance of language for humans is that it makes culture possible. While some other animals have rudimentary forms of culture known as protoculture, only humans have true culture, or complex systems of tools, knowledge, and learned and shared patterns of thought and action. Many animal species live in societies, but only humans live in sociocultural systems or societies organized culturally.

6. Culture is a human achievement with enormous adaptive significance. It allows humans to cope with a great number and variety of survival problems. Culture has now replaced biology as the prime means of human adaptation.

7. The transmission of culture from one generation to another is known as the socialization process. Socialization is a fundamental part of all human experience, yet macrosociologists can explain little about the larger structure of society and of long-term social transformations by invoking this concept. Socialization is mainly a link between the generations, and rather than explaining anything it itself must be explained. Socialization is the transmission of a culture already in existence, and what sociologists most want to know is how and why a particular type of culture came into existence in the first place.

8. Cultures differ enormously, and most humans in all cultures respond to cultural differences ethnocentrically, or by assuming their own way of life to be superior to all others. Social scientists generally agree that ethnocentrism is an unfortunate human trait, and it certainly constitutes an obstacle to meaningful sociological understanding. Many social scientists have adopted the doctrine known as cultural relativism as a means of counteracting ethnocentrism. This doctrine preaches tolerance for cultural diversity and suggests that all cultural traits have value in their own context. While this doctrine may be methodologically useful to social scientists, it does not seem to constitute an adequate ethical philosophy. Indeed, many social scientists, including those who otherwise defend cultural relativism, are sharply critical of such cultural practices as oppression, exploitation, slavery, and various forms of human brutality.

SPECIAL TOPIC: THE SOCIOBIOLOGY CONTROVERSY

One of the newest theoretical strategies in sociology is known as **sociobiology.** As this strategy began to emerge in the middle of the 1970s, it generated one of the more heated of recent controversies in the social sciences. Although the heat has now dissipated considerably, the controversy has not gone away and the issues it addresses are crucial ones.

Sociobiologists attempt to discover the extent to which human social behavior is the result of genetic traits characteristic of the entire human species. In other words, they are interested in identifying the basic features of **human nature.** They base their assumptions on the Darwinian model of biological evolution through natural selection. They believe that as humans evolved from their primate ancestors they inherited certain biological traits from those ancestors that continue to exist in modern humans. These traits are held to have a direct influence on many patterns of social behavior. Sociobiologists do not claim that human social behavior is merely the product of our genetic programming; they recognize that most human activities result from specific forms of learning in particular social and cultural environments. Nevertheless, they argue that human behavior is not entirely learned, and that many aspects of it may be under genetic control.

A well-known example of sociobiological reasoning is found in the work of Lionel Tiger and Robin Fox (1971). Tiger and Fox argue that humans come equipped with a biogrammar: a basic set of biological instructions predisposing them to act in certain ways. They do not regard these instructions as constituting fixed, immutable instincts.

Pierre van den Berghe. Van den Berghe is a professor of sociology at the University of Washington and a major proponent of the sociobiological approach to social life. He believes that sociobiology can be coherently linked with an evolutionary, materialist, and conflict perspective.

Rather, they view them as general behavioral tendencies that are subject to being modified or even neutralized by certain learning experiences. They see the following as the most essential elements of the human biogrammar: (1) the tendency of humans to form strongly hierarchical groups and societies in which the competition for status is of paramount importance; (2) the tendency of males to bond together in political coalitions in which they exercise political dominance and control over females; (3) the tendency of mother and child to form a mutual attachment; (4) the predisposition of humans (especially males) to engage in aggression and violence; (5) the tendency of humans to defend territorial space against intrusions by outsiders.

Tiger and Fox reach these conclusions by drawing analogies between human behavior and the behavior of contemporary nonhuman primates. They note that most nonhuman primates are organized into societies based on status hierarchies with dominance of males over females, and they infer from this that a basic primate biogram has been retained throughout human evolutionary history. The tendency for modern humans to form hierarchical, competitive, and male-dominated social systems is therefore seen as resting essentially in our genes. The same kind of bioevolutionary reasoning is applied by Tiger and Fox in reaching the conclusion that mother-child bonding and the predisposition toward aggression and territoriality are rooted in our biological nature.

Tiger and Fox's arguments are illustrative of one particular version of sociobiological theorizing. Other sociobiologists employ the **theory of kin selection** as the guiding principle in their thinking (E. O. Wilson, 1975). This theory is based on the recent assumption made by many evolutionary biologists that the gene, rather than the organism or species, is the unit on which natural selection operates (cf. Dawkins, 1976). Evolutionary biologists who maintain this assumption claim that natural selection operates to preserve certain genes and maximize their representation in future generations.

Kin selection theory (it might more appropriately be labeled a strategic principle) posits that many forms of behavior result from the attempts of individuals to maximize their **inclusive fitness.** Inclusive fitness is the sum of an individual's own fitness *plus* the fitness present in the genes of all its relatives. A major application of kin selection theory has been to the commonly observed phenomenon of altruism among closely related individuals. For example, the theory holds that when a parent behaves in a self-sacrificial manner toward its offspring it is assisting them to survive and reproduce and therefore leave more copies of its genes in future generations. Such altruistic behavior, then, serves to maximize the parent's inclusive fitness.

The theory of kin selection has been highly successful in explaining many features of animal behavior. It successfully explains, for instance, the extreme altruism characteristic of the social insects (W. D. Hamilton, 1964), as well as altruistic behavior in other animal species (cf. Barash, 1977; van den Berghe, 1978). Some social scientists believe that it can adequately account for several features of human social behavior. Since the theory successfully explains the importance of kinship bonds in many animal species, it has been proposed that it helps to explain the universality of human kinship systems and the great significance that is attached to kinship in so many societies (van den Berghe, 1979). It has also been suggested that it is a promising way of explaining widespread patterns of human sex role behavior (Daly and Wilson, 1978).

A major attack against the theory of kin selection has been made by Marshall Sahlins (1976b). Arguing that this theory is the most important of all the aspects of sociobiology, Sahlins claims that if it can be decisively refuted, then sociobiology will collapse. It is

Sahlins's express aim to provide a complete demolition of kin selection theory. He carries out this aim by drawing on the anthropological literature on human kinship systems.

Kin selection theory predicts that human kinship ties are based on the degree of genetic relatedness. Hence, the closer the genetic relationship, the closer the kinship tie, and the greater the significance of the social relationship resulting therefrom. Sahlins believes that the ethnographic record shows that human kinship systems are actually organized in ways that run completely counter to this prediction. Human kinship, he holds, is organized by culture—by the social definitions used in identifying who is or is not close kin—rather than by nature, that is, by the degree of actual genetic relatedness. Culture, in other words, can make a genetically distant relative a close kinsman and a genetically close relative a distant kinsman. In general, Sahlins concludes that human kinship is not organized according to the degree of genetic relatedness among individuals, as sociobiology predicts. On the contrary, it is unique in being free from determination by natural relationships.

Deserving of special consideration are the political overtones that have accompanied the controversy over sociobiology. There have been charges from a number of quarters that its emphasis on genes is just the latest attempt at scientifically justifying racism, sexism, social and economic inequalities, and a host of other social injustices. These charges have been made most vehemently by a group known as the Study Group of Science for the People, an organization that has done much to turn sociobiology from a scientific into a political issue. There have even been efforts to apply intellectual censorship to Harvard University zoology professor Edward O. Wilson, one of the leading founders of sociobiology. As a climax, at the 1978 annual meetings of the American Association for the Advancement of Science, a meeting at which sociobiology was a major topic of discussion, a member of a political group calling itself the International Committee Against Racism rose from the audience and proceeded to dump a pitcher of water on Edward Wilson's head as he prepared to speak (Pines, 1978). Following this, several demonstrators from the same group made their way to the platform to prevent Wilson from speaking. Such actions clearly point to the politicization of sociobiology and to the emotional intensity that often accompanies discussion of it.

Sahlins's critique of kin selection theory has some merit, but it seems rather exaggerated and extreme in its complete dismissal of sociobiology. Furthermore, the rejection of sociobiology on the grounds that it is politically objectionable is not scientifically or ethically justified and has no place in a democratic society; it is unworthy of responsible scholars who truly understand what intellectual freedom, or, for that matter, science, is all about. Fortunately, this aspect of the sociobiology controversy has diminished greatly. But it is still doubtful that this theoretical approach holds much promise as a suitable *general* strategy for the study of human social life. Most sociobiologists readily admit that the basic differences among human societies are the result of social and cultural factors, and therefore they seldom try to explain societal differences in biological terms (E. O. Wilson, 1977). Most of their efforts are spent attempting to explain the universal or similar features of societies. Even here, however, sociobiology runs into difficulty. A great deal of evidence strongly suggests that such phenomena as social hierarchies, competition, aggression, and territoriality—phenomena put forth by Tiger and Fox as biologically rooted—are the result of social rather than biological causes.

Nevertheless, while sociobiology may not be acceptable as a broad theoretical strategy, it seems to have a contribution to make. It may well be that such universal features of social life as incest avoidance and male political dominance over females have biological causes. (Note, however, that the degree of male dominance over females varies greatly from one society to another, a fact that is scarcely amenable to biological explanation.) Moreover, kin selection theory may account for the fact that all human societies stress kinship relations. (Once again, however, the major differences among kinship systems cannot be understood biologically.) One of the more attractive features of contemporary sociobiological research is its strong commitment to a scientific and comparative approach. Sociobiologists have proposed many interesting hypotheses, some of which may well turn out in the near future to be theoretically meaningful.

As a postscript, it may be worthwhile to ask about the status of sociobiological theory in the early 1990s, some 15 years after it first made its big splash and created the storm of controversy that quickly surrounded it. The answer is not altogether clear, but it appears that among sociologists sociobiology seems almost to have disappeared, at least from clear public view. One no longer hears papers on sociobiology presented at major sociological conferences, and the major theoretical and research journals contain few or no articles making use of this approach. One knows that sociobiology still survives among sociologists (cf. Lopreato, 1984), but it would appear that it does so in a rather subterranean fashion. Among anthropologists, and especially among biologists, sociobiology is considerably more vigorous. Biologists continue to produce important works on the subject, with relevance for human affairs (cf. R. D. Alexander, 1987), as do anthropologists (cf. Betzig, 1986).

What has apparently happened is that sociobiologists have turned increasingly inward. Scorned by the majority of social scientists who have felt threatened, both politically and theoretically, by this approach, many sociobiologists have taken refuge in each other. They have created their own journals and other avenues of scholarly communication. One senses that most sociobiologists want to be left alone to pursue their research away from the kind of storm that once blew around them. Perhaps they feel confident that, in due time and without interference from highly biased "outsiders," they will produce a large body of evidence to support their leading theoretical claims. Sociobiology may be very dormant these days, but it is hardly dead.

FOR FURTHER READING

Chagnon, Napoleon. *Yanomamo: The Fierce People.* Third edition. New York: Holt, Rinehart, and Winston, 1983. A well-known ethnography that provides insight into the nature of culture and vividly depicts the kinds of obstacles that must be overcome in order to gain a scientifically valid understanding of other cultures.

Dobzhansky, Theodosius. *Mankind Evolving.* New Haven: Yale University Press, 1962. A classic introduction to the theory of biological evolution by one of the outstanding contributors to the building of the modern synthesis.

Futuyma, Douglas J. *Evolutionary Biology.* Second edition. Sunderland, Mass.: Sinauer, 1986. A first-rate textbook of evolutionary biology by a leading scholar. Contains excellent discussions of numerous theoretical and empirical questions.

Hatch, Elvin. *Culture and Morality: The Relativity of Values in Anthropology.* New York: Columbia University Press, 1983. An excellent discussion of cultural relativism in social science, with reference to its origins, its proponents and detractors, its strengths and weaknesses, and its current status in social science.

Hockett, Charles F., and Robert Ascher. "The Human Revolution." *Current Anthropology* 5: 135–168, 1964. A plausible and stimulating discussion of human origins with a primary focus on the evolution of language.

Krantz, Grover S. "Sapienization and Speech." *Current Anthropology* 21:773–792, 1980. A strikingly different view of the origin of language from that of Hockett and Ascher.

Lopreato, Joseph. *Human Nature and Biocultural Evolution.* Winchester, Mass.: Allen and Unwin, 1984. A very good, if typically overdone, plea for the relevance of sociobiology by a sociologist keenly aware of its limitations.

Nelson, Harry, and Robert Jurmain. *Introduction to Physical Anthropology.* Third edition. St. Paul, Minn.: West, 1985. An excellent textbook of physical anthropology that provides an intellectually solid and highly readable discussion of the current status of our knowledge of human biological evolution.

Woolfson, Charles. *The Labour Theory of Culture.* London: Routledge & Kegan Paul, 1982. An interesting use of contemporary evidence to defend Frederick Engels's theory of the role of tool use in shaping the nature and development of human culture.

CHAPTER 3

Sociocultural Systems and the Nature of Sociocultural Evolution

This chapter establishes some conceptual and theoretical foundations essential to the study of human social life. It further explores the concept of a sociocultural system by offering a tripartite scheme for classifying the basic components of sociocultural systems. The chapter also begins the study of sociocultural evolution. It discusses the general nature of this process and the various ways in which it may occur. The materialist evolutionary approach to the study of social life, touched on in Chapter 1, is explored more fully. The basic principles of this theoretical strategy are formally stated and discussed, and an attempt is made to demonstrate their usefulness as general theoretical tools.

THE BASIC COMPONENTS OF SOCIOCULTURAL SYSTEMS

The basic unit of macrosociological analysis is a **sociocultural system:** a collection of people who make use of various means of adapting to their physical environment, who engage in patterned forms of social conduct, and who create shared beliefs and values designed to make sense of their collective actions. However, as a starting point for systematic inquiry, it is necessary to break sociocultural systems down into their most essential components. This makes it possible to inquire into the relationships among the components, to see how one or more components may affect the others. Only in this way is it possible to see how sociocultural systems actually work as single functioning wholes.

Numerous ways of compartmentalizing sociocultural systems have been proposed by social scientists. The procedure offered in this book is quite similar to that developed by Marvin Harris (1979), who has presented a compartmentalizing scheme that elaborates on Marx's famous distinction between infrastructure and superstructure (see Table 3.1). This scheme is an extremely useful analytic device for understanding the structure and functioning of sociocultural systems.

Material Infrastructure

The **material infrastructure** consists of the basic raw materials and social forms pertinent to human survival and adaptation. A society's infrastructure is its most basic component in the sense that without it physical survival is literally

Table 3.1 THE BASIC COMPONENTS OF SOCIOCULTURAL SYSTEMS

Ideological superstructure	General ideology Religion Science Art Literature
Social structure	Social stratification (or its absence) Racial and ethnic stratification (or their absence) Polity Sexual division of labor and sexual inequality Family and kinship Education
Material infrastructure	Technology Economy Ecology Demography

impossible. The infrastructure is itself composed of four fundamental subunits:

1. ***Technology.*** **Technology** consists of the information, tools, and techniques with which humans adapt to their physical environment (Lenski, 1970). It consists not merely of physical or concrete tools or objects, but also of knowledge that humans can apply in particular ways. Thus, chairs, plows, and automobiles are elements of technology, but so are such things as knowing how to domesticate wild plants and animals.
2. ***Economy.*** A society's **economy** is the organized system whereby goods and services are produced, distributed, and exchanged among individuals and groups. *Production* refers to such things as what goods are produced, who produces them, what tools or techniques are used in their production, and who owns the basic materials that enter into the process of production. *Distribution* involves the manner in which the items produced are allocated to various individuals and groups within the society. *Exchange* is carried out when individuals and groups transfer valuables to one another in return for other valuables. A society's means of distributing goods and services is generally dependent upon the means by which they are produced.
3. ***Ecology.*** **Ecology** includes the totality of the physical environment to which humans must adapt. It involves such things as types of soils, the nature of climates, patterns of rainfall, the nature of plant and animal life, and the availability of natural resources. In a strict sense, ecology is not a part of a sociocultural system; it is the external environment to which sociocultural systems must adjust. However, since ecological factors are frequently crucial determinants of various aspects of social life, ecology is here treated as a fundamental component of sociocultural systems.
4. ***Demography.*** **Demographic** factors are those involving the nature and dynamics of human populations. The size and density of the population, its growth, decline, or stability, and its age and sex composition are important things to know in studying any society. Demographic factors also include techniques of population regulation or birth control and the intensity with which these are applied.

Social Structure

This component of a sociocultural system consists of the organized patterns of social life carried out among the members of a society, excluding those social patterns that belong to the infrastructure. It is imperative to note that the **social structure** always refers to actual behavioral patterns, as opposed to images or mental conceptions that people have about those patterns. In other words, the social structure consists of what people actually do, not what they say they do, think they do, or think they ought to do. For present purposes, the social structure consists of six subunits:

1. ***Social stratification (or its absence).*** Social stratification refers to the existence within a society of groups of unequal wealth and power. Not all societies have social stratification. In the study of any society, it is crucial to note whether or not it is stratified; if so, the particular nature and degree of stratification must be ascertained.
2. ***Racial and ethnic stratification (or their absence).*** This refers to whether or not there exist within a society groups that may be distinguished by racial or ethnic characteristics, and, if so, whether or not such groups occupy unequal positions with respect to each other. (Racial groups are those that are distinguishable on the basis of observable physical characteristics; ethnic groups are those that exhibit a cultural distinctiveness.) Many societies in human history have not had racial or ethnic stratification. In the past several hundred years, however, racial/ethnic stratification has been a prominent feature of numerous complex societies.
3. ***Polity.*** This refers to a society's organized means of maintaining internal law and order, as well as to its means of regulating or conducting intersocietal relationships. All societies have political systems, although the nature of such systems varies greatly from one society to another.
4. ***Sexual division of labor and sexual inequality.*** This involves the way in which men and women are allocated to specific tasks or roles within the social division of labor. It also includes the way in which and the degree to which men and women occupy positions of unequal rank, power, and privilege within a society. Although the sexual division of labor and sexual inequality are universal, there is great variation among societies in terms of the specific forms these phenomena take.
5. ***Family and kinship.*** All societies have family and kinship systems, or organized sociocultural patterns devoted to mating and reproduction. Once again, however, the specific nature of these systems varies greatly from one society to another. Furthermore, different subcultures within a society often reveal different family and kinship patterns.
6. ***Education.*** Education is any formalized or semiformalized system of cultural or intellectual instruction. Most societies have lacked highly formalized educational systems, but no society has failed to develop some sort of procedure for transmitting knowledge, skills, or values to the next generation.

Ideological Superstructure

The **ideological superstructure** involves the patterned ways in which the members of a society think, conceptualize, evaluate, and feel, as opposed to what they actually do. Whereas the structure refers to behavior, the superstructure refers to thought. The superstructure includes the following subcomponents:

1. ***General ideology.*** This refers to the predominant beliefs, values, and norms characteristic of a society or some segment of a society. **Beliefs** are shared cognitive assumptions about what is true and

what is false. They concern such things as the nature of the universe, what child-training techniques produce children with healthy personalities, what differences exist between men and women, and literally thousands of other things. **Values** are socially defined conceptions of worth. They order our experience of what is good and bad, right and wrong, beautiful and ugly, desirable and undesirable, and so on. **Norms** represent shared standards or rules regarding proper and improper social conduct. They are the do's and don'ts that societies attempt to instill in their members. All societies create beliefs, values, and norms, but the diversity of these phenomena is extraordinary.

2. ***Religion.*** Religion consists of shared beliefs and values pertaining to the postulation of supernatural beings, powers, or forces. Such beings, powers, or forces are generally held to intervene directly in the operation of society, or at least to have some indirect connection with it. Like many of the other components of sociocultural systems, religion is a universal feature of human social life.
3. ***Science.*** Science is a set of techniques for the acquisition of knowledge relying upon observation and experience (i.e., collection of factual evidence, demonstration, proof, etc.). It includes not only the techniques and procedures for producing knowledge, but also the accumulated body of knowledge itself. Conceived in this way, science is not a cultural universal, but has flourished only in certain places at certain times.
4. ***Art.*** Art is a universal component of sociocultural systems. It consists of the symbolic images or representations having esthetic, emotional, or intellectual value for the members of a society or segment of a society. The symbolic images or representations in question are of a physical nature.
5. ***Literature.*** Literature also consists of symbolic images or representations having esthetic, emotional, or intellectual value. However, in this case the images or representations are verbal (oral or written) rather than physical in nature. Conceived in this way, myth, legend, and the plays of Shakespeare all count as literature.

THE NATURE OF SOCIOCULTURAL EVOLUTION

What Is Sociocultural Evolution?

One problem with using the term **evolution** to identify changes that occur in sociocultural systems is that the literal meaning of the term is itself misleading. As Elman Service (1971a) has noted, the term derives from the Latin *evolutis*, meaning an "unrolling." This clearly implies that evolution involves an "unfolding" or a "development," a process whereby a sociocultural system comes to realize the potentialities originally inherent within it. It implies that evolution is movement toward some "goal" or final end state, that societies evolve in much the same way that the embryo matures to become a healthy organism living outside its mother's body. The problem is that sociocultural evolution is not like that at all. As in the case of biological evolution, there is no ultimate "purpose" or "goal" to sociocultural evolution. There is no "unfolding" toward some end state.

In order to avoid misconstruing the nature of sociocultural evolution, it is necessary to stay clear of the literal meaning of the term and the dangers with which it is fraught. As a rough first approximation, we can define **sociocultural evolution** as *a process of change whereby one sociocultural form is transformed into another.* Conceptualized in this way, sociocultural evolution is a process involving *qualitative*, rather than quantitative, change. Quantitative changes are changes from less of something to more of something, or vice versa. Qualitative changes, by contrast, are those in which a new *type* or *form* replaces an old type or form. Of course, qualitative changes are themselves the results of a series of prior quantitative changes. When quantitative changes accumulate over time they eventually result in those kinds of transformations that we term qualitative. Nonetheless, we cannot really speak of evolutionary transformation until the level of qualitative change has been reached. Thus the shift of a society from dependence upon hunting and gathering to dependence upon agriculture for its food supply is an evolutionary change, as is the shift from agriculture to industry. Likewise, the emergence within a society of social class divisions where none existed before is an evolutionary change. The expansion of the number of villages found within a society, however, is not an evolutionary change so long as the new villages are essentially replicas of the old ones.

But there is somewhat more to the notion of evolution than is implied by the idea of qualitative change. Therefore, to complete our definition of sociocultural evolution we need to add that *it is change that exhibits a certain directionality.* What is meant is that sociocultural evolution is patterned change that manifests a trend of a linear nature. For example, changes in the level of technology that increase the sophistication and efficiency of tools and productive techniques signify a directional trend. Such a trend is also indicated by an increase in the level and intensity of class inequality.

Many evolutionists have thought that the chief directional trend in sociocultural evolution is that of increased societal complexity (cf. Parsons, 1966, 1971). Robert Carneiro (1972), for example, has claimed that in fact this is what evolution is—change in a direction of increasing complexity—and that any other use of the concept weakens and debases it. But while it must be acknowledged that growing social complexity is an important dimension of social evolution, there is no warrant for regarding it as the only, or as the most important, dimension. Sociocultural evolution has many dimensions, and thus many directional trends, and we should not restrict ourselves to analyzing a single one.

Sociocultural evolution involves both entire sociocultural systems and the individual components of such systems. What normally occurs is that change begins in one component (or subcomponent) and this change produces changes in the other components. An entire chain of cause and effect is set off that eventually results in the transformation of entire sociocultural systems.

Some scholars have insisted upon a distinction between the terms *history* and *evolution*. Most notable in this regard is Leslie White (1945). White's argument is that history is concerned with unique events or changes, while evolution involves *patterns* of change characteristic of human societies in general. According to this view, to be concerned with history is to limit one's attention to the specific details of historical change going on within any particular society; to be concerned with evolution, however, is to extend one's analysis to the regular and systematic changes characteristic of all or most societies. While there is some justification for White's distinction, it is rather artificial and overdrawn. All changes in sociocultural systems may be regarded as evolutionary to the extent that they involve qualitative and directional transformations of the whole or one or more of the parts. This is true, whether such changes occur in only one society or whether there are similar changes occurring within hundreds of societies (Harris, 1968). However, true to at least the spirit of White's claim, we shall seek an understanding of those major evolutionary transformations that have characterized a large number of the world's societies.

Special care must be taken to avoid identifying sociocultural evolution with progress. This was the great error of the major nineteenth-century evolutionists. These thinkers tended to read into evolution a general record of improvement in human rationality, morality, and happiness, and for this they were justifiably criticized by later scholars. The term *progress* is a moral notion and should not be applied to data gathered in the scientific attempt to understand basic patterns of evolutionary change. Since all societies represent, to one extent or another, adaptive solutions to fundamental human needs, it is an error of the utmost seriousness to assume that some societies are superior to others simply because they occur later in history or because they are more evolutionarily complex.

Parallel, Convergent, and Divergent Evolution

Sociocultural evolution is not a singular, unitary process occurring in the same way in all societies. Like biological evolution, sociocultural evolution has a "dual" character (Sahlins, 1960). On the one hand, it is a process involving the overall transformation of human societies. It exhibits a general character and directional pattern in the case of all societies that undergo it. This process is usually known as *general evolution* (Sahlins, 1960). On the other hand, sociocultural evolution reveals an adaptive diversification along many different lines in many societies. The specific details of evolutionary change commonly differ from one society to another. This pattern of change is typically called *specific evolution* (Sahlins, 1960).

This distinction can be further clarified by introducing three additional concepts: parallel, convergent, and divergent evolution (Harris, 1968). **Parallel evolution** occurs when two or more societies evolve in basically similar ways and at similar rates. Beginning about 10,000 years ago, for example, human communities in various regions of the world independently began to domesticate plants and animals and subsist by agriculture rather than by hunting and gathering. The adoption of agriculture in these communities led to strikingly similar changes in their overall sociocultural patterns. **Convergent evolution** results when societies that have originally been dissimilar evolve in ways that make them increasingly alike. The United States and Japan, for example, have evolved along convergent lines in the past hundred years or so. **Divergent evolution** occurs when originally similar societies evolve along lines of increasing dissimilarity. An excellent example of this phenomenon results from the comparison of Japan and Indonesia (Geertz, 1963). These societies were very similar in the early seventeenth century, but today they are strikingly different: Japan is a modern industrial nation with a high standard of living, while Indonesia is a poor, underdeveloped country. (Some of the reasons for the divergence between Japan and Indonesia will be suggested in Chapter 9.)

These forms of evolution constitute the fundamental ways in which evolutionary transformations have occurred throughout human history, and social-scientific efforts are devoted to studying all of them. However, considerable evidence suggests that parallel and convergent evolution have been much more prominent features of human history than divergent evolution (Harris, 1968). This book therefore gives primary emphasis to parallelism and convergence, while at the same time not neglecting divergent outcomes.

Continuity, Devolution, and Extinction

Sociocultural evolution is a pervasive feature of human social life, and there is no such thing as a society that is completely static or unchanging. Nevertheless, there are numerous examples of societies that have presumably undergone no significant changes for thousands of years. This phenomenon is called **sociocultural continuity.** Many hunting and gathering societies, for instance, have survived into the present, and the majority of them have probably experienced no major change for hundreds or thousands of years.

Just as it is imperative to ask why some societies undergo major transformations, it is necessary to ask why others do not. Sociocultural evolution is an adaptive result of changing conditions. Societies evolve in order to meet new demands and needs. However, societies do not always confront new demands and needs. In such situations, existing sociocultural patterns are adequate for solving the basic problems of human existence, and no evolutionary changes need be undergone. Continuity, then, like evolution, is an adaptive process. Which of these will occur depends upon whether or not the basic underlying conditions necessary to human existence and well-being are changing or remaining the same.

Most human societies are characterized either by relative stability or by evolutionary transformation. In some instances, however, a society may undergo a **devolutionary** change: it may shift back to a form with characteristics of an earlier evolutionary stage. This might mean a decrease in societal complexity, or perhaps a loss of social cohesion. A striking illustration of such an occurrence comes from Colin Turnbull's (1972) description of the Ik of Uganda. The Ik were a hunting and gathering people who experienced economic disaster when their traditional hunting grounds were turned into a game preserve by the Ugandan government. This event precipitated the virtual collapse of the Ik sociocultural system. With the loss of their traditional means of subsistence, and with the shift to agriculture made difficult or impossible, the Ik experienced a substantial decline in population, lost their basis of political cohesion, and even experienced a general erosion of relationships among family members. What resulted was a way of life in which the social ties between all persons were largely broken.

Another example of a devolutionary transformation is the collapse of the Roman Empire in the fifth century A.D. Rome had created a huge empire, which extended all the way from Egypt in the south to the British Isles in the north. The diverse regions of the empire were linked by a marvelous system of roads, and the empire was centralized economically, politically, and militarily. When the empire finally collapsed after a long and slow period of decline, Europe devolved into a vast region filled with by and large economically self-sufficient villages and principalities.

Some societies, of course, come to be extinguished altogether. This process is known as **sociocultural extinction.** Such a fate has happened to numerous hunting and gathering societies in recent times, as well as to various societies of greater evolutionary complexity. A sociocultural system can become extinct either through the complete physical extermination of its members, or through its absorption into another society by means of political conquest. Both of these processes have occurred frequently in human history, especially since the rise of modern capitalism in the sixteenth century. The North American continent, for example, was once filled with hundreds of Indian tribes. With the emergence and expansion of the new American civilization, most of the members of these tribes were killed in bloody wars. Those who remained were eventually herded onto reservations, their aboriginal way of life largely lost.

Sociocultural Evolution as an Adaptive Process

This book emphasizes the adaptive character of sociocultural evolution and therefore makes extensive use of the concept of **sociocultural adaptation.** Unfortunately, the concept of adaptation is a highly contentious one in modern sociology. Some sociologists reject the concept altogether, claiming that it is an inherently functionalist one that has markedly conservative connotations (Zeitlin, 1973; Giddens, 1981). These sociologists recommend that it therefore be discarded. However, such radical surgery is by no means called for. The concept is a useful—indeed, necessary—one that we would be extremely foolish to abandon. What is called for is not abandonment of the concept, but careful clarification of it.

A session of the Roman Senate. The collapse of the Roman Empire and the devolution of Europe into the Dark Ages and feudalism show that not all major social transformations involve increasing sociocultural complexity.

A crucial beginning point is an often overlooked distinction between adaptation and *adaptedness*. Elliott Sober (1984) has argued that this distinction is essential for thinking about biological evolution, and his argument can be extended to sociocultural evolution. The difference between these two concepts is essentially one between the *origins* of a sociocultural trait and the *consequences* of that trait for the individuals (and their progeny) who originated it. We may say that an *adaptation* is a sociocultural trait that has originated as a result of the needs, aims, and desires of individuals. To say that this trait leads to a form of adaptedness, however, is to acknowledge that the trait actually is effective in satisfying the needs, aims, and desires of the individuals who originated it as an adaptation. Now it is usually the case that the two—adaptation and adaptedness—correspond, but there are often exceptions to this general rule, and these exceptions are of great significance for sociological analysis. To illustrate this point, we can consider an adaptation that actually leads to adaptedness, as well as two that do not, at least in the long run.

In India Hindu peasant farmers for many hundreds of years have regarded cattle as sacred beasts that should be protected from slaughter and consumption. This fascinating and often puzzling phenomenon can be regarded as an adaptation originated by Hindu farmers in coping with the unique technological, demographic, economic, and ecological conditions that they faced at an earlier point in history, and that they continue to face (see the Special Topic at the end of the chapter). From all appearances, this adaptation has led to adaptedness in that, given their circumstances, Hindu farmers have been far better off with it than without it. So adaptation and adaptedness correspond.

But consider two other instances of adaptations that lead to different results. In Chapter 9 it is argued that family size tends to be large in many of the poorer countries of the modern world because in these countries most people live by traditional forms of agriculture. Peasant farmers in these societies desire large families because by having many children they are increasing their supply of farm labor, and the more farm workers they have the greater their chance of improving the productivity of the farm and their overall level of economic well-being. Therefore, large family size is an adaptation from the point of view of each peasant couple, and this adaptation may lead to an initial state of adaptedness. However, what is adaptive in the short run for one peasant couple may not be adaptive for all peasant couples in the long run. The aggregate effect of each peasant couple's having a large family is a high rate of population growth for the society as a whole, and the end result of this process is greater population pressure against resources and a lower standard of living for each peasant couple. Thus, what started out as an adaptation paradoxically ends up being maladaptive in the long run. (The biologist Garrett Hardin [1968] has given this process and others like it a graphic name: "the tragedy of the commons.")

Another example of this kind of process involves educational expansion in modern societies. In Chapter 17 it is shown that a major cause of the expansion of modern educational systems is the competition among individuals for educational credentials. Individuals seek these credentials largely for their economic value—for their capacity to be converted into desirable jobs. As more and more individuals attain diplomas and degrees, their value declines simply by virtue of the increased supply of credential holders in the population. What are individuals to do with cheapened degrees? They can either lower their occupational aspirations or they can stay in school longer and get even higher degrees. If many do the latter, then education continues to expand and the occupational value of degrees continues to fall, both of which necessitate a new wave of degree seeking, and the cycle continues. What we have here is a spiraling process that feeds on itself. And it is clearly a process that originated as an adaptation—as a response of individuals toward meeting their needs and desires—but that ends up producing maladaptive consequences in the long run—cheapened degrees, more time spent in school, and so on.

The above examples show that the concept of adaptation is a delicate and subtle one that must be used judiciously. These examples also relate to another caution about the use of the concept: that it not be confused with some notion about what is "good" or "morally desirable." A claim about adaptation is a scientific assessment of how various types of sociocultural patterns originate, persist, and change. A claim about "goodness," by contrast, is completely different. It is a judgment about whether we like or approve of the things that people do. Thus, it is perfectly possible to identify a sociocultural pattern as an adaptation (and as adaptive) and feel a moral repugnance for that pattern. For example, the Yanomamo Indians of South America regularly slaughter one another in deadly wars and kill a given proportion of their female infants, yet such practices can be seen as highly adaptive (Harris, 1974, 1977). To understand this fact is to make a scientific statement, not a judgment of moral desirability.

We also need to be clear about the kind of unit to which the concept of adaptation applies—about just what it is that does the adapting. Some sociologists have assumed that it is an entire sociocultural system. This is especially true of the functionalists and functionalist evolutionists (cf. Parsons, 1966, 1971). But such a notion is misplaced. As argued in Chapter 1, sociocultural systems are not comparable to organisms or individual persons; they do not have needs or desires, and thus they cannot adapt to anything. Since only individual persons have needs and desires, only they can be units of adaptation. Of course, we sometimes speak about whether or not a sociocultural trait is adaptive for a group or even a whole society, but when we do this it is clear that we can only be referring to an aggregate of individuals, and that it is from the point of view of each separate individual that the adaptation or adaptedness is judged.

This leads us to recognize another crucial point strongly emphasized by the conflict theorists: that an adaptive sociocultural pattern may not be equally beneficial for all individuals or groups within a society. It is frequently the case that a pattern that benefits some individuals or groups is maladaptive for others. Indeed, the more evolutionarily complex a society the more this is likely to be the case. Early industrial capitalism, for example, was adaptive for wealthy factory owners, but it was highly maladaptive for the thousands of factory workers who died from exhaustion, malnutrition, and disease (Engels, 1973; orig. 1845). And it is very unlikely that modern world capitalism is adaptive for more than a minority of the world's population (see Chapter 9).

It is extremely important to recognize that it is entirely inappropriate to claim that adaptedness is somehow a quality that increases throughout sociocultural evolution. Many evolutionists have equated sociocultural evolution with improved adaptedness, claiming that evolutionarily later societies have increased their "adaptive capacity." This idea has been promoted most strongly by Talcott Parsons and other functionalist evolutionists, but it has also been endorsed by some materialist evolutionists (cf. Childe, 1936; White, 1959). However, this book strongly rejects such a view, which tends toward ethnocentrism and which is difficult to support by scientifically objective criteria (Granovetter, 1979). New sociocultural forms emerge as adaptations, but these altered adaptations are simply *new* rather than *better* ones.*

Finally, we must acknowledge that not all sociocultural patterns are adaptations, and thus the concept of adaptation does not have universal applicability. But even though we cannot use the concept everywhere and at all times, we are still far better off with it than without it. Indeed, by having a notion of adaptation as a guiding element we will be in a position to identify which sociocultural traits are not adaptations and why they are not.

Biological Versus Sociocultural Evolution

Social scientists have long been interested in the relationship between biological and sociocultural evolution. These processes possess both important parallels and significant differences, and it may be instructive to outline them.

Two basic similarities between these types of evolution can be identified. In the first place, both biological and sociocultural evolution are adaptive processes (again, in the precise sense in which we are using the concepts of adaptation and adaptedness). New biological forms, like new sociocultural patterns, arise largely as adaptations to changing circumstances. Second,

*Actually, in a number of important respects the level of adaptedness clearly *decreases* throughout long-term sociocultural evolution. This will become apparent throughout this book, but Chapter 20 summarizes the most important regressive dimensions of sociocultural evolution.

both forms of evolution have the "dual" character identified by Marshall Sahlins: both exhibit overall directional tendencies along with a variety of radiations along many specific lines.

We could go further and say that the processes of parallel, convergent, and divergent evolution apply to both biological and sociocultural evolution. This would be technically true, but it would also be misleading, because most biological evolution is in fact divergent evolution (the preferred biological term is *cladogenesis*). Most biological evolution involves the adaptive radiation of species at the same phylogenetic level, and evolutionary shifts to new phylogenetic levels are a relatively rare occurrence (Stebbins, 1969, 1974). By contrast, most sociocultural evolution is of the parallel and convergent types. This means that biological evolutionists spend most of their time studying the production of unique life forms, whereas social evolutionists concentrate their energies on the emergence of similar sociocultural patterns in various regions of the world (Sanderson, 1990).

A second difference involves the extent to which sociocultural evolution can be said to be based on a process of natural selection. Since much of sociocultural evolution does involve the selection of adaptive traits, it does involve a kind of natural selection process (cf. Carneiro, 1985). However, this is true only in the most general way. Strictly speaking, the way in which natural selection works in the biological world is quite different from the way it works in social life. The difference involves the source of the variations on which selection operates. We have seen that in biological evolution the variations that are selected for or against—genetic mutations—arise entirely at random. Although some social evolutionists claim that sociocultural variations arise in the same way (Campbell, 1965; Langton, 1979), this is very unlikely. There is overwhelming evidence that most sociocultural innovations are deliberately introduced and are anything but random (Cavalli-Sforza and Feldman, 1981; Hallpike, 1986).

Two other differences between evolution in the two realms are also important. One of these has to do with the pace of change. Sociocultural evolution is extraordinarily faster, even taking into account the first 99 percent of human history (approximately three million years), during which things changed very slowly. In fact, sociocultural evolution has itself evolved, so that the pace of change is now exceptionally rapid. (The extraordinary rapidity of sociocultural evolution is obviously linked to the fact that sociocultural variations are deliberate and purposive rather than random.) Finally, there is a sociocultural evolutionary process known as **diffusion** that has no parallel in the biological world. Diffusion involves the spread of sociocultural traits from one sociocultural system to another. This may occur through deliberate borrowing or through the imposition of a set of traits by a more powerful society on a weaker one. Often diffusion makes up for invention in the sense that a society can take from another what it would otherwise be interested in developing on its own (Ingold, 1986). There is nothing like this process in the world of nature. Organisms cannot borrow genes from each other in order to cope with changing environmental conditions.

THE MATERIALIST APPROACH TO SOCIOCULTURAL STRUCTURE AND EVOLUTION

The most important question about sociocultural systems concerns the causes of their specific features and the changes these undergo. As mentioned in Chapter 1, this book takes a **materialist** approach to the nature of causation. The contemporary materialist approach to the study of social life finds its roots in the "materialist conception of history" of Marx and Engels. However, the modern version of the materialist strategy is a substantial elaboration of their ideas. Like Marx and Engels, contemporary materialists see such material factors as technology and economy as being among the leading causes of social life. But they also expand the notion of material factors to include ecological and demographic variables, and they see these as additional leading causes of sociocultural phenomena. Contemporary materialism is thus a more complex and sophisticated version of the original Marxian form. The most insistent contemporary spokesman for a materialist theoretical strategy is Marvin Harris (1974, 1977, 1979), whose ideas provide the foundation for much of the materialist theoretical argument developed here.

The materialist approach is a general theoretical strategy designed to explain the basic features of sociocultural systems and the parallel, convergent, and divergent evolutionary changes these features undergo. It is also designed to explain sociocultural continuity, devolution, and extinction. In fact, the totality of sociocultural similarities and differences represents its arena of application. Since the materialist approach is a theoretical strategy, there are many specific materialist *theories* that are included within it. Many of these theories will be discussed in the following chapters.

General Nature of the Materialist Approach

The materialist theoretical approach used in this book specifies that a society's infrastructure is the primary cause of its structure, and the structure, in turn, is the primary cause of its superstructure. That is, infrastructural conditions are the primary causes of a society's basic patterns of interpersonal behavior, and these behavioral patterns in turn call forth specific patterns of thought that justify and interpret behavioral realities. Ideas therefore find their origin in the concrete patterns of behavior systematically engaged in by the members of a society, and these patterns of behavior originate in conjunction with the infrastructural conditions whereby people solve the basic problems of human existence.

The materialist approach is, of course, a means of explaining both the structure and evolution of sociocultural systems. As an approach to evolution, it holds that change ordinarily begins in one or more infrastructural factors. Changes within the infrastructure subsequently lead to reverberating changes in both the structure and the superstructure. Hence, changes in modes of thinking ordinarily depend upon prior changes in patterns of behavior, and these latter changes are themselves largely products of prior infrastructural changes.

The materialist strategy holds that infrastructural factors are the primary, but not the only, causes of structural and superstructural phenomena. Indeed, the structure and the superstructure have a partial independence from the infrastructure, and they may occasionally act as causal forces in their own right. However, the impact of structure and superstructure on the infrastructure is much less than is the reverse.

One great advantage of the materialist approach is that it provides a logical set of research

Marvin Harris. Harris taught for many years at Columbia University and is currently a research professor of anthropology at the University of Florida. He is perhaps the most vigorous spokesman for a materialist approach to social life and has done much toward creating his own version of such an approach.

priorities for the study of sociocultural life. As Harris (1979) notes, it directs any investigator to begin the search for the causes of sociocultural phenomena with the examination of infrastructural conditions. It is likely that these conditions provide the clue to explaining the phenomenon in question. If a diligent search fails to reveal the causal impact of infrastructural factors, an investigator is warranted to turn to the examination of structural conditions as possible causes of the phenomenon. Failure to find structural causes in turn licenses the investigator to explore the possibility of superstructural causation. Thus, superstructural causation may be searched for only after the investigator has failed to demonstrate the operation of infrastructural and structural causes. This sort of approach is immensely preferable to those frequently employed by other investigators: reversing the procedure by working from superstructure to structure to infrastructure, or assuming that all three components have a mutual causal influence upon each other.

This brief discussion of the materialist approach is necessarily a somewhat oversimplified account of the nature of causation in sociocultural systems. It does not specify, for instance, which particular infrastructural factor or factors may be most causally important in any given situation. However, it is impossible to make a statement to this effect in the abstract. Depending upon the phenomenon under investigation, any infrastructural factor (or any combination of factors) may be of prime causal importance. In some cases technological factors may be of greatest significance, while in other cases ecological, demographic, or economic factors may assume causal priority. Specification of the precise nature of infrastructural causation can only be done through the investigation of concrete sociocultural phenomena.

Related to the above problem is the fact that causal relationships exist *within*, and not simply among, the sociocultural components themselves. Ecological and demographic factors, for example, are among the primary determinants of the level of technology, and the latter in turn is an important cause of the nature of the economic system (see Chapter 4). Furthermore, the presence of social stratification, itself an element of the social structure, is an important cause of other elements of the structure. Although these problems are noted here, there will be no attempt to build into our abstract materialist formulation all of the causal relationships that exist within and among the basic sociocultural components. To do this would make it unwieldy and hence reduce its usefulness as a general analytic tool.

The Logical Priority of Infrastructure

There are essentially two ways in which a materialist approach to social life can be shown to be preferable to any of the theoretical alternatives that currently exist in the social sciences. One way is to submit the materialist strategy to detailed and rigorous empirical testing against a wide range of sociocultural differences and similarities. If a materialist strategy can successfully explain a large number of these differences and similarities, then the theoretical utility of the approach is at once confirmed. This book takes the position that such rigorous empirical testing has been carried out on a wide enough scale, and with sufficiently satisfactory results, that the usefulness of the approach can no longer be seriously doubted. A materialist approach is unable to explain all relevant sociocultural phenomena, but an approach that could do so does not exist. In any event, the materialist approach has had far greater explanatory success than any of its competitors, and that alone is sufficient justification for its employment as a general theoretical strategy.

The other way of justifying the choice of a materialist strategy rests on logical, rather than empirical, grounds. It is claimed that infrastructural factors have a logical causal priority over structural and superstructural factors. Materialists hold that infrastructural variables take priority because they constitute the fundamental means whereby human beings solve the most basic problems of human existence. Before humans can formulate marriage rules, organize political systems, and construct abstract religious concepts, they must organize the means whereby they will survive. Marx and Engels clearly understood this elementary fact. As Engels put it in his famous eulogy at Marx's graveside (Engels, 1963:188–189; orig. 1883):

> Just as Darwin discovered the law of evolution in organic nature, so Marx discovered the law of evolution in human history; he discovered the simple fact, hitherto concealed by an overgrowth of ideology, that mankind must first of all eat and drink, have shelter and clothing, before it can pursue politics, science, religion, art, etc., and that therefore the production of the immediate material means of subsistence and consequently the degree of economic development attained by a given people or during a given epoch, form the foundation upon which the state institutions, the legal conceptions, the art and even the religious ideas of the people concerned have been evolved, and in the light of which these things must therefore be explained, instead of *vice versa* as had hitherto been the case.

Marvin Harris has argued for the logical priority of infrastructure along similar lines (1979:57):

> Infrastructure . . . is the principal interface between culture and nature, the boundary across which the ecological, chemical, and physical restraints to which human action is subject interact with the principal sociocultural practices aimed at overcoming or modifying those restraints. The order of cultural materialist priorities from infrastructure to the remaining behavioral components and finally to the mental superstructure reflects the increasing remoteness of these components from the culture/nature interface. . . . Priority for theory building logically settles upon those sectors under the greatest direct restraints from the givens of nature. To endow the mental superstructure with strategic priority, as the cultural idealists advocate, is a bad bet. Nature is indifferent to whether God is a loving father or a bloodthirsty cannibal. But nature is not indifferent to whether the fallow period in a swidden field is one year or ten. We know that powerful restraints exist on the infrastructural level; hence it is a good bet that these restraints are passed on to the structural and superstructural components.

THE MAJOR PRINCIPLES OF THE MATERIALIST EVOLUTIONARY THEORETICAL STRATEGY

The materialist evolutionary approach to sociocultural life has certain major principles that serve as the guiding themes throughout the remainder of this book.

The Principle of Sociocultural Adaptation

The **Principle of Sociocultural Adaptation** holds that sociocultural phenomena are adaptive consequences of the basic needs and desires of human beings. This means that social patterns are generally created by humans as rational responses to the fundamental problems that they must solve. When the nature of these problems changes, the responses to them change as well. All of the cautions we discussed earlier about use of the terms *adaptation* and *adaptedness* apply fully to the application of this principle.

The Conflict Principle

The **Conflict Principle** is really derived from a conflict theoretical strategy, but it also typically plays an important role in the thinking of most materialists. It holds that conflict or struggle among individuals and groups over scarce resources is a pervasive occurrence in social life, and that such conflict is an important determinant of basic sociocultural patterns. Conflict most frequently occurs over the material resources that support human existence. Such conflict often leads to social stratification: to the formation of sociocultural patterns in which some groups gain economic and political dominance over others. Emerging patterns of social stratification play a significant role in shaping other aspects of sociocultural life.

The Conflict Principle asserts that people generally act so as to maximize their own interests, whether as individuals or as members of larger social groups. Under many conditions, the attempt to maximize individual or group interest results in overt conflict and structured patterns of economic and political dominance and subordination. These patterns are frequently productive of further conflict and struggle. However, under some circumstances (to be specified in later chapters), the attempt to maximize self-interest takes the form of cooperation and harmony rather than overt conflict. Individuals frequently cooperate with each other because they recognize that such cooperation is essential to their own survival and well-being. This phenomenon has been labeled **antagonistic cooperation** or **enlightened self-interest** (Lenski, 1966).

The Principle of Infrastructural Determinism

The **Principle of Infrastructural Determinism,** the most important of all the principles of the materialist evolutionary strategy, has already been discussed. It holds that infrastructural factors are the primary causes of structural and superstructural arrangements. It is designed to explain the entire range of sociocultural similarities and differences that result from sociocultural continuity, evolution, and devolution.

The Principle of Sociocultural Integration

The **Principle of Sociocultural Integration** refers to the tendency of the major components of sociocultural systems to fit together into a more or less consistent whole. Any particular kind of infrastructure is compatible with only a limited range of structures and superstructures. While it is not possible to make precise predictions about the nature of structure and superstructure from a knowledge of infrastructure, it is certainly possible to indicate the kinds of structures or superstructures that would rarely or never be found with a particular infrastructure. For example, centralized governments are never found among hunting and gathering societies, but all modern industrialized societies have them. Likewise, societies dependent upon simple forms of agriculture for their food supply commonly have elaborate kinship groups known as clans, but such kin groups are never found in modern industrial societies.

SUMMARY

1. A useful way of compartmentalizing sociocultural systems is the tripartite distinction between infrastructure, structure, and superstructure. The infrastructure consists of the raw materials and organizational forms necessary for the production and reproduction of human social life; the structure, of the basic patterns of regularized social behavior characteristic of the members of a society; the superstructure, of the symbols, thoughts, ideas, and ideals shared by individuals as members of society.

2. Sociocultural evolution is a process of directional social change involving the transformation of old social forms into new ones. One important dimension of the directionality of social evolution is that of increasing societal complexity. However, this is only one of several important dimensions.

3. Social scientists generally use the term

evolution to refer to broad changes that have occurred in at least several societies, but it may appropriately be used as well to refer to unique social transformations.

4. Many social scientists believe that sociocultural evolution is necessarily a process of "unrolling," one in which societies pass through stages of development toward some end state or goal. It is also often assumed that this alleged developmental process involves progress or improvement in the human condition. But these connotations of the concept of sociocultural evolution are flatly rejected in the present book.

5. It is necessary to recognize three different types of evolutionary change: parallel, convergent, and divergent evolution. Parallel evolution involves a similar type, rate, and direction of change in several societies; convergent evolution occurs when dissimilar societies become increasingly alike; and divergent evolution occurs when societies change in increasingly dissimilar ways. The first two appear to have been the most prominent types in human history.

6. Not all societies undergo evolutionary modifications. Some remain more or less the same, even for thousands of years, a process known as sociocultural continuity. Many societies have been obliterated altogether due to the encroachment of more powerful societies; this has been a frequent result of the expansion of Western capitalism. Occasionally societies change in a direction of increasing simplicity of organization; this process is known as devolutionary change.

7. Sociocultural evolution is an adaptive process, which means that it occurs as a result of the efforts made by individuals to achieve their needs and wants. Sociocultural traits that arise as the result of adaptations generally produce adaptive—that is, beneficial or favorable—effects on the individuals who originated them. However, in various instances, adaptations may actually lead to maladaptive consequences, at least over the long run and for some individuals and groups.

8. The basic unit of sociocultural adaptation is the individual person, not a sociocultural system. Sociocultural systems do not have needs, desires, or purposes; only individuals do. Hence, only individuals can adapt to anything.

9. Use of the concept of adaptation often leads to the misunderstanding that adaptation is something that improves with sociocultural evolution. Some evolutionists maintain that this is so, but the present book vigorously rejects such a notion. New sociocultural adaptations are more accurately described simply as different, rather than better, social forms.

10. Sociocultural and biological evolution are processes that share both similarities and differences. The main similarities concern their adaptive and their "dual" characters. The basic differences between them involve the pace of evolution; the origin of variations; the fact that most biological evolution is divergent, whereas most sociocultural evolution is parallel and convergent; and the fact that the sociocultural process of diffusion has no parallel in biological evolution.

11. The basic theoretical model of sociocultural structure and evolution used throughout this book is a materialist model. It holds that the material infrastructure constitutes the foundation on which the other components of society are built. Changes tend to occur in it first, and these changes produce reverberating changes in the other components. Those who adhere to the materialist model use it as a starting point for their analyses and are persistent in their search for material causes of social life. Structural and superstructural factors are entertained as possible causal variables only after a conscientious search for material causes has proven fruitless.

12. A materialist model may be justified on empirical or logical grounds. This book attempts to present a large mass of empirical evidence to support the model. But the model may also be justified logically by assuming that material conditions have a priority in the organization of social life because they involve the most fundamental areas of human concern.

13. The basic theoretical principles used in this book are the Principle of Sociocultural Adaptation, which holds that people create social patterns as responses to their needs and desires; the Conflict Principle, which suggests that people generally behave in accordance with their self-interests, and that the social conflict, domination, and subordination that result from this play a major role in shaping social patterns; the Principle of Infrastructural Determinism, which emphasizes the causal priority of the material conditions of social life; and the Principle of Sociocultural Integration, which suggests a minimal consistency among the parts of sociocultural life.

SPECIAL TOPIC: SACRED COWS AND ABOMINABLE PIGS

One of the best-known applications of the materialist evolutionary perspective is Marvin Harris's examination of the origins of religiously based food taboos. Harris has devoted particular attention to explaining why in India the Hindu religion considers the cow sacred and regards beef as forbidden flesh. He has also made a rather thorough study of the ancient Israelites' taboo on the consumption of pork because they viewed the pig as a dirty animal. He believes that these food taboos can best be understood as adaptive responses to the specific constellation of material conditions faced by the populations that adopted them.

It is widely known that a central tenet of Hindu religious ideology is the sanctification of the cow. The cow is regarded as a holy animal, the slaughter and consumption of which is unthinkable. To most Westerners this taboo is a clear case of the irrational mismanagement of resources and is responsible for the perpetuation of widespread poverty and misery on the Indian subcontinent. The whole complex of cow worship is thought to be a classic example of the way in which mystical religious practices lead to undesirable and unnecessary economic results. But Harris (1974, 1977) thinks this is not the case, and in fact believes that the Hindu cow love complex is a rational—indeed, necessary—response to the ecological and economic circumstances in which the great majority of Indian peasant farmers find themselves.

Harris claims that the cow performs vital functions in the context of the Indian ecology and economy, functions that it can perform only if kept alive. Cow dung is particularly valuable to the Indian farmer. It serves as a fertilizer for the fields, as a source of fuel for cooking, and, when mixed with water to form a paste, as an acceptable flooring material for houses. But by far the most useful role played by the cow is that of traction animal for the plowing of fields. Since Indian farmers cannot buy tractors, the cow is the only means by which they can plow. As Harris has argued emphatically, Indian farmers who yielded to temptation in times of particular stress to slaughter their cattle for food would in fact be bringing disaster upon themselves, for they would never be able to plow again. Hence, the cow is far more useful alive than dead to the average Indian farmer. However, since the temptation to slaughter one's cattle during periods of drought or famine was an ever-recurrent problem to most Indian farmers, it was necessary to find a means of removing this temptation. This means, Harris claims, was found in the establishment of a religious taboo deifying the cow and making it an unholy and unthinkable act to kill and consume it. As Harris has put it (1977:147):

Indian sacred cattle. Much misunderstanding has existed concerning their role in Indian social and economic life.

> *The tabooing of beef was the cumulative result of the individual decisions of millions and millions of individual farmers, some of whom were better able to resist the temptation of slaughtering their livestock because they strongly believed that the life of a cow or an ox was a holy thing. Those who held such beliefs were much more likely to hold onto their farms, and to pass them on to their children, than those who believed differently. . . . Cattle had to be treated like human beings because human beings who ate their cattle were one step away from eating each other. To this day, monsoon farmers who yield to temptation and slaughter their cattle seal their doom. They can never plow again even when the rains fall. They must sell their farms and migrate to the cities. Only those who would starve rather than eat an ox or cow can survive a season of scanty rains.*

Just how the cow came to be sanctified in India can be better understood through a sense of historical perspective. As Harris notes, throughout much of Indian history cattle were regularly eaten and there was nothing considered particularly holy about them. He believes that it may not have been until sometime after 700 A.D. that the cow love complex developed into its now familiar form. Regardless of exactly when the cow came to be worshiped in India, we do know that Brahman priests were "for centuries the sacrificers and consumers of animal flesh" (Harris, 1977:145). Under what kinds of conditions would these priests have been transformed from ritual sacrificers of cattle into their ritual protectors? Harris suggests that the answer to this question involves increasing population density and declining standards of living (1977:146):

As population density grew, farms became increasingly smaller and only the most essential domesticated species could be allowed to share the land. Cattle were the one species that could not be eliminated. They were the animals that drew the plows upon which the entire cycle of rainfall agriculture depended. At least two oxen had to be kept per family, plus one cow with which to breed replacements when the oxen wore out. Cattle thus became the central focus of the religious taboo on meat eating. As the sole remaining farm animals, they were potentially the only remaining source of meat. To slaughter them for meat, however, constituted a threat to the whole mode of food production. And so beef was tabooed.

It is also commonly known that modern Judaism bans the eating of pork. Indeed, since the ancient Israelites, Judaism has officially regarded the pig as an abominable animal not suitable for human consumption. But the Jews have hardly been typical in their refusal to eat the flesh of the pig. Pork has been enjoyed for centuries throughout such regions as China and Europe, and the members of many tribal societies not only eat pork but think so highly of pigs that they practically treat them as members of the family (Harris, 1974). Since the members of so many other religions have shown no aversion whatsoever to the consumption of pork, why have the Jews treated it as such an abomination?

Perhaps the most common answer to this question is that the pig is an unclean animal: it wallows in its own excrement and is a carrier of disease. Yet as Harris (1974, 1977) has shown, this explanation is not satisfactory. Pigs are not particularly dirty animals when they live in habitats for which they are well suited. Since pigs cannot sweat, they are better adapted to environments where the temperature does not get too hot. But in dry, hot environments (such as that of the Middle East), pigs have considerable trouble keeping cool, and therefore they wallow in their excrement in order to cool their bodies. Concerning the fact that pigs transmit certain diseases, Harris admits that this is true, but he also notes that other animals that have been widely consumed (such as the cow) are also carriers of disease.

Harris believes that the ancient Israelites forbade pork for reasons that have specifically to do with the ecology of the Middle East. He holds that the consumption of the pig came to be tabooed because the raising of pigs constituted a threat to the entire subsistence system of the ancient Jews (Harris, 1977:132):

The ancient Israelites arrived in Palestine during the early to middle iron age, about 1200 B.C., and took possession of mountainous terrain which had not previously been cultivated. The woodlands in the Judean and Samaritan hills were rapidly cut down and converted into irrigated terraces. Areas suitable for raising pigs on natural forage were severely restricted. Increasingly, pigs had to be fed grains as supplements, rendering them directly competitive with human beings; moreover, their cost increased because they needed artificial shade and moisture. And yet they continued to be a tempting source of protein and fat.

If pigs were ecologically costly, yet continued to be a source of temptation, the solution, Harris argues, would be to forbid the raising and consumption of pigs entirely; and the best way to make such a prohibition stick would be to establish it as a matter of divine interdiction: as a religious taboo. To remove this costly but tempting threat, the pig came to be redefined as an abomination.

Although Harris's theory has been subject to criticism, its plausibility is considerably enhanced by the fact that the ancient Jews shared the pig taboo with many of their neighbors. As Harris notes (1977:135–137):

> *The pig taboo recurs throughout the entire vast zone of Old World pastoral nomadism—from North Africa across the Middle East and Central Asia. But in China, Southeast Asia, Indonesia, and Melanesia the pig was and still is a much-used source of dietary proteins and fats, as it is in modern Europe and the Western Hemisphere. . . .*
>
> *The ancient Israelites even shared their abhorrence of the pig with their mortal enemies, the Egyptians. . . .*
>
> *With the rise of Islam, the ancient Israelite pig taboo was incorporated directly into still another set of supernaturally sanctioned dietary laws. The pig was singled out for special opprobrium in the Koran, and today Moslems are as opposed as Orthodox Jews are to eating pork.*

In other words, it appears to be specifically in those hot, dry regions of the world—regions to which the pig was poorly adapted and where special provisions had to be made for raising it—where the flesh of pigs came to be forbidden. By contrast, wetter, cooler areas of the world better suited to pig raising knew no pig taboo, and pigs were frequently dined upon with gusto in these areas.

Although the pig and the cow have both been the subject of strict religious taboos in which the consumption of their flesh was expressly forbidden, the pig and cow taboos were strikingly different; in India the cow was made holy, whereas the ancient Jews made the pig an abomination. Why this should be so should now be clear, at least if Harris's theories are valid interpretations. The cow was vitally necessary for Indian agriculture, and therefore it came to be sanctified. But the pig among the ancient Jews was of no use as a farm animal and only constituted a threat; hence it came to be defined as an unclean and undesirable creature.

FOR FURTHER READING

Carneiro, Robert L. "The Four Faces of Evolution." In J. J. Honigmann (ed.), *Handbook of Social and Cultural Anthropology.* Chicago: Rand McNally, 1973. A useful discussion of the nature of sociocultural evolution and the various ways in which it has been approached by social scientists.

Harris, Marvin. *Cannibals and Kings: The Origins of Cultures.* New York: Random House, 1977. An absorbing look at the role played by infrastructural factors in shaping the major outlines of sociocultural evolution over the past 10,000 years. A major contribution to materialist evolutionary theory written in a highly readable style.

Harris, Marvin. *Cultural Materialism: The Struggle for a Science of Culture.* New York: Random House, 1979. A passionate and highly persuasive argument for a materialist theoretical approach to the study of sociocultural life by one of the leading social scientists of our time.

Harris, Marvin. *Good to Eat: Riddles of Food and Culture.* New York: Simon & Schuster, 1985. A provocative discussion of food taboos and dietary preferences throughout the world from a materialist perspective. Contains highly informative and captivating discussions of food habits in regard to cattle, pigs, horses, insects, dogs, milk, and people. (The paperback version has been retitled *Sacred Cows and Abominable Pigs*.)

Mann, Michael. *The Sources of Social Power. Volume 1: A History of Power from the Beginning to* A.D. *1760*. Cambridge: Cambridge University Press, 1986. An extraordinarily comprehensive treatment of the major milestones of world prehistory and history. Written from an eclectic theoretical perspective that leans strongly toward a type of Weberianism. A broad evolutionism stressed in the early chapters.

Marx, Karl, and Friedrich Engels. *The German Ideology.* Edited by C. J. Arthur. New York: International Publishers, 1970. (Originally written 1846.) The original statement of the "materialist conception of history" by its founders. Provides the classical intellectual foundations for the contemporary materialist approach.

Sahlins, Marshall. "Evolution: Specific and General." In Marshall Sahlins and Elman Service (eds.), *Evolution and Culture*. Ann Arbor: University of Michigan Press, 1960. A valuable discussion of how sociocultural evolution, like biological evolution, has both "specific" and "general" aspects.

Wenke, Robert J. *Patterns in Prehistory: Mankind's First Three Million Years*. Second edition. New York: Oxford University Press, 1984. An excellent survey of world prehistory.

CHAPTER 4

Preindustrial Modes of Subsistence Technology

In order to survive, all societies must establish technological and economic systems. Technology and economy are very closely related in every society, yet they are by no means the same thing. A society's technology consists of the tools, techniques, and knowledge that its members have created in order to meet their needs and wants. A society's economy, on the other hand, consists of the socially organized way in which goods and services are produced and distributed. This chapter begins the discussion of the evolution of technology, conceived here as *subsistence technology,* or the technology directly related to the getting of a living. Examination is limited to five types of subsistence technology arranged in a general evolutionary order: hunting and gathering, simple horticulture, intensive horticulture, agrarianism or intensive agriculture, and pastoralism.* Of concern are both the nature of these subsistence technologies and the reasons one has replaced another in the evolutionary history of the human species. Industrialism as a mode of subsistence technology is not discussed until Chapter 8.

*Hunting and gathering, horticultural, and sometimes pastoral societies are often known collectively as **primitive societies.** Although some social scientists object to the use of this term, feeling that it is derogatory, there is no reason not to use it from time to time for convenience. The term refers only to the level of technological development, and its usage does not imply any judgment about cultural inferiority.

HUNTING AND GATHERING SOCIETIES

For about 99 percent of their history, humans subsisted entirely by hunting wild animals and gathering wild plant foods. The total monopoly of the hunting and gathering way of life was not broken until some 10,000 years ago, when some societies began to subsist by the practice of agriculture. During the past 10,000 years, **hunting and gathering societies** have grown fewer and fewer in number, and only a handful remain today. Most of these are found in relatively isolated geographical locations, such as the arid and semiarid regions of Australia, the central rain forest and southwestern desert regions of Africa, and the Arctic. It is unlikely that even these will survive more than a few decades longer, and by the early part of the twenty-first century the hunting and gathering way of life is destined to be only a historical relic known to ethnography and archaeology.

Most of what is currently known about hunter-gatherers is based on fieldwork conducted among surviving hunting and gathering groups. It cannot be known with any certainty how similar these groups may be to hunting and gathering societies of prehistoric times. No doubt there are a number of differences, but it is also likely that there are many striking similarities. In any event, the description of the hunting and gathering way of life that follows is based primarily on the results of contemporary ethnographic research.

Hunters and gatherers live in small groups known as *local bands*. These are groups of about 25 to 50 men, women, and children who cooperate with each other in the quest for subsistence. Each local band is a more or less politically autonomous and economically self-sufficient unit. However, many local bands are usually connected by ties of intermarriage into a much larger cultural unit, sometimes known as a **tribe.** A tribe is a network of bands all of whose members share the same cultural patterns and speak the same language. Furthermore, the composition of each local band is constantly shifting. Persons frequently move from one band to another. Such movement may arise from marriage or from a need to create a more even balance between population size and the food supply.

Hunter-gatherers generally depend upon gathering for the bulk of their diet (Service, 1966; Lee, 1968). Richard Lee (1968) has estimated that contemporary hunting and gathering societies derive approximately 65 percent of their diet from gathered foods of all sorts, and he believes that this figure may closely correspond to the subsistence activities of prehistoric hunter-gatherers. Nevertheless, more time is usually spent in hunting activities, and meat is a more highly valued food.

Since hunter-gatherers are food collectors rather than food producers, they must wander over wide geographical areas in search of food. They are thus generally nomadic, and the establishment of permanent settlements is highly unusual.

The technological inventory of hunting and gathering societies is quite limited. The tools and weapons used directly for subsistence typically include spears, bows and arrows, nets, and traps used in hunting, as well as digging sticks used for plant collecting. Tools are crude and simple, generally being made of stone, wood, bone, or other natural materials. There are usually few or no techniques for food storage or preservation, and food is thus generally consumed immediately or within a short span of time.

Hunting and gathering societies are the simplest in structure of all human societies. The division of labor is based almost exclusively on

Hunting and gathering societies are remarkable for their low level of economic specialization.

age and sex distinctions. Primary responsibility for subsistence ordinarily falls to persons who are in middle adulthood, with both young and old members contributing less to the subsistence needs of the group. Hunting is conducted by males, gathering by females. Although women may occasionally engage in the hunting or trapping of small game animals, they are never involved in big game hunting. Likewise, men sometimes share in gathering activities, but they are the principal gatherers in no hunting and gathering society. Hunter-gatherers are notoriously lacking in occupational specialization beyond subsistence tasks. There are no specialized "arrow makers" or "bow makers." Each man makes all of the tools that he needs in the subsistence quest. The women do the same.

The primary unit of subsistence among hunter-gatherers is the family, and hence economic life may be termed *familistic* (Service, 1966). Yet individual families within each local band are linked together into a total economic unit, the local band itself. While individual families produce their own subsistence, they also contribute in significant ways to the subsistence of other families within their band.

Hunter-gatherers are well known for their failure to produce an **economic surplus,** an excess of goods over and above what is needed for subsistence. Until recently it was widely believed that this was due simply to an inability to do so, an inability resulting from a marginal and precarious existence. Contemporary research contradicts this view. Social scientists now generally agree that the failure to produce a surplus is due to a lack of any real need. Since the resources of nature are always there for the taking, nature itself becomes a kind of great storehouse.

The Original Affluent Society

Social scientists used to depict hunters and gatherers in largely negative terms. It was widely believed that they led a precarious and difficult life, one in which people had to work hard and long just to eke out a bare subsistence. As Marshall Sahlins noted two decades ago (1972:1):

> Almost universally committed to the proposition that life was hard in the paleolithic, our textbooks compete to convey a sense of impending doom, leaving one to wonder not only how hunters managed to live, but whether, after all, this was living? The specter of starvation stalks the stalker through these pages. His technical incompetence is said to enjoin continuous work just to survive, affording him neither respite nor surplus, hence not even the "leisure" to "build culture."

Within the past quarter-century social scientists have radically altered this view of hunter-gatherers. Sahlins (1972), for instance, views them as constituting an "original affluent society." By this he means, not that they are rich and enjoy a great abundance of material possessions, but that they are able to satisfy all their material needs and wants with a minimum of effort. To assess Sahlins's claim, we need to look carefully at the standard of living attained by hunter-gatherers and at how hard and long they typically work.

Despite the fact that virtually all contemporary hunter-gatherers exist in marginal environments, these environments often turn out to be surprisingly abundant in resources. For example, Richard Lee (1968) notes that the !Kung San (the "!" stands for a click sound in the language) of southwestern Africa are able to rely on a wide variety of resources of considerable quality. Their most important food source is mongongo nuts, and thousands of pounds of these rot on the ground each year for want of picking. Furthermore, the !Kung habitat contains 84 other species of edible plants, and !Kung gathering never exhausts all the available plant foods of an area. Similarly, James Woodburn (1968) has shown that the Hadza of Tanzania enjoy an exceptional abundance of game, and he thinks it is almost inconceivable that they would die of starvation. It would thus appear that both the !Kung and the Hadza obtain a standard of living that is perfectly adequate in meeting basic human subsistence requirements.

This impression is reinforced by Mark Cohen's (1989) survey of studies of diet and nutrition among many contemporary hunting and gathering groups. Cohen's review of numerous studies suggests to him that most hunter-gatherers generally enjoy diets that are fully adequate in nutrition. Some groups, such as the !Kung, may only barely obtain a sufficient number of calories, but their diets are otherwise abundant in animal proteins and various nutrients. It also seems to be the case that many hunter-gatherers experience seasonal bouts of hunger and food anxiety, and starvation may sometimes occur. However, there is nothing unusual about hunter-gatherers in this respect. Settled agricultural populations also experience such difficulties, and quite likely to an even greater extent.

If hunter-gatherers generally enjoy adequate diets, how long and hard do they have to work to obtain them? A good deal of evidence suggests that many such groups work neither hard nor long. Reviewing data collected on the subsistence activities of the hunter-gatherers of Arnhem Land in northern Australia, Sahlins (1972) notes that these people do not work hard or continuously, that the subsistence quest is highly intermittent, and that plenty of spare time is available. Along the same lines, Lee (1979) has calculated that the average !Kung adult spends only about 17 hours per week in direct food-getting activities. Woodburn (1968) has shown that the Hadza obtain sufficient food with relative ease, and that life for them is anything but a difficult struggle for existence. He believes that they spend less time and energy in obtaining subsistence than do their agricultural neighbors.

Other studies of hunter-gatherer subsistence activities are not as encouraging, at least on the surface. Since Lee's data on !Kung work patterns were collected during the dry season, John Yellen (1977) studied a group of !Kung during the wet season. He found that during this time of the year they worked considerably longer, although exactly how much longer is not clear (cf. Hill, Kaplan, Hawkes, and Hurtado, 1985: Table IV). Yellen's data must serve to qualify those obtained by Lee, but they cannot be taken as undermining the original affluent society thesis. Even if we assume that the !Kung work twice as hard during the wet season as during the dry season, throughout the entire year they spend an average of only about 25 hours per week in direct food-getting activities.

Kim Hill, Hillard Kaplan, Kristen Hawkes, and Ana Magdelena Hurtado (1985) have analyzed the subsistence activities of the Ache of Paraguay. They find that Ache men devote a great deal of time to hunting—perhaps as much as 40 to 50 hours a week—and they conclude from this that Sahlins's depiction of hunter-gatherers as working little is erroneous. This study, however, must be seen in its proper context. The Ache are a tropical forest people, and game is generally thought to be very scarce in such environments (Harris, 1977). It is no wonder, then, that Ache men spend so much time hunting (much of which is spent just looking for game). The Ache are not a good case for making broad generalizations about hunter-gatherer work patterns.

It would seem, when all is said and done, that Sahlins's original affluent society thesis holds up quite well. This appears to be especially true when we realize that most of what we know about the standard of living and the work patterns of hunter-gatherers is based on contemporary groups. Since nearly all of these groups survive in marginal environments, prehistoric hunter-gatherers, most of whom would have existed in much more favorable environments, would have been even better off. It is crucial that we avoid romanticizing the hunting and gathering lifestyle as being some sort of primitive paradise. Clearly that would be a terrible oversimplification. Nonetheless, hunter-gatherers have fared much better than we used to imagine. As Elizabeth Cashdan (1989:26) has concluded, it is now possible to "demolish with confidence the old stereotype that hunter-gatherers had to work all the time simply to get enough food to eat." And it is also possible to demolish with confidence the old stereotype that hunter-gatherers did not eat well.

Among the !Kung, as among all hunter-gatherers, hunting is a crucial economic activity and meat is a highly valued food.

The !Kung San

Some 45,000 San are found scattered throughout the territories of Botswana, Angola, and Namibia in southern Africa. These peoples are divided into several different linguistic groups, one of which is !Kung, spoken by about 13,000 people. Many of these are now either under the direct control of local governments or heavily influenced in their way of life through contact with more technologically advanced peoples. The last of the hunting and gathering !Kung number some 1600 clustered around waterholes in northwestern Botswana.

The ethnographic account that follows is based on a population of 466 !Kung located in the Dobe area of Botswana studied by Richard Lee (1972; cf. Lee, 1979, 1984).

!Kung life is organized around eight permanent waterholes and 14 independent camps. These camps are moved around five or six times a year. The population density is approximately 0.4 persons per square mile, a density typical for hunter-gatherers. The habitat is the Kalahari Desert, a region surprisingly abundant in resources. Nearly 500 species of plants and animals are known and named by the !Kung. The climate is characterized by hot summers with a four-month rainy season and by moderate winters with no rainfall.

The !Kung enjoy a secure existence. They depend primarily on vegetable foods (Lee estimates that about 37 percent of their diet consists of meat). Their most important food plant is the mongongo or mangetti nut, a highly nutritious and superabundant staple. Other major plant foods are also available, but the !Kung tend to eat only those that are more attractive in terms of taste or ease of collection. Game animals are less abundant and predictable. A variety of large antelope is regularly hunted, as are wart hogs and smaller antelopes. Game birds are captured in ingenious snares, and a large tortoise is a great favorite.

The camp or local band is the basic residential unit and the primary focus of subsistence activities. Members of each local group move out each day individually or in small groups to exploit the surrounding area, returning each evening to pool collected resources. Women do the gathering in groups of three to five. The men do the hunting, which is primarily an individual activity. Bows and poisoned arrows serve as effective weapons. Food is extensively shared, although the sharing of meat is more formally organized than the sharing of vegetable foods. Large game is butchered and divided into three portions: about one-fifth remains with the family, one-fifth is cut into strips for drying, and the remaining three-fifths are distributed to closely related households. Meat division is carried out with considerable care. The hunter may call in other men to advise him, or he may even ask his father-in-law to conduct the division. Absolute sharing is the ideal in !Kung camps even though it is seldom attained in practice. It is noteworthy that the most common verbal disputes concern accusations of improper meat distribution and improper gift exchange.

SIMPLE HORTICULTURAL SOCIETIES

The Neolithic Revolution

Although hunters and gatherers have probably known for tens of thousands of years how plants and animals could be domesticated, it was not until about 10,000 years ago that some of them began to live in settled villages devoted to the practice of agriculture. The transition of humankind to an agricultural (technically, horticultural) mode of existence is known as the **Neolithic Revolution.** Actually the term *Neolithic Revolution* is somewhat misleading, since there was not a single revolutionary transition. The transition to agriculture occurred on an independent basis in several different regions of the world and at somewhat different times.

The adoption of agriculture occurred first in the Middle East. The most important domesticated plants were wheat and barley, while the major domesticated animals were sheep, goats, and pigs. The actual process of domestication appears to have followed the emergence of sedentary villages organized around the harvesting of the wild ancestors of wheat and barley. After the initial appearance of agriculture in the Middle East, it spread by diffusion to Europe, although the domesticants involved underwent numerous changes in order to be suitable to the different environmental conditions that Europe presented. It was some time, however, before agricultural communities were common in Europe, and it was not until 5500 B.P. that agriculture was common throughout the British Isles.

Agricultural communities emerged independently in two other areas of the Old World: China and Southeast Asia. Sedentary village life appears to have emerged in China sometime before 6000 B.P., although just how long before is not yet established. The principal domesticants were millet and pigs, with rice and soybeans being added later. Agriculture in Southeast Asia may have originated as early as 9000 B.P. The main domesticants in this region were yams, taro, and rice.

Agriculture was also independently adopted in two regions of the New World: Mesoamerica and Peru. The origins of agriculture in the New World have been dated to around 9000 B.P., although settled village life appears not to have emerged in full bloom until several thousand years later. The most significant New World plant domesticant was maize, the wild ancestor of which was a plant known as *teosinte*. In general, the plant domesticants that have been found in the New World are entirely different from those that developed in the Old World. In addition to maize, these include amaranth, quinoa, lima beans, squash, tomatoes, potatoes, chili peppers, and cacao. In contrast to the Old World, the New World generally lacked domesticated animals, apparently because of a lack of species suitable for domestication. The only domesticated animal of any real significance in the New World was the llama, which was domesticated in Peru around 5500 B.P.

Contemporary Simple Horticulturalists

The first agricultural societies were not based on true agriculture but on simple **horticulture.** A number of **simple horticultural societies** have survived into the modern world. Most of these are found in Melanesia, a chain of islands in the southern Pacific (generally said to include New Guinea), and in various regions of South America. Extensive ethnographic research has been conducted among these societies, and the results of this research provide the basis for the discussion that follows.

Simple horticulturalists live in small villages ordinarily containing from 100 to 200 persons. Although villages substantially larger than this are known to exist, they are not common. Each village is in essence economically and politically self-sufficient. Nevertheless, important inter-village ties do exist. Marriage often takes place between individuals from different villages, and persons residing in separate villages often come together on ceremonial occasions. Members of culturally and linguistically related villages collectively constitute a tribe, a sociocultural unit that may contain tens of thousands or even hundreds of thousands of persons.

Most simple horticulturalists live in heavily forested environments and practice a form of cultivation known as *slash-and-burn* (also known as shifting cultivation). This cultivation technique involves cutting down a section of forest growth and then setting fire to the accumulated debris. The ashes that remain serve as a fertilizer, and usually no other fertilizer is added. The crops are then planted in these cleared plots (usually no more than an acre in size) with the aid of a digging stick, a long pole with a sharpened and fire-hardened end. A given plot may be devoted to a single crop, but a more common practice is to plant several minor crops along with one main staple (Sahlins, 1968). The task of clearing and preparing the plots generally falls to the men, while that of planting and harvesting is typically considered the responsibility of women.

Since wood ashes generally serve as the only fertilizer, slash-and-burn cultivation is associated with short-term soil fertility. Freshly produced ashes are washed away by rain after a year or two, and for this reason a plot of land can only be cultivated for that length of time. It must then be allowed to remain fallow long enough for the forest to regenerate so that new ashes can be produced. The fallow period ordinarily lasts approximately 20 to 30 years. When the forest growth has returned, the process of cutting, burning, and cultivating can begin again.

Because the slash-and-burn system requires lengthy fallow periods, any society practicing it must have much more land at its disposal than it will have under actual cultivation at any given time (Sahlins, 1968). The Tsembaga Maring of New Guinea, for example, had only 42 acres of land under actual cultivation in 1962–1963, but about 864 acres of their territory had been gardened at one time or another (Harris, 1975). Such land use requirements put limits on population density, and tropical forest cultivators often maintain population densities of less than ten persons per square mile (Sahlins, 1968).

Cultivated plants constitute the bulk of the dietary intake among simple horticulturalists. However, a number of simple horticultural societies also possess domesticated animals. Domesticated pigs, for instance, are found throughout Melanesia. But most simple horticulturalists lack domesticated animals, and such groups must rely upon hunting or fishing for their supply of animal protein.

Simple horticulturalists produce more food per unit of land than do hunters and gatherers. Some simple horticulturalists even produce small economic surpluses. Yet it cannot be concluded from these facts that they enjoy a superior standard of living. Indeed, it has been suggested that their standard of living is *inferior* to that of hunter-gatherers (M. Cohen, 1977, 1989) (see the Special Topic at the end of this chapter). They do not consume more calories, and their intake of protein appears to be lower. Furthermore, considerable evidence has accumulated in recent years to show that simple horticulturalists commonly work harder than hunters and gatherers (M. Cohen, 1977). It generally takes more time and energy to clear land and plant, tend, and harvest crops than to collect what nature automatically provides. Thus, simple horticulture is a more intensive system of technology than hunting and gathering, but it does not lead to greater material benefits.

The Yanomamo

The Yanomamo are a South American Indian tribe living in southern Venezuela and adjacent portions of northern Brazil. There are perhaps some 125 widely scattered villages having populations ranging from 40 to 250 inhabitants, with an average village size of about 75 to 80 persons. Several hundred years ago the Yanomamo may have been devoted largely to a hunting and gathering subsistence pattern, and so they may only have recently made the transition to a horticultural existence (Colchester, 1984). Be that as it may, their current subsistence practices nicely illustrate the simple horticultural mode of production. These practices have been described in some detail by Napoleon Chagnon (1983), their principal ethnographer.

The natural environment of the Yanomamo is a relatively dense tropical forest. The land is entirely covered with jungle, even the tops of mountain ridges. The Yanomamo survive in this environment with only a simple technology. All tools and techniques are uncomplicated, and none requires the use of specialized labor. Among the elements of technology the Yanomamo have developed are crude clay pots, bows and arrows, agouti-tooth knives (made from the lower incisor of the agouti rodent), and canoes (which are so crude that they are generally used only once and then discarded).

The Yanomamo are slash-and-burn cultivators. In earlier times, they had only stone axes for clearing the land, but they now have steel axes that have been supplied by local missionaries. Each man clears his own land. Each village has a local headman, and he typically has the largest garden. The headman must produce larger quantities of food as he is expected to give food away at feasts. By far the largest crop is plantains (similar to bananas), and each garden usually contains three or four varieties of both plantains and bananas. A root crop, sweet manioc, is also grown, and this is refined into a rough flour and then converted into a thick, baked bread. Other crops include taro, sweet potatoes, and a palm tree that produces a large crop of fruit. Maize is cultivated as an emergency crop, but it does not figure prominently in the daily diet. Tobacco is another cultivated crop, and the men, women, and children all chew it. Cotton is also grown and is used for making hammocks.

While perhaps 85 percent or more of the Yanomamo diet consists of cultivated plants, the Yanomamo spend almost as much time hunting as they do gardening. Since they have no domesticated animals, they rely exclusively upon hunting (as well as some fishing and the collecting of small animals) for their source of animal protein. Game animals are not abundant, a situation that is typical of tropical forest environments. The most commonly hunted game animals are several species of monkeys, two species of wild pig, armadillos, anteaters, deer, a small alligator, small rodents, and several species of smaller birds. All game animals are shot with arrows. Several varieties of insects, some species of caterpillar, and large spiders are collected and eaten. Wild honey, considered a real delicacy, is collected in large quantities.

Slash-and-burn cultivation among the Yanomamo.

INTENSIVE HORTICULTURAL SOCIETIES

Many of the simple horticultural societies that were ushered into existence by the Neolithic Revolution in due time evolved into **intensive horticultural societies.** No doubt hundreds of intensive horticultural societies have existed during the past several thousand years of human history. Until the influx of the Europeans in the late eighteenth century, such societies were widespread throughout Polynesia, a vast island chain in the southern Pacific that includes the islands of Hawaii, Tahiti, and Tonga, among many others. Prior to the end of the nineteenth century, they flourished throughout large parts of sub-Saharan Africa. South America and Southeast Asia are also regions where numerous intensive horticulturalists were once located. Today, however, few remain. Most of these are found in parts of sub-Saharan Africa, and perhaps in some portions of South America and Southeast Asia.

Like simple horticulturalists, intensive horticulturalists are dependent upon cultivated garden products for the bulk of their food supply, and they cultivate by the slash-and-burn method. Some of them keep domesticated animals, and those that do not engage in hunting or fishing for their supply of meat. Yet intensive horticulturalists differ in several significant ways from simple horticulturalists. One principal difference involves the length of time that land is allowed to remain fallow. Simple horticulturalists generally permit the land to lie fallow for twenty or thirty years before using it again. Intensive horticulturalists, by contrast, shorten the fallow period to perhaps as little as five to ten years, thus cropping a given plot of land more frequently. To compensate for the decrease in soil fertility that accompanies more frequent cropping, intensive horticulturalists further fertilize the soil by adding such things as humus or animal manure.

The shortening of the fallow period has the effect of eventually converting thick forest growth to bush. Land that has been cleared of bush must be prepared for cultivation in a way that is not necessary for land cleared of forest. Thus, many intensive horticulturalists have invented or adopted hoes for the purpose of properly preparing land for cultivation. As Boserup explains (1965:24):

> After the burning of real forest the soil is loose and free of weeds and hoeing of the land is unnecessary. By contrast, when the period of fallow is shortened and, therefore, the natural vegetation before clearing is thin or grassy the land must be prepared with a hoe or similar instrument before the seeds or roots can be placed.

Some intensive horticulturalists employ elements of technology in addition to, or instead of, the ones mentioned above. Polynesian intensive horticulturalists, for example, although they never made use of hoes, did engage in the terracing and irrigation of land. It is clear, then, that intensive horticulturalists have achieved a level of technological development beyond what is typical for simple horticulturalists. It is also clear that people work harder and longer under intensive horticulture. Preparing the land by hoeing and the terracing and irrigation of land are demanding and time-consuming activities. Since people work harder and longer, and since any given area of land is cultivated more frequently, it is obvious why this mode of subsistence technology is referred to as *intensive* horticulture.

Compared to simple horticulture, intensive horticulture is considerably more productive per unit of land. Intensive horticulturalists, in fact, produce sizable economic surpluses, and these surpluses are used to support a class of persons who are freed from direct involvement in agricultural production. In many intensive horticultural societies, the members of this class are regarded, theoretically at least, as the owners of all the land, and in all such societies they direct many economic activities. Their standard of living is higher than that of everyone else. The standard of living of most of the members of intensive horticultural societies is difficult to determine, but it seems likely that it differs little from that typically found among simple horticulturalists. Yet it should not be forgotten that intensive horticulturalists work significantly harder just to achieve approximately the same material results.

Aboriginal Tahiti

Most of the population of aboriginal Polynesia lived on the so-called high islands. These islands are rugged, eroded remnants of great volcanic cones. The arable land is very rich, and it is covered with dense tropical growth. One of these high islands is Tahiti, a member of the Society Islands group. Tahiti is about 35 miles long and about half as wide. In the eighteenth century the island supported a population of approximately 100,000. The description of Tahitian society given here depicts their aboriginal way of life as it is presented by Elman Service (1963).

The Tahitians are sophisticated horticulturalists, considerably more so than groups like the Yanomamo. They make very efficient use of the land for their gardens by terracing hillsides, diverting streams for irrigation, and enriching the soil in various ways. The prime horticultural tool is the simple digging stick. Since there are no metals, they have never developed the metal

The Incas of ancient Peru were one of the most intensive horticultural societies the world has ever known. This illustration depicts Incas harvesting and transporting potatoes.

hoes characteristic of many other intensive horticulturalists.

Tahiti's main domesticated plants were brought from Indonesia, and these include coconut palms, breadfruit trees, taro, yams, sweet potatoes, bananas and plantains, and sugar cane. The most important food is breadfruit, a fruit that is plentiful and nutritious and stores well. The most versatile domesticated plant is the coconut palm. The coconut meat is a nourishing food and coconut milk is used for drinking. Palm leaves are used for thatch, and the fiber is used for the manufacture of mats and baskets.

Fishing is also an important part of the Tahitian subsistence pattern, and the technology available for it is diversified and elaborate. This technology includes basketry traps, many forms of nets, fish poisons, harpoons, and many kinds of hooks and lines. Tahitians of both sexes are excellent swimmers. Women dive for crabs and other shellfish and even capture octopi. Men and boys dive to great depths for pearl oysters, the flesh of which is used for food and the shell for various implements and ornaments. Aside from seafood, the main source of protein is pork, and pigs are carefully fed and tended. Chickens are also raised.

The Tahitian horticultural system is intensive enough to produce a sizable economic surplus, and this surplus is used to support a class of persons known as the *Ari'i:* chiefs and their families. The chiefs and their families live off this surplus and thus have no direct involvement in agricultural production. They also use it to support a set of administrative officials who carry out the daily business of political rule. A good deal of this surplus is also returned to the people through the holding of elaborate feasts.

AGRARIAN SOCIETIES

The first **agrarian societies** arose approximately 5000 to 6000 years ago in Egypt and Mesopotamia and slightly later in China and India. It was not long before agrarian societies were to be found over much of the globe. From the time when agrarian societies first emerged until the present day, the majority of persons who have ever lived have done so according to the agrarian way of life. To the extent that this way of life remains today, it exists largely in substantially altered form in societies that are at least partially industrialized and are part of a worldwide capitalist economy. Hence there are no true agrarian societies left in the world. But what were agrarian societies of the past like?

Agrarian societies rest upon true **agriculture.** Land is cleared of all vegetation and cultivated with the use of the plow and draft animals hitched to the plow. Fields are extensively fertilized, usually with animal manure. When land is cultivated in this fashion, it may be used more or less continuously. Thus, fallow periods are either very short or do not exist. Farmers often crop a given plot of land annually, and in some cases several harvests may be reaped from the same plot of land in a single year.

A number of agrarian societies have existed in areas where rainfall was sufficient to nourish crops. Agrarian societies throughout Europe, for instance, were based on rainfall farming. But in many other agrarian societies, arid or semi-arid climates have made rainfall farming impossible, and farmers have had to construct irrigation systems to water their crops. Farmers in ancient Egypt, Mesopotamia, China, and India, for example, practiced irrigation agriculture.

Agrarian farmers work much harder than do the members of earlier types of societies (cf. Minge-Klevana, 1980). The tasks of clearing land, plowing, sowing and harvesting crops, tending animals, and so on, require extensive labor inputs. Where irrigation systems must be constructed, people work even harder. Because of their efforts, agrarian farmers produce much more per unit of land than do horticulturalists, and much of what they produce constitutes an economic surplus. But their greater efforts and larger surpluses do not yield for them a higher standard of living. Indeed, their standard of living is generally lower, and in some cases much lower, than that enjoyed by the members of horticultural societies. Part of the reason for this apparent paradox is explained at the end of this chapter, but this phenomenon cannot be fully understood until the rise of social stratification is discussed in Chapter 6.

Most members of agrarian societies are **peasants.** They are the primary producers, the persons who farm the land from day to day. Eric Wolf (1966) calls them *dependent cultivators* because they exist in a politically and economically dependent or subordinate relationship to the principal owners of the land. They themselves frequently do not own land, but are merely allowed the use of it. In this sense, they are tenants on the land. In those cases where peasants do own their land, they have far from full control over the dispensation of the produce from this land. But not all of the primary producers in agrarian societies are peasants. Some are slaves. Slaves differ from peasants in that they are legally owned and can be bought and sold. In some agrarian societies—ancient Rome and Greece, for example—slaves actually outnumbered peasants.

Medieval England

Medieval England serves as an excellent example of the agrarian mode of subsistence technology. H. S. Bennett's (1937) study of how English peasants from the twelfth to the fifteenth centuries farmed the land provides the basis for the following discussion.

English peasants lived in an overwhelmingly rural society, one in which there were few, comparatively small cities. The peasants lived in small villages that commonly numbered in the vicinity of a hundred persons. They spent most of their lives doing farm work, much of which was carried out by teams of peasants working cooperatively.

Some peasants farmed the land in a "two-field" fashion. They would work on one field in one year while allowing the other one to remain fallow; then the next year they would reverse the process. Other peasants farmed the land using a "three-field" system. One field would be planted in the autumn with wheat or possibly rye; another would be planted with oats, vetches, or barley the following spring; in the meantime, the third field would lie fallow. The next year the fallow field would be sown with wheat, the first field with oats, vetches, or barley, and the second field would remain fallow, and so on. Naturally, by rotating crops and fields in this manner the peasants were trying to keep the fertility of the soil as high as possible.

Peasants also applied animal manure to the soil to aid in its fertility, but getting enough manure was a constant struggle. There were a number of reasons for this. In the first place, the

Peasants plowing on a medieval European manor.

peasant seldom had enough animals to produce all the manure he needed. Also, peasants did not have unrestricted use of their animals, for their landlords appropriated them on some occasions. Fodder to produce a sufficient quantity of manure was also in short supply. So the peasant did the best he could under difficult conditions, and this meant that he sometimes worked marl or lime into the ground as an additional fertilizer. Numerous animals were kept by peasants, both as means of working the farm and as sources of food. Oxen and cows were extremely important for farm work, and both were used for food and hides. Naturally, cows provided milk as a food product. Sheep were kept for their wool and for food. Pigs were also kept, and they were perhaps the most highly valued of all farm animals, at least as food sources. They had special significance as food sources because they could be economically fed, they put on weight quickly, and they could be efficiently prepared for slaughter.

Farm work for the average English peasant was extremely demanding, and peasants put in many long, hard hours in order to meet their subsistence needs and pay their taxes. The following description of peasant labor should convey just how demanding peasant life really was (Bennett, 1937:82–83):

> Once all this was finished the peasant's labours were not so pressing, and he could turn to the many other secondary jobs waiting to be done. If the land was heavy, draining operations were constantly necessary and worth while; ditches wanted digging out after the winter floods, and the good earth put on to the land again; hedges and enclosures round the little home or any private bit of enclosure required attention, and so on. Then . . . it was time for the first ploughing of the fallow field, and the busy activities in the garden where such vegetables and fruits as were then available were grown.
>
> So the days went by with plenty to occupy men till the end of May. The coming of June saw them making renewed efforts. The haymaking called for all their strength: first, there were the numerous compulsory days which they had to spend in getting in the lord's hay. . . .
>
> With the coming of August the peasant's activities reached their climax. Once again the demands made upon him by his lord were often very heavy. He had to appear in person again and again to gather in the lord's crops—and, although he usually worked one or two days more a week from August to Michaelmas than at other times in the year, this was not enough, and he had to give several extra days of his time as a boon or gift to his lord. And further, he had to come with all his family: everyone able to work, save perhaps the housewife, was pressed into service for so many days. This made the getting-in of his own crops a more difficult and anxious matter, and work during these crucial weeks must have been wellnigh unending.

Thus it was that the medieval English peasant toiled in his fields in a manner that the average hunter-gatherer or horticulturalist would have considered unthinkable.

PASTORAL SOCIETIES

Pastoralism (or pastoral nomadism) originated approximately 3000 to 3500 years ago as a highly specialized subsistence adaptation to arid and semiarid environments. Although occurring later than true agriculture, it is not evolutionarily "higher" or more "advanced" than agriculture, but simply a specific adaptation in regions where the practice of agriculture is impossible or very difficult.

Pastoralists depend upon animal herds for their survival. They tend herds the year round, and move seasonally with their herds in search of pasture (hence the label *pastoral nomadism*). Animals most frequently kept include sheep, goats, camels, cattle, and, in some cases, reindeer. Some pastoral groups depend on a single animal species, whereas others herd a number of different species. Some pastoralists, who are sometimes referred to as "true" pastoralists, practice no agriculture at all. These groups obtain agricultural products for their diet by trade relations with agricultural neighbors. It is not uncommon, however, for pastoral groups to engage in some agriculture in order to supplement the foods they obtain from their animal herds, but this is always distinctly secondary to their herding activities.

Most pastoralists have been located in the dry regions of Asia and Africa: in southwest Asia, northern Africa, and the grasslands of eastern Africa. Sheep, goats, and camels are the most commonly herded animals in Asia and northern Africa, while eastern Africa is famous for cattle herding. Pastoralism is also found in certain northern Eurasian forest regions, and here reindeer herders dominate (Sahlins, 1968).

Pastoralists live and travel in relatively small groups that usually do not exceed 100 to 200 members. Population densities are quite low, usually fewer than five persons per square mile.

Most of what pastoralists eat, of course, comes from their animal herds. They subsist principally on milk, meat, and blood. In eastern Africa, for instance, many pastoral groups have as their major dietary item a mixture of blood and milk obtained from their cattle. Although agricultural products generally supplement the diet, for some groups they do so only to a very small extent.

The Basseri

The Basseri are pastoralists who live in the dry steppes and mountains of southern Iran. Numbering about 16,000 in the entire tribe, they are tent dwellers who move about with their animal herds. Their habitat is hot and dry. Annual rainfall is generally about 10 inches or less, and most of this falls in the winter. The discussion of the subsistent pattern of this group is based on the detailed study by Fredrik Barth (1961).

The Basseri keep a number of domesticated animals, the most important of which are sheep and goats. The products of these animals provide the major part of subsistence. Donkeys are kept for transport and for riding, horses for riding only. Camels are maintained for use in heavy transport, and their wool is also of value. Dogs are used as camp watchdogs. Poultry is sometimes found as a source of meat, but the eggs are not eaten.

The milk obtained from sheep and goats is a most important product. Sour milk is a staple and is processed for storage. Cheese is made, although seldom during the periods of daily migrations. The best cheese is allegedly made during the summer, when the Basseri maintain a stationary residence.

Lambs are slaughtered for meat that is never smoked, salted, or dried, but always eaten fresh. The hides of slaughtered animals are sold in markets and also used as bags for storing water, sour milk, and buttermilk.

Wool is also an important animal product. Felt is made out of lamb's wool, and sheep's wool

A Masai herdsman. The Masai are well-known East African pastoralists who depend upon cattle for their existence and give cattle an important symbolic and ceremonial role in their social life.

and camel hair are sold and used in weaving and rope making. Goat hair is also of value and is spun and woven.

Many agricultural products are included in the typical diet of the Basseri. Part of these are produced by the Basseri themselves; the rest are obtained in trade. Cereal crops like wheat are planted when the tribesmen first arrive in their summer camps, and these are harvested before the departure from the camps. The agriculture performed by the Basseri themselves is very rough, and, in general, disliked and disdained. Therefore, many of the Basseri are reluctant to engage in agricultural activity.

Many of the Basseri's necessities are obtained through trade, Flour, sugar, tea, dates, and fruits and vegetables are obtained exclusively or mainly by trade. Material for clothes, finished clothes and shoes, cooking utensils, and saddles are purchased in markets. For all these items the Basseri exchange clarified butter, wool, lambskins, and some livestock.

THE CAUSES OF THE EVOLUTION OF PREINDUSTRIAL TECHNOLOGIES

We must now consider the crucial question of what accounts for the evolution of preindustrial technologies from one stage to the next.

It was once widely believed by social scientists of all sorts that technology is a self-generating, independent force in its own right. It was thought that technological changes occur as the cumulative result of the inventive powers of the human species. In addition, it was felt that whenever new forms of technology become available, people automatically adopt them because they see the benefits they will bring.

Many social scientists have now abandoned

Table 4.1 PREINDUSTRIAL SUBSISTENCE STRATEGIES

Subsistence strategy	Principal technological characteristics
Hunting and gathering	Hunting of wild animals with the use of spears, spear throwers, bows and arrows, nets, and traps. Gathering of wild plant food using a digging stick. Fishing may be undertaken, and in some environments may be a principal subsistence activity. Division of labor is based mainly on age and sex, with hunters generally males and gatherers generally females. Nomadic bands of 25 to 50 persons follow the supply of game and plants. Labor inputs are normally very low.
Simple horticulture	Small-scale gardening, generally using the slash-and-burn method of cultivation. The men prepare garden sites, but the women are commonly the principal cultivators and harvesters. Gardens are moved frequently, and fallow periods are generally long (20 to 30 years). Labor inputs are typically low.
Intensive horticulture	Small-scale gardening, normally using slash-and-burn techniques but with more frequent and intensive usage of each plot of land and shorter fallow periods (5 to 10 years). May also involve extension of the technological inventory to include metal hoes and the construction of irrigation systems, as well as more extensive fertilization of garden plots. Labor inputs moderate.
Agrarianism	Large-scale intensive agriculture employing the plow and traction animals. Fields are entirely cleared of vegetation and are cultivated permanently or semipermanently. Extensive fertilization to maintain soil fertility. Requires great labor inputs, but is capable of generating large economic surpluses.
Pastoralism	Reliance on animal herds in arid environments not well suited for cultivation of the soil. Herds are moved on a seasonal basis, and thus a nomadic existence is maintained. Some cultivation may be practiced, or vegetable matter may be obtained through trade.

this view of technological change. They embrace instead the view proposed some two decades ago by Ester Boserup (1965, 1981; cf. Wilkinson, 1973). Boserup holds that people have no inherent desire to advance their level of technology. She postulates that people wish to make a living by the simplest and easiest means possible. Their natural inclinations are to meet their subsistent needs with the least amount of work. Since adopting new technologies actually results in people having to work harder, they will not switch to new methods unless special conditions compel them to do so. Boserup believes that the principal condition compelling people to advance their technology is **population pressure.** Population pressure exists when population growth causes people to press against food resources. As the number of mouths to be fed increases, a point is eventually reached at which people begin to deplete their resources and suffer a significant drop in their standard of living. Boserup argues that it is at this point that people will start to intensify production. They adopt new forms of technology and work harder and longer in order to produce more food to feed more people. Simple horticulturalists, for example, may begin to adopt more intensive horticultural techniques. Likewise, intensive horticulturalists may switch to plow agriculture.

It is imperative to realize that Boserup's argument does not assume that the switch to more intensive technologies will lead to the resumption of old standards of living, let alone to an improvement in the standard of living. The evolution from one level of technology to another is generally associated with a deterioration in living standards. Her argument is simply that the adoption of more intensive modes of production is necessary in order to maintain as high a living standard as possible under the imposition of greater numbers.

Mark Cohen (1977, 1985) believes that Boserup's argument is relevant to understanding the origin of agriculture on a worldwide basis. Cohen notes that ancient hunter-gatherers had probably long understood how to domesticate plants and animals, but waited for perhaps tens of thousands of years before putting their knowledge to use. Apparently they saw no benefits to the practice of agriculture, and they probably saw it as a less desirable way of making a living then collecting food from nature's storehouse. Indeed, when contemporary hunter-gatherers are asked by ethnographers why they do not practice agriculture, they usually respond with something like, "Why should we work harder in order to live no better than we're living now?" Richard Lee (1979), for example, asked a !Kung man named /Xashe why the !Kung did not adopt some of the practices of their agricultural neighbors, and /Xashe replied, "Why should we plant when there are so many mongongos in the world?" If, then, ancient hunter-gatherers knew how to plant crops but avoided doing so, what finally compelled some of them to cross the threshold to the agricultural way of life? Cohen believes that the reason was a "food crisis" due to growing population. He holds that hunting and gathering groups in several regions of the world finally outgrew the capacity of their environments to sustain them at an acceptable standard of living. When this occurred, they were forced to start producing their own food in order to stave off the "food crisis." They became willing to work harder, because they now had something to gain from it.

Cohen's theory of the origin of agriculture has not been thoroughly endorsed by modern archaeologists, who are best qualified to judge it. Yet it is extremely plausible in terms of what we know about the attitude of modern hunter-gatherers to the practice of agriculture, and a number of modern anthropologists and archaeologists have developed theories of agricultural origins that give population pressure a significant role (Binford, 1968; Flannery, 1973; Harner, 1970; Harris, 1977). But while there is still a good deal of doubt about the causes of early agriculture, social scientists are more certain about the role of population pressure in leading to the **intensification of agricultural production.** Boserup herself presents considerable evidence that changes in the level of population density precede changes in the mode of economic production. For example, she points to the fact that the population increase in Japan from about 1600 to about 1850 was closely followed by a shift in the intensity of production (1965:61):

> At the beginning of the period dynastic change created internal peace after a period of turbulence, and population grew rapidly, particularly during the first half of the period. From a certain point, the increase of population seems to have caused a reduction of the average size of agricultural holdings and a thorough change of methods. Ploughing with the help of draught animals became more frequent, and double cropping was made possible by irrigation and by the use of purchased night soil and dried fish for fertilizer as a supplement to or substitution for the traditional method of trampling grass, leaves or ashes into the fields.

Boserup also notes that decreases in population density often seem to be followed by an actual *regression* in cultivation techniques. In this regard she writes the following (1965:62–63):

> Latin America is the region which suffered the most from population decline in recent centu-

> ries. In many regions, the population density of pre-Columbian times has never been regained and the Indian population has regressed in agricultural techniques. . . .
>
> . . . Many observers report of apparent technical regression after migrations to less densely populated regions even in cases where the migrations took place at government initiative and were designed to promote the spread of intensive methods to the regions of immigration. In both Tanganyika, Vietnam, Ceylon and India [*sic*] extension service administrations have made the experience that cultivators who used intensive methods in their densely settled home districts give up these methods after they have been resettled in less densely populated districts and given more land per family.

Much additional research has supported the view that population pressure is the basic cause of preindustrial technological evolution. Increasingly intensive systems of agricultural production seem to have arisen as a response to growing numbers in such diverse regions of the world as South America, New Guinea, ancient Mesoamerica, and ancient Mesopotamia (Carneiro, 1968; Clarke, 1966; Sanders, 1972; Adams, 1972).

As noted earlier, although the demographic theory of agricultural intensification has won wide acceptance, some social scientists remain highly critical of it (cf. Bronson, 1972; Cowgill, 1975; B. White, 1982). George Cowgill (1975) and Benjamin White (1982), for instance, argue that the theory incorrectly assumes some natural tendency of human populations to grow. For his part, White claims that population growth is not natural or automatic, but depends on a range of social, economic, and political circumstances. He contends that since there is no inherent tendency for population to grow, then population pressure cannot logically be invoked as a cause of advancements in the level of agricultural technology.

But while it is true that demographic change is influenced by a variety of social factors, it does not follow that there is no inherent tendency for population to grow under most preindustrial conditions. There is considerable evidence that preindustrial peoples devote an enormous amount of attention to attempting to regulate numbers, and this suggests that they are up against potent biological realities (cf. Harris and Ross, 1987). In particular, the widespread existence of female infanticide is powerful evidence of the need people have to control their numbers (Harris and Ross, 1987; Wilkinson, 1973; Cohen, Malpass, and Klein, 1980).

Demographic change interacts in complex ways with the various components of sociocultural systems, but it can hardly be considered some sort of universal cause of sociocultural evolution. More recent evolutionary events, such as the Industrial Revolution or the impoverishment of two-thirds of the population of the contemporary world, have resulted from very different causes. But at the preindustrial level population growth seems to be our best bet as the critical stimulus for the advance of subsistence technology (cf. Johnson and Earle, 1987). At least no one has yet proposed a theory that is as convincing as the theory of population pressure.

SUMMARY

1. Hunting and gathering societies monopolized 99 percent of human history, and some still survive today. The members of these societies survive by hunting wild animals and collecting wild plant and vegetable matter. It was long thought that their members exist at a bare margin of survival, but more recent evidence suggests that they live quite adequately with a minimum of work effort. In fact, it has been suggested that they constitute a kind of "original affluent society."

2. Some human communities in various parts of the world began to adopt agricultural techniques of subsistence some 10,000 years ago. The transition to agriculture is generally known as the Neolithic Revolution. It is now known that the transition to agriculture occurred independently in several different world regions. The development of agriculture was a slow and gradual transition out of hunting and gathering, and it seems that people were actually beginning for the first time to use knowledge that they had long possessed.

3. The earliest agriculturalists practiced a rudimentary form of agriculture known as simple horticulture. Many simple horticulturalists survive today in remote regions of the world, especially tropical forest areas. Simple horticulturalists commonly cultivate land by cutting down forest growth, burning the accumulated debris, and planting crops in the ashes that remain. Such groups generally rotate their gardens frequently and allow previously cultivated plots to remain fallow for long periods.

4. Many past and present societies have used a more intensive form of horticulture. They shorten the fallow period of previously used plots and often make use of additional fertilizers. They might also develop hoes for cultivation, and some have invented techniques like terracing and irrigation of land. Just as simple horticulture is more productive per unit of land than hunting and gathering, intensive horticulture is more productive than simple horticulture.

5. Agrarian societies began to emerge some 5000 to 6000 years ago. The members of these societies practice what some regard as "true" agriculture. This involves cultivating large plots of land with the plow and draft animals and the continuous or semicontinuous usage of land. An agrarian mode of subsistence technology uses the land very intensively, requires enormous labor inputs, and achieves very high levels of economic productivity.

6. Pastoralism is an alternative to agriculture in dry regions not suitable for agriculture. Pastoralists live off their animal herds, especially blood and dairy products. They are nomadic, driving their herds from pasture to pasture as the seasons change. Pastoralists either practice agriculture on a very small scale or avoid it altogether.

7. Social scientists used to treat technological change more or less as a given. People were seen as advancing their level of technology when they knew how to because they obviously sought the benefits of more advanced techniques. This older view is now in serious disrepute. There is much evidence that technological inertia is built into most preindustrial societies. It thus seems that people resist technological advances because they require greater work efforts. Some have theorized that technological advances will only be made under severe population pressure that compels people to change in order to prevent further reductions in their standard of living. One of the great ironies of technological evolution is that it is associated with lower, rather than higher, standards of living.

SPECIAL TOPIC: AGRICULTURAL ORIGINS AND THE DECLINING STANDARD OF LIVING

The notion that cultural progress has accompanied technological advance is a strongly entrenched belief in Western civilization. One aspect of this notion is the belief that technological innovation over the millennia has brought about continuous improvement in the standard of living. Recent research by archaeologists and physical anthropologists into some of the consequences of the transition from hunting and gathering to agriculture, however, sharply challenges this assumption. These scientists have drawn upon the recent technique of paleopathology—the examination of the evidence of biological stress and disease in ancient skeletal remains—to assess the implications for health and nutrition of the adoption of agriculture.

One intriguing paleopathological study has been carried out by the physical anthropologist J. Lawrence Angel (1975). Angel examined some 2,200 human skeletal remains drawn from sites representing the past 30,000 years of human history. Through various painstaking analyses, he estimated the general dietary adequacy of the populations represented by the remains. He found that longevity increased little from 30,000 years ago through the time when complex agricultural systems predominated. For instance, he estimated that hunter-gatherers of 30,000 years ago had a life expectancy of approximately 31 years. By 5000 B.P. the life expectancy was virtually the same; by the early Roman Empire it was only about 37 years; and by late medieval times it was only about 34 years. In addition, Angel found a general decline in body stature over this period, as well as an increase in the incidence of dental disease. These latter findings clearly suggest an overall deterioration in nutritional and health status, especially a notable reduction in protein intake.

A great deal of evidence consistent with Angel's findings has been added in the past few years. At a recent major conference held in Plattsburgh, New York, Mark Cohen and George Armelagos (1984) summarized the paleopathological findings presented by over a dozen physical anthropologists. The participants at the conference "were asked to make comparative statements about the occurrence of as many as possible of a common set of indexes of health, diet, and pathology derived from recent summaries of paleopathological techniques" (M. N. Cohen, 1984:4). The participants addressed questions in regard to such phenomena as life expectancies, the occurrence of indicators of stress that would have disturbed childhood growth patterns, indicators of infection, changes in bone growth indicative of malnutrition, and the prevalence of dental cavities and other oral disease. The skeletal remains on which the paleopathological investigations were performed were drawn from throughout the world. There were eight analyses based on North America, one from Mesoamerica, three from South America, two from Europe, two from the Middle East, one from southern Asia, and one from North Africa.

With few exceptions, these studies strongly point to the conclusion that the standard of living declined with the adoption of agriculture. In regard to infection, most of the studies found that it was a more frequent and severe problem for farming populations than for hunter-gatherers. Evidence regarding chronic malnutrition yields the same result. The investigators looked for the incidence of porotic hyperostosis and cribia orbitalia (porosity of the skull and orbits), bone diseases generally considered good indicators of anemia. Most of the studies showed that these were primarily diseases of agricultural rather than hunting and gathering populations. Other indicators of malnutrition, such as the thinning of long-bone cortices and changes in the skull base and pelvic inlet, were also discovered to be more common in agricultural groups.

Indicators of biological stresses leading to the disruption of childhood growth tell basically the same story as the other indicators. Various defects in tooth enamel are considered good indicators of growth-disrupting stress. Cohen and Armelagos note that ten studies "all report that the frequency and/or severity of this indicator of growth disruption increases in farming and later populations in comparison to hunter-gatherers" (1984:589). Finally, the studies generally show that mean age at death actually declined after the adoption of agriculture, a conclusion even more provocative than Angel's finding in this regard.

The findings reported at the Plattsburgh conference are of major significance for theories of sociocultural evolution inasmuch as they strongly challenge the prevailing wisdom of Western civilization, a wisdom not only of the general member of society but of the majority of social scientists as well. As Cohen and Armelagos comment (1984:594):

> *Taken as a whole, these indicators fairly clearly suggest an overall decline in the quality—and probably in the length—of human life associated with the adoption of agriculture. . . . The studies support recent ethnographic statements and theoretical arguments about the relatively good health and nutrition of hunter-gatherers. They also suggest that hunter-gatherers were relatively well buffered against episodic stress. These data call into question simplistic popular ideas about human progress.*

FOR FURTHER READING

Boserup, Ester. *The Conditions of Agricultural Growth*. Chicago: Aldine, 1965. A highly influential book that postulates that population pressure is the major cause of the advancement of subsistence technologies.

Cohen, Mark N. *The Food Crisis in Prehistory.* New Haven: Yale University Press, 1977. The application of Boserup's hypothesis to explaining the worldwide origin of agriculture.

Dahlberg, Frances. *Woman the Gatherer.* New Haven: Yale University Press, 1981. Valuable essays on the important economic contributions of women in hunter-gatherer societies.

Harris, Marvin, and Eric B. Ross. *Death, Sex, and Fertility: Population Regulation in Preindustrial and Developing Societies.* New York: Columbia University Press, 1987. A major work on the demography of preindustrial societies.

Johnson, Allen W., and Timothy Earle. *The Evolution of Human Societies.* Stanford, Calif.: Stanford University Press, 1987. Excellent discussions of subsistence practices among the main types of preindustrial societies. Proposes population pressure as the basic cause of the advancement of subsistence technology.

Leacock, Eleanor B., and Richard B. Lee (eds.). *Politics and History in Band Societies.* New York: Cambridge University Press, 1982. Recent essays on a variety of hunter-gatherer societies all over the world, with a focus on the political relations between these societies and more technologically advanced cultures.

Lee, Richard B., and Irven DeVore (eds.). *Man the Hunter.* Chicago: Aldine, 1968. The result of a famous symposium on hunters and gatherers, this book provides a variety of important insights into the hunting and gathering way of life.

Minge-Klevana, Wanda. "Does Labor Time Decrease with Industrialization? A Survey of Time-Allocation Studies." *Current Anthropology* 21:279–298, 1980. Contains extensive data on the workloads of preindustrial societies at different levels of technological development.

Price, T. Douglas, and James A. Brown (eds.). *Prehistoric Hunter-Gatherers.* Orlando: Academic Press, 1985. Some valuable archaeological investigations of hunting and gathering societies.

Schrire, Carmel (ed.). *Past and Present in Hunter Gatherer Studies.* Orlando: Academic Press, 1984. Historical, archaeological, and ethnographic accounts of numerous hunter-gatherer societies.

Wilkinson, Richard G. *Poverty and Progress: An Ecological Perspective on Economic Development.* New York: Praeger, 1973. A provocative work that suggests, along the same lines as Boserup, that major advances in subsistence technology result from population pressure, not the desire for greater economic efficiency.

Winterhalder, Bruce, and Eric Alden Smith (eds.). *Hunter-Gatherer Foraging Strategies: Ethnographic and Archaeological Analyses*. Chicago: University of Chicago Press, 1981. A collection of essays applying the recent approach known as optimal foraging theory to the analysis of hunter-gatherer subsistence practices.

Wolf, Eric. *Peasants*. Englewood Cliffs, N.J.: Prentice-Hall, 1966. A valuable overview of peasant life, both in modern times and before the emergence of capitalism and industrialism.

CHAPTER 5

Precapitalist Economic Systems

Every society has an economic system that is closely intertwined with its mode of subsistence technology. Yet there is a crucial difference between economy and technology. Technology involves the tools, techniques, and knowledge that the members of a society possess and use in the process of making a living. Economic activity is impossible without technology, but the economy is something more than the level of technology. The **economy** consists of the *social relationships that organize the production, distribution, and exchange of goods and services in any society.* **Production** is the socially organized process whereby goods and services are created. Questions about who owns the forces of production and how they decide to use these forces are questions about production. **Distribution** is the socially organized process of allocating the goods and services that the society produces—who gets what, how, and why. **Exchange** is the process of transferring valuables in return for other valuables, for example, exchanging gifts or purchasing items in a marketplace.

This chapter discusses those economic systems that existed prior to the development of a worldwide capitalist market economy or, if they exist today, display economic characteristics of a noncapitalist type. A crucial concern of the chapter is to show the ways in which **precapitalist economies** are both similar to and different from modern capitalism.

PRODUCTION-FOR-USE VERSUS PRODUCTION-FOR-EXCHANGE

All goods have two distinct types of value, known generally as use-value and exchange-value. The **use-value** of a good is its direct utility, that is, the benefit it confers upon the user when it is used in the manner for which it is intended. For instance, the use-value of a shoe is its benefit to the wearer as a device that protects the foot, keeps the foot warm and dry, and so on. Likewise, the use-value of an automobile is its utility as a transporting vehicle.

But shoes, automobiles, and all other items also have the type of value called **exchange-value.** The exchange-value of these items is the value of some other item they will fetch when they are exchanged for that other item. For instance, if someone agrees to give to another person 300 pairs of shoes in return for that person's automobile, then the exchange value of the automobile in this situation is 300 pairs of shoes. Put another way, we may say that the exchange-value of the pair of shoes is 1/300 of an an automobile. Exchange-value may be reckoned in terms of other useful goods, or in terms of some medium of exchange, that is, money. In capitalist, market-based societies, exchange-value is almost always calculated in money terms; in precapitalist societies, on the other hand, the exchange-value of goods is as often as not reckoned in terms of other goods rather than in some type of money.

While all goods in all economic systems have both use-value and exchange-value, economic systems themselves tend to be organized around one or the other of these types of value. Precapitalist societies are organized primarily around activities in which the production of goods for their use-value is the sole concern of the producers. In this case, the goods are produced so they can be consumed, not so they can be exchanged for other goods. When this type of activity dominates economic action, then a **production-for-use** economy exists.

Modern capitalism, by contrast, produces a vast quantity of goods primarily for their exchange-value, for the amount of money they will bring to the capitalist producers when they are sold in the market. Of course, these goods have use-value; otherwise no individuals would be interested in purchasing them. But that is beside the point. The *motivation* of modern capitalists to produce them relates to their exchange-value rather than to their use-value. Thus, modern capitalism is a **production-for-exchange** economy, or one in which production-for-exchange takes priority over production-for-use.

It should not be assumed that production-for-use economies do not have production-for-exchange. Indeed they do, at least to some small extent. It is simply that production-for-exchange plays a very secondary role in these types of economies. Nor should it be assumed that production-for-use economies are capable only of meeting the subsistence needs of their members. On the contrary, many precapitalist economic systems produce great wealth and marked economic inequalities among their members. However, the point to be stressed is that such wealth and inequality do not arise from production-for-exchange relationships, but from production-for-use relationships. Only in modern capitalism does the existence of vast wealth and economic inequality result primarily from production-for-exchange relationships. This important point will be developed more thoroughly as the chapter unfolds.

MODES OF OWNERSHIP IN PRECAPITALIST SOCIETIES

When considering how goods are produced in all societies, a vital question concerns who owns the forces of production—that is, who owns those resources that are of greatest significance in carrying out productive activities. In modern capitalism, the vital forces of production are principally owned by a tiny fraction of the population, and this small group of capitalists directs the overall process of economic production. In modern socialist societies, such as the Soviet Union, ownership of the productive forces resides in the government, which claims to direct production for the general good of society. Thus, in both modern capitalism and socialism the production process is strongly determined by those persons or groups who are the owners of crucial resources.

In precapitalist societies as well, economic production is shaped by the desires and choices of the owners of the productive forces. It is useful to distinguish four broad modes of ownership in precapitalist societies: primitive communism, lineage ownership, chiefly ownership, and seigneurial ownership. These types are not exhaustive of all modes of property ownership in precapitalist economies, and there are important variations within each type, but they are more or less representative of the ways in which property ownership is organized in the precapitalist world.

Primitive Communism

In the middle of the nineteenth century, Karl Marx speculated that the earliest mode of economic life in human history was what he termed **primitive communism.** By primitive communism, Marx meant a type of society in which people subsisted by hunting and gathering or by simple forms of agriculture, and in which all of the vital resources of nature were held in common. Private ownership of resources by individuals or small groups was not found, he thought, in this type of society.

Although many social scientists over the years have challenged Marx's view on this matter, contemporary social science provides considerable evidence that Marx was basically correct. The vast majority of hunter-gatherers studied by modern anthropologists display a mode of resource ownership that can be adequately characterized by Marx's notion of primitive communism. While much economic activity among hunter-gatherers is centered around the family, all individuals in such societies have equal access to those resources of nature that are necessary for their subsistence. No person among hunting and gathering bands may be deprived by any other person or group of an equal opportunity to hunt game, collect plants, use a waterhole, or camp on the land. Everyone thus owns these resources collectively (it is sometimes said that since everyone has an equal right to their use, *no one* owns them). In fact, some hunter-gatherers do not even restrict the ownership of resources to their own local band; instead, they provide equal access to resources to all other individuals and groups who may have need for them (Woodburn, 1968). Even in those instances where resources may be "owned" privately by individual families, there are typically no restrictions placed against other families *using* these resources. Among the !Kung, for instance, waterholes are frequently said to be "owned" by individual families, but these families do not prevent other families from using them (Lee, 1968, 1972).

It is true that among hunter-gatherers items such as jewelry and art objects are owned privately, but this fact does not invalidate the claim that primitive communism is the principal ownership mode of hunting and gathering peoples. Jewelry and art objects are not a part of the forces of production, as Marx called the vital resources necessary to economic production. Rather, they are items of what is more appropriately referred to as *personal property.* Since they are not used in the productive process, the nature of their ownership is irrelevant to the Marxian thesis of primitive communism. Even then, we find that these items of personal property are seldom kept for long as private objects. Instead, they continually circulate among members of the group, and thus their use is community-wide.

Lineage Ownership

Among many small-scale horticultural peoples, primitive communism in the strict sense ordinarily does not prevail. Instead, most low-energy horticulturalists have a mode of property ownership that can best be designated **lineage ownership.** Lineage ownership occurs when large-scale kinship groups, known as lineages (or sometimes as clans), hold property in common. Of course, in such societies the most important form of property is land. When lineages own land in common, individual members of the group participate in the use of lineage land only because they are lineage members. Their right to the use of this land is only granted by the lineage itself as a corporate body; the leaders of the lineage, acting as representatives of the lineage as a whole, bestow these rights.

Lineage ownership is similar to primitive communism in that it is not a private form of property holding. Property is still held and used communally. But there is an important difference between lineage ownership and primitive communism. Lineage ownership is more exclusive or more restrictive inasmuch as it makes ownership and use of valuable resources dependent on kinship group membership. In societies resting on lineage ownership, not all members of the society have equal access to the forces of production, even though all members of the same lineage do. Lineage ownership is thus a small step away from primitive communism and toward private ownership. Still, it is closer to primitive communism than to private ownership, since in true lineage ownership the lineages themselves have relatively equal access to resources.

Chiefly Ownership

Chiefly ownership is an evolutionary variation on the theme of lineage ownership. It is ordinarily found among more intensive horticultural societies, although it has been known to exist in a few atypical hunting and gathering societies. Chiefly ownership prevails when a powerful individual—a chief—who is the head of a lineage, of an entire village, or of a vast network of integrated villages, claims personal ownership of the land within his realm and attempts to deprive those persons living on this land of full rights to its use. In order to use the land, these persons must observe certain restrictions on their production, such as turning over a part of their harvests to the chief.

Actually, the ownership of all the land within his realm by a chief is to a certain extent a fiction. The ownership rights of the chief are not as "real" as they are often made out to be. The Kpelle of Liberia in West Africa are intensive horticulturalists with a chiefly mode of ownership, yet the ownership rights of the chief are quite limited. As James Gibbs explains (1965: 200–201):

> Formally, land is said to be "owned" by the paramount chief, who divides it into portions for each town in the chiefdom, using for boundaries cottonwood and kola trees, creeks and hills. Each town chief divides the land for his town into segments for each quarter, using similar boundaries. These portions, in turn, are further split . . . into parcels for each of the "families" or unnamed lineages. . . .
>
> Because each man in the lineage is entitled to the use of a portion of the land, the lineage head cannot refuse to allot a piece of it to each household head in the lineage. Once land is parceled out, it stays within the lineage and reverts to the quarter elder or other original "owner" only when a lineage dies out or some other unusual event occurs. Thus, although a town chief, a quarter elder, or a lineage head is, like a paramount chief, called "owner of the land," each is really a steward, holding the land for the group he represents.
>
> Actually, in everyday situations, the head of the household to whom lineage land has been allocated is spoken of as the owner of the land. He decides which bit of "his" land he will work during a given year and which portions he will allow to lie fallow. Most farms are individually owned by the heads of the households and are worked with the help of the farmer's household group and cooperative work groups.

Thus, even though chiefs are the official owners of the land among the Kpelle, the powers of these chiefs appear to be significantly restricted. Since ordinary individuals make most of the daily decisions regarding the actual productive use of the land, these individuals are, in a sense, also its "owners."

Seigneurial Ownership

Although chiefly ownership represents a significant movement in the direction of private ownership, it has many of the characteristics of lineage ownership and is by no means a true mode of private ownership. True private ownership is reached with the evolution of **seigneurial ownership.** Seigneurial ownership prevails when a small class of persons, generally known as landlords (*seigneurs* in French), claims private ownership of vast tracts of land on which there live and work peasants or slaves who pay rent, taxes, and labor services to these lords. There is nothing fictitious about this type of ownership, since landlords have the power to deprive others of the unrestricted use of land, and these other persons frequently do *not* make the day-to-day decisions about how the land is to be productively used.

Seigneurial ownership has been most characteristic of large-scale agrarian societies, although it has occasionally been found among some especially intensive horticulturalists. It is clear that it is associated with a very intensive mode of agricultural production. In medieval Europe, under the politico-economic system known as feudalism, seigneurial ownership prevailed for many centuries between the fall of the Roman Empire and the rise of modern capitalism. Following Max Weber (1978; orig. 1923), Eric Wolf (1966) has called the type of seigneurial ownership characteristic of medieval Europe **patrimonial ownership.** In this type of ownership, land is privately owned by a class of landlords who inherit it through family lines and who personally oversee its cultivation. Wolf has identified another type of seigneurial ownership that he calls **prebendal ownership.** Prebendal ownership exists when land is owned by a powerful government that designates officials to supervise its cultivation and draw an income from it. As Wolf notes, prebendal ownership was "characteristically associated with strongly centralized bureaucratic states—such as the Sassanid Empire of Persia, the Ottoman Empire, the Mogul Empire in India, and traditional China. The political organization of these empires attempted to curtail heritable claims to land and tribute, and asserted instead the eminent domain of a sovereign, a despot, whose claims overrode all inferior claims to domain" (1966:51).

Ownership Versus Control

The evolution of property rights has been a steady movement away from communal rights toward private rights, from the right of everyone to use vital resources to the right of only a few to the full use of these resources. But to be clear as to just what the important dimension of ownership is, it is important to avoid a narrow, legalistic conception of ownership, of ownership as "title." Rather, what is important is not "title" but *control.* For example, among the !Kung individual families "own" waterholes, that is, have a "title" to them. But this ownership in the sense of "title" means little, since these families have no capacity or inclination to deprive other families of using the waterholes. Thus, among the !Kung the control over waterholes is communal, and that is what is important. In a similar vein, in medieval Europe there were numerous free peasants who owned their own land, that is, who had "title." Yet these peasants were effectively deprived of full control over their own land, since the landlord class held the administrative right to levy taxes against these peasants and to control them in other ways as well. Thus, the peasants owned their land, but the landlords heavily controlled it. Again, it is control that determines just what transpires within a system of production, and when ownership and control do not correspond, it is the latter to which social scientists must attend.

MODES OF DISTRIBUTION IN PRECAPITALIST SOCIETIES

The evolution of modes of property ownership in precapitalist societies is closely associated with the evolution of modes of resource distribution. The more privatized the system of ownership, the more unequal the system of distribution. It is useful to think of four major modes of distribution in precapitalist societies: reciprocity, pure redistribution, partial redistribution, and surplus expropriation.

Reciprocity

Reciprocity is the obligation to repay others for what they have given to or done for us, or the overt act of repaying others. Two distinct types of reciprocity, known as balanced and generalized reciprocity, exist. **Balanced reciprocity** occurs when individuals are obligated to provide equivalent and, frequently, immediate repayment to others. Balanced reciprocity can be identified by the fact that individuals deliberately and openly calculate what they are giving each other and openly declare the nature of the repayment to be made. Each party to the transaction expects to benefit in some way, but there is a clear expectation of mutual benefit and a lack of "exploitation."

Generalized reciprocity occurs when individuals are obligated to give to others without expecting any immediate or equivalent repayment. As opposed to balanced reciprocity, generalized reciprocity does not involve any direct or open agreement between the parties involved. There is a general expectation that equivalent repayment of a debt shall be made, but there is no particular time limit set for the repayment, nor is there any specification as to just how the repayment shall be made. The terms of repayment in generalized reciprocity are notoriously vague.

Marvin Harris (1974) has noted that one can tell whether generalized reciprocity is the prevailing mode of distribution by noticing whether people say "thank you." As Harris (1974:124) puts it, when generalized reciprocity is the distributive mode

> it is rude to be openly grateful for the receipt of material goods or services. Among the Semai of central Malaya, for example, no one ever expresses gratitude for the meat that a hunter gives away in exactly equal portions to his companions. Robert Dentan, who has lived with the Semai, found that to say thank you was very rude because it suggested either that you were calculating the size of the piece of meat you had been given, or that you were surprised by the success and generosity of the hunter.

One might also say that it is rude to say "thank you" when generalized reciprocity is the distributive mode because under such circumstances giving things away to others is a social obligation, not an act of kindness.

While generalized reciprocity occurs to some extent in all societies (it occurs among friends and family members in our own society, for instance), it constitutes the very essence of economic life among hunters and gatherers, where it is most frequently found. Hunting and gathering peoples are famed for their extensive food-sharing. Individuals constantly give food to others and receive food in return. When a man returns to camp with an animal that he has killed, he will divide it into portions and then give these away, typically first to members of his family and then to other members of the band. Similarly, women constantly give away portions of food they have gathered. When a hunter gives meat to others he expects only that he will probably be repaid in some way at some time. The hunter may give to others time after time without any repayment taking place and without any mention being made of this fact. He understands that the chances are excellent that his acts will eventually be reciprocated. A failure to reciprocate only becomes a cause for concern and conflict when it appears that one person is "freeloading" off another.

Where generalized reciprocity is a pervasive feature of economic life, sharing and individual humility become compulsory social habits. As

Meat distribution among the !Kung must be handled delicately and is governed by powerful social norms of reciprocity.

Richard Lee comments in regard to the !Kung (1978:888):

> The most serious accusations that one !Kung can level against another are the charge of stinginess and the charge of arrogance. To be stingy or "far-hearted" is to hoard one's goods jealously and secretively, guarding them "like a hyena." The corrective for this in the !Kung view is to make the hoarder give "till it hurts," that is, to make him give generously and without stint until everyone can see that he is truly cleaned out. In order to ensure compliance with this cardinal rule, the !Kung browbeat each other constantly to be more generous and not to set themselves apart by hoarding a little nest-egg. . . .
>
> But as seriously as they regard the fault of stinginess, the !Kung's most scathing criticisms are reserved for an even more serious shortcoming: the crime of arrogance. . . . A boasting hunter who comes into camp announcing "I have killed a big animal in the bush" is being arrogant. A woman who gives a gift and announces her great generosity to all is being arrogant. Even an anthropologist who claims to have chosen the biggest ox of the year to slaughter for Christmas is being arrogant. The !Kung perceive this behavior as a danger sign, and they have evolved elaborate devices for puncturing the bubble of conceit and enforcing humility. These leveling devices are in constant daily use, minimizing the size of others' kills, downplaying the value of others' gifts, and treating one's own efforts in a self-deprecating way. "Please" and "thank you" are hardly ever found in their vocabulary; in their stead we find a vocabulary of rough humor, backhanded compliments, put-downs, and damning with faint praise.

One possible reason generalized reciprocity is the dominant distributive mode among hunter-gatherers is that it is due to a "natural" tendency to share found among peoples who have yet to develop the corrupting influences of private property. Yet this explanation seems dubious because it paints an unduly romantic picture of hunter-gatherers. The explanation is more likely to be found in the necessity of close forms of cooperation among the members of such groups. Hunters and gatherers intimately depend on one another for survival. While resources are typically not highly scarce in a general sense, they are notoriously subject to marked fluctuations in availability. Thus a man may encounter a long run of bad luck in hunting. If others do not give meat to him during this time, he must go without. They give meat to him because they know that they too will eventually have their turn with bad hunting luck, during which time they will expect to receive meat from him. Therefore to give regularly to others is to help ensure one's own well-being in the long run (Weissner, 1982; Cashden, 1985). Generalized reciprocity is thus a special instance of the phenomenon we earlier identified as *enlightened self-interest.* There can be nothing surprising in the fact that hunters and gatherers show great disdain for the occasional individual who is competitive, selfish, and boastful. Such a person is a direct threat to the economic well-being of others and must be subjected to severe pressure to change his or her ways.

Pure Redistribution*

Another process whereby goods are circulated in precapitalist societies is known as **redistribution.** When redistribution occurs, products are funneled from individual households to a central source and then returned to those households in some sort of systematic manner. Redistribution differs from reciprocity in that redistribution is a more formalized process involving the movement of goods into the hands of some person or group that serves as the focal point for their reallocation.

Two types of redistribution may be identified: pure and partial (Moseley and Wallerstein, 1978), sometimes called egalitarian and stratified (Harris, 1975). In **pure redistribution,** the redistributive process is complete in the sense that the redistributive agent reallocates all goods and keeps no extra portion for himself. Thus pure redistribution is associated with economic equality. In **partial redistribution,** the redistributive process is incomplete inasmuch as the redistributive agent keeps a portion of goods for himself. Thus partial redistribution is associated with economic inequality.

Pure redistributive economies, which are most commonly associated with small-scale horticulturalists, work somewhat differently from one society to another. One version of a redistributive economy is widespread among simple horticultural groups in Melanesia. These societies contain extremely ambitious men known as **big men.** Big men are individuals who seek prestige and renown through their roles as organizers of economic production. The typical aspiring big man begins his career by cultivating larger gardens and raising bigger pig herds. He does this by drawing on the help of close relatives and neighbors, who themselves have a stake in his success. If he is successful at his attempts to increase the productivity of his own gardens and herds, he will eventually have accumulated enough foodstuffs to hold a large feast, at which time these foodstuffs will be redistributed to other village members. Prestige and some renown fall upon him through the holding of a successful feast. But there are usually other individuals in his village with the same aspirations holding feasts of their own. If

*This section owes much to Harris (1974:111–130).

he is consistently able to hold larger feasts than those held by his competitors, he is generally recognized as the village big man and given considerable prestige. But should he falter at this task, his status is quickly lost, and he will be replaced by one of the competitors who has outdone him. Also, he is expected to be generous in his distribution of products and must place considerable emphasis on the welfare of the entire village. Big men who are not sufficiently generous and keep too much for themselves are frequently killed.

The quest for high status on the part of aspiring Melanesian big men has definite economic consequences. Such a quest strongly enhances economic productivity, leading to a general increase in the quantity of garden products, domesticated animals, fish, and other economic products (Oliver, 1955). The circulation of goods is also substantially increased, as feast preparation involves numerous exchanges of goods and services. In addition, there is typically a notable increase in the consumption of many goods by the members of the entire village (Oliver, 1955). The process of competitive feasting is, then, a vital part of the economic systems of Melanesian horticulturalists.

The Kaoka-speakers, a simple horticultural group in Melanesia, are characterized by a classic big-man redistributive system (Hogbin, 1964). The native expression for a leader of prestige and renown is *mwane-kama*, which literally means "man-big." The natives generally agree that there is at any given time only one real big man to a village. He is usually a man over 40 years old who carries himself with assurance and dignity, lives in the most solidly built house, extends extraordinary hospitality, and is shown deference by the villagers.

To win the support of relatives and neighbors in order to launch a career toward bigmanship, a man must be forceful, even-tempered, tactful, industrious, and a good organizer. A man's ambition to pursue such a career usually becomes apparent in his early thirties. When a man intends to strive toward bigmanship, he begins by cultivating larger gardens, a task for which he enlists the aid of close relatives. He also attempts to increase the size of his pig herd. When in time his gardens are flourishing and he has perhaps ten fat pigs and several smaller ones, the man makes it known that he wishes to build a new dwelling, one that is larger and better built than usual. This move is usually taken as a public declaration that he is a candidate for the highest honors of the village. The celebration to mark the end of the job, what the Kaoka-speakers call "the feast-to-remove-the-splinters," is highly elaborate.

One such feast was that of Atana, a man who was already notable but not as yet a rival to the acknowledged village big man. Toward this feast, Atana and his immediate kinsmen contributed 250 pounds of dried fish, 3000 yam cakes, 11 bowls of yam pudding, and 8 pigs. Other villagers attending the feast also brought along additional foodstuffs. When these were added to what was provided by Atana and his kinsmen, the final count was 300 pounds of fish, almost 5000 yam cakes, 19 bowls of pudding, and 13 pigs. It was then Atana's task to redistribute this food to all those who were in some way connected with the feast. By the time he was finished, he had made 257 separate presentations, and only the remnants were left for him. The Kaoka-speakers considered this to be the proper result. As they said, "the giver of the feast takes the bones and the stale cakes; the meat and the fat go to others."

Further progress toward village bigmanship requires that there be more and bigger feasts. If a man can continue to do this, he is eventually likely to become the village big man. If he does succeed, however, he can never rest on his laurels. As soon as the size of his gardens and pig herds begins to shrink, he subsides into insignificance. He is always faced with competitors who are waiting to take his place should he be unable to maintain a sufficiently intense level of economic productivity.

What accounts for the evolution of such redistributive systems? Harris (1974, 1977) argues that the big man is an *economic intensifier:* His role is to increase the level of production beyond what it would otherwise be. Harris believes that this increase in the level of production has adaptive significance for small-scale horticultural groups. As he explains (1974:118): "Under conditions where everyone has equal access to the means of subsistence, competitive feasting serves the practical function of preventing the labor force from falling back to levels of productivity that offer no margin of safety in crises such as war and crop failures."

Michael Harner (1975) offers a similar, yet slightly different, explanation. He theorizes that big-man systems are products of labor scarcity. Where people cultivate the land by simple horticultural methods, vast tracts of land are usually available, and it is labor, rather than land, that is a scarce resource. Under conditions of labor scarcity, the role of big man arises as the principal mechanism for the attainment of power and prestige. Thus Harner focuses on the evolution of the big-man system from the point of view of benefits to the individual, whereas Harris's explanation stresses the society-wide benefits of the big-man system. Nonetheless, their explanations appear complementary rather than contradictory; that is, in this particular situation, the individual's selfish interests and everyone's economic needs are simultaneously satisfied through the same social activities.

Given Harris's explanation of the big-man system, it is easy to see why big men are not found among hunter-gatherers. Big men in hunting and gathering societies would be economically maladaptive, for they would exploit the resources of nature beyond their natural recovery points and thus destroy the ecological and economic foundation of hunter-gatherer society (Harris, 1974). Thus, the very personalities that may be highly beneficial for many horticultural societies would produce disastrous consequences for hunters and gatherers.

Partial Redistribution

Partial redistributive systems are most commonly found in societies in which intensive horticulture is the technological mode and chiefly ownership the prevailing mode of property rights. Chiefly ownership is a vital aspect of partial redistribution.

Marshall Sahlins (1963) highlights the important differences between pure and partial redistribution by comparing the distributional systems of Melanesian and Polynesian societies. As he notes, most Melanesian societies have had small-scale horticulture and big-man systems, whereas most Polynesian societies have been characterized by more intensive horticulture and partial redistribution.

Melanesian big men are persons who *seek prestige and renown* through the holding of elaborate feasts. They have little real power over their constituents, however, and their prestige and renown quickly disappear when their elaborate feast giving declines. By contrast, Polynesian chiefs are *installed in office* through a system of hereditary succession. These chiefs exercise considerable power over their followers, and they hold substantial economic leverage over the large mass of ordinary folk. One of their primary aims is the production and maintenance of a constant economic surplus. They accomplish this by compelling the people to give up a portion of their harvests. This leads to the formation of a "public treasury," a great storehouse over which the chief exercises control. The uses to which this storehouse is put are many. Chiefs support themselves and their families from it. They also use it for such things as providing lavish entertainment for visiting dignitaries, initiating major public projects such as irrigation works, building temples, sponsoring military campaigns, and supporting a vast range of political functionaries and administrative officials. In addition, portions of the storehouse are redistributed to the people as the need arises, and chiefs are expected to be generous with it. Those who are not sufficiently generous or who make excessive demands on the people's harvests are sometimes put to death.

Polynesian partial redistributive systems are redistributive in the sense that they involve a continual flow of goods between the chiefs and the people. In this case, however, the flow of goods is an unequal flow: The people clearly give more than they receive in return. While clearly similar in principle to the pure redistributive systems of small-scale horticulturalists, these intensified redistributive systems of more advanced horticulturalists are different in that they serve to promote a system of economic inequality. As such, they constitute a notable evolutionary development beyond the pure redistributive level.

Michael Harner (1975) has suggested that the key factor behind this significant evolutionary outcome is land scarcity. When population pressure forces small-scale horticultural groups to adopt more intensive methods of cultivation, it is clear that land is becoming a scarce resource. Indeed, that is precisely why each particular unit of land must be cultivated more intensively. Land scarcity, in Harner's view, results in increased competition over valuable land, and some persons end up with greater access to land than others. Former big men, with a relatively weak power base resting on their own efforts and the voluntary assistance of their followers, turn into chiefs, persons whose power base is made much stronger by their control over land.

Tribal chief in Ghana, with his retinue of attendants. In many African horticultural societies, chiefs play a major role as economic organizers and redistributors of wealth.

The Potlatch*

The Northwest Coast of North America, an area that stretches from northern California to northern British Columbia, has in recent centuries been populated by Indian tribes who practiced a fascinating and seemingly bizarre custom known as the **potlatch.** The potlatch, which reached its highest level of development among the tribe known as the Kwakiutl, was an elaborate giveaway feast held by village chiefs as a means of validating and reinforcing their high social and political status. The highest status went to those chiefs who could give away the most property and by doing so compel other chiefs to give away their property too.

A potlatch worked more or less in the following manner. The chief of one group would announce that he was holding a potlatch and publicly invite another chief and his followers weeks in advance of the big occasion. Elaborate preparations would then be made for the potlatch. The host chief would assemble a vast array of valuables, including fish, fish oil, berries, animal skins, blankets, and many other valuables (Harris, 1974). At the appointed time the visiting group would arrive, and serious feasting would begin. When the feasting itself had con-

*This section owes much to Harris (1974:111–130).

cluded, the host chief would begin the process of presenting gifts to the visitors. The more gifts he was able to bestow upon them, in the viewpoint of the Northwest Coast tribes, the greater he was and the more honor and respect he deserved. As the host chief gave away his valuables, he would sing and chant about his greatness. Ruth Benedict records the following speech made by a Kwakiutl chief (1934:191):

> I am the first of the tribes,
> I am the only one of the tribes.
> The chiefs of the tribes are only local chiefs.
> I am the only one among the tribes.
> I search among all the invited chiefs for greatness like mine.
> I cannot find one chief among the guests.
> They never return feasts,
> The orphans, poor people, chiefs of the tribes!
> They disgrace themselves,
> I am he who gives these sea otters to the chiefs, the guests, the chiefs of the tribes.
> I am he who gives canoes to the chiefs, the guests, the chiefs of the tribes.

The most successful potlatches were those in which a chief would give away all his property and, to demonstrate his true greatness, pour oil on his house and burn it to the ground. Thus the potlatch sometimes reached extreme and bizarre proportions. The successful potlatch not only brought greatness to the host chief, but it heaped shame upon the visiting chiefs unless they were able to reply with even greater potlatches of their own. Thus chiefs to whom much property had been given were highly motivated to organize future potlatches, at which time they could banish their shame and reassert their own greatness.

The potlatch has been the subject of considerable theoretical work attempting to make sense of it. A well-known older theory is that of Ruth Benedict (1934). She has argued that the entire culture of the Kwakiutl and related Northwest Coast tribes was the product of the "obsessive, megalomaniacal desires" of the chiefs (1934:193): "The whole economic system of the Northwest coast was bent to the service of this obsession." But this essentially psychological theory is thoroughly inadequate, since it offers no clues as to why Northwest Coast chiefs acquired their fanatical personalities.

More recent scholarship has attempted to explain both the fanatical personalities of the Northwest Coast chiefs and the potlatch itself by examining the ecological conditions of Northwest Coast society. One theory that has been widely endorsed is Stuart Piddocke's (1965).

It has been commonly believed that the Northwest Coast tribes lived amidst great material abundance due to the extraordinarily productive nature of their environments. Although possessing only a hunting and gathering technology, these tribes were said to be able to support large populations because the environment assured continuous plenty. But as Piddocke points out, this picture of material abundance on the Northwest Coast is highly misleading. He believes that the level of abundance has been overestimated and that, in addition, there was sharp regional variation and seasonal fluctuation in both plant and animal resources. Some areas would have more than they needed, whereas others would frequently suffer from considerable resource scarcity; by the same token, sharp seasonal fluctuations meant that groups could not always count on a steady and continuous subsistence. Piddocke (1965:247) thus reports that "it [the abundance] was great enough to support a population larger than the usual size reported for hunting and gathering societies; but this population lived sufficiently close to the margins of subsistence so that variations in productivity which fell below normal could threaten parts of the population with famine and death from starvation."

On the basis of these considerations, Piddocke's theory is that the potlatch system arose as a specialized type of redistributional mechanism designed to even out sharp regional and seasonal variations in resources, and thus contribute to the survival and well-being of entire groups (Piddocke, 1965:245):

> Without the distribution of food from wealthier groups to poorer ones, the latter would often have died of hunger. . . .
>
> . . . Through this exchange system, the effects of variations in productivity were minimized, and a level of subsistence was maintained for the entire population. . . .
>
> . . . In this system food could be exchanged for wealth objects, such as blankets, slaves, and canoes; and wealth objects exchanged in turn for increased prestige. . . .
>
> . . . The desire for prestige and the status rivalry between chiefs directly motivated potlatching and so indirectly motivated the people to continue the system of exchanges; and the continuation of these practices ensured the survival of the population.

Although Piddocke's theory may explain much of what went on in the potlatches, how do we account for the extremes the potlatch sometimes reached, such as chiefs burning down their own houses? Piddocke suggests that the aboriginal potlatch was not characterized by such extremes of behavior, and that these only arose after European influence began pouring great wealth into the Northwest Coast economy. Peter Farb explains further (1978:158):

> It must be remembered, though, that the potlatches observed in the nineteenth century were outlandish exaggerations of the indigenous tradition, the result of contacts with Whites. The Whites, in their scramble to obtain sea-otter and fur-seal pelts, pumped vast amounts of fresh wealth into the Northwest Coast societies. The potlatch simply could not handle the sudden flood of mass-produced fabrics, guns, kitchen utensils, metal tools, cheap jewelry, and other products of industrialized Europe and the United States. So one cause for the explosion of the potlatch was a deluge of White wealth.

Another cause of the explosive growth of the aboriginal potlatch was the severe depopulation of the Northwest Coast tribes resulting from European-induced diseases and warfare. Thus "the numerous deaths left open more noble titles than there were persons of high rank to bear them" (Farb, 1978:158). This created widespread competition among the tribesmen to rise to these positions of high rank, and the potlatches were highly exaggerated as a result (Farb, 1978).

Thus the Northwest Coast potlatch does not seem to be a bizarre and inexplicable phenomenon at all. Rather, it appears to be a specialized type of redistributive system containing elements of both pure and partial redistribution.

Surplus Expropriation and Exploitation

Surplus expropriation is a distributive mode most generally found in agrarian societies organized in terms of a seigneurial system of property rights. It occurs when a class of landlords compels another class of dependent economic producers to produce a surplus from their fields and hand this surplus over to them. The surplus is handed over in the form of rent, taxation of various sorts, and various types of labor services.

Some students of precapitalist economies, notably the economic historian Karl Polanyi (1957), do not distinguish between expropriation and partial redistribution. Instead, they use the concept of redistribution to cover both types of economic activity. Yet this seems a serious mistake and at the very least highly misleading. There are several crucial differences between expropriation and partial redistribution, two worth noting here. First, landlords have considerably greater power than chiefs, and they use this power to place many more economic burdens upon peasant producers than chiefs are capable of placing on their followers. Second, the flow of goods and services between peasants and lords is substantially more unequal than is the flow of valuables between chiefs and commoners. The flow of valuables between peasants and lords can scarcely be described as redistribution, since there is little counterflow from lords to peasants; indeed, the flow of valuables is largely in one direction only: from peasants to lords. Although there may be in some situations a fine line between partial redistribution and expropriation, in most cases it is not difficult to tell whether redistribution or expropriation is operating within a society.

Under medieval European feudalism, surplus expropriation was the dominant distributive mode. Peasants owed landlords a specified rent for the use of the landlord's land that they paid either as a portion of their harvests (rent in kind), or by money (cash rent), or some combination of the two. In the earlier days of the feudal period, rent in kind was the standard form of rent payment; but as the feudal system evolved in the later Middle Ages cash rent began to replace rent in kind. Since the peasant was thus producing both for himself and for his landlord, he had to increase his own toil as well as that of his family in order to meet these economic demands placed upon him. Peasants also had economic burdens in the form of taxes. For instance, peasants had to pay a tax to grind their grain in the lord's mill, another tax to bake their bread in the lord's oven, and yet another to fish in the lord's fishpond. (Since peasants did not own these items, they fell into this sort of dependence on their lords.) A third type of economic burden placed on medieval European peasants was that of labor services. Peasants were required to spend so many days working on the lord's demesne (his home farm, or personal land on which he, and not his peasants, lived), tilling the soil and tending the animal herds. This burden often became very oppressive and left the peasant little time to provide for his own family's subsistence by working his own lands.

In ancient Rome a vast system of surplus expropriation also existed, but this system rested primarily on slave rather than peasant labor. The huge supply of slaves on which Rome relied was acquired by political conquest of foreign lands. Slave labor was much cheaper than peasant labor and therefore was the principal labor mode in Roman society (Cameron, 1973). There were many great Roman estates that had large slave gangs working on them; Pliny, for instance, mentions one estate that had 4117 slaves (Cameron, 1973). Where slavery rather than serfdom is the principal labor mode, the system of surplus expropriation is more direct and obvious. For example, to calculate their economic gain, the Roman landowners simply had to determine the amount of wealth their slaves produced for them and subtract from this the cost of acquiring and maintaining a slave labor force.

Many scholars have applied the term **exploitation** to the relationships between lords and peasants, masters and slaves, and, to some extent, chiefs and commoners. At the same time, others have objected to the use of this term. George Dalton (1974), for instance, has argued that the term is a highly prejudicial and emotion-ridden one that is used by those who do not like a particular economic system simply to condemn it. Since Dalton believes that the term is used merely to register disapproval rather than to engage in scientific analysis, he recommends that it be dropped from the vocabulary of social scientists. Dalton does suggest, however, that if the term is to be used, then it should be made to depend upon people's subjective judgments of whether or not exploitation is taking place—that is, of whether or not they themselves are being exploited. As Dalton explains (1972:391n):

> Are present-day Americans (and Russians) "exploited" by definition because we are forced under threat of legal penalty to pay one-third of our income to federal, state, and local govern-

> ments? I suggest that whether or not "exploitation" exists in such situations should be made to depend on the tax or tribute payers' subjective reactions to such obligatory payments upwards; when U.S. (or, presumably, Soviet) citizens approve of the quantity and quality of public services they receive back for their tax money, they do not feel exploited.

Dalton thus believes that objective definitions and calculations of exploitation are not possible and that exploitation can only be said to exist if people think it does. In other words, if a peasant does not *feel* exploited by his lord, then he isn't.

Dalton's wholly subjective approach to the problem of exploitation is unacceptable. Saying that exploitation does not exist when people do not feel exploited is very much like saying that people are not suffering from heart disease if they think they aren't. Like heart disease, exploitation is an objective phenomenon, and hence must be conceptualized and measured by objective criteria, not by people's subjective thoughts and feelings (Moore, 1966; Zeitlin, 1973).

The following objective definition of exploitation is offered here: *Exploitation exists when one party is compelled to give to another party more than it receives in return.* Two aspects of this definition must be emphasized. First, exploitation obviously occurs only when two parties to a relationship receive unequal benefits as the result of that relationship. Second, the unequal benefits must occur because one of the parties is being compelled to give or do something. That is, one party does not voluntarily enter the relationship, or, if there is voluntary entrance into the relationship, it is because alternative relationships would produce no improvement in that party's economic situation.

This definition of exploitation is somewhat easier to state, unfortunately, than to apply. Nonetheless, it can be applied with reasonable success. Dalton (1972) suggests that no objective assessment of the fairness of the flow and counterflow of goods and services between lord and peasant can be made. But this viewpoint seems unduly pessimistic. While it is perhaps difficult to do, it is by no means impossible. The products and services that peasants give to lords have already been noted. What do lords give in return to peasants? As Dalton (1972) himself mentions, they offer military protection against invaders, police protection against robbery, juridical services to settle disputes, feasts at special holidays, food on days when peasants work on the lord's demesne, and emergency food provisions. Dalton argues that there is no way to tell whether or not this set of exchanges is fair or unfair, exploitative or nonexploitative (except by appealing to the thoughts and feelings of the peasants).

But what is the one resource that lords never give to peasants? As Harris (1980) points out, it is the free and unrestricted use of land. Were they to do this, the relationship between lord and peasant would not be economically unbalanced, for peasants would then have no obligations to provide rent, taxes, and services to lords and undoubtedly would not do so. The economic situation of peasants would thus improve, while that of lords would deteriorate. In other words, even though lords provide valuable goods and services to peasants, they do not provide unrestricted access to the resource that is of greatest value in agrarian societies. Thus, it seems fair to conclude that peasants receive unequal benefits as the result of their relationship with lords, that they do so under a particular type of compulsion, and that they enter the relationship involuntarily or because alternatives are no more (and quite possibly less) attractive. It therefore seems reasonable to conclude that peasants are exploited by landlords.

Are, then, commoners exploited as well by chiefs? Probably they are, at least to some degree, although it appears that the level of exploitation is substantially less than in the landlord-peasant relationship. In fact, it seems fair to suggest that the very beginnings of exploitation, in an evolutionary sense, are to be found in intensive horticultural societies with chiefly modes of ownership and partial redistributive systems. Big-man and other pure redistributive systems, as well as systems of balanced and generalized reciprocity, are notable for their lack of any genuinely exploitative elements. In fact, these appear to be the only types of economic systems in which exploitation does not appear as a structured part of everyday social life.*

THE EMERGENCE OF ECONOMIC MARKETS

That economic institution known as the **market** exists when people offer goods and services for sale to others in some more or less systematic and organized way. It is important to distinguish between the terms *market* and *marketplace*. A **marketplace** is a physical site where goods and services are brought for sale and where buyers assemble to purchase these goods and services. In precapitalist societies, marketplaces are physical sites found at a small number of designated locations within the society. But in modern capitalism, the marketplace is "diffuse," that is, spread pervasively throughout society. The market, by contrast, is not a physical place, but a social institution, or a set of social relationships organized around the process of buying and selling valuables.

Societies in Relation to the Market

Paul Bohannan and George Dalton (1962) have distinguished three kinds of societies with respect to their relationship to the market: marketless societies, peripheral market societies, and market-dominated societies.

*In later chapters we shall inquire as to whether modern capitalist and socialist economies operate according to exploitative principles.

Marketless societies have neither markets nor marketplaces. Although there may be a few economic transactions based on buying and selling, these are casual and few and far between. Since marketless societies have no markets, subsistence is not provided by market principles, but by the mechanisms of reciprocity or redistribution. The !Kung, the Kaoka-speakers, and the Yanomamo are marketless societies, as are indeed the vast majority of hunter-gatherer and horticultural groups.

Peripheral market societies have marketplaces but market principles clearly do not serve to organize economic life. In such societies, people may frequently be involved in marketplace activity, either as buyers or sellers, but this activity is a very secondary economic phenomenon. People do not receive their subsistence through marketplace activities, but through reciprocity, redistribution, and expropriation. In peripheral market societies, "most people are not engaged in producing for the market or selling in the market, or those who are so engaged are only part-time marketers" (Bohannan and Dalton, 1962:7).

Peripheral markets are found quite frequently among intensive horticulturalists, and almost universally in agrarian societies. The Aztecs, highly intensive horticulturalists who dominated Mexico during the fifteenth and sixteenth centuries, had peripheral markets of considerable scope and significance (Beals and Hoijer, 1971). In each city throughout the Aztec Empire there existed large markets, and these markets were connected to each other and to the Aztec capital city of Tenochtitlán by a system of traveling merchants. A huge market located in a suburb of Tenochtitlán took place every fifth day. Potential buyers came to this market from miles around to buy the many and varied goods that were offered in it: gold, silver, jewels, clothing, chocolate, tobacco, hides, footwear, slaves, fruits and vegetables, salt, honey, tools, pottery, household furnishings, and many other items.

A seventeenth-century London fair.

Peripheral markets were also significant in medieval Europe (Heilbroner, 1985). Markets in the small cities of medieval Europe were places where peasants would bring some of their harvests for sale. Merchants and artisans who lived in these cities, however, were more important to the life of the marketplace. These merchants and artisans manufactured goods to be sold in the markets and made their livings from such sale. Medieval Europe also had a special kind of marketplace activity known as a *fair*. This was a type of traveling market, held usually once a year, to which merchants from all over Europe came to sell their products. The fair combined social holiday, religious festival, and intense economic activity. At some of these fairs, merchants brought a considerable variety of products for sale, such as silks, horses, drugs, spices, books and parchments, and many other items (Heilbroner, 1985).

Market-dominated societies have both markets and marketplaces (i.e., "diffuse" marketplaces), and the market principle—the principle of buying and selling goods according to the forces of supply and demand—governs all important decisions in regard to production, distribution, and exchange. In these societies, various types of reciprocity and redistribution may be found, but they are of very minor significance indeed. The only genuine market-dominated societies are those characterized by modern capitalism. Since we shall examine market-dominated societies in detail later in this book, the rest of the discussion in this section of the chapter concerns peripheral market societies. Our focus is on the kind of highly developed peripheral market activity characteristic of most agrarian societies and typically located in cities.

Aspects of the Market in Precapitalist Societies

Manufacturing and the Guilds In precapitalist societies in which manufacturing occurs as a substantial economic activity, it is a small-scale undertaking, generally confined to the homes of artisans or to a few small shops located in the marketplaces (Sjoberg, 1960). Even the largest workshops in precapitalist societies would be quite small by modern standards of manufacturing. With no mass market for goods, and thus strict limits upon the formation of capital, productive units must necessarily remain small.

Precapitalist forms of specialization occur in regard to the product rather than the production process. Each craftsman fashions an entire product himself, from beginning to end. As Gideon Sjoberg notes: "Specialization in product is often carried to the point that the craftsman devotes his full time to producing items made from a particular raw material; thus we have goldsmiths, coppersmiths, silversmiths, silk weavers, wool weavers, and so on, each with their own guild" (1960:197). In addition, the precapitalist craftsman typically functions as his own merchant in selling the final product.

In virtually all large-scale precapitalist societies with significant manufacturing sectors, craftsmen and merchants are organized into work organizations known as *guilds.* Guilds are specialized by occupation; they include as their members all persons who perform the same

A parade of the Butchers' Guild in Nuremberg, Germany, in 1658. The object being carried is a 460-yard sausage. Throughout the Middle Ages, and even into early modern times, guilds were important organizations designed to promote the economic interests of craftsmen and merchants.

occupation or highly specialized branch of an occupation. Sjoberg (1960), for instance, lists the following guilds in just one precapitalist city, Beijing in the 1920s: carpenters (Sacred Lu Pan Society), shoe fasteners (Sewers of Boots and Shoes Guild, or Double Thread Guild), tinkers (Clever Stove Guild), clock stores (The Clock Watch Commercial Guild Association), leather stores (Five Sages Hide and Skins Guild), vegetable merchants (Green or Fresh Vegetable Guild), barbers (Beautify the Face Guild), and waiters (Tea Guild).

The most important function of guilds is creating and maintaining a monopoly over a specific type of economic activity: "The right to pursue almost any occupation concerned with manufacturing or trade, or even services, is possible only through membership in the guild that controls it" (Sjoberg, 1960:190). In exercising their monopolistic control over occupations, guilds engage in a variety of activities. As Sjoberg points out, they determine the selection of personnel for an occupation; train members for their work, usually through a master-apprentice relationship; set standards of workmanship for their members; control the output generated by their members; protect their members from excessive restrictions that might be placed upon them by governmental or religious bodies; and assist their members in establishing shops or purchasing the raw materials they need to complete their work.

Clearly guilds play a crucial role in the lives of precapitalist craftsmen and merchants. Indeed, they are roughly comparable in their basic aims to our modern-day labor unions and business and professional organizations.

Price Determination in Precapitalist Markets In modern capitalism, prices for goods and services are determined by abstract supply and demand forces. Individuals may expect to go into stores and find fixed prices already attached to items. Prices in precapitalist settings, however, are not established in this way, but are set by what is usually called *haggling*. Haggling occurs when a potential purchaser asks a merchant how much he wants for an item, the merchant replies, and then the purchaser offers a counterprice, which is usually much lower than that mentioned by the merchant. The seller and buyer then negotiate (haggle over) the price until eventually an agreement is reached or the buyer leaves in disgust. Sjoberg adds the following about the haggling process (1960:205):

> In the process the verbal duel may wax violent. Usually the customer belittles the item in question and tries to evince little interest in purchasing it, while the seller uses counterarguments to persuade the customer to buy it at the asking price. Occasionally friends, even strangers, will join in, interposing remarks as to the probable worth of the article. Not only does the skill of the participants enter into the final figure, but the relationship of the buyer to the seller is a decisive factor. Friends are likely to obtain goods at favored prices.

Haggling is the typical mode of price determination in societies where mass markets do not exist and thus where sellers and buyers have little "knowledge of the market" for any given item. In addition, since haggling can take up large amounts of time, time must not be a valuable and scarce resource, as it is in modern capitalism. Therefore, haggling can only occur in settings in which people are seldom in a hurry to accomplish their everyday tasks (Sjoberg, 1960).

Nonrationality of Economic Activity Modern capitalism is a supremely rational type of economic system in the sense that there are a variety of sophisticated techniques used in the conduct of business—techniques designed to maximize economic productivity and growth. Thus, modern capitalists use advanced forms of accounting, finance, workplace organization, and marketing in the conduct of their business activity, and these procedures are crucial to their success.

In precapitalist markets, however, such a rational organization of economic activity is largely absent (Sjoberg, 1960). This nonrationality (not to be confused with "irrationality") of economic activity is expressed in numerous ways. For one thing, artisans and merchants commonly do not adhere to fixed work schedules closely regulated by the clock. On the contrary, they often start work at different hours in the morning and stop work at different times later in the day, according to the nature of other noneconomic activities in which they are engaged. In addition, precapitalist manufacturing is characterized by little synchronization of effort. Workers in one sector of manufacturing have little knowledge of what is happening in other sectors, and they make little if any effort to coordinate their activities with the activities being undertaken in these other sectors. Finally, the marketing of goods in precapitalist societies is subject to little standardization. For example, merchants seldom grade or sort their products, and there is little standardization of weights and measures. As Sjoberg notes, this lack of standardization is linked to the absence of a mass market and thus to the highly personalized nature of market activity.

A Reflection

Although these views about the role of the market in human societies have been widely accepted by comparative social scientists, in recent years some social scientists have strongly challenged them. Kajsa Ekholm and Jonathan Friedman (1982), for example, have suggested that market activities and production-for-exchange have played a much greater role in earlier societies than has generally been recognized. They oppose the traditional division of "the world's history into distinctive market/nonmarket or capitalist/pre-capitalist systems," and maintain the "point of view that there exists a form of 'capitalism' in the ancient world" (1982:87–88). In other words, Ekholm and Friedman object to the very conceptualization of peripheral market societies, or at least claim that this conceptual category does not apply as broadly as ordinarily thought.

Ekholm and Friedman do not claim that there are no differences between ancient societies and modern capitalism; they argue simply that the differences are less great than we have been taught to believe. It is too early to tell for sure, but it is quite possible that they are onto something. Perhaps traditional scholarship has underestimated the extent and importance of exchange relationships in ancient horticultural and agrarian economic systems. And perhaps these relationships were similar to some aspects of modern capitalism. Nonetheless, one senses that Ekholm and Friedman are going too far in their claim. Before the sixteenth century in western Europe, production-for-use relationships still dominated economic life, and the exchange relationships that did exist should not be compared too closely with those of the modern capitalist world. The traditional analysis therefore still stands, even though it may need to be somewhat modified.

SUMMARY

1. All societies have economies, or means of organizing the production, distribution, and exchange of goods and services. Two fundamentally different types of economic activity are production-for-use and production-for-exchange. Although both forms of economic activity are found in precapitalist societies, production-for-use is clearly dominant. In modern capitalism, though, production-for-exchange overwhelmingly displaces production-for-use.

2. Several modes of resource ownership can be distinguished in precapitalist societies and viewed from an evolutionary perspective. In

Table 5.1 OWNERSHIP, DISTRIBUTION, AND EXCHANGE IN PRECAPITALIST SOCIETIES

Mode of subsistence technology	Mode of ownership	Mode of distribution	Mode of exchange
Hunting and gathering	Normally, primitive communism. The vital resources that sustain life are owned by the entire community, and no person may deprive others of the full right to use these resources.	Generalized reciprocity. Sharing and generosity are pervasive and are compulsory social habits.	Although some exchange does occur, markets and marketplaces are generally absent.
Simple horticulture	Typically, lineage ownership. This is a variation on primitive communism in which resources are communally owned, but the owning group is a kinship group rather than the entire community.	Pure or egalitarian redistribution. Goods are funneled into the hands of a leader, who is responsible for reallocating them to the entire community in an essentially egalitarian fashion.	Again, marketless societies, as above.
Intensive horticulture	Usually chiefly ownership. Powerful chiefs claim ownership of vast tracts of land and exert considerable control over how this land is used. However, the primary producers who live on the land retain substantial decision-making power over the day-to-day cultivation activities.	Partial or stratified redistribution. Goods are funneled into the hands of a centralized social group, but this group retains a large portion of these goods for its own subsistence and for building and maintaining a governmental administrative apparatus. Some reallocation, though, does occur.	Peripheral market societies. Markets exist and may have considerable importance, but are distinctly secondary to production-for-use activities.
Agrarianism	Typically, some type of seigneurial ownership. Land is owned and controlled by a private class of landlords, or by a powerful governmental apparatus functioning in the role of landlord. Landlords exert enormous power over the primary producers (peasants) who cultivate the land and impose severe penalties on them for the use of this land.	Surplus expropriation. A highly imbalanced and exploitative relationship exists between landlords and the primary producers. Landlords extract surplus through rent, taxation, demands for labor services, and other mechanisms.	Peripheral market societies, but with greater importance of market activities. In some cases—e.g., ancient Rome—market exchange becomes very important. Exchange activities often strongly promoted by elaborate intersocietal networks of trade.

hunting and gathering societies, primitive communism predominates. In most simple horticultural societies, a communal pattern of ownership prevails, but ownership is restricted to the members of particular kinship groups (lineage ownership). The beginnings of private property are found with the emergence of chiefly ownership in more advanced horticultural societies. In agrarian societies a highly restrictive form of ownership known as seigneurial ownership prevails. Here a tiny class of landlords claims ownership of land and imposes various penalties on the huge class of peasants who must have access to this land. There is a clear trend toward the evolution of increasingly private and restrictive modes of ownership.

3. Generalized reciprocity is a mode of resource distribution in which individuals give to others without any expectation of equivalent or immediate repayment. This form of behavior is characterized by strong demands for generosity, cooperation, and hospitality. Generalized reciprocity is at the center of the economic behavior of most hunter-gatherers.

4. Horticultural societies commonly emphasize redistributive modes of resource allocation. Pure redistribution prevails when individuals such as "big men" return to everyone the goods they have accumulated. Partial redistribution exists in more advanced horticultural societies and generally involves the activities of more powerful political leaders who redistribute only a portion of what they accumulate.

5. The famous potlatch of the Northwest Coast tribes can be understood as a specialized system of economic redistribution having characteristics of both pure and partial redistribution. This system seems to have arisen as a result of the unique ecology of the region.

6. Surplus expropriation exists in agrarian societies. Here the powerful owners of the land compel those who cultivate it to produce large economic surpluses and turn them over to the owners.

7. Economic exploitation exists when one party compels another party to give up more than it receives in return. Exploitation should be seen as an objective phenomenon, not as something subjectively dependent on people's feelings about their situation. Where reciprocity and pure redistribution prevail, exploitation does not exist. Exploitation exists to some extent where partial redistributive systems are found, and it is a fundamental feature of economic life in agrarian societies with their seigneurial ownership and surplus expropriation.

8. Markets exist in many precapitalist societies, but they do not dominate economic activity. In more advanced precapitalist societies, though, markets are usually of considerable economic significance. Yet even in these markets economic activity is organized in ways different from the elaborate market economy of modern capitalism. The extraordinary "rationality" of modern capitalism is largely absent from precapitalist economic systems.

SPECIAL TOPIC: THE SUBSTANTIVISM-FORMALISM CONTROVERSY

For many years a debate has raged among social scientists concerning the best way to study precapitalist economic systems. Although this debate has died down considerably in the past few years, it continues nonetheless and the issues it raises are crucial ones. The debate in question is between two viewpoints or schools of thought that are commonly identified as **substantivism** and **formalism.**

The substantivists assert that there is a qualitative gulf between capitalist and precapitalist economies and that each must therefore be studied using different concepts and approaches. Modern economic theory, they claim, was developed by economists in Western capitalist societies specifically to study economic behavior in those societies. It therefore has no application to the study of primitive and peasant economies. Modern Western economic theory emphasizes that people attempt to "maximize" or "economize" under conditions of scarcity. That is, they rationally calculate how to achieve certain desired economic ends, these ends being the best they can do, economically speaking, in a given situation.

The substantivists believe that individuals in precapitalist societies do not attempt to "maximize" or "economize." Indeed, their economic decisions are said to be based not on the rational calculation of economic ends, but on consideration of kinship group affiliation, religious prescriptions, or political or other group loyalties. The substantivists therefore claim that economic behavior in primitive and peasant societies is "embedded in," and actually frequently shaped by, the other social arrangements of those societies.

The substantivist position is that misleading if not highly erroneous results will be produced if Western economic theory is applied to understand precapitalist economies. The substantivists therefore recommend that social scientists who study such economies suspend their Western assumptions about typical economic behavior. This would help alert them to the existence of economic assumptions held and forms of behavior practiced by people in precapitalist societies that are distinctively non-Western in character. In turn, more accurate descriptions and explanations of precapitalist economies would thereby result.

The formalists have responded to these pronouncements by agreeing that capitalist and precapitalist economies are by no means identical, either ideologically or behaviorally. Yet they claim that "maximizing" and "economizing" under conditions of scarcity are universal phenomena and thus characteristic of the behavior of persons in precapitalist as well as capitalist economies. They therefore believe that the concepts and principles of modern Western economic theory can be applied to primitive and peasant economies. The formalists base much of their argument on the concept of "scarcity." For example, Scott Cook, a well-known formalist advocate, argues the following (1966:333–334):

> *Although frequently denying the universal relevance of scarcity as a conditioning factor in economic action, the substantivists have never, to my knowledge, provided an ethnographic example of an empirical economy in which scarcity was without implications for economic decision-making (i.e., economizing). Nor . . . have they formulated a counter-postulate which better serves economic analysis than that based on the notion of "scarcity". . . .*
>
> *Economists reject the thesis . . . that scarcity is solely a function of social organization. . . . The basic assumption which economic analysis makes about the physical world is that the resources which it provides for human utilization are scarce (i.e., limited in relation to the demand for them). It is because of this scarcity that goods have to be shared out among the individual members of a social group, and it is the role of an economic system to perform this "sharing out" task. From the economist's point of view, if there were no scarcity and consequently no need for goods to be shared out among individuals, there would be no economic system.*

There are strengths and weaknesses to both of these theoretical positions. On the substantivist side, George Dalton (1967) has provided an illustration of the errors that sometimes result when Western economic assumptions are employed in the analysis of a primitive economic system.

In the early part of this century W. E. Armstrong, a Western economist, studied the monetary system found among the Rossel Islanders, a horticultural society in the southern Pacific (Armstrong, 1924, 1928; discussed in Dalton, 1967). The Rossel Islanders have a type of money consisting of shells known as *ndap* shells. There are 22 named classes of *ndap* shells, apparently arranged in a kind of hierarchy, and Armstrong numbered each of these classes from 1 to 22 (the higher the number, the greater the value of the shell).

Armstrong believed that Rossel Island shell money was essentially equivalent to Western money. He claimed that it was a medium of commercial exchange, a standard of value, and a standard of payment. Furthermore, debts were said to be calculated and goods and services priced in terms of shells of specific classes. However, Armstrong did note an odd feature of this monetary system: the classes of shells were not convertible into each other. For example, a no. 18 shell was needed in exchange for a pig, but a man lacking such a shell could not obtain a pig with, say, a no. 14 shell and a no. 4 shell. Likewise, a no. 20 shell was not said to be worth 20 no. 1 shells, and thus 20 no. 1 shells could not be used to obtain something which required a single no. 20 shell. Armstrong viewed this unique feature of the Rossel Island monetary system as essentially nothing more than a native quirk, and as an inefficiency in their system compared to the Western monetary system.

Dalton argues that Armstrong's analysis was faulty because he could only think of Rossel Island money from the standpoint of Western money. Dalton makes two significant points against Armstrong's analysis. First, he indicates that not all *ndap* shells functioned as media of commercial exchange; rather, only the shells of the lowest few classes served this function. Second, Dalton claims that Armstrong's Western market-oriented conception of what money is led him to do something that the Rossel Islanders themselves do not do, and that is to number the shell classes from 1 to 22. By numbering them Armstrong was implicitly suggesting that the shell classes ought to be convertible into one another, thus giving a false impression of a basic similarity between *ndap* shell money and Western money.

Dalton goes on to point out some additional features of the Rossel Island money system not appreciated by Armstrong. The shells numbered from 18 to 22 stand clearly apart from all the others. Indeed, they are treasure items, with individual names and histories attached to them, that are used to validate important social events. In addition, they have a certain sacred quality about them, and are handled with great care and reverence. Thus they are not media of commercial exchange at all. A no. 18 shell is a necessary part of bridewealth payment, for instance, while a no. 20 is a necessary part of indemnity payments to the relatives of a man who has been ritually murdered.

From the above case it is clear that the substantivists are sometimes correct when they suggest that inaccurate results may be produced when precapitalist economies are analyzed from the standpoint of Western economic concepts and principles. Yet this does not mean that the substantivist position must be endorsed. In fact, substantivism suffers from two crucial weaknesses. One is its claim that economic behavior in precapitalist societies is often or largely motivated by noneconomic considerations; the other is its general denial of the usefulness of the notion of scarcity (Dowling, 1979).

The real strength of the formalist position is its avowal that scarcity is not only universal, but also plays a significant role in shaping economic behavior in all societies (cf. Dowling, 1979). At the same time, caution is especially called for when considering the formalist concept of "maximization," for the members of precapitalist societies may not maximize in quite the same way as the members of capitalist societies. In capitalist societies, maximization commonly takes the form of individuals attempting to increase their supply of money and goods to ever higher levels, while in precapitalist societies maximization takes other forms. For instance, it might take the form of maximizing the supply of leisure time rather than the supply of material items. In addition, people do not always try to truly maximize their outcomes. As the eminent economic theorist Herbert Simon (1976) has pointed out, people are often content with merely a satisfactory, rather than a maximum, level of reward. They may be "satisficers" rather than "maximizers."

In this book we have adopted neither a formalist nor a substantivist position. Rather, we have taken a position that contains features of both perspectives, a position known as **cost/benefit analysis** (Harris, 1977, 1979). Cost/benefit analysis suggests that economic decisions in all societies are made by individuals and groups deliberately weighing the benefits of a certain undertaking against its known or assumed costs. When the benefits outweigh the costs a course of action will be taken, but when the costs exceed the benefits people will generally avoid that course of action.

Cost/benefit analysis has been employed throughout this chapter and the last. It suggests, for example, that hunter-gatherers will not switch to an agricultural mode of production when they perceive the extra work load to bring them no significant improvement in their standard of living; that hunter-gatherers will share food extensively under conditions in which resources are generally abundant but display marked seasonal and regional fluctuation; that big men will arise in societies experiencing labor scarcity as a means of motivating people to bring their economic productivity up to more acceptable levels; that landlords will exploit peasants when their control over land allows them to, and that peasants will frequently resist this exploitation by organizing themselves into movements of rebellion; and that buyers and sellers in precapitalist markets will haggle in an effort to maximize their economic situation.

Thus self-interest and deliberate calculation of costs and benefits govern the economic actions of people everywhere, and their economic arrangements are products of the operation of self-interest under definite kinds of material and historical conditions. Yet it cannot be forgotten that these conditions differ widely from one place to another and from one time to another, and thus numerous and highly diverse systems of economic action have evolved among the members of the human species.

FOR FURTHER READING

Bohannan, Paul, and George Dalton (eds.). *Markets in Africa.* Evanston, Ill.: Northwestern University Press, 1962. A collection of essays on peripheral markets in a variety of African societies. Includes a useful introduction by the editors.

Dalton, George. *Tribal and Peasant Economies.* Austin: University of Texas Press, 1967. A well-known collection of previously published articles and essays on numerous aspects of precapitalist economic life. Discussions of, among other things, primitive money, chiefly forms of landownership, trade, the manorial economy of medieval Europe, and varieties of peasantry.

Harris, Marvin. *Cows, Pigs, Wars, and Witches: The Riddles of Culture.* New York: Random House, 1974. The chapter entitled "Potlatch" contains not only an analysis of that phenomenon, but also a general analysis of reciprocity and redistribution in primitive societies.

Harris, Marvin. *Cannibals and Kings: The Origins of Cultures.* New York: Random House, 1977. Additional discussions of redistribution, plus discussions of the evolution of economic systems from pure redistribution to expropriation.

Hodges, Richard. *Primitive and Peasant Markets.* Oxford: Blackwell, 1988. A recent work on market exchange in precapitalist societies.

LeClair, Edward E., Jr., and Harold K. Schneider (eds.). *Economic Anthropology: Readings in Theory and Analysis.* New York: Holt, Rinehart, and Winston, 1968. An anthology containing several useful articles on precapitalist economies. Especially valuable are several articles concerned with the formalism-substantivism debate.

Lee, Richard B. *The !Kung San: Men, Women, and Work in a Foraging Society.* New York: Cambridge University Press, 1979. A comprehensive study of a hunting and gathering society, with a major focus on economic life. Considerable attention is given to technology, the work roles of men and women, ownership patterns, and recent economic changes due to contact with more advanced societies.

Plattner, Stuart (ed.). *Economic Anthropology.* Stanford, Calif.: Stanford University Press, 1989. A recent textbook that explores economic behavior throughout the whole range of precapitalist societies.

Popkin, Samuel L. *The Rational Peasant.* Berkeley: University of California Press, 1979. A well-known study of peasant economic life from a perspective much like that of the formalists.

Sahlins, Marshall. *Stone Age Economics.* Chicago: Aldine, 1972. A well-known work on precapitalist economic systems written from a perspective different in important respects from that of the present book.

Scott, James C. *The Moral Economy of the Peasant.* New Haven: Yale University Press, 1976. A celebrated study of peasant economic life from an essentially substantivist perspective.

CHAPTER 6

The Origin and Evolution of Social Stratification

This chapter begins the discussion of social stratification, a phenomenon of central concern to sociologists, comparative macrosociologists especially. It explores the way in which social stratification originates and is intensified in human societies, and examines the nature of stratification (or its absence) in hunter-gatherer, horticultural, and agrarian societies. The principal theories offered to account for the origin and evolution of stratification are compared and contrasted and their general explanatory power is assessed. The extremely important issue of the nature of stratification in industrialized societies is postponed until Chapter 10.

THE NATURE OF SOCIAL STRATIFICATION

An important distinction must be drawn between the concepts of **social inequality** and **social stratification.** Failure to make this crucial distinction has led to much confusion among sociologists as to whether social stratification is actually a universal feature of social life.

Social inequality refers to *the existence of differential degrees of social influence or prestige among individual members of the same society.* There are two important facets of this definition. First, social inequality refers only to distinctions among individuals in terms of **social influence**—the degree to which the actions of an individual will be followed or copied by others; or **prestige**—the degree to which an individual is accorded honor or respect. Thus, inequality *does not refer to differential degrees of power and wealth.* Inequality can and does exist in human societies without any differential access of individuals or groups to wealth or to the resources of nature that sustain life. Second, social inequality implies *an inequality among individuals, not among discrete groups.* Where only inequality prevails, individual persons attain differential social standing, but they do so only as individuals, not as members of groups. Indeed, the fact of mere inequality implies the absence of distinct groups that are differentially ranked. Thus conceived, social inequality is a universal feature of human societies, for there is no record of a society that fails to make at least some evaluative distinctions among some individuals.

In contrast to social inequality, social stratification involves *the existence within a single society of two or more differentially ranked groups, the members of which control unequal amounts of power, privilege, and prestige.* This definition of stratification closely follows the conception of stratified society developed by the anthropologist Morton Fried. As Fried notes, "A stratified society is one in which members of the same sex and equivalent age status do not have equal access to the basic resources that sustain life" (1967:186). The key notion contained in Fried's definition is **differential access to resources.** This clearly goes beyond the fact of simple inequalities in influence or respect and into the realm of fundamental inequities in **power** and **privilege.** Power involves the capacity of some persons to command the actions of others, even against their will and despite their resistance. Privilege refers to wealth and other material benefits and opportunities. Differences in prestige also are a part of stratification systems, and it is usually the case that in stratified societies inequalities of prestige derive from inequalities of power and privilege.

Another crucial characteristic of stratification is that *it involves not individuals, but groups.* The degree of power, privilege, and prestige that individuals have in stratified society depends on their membership in actual social groups, not on their personal characteristics. These differentially ranked groups constitute **social strata** (singular = **stratum**), or layers of the overall sociocultural system, and they have a strongly hereditary character. Hence in stratified societies individuals are born into a particular social stratum that gives them a social position and identity regardless of their own personal characteristics. This hereditary quality of stratification clearly sets it apart from inequality. In unstratified societies, the inequalities that emerge (beyond those based on age and sex) are due mainly to individual effort and ability, rather than to hereditary social placement.

Stratification is by no means a universal characteristic of human societies. While there is no such thing as a society in which all persons are perfectly equal, there have been many societies lacking stratification. Stratification tends to be found for the first time among those societies that have evolved to an intensive horticultural level of technological development (although it is occasionally found below this evolutionary stage). Yet despite the fact that stratification has not been universal, it has been a common feature of many societies, and it is indeed universal among all complex societies.

SOCIAL STRATIFICATION IN EVOLUTIONARY PERSPECTIVE

A brief synopsis of the evolution of stratification in preindustrial societies is presented in Table 6.1. This synopsis may be useful in approaching the discussions that follow.

Inequality Without Stratification: Hunting and Gathering Societies

Generally speaking, hunting and gathering societies are unstratified. Their economies are characterized by generalized reciprocity, by an intense sharing and cooperativeness among all members. Hunter-gatherers generally exhibit "primitive communism": Ownership (or at least right of use) of basic resources is communal, and no individual is deprived of access to the resources of nature that sustain life and well-being. Hunting and gathering societies are not characterized, therefore, by any fundamental inequalities of privilege, and no social strata can be said to exist.

Yet the absence of social strata does not mean that perfect equality prevails among all the members of hunter-gatherer societies. Inequalities do exist. These are mainly inequalities of prestige or social influence and are typically based on such factors as age, sex, and certain personal characteristics. As is common throughout the world, men tend to have higher status

Table 6.1 THE EVOLUTION OF SOCIAL STRATIFICATION IN PREINDUSTRIAL SOCIETIES

Type of society	Nature of social stratification
Hunting and gathering	Typically, no stratification. Inequalities of privilege generally absent. Mild inequalities exist based on age, sex, and personal characteristics, such as courage and hunting skill, but these are inequalities of prestige and influence only. General equality permeates entire society.
Simple horticultural	Typically, no stratification. Inequalities of privilege generally absent. Inequalities based on age and sex exist. Outside of sexual inequality, main form of inequality is personal prestige and renown accumulated by redistributor big men. These are frequently "rank" societies in Fried's sense of the term.
Intensive horticultural	Typically, first emergence of genuine stratification. Common pattern is division of society into three social strata (chiefs, subchiefs, commoners). Power and privilege of chiefs limited by people's demands for their generosity. Redistributive ethic still prevails, preventing extreme stratification.
Agrarian	Typically, extreme stratification. Bulk of population is a subjugated and exploited peasantry. Rulers and governing classes possess great wealth and power. Serfdom and slavery are most common forms of subordination of bulk of the population. Caste system of unique nature in southern Asia. Poverty and suffering are widespread. Placement of individuals in class structure is largely by birth, but some mobility does occur.

than women among hunters and gatherers, and, likewise, the older members of society are often given more honor and respect than the younger ones. In addition, the possession of certain personal traits is generally a basis for the acquisition of prestige. Men who are particularly skilled hunters, who show special courage, or who are thought of as having great wisdom are often accorded high prestige. Such individuals typically assume leadership functions because they are deemed to be worthy of the trust and confidence of others.

However, men of prestige and influence among hunter-gatherers are no more than "firsts among equals," and they typically have no special privileges not available to others. It must also be noted that the acquisition of prestige and influence comes from an individual's own abilities and efforts, not from any mechanism of social heredity. Prestige is both personally gained and personally lost. Individuals must continually justify such honor, and should their abilities or efforts fail them, their status will fall and others will replace them. Thus, hunting and gathering societies permit virtually complete equality of opportunity for individuals to gain high status. In such societies, talent, effort, and social reward are closely aligned, a fact that sets them sharply apart from highly stratified societies.

It must be stressed that the degree of prestige that can be gained among hunter-gatherers is very mild when compared to the nature of prestige in other societies. Hunter-gatherers loathe boasting and self-glorification, and they use strong sanctions against those persons who come to think too highly of themselves. Their emphasis is clearly on communal well-being and general social equality. In this sense they are quite aptly described as *egalitarian* societies.

Yet not all hunter-gatherers have been egalitarian, for some have been characterized by considerable inequalities in privilege. By far the best examples of stratified hunting and gathering societies are those Indian tribes that have inhabited the Northwest Coast of the United States. Although there has been some disagreement as to the actual nature and extent of the inequalities present, a number of anthropologists believe that the Northwest Coast was characterized by an exploitative class system. Anthropologist Eugene Ruyle (1973), for instance, makes a strong claim for the existence of a ruling class, rent or taxation, and slavery. These societies have been famous among social scientists for their elaborate competitive feasts known as potlatches, a phenomenon encountered in the last chapter. During their potlatches Northwest Coast chiefs would attempt to shame rival chiefs by giving away large quantities of wealth and ranting and raving about their own greatness. Among the Kwakiutl, for example, chiefs seemed obsessed with maintaining and enhancing their high status.

Clearly the pattern of stratified life and status seeking in the Northwest Coast region is highly unusual for a hunting and gathering society. But the Northwest Coast tribes were atypical hunter-gatherers. They lived in unique environments and had levels of population density highly uncharacteristic of other hunting and gathering groups. Their uniqueness should not be allowed to detract from a proper understanding of what is ordinarily found at the hunting and gathering stage of social life—pervasive social and economic equality.

Inequality Without Stratification: Simple Horticultural Societies

Simple horticultural societies have greater opportunities than hunter-gatherers for the creation of various social inequalities. Greater inequalities are indeed characteristic of simple horticulturalists, but these are not inequalities of privilege or wealth. Rather, they are inequalities of prestige. For this reason, simple horticultural societies are not stratified but are frequently examples of what Morton Fried (1967) has termed **rank societies.** As Fried defines it, "A rank society is one in which positions of valued status are somehow limited so that not all those of sufficient talent to occupy such statuses actually achieve them" (1967:109). Put another way, rank societies establish a prestige ranking system characterized by a limited number of high status positions that confer no special material advantage.

As discussed in Chapter 5, simple horticultural societies generally display economies resting upon egalitarian (or pure) redistribution. The prestige ranking system of such societies is intimately connected with this redistributive pattern. In many simple horticultural societies, individuals who work hard, make sacrifices, and solicit the help of their kinsmen are ultimately able to accumulate a considerable number of products from their gardens and animal herds. This fund of valuables may be used for the holding of large feasts, at which time a general redistribution of the products is made. Individuals who repeatedly demonstrate their prowess in holding successful feasts come to be persons of high rank: They come to be held in considerable respect, envy, and sometimes even awe. As noted in the last chapter, these individuals acquire the status of "big men."

Big men typically have many rivals who wish to oust them from their high rank. Although a society may have only one genuine big man, there are likely to be other persons who are also held in high regard. High rank must be earned through talent and effort; it cannot be acquired hereditarily. To become a big man, a number of personal qualities are necessary. Perhaps paramount among these is generosity. Big men accumulate wealth, but they do not gain their status through hoarding it; rather, prestige comes to them through their generous distribution of this wealth to others. Individuals who hoard their wealth rather than give it away are looked upon with great disfavor. Rank societies are therefore strongly antagonistic in principle

A Melanesian big man, Soloman Islands. A big man holds a high social rank, but this position confers no material advantage over others.

to the existence of differential material advantage, and they contain strong built-in pressures working to prevent such a development. In this way, a system of ranking works to serve the common good (through the redistributive actions of persons of high status) while at the same time preventing the formation of differentially advantaged social strata.

The Siuai of Bougainville in the Solomon Islands are simple horticulturalists with a ranking system of the type envisioned by Fried (Oliver, 1955). Among the Siuai, individuals must possess a number of qualities in order to attain high rank. One of these, of course, is the possession of a considerable supply of valuables available for redistributive feasting. But mere possession of wealth does not by itself guarantee high rank. Men are also expected to be generous with this wealth, to be willing to distribute it to others. The Siuai actively dislike individuals who are miserly with their wealth, and they take a generally negative attitude toward selfishness. Selfishness in a spouse is a basis for divorce, and miserly men who do not aid their kinsmen in times of need are referred to as "stone-hearts." Misers are often feared and suspected of sorcery, are rarely liked, and cannot advance to positions of high rank and leadership. By contrast, generous men are universally liked and respected and, contingent upon their successful feast giving, have good opportunities for attaining high rank. Men who give frequent feasts that are well attended generally gain renown for themselves.

In recognition of the accomplishments of successful feast givers, the Siuai heap considerable praise upon these men of high rank. They also show much respect for a high-ranking individual's name and person. He is generally not addressed by name, but usually called instead by a kinship term or simply *mumi* ("big man"). Even in reference his personal name may not be used, and on these occasions he may be referred to by the name of his clubhouse or by the name of one of his assistants. The respect given his name typically continues even after his death. High-ranking persons are also usually given considerable deference. As the Siuai's principal ethnographer, Douglas Oliver, comments (1955:401):

> Leaders are usually spared menial jobs; others fetch water for them, and climb palms to get coconuts and areca nuts for their refreshment. Boisterous talk usually becomes quieter when a leader approaches, and boys leave off roughhousing. In fact, one of the sternest lessons impressed upon a child is to stay away from a leader, or else remain quiet in his presence. ("Never play when a mumi is nearby; you might disturb him or hit him with your toys.") Females, especially, appear awed near the great men, often looking shyly to the ground. Men usually wait for a leader to open conversations, and take their cues from him concerning when to laugh, to commend, or to decry.

> No supernaturally sanctioned taboos surround a leader's person in order to insulate him from plain physical contact with other natives, but few people would assume enough familiarity with him to place a friendly hand on his shoulder—a common gesture among equals.

Oliver's comments make clear the social meaning of rank in Siuai society. As a fairly typical example of the structure of inequality in most simple horticultural societies, the Siuai effectively demonstrate the nature of a system of ranking in the absence of stratification. Such a ranking system represents a definite evolutionary movement beyond the typical pattern of inequality prevalent among hunter-gatherers, where no man could be shown the kind of deference given to a Siuai mumi. On the other hand, Siuai mumis would themselves be in awe of the attainments of their chiefly counterparts in truly stratified societies.

Intensive Horticultural Societies and the Emergence of Social Stratification

Social stratification generally emerges with the transition to intensive horticultural societies. These societies frequently exhibit hereditary social strata or classes, the true mark of stratified society. Three main social strata (consisting roughly of chiefs, subchiefs, and commoners) are a common pattern. Thus what appear only as differences of rank or status among simple horticulturalists are transformed among intensive horticulturalists into genuine inequalities involving differential access to the basic resources of nature. Appearing on the scene are separate groups of persons distinguished by their differences in social rank, power, dress and ornamentation, patterns of consumption of luxury and other goods, direct involvement in economic production, availability of leisure time, and general styles of life. Membership in such groups is hereditary, and the placement of individuals in the stratified order is largely unrelated to individual talents or efforts. Social status is determined by a person's genealogical relationship to the chief or king.

Yet because chiefs and commoners are related through kinship ties, the stratification system has definite restraints placed upon it. Kinship ties function to soften the nature and consequences of inequality, and chiefs are still expected to be generous with their wealth and to have a concern for the common good. As Lenski (1966) notes, the "redistributive ethic" still prevails in such societies, preventing too great a use of the surplus for the chiefs own ends. Although members of the chiefly class enjoy substantial (and often great) privilege, chiefs are still regarded as "great providers" who must constantly consider the needs and wishes of their distant kinsmen in the commoner class.

Stratification systems of this type have been found among many of the intensive horticultural societies of sub-Saharan Africa as they existed in the eighteenth and nineteenth centuries. Here the familiar three-class system of stratified life was frequently found (Lenski, 1966). The dominant class consisted of a small minority of powerful and privileged persons who lived off the economic surplus generated from below. An intermediate class of officials and specialists served the fancies of the dominant class and carried out some of the lesser functions of political rule. The lowest class consisted of the large majority of ordinary people who were charged with producing enough economic goods to support the other two classes.

Chiefs or kings in some of these societies were treated with great respect and were often exalted and deified. In Dahomey, for instance, extreme acts of deference were shown the king. Even his ministers of state were expected to grovel in the dust in his presence, all the while throwing dirt over their heads and bodies (Lenski, 1966). Also, "No one could appear in his presence with his shoulders covered, or wearing sandals, shoes, or hat. No one could sit on a stool in his presence; if they sat, they were obliged to sit on the ground" (Lenski, 1966: 154). Dahomean kings also possessed great wealth, both in the form of property and wives. They were nominally regarded as the owners of all property within the kingdom, were permitted to engage in incestuous marriages, controlled all appointments to public office, and approved the inheritance of property. Such exalted figures also possessed literally life-and-death power over their subjects, for persons who displeased the king could be (and often were) put to death.

Even though considerable stratification among such African horticulturalists did exist, such societies were still permeated by a basic redistributive ethic. Among the Southern Bantu, for example, a chief was expected to be generous, and a failure to display such behavior was cause for a sharp decline in his popularity. As Lenski notes (1966:165):

> Though he is the wealthiest man in his tribe, he cannot use his wealth solely for the satisfaction of personal needs and desires. He is obliged to provide for the support of his ministers and courtiers. He must entertain all those who come to visit him. On great public occasions he is expected to slaughter many of his cattle and provide beer and porridge for all who gather at his village. He lends cattle, supports destitute widows and orphans, sends food to sick people and newly confined mothers, and in time of famine distributes corn from his own granaries or, if this is insufficient, purchases supplies from neighboring groups.

Similar systems of stratified life have also existed among many of the aboriginal societies of Polynesia. Aboriginal Hawaii affords an excellent example from this region of the world. According to the description given by Marshall Sahlins (1958), Hawaii was divided into three

A reconstruction of Tenochtitlán, the capital city of the Aztecs of ancient Mexico. The Aztecs were a very intensive horticultural society with an elaborate system of stratification.

main social strata: the "high chiefs" and their families, local stewards who administered the various domains of a chiefdom, and commoners. A paramount chief managed the use of lands throughout an entire island. This chief had the right to redistribute all lands upon his accession to office. In addition, he could alienate the land of any lower-ranking manager and transfer it to someone else. Commoners could be dispossessed from land for such reasons as hoarding surplus production, failure to contribute labor for the construction of irrigation works, and failure to make one's household plot adequately productive. High chiefs and local stewards also controlled and supervised access to water used in irrigation. Local stewards directly supervised household economic production, making sure that the land was being cultivated. In general, persons of high status could call upon those of lower rank for the performance of various labor services; commoners, of course, were the major source of labor for communal projects. Refusal by a commoner to comply with a demand for labor could result in his being put to death. It is clear that the major responsibilities of labor and economic production were carried out by the commoner class, and high chiefs and their families were freed from direct involvement in subsistence production. In this sense, chiefs constituted a kind of primitive "leisure class," putting others beneath them to work.

The stratified nature of Hawaiian society is also indicated by the existence of class differences in consumption patterns. Though differences in food consumption between classes were not prominent, certain choice foods were reserved for high chiefs. The chiefly redistributive ethic guaranteed an adequate food supply for all, and commoners have been described as "prosperous." With regard to the consumption of luxury goods, however, the matter is different. Luxury goods were often confined to high-status persons and served as insignia of rank. The use of certain luxury items for dress and ornamentation was restricted to high chiefs, and the quality of housing was highly associated with rank.

The Hawaiian paramount chief was considered divine. Because of the aura of sanctity that surrounded him, a series of elaborate taboos existed concerning contact with him, violation of which could result in death. For example, it was prohibited to let one's shadow fall on the paramount's house or possessions, to pass through his door ahead of him, or to put on his robe. Commoners were generally prohibited from touching anything used by the chief. In his presence, others were expected to prostrate themselves on the ground in a demonstration of extreme humility. When he traveled, people were warned of his coming so they could properly prepare themselves.

Social Stratification in Agrarian Societies

With the transition from intensive horticultural to agrarian societies, the limitations formerly placed on the stratification system were removed. The disappearance of the chiefly redistributive ethic and the removal of kinship ties between the members of different social classes were connected with the emergence of extreme forms of social stratification in which the majority of persons were frequently thrown into conditions of extreme poverty and degradation. One of the most striking characteristics of agrarian societies was the immense gap in power, privilege, and prestige that existed between the dominant and subordinate classes. Indeed, agrarian societies are by far the most highly stratified of all preindustrial societies. Unless otherwise noted, the following discussion is based on the description of agrarian stratification provided by Lenski (1966).

Agrarian stratification systems generally contained the following social strata: (1) a political-economic elite consisting of the ruler and his royal family and a landowning governing class; (2) the retainer class; (3) the merchant class; (4) the priestly class; (5) the peasantry; (6) artisans; and (7) expendables. While the first four of these strata may be considered privileged groups, the privileged segment of greatest significance in all agrarian societies was, of course, the political-economic elite: the ruler and the governing class. Likewise, while peasants, artisans, and expendables were all highly subordinate classes, the peasantry, since it constituted a majority of the population, was far and away the primary subjugated class.

The ruler in agrarian societies—monarch, king, emperor, or of whatever title—was that person who officially stood at the political head of society. The governing class consisted of those persons who were ordinarily the primary owners of land and who received the benefits that accompanied such ownership. But in fact both the ruler and the governing class tended to be both major landowners and major wielders of political power, and there were vital connections between these two segments of the elite. Taken together, they typically comprised no more than one or two percent of the population while receiving approximately half to two-thirds of the total wealth. The specific relationship between ruler and governing class varied from one agrarian society to another. In some societies, the power and wealth of the ruler was considerably diminished at the hands of the governing class, and the governing class itself was the primary holder of political power. This situation was found, for instance, in medieval Europe. In other agrarian societies, such as Ottoman Turkey or Mughal India, political power was highly concentrated in the hands of the ruler, and the ruler himself was the largest landowner. Under this situation, the prerogatives of the governing class (in terms of power, ownership and control of land, and wealth) were substantially reduced.

Regardless of the specific relationship between ruler and governing class, each typically enjoyed a considerable (and often enormous) amount of power, privilege, and prestige in comparison to other classes. A majority of the huge economic surplus generated within agrarian societies almost always found its way into the hands of the entire politico-economic elite. The rulers of agrarian societies have generally controlled great wealth. By the end of the fourteenth century, for example, English kings had an average income of approximately £135,000 a year, an amount that was equal to 85 percent of the combined incomes of the 2200 members of the nobility and squirearchy. Rulers of some of the great agrarian bureaucratic empires have fared much better than this. Xerxes, emperor of Persia in pre-Christian times, is said to have had an annual income that would have totaled $35 million by modern standards. Similarly, the annual income of Suleiman the Magnificent of Turkey was judged to have equaled $421 million; the figures for Akbar the Great of India and his successor, Aurangzeb, are estimated at $120 million and $270 million, respectively. As for the wealth of the governing class, Lenski estimates that this class probably received on the average at least one-quarter of the total income of most agrarian societies. In late nineteenth-century China, for instance, the Chinese portion of the governing class (that is, excluding the Manchu segment of this class) received approximately 645 million taels per year in total income, a figure that amounted to 24 percent of the gross national product. Averaging out to about 450 taels per family head, the Chinese segment of the governing class had an annual income roughly 20 times that of the remainder of Chinese society.

Standing directly below the ruler and governing class in agrarian societies was that social stratum that has been termed the retainer class. This class consisted of such functionaries as government officials, professional soldiers, household servants, and other persons who are directly employed to serve the ruler and governing class. Lenski estimates that the retainer class probably constituted around five percent of the population of most agrarian societies. A crucial role of this class was to mediate the relations between the elite and the common people. As Lenski notes, it was various officials of the retainer class who actually carried out the day-to-day work necessary for transferring the economic surplus into the hands of the ruler and governing class. The actual privilege and social status of members of the retainer class varied considerably. While certain members of this class enjoyed greater privilege than some lower-ranking members of the governing class, others of the class often enjoyed no special measure of privilege; their overall standing in society has been perhaps only slightly better than that of the average peasant. On the average, however, members of the retainer class tended to share to a significant degree in the benefits of the wealth controlled by their employers. While the retainer class was in effect a service class, its general position in society was clearly nearer that of the privileged than of the disprivileged.

Also standing among the privileged segments of agrarian societies was the merchant class. Merchants, of course, engaged in commercial activity and were a vital part of the agrarian urban economy. The merchant class was often of great value to the ruler and governing class, since merchants dealt in many of the luxury goods that were purchased by the elite. Although many merchants remained poor, quite a number amassed substantial wealth, and a few were wealthier than some members of the governing class. Yet despite these material benefits, merchants were frequently accorded very low prestige. In the traditional status-ranking systems of China and Japan, for instance, merchants were placed near the very bottom of the social scale, ranking even below peasants and artisans. In medieval Europe merchants fared somewhat better, but they were still regarded as highly inferior to the governing class. Merchants appear to have been well aware of their low status, and many strove to raise their status to the level of the governing class by imitating its lifestyle.

Although the priestly class in agrarian societies was often internally stratified, in general it is appropriate to consider it a privileged stratum. Indeed, priests have frequently commanded substantial wealth in many agrarian societies, and it has been a common pattern for them to be close allies of rulers and governing classes. In Egypt in the twelfth century B.C., for example, as well as in eighteenth-century France, priests owned 15 percent of the land. In pre-Reformation Sweden the Church owned 21 percent of the land, while in Ceylon, Buddhist monasteries are said to have been in control of about one-third of the land. This privileged status of the priestly class as a whole no doubt resulted from the political alliances typically forged between priests and rulers and governing classes. The latter two groups have commonly sought priestly support for their oppressive and exploitative activities. Priests have therefore been properly rewarded for their aid to these dominant groups. However, it must not be overlooked that the privilege of the priestly class was typically insecure. The holdings of this class were often stripped away by acts of confiscation by the political elite, indicating that the economic alliance between the priesthood and the elite was often a shaky one. In addition, it is imperative to recognize that not all priests were wealthy and of high rank. In medieval Europe, for instance, priests were divided into an upper and lower clergy. While the upper clergy lived in a privileged style consistent with their noble background, members of the lower clergy—parish priests directly serving the common people—lived in a style resembling that of the common people themselves.

In most agrarian societies the bulk of the population has consisted of peasants. As a class, peasants have occupied a distinctly inferior social, economic, and political status. Economically, their lot has generally been a miserable one, although the specific degree of their exploitation has varied from one society and one time to another. A major burden placed upon all peasants has been taxation, the principal means of separating the peasant from his surplus product. The oppressiveness of taxation has varied considerably. During the Tokugawa era in Japan, the rate of taxation of the peasantry varied from as little as 30 percent to as much as 70 percent of the crop. In China, approximately 40 to 50 percent of total peasant agricultural production was commonly claimed by landowners. In pre-British India, peasants apparently handed over from one-third to one-half of their crops to both Muslim and Hindu rulers. In Babylon during the time of Hammurabi, taxes ranged from one-third to one-half of the crop. In Ottoman Turkey, the tax rate varied from 10 to 50 percent. In sixteenth- and seventeenth-century Russia, the rate was 20 to 50 percent. In a number of agrarian societies, multiple forms of taxation have existed. One of the most striking illustrations of a system of multiple taxation comes from the period of Ottoman rule in Bulgaria. Here the Turks imposed nearly 80 different kinds of taxes and obligations upon the peasantry. One such tax was known as the "tooth tax," a levy placed on a village by the Turks after they had eaten and drunk there. In official terms, the tax was said to compensate the Turks "for the wear and tear sustained by their teeth during the meal" (Lenski, 1966:269). Incredible as such a tax seems, it does indicate the lengths to which many agrarian elites have gone to benefit themselves at the expense of the bulk of the population.

In addition to the burdens of taxation, peasants were also subjected to other hardships. One of these was the **corvée,** or system of forced labor. Under this system, peasants were obligated to provide so many days of labor either for their lord or for the state. In medieval Europe, for example, peasants were obligated to work on their lord's land a specified number of days per week throughout the year. During the building of the Great Wall in China, some peasants were kept on forced labor projects nearly their entire adult lives. Peasant hardships did not end with the burdens of taxation and forced labor. If the peasant's lord operated a mill, oven, or wine press (and he frequently did), the peasant was under obligation to use them and to compensate the lord handsomely for such use. In some agrarian societies, the lord could take anything he desired from a peasant's personal property, and he could do so without payment. In medieval Europe, when a man died, his lord could claim his best beast. Furthermore, if a man's daughter married off the manor or without the lord's permission, the girl's father could be fined.

Landlords and peasants were the two great social classes of medieval Europe, as they are in all agrarian societies.

It should be obvious that the life of the average peasant was an extremely difficult one. By and large, life was lived with but the barest necessities for existence. The peasant diet was generally a poor one in terms of the quantity, variety, and nutritional adequacy of the food. Household furniture was extremely meager, and most peasants slept on straw-covered earthen floors. Sometimes conditions became so bad that a living was no longer possible and peasants had to abandon the land and attempt to sustain themselves by other means.

In addition to the severe economic deprivation typically suffered by peasants, the peasantry occupied a very low social status in all agrarian societies. A great gulf separated the lifestyles of peasants and the elite. The elite (and, to varying degrees, other classes as well) regarded peasants as extreme social inferiors, frequently conceiving of them as something less than fully human. In some agrarian societies, peasants were formally classified in various documents as belonging to roughly the same category as the livestock. Lacking all but the barest necessities of life, and deprived of any opportunity to pursue even such unremarkable amenities as an education or the cultivation of good manners, the peasantry stood in stark contrast to the privileged elite, where the social trappings of high status were a fundamental part of everyday life.

Standing below the peasantry in the agrarian stratified order were two other classes. One of these consisted of artisans, or trained craftsmen, a class that Lenski estimates probably represented about three to seven percent of the population in most agrarian societies. Artisans were mainly recruited from among the ranks of the dispossessed peasantry. Although the incomes of peasants and artisans overlapped, artisans were generally worse off economically than most peasants. Many apparently lived in destitute circumstances on the verge of starvation. At the very bottom of virtually every agrarian society could be found a class of "expendables." Constituting approximately five to ten percent of most agrarian populations, these persons were found in urban areas. Their ranks were filled by beggars, petty thieves, outlaws, underemployed itinerant workers, and other persons who, as Lenski has noted, were "forced to live solely by their wits or by charity" (1966:281). Members of this class suffered from extreme economic deprivation, malnutrition, and disease, and had a very high death rate. The sons and daughters of poor peasants who inherited nothing often fell into this extraordinarily hapless class.

One's class position in all agrarian societies was overwhelmingly determined by social heredity. Most persons died as members of the class into which they were born. This does not mean, however, that social mobility was impossible or nonexistent in such societies, and a small amount of it did occur. Occasionally a person rose to the ranks of one of the privileged classes. Nevertheless, such upward movement seldom occurred; far more common was downward mobility. As noted above, children who inherited nothing from their poor peasant parents were often forced into either the artisan or expendable class in order to maintain any sort of existence at all. Thus, the possibility of improving one's disadvantaged position in an agrarian society was greatly limited.

THEORIES OF THE ORIGIN OF SOCIAL STRATIFICATION

The Functionalist Evolutionary Theory

A number of theories have been proposed by social scientists to account for the developments recounted in the preceding pages. One very well-known theory of the origin of stratification is the functionalist evolutionary theory of sociologist Talcott Parsons (1966, 1977). Parsons regards social evolution in general as resulting from an inherent tendency that societies have for increasing what he calls their "adaptive capacity." This involves their ability to respond effectively to the environment and to handle the various problems that are always posed by the fact that humans must live in social groups. Societies have been evolving over the millennia, Parsons believes, toward higher and higher forms of adaptive capacity. Thus more contemporary societies handle the problems of social organization more efficiently than did earlier forms of social life. Parsons sees the emergence of stratification as a crucial aspect of the evolution of increased adaptive capacity in social life. It is for him an "evolutionary breakthrough," a great accomplishment bringing about various forms of social progress.

Stratification has such significance for Parsons because he believes that it allows societies to overcome the limitations placed upon them by social equality. When everyone is treated equally, no individual will have the motivation to assume important leadership roles necessary for a society to deal with many of the important problems and challenges it must face. With the emergence of stratification, though, some individuals will be inclined toward assuming these leadership roles because they know they will be rewarded for doing so with a superior measure of privilege and prestige. Stratification is thus a necessary device whereby societies begin to centralize many of their activities in order to solve problems and meet challenges with which they would otherwise be unable to deal. The more pressing these problems and challenges are, the greater the need for stratification.

There are numerous difficulties with this interpretation of the origin of stratified social life. In the first place, Parsons's concept of "increased adaptive capacity" is highly questionable. Parsons is suggesting that more contemporary and more complex societies are really superior in their organizational effectiveness to earlier societies. This judgment reeks of ethnocentrism. While it is certainly the case that more contemporary societies have *different* adaptive mechanisms (that is, different infrastructural, structural, and superstructural arrangements) from those found in earlier societies, most sociologists find little empirical support for the claim that these mechanisms are superior. Parsons has fallen into the trap of ethnocentrism that so characterized the nineteenth-century evolutionists—one that many twentieth-century evolutionists have been especially careful to avoid.

A second difficulty with Parsons's theory is that, in stressing the alleged benefits to society of the emergence of stratification, it seems to overlook entirely the negative social consequences of stratification. These consequences include, among other things, the oppression, exploitation, and misery suffered by the lower strata. Indeed, one of the most significant consequences of the rise of stratification is an increase in the degree of conflict in social life. It is extremely difficult to see how these phenomena can be regarded as examples of "increased adaptive capacity."

Lenski's Surplus Theory

The sociologist Gerhard Lenski (1966) has presented another well-known theory of stratification, but one that has a strong materialistic and conflict-theoretical orientation. It therefore stands in sharp contrast to Parsons's theory. Although this theory has been known by a variety of names, we shall refer to it here as the *surplus theory.* The theory is represented diagrammatically in Figure 6.1.

Lenski's theory assumes that humans are essentially self-interested creatures who strive to maximize their own well-being. Individuals behave largely according to a principle of enlightened self-interest, cooperating with each other when it can further their interests, and struggling with each other when that seems the avenue to the satisfaction of their interests. The theory also assumes that the objects individuals seek are always scarce relative to the desire for them, and that individuals are unequally endowed by nature to compete for the attainment of scarce objects.

Lenski believes that basic equality will prevail in those societies in which cooperation is essential to the satisfaction of individual interests. People will share with each other when such sharing is to the long-run benefit of the sharers. When this condition is not met, conflict and stratification are expected to arise. This condition is not met when a society produces an economic surplus. When a surplus becomes available, a struggle for control of it seems inevitably to arise, and the surplus ends up largely

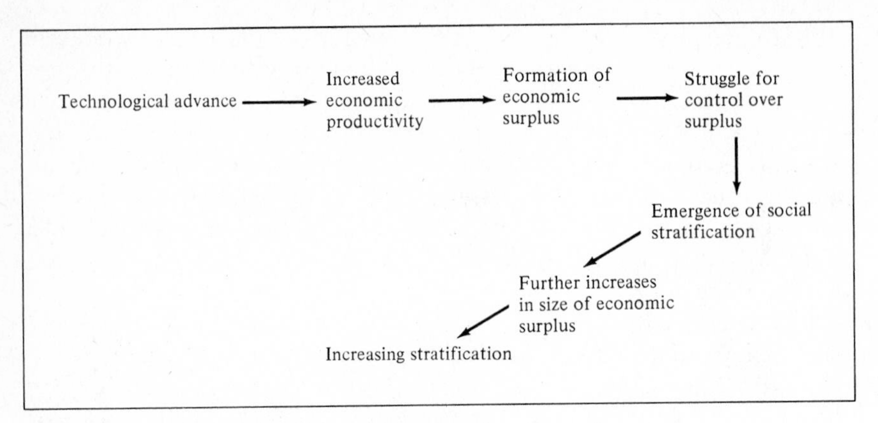

Figure 6.1 Lenski's surplus theory of the origin of social stratification.

in the hands of the most powerful individuals and groups.

Surplus economic production, then, is the key to the development of stratification, and the larger the surplus, the greater the extent of stratification. What determines the size of the surplus? According to Lenski, it is a society's technological capacity. There should thus be a very close association between a society's degree of technological development and its degree of stratification. The simplest societies, such as hunter-gatherers and simple horticulturalists, should be characterized by little or no stratification. With technological advance, substantial economic surpluses arise and the struggles over these should produce increasing stratification. Thus, intensive horticultural and agrarian societies should display proportionately increasing levels of stratification.

The empirical data discussed earlier on the evolution of stratification are certainly strongly consistent with Lenski's theory. Yet there are some significant problems with the theory, and the close association between technological development and stratification pointed to by Lenski seems to mislead us theoretically. Although highly correlated with stratification, technological development may not be the actual causal factor.

The major difficulty with Lenski's theory involves his assumption about the origin of an economic surplus. Lenski appears to assume that economic surpluses are more or less automatic results of technological advance. Yet this cannot really be the case. Technological advance makes surpluses possible; however, as Ester Boserup (1965) points out, people will not automatically desire to produce them because to do so involves more work for questionable results. (The discussion in Chapter 4 suggested that people are highly motivated to resist technological change in order to prevent increases in the workload.) If people are not naturally inclined to produce surpluses, then the question arises as to how they can originate at all. The answer would seem to involve political compulsion: People produce surpluses because other people compel them to do so. And if this is the case, then stratification, at least in the sense of differential power, already exists. Surpluses, then, actually follow closely upon the heels of the development of stratification (cf. Elster, 1985:169). To see how this can happen, and to see what is ultimately behind such a process, the so-called *scarcity theory of stratification* must be examined.

The Scarcity Theory

The presentation here of the scarcity theory of stratification is derived from suggestions made in the work of Michael Harner (1970), Morton Fried (1967), and Rae Lesser Blumberg (1978). This theory is represented diagrammatically in Figure 6.2.

The scarcity theory holds that the basic cause of the emergence and intensification of stratification is population pressure. The following scenario may be imagined for purposes of illustrating the theory. Population pressure against resources has eventually led hunter-gatherers to begin adopting agricultural modes of subsistence. Agriculture eventually entirely displaces hunting and gathering. The "primitive communism" of hunter-gatherers gives way to the ownership of land by large kinship groups, but nonetheless ownership is still largely communal rather than private. However, further increases in population pressure cause horticulturalists to become more concerned about landownership. Increasing **scarcity** in the availability of land suitable for cultivation leads some families to increased "selfishness" in landownership, and some families begin to own more land than others. Additional population pressure leads to still greater "selfishness" in landownership, and eventually private relations of production (in the Marxian sense) emerge out of what was originally communal ownership. Differential access to resources now exists, and one group may compel others to work harder in order to produce economic surpluses off which the owning group may live, a group that is now emerging as a primitive "leisure class." Since technological advance has accompanied population pressure and declining standards of living, surpluses are now technologically feasible. With additional advances in population pressure and technology, differential access to resources becomes even more severe, and stratification intensifies under greater political compulsion by owning groups.

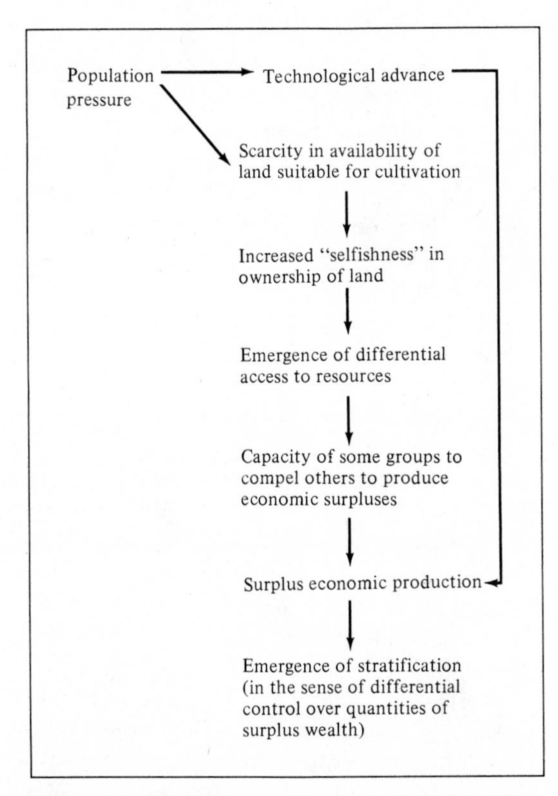

Figure 6.2 Scarcity theory of the origin of social stratification.

The scarcity theory holds that something probably very much like this process has happened in human history, no doubt not just once, but many times. It is important to see that the scarcity theory and the surplus theory are similar in some ways. Both are materialistic, conflict-oriented theories that are strikingly different from the functionalist evolutionary interpretation. But whereas the surplus theory regards technological advance as the basic cause of the development of stratification, the scarcity theory claims that the causal relationship between technology and stratification is illusory. It holds that both are results of population pressure and the scarcity of resources that this produces. The scarcity theory is favored in this book because the surplus theory is contradicted by Boserup's interpretation of the causes of technological change and the data that support her interpretation, yet the scarcity theory fits Boserup's claim very nicely.

It is important to realize that, once initiated, stratification has, so to speak, a "life of its own." Lenski himself recognizes this and stresses it. That is to say, once there emerge in society groups with differential access to the means of production, advantaged groups are highly motivated to maintain their advantage, and enhance it if possible. Thus stratification systems tend to be inherently self-perpetuating and self-enhancing.

SUMMARY

1. All societies are characterized by social inequality, or differentials among individuals in their levels of prestige and social influence. Many societies, though, go considerably beyond social inequality and establish social stratification, or hierarchies of hereditary social groups having unequal levels of social power and privilege.

2. In hunting and gathering societies inequality generally prevails in the absence of stratification. Individuals in such societies generally possess equal access to the resources of nature that sustain life. Equality is reinforced by strong norms compelling people to share and punishing them for failure to do so. The inequalities in hunter-gatherer societies are generally those of prestige and influence only, with the most skilled and courageous hunters and the wisest leaders commanding the most respect.

3. Simple horticultural societies commonly lack stratification as well. Many of them are examples of rank societies, or those in which a few individuals are accorded very high levels of respect. These individuals, though, do not inherit their positions but attain them competitively through their efforts as economic organizers. The superior prestige of village leaders does not translate into superior power and privilege.

4. Genuine stratification tends to emerge for the first time in more intensive horticultural societies. Many of these societies have stratification systems in which unequal groups composed of chiefs, subchiefs, and commoners are found. Chiefs and subchiefs have considerable control over economic production, and the large commoner class has a number of restrictions placed on its ownership and use of land.

5. Stratification reaches extreme proportions in agrarian societies. The two main social classes are landlords and peasants, but a number of other classes exist as well. These include merchants, priests, artisans, and "expendables." The extreme differences in power and privilege between different social classes is accompanied by major differences in styles of life and in levels of prestige.

6. One well-known interpretation of the origin of stratification is the functionalist evolutionary theory of Talcott Parsons. Parsons has theorized that stratification arose in human history in order to serve crucial societal needs. Societies with stratification could function more effectively than those without it. By rewarding some individuals more highly than others, societies could motivate those persons to assume important positions of societal leadership and thus direct the affairs of society in a more effective way.

7. The materialist evolutionary view suggests a sharply opposing interpretation. One version of this view is the surplus theory of Gerhard Lenski and others. Lenski sees stratification arising through the creation of economic surpluses, themselves produced by technological advance. When surpluses exist, individuals and groups struggle over their allocation, and some groups will win out over others. The bigger the surplus, the more severe the struggles and the more elaborate the stratification system.

8. An alternative materialist interpretation is the scarcity theory. This theory holds that population growth is the main engine of the rise of stratification. Population growth produces scarcity in resources, and with increasing resource scarcity individuals turn from more communal to more private modes of ownership. As some individuals gain control over resources, they gain the capacity to compel others to engage in surplus production. Owning groups take away (expropriate) this surplus and use it as the source of their own livelihoods.

SPECIAL TOPIC: A NEW PERSPECTIVE ON THE CASTE SYSTEM

The term **caste** generally refers to an especially rigid form of stratification characterized by the existence of endogamous (in-marrying) social strata that practice ritual avoidance of one another and out of which mobility is said to be impossible. While a number of societies have been said to have caste or castelike systems, by far the best-known (and perhaps the only true) caste system is the one that has prevailed among the Hindus of India for some 2000 years or more. In Hindu ideology, the caste system is said to operate such "that each person is assigned a place in society at birth, that contact between different ranks is 'impure,' that intermarriage between castes is forbidden, and that every social act is governed by caste rules" (McCord and McCord, 1977:30).

Five main castes have constituted the structure of Indian society: (1) *Brahmans,* or priests and landowners; (2) *Kshatriyas,* or warriors and political leaders; (3) *Vaisyas,* or workers performing agricultural and mercantile functions; (4) *Sudras,* or servants, menial laborers, and peasants; and (5) *Harijans,* or "untouchables," persons regarded as impure and degraded. The five major castes, or *varnas,* though, are not the basic functional units of the caste system. These units are the *jatis,* or subcastes. Each major *varna* is subdivided into hundreds of *jatis,* and there are several thousand *jatis* throughout India. An individual's *jati* is the social group that regulates all aspects of his or her everyday social life: It places the individual within the economic division of labor; it regulates marriage and family life; it coordinates religious ritual; it enforces caste taboos and imposes sanctions for their violation; and so on.

The Hindu caste system is undoubtedly the most elaborate and rigid form of stratification the world has ever known. It is also probably one of the least understood social phenomena in all of social science. Many attempts have been made over the decades to explain the origins of this unique system, but consensus among theoreticians is yet to be achieved. Because so much of Indian history is shrouded in mystery, it is unlikely that a really satisfactory solution can be given to so large and complex a problem.

A more limited and manageable question is the extent to which the caste system is, like other complex stratified orders, closely associated with economic exploitation. The traditional view has been to conceptualize the caste system as an elaborate status system that rests basically upon a widespread social consensus. The members of all castes, it has been asserted, view the caste system positively because they see it as promoting the interests of all groups within Indian society and thus as contributing to a

The Indian caste system in operation.

fundamental social harmony. Yet in recent years this traditional view has been seriously challenged. As Joan Mencher has remarked (1974:470):

> *For a long time, studies of India have focused on caste as a system of interdependence and reciprocity rather than one of exploitation. But it is hard to see it as being any more interdependent than any other stratification system. Indeed, looking at India from the viewpoint of the bottom layers of the hierarchy can shed a very different light on the way in which the social structure has functioned and on the forces that have kept it functioning. It can show in what ways Indian society, though superficially different from other stratified societies, also shares many things with traditional stratified societies the world over.*

On the basis of several years of field study in India, Mencher has tried to show how the caste system works to the disadvantage of lower-caste groups, especially Harijans (who make up about 15 percent of Indian society). Harijans, she believes, suffer from two main disadvantages: economic exploitation and a stigmatized identity. Harijans in the villages where Mencher lived were poorer than the members of all other castes, and possessed the least land for cultivation. As she points out (1980:265–266):

> *While not all of the landless laborers are by any means untouchables, it is certainly clear that being an untouchable carries additional burdens along with it. In a sample of five villages in Chingleput District studied in 1967, 85% of the Paraiyans [untouchables] had less than 1 acre of land, and derived their main income from agricultural labor; whereas this was the case with only 56% of the Naickers (the other large agricultural community in this region). . . . In a larger sample of eight villages surveyed in 1971, 94% of the Paraiyans owned 1 acre or less; 54% of Naickers owned 1 acre or less. . . .*

> *In the village in Kerala where I was working in 1971, none of the Cherumakkal [untouchable] families owned over 1 acre of land, whereas among other castes that furnish agricultural laborers, there are a sizeable number of people having modest though adequate landholdings. In general many villages in Kerala have a few Harijans who own a little over 1 acre of land. . . . Nonetheless, the vast majority of Harijans in Kerala are landless, apart from a few cents of land (1 cent = .01 acre) around their house site. . . .*
>
> *Thus it should be clear from the outset that a very high percentage of rural Harijans belong to the lowest social class in the economic system.*

Mencher devotes particular attention to the problem of stigmatized identity among Harijans. Harijans are generally perceived by members of higher castes as impure and degraded, indeed, as "polluting." They are made aware of this social identity in numerous ways: Members of higher castes frequently object to their wearing clean clothes, sandals, or pressed shirts in public; they are often made to walk alongside a bullock cart rather than allowed to ride on it; they may be compelled to eat their meals in the road outside their employer's compound; when out of necessity Harijans in one particular village began to take water from a nearby pump, the pump's high-caste owner put cow dung in the water; in central Kerala, Harijans commonly use demeaning terms of self-reference (e.g., *adiyan,* "slave") when conversing with members of certain higher castes; Harijans are generally forbidden to enter local temples, and in some cases are not allowed to use private temples and bathing pools. Mencher points out that although there are laws against many of these practices, high-caste landowners may use economic sanctions against those who violate these traditional caste rules. In other words, they simply do not hire the offending parties.

Mencher firmly believes that Harijans do not accept their stigmatized identity as legitimate and deserved. On the contrary, there is considerable evidence that they deeply resent it. Moreover, Mencher has collected ample evidence that Harijans view their poor economic situation as resulting from economic exploitation by wealthy landowners. When she questioned Harijans about why they thought their economic situation was the way it was, they often referred to the concentration of landownership among members of higher castes, or specifically mentioned the ability of higher-caste persons to use force against them. On the basis of Harijans' remarks and her own observations, Mencher concludes (1980:291):

> *What people so often fail to understand is the extent to which power relations dominate life in Indian villages. Fear of oppression and of the use of brute force has dominated people's minds and hearts much more than appears in traditional pictures of Indian village life. . . . If this is true now, one can easily imagine the situation of untouchables in the past, in a village dominated by one or two wealthy families. Even where the landlord may appear cordial and sympathetic, village Harijans know how easily friendliness has turned to hate and oppression elsewhere, and carefully control their behavior.*

FOR FURTHER READING

Berreman, Gerald D. (ed.). *Social Inequality: Comparative and Developmental Approaches.* New York: Academic Press, 1981. A good collection of articles on numerous aspects of stratification in a diverse range of societies.

de Ste. Croix, G.E.M. *The Class Struggle in the Ancient Greek World.* Ithaca, N.Y.: Cornell University Press, 1981. An extraordinary and much praised analysis of the class structure of ancient Greece and Rome, with a proper focus on the role of slavery in the economic life of antiquity. The first, and perhaps still the only, Marxian study of the ancient world.

Fried, Morton. *The Evolution of Political Society.* New York: Random House, 1967. An interesting treatment by a leading anthropologist of the evolution from "egalitarian" through "rank" to "stratified" societies. Suggests that population pressure and attendant scarcity are the causal forces in the emergence of stratified society.

Harner, Michael. "Population Pressure and the Social Evolution of Agriculturalists." *Southwestern Journal of Anthropology* 26:67–86, 1970. An intriguing study that tries to show that population pressure is the basic cause of the origin and evolution of stratification. Uses a large sample of the world's societies.

Lenski, Gerhard E. *Power and Privilege: A Theory of Social Stratification.* New York: McGraw-Hill, 1966. An important work in which the author presents his surplus theory of the origin of stratification. Also presents a vast array of valuable data on the nature of inequality and stratification throughout the entire evolutionary range of human societies.

Patterson, Orlando. *Slavery and Social Death: A Comparative Study.* Cambridge, Mass.: Harvard University Press, 1982. An unusually comprehensive study of slavery in the world's societies. Discusses all manner and type of slavery, and emphasizes the status- and honor-conferring aspects of slavery over its economic dimensions. Quite valuable and insightful despite being marred by a kind of idealist approach.

Sahlins, Marshall. *Social Stratification in Polynesia.* Seattle: University of Washington Press, 1958. A dated but still interesting study of the variations in stratified social life found among the major aboriginal Polynesian societies. Puts forth an essentially surplus interpretation of the evolution of stratification.

CHAPTER 7

The Origins of Modern Capitalism

This chapter begins the discussion of perhaps the greatest social transformation in human history: the transition from the medieval feudal economy in western Europe to the capitalist mode of production. Attention is focused on the early development of capitalism prior to the Industrial Revolution, the period from the early sixteenth century to the middle of the eighteenth century. Considerable attention is given to the various theories that attempt to explain why the feudal mode of production collapsed and a capitalist system replaced it. The development of capitalism from the Industrial Revolution to the present day is the subject of the next chapter.

THE FEUDAL MODE OF PRODUCTION

The system of economic life that prevailed in western Europe from approximately the collapse of the Roman Empire until the advent of modern capitalism was known as **feudalism.** Feudalism was especially characteristic of France, Germany, and the British Isles, although it existed in other parts of western Europe as well. The basic unit of economic production under feudalism was the **manor.** The manor was overseen by a powerful feudal landlord and cultivated by numerous peasants. The average peasant held perhaps as much as 30 acres of land on which he lived and that he cultivated for his own living. The land held directly by the lord for his own use was known as the **demesne.** As seen in the two preceding chapters, the relationship between lord and peasant was a highly unbalanced and exploitative one. The peasant owed the lord so many days of work on the demesne, and he also had to pay dues of various sorts. For instance, he often rendered certain food products and paid certain fees, such as those exacted by the lord when the peasant used his winepress, his oven, or his grinding mill.

Just how different the feudal system was from modern industrial society can be seen in the following remarks about feudalism by Douglass North and Robert Thomas (1973:11):

> Thus the customs of the manor became the unwritten "constitution," or the fundamental institutional arrangement of an essentially anarchic world, most properly viewed as small isolated settlements, frequently in the lee of a fortified place and surrounded by wilderness. The wooden or earth castle, the knight, and the relatively self-sufficient manor had emerged as

the most viable response to the collapse of order and the recurrent invasions of Norsemen, Moslems, and Magyars. While the terror of foreign marauders had declined by the middle of the tenth century, the land seethed with continual warfare and brigandage, as the power of local lords waxed and waned. Feudalism provided a measure of stability and order in this fragmented world. . . .

Commerce between different parts of Europe had always been potentially of mutual benefit, since the variety of resources and climatic conditions induced differentiation of crops and livestock. But trade had been sporadic because so many dangers within the wilderness beset the traveling merchant. As peace and security now revived, so did the profitability of exchanging varied products. In response, towns were taking form in the more densely settled areas either under the protection of a lord or as independent entities with their own walls, government, and military defense. Here skills and crafts flourished, providing "manufactured" goods to trade for the needed food and raw materials from the countryside.

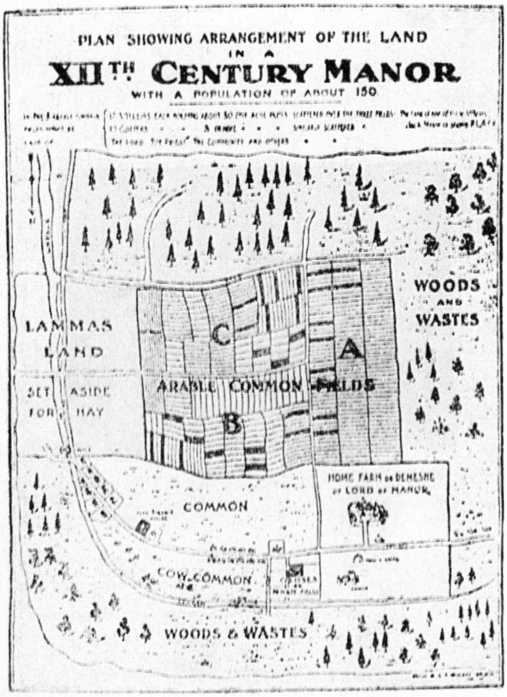

A map of land allocation on a twelfth-century English manor.

It is clear that the feudal economy was overwhelmingly one of production-for-use. The basic economic relationship was that between landlord and peasant, the latter producing for them both. Life was tied securely to the soil and was very plain and simple—especially for the peasant, but for the lord as well. Production-for-exchange played little role in economic life. Markets existed, but they were of limited significance. Towns existed and became more prominent as feudalism advanced, but the individuals and groups who lived and worked there—merchants and artisans primarily—had little impact on the functioning of the feudal economy. Trade also existed, but until the eleventh and twelfth centuries it was primarily local and very limited in extent of items traded.

This relatively simple economy persisted for hundreds of years in medieval Europe, but by the beginning of the fourteenth century it entered a period of crisis from which it was not to recover. The crisis led to two major attempts by the feudal nobility to improve its declining economic fortunes: leasing out the demesne to tenants who paid a money rent and who began to farm the land in the manner of a capitalist enterprise, and enclosing land for the pasturing of sheep. These new forms of landholding and land use spelled the end of the old feudal system and were among the earliest signals of the beginnings of the transition to a capitalist mode of economic production.

THE RISE OF THE CAPITALIST MODE OF PRODUCTION

The Nature of Capitalism

With the breakdown of feudalism, production-for-exchange slowly began to replace production-for-use as the principal type of economic activity throughout western Europe. At some point in this transition, the system we call **capitalism** began. But exactly when capitalism began is a question that can only be answered when we know what capitalism *is*. Contemporary scholars disagree in their answers to this fundamental question.

One of history's most prominent students of the capitalist system was Karl Marx. Marx was relatively clear as to just what capitalism was and when it began in European history. Although he conceived it as a type of economy in which people ran companies in an effort to earn **profits,** he knew that this sort of thing had existed for thousands of years, and he did not refer to these earlier modes of economic behavior as capitalist. Capitalism involved something more than merely the search for profits.

For Marx, capitalism was a type of economic system in which some individuals owned vital productive resources that they used in an effort to make the maximum profit. These individuals, whom Marx referred to as the **bourgeoisie,** employed another group of persons, whom Marx called the **proletariat,** who through their labor produced goods that the capitalists could exchange in the market for a profit. The capitalist was able to earn a profit because he paid the worker less than the full value of the goods that the worker produced. Marx was quite clear in his belief that the profits of the capitalist did not arise through the simple process of the exchange of goods—through mere buying and selling. Rather, profits were generated through the process of production itself, and the act of selling goods only served to realize the profits that were already there in the creation of the product by the worker.

In Marx's view, then, capitalism required the existence of a class of workers who sold their labor power to capitalists for wages. Only through the exploitation of workers by capitalists in the wage relationship could profits be generated. Marx thus identified the beginnings of the capitalist mode of production with the Industrial Revolution in England in the middle of the eighteenth century, because it was not until this time that wage labor and the factory system became prominent economic phenomena.*

Of course, Marx was well aware that the vigorous search for profits began in western Europe long before the Industrial Revolution. Beginning as early as the late fifteenth century, some European nations embarked on colonial expeditions in which the search for profits was of paramount significance. And during the seventeenth century the search for profits was an obsession of governments throughout Europe. Yet Marx argued that the mode in which profits were realized in these centuries was fundamentally different from the mode in which they were obtained after the Industrial Revolution. Before the Industrial Revolution, profits were obtained through exchange rather than production relationships: through buying and selling rather than through the exploitation of a class of wage workers. A company could make profits by buying a product in one region of the world and selling it in another region in which a greater price could be asked. Marx identified this type of economic activity as a sort of capitalism, but he called it **merchant capitalism** in order to distinguish it from the **industrial capitalism** of a later era. Only industrial capitalism was a "true" system of capitalism for Marx.

Some contemporary social scientists believe that Marx's distinction should be strictly maintained. Eric Wolf (1982), for example, identifies the emergence of capitalism only with the Industrial Revolution, referring to the preindustrial period between the fifteenth and eighteenth centuries as a transitional period in which there was a "search for wealth," not a "search for profits." In fact, Wolf goes a step

*The reader wishing a somewhat more detailed analysis of the Marxian conception of capitalism may turn to the appendix to Chapter 8.

beyond Marx when he asserts (1982:79): "There is no such thing as mercantile or merchant capitalism. . . . There is only mercantile wealth. Capitalism, to be capitalism, must be capitalism-in-production."

Other social scientists, including many Marxists, hold a different view. Most notable among these is Immanuel Wallerstein (1974a,b). Wallerstein rejects Marx's distinction between merchant and industrial capitalism and claims that capitalism is simply production in a market in which the aim of the producers is to realize the maximum profit. For Wallerstein, it does not matter whether there are wage workers or not. Indeed, for him several types of coercive, non-wage labor have existed within the capitalist mode of production. What is crucial about capitalism for Wallerstein is that the maximum accumulation of profits over time be the guiding aim of economic activity. Wallerstein believes that this requires the exploitation of workers, but that this exploitation may take a variety of forms, not just the exploitation of wage laborers. Given his conception of capitalism, Wallerstein sees it originating in the late fifteenth century with the rise of European colonialism.

This book is more sympathetic to Wallerstein's point of view but frankly recognizes that the Industrial Revolution of the eighteenth century dramatically changed the nature of capitalism. Indeed, it inaugurated a phase of capitalist development that was in certain crucial respects qualitatively different from anything that had previously existed. In siding with Wallerstein, we can scarcely overlook this important fact.

The Early Capitalism of the Fifteenth and Sixteenth Centuries

One of the most famous historical analyses of the formation of capitalism is Maurice Dobb's *Studies in the Development of Capitalism* (1963). Dobb conceives of the early development of capitalism primarily in terms of the expansion of the economic activity and social power of urban merchants. During these two centuries, merchant capital rather than industrial capital was the order of the day. This fact leads Dobb to ask about the source of the profits earned by merchant capitalists. Dobb answers his own question in the following way (1963:88):

> The explanation we are seeking is evidently twofold. In the first place, so much commerce in those times, especially foreign commerce, consisted either of exploiting some political advantage or of scarcely-veiled plunder. Secondly, the class of merchants, as soon as it assumed any corporate forms, was quick to acquire powers of monopoly, which fenced its ranks from competition and served to turn the terms of exchange to its own advantage in its dealings with producer and consumer. It is evident that this twofold character of commerce at this period constituted the essential basis of early burgher wealth and of the accumulation of merchant capital.

Thus European economic activity in these centuries was increasingly dominated by urban merchants who were operators of trading companies. These merchants were gaining increasing power in the towns. Indeed, Dobb variously refers to them as constituting a "burgher oligarchy" and a "new merchant aristocracy." Many of the trading companies were highly exclusive organizations, and entry into them often required especially stiff entrance fees. In the sixteenth century such companies were common in the British Isles. As Dobb comments (1963:113–115):

> By the middle of the sixteenth century British merchants had ventured sufficiently far afield, both across the North Sea and into the Mediterranean, to inaugurate some five or six new general companies, each possessing privileges in a new area. The year 1553 saw the foundation of the Russia Company (which two years later received a charter giving it a monopoly) as the first

An early capitalist market in sixteenth-century Antwerp.

company to employ joint stock and to own ships corporately. . . . In 1557 Jenkinson, a servant of the company, journeyed as far as Persia and Bokhara, and in 1567 the company obtained the right to trade across Russia through Kazan and Astrakhan. . . . In 1578 the Eastland Company was chartered "to enjoy the sole trade through the Sound into Norway, Sweden, Poland, Lithuania (excepting Narva), Prussia and also Pomerania, from the river Oder eastward to Dantzick, Elbing and Königsberg; also to Copenhagen and Eisinore and to Finland, Gothland, Barnhold and Oeland." . . . The year before the foundation of the Eastland Company, a number of members of the Merchant Adventurers founded the Spanish Company to monopolize the lucrative trade in wine, oil and fruit with Spain and Portugal, and to secure powers under charter to exclude competitors.

Although merchant capital dominated in the fifteenth and sixteenth centuries, some early forms of industrial capital did begin to appear. In England the first forms of industrial capital emerged in the textile, leather, and smaller metal trades during the sixteenth century. Industrial capital arose even earlier in the Netherlands and in some Italian cities, perhaps as early as the thirteenth century. For instance, in "Florence in 1338 there were said to be as many as 200 workshops engaged in cloth manufacture, employing a total of 30,000 workmen or about a quarter of the whole occupied population of the city" (Dobb, 1963:157). There were few factories during these times, and most industries were of the type frequently known as cottage industries (see the Special Topic at the end of this chapter). In these industries, workers remained in their homes and produced goods under the general supervision of capitalists who supplied the raw materials and paid wages to the workers. The real development of the factory system was to await the eighteenth century.

The Seventeenth Century and Mercantilism*

The form taken by capitalism in the seventeenth century is commonly referred to as **mercantilism.** Mercantilist economic policies were practiced by all the major European capitalist nations of the day. These policies involved governments' granting of monopolies to trading companies so that the companies could benefit from trade between the European nation and its colonies elsewhere. Monopolies for trading companies were not new to the mercantilist era, but the specific economic context in which these monopolies were granted—that of colonial trade—was.

Mercantilist practices created an economic situation in which manufacturers in the European country could receive extremely favorable terms of exchange for their products. Efforts were undertaken to prevent the colonies from manufacturing items that would compete with those being produced in the home country. Moreover, every effort was made to encourage the import of raw materials from the colonies to the home country, the raw materials to be brought in at low prices, turned into manufactured goods, and then sold at very high profits.

The great mercantilist trading companies of the seventeenth century were established in the Netherlands, England, and France. In 1602 the Dutch East India Company was formed. This company acquired a monopoly on trade with India, forbidding the English, the Portuguese, and the French to engage in such trade. The company had an army of nearly 12,000 men and a navy of between 40 and 60 ships. It brought into Europe each year between 10 and 12 million florins worth of goods.

*Unless otherwise noted, much of this section is attributable to Beaud (1983).

Between 1619 and 1663 the Dutch came to dominate the routes of the Far East. From 1648 to 1650 they imported from this area pepper and spices in quantities constituting 66 percent of all purchases and, in the same period, textiles totaling 14 percent of all purchases. They also began sugarcane production in Java. On the home front, the Netherlands established important processing industries, such as wool and linen processing; diamond cutting; and the dyeing, weaving, and spinning of silk. Other industries included sugar refining, brewing, distilling, tobacco and cocoa refining, and lead working.

England became a major rival of the Netherlands during the seventeenth century. In 1600 the English East India Company was formed under a charter from Queen Elizabeth, and within 15 years the company had established more than 20 trading posts. These were located in India, certain islands in the Indian Ocean, Indonesia, and in Hiratsuka, Japan. Between 1610 and 1640 England's foreign trade increased by ten times. English kings "distributed privileges and monopolies, regulated and organized the control of manufacturers, prohibited the export of wool, and raised taxes on imported French and Dutch fabrics; Acts of Parliament went so far as to make obligatory the use of woolen cloth for mourning clothes" (Beaud, 1983:28–29). Moreover, especially vigorous mercantilist practices were carried out under the guidance of the statesman Oliver Cromwell. He issued a navigation act specifying that "European goods could be transported only on English ships or on ships belonging to their country of origin; products from Africa, Asia, or America could be imported only on ships of England or the colonies" (Beaud, 1983:29).

Mercantilist policies were also prominent in France. Cardinal Richelieu, Louis XIV, and Jean Baptiste Colbert were the principal governmental personages associated with French mercantilism. Under Cardinal Richelieu, who was called upon to handle royal finances in 1624, various protectionist measures were established. These involved such things as a protective tariff on textiles in 1644 and a 50 cent per ton tax on foreign ships in 1659. But mercantilism in France reached its apex between 1663 and 1685 under Louis XIV and his chief economic minister, Colbert. For these men, the trading companies were regarded as the armies of the king, the manufacturers of France as his reserves (Beaud, 1983:39):

> [Colbert] watched over the establishment of more than 400 manufactures. There were "collective" works which brought together several artisan centers which benefited as a group from conferred privileges. . . . There were "private" works, individual enterprises (Van Robais in Abbeville), or large companies with branches in several provinces, especially in mining and metallurgy . . . and woolen goods. Finally there were royal manufactures, which were the property of the sovereign. . . . The counterpart to the privileges (monopolies, of production or of sale, exemptions and financing) was strict controls (norms, quantity, quality). These policies developed luxury and export production (tapestries, porcelain, glassware, luxury fabrics) as well as basic production (iron working, paper making, armaments) and products for common consumption (woolen and linen fabrics, etc.). . . .
>
> State policy extended to commerce as well as production. The French East Indies Company (1664) received a fifty-year monopoly on trade and navigation in the Indian Ocean and the Pacific Ocean.

Immanuel Wallerstein. Wallerstein is a professor of sociology at the State University of New York at Binghamton and directs the Fernand Braudel Center for the Study of Economies, Historical Systems, and Civilizations. The first three volumes of his work *The Modern World-System* have profoundly influenced our understanding of the developement of the modern capitalist world.

Capitalism as a World-System

A rather different view of the historical development of capitalism has been presented in Immanuel Wallerstein's *The Modern World-System* (1974a, 1980, 1989). There are two major ways in which Wallerstein's view of the development of capitalism differs from Dobb's. In the first place, Wallerstein de-emphasizes just those phenomena on which Dobb concentrates—those involving the expansion of the urban bourgeoisie—and views early capitalism as primarily connected with the agricultural realm. For Wallerstein, the early capitalism of the preindustrial period is principally *agricultural capitalism.* Second, and even more important, Wallerstein regards capitalism as constituting what he calls a **world-system.** This notion represents Wallerstein's distinctive contribution to our understanding of the emergence of the capitalist mode of production.

A world-system is defined by Wallerstein as any relatively large social system having three principal characteristics: (1) a high degree of autonomy; that is, the system is self-contained in the sense that it does not depend for its existence on something outside it; (2) an extensive division of labor, there being a high degree of specialization of economic roles within the system; and (3) a multiplicity of cultures, or the existence of different groups adhering to different traditions, speaking different languages, and so on.

Wallerstein identifies two basic types of world-systems: world-empires and world-economies. A **world-empire** is a world-system that is politically centralized and unified, every group within the empire being subordinate to one political center. Ancient Rome and classical China and India, for example, were organized according to this type of world-system. A **world-economy** is a world-system that lacks political centralization and unification. It therefore contains not only a multiplicity of cultures, but a multiplicity of sovereign political units as well. In the past there may have been numerous world-economies, although all of these either collapsed or quickly became converted into world-empires. In the modern world, however, there is only one world-economy: the capitalist world-economy, which has existed from the sixteenth century to the present day. Although Wallerstein notes that there have been attempts to turn this world-economy into a world-empire (most notably by Spain in the sixteenth century), these attempts have failed, and capitalism to this day has remained a politically decentralized system. Wallerstein holds that this political decentralization has greatly contributed to the long-term persistence of capitalism, inasmuch as empires tend to stifle innovation and individual creativity, factors that are basic to the capitalist organization of production.

But what exactly is a world-economy? What integrates it, or holds it together? Rather than being integrated by an overarching political structure, the capitalist world-economy is held together by a set of economic relationships: relationships of production and exchange of valued goods and services. In this sense the world-economy does not have the "tightness" of integration of a world-empire, but is a rather loosely structured network of economic relationships. These relationships involve extensive geographical and labor specialization. On the basis of such specialization, Wallerstein identifies three basic types of economic units that compose the world-economy.

The **core** consists of those regions and nation-states that dominate the capitalist world-economy and expropriate the bulk of the surplus produced within it. In the core are found those societies that are the most economically advanced or developed, that have the greatest degree of technological advancement, and that have the strongest governments and military structures. In the core, **wage labor**—work performed by employees bargained for by employers in a labor market—predominates. Wallerstein suggests that this is the case because work in the core is more highly skilled than work elsewhere, and more highly skilled work can be done more efficiently (i.e., more profitably) when wage labor is employed. The wealthiest capitalists within the entire world-economy are to be found residing in the core, establishing economic enterprises there and in other parts of the world-system.

The **periphery** is that segment of the world-economy that is most extensively subjected to surplus expropriation by the core. There is an intimate economic relationship between the core and the periphery. This relationship is one in which the core dominates the periphery, which in turn becomes economically dependent on the core. The periphery has in most respects those characteristics that are the reverse of what we find in the core. The societies and regions of the periphery are those that are least economically developed, have the lowest level of technological advancement, and have the weakest governments and military units (or no sovereign governments or military units at all). Forced labor, rather than wage labor, predominates here (or at least has done so historically). **Forced labor** is any system of labor in which workers are not legally free to sell their labor in a market and are therefore politically compelled by members of some other group to work for them. The main historical types of forced labor have been slavery and serfdom. Under slavery, workers are owned outright and are under the complete political control of their owners. Under serfdom workers are tied to specific parcels of land from which they have no freedom to move away. Wallerstein believes that since most work in the periphery is unskilled compared to work in the core, forced labor systems are more suitable because they are less costly.

The **semiperiphery** is that segment of the world-economy that operates between the core and the periphery. Wallerstein conceives of it as both an exploiter and as itself being exploited: It is an exploiter of the periphery, but it is exploited by the core. The societies of the semiperiphery are more technologically and economically advanced than those of the periphery, but less so than those of the core. They have stronger governments and military units than those found in the periphery, but weaker governments and military units than those possessed by core societies. Another way of characterizing the semiperiphery is to say that it contains features of both core and peripheral societies. For example, semiperipheral societies, at least historically, have combined wage labor with certain types of forced labor. They thus carry out certain economic activities that are typical of core societies in conjunction with other economic activities characteristic of the periphery.

It is crucial to see that for Wallerstein capitalism is a vast system of surplus expropriation that goes on not only within regions, but *between* them as well. Marx focused his attention on the surplus expropriation that went on within core societies, using England as a model. Wallerstein, though, has broadened the Marxian model of capitalism to a worldwide level. He recognizes with Marx that capitalists exploit workers within the developed European nations, but he goes a step further in asserting that there are crucial relations of economic exploitation that go on between nations, that is, primarily between core and periphery. Wallerstein views the periphery as having a vital role to play in the capitalist world-economy. Peripheral societies are primarily organized by capitalists in the core to serve as raw-material-producing units whose products can be exported to the core and turned into finished goods. Regions selected for peripheral development will be those that are most geographically suited for the production of certain raw materials at a certain time. (The relationship between core and periphery will become clearer in due course, especially in Chapter 9 when the problem of economic development and underdevelopment is discussed.)

It is also important to see that Wallerstein's notion that capitalism has constituted a world-system from its very inception is a rather revolutionary idea. Before Wallerstein, all analysts of capitalism, including Marx himself, limited their analyses to individual nation-states. But Wallerstein believes that the proper unit to deal with in analyzing capitalism is the world-system as a whole. He argues that one cannot understand what goes on in any single part of the world-system without understanding what is simultaneously going on in other parts of that system, indeed in the world-system as a whole. He believes that in order to understand the modern world from about 1500 on, societies can no longer be viewed as separate, independent units. Instead, they must be viewed in terms of their participation in or connection with a world-economy. This is a very bold idea, and the extent to which Wallerstein is correct is still hotly debated (cf. Skocpol, 1977; Brenner, 1977; Zolberg, 1981). Certainly one must be careful about pushing Wallerstein's world-system concept too far. However, whatever its limitations, the concept does appear to be a vital one for understanding the modern world and its evolution over the past five centuries.

The Capitalist World-Economy from the Sixteenth to the Eighteenth Centuries

Since its inception in the fifteenth century, the capitalist world-economy has been undergoing continual *expansion* and *evolution*. By saying that it has been expanding, we mean that it has been increasing its geographical range to cover wider and wider areas of the globe (see Figures 7.1 and 7.2). By saying that it has been an evolving system, we mean that its various components—core, periphery, and semiperiphery—have been changing their structure as parts of the whole. As we will see in the next two chapters, capitalism is now a vastly complex and technologically sophisticated system that covers most of the globe. But, as a world-system, what was it like during its early stages?

The first European nations to make a bid for core status in the sixteenth century were Spain

This old woodcut shows slaves processing sugar cane in early Iberian America, an activity that was extremely common in the capitalist periphery during its early stages.

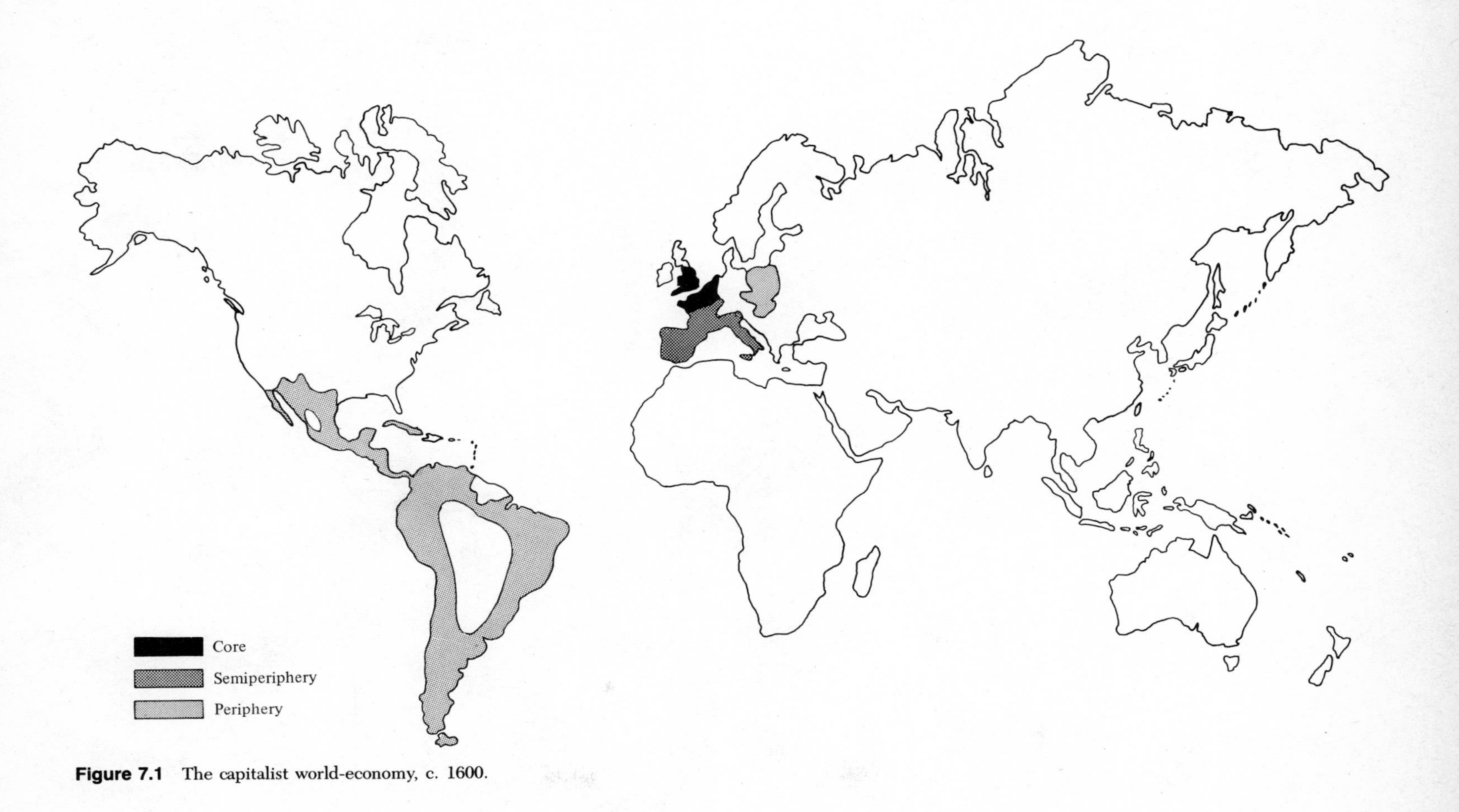

Figure 7.1 The capitalist world-economy, c. 1600.

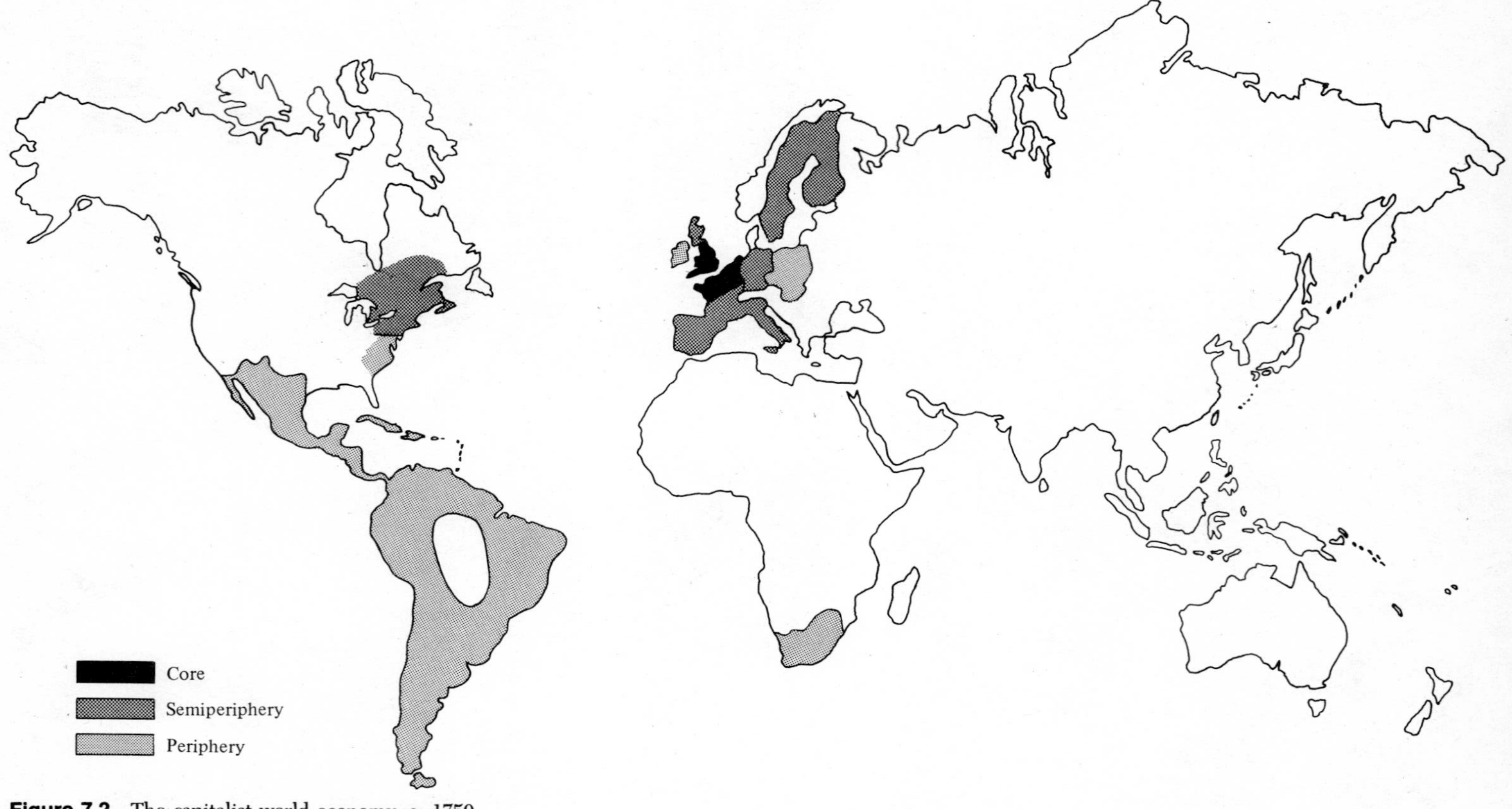

Figure 7.2 The capitalist world-economy, c. 1750.

and Portugal. These were the first European societies to engage in colonial expeditions in other regions of the world. Spain, in fact, attempted to turn the capitalist world-economy into its own world-empire—an attempt that failed. By the late sixteenth century it was clear that these societies would no longer be at the head of the world-economy. Their places were taken by the Netherlands, England, and France, the main core societies from the late sixteenth century on. Of these, the Netherlands was initially dominant. In these societies the principal economic activity was capitalist farming. Nobles increasingly leased their land out to tenants for a money rent and the land came to be farmed for profit. Many former nobles and peasants were converted into capitalist farmers. Much land was also turned over to the grazing of sheep, giving rise to an important woolen industry in England. Cottage industries were also of growing significance in these core societies.

The periphery in the sixteenth century consisted of two major world regions: Iberian (Hispanic and Portuguese) America and eastern Europe. In Hispanic America, the Spaniards had established important colonies given over to large-scale agriculture and, more importantly, to gold and silver mining. Forced labor systems established by the Spaniards produced large quantities of gold and silver ore, which were exported back to Europe to be turned into coinage. The influx of these precious metals contributed in a major way to the expansion of the money supply in Europe and thus had a great impact on the world-economy. In Portuguese America (Brazil), sugar plantations were established and came to depend on extensive slave labor imported from Africa. Sugar became a commodity greatly valued in Europe for sweetening coffee and making chocolate. In the other major peripheral region, eastern Europe, large-scale grain farming was the primary economic activity. This was carried out under a forced labor system that was essentially like the serfdom of earlier days. The peasant-landlord relation still prevailed, but peasants were producing for a world economic market, not simply for their lords. During the sixteenth century, eastern Europe, Poland especially, was a major exporter of grain to western Europe.

The semiperiphery in the sixteenth century was located in Mediterranean Europe, primarily in Italy and ultimately in Spain and Portugal. Sharecropping was the principal form of agricultural labor, and industry mainly involved the production of high-cost products, such as silks.

After the middle of the seventeenth century, England began to replace the Netherlands as the major core society, due in large part to the military defeats the English imposed on the Dutch. France also began to supersede the Netherlands, but the French did not attain the degree of success that the English did. During this time, several new societies entered the periphery. The most important of these were the U.S. South, a slave colony of England devoted to the production of numerous agricultural goods; and the slave societies of the West Indies, established primarily under the influence of the British and the French. The Caribbean slave-plantation societies were devoted heavily to sugar production. The semiperiphery at this time also expanded to include Sweden, Prussia, and the U.S. North.

EXPLAINING THE TRANSITION TO CAPITALISM

Explaining the transition from feudalism to capitalism involves giving answers to two closely related questions: Why did the old feudal system enter a crisis and collapse, and why was a capitalist economy the type of system that replaced it? Numerous theories attempting to answer these questions have been proposed by social scientists and historians, but little consensus has emerged among scholars. The various theories can be grouped into four main categories: (1) Weberian theories, (2) Marxian theories, (3) world-system theories, and (4) demographic theories.

Weberian Theories

Perhaps the most famous explanation of the transition to capitalism is that given by Max Weber in his book *The Protestant Ethic and the Spirit of Capitalism* (1958; orig. 1905). This book was at least partly motivated by Weber's belief that Marxian historical materialism was too one-sided and needed to be counterbalanced by a greater stress on the casual role of ideas in historical change. One of Weber's lifelong interests lay in understanding the growth of the system of rational capitalism in the West. He was especially concerned to determine why capitalism arose in this area of the world on such a massive scale and yet lay so dormant and undeveloped in the Eastern world. Weber by no means dismissed the significance of economic factors in the transformation of the West, but he emphasized the causal role that was played, he thought, by the Protestant Reformation. He saw the Reformation as a critical stimulus and deduced that the absence of such a religious transformation in the East prevented any substantial development of capitalism there.

Weber thought that Protestantism, and particularly its Calvinist branch, offered a doctrine of human salvation that departed strongly from that espoused by the Catholic Church. Instead of emphasizing faith in God alone as the key to salvation, Calvinism promoted a more individualistic and personal means of gaining salvation. This was embodied in what Weber called the *Protestant ethic*. This ethic emphasized that hard work and worldly success were favorable to God and, if not a direct route to salvation, then at least a signal from God that one had been saved. Success in the world of business through one's own efforts was thus the avenue to the heavenly afterlife. Weber thought that this new religious orientation changed people's attitude toward the world into one emphasizing greater rational control and manipulation of it, and that such a change had a direct carryover into the economic world. By worshiping God and guaranteeing their salvation, people were also inadvertently creating a new economic system based on the rational pursuit of profit. Weber was quick to emphasize that capitalism did not develop out of Protestantism alone; but without such a religious value system, he felt, capitalism would not have developed as it did. Protestantism tipped the balance, as it were, for Western capitalist development.

Although this thesis is widely accepted today by many social scientists, it has received abundant criticism from others and there appear to be some solid grounds for abandoning it. The Swedish economic historian Kurt Samuelsson (1957) has rejected the thesis completely, arguing that Weber's supporting evidence was faulty and that there was never any close connection between Protestantism and capitalism. This view of Weber's argument, however, seems rather overdrawn; it appears clear that Protestantism and capitalism have been historically linked. Yet this does not demonstrate the causal impact of Protestantism upon capitalism, for the relationship between the two may have been quite the other way around: capitalism may have promoted changes in Protestantism. Such a view is in fact held by H. M. Robertson (1959), another economic historian, who has argued that what we today call the Protestant ethic was strongly influenced by the steady spread of capitalism. Robertson believes that religion came to be gradually accommodated to the new economic system so that it could more adequately serve the needs of economically dominant groups.

Further skepticism regarding Weber's thesis is warranted due to the fact that capitalism was able to prosper in staunchly Catholic countries. France, for example, was one of the major core powers of the world-economy from the seventeenth century on. Moreover, an early form of rational capitalism developed in pre-Reformation Italy (J. Cohen, 1980).

In his more mature work Weber seems to have moved in a different direction in explaining the origins of capitalism (R. Collins, 1980). In his *General Economic History* (1927), he appears to relegate the Protestant ethic to a relatively minor role in capitalist development and to stress other factors, especially the modern nation-state, as of greater causal significance. As Randall Collins comments (1980:931–932):

> The state . . . is the factor to which he gave the most attention; . . . [it is] the key to all of the *institutional* structures of rational capitalism. Only the West developed the highly bureaucratized state, based on specialized professional administrators and on a law made and applied by full-time professional jurists for a populace characterized by rights of citizenship. It is this bureaucratic-legal state that broke down feudalism and patrimonialism, freeing land and labor for the capitalist market. It is this state that pacified large territories, eliminated internal market barriers, standardized taxation and currencies. It is this state that provided the basis for a reliable system of banking, investment, property, and contracts, through a rationally calculable and universally applied system of law courts.

In fact, Weber appeared to come very close to a view that has been promoted by Wallerstein: that it was the politically decentralized character of capitalism that allowed it to prosper and develop. Weber wrote of modern cities (1927:337; quoted in Collins, 1980:940; emphasis added):

> [They] came under the power of competing national states in a condition of perpetual struggle for power in peace or war. This competitive struggle created the largest opportunities for modern Western capitalism. The separate states had to compete for mobile capital, which dictated to them the conditions under which it would assist them to power. Out of this alliance of the state with capital, dictated by necessity, arose the national citizen class, the bourgeoisie in the modern sense of the word. Hence it is the closed national state which afforded to capitalism its chance for development—*and as long as the national state does not give place to a world empire capitalism will also endure.*

This last statement reveals, as Collins has noted, a remarkable anticipation of Wallerstein.

This later theory of Weber's should also be regarded with considerable skepticism. Most important, it begs the question as to what gave rise to the modern nation-state. Weber's answer was that the bureaucratic state was "the most efficient means of pacifying a large territory" (Collins, 1980:932). But this is unacceptable, because it does not explain why such a state did not arise at an earlier period to pacify large territories. There is no need to deny the connection between the rise of capitalism and the emergence of the modern bureaucratic state, but it is just as logical (if not more so) to regard the modern state as the *outcome* of capitalist development (see Chapter 12).

In recent years a number of scholars have kept the spirit of Weber alive by offering neo-Weberian interpretations of a highly eclectic nature. Daniel Chirot (1985, 1986), for example, claims that the main causal factors in the rise of capitalism were Europe's unique geographical conditions, the highly decentralized character of the European feudal system, and the increasing rationality that law and religion came to adopt in the later feudal period. John Hall (1985) and Michael Mann (1986) offer similar interpretations but give particular emphasis to the role of religion. Both go considerably beyond Weber's original Protestant ethic thesis in giving not only Protestantism, but Christianity in general, a major causal role in the rise of capitalism. Mann views Christianity as containing an ideology or spirit that he refers to as "rational restlessness," and he believes that this ideology uniquely stimulated a strong attitude toward economic growth.

Although these neo-Weberian arguments often contain major insights, to my mind they unnecessarily complicate our search for a coherent understanding of the European capitalist transition. They make too many factors important and fail to give us a proper understanding of the relative contributions of the factors. Moreover, serious questions can be raised about some of the proposed factors, such as Christianity. As we shall see in a moment, there was another civilization that underwent a transition from feudalism to capitalism at roughly the same time as Europe. This was Japan, and it was anything but a Christian civilization. Finally, to claim, as Chirot does, that Europe made the transition to capitalism because of a unique spirit of rationality begs the question as to the origin of this rationality. Until we have correctly understood what made Europe more "rational" than other civilizations, we cannot legitimately invoke this as a cause of Europe's rise.

Marxian Theories

Marxists emphasize class and economic forces in bringing about the transition from feudalism to capitalism. Yet there is no general Marxian theory of this problem, for Marxists disagree significantly with one another over the issue. Perhaps the two most famous Marxian theories are those of Maurice Dobb (1963) and Paul Sweezy (1976).

Dobb's theory holds that it was the internal contradictions or conflicts within the feudal mode of production that eventually tore it apart. These conflicts revolved around the exploitative relationship between landlord and peasant. In the thirteenth and fourteenth centuries, the demands placed upon the peasants by the landlords increased sharply. The increasing exploitation of the peasantry resulted from several factors: an increase in the size of the noble class, increasing expenses resulting from war and the Crusades, and the growing extravagance and status competition among noble families. The increase in the demands placed upon the peasantry caused a mass migration from the manors, an exodus "which was destined to drain the system of its essential lifeblood and to provoke the series of crises in which feudal economy was to find itself engulfed in the fourteenth and fifteenth centuries. This flight of villeins from the land often assumed catastrophic proportions both in England and elsewhere" (Dobb, 1963:46).

Paul Sweezy rejects Dobb's view that the end of feudalism was brought about by forces internal to it. Sweezy believes that feudalism was a largely stagnant mode of production that required some external force to dissolve it. Thus the major changes it began to undergo in the thirteenth and fourteenth centuries, such as the growing need for revenue on the part of the nobility and the consequent increased pressure on the peasantry, were actually generated by forces outside the feudal system proper. Sweezy argues that the main external factor that caused severe disruptions within feudalism and led to the adoption of a capitalist mode of production was the revival of long-distance trade between Europe and other world regions. Long-distance trade had a dissolving effect on feudalism for several reasons. For one thing, it brought a more rational system of production into play alongside feudalism, a system that brought "the feudal estates within the orbit of the exchange economy" (Sweezy, 1976:42). In addition, the strong presence of a system based on exchange-value tended to turn the economic outlook of the producers in a more "businesslike" direction. It became desirable to seek wealth in the form of money rather than in terms of perishable goods, and ultimately wealth seeking became an end in itself. Finally, the revival of trade increased the importance of the towns, which became magnets pulling the peasants away from the increased pressures they were experiencing in the countryside.

Sweezy's interpretation has an important contribution to make, but only in the context of other theories. Taken by itself, it is unacceptable. For one thing, it greatly undervalues the extent to which European feudalism was an internally dynamic mode of production, and thus it exaggerates the role of factors outside Europe. Moreover, there is a curiously ethnocentric quality to Sweezy's argument. He appears to assume that the mere existence of a system of production-for-exchange would have been sufficient to pull feudal lords away from their traditional production-for-use economy. He repeatedly implies that feudalism was an economic system that was inferior to capitalism, and that this inferiority would have been apparent to the feudal lords themselves.

The difficulties with Sweezy's theory push us back toward Dobb's interpretation. Dobb has made a vital contribution in focusing on the internal difficulties of the feudal system. Contrary to Sweezy, considerable evidence has emerged in recent decades to indicate that feudalism was not a stagnant mode of production, and that it quite definitely had a dynamic quality that had much to do with its internal characteristics. Dobb sees the feudal dynamic as rooted in the increasing exploitation of peasants by landlords, and there is much truth in this. However, Dobb does not offer a convincing explanation for this increase in exploitation. At one point he hints that this may have been linked to demographic changes, but he does not really follow up on this point. We shall return to the point in our discussion of demographic theories.

World-System Theories

Some of the most recent and provocative theories of the rise of European capitalism use a world-system approach similar to Wallerstein's (Schneider, 1977; Ekholm, 1981; Abu-Lughod, 1988, 1989). These theories resemble Sweezy's in emphasizing factors external to Europe, but they go considerably further.

The most elaborate of these theories is that of Janet Abu-Lughod (1988, 1989). Abu-Lughod suggests that from about the thirteenth century Europe was part of a gigantic world-system that included Asia and Africa. This "Afro-Eurasian" world-system was centered on long-distance trade and had a strongly capitalistic character. At this time Asia was at least on a par with Europe, and in some respects was actually in a more favorable position. Asia was, in a sense, a kind of core and Europe was a kind of periphery. Abu-Lughod claims that to understand how this all changed in the coming centuries we need to look, not at the internal features of Europe or Asia, but to the relations between them. The rise of Europe was just as much the fall of Asia, and the two cannot be separated. This shift was due to the rupturing of trade relations between the eastern Mediterranean and the Orient and a corresponding deepening of trade links between the Mediterranean and northwest Europe.

It has become clear that there was extensive economic interaction between Europe and Asia after about A.D. 1000 and that this interaction contributed to the capitalist takeoff in Europe (cf. McNeill, 1982). However, like Sweezy's theory, the world-system theories overrate this interaction and in the process greatly underplay the extent to which feudalism had an internal dynamic. But further questions arise. Was there really an "Afro-Eurasian" world-system in any meaningful sense of the concept of a world-system? And, even if there was, why were the relations between the parts of this system more important than the relations within the parts, especially the European part? World-system theories have yet to offer a convincing answer to this latter question. And, in ignoring or downplaying the internal characteristics of feudalism, such theories seem to miss what is perhaps the most important reason for the capitalist transition.

Demographic Theories

Many students of the transition from feudalism to capitalism have stressed the role of demographic factors in leading to the crisis and ultimate breakup of the feudal system (Postan, 1972; Wilkinson, 1973; North and Thomas, 1973; P. Anderson, 1974a:197–199; Le Roy Ladurie, 1974). The general arguments of these scholars are approximately as follows. During the twelfth and thirteenth centuries, population was growing significantly in western Europe and beginning to be a substantial problem. As densities rose, declining yields set in, and new and marginal lands were increasingly settled and cultivated. By the end of the thirteenth century, a crisis of overpopulation had more or less been reached. Famine became more and more common. But this crisis of overpopulation produced, as it were, its own cure. Beginning in the early fourteenth century, population actually began to decline because of severe famines that led to malnutrition, disease, and, ultimately, death. By the middle of the fourteenth century, in 1348–1350 to be precise, the Black Death swept Europe and accelerated population decline. The plague returned again and again to many parts of Europe throughout the second half of the fourteenth century and in the early fifteenth century. Population continued to decline until approximately 1450, when it began once again to increase. Thus western Europe experienced significant, and in some cases continuous, population decline over a 150-year period.

This population decline had severe consequences for the feudal economy. As population declined, landlords were faced with fewer and fewer peasant workers, and eventually severe labor shortages resulted. This caused a fall in

The Demon of the Plague. This German woodcut of 1540 was designed to symbolize the Black Death.

feudal revenues and necessitated a dramatic response on the part of the nobility to prevent further declines in their incomes. This decline in feudal revenues is in essence the "crisis of feudalism" referred to earlier. As mentioned at that time, the landlords responded to their economic difficulties in two ways: by leasing out their demesnes to be run as capitalist farms, and by enclosures of land. As Michael Postan (1972:105) comments, "The letting-out of the demesne in parcels had now become one of the ways of arresting the decline of profits."

Conclusions

The demographic interpretation seems to point to an especially significant internal feature of feudalism that gave it a dynamic quality. However, two questions still remain to be answered. First, if demographic changes were the principal cause of the feudal crisis, why did this crisis get resolved in the way it did (Mann, 1986)? In other words, why did the landlords respond to their declining economic fortunes by changing the economic system rather than by increasing their repression and exploitation of the peasantry? Second, why was the new type of economic system that the feudal lords brought about a specifically *capitalist* system?

In answering the first question, we need to recognize that feudal lords did indeed engage, as Dobb has well recognized, in increasing repression and exploitation of the peasantry. However, as Michael Mann (1986) has pointed out, this was only a temporary solution to their economic problems. Eventually, the lords began to see that it was easier to improve their economic fortunes by shifting toward a more capitalistic system of production. And why was this an easier solution? As Mann suggests, it was because of the increasing presence of a market economy, a presence that resulted from the increased role of long-distance trade between Europe and Asia. This puts us back in the camp of Sweezy and the world-system theorists, but within the context of a full consideration of the internal evolution of the feudal system. In other words, we can say that the transition from feudalism to capitalism resulted from a historical coincidence of two great forces: the internal crisis of feudalism that was generated by demographic collapse, and the increasing involvement of Europe within a market-oriented economy that included Asia.

In terms of explaining why it was a specifically capitalist system that feudalism turned into, there is wide agreement that the answer has to do with the political character of feudalism (cf. Wallerstein, 1974a; Mann, 1986; Hall, 1985; Chirot, 1986). Unlike most other agrarian civilizations, feudalism was politically decentralized. Other civilizations, such as China and India, were dominated by large bureaucratic states. In these civilizations there could have been little incentive for the kind of individual entrepreneurship that we associate with capitalism, because the state was so powerful that it crushed such efforts from the beginning. But European feudalism lacked such strong states, and therefore the political atmosphere was favorable to individual innovation.

These conclusions are reinforced when we recognize that in Japan something very similar occurred. According to Perry Anderson (1974b), between the fifteenth and nineteenth centuries Japan had a feudal system strikingly similar to European feudalism (and, in fact, was the only other civilization in world history to have had such a system). After about the middle of the seventeenth century this system underwent a remarkable degree of commercialization (cf. P. Anderson, 1974b; Halliday, 1975). Agricultural products were increasingly marketed, and urban mercantile activity expanded vigorously. By the middle of the nineteenth century Japan was, in economic terms, a substantially capitalist society, even if it remained basically feudal in a social and political sense. It is likely that the politically decentralized character of Japanese feudalism played a crucial role in facilitating this transition toward capitalism. And the "crisis of Japanese feudalism" of which Anderson (1974b) speaks may well have been linked to demographic changes (Boserup, 1965). Moreover, external trade played no role at all in the initial transition, because between 1638 and 1853 Japan maintained a policy of strict isolation from the rest of the world (Mutel, 1988). It was not until after the middle of the nineteenth century that Japan rejoined the world-economy and experienced even further economic growth as the result of participation in that economy.*

*A more elaborate discussion of these conclusions can be found in Sanderson (in press).

Table 7.1 THEORIES OF THE TRANSITION FROM FEUDALISM TO CAPITALISM

Theory	Characteristics	Evaluation
Weberian theories	Weber's original Protestant ethic thesis emphasized the religious values created by the Protestant Reformation in stimulating the development of Western capitalism. Weber later downplayed the role of Protestantism and gave the modern rational state the key role. Neo-Weberian theories tend to emphasize an eclectic combination of factors—such as geography, politics, and religion—and to downplay economic factors (or at least to treat economics only as one factor among many).	Some Weberian theories contain important insights, but in general these theories contain several fatal flaws and contribute little.
Marxian theories	Emphasize class struggle and other economic forces as essential to the breakdown of feudalism and the rise of capitalism. There are numerous Marxist theories of the transition, some of which are radically opposed. Dobb's classic Marxian theory emphasizes increasing exploitation of peasants by landlords. This drove peasants off the land and into the towns, where they contributed to the expansion of urban mercantile activity. Sweezy's theory denies an internal dynamic to feudalism and emphasizes the revival of long-distance trade between Europe and Asia as leading to capitalism.	Sweezy's theory exaggerates factors external to Europe, and incorrectly perceives feudalism as having no internal dynamic. Dobb's theory properly recognizes an internal dynamic to feudalism, but only partially perceives what this dynamic is.
World-system theories	Suggest that focus on the internal character of Europe is an unjustified form of "Eurocentrism." It was not anything internal to Europe, but the economic and political relations between Europe and Asia that led to a shift toward capitalism. The rise of the West was part and parcel of the fall of the East. Trade relations between the Mediterranean and northwest Europe deepened at the same time that there was a rupturing of relations between the Mediterranean and the Orient.	Correctly give an important role to the economic relations between feudal Europe and Asia, but, like Sweezy's theory, fail to appreciate the internal features of feudalism that gave it an impetus to breakdown and transformation.
Demographic theories	Hold that population growth in feudal Europe by the thirteenth century had led to severe overpopulation. This ultimately led to famine and disease and to a catastrophic population collapse. The thinning of population led to severe labor scarcity from the standpoint of the feudal lords, and thus to the lords' declining economic fortunes. The lords responded to this economic crisis by shifting their economic actions in a more capitalistic direction.	Contain the key to understanding the internal dynamic of feudalism. But need to be combined with the argument of Sweezy and the world-system theorists in order to understand the precise historical conjuncture that produced the beginnings of the modern capitalist world.

SUMMARY

1. The feudal economy of western Europe was a production-for-use economy organized around the manor. Landlords subjugated a peasantry who cultivated for their own subsistence and rendered taxes, rent, and labor services to their lords. Production-for-exchange played little role in economic life. Although towns and trade existed, they had little impact on the functioning of the feudal economy.

2. This system was eventually replaced by the capitalist mode of production. The capitalist system is one in which the selling of commodities for maximum profit is the essence of economic life. Marx and many other Marxists view capitalism as based on the wage-labor relationship and as developing with the Industrial Revolution in the late eighteenth century. They distinguish between industrial capitalism (or "true" capitalism) and a type of capitalism known as merchant capitalism that existed between the sixteenth and eighteenth centuries. Others reject the distinction between merchant and industrial capitalism and date capitalist origins from the sixteenth century.

3. A major effort to interpret the historical development of capitalism has been made by Wallerstein. Wallerstein sees capitalism as a world-system that has always had a complex division of labor along both occupational and geographical lines. This world-system has been geographically expanding for several hundred years and is now nearly worldwide in scope.

4. Wallerstein divides the capitalist world-system into core, peripheral, and semiperipheral nations and regions. Core areas are politically and economically dominant and engage in extensive surplus extraction from peripheral regions they create in order to exploit. Core regions are the most technologically and economically advanced. Peripheral regions have historically functioned in the world-economy as raw-material-producing areas whose products are desired by the core. Semiperipheral nations and regions are economically between core and peripheral nations and regions and have many of the characteristics of both.

5. For Wallerstein capitalism began in the sixteenth century with the emergence of Spain and Portugal as colonially expanding European powers. When they declined, their place was taken by the Netherlands, England, and France. These nations dominated the world-system by the middle of the seventeenth century. The major peripheral regions during this period were Iberian America and eastern Europe. The semiperiphery consisted of Mediterranean Europe.

6. The seventeenth century has been known as the age of mercantilism. In this era governments granted monopolies to companies to engage in international trade. Huge profits were earned by the major European core powers through trade with their colonies elsewhere in the world.

7. Numerous theories have been proposed to explain the transition from feudalism to capitalism. Most important, these include Weberian theories, demographic theories, world-system theories, and several different kinds of Marxian theories. The leading assumptions of these theories, and an evaluation of their explanatory value, can be found in Table 7.1.

SPECIAL TOPIC: INDUSTRY BEFORE THE INDUSTRIAL REVOLUTION

The Industrial Revolution of the late eighteenth century unleashed industrial activity on a massive scale and converted European capitalism into a highly urbanized, manufacturing-oriented economic activity. Yet in the principally agrarian life of Europe before the

Industrial Revolution, industry was not lacking. Indeed, a good deal of it existed. But it was organized very differently from the later industry that developed under industrial capitalism.

The French social historian Fernand Braudel (1982) has distinguished four forms of industrial activity in early capitalist Europe. At the simplest level were *family workshops.* There were countless numbers of these tiny industrial units throughout Europe. Each workshop was normally headed by a master tradesman and contained two or three journeymen and an apprentice or two. The division of labor was very simple or there was none at all. Braudel includes in this category the cutler, the nail maker, the village blacksmith, the cobbler, the goldsmith, the locksmith, and the lacemaker, as well as the baker, the miller, the cheesemaker, and the butcher.

A second type of industrial activity might be termed the *dispersed factory.* In this type of arrangement, workshops were scattered over possibly wide areas yet connected to one another. A merchant entrepreneur served as a kind of director or coordinator. This entrepreneur provided raw materials to the individual workshops, ensured that the work got done, made payments of wages to the workers, and marketed the finished product. This category of industry was perhaps most commonly found in textile manufacturing, but it was also associated with cutlery, nail making, and iron working.

A third category of industry involved *concentrated manufacture,* or the *manufactory,* a form that represented a significant break with the first two types. Rather than remaining in their own homes, workers came together under one roof to complete a series of tasks. A division of labor ensued, leading to an increase in the level of productivity. This type of work organization had penetrated textile manufacturing to some extent, and was also found in connection with brewing, tanning, glassworking, and a number of other industries.

The fourth type of industrial activity was very similar to the third, but was distinguished by the level of technology employed. In manufactories, work was done primarily by hand, but in the fourth category—*factories*—work was accomplished through considerable reliance upon machinery. Of course, factories did not become a significant feature of capitalism until the late eighteenth and early nineteenth centuries, but they existed to some extent nonetheless. As Braudel comments (1982: 301–302):

> *I would regard the typical* modern *mine of the sixteenth century for instance, such as existed in central Europe . . . as an example, and an important one, of mechanization, even if steam was only introduced two hundred years later and then only very slowly and grudgingly. . . . Other examples are the naval yards of Saardam near Amsterdam in the seventeenth century, with their mechanical saws, their cranes, their mast-erecting machines; and so many little "factories" using hydraulic wheels: paper-mills, saw-mills or the sword-works in Vienne in the Dauphine, where the grindstones and bellows were mechanically operated.*

The most famous form of industrial activity throughout preindustrial Europe was what in Germany came to be known as the *Verlagssystem,* more commonly known as the **putting-out system,** or sometimes simply as **cottage industry.** This is a version of the second category of industry discussed above. In the *Verlagssystem,* a merchant served as "the middleman between the producer of raw materials and the artisan, between the artisan and the purchaser of the finished product, and between his local town and foreign markets" (Braudel, 1982:318). As Braudel notes, this merchant "had one foot in the town and the other in the country" (1982:318). The merchant organized industrial activity by providing workers with raw materials and an initial wage and then placing an order for a certain quantity of finished products. Workers remained in their homes to manufacture the products. The merchant paid the remaining wages when the products were turned over to him, and he saw to the selling of the products in the available markets.

The putting-out system developed very early in preindustrial Europe, even before the sixteenth century. Although it was originally named by the Germans and first analyzed by German historians, it was not invented in Germany. Braudel suggests that it probably originated in the Netherlands and in Italy, perhaps as early as the thirteenth century. It soon spread throughout Europe.

Although many forms of industry were organized by the *Verlagssystem,* the principal industry with which it was associated was textile manufacturing. Braudel gives us a concrete picture of the *Verlagssystem* as applied to lace manufacture in eighteenth-century Germany (1982:318):

> *In the month of June 1775, an observant traveller crossing the Erzgebirge from Freyberg to Augustusberg, journeyed through the string of mountain villages where cotton was spun and lace made. . . . Since it was summertime, all the women were sitting outside on their doorsteps; under a lime tree, a circle of girls sat round an old grenadier. And everyone, including the old soldier, was hard at work. It was a matter of life and death: the lacemaker's fingers only stopped for a moment to pick up a piece of bread or a boiled potato sprinkled with salt. At the end of the week, she would take her work either to the local market (but that was the exception) or more probably to the* Spitzenherr, *the "lord of the lace," who had provided her with thread and patterns from Holland and France, and who had placed an advance order for her work.*

This system is an excellent example of a type of productive activity that was different in its very essence from the one that came to dominate after the Industrial Revolution. The organization of work associated with industrial capitalism was completely absent, and the workers retained their traditional craft skills. The merchants' concerns were limited to the marketing of the final product and did not involve attempts to alter the production process. Thus, the putting-out system was a classic form of merchant capitalism. As Braudel comments (1982:321):

> *These putting-out networks are the first hard evidence of a merchant capitalism which was intended to dominate though not to transform craft production. What interested these merchants was undoubtedly marketing. Thus conceived, the* Verlagssystem *might concern itself with any branch of production as soon as a merchant could see any benefit to himself in controlling it.*

FOR FURTHER READING

Aston, T.H., and C.H.E. Philpin (eds.). *The Brenner Debate: Agrarian Class Structure and Economic Development in Pre-Industrial Europe.* Cambridge: Cambridge University Press, 1985. A collection of famous essays centering around the recent controversy generated by Robert Brenner, a historian highly critical of Wallerstein and the demographic theorists. Reprints Brenner's 1976 article, which offers a class-based Marxian account of the transition to capitalism, and the essays criticizing Brenner.

Beaud, Michel. *A History of Capitalism, 1500–1980.* New York: Monthly Review Press, 1983. A valuable general sketch by a French Marxian economist of the historical development of capitalism.

Braudel, Fernand. *Civilization and Capitalism, 15th–18th Century.* New York: Harper & Row, 1981–1984. An extraordinary economic history of capitalism before the Industrial Revolution by an eminent French historian who has had a great influence on Wallerstein. Volume 1, *The Structures of Everyday Life,* explores such basic aspects of human material existence as population, housing, food and drink, and technology. Volume 2, *The Wheels of Commerce,* examines many intricate details of economic exchange and commerce. Volume 3, *The Perspective of the World,* is the most theoretical of all the volumes and examines the early history of capitalism from a perspective similar to Wallerstein's world-system approach.

Hall, John A. *Powers and Liberties: The Causes and Consequences of the Rise of the West.* Berkeley: University of California Press, 1985. A noted neo-Weberian effort to explain the rise of Western capitalism, as well as why capitalism did not develop originally in China, India, and Islamic civilization.

Kriedte, Peter. *Peasants, Landlords and Merchant Capitalists: Europe and the World Economy, 1500–1800.* Cambridge: Cambridge University Press, 1983. A good brief treatment of the development of capitalism during its early centuries.

Mann, Michael. *The Sources of Social Power. Volume 1: A History of Power from the Beginning to* A.D. *1760.* Cambridge: Cambridge University Press, 1986. Several chapters near the end treat in considerable detail the rise of modern capitalism. Adopts basically a Weberian perspective and locates the roots of capitalism several centuries earlier than most treatments.

Wallerstein, Immanuel. *The Modern World-System: Capitalist Agriculture and the Origins of the European World-Economy in the Sixteenth Century.* New York: Academic Press, 1974. An outstanding, but highly controversial, work on the emergence of capitalism by a noted sociologist. The first of four planned volumes on the development of capitalism from Wallerstein's world-system perspective. Already a modern classic, it is essential reading for anyone interested in the general history of capitalism.

Wallerstein, Immanuel. *The Modern World-System II: Mercantilism and the Consolidation of the European World-Economy, 1600–1750.* New York: Academic Press, 1980. The second volume of Wallerstein's planned four-volume opus.

Wolf, Eric. *Europe and the People Without History.* Berkeley: University of California Press, 1982. An absorbing historical analysis of capitalism in which the author gives special emphasis to the impact of capitalism on the precapitalist societies that fell under capitalist influence.

CHAPTER 8

Capitalism and Socialism Since the Industrial Revolution

Immanuel Wallerstein (1984d) has claimed that there have been three great trends in the evolution of the capitalist world-economy: increasing mechanization of production, increasing commodification of the factors of production, and increasing proletarianization of the labor force. Increasing **mechanization** involves the increasing application of advanced technology, especially machinery, to production tasks. The level of **commodification** of the factors of production advances when land, labor, technology, and other productive forces increasingly come to be regulated by the market and by considerations of their exchange-value. Increasing **proletarianization** results when a larger percentage of the work force is compensated in the form of wages. Taken together, these three trends mark what is known as a "deepening" of capitalist development. This chapter and the next explore the deepening of capitalism over the past two centuries. Of particular concern in the present chapter is what has been called the Industrial Revolution: what it was, when and why it occurred, and what its consequences were for the capitalist system. The chapter also explores the evolution and expansion of capitalism from the late nineteenth century to the present, and takes a close look at the impact of evolving capitalism on the nature of work. After 1917, and particularly after 1945, some capitalist societies began efforts to withdraw from the capitalist system and to establish socialist economic forms. The nature and significance of these efforts is also a major topic of the chapter. An appendix presents the rudiments of Karl Marx's conception of how exploitation occurs within capitalism.

THE INDUSTRIAL REVOLUTION AND THE EMERGENCE OF INDUSTRIAL CAPITALISM

The Industrial Revolution and Its Causes

The Industrial Revolution involved the transformation of a technology resting heavily on human and animal labor into a technology characterized by *machines* (Landes, 1969). Along with this came the transition from a heavy reliance on agricultural production to a reliance on the manufacture of goods for sale in the context of a factory system. The Industrial Revolution was, at bottom, a revolution in technology; it created, nevertheless, new and profound changes in the very economic structure of society, bringing new methods of production and exchange of goods, and profound changes in the organization of labor.

The Industrial Revolution began in England during the second half of the eighteenth century, its first phase typically dated from about 1760 to 1830 (Landes, 1969). This initial phase of **industrialization** was characterized by the great expansion of the textile industry and by major developments in the manufacture of iron and the mining of coal. The textile industry, especially the manufacture of cotton cloth, was advanced through the invention of the spinning jenny, the water frame, the power loom, and the cotton gin. The growth of textile manufacture spurred the development of the factory system. The invention of the steam engine was also an important part of this process, as it was used to power the heavy machinery housed in the textile factories. Textiles formed a vital part of the English economy and were a major export in the international capitalist system.

The iron industry also underwent significant expansion in the first phase of industrial development. Iron was increasingly in demand for the manufacture of steam engines and machine tools; machine tool production itself became a significant feature of the English economy. The increasing manufacture of these products, in turn, caused an increase in the demand for coal and the expansion of the coal-mining industry.

Industrial technology was soon to be found in several other parts of Europe during the nineteenth century, especially in France, Belgium, and Germany. The United States also began to emerge as a major industrial society during this

Cotton manufacturing in a Lancashire cotton mill, 1834. The manufacture of cotton cloth was the spearhead of the English Industrial Revolution.

time. By the late nineteenth century, both Russia and Japan had begun to industrialize.

The Industrial Revolution created a new mode of economic production, *industrial capitalism.* As indicated in the last chapter, industrial capitalism differs from other forms of capitalism in that it involves the earning of profit through the exploitation of wage-workers. The establishment of industrial capitalism on a major scale thus required the reorganization of the work force into the factory system, and the factory became the basic social unit of capitalist production. Michel Beaud has said the following in regard to the emergence of industrial capitalism (1983:83):

> During the nineteenth century it was chiefly through the establishment of mechanized industry that the capitalist mode of production was extended. The "mills" which had begun to be built in England at the end of the eighteenth century became more widespread, not only in England itself, but in Belgium, France, Switzerland, Germany, and the United States. The development of these mills was particularly striking in the "driving" sectors of the time: textiles and metallurgy. Men who had previously been traders or merchants, as well as foremen and the sons of artisans, became manufacturers and availed themselves of a labor force that had become available through the transformation of the countryside or through immigration. These laborers were employed with the intention of extracting the maximum, and it was in conditions of misery and unbearable oppression that the original core of the modern working class was formed.

Obviously, industrialization did not end with these technological and economic developments. Rather than as an event or a series of events, industrialization is best thought of as a continuous process that has existed down to the present time. In the middle of the nineteenth century, further technological innovations emerged and existing technologies were elaborated and applied to capitalist production on a wider scale. For instance, the steam engine came to be applied to transportation. It was used to create the first steam railway and was applied as well to navigation with the invention of the steamboat. It was during this time that railroads began to emerge as an extremely significant aspect of capitalist investment (Dobb, 1963:296–297):

> In the '40's and '50's of the century there arrived on the scene a novel activity which, in its absorption of capital and of capital goods, surpassed in importance any previous type of investment-expenditure. Even when we label these decades of the mid-nineteenth century "the railway age," we often fail to appreciate to the full the unique strategic importance of this period. Railways have the inestimable advantage for Capitalism of being enormously capital-absorbing; in which respect they are only surpassed by the armaments of modern warfare and scarcely equalled by modern urban building.
>
> . . . The 2,000 miles of railway line opened in the United Kingdom in 1847–8 must have absorbed nearly half a million tons of iron for rails and chairs alone, or one quarter of the iron output of that date; and . . . railway expenditure gave employment to 300,000 "on and off the lines" in the peak year. By 1860 some 10,000 miles of railway had been laid in Great Britain and Northern Ireland: a figure which was to increase by half again between 1860 and 1870.
>
> . . . Close on the heels of the British railway boom of the '40's came continental railway building; and following this there yawned the even larger maw of American railroad construction.

By the turn of the twentieth century, the automobile, electrical, and petroleum industries were becoming important features of life in industrial societies (Lenski, 1970). By World War II, the aviation, aluminum, and electronics industries were achieving major economic significance (Lenski, 1970). Recent years have witnessed such notable technological developments as the harnessing of nuclear energy and the manufacture of highly sophisticated computers on a major scale. And it takes no particularly acute vision of the future to see that such developments are probably only the very beginning of a series of enormous technological accomplishments.

This picture of the Industrial Revolution is highly schematic, but it should nonetheless serve to make clear just how significant were the technological changes that were taking place. These changes were to produce major changes in the structure of social life throughout virtually the entire world. But why did the Industrial Revolution occur when and where it did? Indeed, why did it occur at all?

Some scholars have seen the Industrial Revolution as rooted in population pressure (Wilkinson, 1973; Boserup, 1981). They thus see industrialization as simply another technological advance that, like earlier technological advances such as the Neolithic Revolution or the emergence of the plow, is rooted in the desire to stave off declining standards of living produced by increasing numbers. It is unlikely, though, that industrialization can be explained by demographic growth. We are dealing here with a technological change far different from the technological changes of earlier eras.

A much better explanation is that the Industrial Revolution was the logical and predictable outcome of the evolving European world-economy (Wallerstein, 1989). By the middle of the eighteenth century, England had clearly emerged as the dominant power within this economy. England had expanded its import and export markets throughout the capitalist system and had concentrated within itself enormous quantities of wealth. This wealth became essential as capital to be used in financing factories and machinery, and thus England was in a uniquely favorable financial position to engage in industrial development. But as Eric Hobsbawm (1968) has pointed out, capitalism has no inherent bias toward technological innovation for its own sake. It only has a bias toward increased profitability and will innovate only when it is profitable to do so. With this insight, it is easy to see why England was strongly oriented toward major industrial development. Industrialization permitted increasing productivity and lowered costs, which in turn allowed for the expansion of England's existing domestic and foreign markets and for the creation of new ones. The result was the increasing accumulation of capital on a grand scale. As Hobsbawm has put it (1968:38):

> The Industrial Revolution was generated in these decades—after the 1740's, when this massive but slow growth in the domestic economies combined with the rapid—after 1750 extremely rapid—expansion of the international economy; and it occurred in the country which seized its international opportunities to corner a major share of the overseas markets.

The Industrial Revolution was thus the historical product of the European capitalist world-economy, and it was initiated by the nation that was best suited economically to bring it about. This fact also helps explain why the Industrial Revolution occurred when it did rather than much earlier or later. It could not have occurred much earlier since its emergence closely depended upon the creation and substantial expansion of a capitalist world-economy. Its occurrence at some much later time was also most unlikely, since industrial technology was an important—indeed, an essential—component of an expanding economic system fundamentally committed to unlimited growth.

It is also important to see why the Industrial Revolution did not occur outside Europe. Of all the non-European societies, China was in one sense the most likely to have had an industrial revolution. As Wallerstein (1974a) has pointed out, in 1500 China was technologically at least as advanced as, if not more advanced than, western Europe (cf. McNeill, 1982). But by 1800 western Europe had far surpassed China. This demonstrates that technological change is surely not an autonomous process, occurring for its own sake. Rather, it depends upon particular conditions. Western Europe, and England especially, had precisely those conditions logically leading to major technological innovation. But what did China have (or not have) that impeded major technological advance? For one thing, it was not organized around a capitalist mode of production in the eighteenth century. In addition, it had an imperial bureaucratic state that did not depend upon technological advance for its enrichment and that actively squashed many technological innovations because of their potential economic threat (Wallerstein, 1974a). Imperial China was thus very poorly situated to experience the world's first industrial revolution.

The Industrial Revolution in World-System Perspective

In the third volume of his *The Modern World-System* (1989), Wallerstein has suggested that the notion of the Industrial Revolution is something of a myth, or at least that the way in which most scholars have spoken of these changes is highly misleading. Wallerstein is essentially making three closely related points: first, that the changes were not as dramatic or as revolutionary as commonly thought; second, that the so-called Industrial Revolution is not some sort of great dividing point between the past and the modern world; and finally, that what we call the Industrial Revolution was part and parcel of the evolution of the world-economy as a whole, not of individual societies within it.

As noted earlier, Wallerstein has argued that one of the great evolutionary trends of the capitalist world-economy is increasing mechanization. This occurs throughout the entire system, but is carried out faster and far more extensively in core societies. Increasing mechanization has gone on continuously, even if not smoothly, throughout the history of capitalism. From this perspective, the Industrial Revolution of the eighteenth century was simply one phase in this evolutionary process, and therefore not really revolutionary at all. Considerable mechanization had occurred in earlier centuries, especially during the period 1540–1640 (cf. Nef, 1964). All of this means that the "great divide" in world history is not the Industrial Revolution, as many social scientists argue, but the transition to capitalism that occurred some three centuries earlier.

In addition, if the Industrial Revolution was simply part of the evolution of the capitalist world-economy as a whole, then we have to use the entire system as a reference point in understanding why it occurred. In this regard Wallerstein insists that what we call the Industrial Revolution occurred in certain core societies during what he terms "the second era of great expansion of the capitalist world-economy" (Wallerstein, 1989). Capitalism was born in the fifteenth and sixteenth centuries and expanded throughout a significant portion of the globe during that time. Then, in the seventeenth century, it continued to expand, but at a much slower rate than earlier (Wallerstein, 1980). After about 1730, it entered a third phase, which was its second phase of rapid expansion. By the end of this phase—sometime during the middle of the nineteenth century—it had come to cover a large portion of the globe (most of it by the end of that century; see Figure 8.1). And it was during this third phase that extensive industrialization occurred within the major core societies, and for reasons that have already been explained.

To my mind, Wallerstein's overall position is basically correct, but with the important qualification that he underestimates the extensiveness of the technological and economic changes after the middle of the eighteenth century. To be sure, increasing mechanization has been a continuous process in the history of capitalism, but it has also been very sporadic and uneven. It is an exaggeration to imply that the technological changes before 1760 were on the same scale as those that occurred after that time. Therefore, while many scholars may overrate the significance of the Industrial Revolution, Wallerstein is underrating its significance.

Some Social Consequences of Industrialization

In fact, industrial development has had enormous consequences for the organization of social life, and virtually every aspect of social life has been touched by it. One of the most fundamental consequences of industrialization has been an enormous increase in economic productivity, an increase on a scale totally unprecedented in human history. To take a simple example, in 1750 the import of raw cotton for spinning amounted to £3 million, but by 1784 the figure had climbed to £11 million, by 1799 to £43 million, and by 1802 to £60 million (Heilbroner, 1972). Likewise, the production of pig iron increased dramatically from 68,000 tons in 1788 to 1,347,000 tons in 1839 (Heilbroner, 1972). Moreover, the productivity of labor has increased continuously from these early days of industrial capitalism to the present and is far greater today than it was in the early nineteenth century.

A second consequence of industrialization, already touched upon, was the creation of an industrial proletariat within the core capitalist societies. This was the first great wave of proletarianization in the history of capitalism. This proletariat consisted of the mass of workers—men, women, and children—who worked in the factories. In the early days of industrial capitalism, these workers labored under conditions of severe hardship. They were brutally overworked in the factories and paid extremely low wages, in many cases barely enough to keep them alive. They lived in overcrowded slums and suffered frequently from malnutrition and disease. Many of them were children, who could be paid even lower wages than adult men and women. The situation in industrial England in the first half of the nineteenth century was one characterized thus by the exploitation and degradation of a large mass of the population. It was precisely this situation that led to Marx's (1967; orig. 1867) scathing critique of capitalism. In his famous study of the working class in nineteenth-century Manchester, Friedrich Engels noted (1973:240; orig. 1845):

> Everywhere we find permanent or temporary suffering, sickness and demoralization all springing from the nature of the work or from the circumstances under which they are forced to live. Everywhere the workers are being destroyed. Slowly but surely they are ceasing to be human beings, either physically or morally.

Also commenting on life in the English factory towns, Eric Hobsbawm writes (1968: 67–68):

> And what cities! It was not merely that smoke hung over them and filth impregnated them, that the elementary public services—water-supply, sanitation, street-cleaning, open spaces, etc.—could not keep pace with the mass migration of men into the cities, thus producing, especially after 1830, epidemics of cholera, typhoid and an appalling constant toll of the two great groups of nineteenth-century urban killers—air pollution and water pollution, or respiratory and intestinal disease. It was not merely that the new city populations, sometimes entirely unused to non-agrarian life, like the Irish, pressed into over-crowded and bleak slums, whose very sight froze the heart of the observer. "Civilization works its miracles," wrote the great French liberal de Tocqueville of Manchester, "and civilized man is turned back almost into a savage."

A third consequence of industrialization has also occurred within the realm of work: the increasing specialization of labor. This phenomenon, whereby the worker has increasingly become a small cog in a large machine, has developed especially rapidly and extensively since the late nineteenth century. In the view of Karl Marx, this growing specialization of labor made work more and more meaningless and stifling for the worker. This was another feature of industrial capitalism that led him to be extremely critical of it. In a very real sense, the increasing specialization of labor signifies all three major trends of capitalist evolution. It results from a combination of proletarianization and mechanization, and it leads to the increasing commodification of work and the worker. We shall have more to say about this process shortly.

A fourth consequence of the emergence of industrial capitalism has been the extensive urbanization of society. Social life has shifted from the rural countryside to cities, many of them of vast scale. As Heilbroner (1972) notes in regard to the urban development of the United States, in 1790 only 24 towns and cities exceeded 2500 citizens, and collectively these towns constituted only 6 percent of the total population. But by 1860, 20 percent of the population was located in the 392 largest cities, and by 1970, much of the Eastern seaboard had evolved into practically one gigantic city containing more than 60 percent of the total population of the country.

A fifth and final consequence of industrialization to be noted is demographic in nature. Industrialization has generally produced what is called the **demographic transition** (Harris and Ross, 1987; cf. Handwerker, 1986). This involves, initially, a lowering of the mortality rate because of improvements in sanitation, health care, and so on. People begin to live longer, healthier lives. The fall in the death rate is eventually followed by a dramatic decrease in the birth rate. Children are a strong economic asset in societies dominated by agricultural production, as they can be put to good use as farm

Pittsburgh, Pennsylvania. Extensive urbanization has been one of the most profound consequences of the rise and growth of the capitalist mode of production.

workers. People in agrarian societies are thus generally motivated to have large families. But in industrial societies children become economic liabilities. As this occurs, people are motivated to reduce their family size. Instead of having six or eight children, they have two or three and invest more in each child. This sharp reduction in the birth rate has led to much lower rates of population increase in industrial societies than in societies still having a large agricultural population (Harris and Ross, 1987). (For some comparative statistical data on population growth rates in the world's societies, see Table 9.1 in Chapter 9.)

INDUSTRIAL CAPITALISM SINCE THE LATE NINETEENTH CENTURY

By the last quarter of the nineteenth century, the capitalist world-economy was dominated by four core societies (see Figure 8.1): the United Kingdom, the United States, Germany, and France (Chirot, 1986). These four societies were the most highly industrialized and urbanized societies in the world. In 1900 they collectively produced approximately three-quarters of all the world's manufactured goods, despite having only about one-eighth of the world's population (Chirot, 1977).

According to Daniel Chirot (1986), membership in the capitalist core was also held by five other societies: the Netherlands, Belgium, Switzerland, Sweden, and Denmark. These five societies were substantially overshadowed economically by the four main core powers. The semiperiphery at this time consisted mainly of Spain, Austria-Hungary, Italy, Russia, and Japan (Chirot, 1986). The periphery consisted of Portugal, China, the Ottoman Empire, the Eastern European countries, and all or nearly all of Latin America, Asia, and Africa (see Figure 8.1).

World capitalism around the turn of the twentieth century had a number of crucial features that cannot be overlooked. One of these was the relative decline of Britain in the world economy and the relative rise of several other nations, especially the United States. As Beaud (1983) notes, Britain's share of world industrial production fell from 32 percent in 1870 to 14 percent just before World War I, and then to only 9 percent by 1930. At the same time the U.S. share of world production was increasing. In 1870 the United States produced 23 percent of the world's goods; by the eve of World War I it was producing 38 percent; and its share of world production had climbed to a full 42 percent by 1930. By the early twentieth century the United States had clearly replaced Britain as the world's major core power.

Another crucial feature of world capitalism at this time was its entry into a new phase of capitalist development, what has often been termed **monopoly capitalism.** Under monopoly capitalism, the competitive character of capitalism is increasingly reduced as capitalist companies grow in size and in their concentration of capital. Large corporations begin to dominate the market and drive out smaller producers by ruining them economically and then swallowing them up. Eventually a few giant corporations dominate the market for many industries. Beaud sums up the extent to which capital was being centralized in the hands of fewer and fewer companies during this time (1983: 136–137):

> Everywhere, the average size of business establishments and industrial companies increased. . . . In times of crisis mergers took place which benefited the most powerful companies; thus during the period 1880–1918 in Britain, 655 companies "disappeared" into 74 merger companies.
>
> Above all, unprecedented concentrations of capital occurred, under the direction of a capitalist or of a family; trusts or groups very quickly came to dominate an entire industrial sector within a nation, especially in the United States and in Germany. In the United States in 1908,

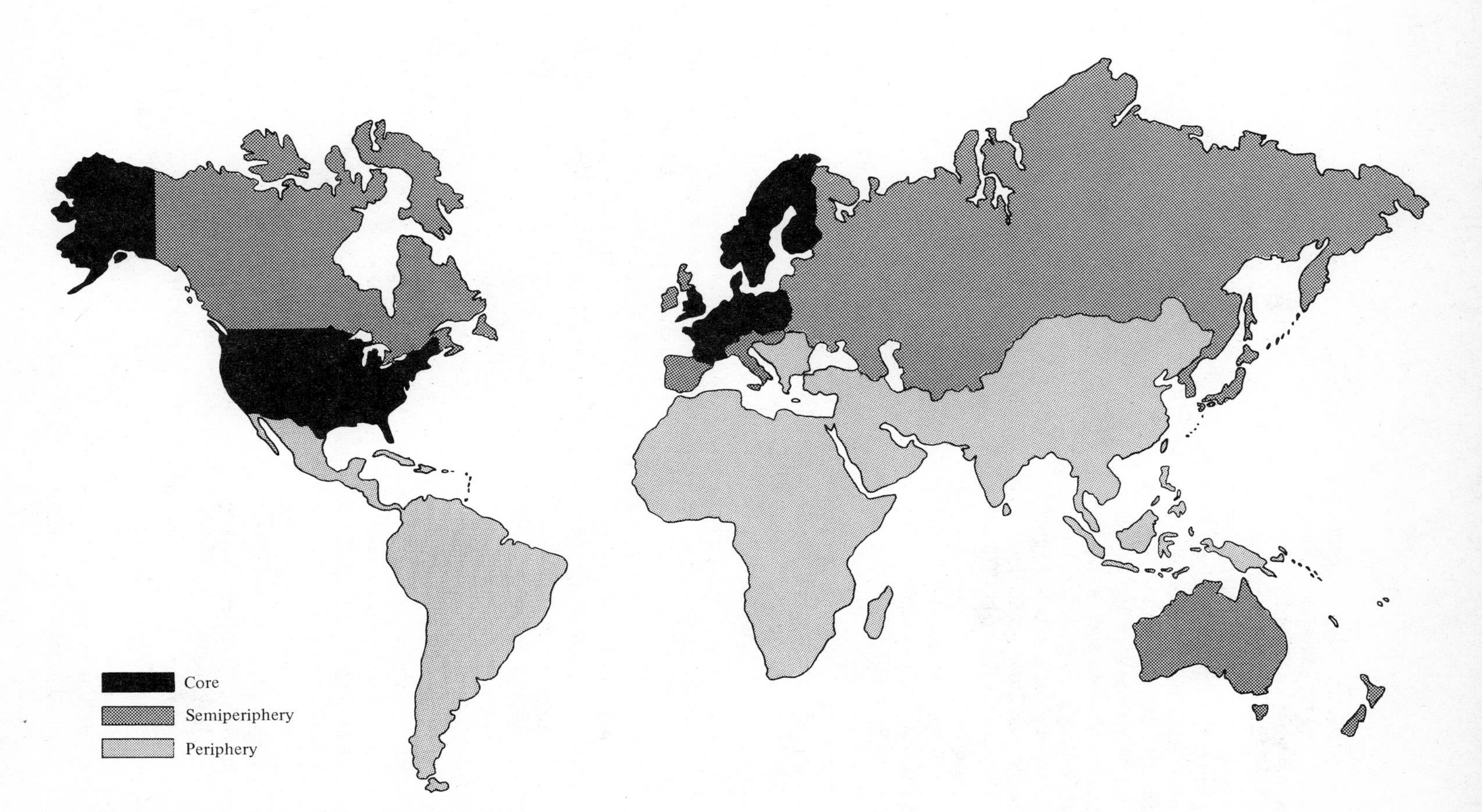

Figure 8.1 The capitalist world-economy, c. 1900.

the seven largest trusts owned or controlled 1,638 companies. By 1900, the percentage represented by the trust included 50 percent of textile production, 54 percent of the glassmaking industry, 60 percent of the book and paper industry, 62 percent of the food industry, 72 percent of the liquor industry, 77 percent of nonferrous metals, 81 percent of the chemical industries, and 84 percent of iron and steel. These included companies such as the United States Steel Corporation, founded by J. P. Morgan and E. H. Gary, which incorporated the Carnegie steel mills, and Standard Oil, founded in 1870 by J. D. Rockefeller, which in 1870 refined only 4 percent of American petroleum but by 1879 controlled 90 percent of the American refineries, and by 1904 controlled 85 percent of the domestic business and 90 percent of the export business as well.

In Germany the Krupp industrial empire employed 7,000 workers in 1873, and 78,000 in 1913; the AEG electrical industry, through an astonishing process of concentration, by 1911 controlled 175 to 200 companies, and employed more than 60,000 workers.

The emergence of monopoly capitalism was also characterized by a substantial increase in foreign investment by the core capitalist nations. Foreign investments quadrupled in Britain from the early 1890s to the early 1910s. In Germany, such investments doubled between 1883 and 1893, and then doubled again between 1893 and 1914. In France, they tripled between 1880 and 1914 (Beaud, 1983). About half of the foreign investments of the core powers were made outside Europe and North America. Latin America accounted for 19 percent, Asia for 16 percent, Africa for 9 percent, and Oceania for 5 percent (Beaud, 1983).

By the middle of the twentieth century, a new economic unit had become prominent in the capitalist world-economy: the **multinational corporation** (Barnet and Müller, 1974). The multinational corporation is today the central economic entity within world capitalism (Bornschier and Chase-Dunn, 1985). A multinational corporation is a company that has branches of production in more than one country. Long before the rise of such a corporation, capitalists *sold* their products in a world market, but the rise of the multinational corporation marked the emergence of international *production*.

The huge importance of the multinational corporations can be gleaned from a comparison of their sales with the gross national products (GNPs) of some smaller European nations (Heilbroner, 1972). For instance, in the late 1960s General Motors had a sales level exceeding each of the GNPs of Belgium, Switzerland, Denmark, Austria, Norway, Greece, and Portugal. Similarly, the sales of Standard Oil of New Jersey exceeded the GNPs of all these countries except for those of Belgium and Switzerland.

The multinational corporation is only the latest in a series of strategies used by capitalists in the historic process of capital accumulation. By internationalizing production, capitalists are able to overcome certain barriers imposed on their accumulationist activities. One of these barriers is the existence of tariffs on imports. By locating a branch of their company in a foreign country, capitalists are able to produce and sell their products directly in that country and avoid costly tariffs.

In the capitalist world-system today the great core powers are the United States, West Germany, France, and Japan. Although the United States is still the leading core power, its dominance is not as great as it once was. Most of the rest of Western Europe, Canada, and Australia are also members of the core. The semiperiphery principally consists of European nations such as Spain, Italy, and Greece; some of the better-off less-developed countries, like Argentina, Venezuela, South Africa, and Taiwan; and the resource-rich OPEC countries of the Middle East. The periphery consists of the rest of the less-developed world in Africa, Asia, and Latin America (see Figure 8.2). (The next chapter will provide a close look at these nations

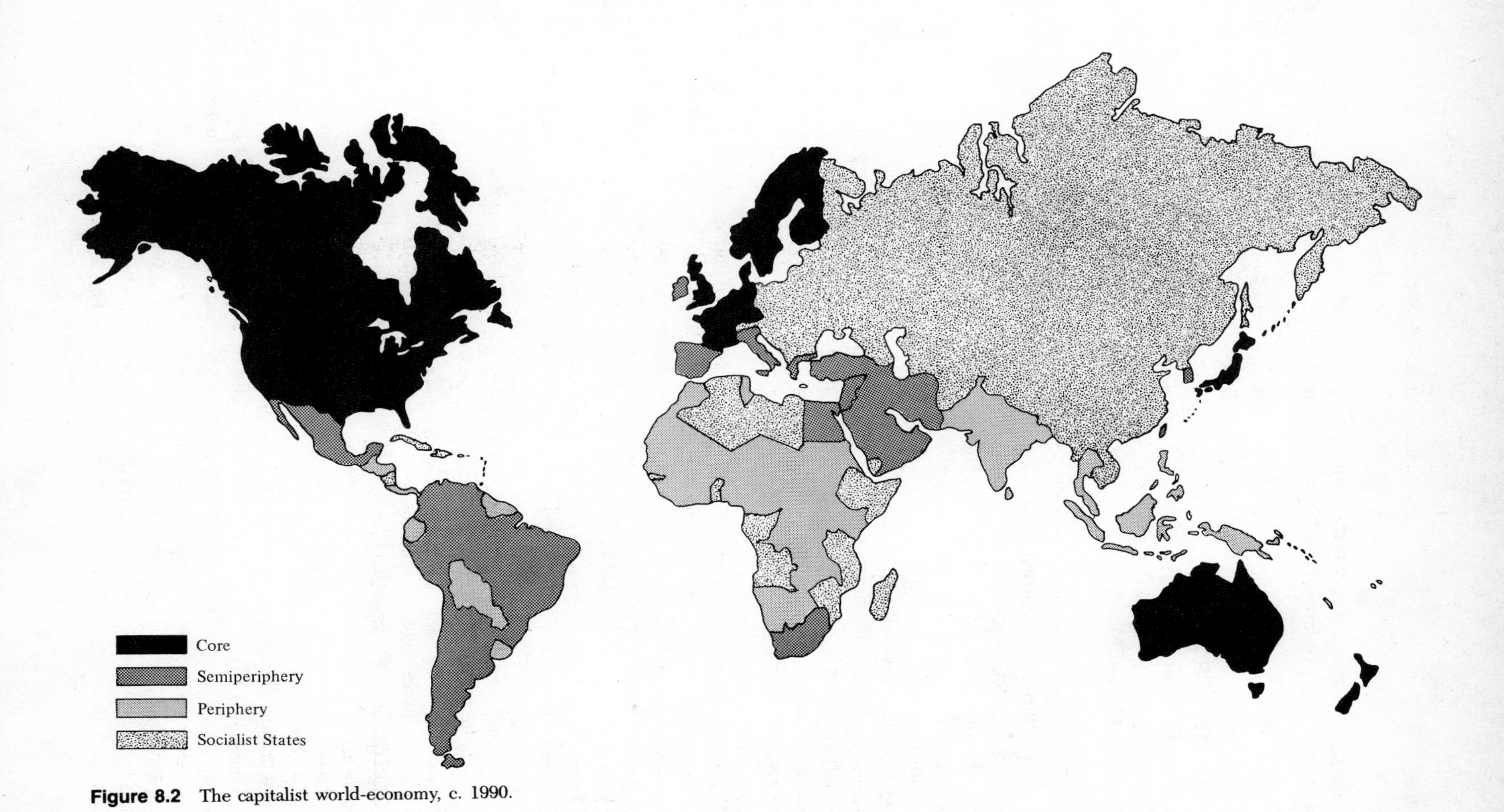

Figure 8.2 The capitalist world-economy, c. 1990.

of the contemporary capitalist periphery and semiperiphery, with an eye to explaining their low levels of economic development.)

THE LABOR PROCESS UNDER MONOPOLY CAPITALISM

Marx's Theory of Human Nature and Alienation

The work process has been thoroughly transformed under industrial capitalism, and especially under the monopoly phase of capitalist development. Some of Karl Marx's most important philosophical insights are especially relevant to understanding the nature and implications of this extraordinary transformation.

In some of his earliest writings, Marx (1963; orig. 1844) speculated about what distinguished humans from all other species. Marx characterized humans as *Homo faber*, Man the Worker. Humans are most distinctive, he thought, in that they produce their own means of subsistence. Only humans act on their physical environment and transform it according to their own purposes. It is true, of course, that bees build hives, beavers dams, and birds nests. Yet these animals are not engaged in productive activity in the Marxian sense. Their actions follow directly from instinct, from biological programming rather than from conceptualization and intent. In a famous passage, Marx wrote that what distinguishes the worst of architects from the best of bees is that the architect raises his structure in his imagination before he constructs it in reality.

Given that humans are most characterized by their capacity for productive activity, it followed for Marx that work must be more than a mere means to an end. It must be as well an end in itself, a means by which humans gain meaning and satisfaction in life. In performing the labor that they have already conceptualized, humans realize their true nature and feel fulfilled and gratified. In fact, for Marx, work was not simply one means among others for achieving meaning and purpose. It was *the* principal means by which humans achieved meaning and fulfilled their true nature. (cf. Sayers, 1988).

For Marx, whether humans will actually be able to realize their human nature through their labor depends on the organization of society. Implicit in his writings is the notion that throughout most of history people have actually lived under conditions in which they could work in a self-fulfilling way. Primitive hunters, stalking and killing game and bringing it back to camp to divide for all, are fulfilled workers. Agrarian craftsmen, designing their products and producing and selling them to others, are also achieving their basic nature. Even typical peasants, despite their oppression and exploitation, are fulfilled workers in a very basic sense. They work in harmony with nature and the seasons, have considerable self-determination in their work activities, and live off what they produce. Of course, slaves in agrarian societies were undoubtedly not fulfilled workers, their human nature being deformed by their conditions. But such workers would generally be exceptions to the rule in the precapitalist world.

When social conditions do not permit humans to realize their nature through work, Marx speaks of the emergence of a pathological condition of **alienation.** When workers are alienated, they do not receive meaning and gratification from their work, but find only frustration and emptiness. They are, in the strictest Marxian sense, dehumanized workers. Marx seemed to regard industrial capitalism as that economic system most productive of alienated labor. Alienation is characteristic of capitalism because of the peculiar character of the capitalist division of labor. This division of labor involves a marked separation between the conceptualization and the execution of work. Typical factory workers carry out tasks conceptualized by others. In addition, the work process is broken down into separate, isolated steps, and workers typically perform only one or a few of these. Moreover, they lose control over the dispensation of the products they make, these products being owned by someone else and sold by their owners in a market. Because of these aspects of the organization of work, workers can feel no identification with the products they help to make nor any truly meaningful participation in the work process. Their work produces sadness, frustration, and a sense of meaninglessness instead of fulfillment.

Work in Preindustrial Societies

Close examination of the labor process in preindustrial societies gives strong confirmation to Marx's notion that the nature of work in those societies is largely unalienating. Recall the discussion of the basic nature of work activities among hunter-gatherers, horticulturalists, and pastoralists. It is virtually inconceivable that workers in such societies are alienated laborers, given the extremely simple and unspecialized nature of most work and the extraordinarily high levels of self-direction involved. Or consider once again the nature of work in agrarian societies. With the exception of slavery, there is little in the conditions of work that would produce alienation. The following comments by Keith Thomas strongly suggest the absence of alienated labor in preindustrial societies (1964:51–53):

> The most obvious contrast to the working habits of the modern industrial world is provided by the primitive societies with which pre-historians and anthropologists are familiar. Here the distinction between work and leisure is not one which it is possible to draw. Life in such a world follows a pre-determined pattern in which work and non-work are inextricably confused. . . . In these societies there are no clearly defined periods of leisure as such, but economic activities, like hunting or market-going, obviously have their recreational aspects, as do singing or telling stories at work. . . . Finally work is not regulated by the clock, but by the requirements of the task.
>
> It seems to me that there are a number of respects in which the agrarian life of medieval Western Europe continued to display some of these more primitive features. The close relationship between the agricultural cycle and the liturgical year, with its blessings and processions, shows that the association between technique and ritual was still very close, just as do the ceremonies of the craft guilds with their oaths and initiations. Work was still discontinuous, for the agrarian year was punctuated by the feasts of the church and, for climatic reasons, virtually all medieval industries had a seasonal character. . . .
>
> The recreational activities of the Middle Ages recall the old primitive confusion as to where work ended and leisure began.

Alienation and Modern Capitalism

There is also much evidence to suggest considerable validity to the Marxian view of the alienating consequences of modern capitalism. One of the most important analyses of alienation to appear in recent years is that of Harry Braverman (1974), a firm adherent of the Marxian conception of alienation. Braverman's main concern is not with work under early industrial capitalism, which he clearly acknowledges was often subject to the brutal despotism of factory managers and foremen. Rather, his concern is principally with the transformation of work since the beginning of monopoly capitalism.

Braverman holds that since the late nineteenth century a central concern of capitalists has been to gain control over the work force and the work process. They have done this primarily through the implementation of the brainchild of Frederick Winslow Taylor, an organizational system known as *scientific management*. According to Braverman, scientific management in one mode or another still guides the organization of work under modern capitalism—and in fact does so even more pervasively with each passing year.

In Taylor's formulation, scientific management has three basic principles. The first involves the separation of the work process from the skills of the worker. The work process is to be organized so that it does not depend on the knowledge and craftsmanship of the workers. The practices of management, and not the abilities of workers, determine how work is done. The second principle Braverman refers to concerns the separation of conception from execution. Quoting Taylor, Braverman notes that this principle demands that "all possible brain work should be removed from the shop and centered in the planning or laying-out department." The third principle involves management's gaining a monopoly over knowledge in order to control every step of the work process. Once again Braverman quotes Taylor's statement of this principle: "Perhaps the most prominent single element in modern scientific management is the task idea. . . . This task specifies not only what is to be done, but how it is to be done and the exact time allowed for doing it."

Braverman believes that the implementation of scientific management practices has had disastrous consequences for workers. Modern workers scarcely resemble the contented craftsmen of earlier times. They are inevitably alienated by a system that vigorously destroys craftsmanship, reduces work to a few small, highly repetitive, and routinized actions, and makes it impossible for them to think out the performance of their tasks. Workers lose their basic humanity and are turned into automatons. Moreover, Braverman argues that the dehumanization of the work process has not only been occurring in regard to factory work, but has invaded most forms of office work as well.

Cadillac assembly line, Detroit. Automobile assembly lines represent the most vigorous application of Taylorism to the capitalist workplace.

Although highly plausible, Braverman's argument remains more or less at the theoretical level. It still must be conclusively demonstrated that workers actually *feel* alienated as a result of the modern organization of the workplace. A study that sheds considerable light on this issue is Robert Blauner's classic *Alienation and Freedom* (1964). Blauner studied American workers' reactions to their work in several different kinds of workplace environments. He found that automobile assembly line workers had relatively high levels of alienation, but that workers in a printing shop had relatively little alienation. These findings are just what would be expected from Braverman's analysis. Automobile companies under contemporary capitalism have carried the Taylorist techniques of workplace organization as far as or farther than has any other industry. By contrast, the printing shop that Blauner studied had retained many old-fashioned modes of organization: Workers had considerable personal control over their work, were expected to be involved in the conceptualization of much of what they did, retained skills necessary to the performance of their work, and had considerable variety in the work they performed.

Blauner also found low work alienation among workers in a chemical plant. In one sense, this finding does not entirely fit with Braverman's interpretation of modern capitalism, since the chemical workers spent most of their time watching over machines that did the work (and thus had little in the way of traditional craft skills). Yet in another equally important sense there is neither anything surprising about Blauner's finding nor anything about it that contradicts Braverman's analysis. The chemical workers had considerable variety in their jobs, a great deal of freedom to control their own work activities, and, most important, considerable responsibility to make sure that the technology they supervised was working properly. As Blauner emphasizes, the jobs of these workers substituted responsibility for craft skills, and this helped to give them an important sense of gratification and self-fulfillment in their work.

THE EMERGENCE OF STATE SOCIALIST ECONOMIES

The Origin and Nature of State Socialism

The world's first socialist society emerged in 1917 when Russia underwent the Bolshevik Revolution and became the Soviet Union. Other socialist societies emerged fairly soon thereafter. Yugoslavia became socialist by revolution in 1945. Between 1945 and 1948 Poland, East Germany, Czechoslovakia, Hungary, Romania, and Bulgaria were turned into socialist societies through occupation by the Soviet army (Chirot, 1986).*

These societies are perhaps best termed **state socialist** because of the strong role that the government plays in the direction of the economy. In the classical exemplar of state socialism, the Soviet Union, private property has been almost completely eliminated, with the exception of consumer goods. Thus, one can own one's own house, car, or wardrobe privately (as items of personal property), but one cannot privately own the means of economic production. Most of the industrial sector and part of the agricultural sector have been nationalized. Indeed, all sectors of the economy, except for small plots of land cultivated by collective farmers, have been brought under the control of national economic planning. The very core of the Soviet economy is its state sector; all major industries are state owned and operated in the areas of mining, heavy construction, railroads, communications, power production, urban retailing, large cooperative farms, and others. The major means of production are thus publicly owned, and all employees work for the

*This chapter deals only with those socialist societies that have experienced substantial industrialization.

state. Whatever private enterprise exists, such as small-scale artisans selling their products or individual peasants operating small farms in remote areas, is very limited (Gruchy, 1966; Lane, 1985). (Recent changes in the economic organization of the Soviet Union are explored in the Special Topic at the end of the chapter.)

The Eastern European state socialist societies are more or less based on the Soviet model, but they have a tendency to be somewhat more open to capitalist economic activity. This is especially the case in Yugoslavia, which in the early 1950s began an experiment in "market socialism." This involved retaining a basic state socialist economy but allowing considerable development of capitalist businesses alongside socialist operations. Today Yugoslavia has more consumer goods available to its citizens than does any other state socialist society (Chirot, 1986).

Industrialization in the state socialist societies has taken place under the close control of the state (Gershenkron, 1962). In the Soviet Union, the major drive toward industrialization occurred from the late 1920s through World War II under the leadership of the Stalinist regime. In a very short time the Soviet Union was transformed from a largely agrarian society into one of the world's major industrial societies. The speed of industrialization in the Soviet Union, and the fervor with which the Soviet leaders carried it out, took a terrible human toll. Several million peasants were either killed or sent to labor camps in order to make the transi-

Workers in the Soviet Union making welding equipment. The Soviet Union is an industrial society with a division of labor and an occupational structure quite similar to those found in Western capitalist societies.

tion from agriculture to industry. This was one of the sorriest sagas in human history.

Today the major state socialist industrial societies closely resemble the industrial capitalist societies in important respects. To a large extent, industrialization has created marked similarities in the basic social patterns of both types of society. However, the state socialist world, although it has made considerable progress in this regard, has yet to achieve the truly high levels of economic prosperity characteristic of modern capitalism. The GNPs of the state socialist societies are still generally only about a third to a half as high as those of the industrial capitalist nations (see Table 9.1 in Chapter 9).

State Socialism and the Capitalist World-Economy

The relationship between the socialist states and the capitalist world-economy has been the subject of recent and intense debate, especially among Western Marxian social scientists. Christopher Chase-Dunn (1982), for instance, argues a position that has become popular among Wallersteinian world-system theorists in recent years. He holds not only that the state socialist nations have close economic ties with world capitalism, but, indeed, that the socialist states are integral parts of the capitalist world-economy. The position they occupy in the world-system is in the semiperiphery. The socialist states have this role, Chase-Dunn claims, because they engage in commodity production for a world market and have important dealings with the capitalist multinational corporations. It is thus Chase-Dunn's view that the socialist societies are not really socialist at all. Rather, they are essentially capitalist societies whose governments are led by socialist political movements.

At the opposite extreme from Chase-Dunn is Albert Szymanski (1982). Szymanski argues that the state socialist nations are thoroughly socialist. They have economies that are geared only to production-for-use and not to production-for-profit. Moreover, the state socialist economies are basically autonomous from Western capitalism, the economic exchanges between the capitalist and socialist nations being mainly of a nonessential or luxury nature.

Szymanski offers the following lines of evidence to support his position (his analysis is based almost entirely on the case of the Soviet Union). First, the agreements with Western capitalists that the Soviet Union enters into—agreements that involve various exchanges of goods or technology—are made on the Soviet Union's own terms. These agreements cannot significantly affect economic processes within the Soviet Union because they do not involve any direct investment or management rights for capitalists in Soviet enterprises. Second, although the state socialist societies invest in both core and peripheral capitalist societies, these investments are extremely small in comparison to those of the advanced capitalist nations. For example, in 1978 U.S. investments in the peripheral capitalist countries exceeded Soviet investments in those countries by a factor of 2200. Third, the state socialist societies trade far more among themselves than with the advanced capitalist societies. For instance, in 1978 about 60 percent of Soviet trade occurred with the other state socialist nations, but only 28 percent of its trade was with the core capitalist nations. Moreover, in the same year only about 4 percent of the trade of the core capitalist societies was with the socialist states. Finally, if there were a close economic tie between the socialist and capitalist countries, the economic fluctuations so characteristic of capitalism should be reflected in similar fluctuations in the socialist nations. However, the correlation between the capitalist and socialist societies in this regard is not strong. Indeed, "the period of the most rapid industrial growth in the USSR, 1928–1941, coincided with the period of the most protracted and deep depression in the modern history of capitalism" (Szymanski, 1982:75).

The disagreement between Chase-Dunn and Szymanski is a complex one that involves a wide range of issues, and it is therefore difficult to resolve in a definitive way. Indeed, this disagreement is only part of a much larger discussion about the nature of the economic systems in the Soviet Union and Eastern Europe (cf. Sweezy, 1980; Lane, 1985: Chapter 3). On Szymanski's side, it must be recognized that the state socialist societies do have economies that are different in important ways from Western capitalism. The state socialist societies have no private capitalist class engaged in profit maximization as an end in itself; they make use of centralized economic planning to a degree that is unheard of in Western capitalism; and they, the Soviet Union in particular, have made relatively minimal use of market mechanisms to guide economic decisions. Thus, the state socialist societies obviously do have some important characteristics that we normally associate with a socialist mode of economic organization (Gorin, 1985; Davis and Scase, 1985).

On the other hand, Szymanski clearly errs in regarding the state socialist societies as having essentially fulfilled the expectations of Marx and Engels regarding the content of socialist society. The plain and simple truth is that the Soviet Union and Eastern Europe depart markedly from the classical Marxian conception of socialism. Although Marx did not spell out in any detail what he thought the future socialist society would look like, we know some of the basic things he had in mind. For one, he was thinking of a society with a level of economic equality much greater than that which currently prevails in the Soviet Union and Eastern Europe (see Chapter 10). For another, he thought of socialism as being relatively democratic in nature, as giving everyone a strong voice in the whole process of social and economic planning. The politically repressive character of modern state socialism shows that this expectation is not even remotely realized. Finally, and in some ways most significantly, there is the fact that Marx conceived of genuine socialism as being built around production-for-use rather than production-for-exchange. Contemporary state socialist societies do not live up to this expectation, either, as their economies are devoted greatly to the production of commodities—goods that are designed to augment the value that they originally had when created. In sum, it is a serious error to refer to contemporary socialist states as "Marxist states." Although these states have historically characterized themselves as Marxist, this is at best only a very partial truth.

This brings us back to Chase-Dunn's position. It is important to understand that he is not claiming that the state socialist societies are literally capitalist in the same way that Western capitalist societies are. He recognizes that the socialist societies have had unique forms of internal economic organization. His position springs from his world-system outlook. The state socialist societies have been, he claims, important experiments in socialism that have largely failed because these societies have been greatly constrained by the existence of the capitalist world-economy (Chase-Dunn, 1989a). Socialist societies have great difficulty surviving within a capitalist world-system; they are compelled to interact to some extent with that system, and as this happens they tend to be drawn back increasingly toward a capitalist mode of operation. Thus, the Soviet Union and Eastern Europe have become gradually reincorporated into the capitalist world-economy and have lost most of whatever socialist content they once possessed. There is a good deal of evidence to show that this is precisely what has been happening over the past two or three decades, and more rapidly and substantially in Eastern Europe than in the Soviet Union itself (Frank, 1980; Abonyi, 1982; Rossides, 1990). Andre Gunder Frank (1980), for example, has shown in considerable detail the extent to which the state socialist societies have reinserted themselves into global capitalism. Since the early 1970s they have begun to trade with Western capitalism much more vigorously, and many important financial and industrial agreements have been established. Frank's analysis ends in 1979, but it looks as though the process of reintegration he described for the decade of the 1970s has accelerated throughout the 1980s. Indeed, it appears that this process is currently growing by leaps and bounds (cf. Aganbegyan, 1989) (see the Special Topic at the end of the chapter).

In the end, then, Chase-Dunn's position turns out to be the more valid and enlightening one. The state socialist societies had only a limited Marxian socialist content to begin with and are now in the process of losing most of what they had. This conclusion has implications for a final important question: Have the socialist countries ever had relations among themselves comparable to the relations among more and less developed capitalist countries? To the extent that there ever was a separate socialist world-system, it seems clear that this system never structurally resembled the capitalist world-system (Chase-Dunn, 1982; Chirot, 1986). In other words, the Soviet Union never acted like a socialist "core" that exploited its Eastern European neighbors, or less developed socialist countries such as Cuba. The Soviet Union is not dependent upon other socialist countries for its essential raw materials. In fact, it has played an important role in *exporting* raw materials to other socialist countries (Chirot, 1986). Moreover, the Soviet Union has historically acted in ways that have apparently been designed to help less developed socialist countries enhance their economic development. For example, it has paid Cuba well above the world market price for Cuban sugar (Eckstein, 1986). While it is true that the Soviet Union has engaged in political and military domination over the Eastern European states, as well as over many less-developed socialist countries, this domination is not comparable to the economic domination that some nations exert over others within the world capitalist system.

Does Alienated Labor Exist Under State Socialism?

A question not raised in the earlier discussion of alienation under modern capitalism is the extent to which alienation is a product of capitalism or of *industrialism and bureaucracy.* Numerous social scientists have argued that alienation is not so much the product of the capitalist ownership of production as of modern industrial and bureaucratic techniques of workplace organization that are just as characteristic of modern socialist societies as they are of capitalism. Max Weber, for instance, thought that a future socialist society could not abolish alienation since this condition was a product of bureaucracy, and socialism would require at least as much bureaucracy as capitalism.

Unfortunately, there are no solid data to answer definitively the question of whether or not alienated labor is a basic characteristic of contemporary state socialism. Still, there is good reason to answer this question affirmatively. The state socialist societies seem to have adopted Taylorist methods of workplace organization about as thoroughly as have the capitalist societies (Lane, 1987). It would appear that Braverman's theoretical analysis of alienation can logically be extended to state socialism. In a similar vein, some intellectuals in state socialist societies see alienated labor resulting from the fact that labor is still a commodity in these societies, something to be bought and sold for a price in much the same way it is under capitalism (cf. Israel, 1971). The Polish philosopher Adam Schaff, for instance, concludes (1965:168; cited in Israel, 1971:240):

> In all forms of socialist society known to us at present, different types of alienation occur. This means that it is not automatically true that the abolition of private ownership of the means of production leads to the disappearance of alienation.

The likely persistence of significant levels of alienated labor in state socialist society is just one more difference between state socialism and the classical Marxian notion of socialism. Marx thought that alienation would disappear under socialism because there would be a radical change in the specialization within the division of labor. Although specialization by type of work would exist, workers would become "jacks of all trades," sharing thoroughly in the most and least pleasant forms of work. Moreover, work would lose its character as a commodity, and workers would be compensated according to their needs. Such qualities are scarcely characteristic of contemporary state socialism.

The Democratic Socialism of Scandinavia

Mention must also be made of the variety of socialism that has arisen in the Scandinavian nations, primarily in Sweden, Denmark, and Norway. (This variety has also arisen, although to a lesser extent, in such Western European nations as England and the Netherlands.) Actually, the Scandinavian nations are not socialist at all, at least not in any economic sense. Their economies are still overwhelmingly capitalist. The great bulk of the means of production is privately owned and production takes place for profit. There has, however, been some nationalization. Some heavy industries and utilities are owned and operated by the government.

The Scandinavian societies are only really "socialist" in a political sense. Beginning in the 1930s, socialist political parties came to occupy a dominant place in the government, and they still do today. These parties have had the express aim of reforming the economy so as to make it more just and egalitarian. Although production can take place for profit in most spheres of economic life, the government considers that private companies should have a strong concern for the national interest. It has entered into close collaboration with private business in order to manage the economy for the public good. The state closely watches over and helps to regulate prices, wages, interest rates, and so on.

The Scandinavian version of "socialism" is even more removed from the classical Marxian conception of socialism than is state socialism. Marx held that capitalism was incapable of being reformed, and that socialism necessarily involved the complete abolition of private property and the collective ownership of the means of production. He would have taken a very dim view of any social experiment designed merely to reform the capitalist system. (In Chapter 10 we will examine the degree to which this experiment has been successful.)

SUMMARY

1. The Industrial Revolution began in England in the second half of the eighteenth century. By the nineteenth century it had spread to other Western European countries and to the United States. It was a massive economic and technological transformation in which machines and the factory system came to dominate production. Industrial capitalist society was the child of this massive change.

2. The Industrial Revolution occurred as a major phase in the development of the capitalist system. It was inaugurated by capitalists as a means of greatly expanding their productivity and lowering their operating costs. In effect it established a fundamentally new means whereby capitalists could earn profits: by extracting surplus value at the point of production. Industrialization developed earliest in the most economically advanced capitalist societies.

3. Some major consequences of industrialization have been an enormous increase in the productivity of labor, the creation of a large and socially significant urban proletariat, an increase in the specialization of labor, the extensive urbanization of society, and a marked decline in the rate of population growth because of a decline in the birth rate.

4. In the late nineteenth century capitalism entered a monopoly phase. This involved the emergence of the large corporation as the basic economic unit and a corresponding reduction of the competitive character of economic life. Monopoly capitalism also involved extensive investment of advanced capitalist nations in poorer regions of the world.

5. The capitalist world-system today is approximately as follows: The major core nations are the United States, West Germany, France, and Japan; the periphery consists of the poorest nations of Asia, Latin America, and Africa; and the semiperiphery includes some of the less-developed European nations, as well as some of the better-off nations in Latin America, Asia, and Africa.

6. Marx theorized that one of the more destructive effects of industrial capitalism was the alienation of the worker. Marx thought that work was a means of human self-realization, and that the capitalist organization of work destroyed the capacity of the worker to find meaning in his tasks. Recent research suggests that alienation has been a progressive feature of the development of monopoly capitalism in the twentieth century.

7. State socialist societies arose in the Soviet Union in 1917 and in much of eastern Europe after World War II. Much debate currently rages about the specific economic character of these societies. Some sociologists see them as simply an alternative version of capitalist commodity production, while others believe they have uniquely socialist features. In recent years it appears that they have increasingly lost their socialist content and have moved toward closer integration into the capitalist world-economy.

8. The economic systems of the state socialist societies should not be confused with the allegedly socialist economies of Scandinavia. The Scandinavian economies are fundamentally capitalist in the sense that private production for profit is the basis of economic life. The Scandinavian version of "socialism" is an attempt to reform capitalism through political measures while leaving the economy basically intact.

9. It is likely that alienation is as characteristic of state socialism as it is of Western capitalism. Alienation may be as closely linked to the nature of technology and bureaucracy as it is to the ownership of the means of production.

SPECIAL TOPIC: *PERESTROIKA* AND ITS SOCIOLOGICAL SIGNIFICANCE

In the past few years the Soviet Union has begun to embark on a series of social, political, and economic reforms. These reforms began with the rise, in the spring of 1985, of Mikhail Gorbachev to the position of General Secretary of the Communist Party, the most powerful political office in all of Soviet society. Not long after coming to power, Gorbachev began to pursue two types of reform, known respectively as *perestroika* and *glasnost. Glasnost,* which is usually translated as "openness," involves a greater commitment to honesty and to frank discussion on the part of government officials of the problems facing Soviet society, as well as to admitting current flaws and past mistakes. The policy of *glasnost* also permits greater freedom of individual expression, both political and otherwise, and allows more latitude to the press in publishing facts and presenting opinions.

Perestroika, on the other hand, involves a specifically economic set of reforms. It is, literally, a "restructuring" of economic life (cf. Gorbachev, 1987). There are several important aspects of this restructuring, but the most fundamental are the following (Lapidus, 1988; Kushnirsky, 1988; Leggett, 1988; Zemtsov and Farrar, 1989):

1. While centralized economic planning is to be maintained as a guiding policy, individual firms are being given increased responsibility to make decisions about their production activities. These firms must now compete with each other, with the level of profitability being the main criterion for success. Firms that are not sufficiently profitable will be eliminated. Moreover, managers of firms are increasingly to be elected, rather than simply rising to power through the political patronage system that has traditionally been in effect.

2. The wage structure is being overhauled so as to generate greater wage differentials. This is designed to serve as an incentive for workers to work harder and better. As a further incentive, workers can now be fired for poor work and excessive absenteeism. With this reform, unemployment becomes a reality for the first time since the early years of Soviet society.

3. New joint ventures with Western firms are being undertaken. These ventures are designed primarily to attract Western capital and enhance the production of consumer goods.

What all of these changes have in common is obviously a recognition of the limitations of centralized economic planning, and thus an increased reliance on the market (Lapidus, 1988; Aganbegyan, 1988, 1989). The changes are designed to shift the Soviet economy in a more "capitalistic" direction, a move that would not surprise Wallerstein and the world-system theorists since they see the Soviet Union as already substantially capitalistic.

Many recent commentators on *perestroika* have addressed the question of whether it involves a truly radical set of economic changes, or is simply a relatively minor tinkering with the existing system. Although some see Gorbachev's reforms as involving some fundamental departures from current economic practices (Lapidus, 1988; Aganbegyan, 1989), the prevailing opinion seems to be that *perestroika* involves a relatively mild set of reforms (Kontorovich, 1987; Zemtsov and Farrar, 1989; Leggett, 1988; Mandel, 1989). Ilya Zemtsov and John Farrar, for example, have suggested that "in terms of their real content, Gorbachev's economic changes to date have to be assessed as only tinkering with the fringes of the system" (1989:81). And Robert Leggett has claimed that "the overwhelming consensus of Western experts who have analyzed the changes in the Soviet economy under Gorbachev is that they do not constitute much real reform" (1988:35). Leggett concludes that Gorbachev's reforms do not really differ in principle or substance from the variety of reform efforts that the Soviet Union has undertaken since the 1950s.

Regardless of the extent of the proposed changes, the fact that they have captured world attention, and that they are being extensively analyzed by Western social scientists, indicates that there is something significant about them. Obviously, the two most important questions about them concern why they are occurring at this particular time, and whether they are likely to succeed in bringing the Soviet Union what it is seeking.

In terms of the first question—why *perestroika,* and why *perestroika* now?—it is clear that at least part of the answer involves the economic and social crisis that the Soviet Union is currently facing, a crisis that has only recently become apparent to many Western observers (Leggett, 1988; Lapidus, 1988; Zemtsov and Farrar, 1989; Kaneda, 1988; Mandel, 1989). This crisis involves severe economic deterioration and an accompanying demoralization of many segments of Soviet society. Robert Leggett (1988) and Tatsuo Kaneda (1988) summarize the dimensions of the problem:

> *Growth has been trending downward for several decades as the economy experienced repeated harvest failures, bottlenecks in industry, shortages of energy and labor, and chronically low productivity. GNP growth during the 11th Five-Year Plan (1981–85) had its worst showing of any five-year period since World War II.*
>
> . . .
>
> *Meanwhile, improvements in living standards have tapered off as a result of the worsening performance of the economy, and popular discontent has grown. The latter has manifested itself in declining worker morale, more materialistic attitudes, an increase in "deviant" and "delinquent" behavior by Soviet youth, rising crime rates, alcohol and drug abuse, and a rising anti-Russian nationalism among ethnic groups (Leggett, 1988:23, 25).*
>
> *Soviet leaders face the wastefulness of their entire economy; a decrease in the Soviet capacity for technological development; dependency on the technological progress of the West; a drop in international competitiveness; chronic shortages of basic necessities; the existence of black markets; widespread bribery and corruption; growing debt; feelings of alienation and habitual drinking among the people, who avoid work and whose rates of illness and mortality are increasing (Kaneda, 1988:81).*

Zemtsov and Farrar (1989) and Ernest Mandel (1989) view the reformist motives of Gorbachev and his supporters among the Soviet political elite as being rooted in a strategy of elite self-preservation. Zemtsov and Farrar see *perestroika* as stemming from the elite's desire to change the Soviet system enough for it to function more effectively, but not so much that its power within the system would be significantly threatened. Mandel is more explicit. He views Gorbachev and his supporters as recognizing the threat to the elite that the current economic and social crisis represents, and thus as being motivated to implement reforms in order to avert an explosive situation in the near future. As he puts it, "Gorbachev represents the response of the modernist wing of the bureaucracy to the threat to the stability of its rule represented by this crisis and by the rise of public awareness" (1989:xi).

This interpretation, though, seems too narrow. As suggested in the main text, in recent decades the Soviet Union has begun to reinsert its economy into the capitalist world-economy. As it has moved in an increasingly capitalist direction, it has begun to act more and more in the manner of a traditional capitalist state in the international economic arena. That is, it has been using that arena as a means of advancing its economic position with respect to other states. The economic crisis it is currently experiencing may be due to more than just inefficiencies in its own internal economic organization. The crisis may also result from the inadequacy of certain competitive economic strategies within the international economic arena.

This line of reasoning is strongly confirmed by Abel Aganbegyan's *Inside Perestroika: The Future of the Soviet Economy* (1989). Aganbegyan, who is Mikhail

Mikhail Gorbachev holding a news conference at the Soviet Embassy in Washington, D.C., during his visit in December of 1987. Since Gorbachev came to power in 1985, the Soviet Union has begun a series of dramatic economic reforms that are bringing it much nearer to full integration into the capitalist world-economy.

Gorbachev's principal economic advisor, makes clear the extraordinary extent to which the Soviet Union now wishes to compete in the capitalist world-economy at the level of a major economic power. According to Aganbegyan, a key feature of *perestroika* involves an economic shift toward export promotion. The Soviet Union is reorganizing itself so as to be able to manufacture and sell commodities competitively in the world market. As Aganbegyan has put it (1989:186):

> *The Soviet Union will specialize increasingly in the export of industrial goods, particularly machinery, equipment and chemicals, and also of a large selection of services. Even in the export of raw materials we shall emphatically try to sell them in processed form. . . . We have elaborated a special long-term programme for developing our export base for the future. This is founded on the specialization and industrialization of our exports, and its aim is to ensure that this considerable structural change in exports will be achieved.*

For the world's most prominent socialist state, this is an extraordinary departure from past economic practices, and it surely indicates a pronounced shift in the economic outlook and interests of a sizable segment of the Soviet elite. It also suggests, as Aganbegyan is at pains to point out, that *perestroika* is no mere economic tinkering. Gorbachev and his supporters seem to be doing much more than just repairing the flaws in the Soviet economy. They seem to be completing the shift, begun some time before them, of the Soviet Union toward full-fledged participation in the world capitalist system. Should any doubt remain that this is what is happening, we need only quote Aganbegyan once again (1989:175–176):

> *We have begun to look at our own country as an indivisible part of the whole world of nations and our economy as a part of the world economy. We have analysed the situation and come to the conclusion that our level of foreign trade, our position in the world market, does not correspond to the economic, scientific and technological potential of our country. From this we have drawn the inevitable conclusion that we must become more involved in the international division of labour, in the system of world economic relations.*

What are the prospects for *perestroika?* Mandel has suggested four possible outcomes. First, the reforms will be allowed to continue and will produce many of the results Gorbachev is seeking. Second, the impetus generated by *perestroika* will cause Gorbachev to be outflanked by reformers far more radical than he, who would attempt to make even more fundamental changes in the Soviet system. Third, the reform efforts will not work, and as a result there will be political purges within the party, including possibly the elimination of Gorbachev. Finally, failure of the reform efforts to work quickly enough will produce severe discontent within the working class, which will become highly politicalized. As a result, a "new political leadership will emerge from the working class and from the socialist intelligentsia which will help the masses in the achievement of their fundamental objectives. The political revolution, in the classical Marxist sense of the term, will triumph" (Mandel, 1989:xvi).

Mandel believes that, of these four possible outcomes, the first is the least likely and the third and fourth the most likely. As a politically committed Marxist intellectual, Mandel obviously favors the fourth outcome. I myself think that the first two outcomes are the most likely. Of course, a reaction against Gorbachev is always possible, but it seems that the economic changes that have already occurred within the Soviet Union are so profound that a turning back of the clock is unlikely. Because of these changes, a substantial segment of the Soviet elite now either supports Gorbachev's overall strategy or wants to go even further than he does. I will not be surprised if, by the turn of the next century, the Soviet economy has changed dramatically.

APPENDIX: MARX'S THEORY OF CAPITALIST EXPLOITATION

One of history's most famous analysts of capitalism was Karl Marx. In his great three-volume work *Capital* (1967; orig. 1867), he provided an extremely detailed critical analysis of capitalism, focusing primarily on its basic laws of functioning and the cyclical fluctuations to which it is especially subject. The best-known part of his work is his theory of capitalist exploitation developed in the first volume. This is generally known as the **theory of surplus value.**

For Marx, capitalism involves two essential elements. First, it is based on the buying and selling of *labor power* (the capacity of the individual to work), and thus labor is a commodity. Second, it is a system in which entrepreneurs engage in commodity production in order to realize the maximum *profit,* and in order to increase over time the quantity of profit. This second feature Marx refers to as the **accumulationist** character of capitalism.

Modern capitalism differs appreciably, Marx thought, from earlier forms of commodity production, which are often mistakenly called capitalist. These earlier forms Marx referred to as **simple commodity production.** In simple commodity production, producers generate a commodity, exchange it for an equivalent amount of money, and then use this money to purchase an equivalent amount of some other commodity. Simple commodity production is thus represented by the formula C–M–C. In capitalist production, a producer starts with a given amount of money (his or her capital), used to organize business activity that will generate a commodity the producer then sells on a market for another sum of money. But this second sum of money exceeds in value the sum that the capitalist started with. Capitalist production may therefore be represented by the formula M–C–M′. The increase in the value of the capitalist's money—the difference between M′ and M—Marx refers to as **surplus value,** a portion of which is the capitalist's profit. One of the most significant of all of Marx's theoretical contributions was to explain how surplus value originates.

Marx was emphatic that surplus value could not originate from the mere circulation of commodities, that is, from buying and selling. This is because commodities sell at their values, and the market will therefore always determine that exchanges of commodities will be equivalent. Surplus value, then, does not originate in the relationship between buyer and seller, or producer and consumer. But, Marx argued, there is one commodity that can be purchased at less than its value: labor power. If capitalists pay less than the full value for the labor power they buy, they can sell the commodities this labor power generates for more than it takes to generate them. Marx therefore concludes that surplus value originates in the wage relationship between capitalists and workers. The surplus value is already in a commodity when it reaches the market, and the act of selling it only realizes or actualizes the surplus value already there.

A worker who is hired by a capitalist takes just so long to turn out a quantity of commodities equal in value to what the capitalist pays him. This length of time Marx calls *necessary labor time.* If the worker stopped working after he had completed his necessary labor time, there could be no surplus value and no profit for the capitalist. But the capitalist keeps the worker working beyond the necessary labor time. If the necessary labor time is, say, five hours, but the worker is required to work an eight-hour day, then the worker is working three hours beyond the necessary labor time. This time Marx calls *surplus labor time.* The value of the commodities the worker is able to produce in this time is completely for the benefit of the capitalist, and this value is surplus value.

The reason capitalists can purchase labor power at less than its full value is that they have economic power. They own the means of production, and workers are forced to sell them their labor power in order to survive, and they must do so on terms set by capitalists.

Since the aim of capitalist production is the accumulation of capital, capitalists must always attempt to keep the price of labor power as low as possible. As the price of labor power rises, capitalists' profits must fall. Thus the relationship between capitalists and workers is an inherently antagonistic one, since workers' gains are capitalists' losses, and vice versa.

Marx therefore identifies the exploitative mechanism of the capitalist mode of production as the wage relationship. He stresses that this relationship obscures the exploitation actually taking place under capitalism, and it promotes the claim that exploitation does not exist at all within capitalism ("a fair day's work for a fair day's pay"). Marx also points out that this exploitative mechanism in capitalist society radically distinguishes it from the exploitative character of precapitalist societies. In precapitalist societies, exploitation is not "purely economic," but occurs in the context of state political and military power in a way that is fairly obvious to everyone.

Marx's account of the origins of profit remains highly controversial, and not even all Marxists accept it (cf. Roemer, 1982a,b). Conventional economists generally criticize it on the grounds that labor power can be only one source of value among others, and thus only one of several determinants of profits. Yet in a sense this criticism is beside the point. Even if it must be conceded that labor power is only one of several sources of profit, it is an especially crucial one. Even if the theory of surplus value is only partially valid, it contains an enormous insight, and that is that capitalists are constantly preoccupied with cheapening the cost of labor power. From a sociological point of view, this means that social struggles or antagonisms between capitalists and workers are built into the basic functioning of capitalism, and such struggles have to be understood in order for one to grasp the overall character and dynamics of capitalist society.

FOR FURTHER READING

Beaud, Michel. *A History of Capitalism, 1500–1980.* New York: Monthly Review Press, 1983. Contains some very informative material on the emergence and development of industrial capitalism.

Braverman, Harry. *Labor and Monopoly Capital: The Degradation of Work in the Twentieth Century.* New York: Monthly Review Press, 1974. An excellent work in which the author analyzes in depth the transformation of the workplace in capitalist society since the late nineteenth century. A major extension of the Marxian conception of alienation.

Chase-Dunn, Christopher (ed.). *Socialist States in the World-System.* Beverly Hills, Calif.: Sage, 1982. A provocative set of essays in which a number of contemporary Marxian scholars debate the nature of contemporary state socialism and its relationship to the capitalist world.

Chase-Dunn, Christopher. *Global Formation: Structures of the World-Economy.* Oxford: Blackwell, 1989. An extremely comprehensive extension and reformulation of Wallersteinian world-system theory. An outstanding work that applies world-system concepts and principles in considering a vast range of issues in the contemporary world-system, its past and its future.

Chirot, Daniel. *Social Change in the Modern Era.* Orlando: Harcourt Brace Jovanovich, 1986. Despite an unconvincing Weberian approach to the origins of the modern world, a very good treatment of many of the most basic social, economic, and political changes in the capitalist world-economy since the early nineteenth century, and especially since 1900. Also contains a good analysis of contemporary state socialism. (An earlier version of this book was published in 1977 under the title *Social Change in the Twentieth Century.* It is substantially different in parts, owing more to Wallerstein, and can still be valuably consulted.)

Davis, Howard, and Richard Scase. *Western Capitalism and State Socialism: An Introduction.* Oxford: Blackwell, 1985. A very good and easily understood treatment of the basic socioeconomic character of contemporary Western capitalist and state socialist societies.

Hobsbawm, E.J. *Industry and Empire.* New York: Pantheon Books, 1968. A valuable study by an eminent British Marxist historian of the Industrial Revolution in England and the development of the English economy since that time.

Lane, David. *Soviet Economy and Society.* New York: Blackwell, 1985. Some important discussions of various dimensions of Soviet economic life.

Mandel, Ernest. *Beyond Perestroika: The Future of Gorbachev's USSR.* London: Verso, 1989. One of the most important books yet written on the economic reforms currently going on in the Soviet Union.

Shannon, Thomas Richard. *An Introduction to the World-System Perspective.* Boulder, Colo.: Westview, 1989. The first textbook on world-system theory. An excellent and very succinct summary of the leading features of world-system theory and the critical reaction to it.

Sweezy, Paul. *The Theory of Capitalist Development.* New York: Monthly Review Press, 1942. Perhaps the best general secondary treatment available of the full scope of Marx's theory and critical analysis of capitalism. The author is an eminent Marxian economist and is exceptionally well qualified for the task at hand.

Thompson, Paul. *The Nature of Work: An Introduction to Debates on the Labor Process.* London: Macmillan Press, 1983. A good overview of the critical discussion that has centered around Braverman's work as well as around other important recent contributions to the analysis of work under modern capitalism.

Wallerstein, Immanuel. *The Modern World-System III: The Second Era of Great Expansion of the Capitalist World-Economy. 1730–1840s.* San Diego: Academic Press, 1989. The long-awaited third volume of Wallerstein's multivolume work on the history of the capitalist world-economy.

CHAPTER 9

Capitalism and Economic Underdevelopment

Sometime after the end of World War II social scientists began to speak of three "worlds." These worlds represented social, economic, and political categories into which contemporary societies could be placed. The First World consisted of the industrially advanced capitalist nations, which had parliamentary democratic forms of government: the United States, Canada, England, France, the Netherlands, Sweden, most of the rest of western and northern Europe, and also Australia and Japan. The Second World was industrially advanced, or at least on the path toward industrial development, but the societies of this category had socialist economies and totalitarian forms of government. Included in this category were the Soviet Union and the Eastern European socialist states. The rest of the world, not counting primitive or preliterate cultures, was the Third World. This world consisted of the poor, technologically backward, economically underdeveloped societies constituting most of Latin America, Africa, and Asia.

Having conceptualized something called a Third World, social scientists proceeded vigorously to study it. Many kinds of social scientists became involved in investigations focusing on different aspects of life in the Third World. Yet the overriding question for most investigators was why the societies of the Third World had failed to achieve the levels of technological and economic development, as well as the social patterns, so characteristic of the First World, and to some degree, of the Second.

This question is the focus of the current chapter. After discussing the nature of underdevelopment, this chapter proceeds to examine the major theories that social scientists have proposed to explain underdevelopment. These theories are critically assessed in light of the most recent evidence that social scientific research has been able to produce. The chapter concludes by using some of the most recent theoretical insights as a basis for asking what the future holds for the underdeveloped world.

THE NATURE OF UNDERDEVELOPMENT

Social scientists first called the societies of the Third World "backward nations," but later abandoned this expression as derogatory, adopting instead the expressions "underdeveloped nations," or "underdevelopment." Although these terms have also been criticized and others proposed, they have stuck and continue to be used by most social scientists. To understand exactly what is meant by underdevelopment, or by an underdeveloped nation, a useful first step is to distinguish between underdevelopment and *un*development (Frank, 1966). **Undeveloped societies** may be regarded as those outside the framework of a capitalist world-economy that have not yet gotten beyond a preindustrial stage of technological development and a precapitalist stage of economic development. Societies surviving by hunting and gathering, horticultural, pastoral, or agrarian methods of production and having some sort of production-for-use, premarket economy are referred to as *undeveloped*. The term *underdevelopment* is reserved for societies incorporated into a capitalist world-economy and functioning within it in some way. **Underdeveloped societies** may thus be regarded as the least technologically and economically advanced members of the modern world-system.

The most commonly used measure of economic development is a nation's per capita Gross National Product (GNP), which is the total value of goods and services it produces per person in a given year. This and other measures of underdevelopment are represented in Table 9.1. It can be seen that most of the underdeveloped nations have per capita GNPs that are strikingly low when compared to those of the developed nations. All of the African nations shown in Table 9.1, for instance, have per capita GNPs of less than $1,000. These levels of economic productivity are low indeed when compared with those of the developed nations, where the per capita GNP averages approximately $14,000 per year for the capitalist countries and nearly $8,000 per year for the state socialist countries. Most Asian nations are at about the same level of economic productivity as contemporary African societies. The productivity levels of the Latin American nations are notably higher, but even these compare very unfavorably with those of the developed world.

Two apparent anomalies in Table 9.1 are Kuwait and Qatar, contemporary nations with especially high per capita GNPs. Kuwait, in fact, has one of the highest per capita GNPs in the entire world. Such facts, however, do not indicate that these nations are misclassified. Brief examination of the other measures of underdevelopment shown in Table 9.1 reveals that Kuwait and Qatar are in these respects essentially like the other underdeveloped nations. Moreover, these extremely high per capita GNPs are relatively recent phenomena, the result of oil exportation to the developed world. Kuwait and Qatar have yet to develop the kind of industrialized, manufacturing economy characteristic of the developed nations. In addition, these high GNP levels have not resulted in a general diffusion of income and wealth throughout the population. The role of Kuwait and Qatar as oil exporters has yet to produce significant society-wide benefits in raising general living standards. The vast majority of this income and wealth remains for the benefit of a few extremely rich and powerful families.

The general measure of technological advance used in Table 9.1 is the number of scientists, engineers, and technicians employed in research and experimentation. The developed countries average nearly 450 scientists, engineers, and technicians engaged in research per 100,000 population. But the underdeveloped nations average only about 35 research and experimental personnel per 100,000 population.

In most of the underdeveloped world today, agriculture is still the dominant economic activity, and peasants outnumber workers of any other type. Most of these peasants farm small plots of land using techniques inherited from their ancestors thousands of years ago. Although industrialization has developed to some extent in all underdeveloped nations, in many it has not proceeded very far. In many of the underdeveloped nations shown in Table 9.1, half or more of the population is engaged in agricultural pursuits, and in some of these na-

Table 9.1 SOCIAL, DEMOGRAPHIC, AND ECONOMIC CHARACTERISTICS OF SELECTED CONTEMPORARY NATIONS AT DIFFERENT LEVELS OF ECONOMIC DEVELOPMENT

	POP	RNI	IMR	LFA	GNP	SCE
			Developed capitalist nations			
Denmark	5.1	0.0	8.4	7	15,010	348
Sweden	8.5	0.2	5.7	6	15,690	562
United Kingdom	57.3	0.2	9.1	3	10,430	284
France	56.1	0.4	7.6	9	12,860	411
West Germany	61.5	−0.1	8.3	6	14,460	396
Netherlands	14.9	0.4	7.6	6	11,860	387
Canada	26.3	0.8	7.9	5	15,080	192
United States	248.8	0.7	9.9	4	18,430	293
Australia	16.8	0.8	8.8	7	10,900	216
Japan	123.2	0.5	4.9	11	15,770	510
			Developed state socialist nations			
USSR	289.0	1.0	25.0	20	8,375	507
Czechoslovakia	15.6	0.2	13.1	13	8,298*	677
East Germany	16.6	0.1	8.7	11	9,769*	1,188
Poland	38.2	0.6	17.5	29	6,159*	287
Hungary	10.6	−0.2	17.3	18	7,277*	386
			Underdeveloped nations			
Latin America						
Mexico	86.7	2.4	50.0	37	1,820	—
Nicaragua	3.5	3.5	69.0	47	830	—
Bolivia	7.1	2.6	110.0	46	570	—

Peru	21.4	2.1	69.0	40	1,430	26
Brazil	147.4	2.0	63.0	31	2,020	24
Venezuela	19.1	2.4	36.0	16	3,230	44
El Salvador	5.1	2.7	62.0	43	850	34
Africa						
Egypt	54.8	2.8	93.0	46	710	54
Nigeria	115.3	2.9	122.0	68	370	4
Senegal	7.2	2.6	135.0	81	510	8
Kenya	24.1	4.1	76.0	81	340	3
Tanzania	26.3	3.6	111.0	86	220	—
Zaire	34.9	3.1	103.0	72	160	—
Asia						
Kuwait	2.1	2.8	15.6	2	14,870	115
Qatar	0.4	2.7	31.0	—	12,360	14
Iran	53.9	3.4	93.0	36	3,504*	5
India	835.0	2.2	96.0	70	300	13
Indonesia	184.6	2.0	83.0	57	450	18
China	1,103.9	1.4	44.0	74	300	—
Taiwan	20.0	1.1	6.9	—	2,969*	—
South Korea	43.1	1.3	30.0	36	2,690	125

Legend: POP = total population in millions (1989); RNI = annual percentage of population increase (various points since 1980); IMR = infant mortality rate, calculated as annual number of deaths to infants under one year of age per 1000 live births (various points since 1980); LFA = percentage of the labor force engaged in agriculture (1980); GNP = Gross National Product per capita calculated in U.S. dollars (1987); SCE = number of scientists, engineers, and technicians engaged in research and experimental development per 100,000 population (years vary from 1975 to 1984).

Sources: Data in columns 1, 2, 3, and 5 are from *World Population Data Sheet*, Washington, D.C.: Population Reference Bureau, 1989; data in column 4 are from the World Bank's *World Development Report 1988*, New York: Oxford University Press, 1988, Table 31; data in column 6 are from the United Nations's *1985/86 Statistical Yearbook*, New York: United Nations, 1988, Table 57 (recalculated). Data marked with an asterisk (*) come from U.S. Bureau of the Census, *Statistical Abstract of the United States*, Washington, D.C.: U.S. Government Printing Office, 1988, Table 1387.

A peasant plowing a rice paddy in contemporary Thailand. In most underdeveloped countries the peasantry still constitutes the largest part of the population, and the agricultural methods and tools that peasants use are much the same as those used by their ancestors for thousands of years.

tions the proportion approaches or exceeds three-quarters. In contrast, the figures for the developed countries indicate that less than 10 percent of the population is agriculturally employed in virtually all developed nations, and in some nations (such as the United States and the United Kingdom) only a minuscule segment of the population makes its living from agricultural work.

Yet underdevelopment involves considerably more than low levels of technological and economic development. It also involves important social dimensions. Social and economic inequality is an especially important characteristic of underdeveloped societies. In most underdeveloped societies, wealth is enormously concentrated in the hands of a few, and tiny elites generally dominate the manufacturing and agricultural sectors of the economy. In Brazil, for instance, 0.5 percent of the adult population owns half of the private lands (Anderson and Gibson, 1978), a situation that is much the same throughout Latin America and the underdeveloped world generally. What is true of the inequality of wealth also holds for income inequality. As Table 9.2 reveals, income inequality in underdeveloped nations is notably higher than in the industrialized countries.

Yet these data on income inequality, useful as they may be, do not tell what we really want to know about underdeveloped nations: what is the standard of living for the majority of the population? Table 9.3 shows the percentage of the population of each underdeveloped country that falls below $75 (in 1969 dollars) in annual per capita income. The standard of living in most underdeveloped nations is very low, especially in Asia and Africa, where about half of the population is living on less than $75 per person per year. Even in Latin America, where general living standards are considerably higher, much of the population is existing at a very low standard of living.*

Underdeveloped societies also stand out because of their demographic features. They are growing at a rate approximately six to seven times as fast as the developed nations (see Table 9.1). This greater rate of growth is primarily attributable to the fact that birth rates remain

*The data in Table 9.3 are based on income received from economic activities that take place within the context of an economic market, such as wage work or the selling of products in local markets. These figures underestimate the real income available to peasant farmers, much of which is provided by subsistence farming. Nonetheless, the figures in Table 9.3 still demonstrate markedly low living standards in the underdeveloped world.

Table 9.2 INCOME INEQUALITY IN DEVELOPED AND UNDERDEVELOPED NATIONS

Nation	Income share of top 10%[a]	Income share of bottom 20%[b]	Ratio of top 10% to bottom 20%	Year[c]
		Developed nations		
United Kingdom	23.4	7.0	3.3 : 1	1979
Belgium	21.5	7.9	2.7 : 1	1978–79
Netherlands	21.5	8.3	2.6 : 1	1981
France	26.4	5.5	4.8 : 1	1975
Australia	30.5	5.4	5.6 : 1	1975–76
West Germany	24.0	7.9	3 : 1	1978
Denmark	22.3	5.4	4.1 : 1	1981
Japan	22.4	8.7	2.6 : 1	1979
Sweden	28.1	7.4	3.8 : 1	1981
Canada	23.8	5.3	4.5 : 1	1981
United States	23.3	5.3	4.4 : 1	1980
Switzerland	23.7	6.6	3.6 : 1	1978
Averages	24.2	6.7	3.6 : 1	
		Underdeveloped nations		
Bangladesh	29.5	6.6	4.5 : 1	1981–82
India	33.6	7.0	4.8 : 1	1975–76
Kenya	45.8	2.6	17.6 : 1	1976
Zambia	46.4	3.4	13.6 : 1	1976
Sri Lanka	34.7	5.8	6 : 1	1980–81
Indonesia	34.0	6.6	5.2 : 1	1976
Philippines	37.0	5.2	7.1 : 1	1985
Ivory Coast	43.7	2.4	18.2 : 1	1985–86
Egypt	33.2	5.8	5.7 : 1	1974
Thailand	34.1	5.6	6.1 : 1	1975–76
El Salvador	29.5	5.5	5.4 : 1	1976–77
Peru	42.9	1.9	22.6 : 1	1972
Turkey	40.7	3.5	11.6 : 1	1973
Brazil	50.6	2.0	25.3 : 1	1972
Malaysia	39.8	3.5	11.4 : 1	1973
Mexico	40.6	2.9	14 : 1	1977
South Korea	27.5	5.7	4.8 : 1	1976
Trinidad and Tobago	31.8	4.2	7.6 : 1	1975–76
Hong Kong	31.3	5.4	5.8 : 1	1980
Averages	37.2	4.5	8.3 : 1	

[a]Proportion of the total national income received by the top 10% of the population.
[b]Proportion of the total national income received by the bottom 20% of the population.
[c]Year in which the data for these computations were collected.

Source: World Bank, *World Development Report 1988*. New York: Oxford University Press, 1988, Table 26.

Table 9.3 ESTIMATES OF POVERTY LEVELS AMONG UNDERDEVELOPED COUNTRIES

Country	Population below $75 annual per capita income	
	Millions	% of total population
	Latin America	
Ecuador	3.5	58.5
Honduras	1.0	38.0
El Salvador	.6	18.4
Dominican Republic	.7	15.9
Colombia	5.6	27.0
Brazil	18.2	20.0
Jamaica	.3	15.4
Guyana	.1	15.1
Peru	3.3	25.5
Costa Rica	.1	8.5
Mexico	8.7	17.8
Uruguay	.2	5.5
Panama	.2	11.0
Chile	N	N
Venezuela	N	N
Argentina	N	N
Puerto Rico	N	N
Totals	42.5	17.4
	Asia	
Burma	19.2	71.0
Sri Lanka	7.8	63.5
India	359.3	66.9
Pakistan	64.7	57.9

Thailand	15.4	44.3
Korea	5.3	17.0
Philippines	11.2	30.0
Turkey	8.2	23.7
Iraq	3.1	33.3
Taiwan	2.0	14.3
Malaysia	1.6	15.5
Iran	4.2	15.0
Lebanon	.1	5.0
Totals	502.1	56.4
	Africa	
Chad	2.7	77.5
Dahomey	2.3	90.1
Tanzania	9.3	72.9
Niger	2.3	59.9
Madagascar	4.7	69.6
Uganda	4.1	49.8
Sierra Leone	1.5	61.5
Senegal	1.3	35.3
Ivory Coast	1.4	28.5
Tunisia	1.6	32.1
Rhodesia	1.9	37.4
Zambia	.3	7.5
Gabon	.1	23.0
South Africa	3.1	15.5
Totals	36.6	43.6
Grand total	583.2	47.9

Source: Montek S. Ahluwalia, "Income Inequality: Some Dimensions of the Problem." In Hollis Chenery (ed.), ***Redistribution with Growth***. New York: Oxford University Press, 1974, Table I.2, p. 12. Data are for 1969; N = negligible.

high in the underdeveloped world, especially among peasant farmers who desire large numbers of children as farm workers (Harris and Ross, 1987). The underdeveloped nations currently constitute about three-fourths of the world's population, but because of their rapid growth rates a greater and greater percentage of the world's population will live in these nations in the years ahead. Rapid population growth is creating increasingly severe problems in the underdeveloped world, and for some Asian and African nations population growth has created problems of crisis proportions. (At the end of this chapter the demographic problems of many underdeveloped societies are examined more closely.)

A final characteristic of the underdeveloped world that is important to note involves general standards of nutrition and health. One of the most useful measures of a nation's overall nutritional and health status is its infant mortality rate. As can be seen from Table 9.1, infant mortality rates are dramatically higher in underdeveloped countries. Whereas the developed capitalist nations have infant mortality rates of approximately 8 per 1000 births, and the developed state socialist nations have rates of around 15 to 20 per 1000 births, many of the underdeveloped nations have rates that approach or exceed 100 per 1000 births. Infant mortality rates are especially high in Asia and Africa but are also quite high throughout Latin America.

Much of what has been surveyed from a statistical point of view can be summarized and seen more vividly by imagining what daily life is like for a more or less typical member of a more or less typical underdeveloped nation. Robert Heilbroner's attempt to evoke such a daily life imaginatively is worth quoting in its full detail (1963:23–27):

> We must conjure up in our mind's eye what underdevelopment means for the two billion human beings for whom it is not a statistic but a living experience of daily life. . . .
>
> It is not easy to make this mental jump. But let us attempt it by imagining how a typical American family . . . could be transformed into an equally typical family of the underdeveloped world.
>
> We begin by invading the house of our imaginary American family to strip it of its furniture. Everything goes: beds, chairs, tables, television set, lamps. We will leave the family with a few old blankets, a kitchen table, a wooden chair. Along with the bureaus go the clothes. Each member of the family may keep in his "wardrobe" his oldest suit or dress, a shirt or blouse. We will permit a pair of shoes to the head of the family, but none for the wife or children.
>
> We move into the kitchen. The appliances have already been taken out, so we turn to the cupboards and larder. The box of matches may stay, a small bag of flour, some sugar and salt. A few moldy potatoes, already in the garbage can, must be hastily rescued, for they will provide much of tonight's meal. We will leave a handful of onions, and a dish of dried beans. All the rest we take away: the meat, the fresh vegetables, the canned goods, the crackers, the candy.
>
> Now we have stripped the house: the bathroom has been dismantled, the running water shut off, the electric wires taken out. Next we take away the house. The family can move to the toolshed. It is crowded, but much better than the situation in Hong Kong, where (a United Nations report tells us) "it is not uncommon for a family of four or more to live in a bedspace, that is, on a bunk bed and the space it occupies—sometimes in two or three tiers—their only privacy provided by curtains."
>
> But we have only begun. All the other houses in the neighborhood have also been removed; our suburb has become a shantytown. Still, our family is fortunate to have a shelter; 250,000 people in Calcutta have none at all and simply live in the streets. Our family is now about on a par with the city of Cali in Colombia, where, an official of the World Bank writes, "on a hillside alone, the slum population is estimated at 40,000—without water, sanitation, or electric

light. And not all the poor of Cali are as fortunate as that. Others have built their shacks near the city on land which lies beneath the flood mark. To these people the immediate environment is the open sewer of the city, a sewer which flows through their huts when the river rises."

And still we have not reduced our American family to the level at which life is lived in the greatest part of the globe. Communication must go next. No more newspapers, magazines, books—not that they are missed, since we must take away our family's literacy as well. Instead, in our shantytown we will allow one radio. In India the national average of radio ownership is one per 250 people, but since the majority of radios is owned by city dwellers, our allowance is fairly generous.

Now government services must go. No more postman, no more fireman. There is a school, but it is three miles away and consists of two classrooms. They are not too overcrowded since only half the children in the neighborhood go to school. There are, of course, no hospitals or doctors nearby. The nearest clinic is ten miles away and is tended by a midwife. It can be reached by bicycle, provided that the family has a bicycle, which is unlikely. Or one can go by bus—not always inside, but there is usually room on top.

Finally, money. We will allow our family a cash hoard of five dollars. This will prevent our breadwinner from experiencing the tragedy of an Iranian peasant who went blind because he could not raise the $3.94 which he mistakenly thought he needed to secure admission to a hospital where he could have been cured.

Meanwhile the head of our family must earn his keep. As a peasant cultivator with three

This dwelling in Colombia, South America, shows how wretched life can be for many of the members of the underdeveloped world.

acres to tend, he may raise the equivalent of $100 to $300 worth of crops a year. If he is a tenant farmer, which is more than likely, a third or so of his crop will go to his landlord, and probably another 10 percent to the local moneylender. But there will be enough to eat. Or almost enough. The human body requires an input of at least 2,000 calories to replenish the energy consumed by its living cells. If our displaced American fares no better than an Indian peasant, he will average a replenishment of no more than 1,700–1,900 calories. His body, like any insufficiently fueled machine, will run down. That is one reason why life expectancy at birth in India today averages less than forty years.

But children may help. If they are fortunate, they may find work and thus earn some cash to supplement the family's income. For example, they may be employed as are children in Hyderabad, Pakistan, sealing the ends of bangles over a small kerosene flame, a simple task which can be done at home. To be sure, the pay is small: eight annas—about ten cents—for sealing bangles. That is, eight annas per *gross* of bangles. And if they cannot find work? Well, they can scavenge, as do the children in Iran who in times of hunger search for the undigested oats in the droppings of horses.

And so we have brought our typical American family down to the very bottom of the human scale. It is, however, a bottom in which we can find, give or take a hundred million souls, at least a billion people. Of the remaining billion in the backward areas, most are slightly better off, but not much so; a few are comfortable; a handful rich.

Of course, this is only an impression of life in the underdeveloped lands. It is not life itself. There is still lacking the things that underdevelopment gives as well as those it takes away: the urinous smell of poverty, the display of disease, the flies, the open sewers. And there is lacking, too, a softening sense of familiarity. Even in a charnel house life has its passions and pleasures. A tableau, shocking to American eyes, is less shocking to eyes that have never known any other. But it gives one a general idea. It begins to add pictures of reality to the statistics by which underdevelopment is ordinarily measured. When we are told that half the world's population enjoys a standard of living "less than $100 a year," this is what the figures mean.

Heilbroner wrote these words more than a quarter of a century ago, but there is no reason to suspect that they apply any less to today's world. Indeed, they may apply even more forcefully to the 1990s, since the gap between the developed and the underdeveloped nations has actually been increasing rather than decreasing. Only a handful of the underdeveloped nations of 25 years ago have made significant strides toward economic development, and many have actually been experiencing even greater poverty and misery. How can we explain not only this historical problem of underdevelopment, but the marked failure of most of the underdeveloped world to move toward the status of the developed nations?

THE MODERNIZATION APPROACH TO UNDERDEVELOPMENT

Social scientists have developed three principal theoretical approaches to the problem of underdevelopment: **modernization theory, dependency theory,** and **world-system theory.** In many ways world-system theory is a more flexible version of dependency theory, and so these two approaches are very similar. They stand sharply opposed, however, to modernization theory, and in fact originally emerged as alternatives to that approach.

The General Nature of Modernization Theory

Modernization theory is a very broad theoretical strategy that includes a variety of complementary, but also competing, theories. By and large, it is a specialized version of an even broader theoretical strategy, the functionalist evolutionary approach to sociocultural evolution (A. D. Smith, 1973; Sanderson, 1990). The diverse theories that coexist within the modernization approach are united by two fundamental assumptions. First, underdevelopment tends to be seen as an "original state," as a state of society that has always existed in some form or another. Modernization theorists tend to conceive underdevelopment as a social and economic process that long predates the emergence of modern capitalism. Indeed, they suggest that it was only with the rise of modern capitalist societies that underdevelopment was first overcome, despite the fact that many contemporary nations have not yet been able to reach this developmental stage. For the modernization theorists, then, such societies as the Yanomamo, the Aztecs, and medieval England were or are underdeveloped in much the same way that contemporary Brazil, Thailand, and Nigeria are. This view is in sharp contrast to the point made earlier about development and underdevelopment being meaningful concepts only when they are applied to nations incorporated into a capitalist world-economy.

A second major assumption of modernization theory is that underdevelopment results from any of a number of internal deficiencies of a society. This notion is the counterpart to the claim that development results from certain special qualities of those societies having achieved it, qualities that set them apart from the rest. Three broad kinds of internal deficiencies are proposed by modernization theorists as causes of underdevelopment. One of these is insufficient capital formation. Many economists argue that underdeveloped societies have been unable to generate an amount of capital sufficient to get them to a "takeoff point": a point at which they could begin rapidly growing economically.

Other modernization theorists have mentioned outdated business techniques and practices as factors preventing economic development. They suggest that underdeveloped societies commonly do not have the modern rational techniques of marketing, accounting, finance, sales, and so on, that are so common in the developed nations. The failure of such societies to adopt these modern rational business practices keeps their productivity and profit rates low and prevents significant development within them.

Finally, more sociologically oriented modernization theorists stress that underdeveloped societies generally lack the kind of consciousness or mentality—the kind of outlook on the world—that promotes development. Development is said to occur when people adopt rational, future-oriented value and ethical systems, and religions or philosophies that embody these kinds of values and ethics. It is alleged that most people in underdeveloped countries are governed by attitudes and values stressing the past and the importance of custom and tradition. Moreover, they are often caught up in religions that emphasize that human suffering can only be changed in the afterlife and that attempting to change the secular world is futile. Thus people are rendered fatalistic and generally accept their situation in life rather than make rational efforts to change it. When people remain passive in regard to changing their situation, their underdeveloped state is perpetuated.

Rostow's Evolutionary Interpretation

Perhaps the best-known modernization theory is that of the economist W. W. Rostow (1960). According to Rostow, economic development involves the passage of a society through five evolutionary stages: the stage of traditional society, the stage of the preconditions for takeoff, the takeoff stage, the drive to maturity, and the age of high mass consumption. All underdeveloped societies are in the stage that Rostow calls traditional society. This stage includes "the whole pre-Newtonian world: the dynasties in China; the civilization of the Middle East and the Mediterranean; the world of medieval Europe" (Rostow, 1960:5). Moreover, traditional societies are also "post-Newtonian societies which, for a time, remained untouched or unmoved by man's new capability for regularly manipulating his environment to his economic advantage" (1960:5). In these societies, agriculture is by far the dominant economic activity, and political power generally rests with those who control the land. It is possible for there to be increases in economic productivity, but because of the inaccessibility of modern science there are strong limitations placed upon such increases. Family membership generally plays a powerful role in the life of each individual. The value system of traditional societies is generally oriented around a kind of long-run fatalism. Although people believe that their efforts to improve their lot can make some difference in the short run, most persons believe that the lives of their grandchildren will be more or less the same as the lives lived by their grandparents.

Societies begin the transition out of traditional society when they acquire the preconditions for takeoff. During this stage, a society acquires the social, political, economic, and ideological conditions that promote economic growth. The idea spreads that economic progress is not only possible, but a necessary condition for a proper life. Education broadens and becomes more closely linked to the particular nature of modern economic activity. New types of personalities emerge, individuals who are willing to take risks in order to achieve modernization. Banks and other capital-mobilizing institutions appear, and the scope of investment and commerce increases significantly. Modern manufacturing enterprises using the latest technological methods appear. Changes also take place in the political realm, particularly in terms of building an effective centralized government.

The takeoff itself is achieved when a society has reached the point where it can carry on sustained economic growth. Old forms of resistance to economic growth are at last overcome, and growth becomes an inherent feature of the society. The takeoff requires substantial capital development. In this stage "the rate of effective investment and savings may rise from, say, 5 percent of the national income to 10 percent or more" (Rostow, 1960:8).

The drive to maturity involves a long period of sustained economic progress in which the society attempts to apply its new technological capacity to a wider and more diverse range of economic activities. The economy moves well beyond the original industries which promoted its takeoff. During this stage, Rostow estimates that approximately 10 to 20 percent of the national income is reinvested. He believes that the drive to maturity takes on the order of 60 years to achieve, counting from the beginning of the takeoff phase.

The age of high mass consumption is reached when many of the leading sectors of the economy shift toward the production of consumer goods and services. Per capita income is high enough for individuals to consume at a level that is notably beyond their basic needs for food, shelter, and clothing.

Rostow's analysis of economic development is less a theory than a description of the stages through which he believes societies must pass in order to obtain development. However, he does give some attention to the problem of what prompts a society to move beyond the traditional society stage. The factor he gives greatest weight to is what he calls "reactive nationalism," a phenomenon that results from "the affront to national dignity caused by the intrusion of a foreign power." Rostow believes that the real or perceived threat of humiliation by a foreign power has played a role at least as important as the profit motive in motivating leaders to modernize their society so as to handle the foreign threat.

Although Rostow's analysis focuses more on the causes of development than those of underdevelopment, there is clearly implied in his work a theoretical conception of underdevelopment. Underdeveloped societies are those that have not passed beyond the stage of traditional society. They have yet to experience those crucial stimuli that prompt people to want to reorganize their society so that self-sustaining economic growth can be realized. Underdeveloped societies lack the social patterns, political structures, and values that promote economic progress. Instead, the traditional features of these societies lead to a perpetuation of historically low levels of economic productivity.

Despite its considerable fame, Rostow's analysis of development and underdevelopment is not particularly impressive. The vast majority of his discussion is taken up with detailed descriptions of his stages, especially the last four. This sort of detailed description is of limited use. As Baran and Hobsbawm (1973) have pointed out, once a takeoff stage has been posited, the stages that precede and follow it are logically implied by it. Thus, the identification of these stages tells us little that we do not already know. Moreover, simply "pigeonholing [an underdeveloped society] in one of Rostow's 'stages' does not bring us any closer to an understanding of the country's economic and social condition or give us a clue to the country's developmental possibilities and prospects" (Baran and Hobsbawm, 1973:51). In other words, it gives us no insight into what the causes of development and underdevelopment are.

Even when Rostow does set forth a mechanism that is supposed to prompt development, his analysis seems on shaky ground. Surely something much like what Rostow calls "reactive nationalism" has occurred many times in human history prior to the development of modern capitalism and industrialism. Yet such occurrences did not lead to the kind of economic development that Rostow is talking about. It is perhaps the case that the kind of reactive nationalism Rostow has in mind is somehow different from other historically earlier types. But if this is the case, Rostow does not say so.

The Failures of Modernization Theory

The critical stance toward Rostow's particular interpretation may be extended to modernization theory in general. By and large, it has failed to produce an acceptable interpretation of the conditions that stimulate development and of those that establish obstacles to it. One major failing of the modernization theorists lies in the concept of "traditional society." For most modernization theorists, underdevelopment means that a society remains a "traditional society," and development is the process whereby traditionalism is transcended and replaced with "modernism": a rational set of beliefs, values, and social patterns that stress human manipulation of the environment directed toward self-sustaining economic and technological progress. A major difficulty with the concept of traditional society is the global character it takes on in the eyes of the modernization theorists. Traditional societies include not only ancient Rome, medieval Europe, and classical China, but also contemporary Kenya, Chile, and India. These societies differ dramatically in terms of a whole range of social, technological, economic, and political patterns, yet the concept of traditional society is used to cover them all. Can a concept that is applied so globally, and that ignores crucial differences among societies, really be a useful one?

There is another crucial difference among the societies mentioned above: their relationship to world capitalism. Ancient Rome, medieval Europe, and classical China were all historic civilizations that existed before the development of European capitalism; but contemporary Kenya, Chile, and India are all nations that have been subjected, at one time or another and in one form or another, to European colonialism. This suggests another major weakness of modernization theory: its virtual neglect of the economic and political relations that have historically existed between contemporary underdeveloped nations and the nations of the developed world (Frank, 1967). It is difficult to see how social scientists can justify paying little or no attention to these relations when formulating theories of underdevelopment.

As important as these weakness are, the real failing of modernization theory has been its inability to predict successfully the way development can be produced. Various modernization theorists have served as advisors to governments in developed nations and have made numerous recommendations regarding methods by which development in the Third World can be stimulated. In general, they recommend closer contact between the developed and the underdeveloped countries. Greater capital investment in the Third World, or large amounts of foreign aid to poor countries, are among the most frequent recommendations that have been made. Also, sociologically sensitive modernization theorists commonly recommend that underdeveloped countries should seek to imitate the social patterns of the advanced industrial nations. Yet despite the implementation of these recommendations, in some cases on a grand scale, most of the underdeveloped nations have not been developing as the modernization theorists have predicted. The economic gap between the developed and the underdeveloped countries is actually larger today than it was several decades ago, and the extent of poverty and misery in the Third World has conceivably been growing rather than lessening. Such facts scarcely speak well for modernization theory.

Despite the severe criticism that it has received, modernization theory has never died out. Not only does it still survive, but it probably is still the most widely embraced of the theoretical approaches to underdevelopment, at least outside of sociology (cf. Apter, 1987). Nevertheless, it must share theoretical attention with the approaches that came to challenge it in the 1960s, the first of which was dependency theory.

THE DEPENDENCY APPROACH TO UNDERDEVELOPMENT

Dependency theory was first developed in Latin America and came to the attention of North American and European social scientists largely through the writings of the American-educated economist Andre Gunder Frank (1966, 1967, 1969). By the mid-1970s this approach had become very popular, especially among sociologists. In many ways dependency theory is a specialized offshoot of the Marxian theory of capitalism.

The General Nature of the Dependency Approach

The basic underlying assumptions of the dependency approach stand in stark contrast to those of modernization theory. Rather than conceiving underdevelopment as an "original state," as something characteristic of a "traditional society," underdevelopment is viewed as something created within a precapitalist society that begins to experience certain forms of economic and political relations with one or more capitalist societies. Underdevelopment is not a product of certain internal deficiencies, as modernization theory holds. It results not from the absence of something, but from the *presence* of something. Thus dependency theory would not regard India in 1700 as an underdeveloped society. At this time it was an agrarian, precapitalist empire. But by 1850 it was well on the road to becoming underdeveloped due to its relationship to British capitalism.

The root cause of underdevelopment in the dependency perspective is **economic depen-**

dency. Economic dependency exists when one society falls under the sway of some foreign society's economic system, and when the first society's economy is organized by persons in the foreign society so as to benefit primarily the foreign economy. Economic dependency implies that there are relations of economic domination and subordination between two or more societies.

The concept of dependency as an explanation for economic underdevelopment has been developed most prominently by Andre Gunder Frank (1966, 1979) and Samir Amin (1974). For Frank the concepts of development and underdevelopment have meaning only when applied to nations within the capitalist world-economy. Frank envisions this world-economy as being divided into two major components, *metropolis* and *satellite*. (These concepts are basically equivalent to Wallerstein's concepts of core and periphery.) The flow of economic surplus in the world-economy is from the satellite (or periphery) to the metropolis (or core), and the world-economy is organized to make this happen. The underdeveloped nations therefore have become and remain underdeveloped because they are economically dominated by developed capitalist nations that have continuously been extracting wealth from them. Frank has called this process the *development of underdevelopment* (1966). In this view, the development of the rich nations and the underdevelopment of the poor ones are but two sides of the same coin; underdevelopment of some nations has made development for others possible. The primary victims of this process are the vast majority of peasants and urban workers of the underdeveloped world itself. And who benefits from such a system? The members of developed nations certainly do, since their standard of living is raised substantially. But the greatest benefits go to capitalists in the metropolitan countries, as well as to the agricultural and industrial elites of the satellite countries. The latter have close economic and political ties to the metropolitan elite and play a crucial role in maintaining the situation of economic dependency.

Amin's formulation of the dependency concept is quite similar to Frank's. However, he goes somewhat further and suggests abandoning the terms development and underdevelopment and replacing them with the terms *capitalist formations of the center* and *capitalist formations of the periphery*. These concepts correspond, respectively, to what we are in the habit of calling the developed and the underdeveloped nations. Amin believes that the recommended change in terminology is more than just a semantic exercise. He argues that the new concepts more precisely identify the kinds of economic structures found among societies within the modern world-economy.

Amin argues that the capitalist formations of the center are characterized by **articulated economies.** Articulated economies are those whose multiple sectors are closely interrelated such that development in any one sector stimulates development in all of the other sectors. Articulated economies are therefore coherent and integrated wholes. The capitalist formations of the periphery, on the other hand, have **disarticulated economies.** These are economies whose sectors do not closely interrelate. Development in any one sector may be unable to stimulate the development of other sectors. Those sectors that are most developed in disarticulated economies involve the production of raw materials for export to the capitalist center. Moreover, disarticulation results from foreign control of the economy. Capitalists of the center have important connections with those peripheral capitalists who control raw-materials production.

What disarticulation really means, Amin argues, is that the kind of development characteristic of the advanced industrial societies cannot occur. When a society's economy becomes disarticulated due to foreign economic control, attention is directed to the development of those economic activities that benefit central capitalists. Those activities that would involve production for the overall benefit of the domestic economy are consequently neglected. The following discussion by Amin conveys more completely his concepts of articulation and disarticulation (1974:16–19):

> An advanced economy forms a coherent whole, made up of sectors that carry out substantial exchanges between themselves, what may be called "interindustrial" or "intersectoral" exchanges. Thus, these sectors appear complementary, solid with each other, so to speak: the extractive and power industries provide the basic industries with their chief raw materials, and these industries support, through the capital goods and semi-finished goods that they produce, light industries and modernized ("industrialized") agriculture, which, in their turn, provide the ultimate consumer goods. An underdeveloped economy, however, is made up of sectors that carry out only marginal exchanges among themselves, their exchanges being made essentially with the outside world. Some of these sectors are made up of a few large-scale enterprises—often foreign, and dependent on great international businesses—the governing centers of which are outside the underdeveloped economy. The different kinds of mineral wealth exploited by these great concerns—metals, oil, etc.—are not destined to supply domestic industries on the spot, but are exported in order to supply complex industrial groups in the advanced countries.
>
> . . .
>
> The disarticulation of the economy prevents the development of any one sector from having a mobilizing effect upon the rest. Any such effect is transferred abroad, to the supplying countries: the sectors of the underdeveloped economy appear as extensions of the dominating advanced economy. In turn, this disarticulation and its corollary, the unevenness in productivity, are reflected in the distribution of the gross internal product and of investments, which is very different from that which is typical of the advanced countries.
>
> External dependence is at once the origin and the result of this situation. It appears first of all on the plane of external trade. The trade of the underdeveloped countries, whether taken individually or jointly, presents this distinctive feature, that not only are the exports of these countries largely made up of (mineral and agricultural) primary products, and their imports of manufactured goods, but also, and above all, this trade is carried on essentially with the advanced countries, whereas the trade of the advanced countries is essentially carried on among themselves.
>
> . . .
>
> As economic growth proceeds, none of these factors by which the structure of the periphery is distinguished lessens; on the contrary, each increases. Whereas at the center, growth *is* development—that is, it has an integrating effect—in the periphery growth is *not* development, for its effect is to disarticulate. Strictly speaking, growth in the periphery, based on integration into the world market, is *development of underdevelopment.*

Amin's analysis hammers just one more nail into the coffin of modernization theory's "traditional society." India after the arrival of the British developed a disarticulated economy, but no such phenomenon existed before the British came. British colonialism thus created an underdeveloped society where none had existed before.

Types and Varieties of Economic Dependency

The concept of dependency can be understood more thoroughly by examining its various forms. Theotonio Dos Santos (1970) has suggested three historical forms of dependency through which the now-underdeveloped nations have passed. The first of these he calls *colonial dependence.* Under this form of dependency, which began as early as the sixteenth century in some parts of the world, European capitalist powers colonized precapitalist regions and established a monopoly over land, mines, and labor. Surplus wealth was extracted from these regions by means of European control over trade relations. The economic character of these colonized regions was powerfully shaped by their subordination to European nations.

A second historical form of dependency identified by Dos Santos is *financial-industrial dependence*. This form of dependence began in the late nineteenth century. It was characterized by the expansion of European industrial capital (as opposed to the earlier merchant capital) into the backward regions of the world. This form of dependence was part and parcel of the monopoly phase of capitalist development. Financial-industrial dependence involved heavy investment of big capitalists in the world's backward regions mainly for the purpose of producing raw materials to be exported back to the core nations.

The most recent form of dependency is termed by Dos Santos *the new dependence*. This kind of dependence is a post-World War II phenomenon and involves the emergence of multinational corporations that engage in extensive economic investment in Third World countries.

In addition to this concern about the forms of dependency, there is the question of how dependency creates and perpetuates underdevelopment. Dependency theorists do not agree on the precise mechanisms whereby this occurs. Several different mechanisms through which dependency induces underdevelopment have been proposed by various theoreticians, and more than one is sometimes proposed even by the same theorist. Four possible dependency mechanisms are most frequently suggested in the current dependency literature (Chase-Dunn, 1975; Delacroix and Ragin, 1981; Barrett and Whyte, 1982):

1. ***Exploitation through repatriation*** It is often suggested in dependency writings that foreign firms reinvest only a portion of their profits derived from Third World investments in the Third World itself. The bulk of these profits is shipped home (repatriated) for the benefit of the investing nation.
2. ***Elite complicity*** A common theme in dependency writings is the claim that the rich capitalists of Third World countries enter into various types of agreements with rich core capitalists to maintain the status quo of the underdeveloped country. This occurs because the elites of both countries benefit from the prevailing economic situation.
3. ***Structural distortion*** Some dependency theorists argue that economic dependency leads to a distortion of the economy in the underdeveloped nation. This distortion then creates severe barriers to economic development. This argument, for example, is the kind made by Amin when he speaks of the disarticulation of the economy that results from the dependence of Third World countries on the capitalist center.
4. ***Market vulnerability*** It is sometimes argued that the peripheral nations are especially harmed by world market conditions. World demand for the primary products of peripheral countries tends to decline over time, and this decline is aggravated by price fluctuations for primary products.

These four ways in which dependency can induce underdevelopment should not be thought of as mutually exclusive. It is entirely possible that underdevelopment could result from more than one mechanism operating at the same time, or even from the simultaneous operation of all of them.

Recent Empirical Explorations of Dependency Theory

In recent years numerous sociologists and other social scientists have conducted empirical investigations designed to test the basic claims of dependency theory. These studies generally examine a large number of the world's nations and employ the most advanced and sophisticated statistical procedures. A work by Volker Bornschier, Christopher Chase-Dunn, and Richard Rubinson (1978) attempts to synthesize the results of 16 such studies (cf. Rubinson and Holtzman, 1981).

Five of the studies examine the effects of economic dependence on economic inequality. All five show that dependence is associated with greater inequality. More specifically, five studies demonstrate that investment dependence—investment by foreign firms in a society's domestic economy—increases economic inequality. Similarly, two studies show that aid dependence—provision of economic aid by one country to another—also is associated with inequality.

Of greater concern to Bornschier et al. are the findings of these studies in regard to economic growth (most of the studies examine economic growth from about 1960 until the early 1970s). Initial examination of the studies indicated that some found that investment and aid dependence promoted economic growth, while others found such dependence retarded economic growth. Bornschier et al. have gone on to scrutinize these studies to determine what would have produced such apparently contradictory findings. They have shown that the findings of each study are closely linked to the way dependence is conceptualized and measured. By and large, the studies that show that foreign investment promotes economic growth conceptualize and measure investment in terms of *recent flows of investment capital*. By contrast, those studies demonstrating that foreign investment retards growth conceptualize and measure investment in terms of *long-term stocks of foreign investment*. Bornschier et al. believe this finding to be of great substantive significance. On the basis of it, they conclude that "the immediate effect of inflows of foreign capital and aid is to increase the rate of economic growth, while the long-run cumulative effects operate to reduce the rate of economic growth" (1978:667). Moreover, they go on to say (1978:667–668):

> These results tend to confirm the hypothesis that current inflows of investment capital and aid cause short-term increases in growth due to the contribution to capital formation and demand as foreign corporations purchase land, labor, and materials and start production, while the long-run structural distortions of the national economy produced by foreign investment and the exporting of profits tend to produce negative effects over time. We conclude, then, that the effect of short-term flows of investment and aid has positive effects on growth, but that their cumulative effect over time is negative. Many of the seemingly contradictory findings of these studies can be reconciled under this proposition.

In more recent work, Bornschier and Chase-Dunn (1985) have expanded this line of inquiry to include a greater number of studies (36 rather than 16), and reach the same basic conclusions. Moreover, using a sample of 103 nations, they have gone on to conduct new original research on the developmental effects of short-term capital flows versus long-term stocks of capital. They regard this original research as eliminating some of the flaws of the earlier studies. Once again, the same basic conclusions are forthcoming, the most important of which is that long-term penetration of foreign capital hinders a country's chances of economic development.

The Effects of Economic Dependency and Its Avoidance: Some Historical Case Studies

It is clear that the studies discussed above offer strong support for the overall argument of dependency theory. However, as useful and important as they are, these studies have some definite limitations. Perhaps the most important of these is the restricted time span they explore. Most of the studies examine economic growth within a time span of only 10 to 15 years. Moreover, all the studies concentrate on economic growth since the late 1950s or later. Yet the Third World countries being explored in these studies were already underdeveloped by that time, and dependency theorists would argue that this underdevelopment was the result of a long-term historical process of economic dependency of one sort or another. To carry out a genuinely meaningful test of dependency theory, then, a long-term historical perspective on underdevelopment is needed. This can be accomplished through the use of two carefully selected historical comparisons: the economic divergence of China and Japan since the nineteenth century, and the differential economic outcomes that have occurred in the Americas over the past few centuries.

China and Japan A historical comparison of China and Japan seems especially appropriate inasmuch as Japan is today the only nation in Asia to have become an economically developed, industrialized country. In her book *Japan, China and the Modern World Economy* (1977), Frances Moulder suggests that a major reason Japan became developed and China did not was the incorporation of China into the capitalist world-economy as a peripheral society.

According to Moulder, China first came to be incorporated into the world-economy as a trading partner of Great Britain. For centuries China had engaged in a luxury trade with Europe, but in the late eighteenth and early nineteenth centuries the trade relations between China and Europe underwent a major change. Trade between China and Britain became a trade in staples rather than in luxury items. As tea became a staple item in Britain, nearly all of the tea that the British imported came from China in the first half of the nineteenth century. This import was a very important source of revenue for the British government. "In 1855, for instance, about 10 percent of the gross revenue of the British government was derived from duties on imported tea" (Moulder, 1977:99). In addition, an interesting trade network developed among Britain, China, and India. The British found a market in China for the raw cotton they were producing in India and thus exported much of this cotton to China. Moreover, after the middle of the eighteenth century the British gained control of opium production in India and substantially increased its output. They eventually succeeded in addicting a portion of the Chinese population to opium and thus developed a vast opium market in China, a market supplied, of course, by Indian opium.

Another aspect of Britain's trade with China involved the development of Britain's textile industry. As British cotton textile production increased, there was increasing concern to find foreign markets for the sale of these products, and China was seen as an important market. In their development of China as an export market for British cotton goods, it was necessary for Britain to deprive the Chinese of a home market for their own textile industry. British rather than Chinese manufactures increasingly came to be sold in China. By the late nineteenth century, other industrializing nations, such as France, the United States, and Germany, began to follow Britain's lead and sell a portion of their manufactures in China. By the end of the nineteenth century China's consumption of Western goods was substantial.

The incorporation of China into the world-economy involved foreign investment as well as trade. Shipbuilding became an important form of foreign investment, "and by the 1930s over half the tonnage built in China was the work of foreign-controlled firms" (Moulder, 1977:113). This industry was primarily controlled by the British. But the most important form of foreign investment in China involved railroads and mining. As Moulder notes (1977:114):

> Since the 1860s, Western merchants and statesmen continually sought out Chinese officials and urged railroad and mine construction. They offered to construct railways and to open mines or to lend the money to the government to do so. . . .
>
> The Sino-Japanese War marked the end of the government's ability to resist foreign investment in railroads and mines, as it had in manufacturing. After 1895 the Chinese government was forced to grant railway and mining concessions to various Western nations and Japan (a concession granted the sole right to construct railroads or open modern mines within a specified territory). France received railway concessions in various places on the borders between Indochina and China, Russia obtained concession in Manchuria and Liaotung (whose railways ultimately came under control of Japan), the Germans in Shantung (which also came under control of Japan after World War I), and the English in the Canton area.
>
> By 1911, 41 percent of the railway mileage in China was owned by foreigners and the remainder had largely been built by the Chinese government with foreign loans. . . .
>
> Numerous mining concessions were granted from 1896 to 1913 to the British, Germans, Russians, French, Americans, Belgians, and Japanese.

Japan's experience with European capitalism has been very different. In 1638 Japan initiated a policy of political, social, and economic isolationism. For more than two centuries Japan had very little contact with western Europe. For a number of reasons Japan, unlike its Asian neighbors, never fell victim to colonization (or foreign economic penetration). During this

Contemporary Tokyo. Japan is by far the most economically developed and prosperous society in the non-Western world and is on the verge of becoming the world's most economically dominant nation. There are many reasons for Japan's success, but an especially important one has been Japan's historical isolation from the European world-economy from the early seventeenth to the mid-nineteenth century.

time the economic relations between Japan and the West were limited to some minor and closely regulated forms of trade. After the middle of the nineteenth century, Japan reversed its isolationist policy and began opening up to Western contact and influence. However, the nature of its economic relationship to the West even after this time has been very different from China's. Although trade with the West did increase, and some foreign investment did develop in Japan, these never approached the levels reached in China. In this regard, Moulder concludes (1977:145):

> China was tightly integrated as a satellite of the Western world economy throughout the nineteenth century and Japan was not. In China, an important trade in staple products developed, as well as a large and interrelated body of investments. In Japan, trade remained peripheral to the Western economies and their investments in Japan were few and isolated.

Thus Moulder sees China's heavy incorporation as a peripheral segment of the world-economy and Japan's relative lack of peripheralization as a crucial factor leading to the divergent economic outcomes observable today. In other words, it is the emergence of economic dependency in China and the failure of dependency to develop in Japan that lie, respectively, behind modern China's underdevelopment and modern Japan's development.

The Americas Andre Gunder Frank (1979) has given particular attention to explaining the historical underdevelopment of Latin America and the development of North America. Within this latter category he has tried to explain why it was the northeastern states of the United States that led the way into economic development in the nineteenth century, whereas the U.S. South experienced its own form of underdevelopment and did not begin to develop until much later.

According to Frank, Latin America's current underdevelopment is the historical legacy of centuries of dependent development—of the development of underdevelopment. Much of Latin America fell under European colonial domination from the sixteenth century on. Contemporary Mexico and Peru, for instance, were colonized in the sixteenth century by Spain. Although the Spaniards first imposed slavery on the indigenous population, this was quickly abandoned. It was replaced by a form of labor control known as the *encomienda*. Under this system (Frank, 1979:45):

> Indians of designated communities were assigned to particular Spaniards, who did not receive ownership of their persons, lands or other property, but were authorised to exact tribute in personal services, goods and money from them. This tribute was the principal source of the Spaniards' capital, and the *encomenderos* invested it in a variety of mining, agricultural, commercial and other enterprises, such as further conquests, that permitted the realisation of this tribute for shipment abroad and for further capital accumulation in Mexico itself.

The *encomienda* was soon replaced by a labor system known as the *repartimiento*. This was similar to the *encomienda* but more flexible. Under the *repartimiento* a state official would assign a certain number of man-days of labor to particular Spaniards. Beginning in the late sixteenth century, this system was itself replaced by the *hacienda* system. In this system, Indians were tied to particular Spaniards through a form of debt, and these Indians had to work for their overlords until such debts were repaid. The *hacienda* system was generally organized so that it was virtually impossible for debts to be repaid, and thus the Spaniards were more or less assured of a continuous supply of cheap labor.

In Brazil, under the direction of the Portuguese, a slave plantation system was established using imported Africans as slaves. This system prevailed from the sixteenth until the late nineteenth century. Slave plantation systems prevailed as well in the Caribbean, where they were established by the British, the French, the Dutch, and the Spaniards.

In North America, suitable geographical conditions favored the establishment of a slave society in the Southern colonies of the United States. Slavery using imported Africans as workers prevailed there from the late seventeenth century until the middle of the nineteenth century. Frank believes that this slave society, as well as those in Latin America, functioned as a vital part of the capitalist world-economy. It served in the first half of the nineteenth century, for instance, as a major producer of raw cotton, a product that fed the flourishing textile industries of Britain and the U.S. North. It was therefore an important part of the capitalist periphery.

But what of the U.S. North itself? What prompted it to take off into enormous industrial development beginning around 1830? Frank notes that the original Northern colonies were not highly regarded by the British. Unlike the Southern colonies, they did not have a long growing season and were not deemed to be particularly suitable for large-scale agricultural production. This low assessment of the economic value of the Northern colonies led to what Frank calls their "benign neglect." They were never peripheralized or made an economic dependency of some European country, as were the Southern colonies and much of Latin America. Instead, the U.S. North became a *settler colony,* a region settled by a foreign country but then left more or less alone economically. The U.S. North was in the seventeenth and eighteenth centuries largely a society of small independent farmers and craftsmen, very different indeed from its neighbors in the U.S. South and Latin America.

Frank is suggesting, then, that the U.S. North was not constrained by a foreign power, and thus was free to develop its own resources for itself rather than for the benefit of someone else. But what could have stimulated the enormous development it did experience? Frank argues that it was the North's unique role in world capitalist trade networks, a role no doubt conditioned by its geographical location, that was responsible (Frank, 1979:61):

> The North-eastern colonies came to occupy a position in the expanding world mercantile capitalist system and in the process of capital accumulation which permitted them to share in the latter as a sub-metropolis of Western Europe in the exploitation of the South, the West Indies, and indeed of Africa and indirectly of the mining regions and the Orient. This privileged position—not shared by others in the New World—must be considered as contributing crucially to the economic development of the North-east during colonial times and to its successful political policy of Independence and further development thereafter. This privileged position and role impinged on northern transport, mercantile and financial participation in southern and western export (and import) trade; the North-east's advantageous participation in the West India trade, the slave trade and indeed world trade; north-eastern manufacturing development, largely for export; and in the associated capital accumulation and concentration in northern cities.

In sum, Frank is persuasively suggesting for the Americas what Moulder argued in the case of China and Japan: that underdevelopment is the historical outcome of a situation of economic dependency, whereas development requires (at the very least) economic autonomy.

FROM DEPENDENCY THEORY TO THE WORLD-SYSTEM

Despite its superiority to modernization theory in explaining historical and contemporary patterns of underdevelopment, dependency theory has certain weaknesses that cannot be overlooked. By the late 1970s these weaknesses had begun to be noticed even by many of this approach's most enthusiastic supporters, and today dependency theory is regarded as a flawed, if still highly useful, perspective. Of the objections that have been raised against it, the most important are essentially as follows (Roxborough, 1979; Hoogvelt, 1982; Leys, 1982; Blomstrom and Hettne, 1984):

1. In spite of its severe criticism of modernization theory's failure to place contemporary underdeveloped societies in their historical context, in its own peculiar way dependency theory is also ahistorical. While it gives great attention to the historical relationship of underdeveloped societies to the capitalist core, it tends to ignore the precapitalist history of these societies. This history is very important, however, in conditioning the way in which a particular precapitalist society will be incorporated into the capitalist system and the results of that incorporation (Chase-Dunn, 1989a; Lenski and Nolan, 1984).
2. Dependency theory tends to overgeneralize about contemporary underdeveloped nations. It assumes that their dependent status renders them all essentially alike. Yet there are important differences among these nations with respect to such things as class structures, political systems, and geographical and demographic size, and these differences play a role in shaping a nation's current development level and future developmental prospects. Another way of putting this is to say that dependency theory concentrates too much attention on the external relations between an underdeveloped society and the capitalist core, and not enough attention on its internal characteristics.
3. Dependency theory is too pessimistic in asserting that economic dependency makes economic development impossible. This is contradicted by the experience of a number of countries in recent decades. For example, Brazil underwent substantial economic growth between the mid-1960s and the mid-1970s, and East Asian countries like Taiwan and South Korea have experienced very rapid growth since the 1950s.
4. Dependency theory's main policy recommendation for the underdeveloped countries—breaking out of the capitalist system by socialist revolution—has produced little. The vast majority of the Third World countries that have opted for socialism in recent decades have failed to generate any real developmental impetus; in fact, their record is inferior to that of several countries that have remained capitalist.

These criticisms have considerable force, but it needs to be understood that they are directed more to some dependency theorists than to others. It is essential to distinguish two rather different strands of dependency theory (Bornschier and Chase-Dunn, 1985), what might be called "strong"and "weak " dependency theories.

The strong version of dependency theory is associated primarily with the works of Frank and Amin discussed earlier. It sees economic dependency as always generating the development of underdevelopment, and thus as rendering development impossible (or at least extremely difficult) so long as it continues. The weak version is associated mainly with Fernando Henrique Cardoso (1982; Cardoso and Faletto, 1979) and Peter Evans (1979; cf. Bornschier and Chase-Dunn, 1985). It does not assume that dependency must always lead to the development of underdevelopment. Under some circumstances there can occur what Cardoso has called "associated dependent development," or simply "dependent development." This is a type of economic growth that occurs primarily as the result of extensive investment in manufacturing industries by multinationals. Weak dependency theorists insist that in recent decades a new form of dependency has grown up alongside the old form. In the older, or "classical," dependency, core countries use peripheral countries as sources of investment in raw agricultural and mineral products. But in the new dependency, investment occurs within the industrial sector. And this form of dependency, it is argued, is not incompatible with certain amounts of economic development.

It is obvious that the weak version of dependency theory is much more flexible than the strong version, and thus largely free from the criticisms cited earlier, especially the third. Dependency and development can go together. However, it is vital that this point not be overinterpreted. It seems clear that the kind of development that occurs under the new dependency is quite different from the kind that has occurred within the core capitalist countries. For one thing, it has not gone nearly as far, and for another it has some peculiarities not associated with development in the core. Contemporary Brazil, which both Cardoso and Evans take as the leading exemplar of dependent development, illustrates both of these points. After about the mid-1960s Brazil experienced a spurt in economic growth that occurred simultaneously with extensive multinational industrial investment. This growth was so rapid that many observers began to speak of a "Brazilian miracle" (Skidmore and Smith, 1989). However, by about the middle of the 1970s this growth had slowed greatly, and today it has virtually stopped altogether. Brazil's current per capita GNP is still meager when compared with the per capita GNPs found in the core (see Table 9.1). Moreover, the economic growth that did occur in this period has benefited only a small segment of the population, perhaps less than 20 percent. Income inequality has increased sharply, and there is now a great gap between persons working in the modern industrial and service sector and those still living and working in traditional occupations (Skidmore and Smith, 1989) (Brazil now has one of the most unequal income distributions in the world). To make matters worse, to finance its dependent development Brazil borrowed huge sums of money from core financial institutions, and now it has accumulated a huge foreign debt that is a severe obstacle to further economic growth (cf. World Bank, 1988).

It is but a short step from the theory of dependent development to a full-blown world-system theory of underdevelopment. Wallerstein has claimed that it is the capitalist world-system as a whole that develops, not particular societies. He acknowledges that internal characteristics of societies matter, but they exert their effects only in the context of a society's position within the world-system at a particular time in history. As the world-system evolves, there is increasing polarization between core and periphery, and it is difficult for less-developed nations to improve their status, or at least improve it very much. However, at particular historical junctures opportunities are created for some countries to move up. Wallerstein (1979b) proposes three basic strategies that nations can adopt to accomplish this: "seizing the chance," "development by invitation," and "self-reliance."

During periods of contraction of the world-economy, core countries may be in a weakened economic position. If so, peripheral or semiperipheral countries may be able to use aggressive state action to improve their position. This is the strategy of seizing the chance. Wallerstein suggests that Russia adopted this strategy in the late nineteenth century, and that it was employed by Brazil and Mexico during the 1930s.

Development by invitation, by contrast, occurs during periods of expansion of the world-economy. During these periods, "space" or "room" is created for some countries to move up because there is an increased level of demand for commodities on the world scale. Underdeveloped countries with just the right internal characteristics (especially geopolitical circumstances) may be treated unusually favorably by core countries. As a result they may be able to use the resulting economic advantages to inaugurate a developmental surge. Wallerstein suggests that Scotland followed this developmental strategy in the late eighteenth century. Perhaps the best recent exemplars of the strategy are the East Asian countries of Taiwan and South Korea (see the Special Topic at the end of the chapter).

Some countries, though, may see their best chance for economic development resting on withdrawal from the world-system and adoption of some version of socialism. No doubt the most successful employment of this strategy has been by Russia (the Soviet Union), beginning in 1917.

Despite the differences between world-system theory and classical dependency theory, it is clear that the former is only a version of the latter. Wallerstein stresses what he calls "limited possibilities" for transformation of underdeveloped countries within the world-economy. In point of fact, most countries don't move up, and those that do don't move very far. They move from the periphery into the semiperiphery, or from a lower to a higher semiperipheral position. There is no example of a country's ever having been truly peripheral and moving from that position all the way into the core. Since most nations continue to stagnate rather than move up, and since there is increasing polarization within the system, Wallerstein is not optimistic about the fate of the underdeveloped countries within a capitalist context. For him, the only real solution to the problems of the underdeveloped world is a long-term one: the ultimate worldwide collapse of capitalism and its replacement by a socialist world-government.

THE FUTURE OF THE UNDERDEVELOPED WORLD

According to world-system theory, the gap between the developed and the underdeveloped countries is not decreasing. Wallerstein (1983) takes the strongest stance of all the world-system theorists. He maintains that the gap has been widening ever since the beginnings of capitalism and will continue to widen in the future. Moreover, he is asserting that this widening gap is absolute rather than relative. In other words, it is not merely that the developed countries are increasing the size of their lead over the underdeveloped countries, while the underdeveloped countries stagnate or improve slightly. On the contrary, Wallerstein argues that the absolute condition of the underdeveloped countries has been deteriorating and will continue to do so. This argument is known as the **thesis of absolute immiseration.**

Another world-system theorist, Christopher Chase-Dunn (1989a), has questioned this thesis and maintained that the widening gap is only relative. This is a very complex problem, and it is difficult to say which position is correct. On the side of the **relative immiseration thesis,** we can note that in recent decades underdeveloped countries have experienced declines in their infant mortality rates, increases in longevity, and at least small (in some cases substantial) increases in per capita Gross National Product. However, Wallerstein questions making this kind of easy argument, claiming that, although members of Third World countries "are more likely to survive the first year of life (because of the effect of social hygiene undertaken to protect the privileged), I doubt that the life prospects of the majority of the world's population *as of age one* are greater than previously; I suspect the opposite is true. They unquestionable work harder—more hours per day, per year, per lifetime. And since they do this for less total reward, the rate of exploitation has escalated very sharply" (1983:101).

Regardless of which version of the immiseration thesis is correct, the fact is that the current plight of the Third World remains extremely serious. And in terms of how we view the near to medium-term future of the Third World, it matters little whether its overall condition is deteriorating or improving just slightly. In either case, there is little cause for optimism about major economic transformations.

To make matters worse, there is an additional problem that the Third World nations face that will probably play a major role in shaping their fate in the near future: the problem of population growth. As noted earlier in the chapter, the underdeveloped nations have population growth rates approximately six to seven times as high as those of the developed nations. The reason has nothing to with ignorance on the part of members of the Third World societies about birth control. Rather, Third World peasants (who are by far the largest economic group in underdeveloped countries) have a strong economic desire to keep their birth rate high. Large numbers of children are important to the economic well-being of peasants, since children play important roles as farm laborers (Harris and Ross, 1987; B. White, 1976, 1982).

However, even though having many children is an economically adaptive strategy from the point of view of any given peasant family in the short run, in the long run such a practice may have severe consequences for people in the Third World (cf. B. White, 1976). Rapid population growth is just one more problem that the Third World countries face in their efforts to develop, since such growth helps to undermine whatever economic advances otherwise occur. Some Third World countries, India and Bangladesh being perhaps the best examples, have already suffered profound economic consequences because of overpopulation. Famine has

A family in Tanzania. For economic reasons, family size is generally much larger in the underdeveloped world than in the more developed countries. Although the decision to have many children is rational from the perspective of a family's short-run economic interests, the aggregate demographic consequences of these individual decisions are highly maladaptive for many Third World nations.

been a recurrent problem in some African nations in recent years. And the problem of population growth threatens to get much worse in the years ahead. As Daniel Chirot (1977) has suggested, unless the underdeveloped nations can gain control of their population growth rates, the future for them looks very dismal. Yet it will be difficult for them to begin lowering these rates unless they experience the kinds of economic improvements that will give peasant farmers enough incentive to reduce their family size. The underdeveloped nations therefore seem to be caught in a vicious economic and demographic trap. The likely consequences of this trap are not only disheartening, but are cause for alarm. These include drastic declines in living standards, the emergence of extremely high levels of resentment against the developed nations, and the explosive political violence that would inevitably follow (including the distinct possibility of nuclear attack) (Chirot, 1977).

Although the picture painted here is a pessimistic one, despair or fatalism is by no means called for. Sociologists and other social scientists have learned to take demographic projections with a large grain of salt because they are frequently off the mark. Although the short-term future of the underdeveloped countries looks gloomy, the possibility remains that in the slightly longer term these societies will somehow find the means to control their population growth and be able to avoid economic and political catastrophe. Indeed, some underdeveloped countries, most notably China, currently do show signs of bringing their rate of population increase down to manageable proportions. It is entirely possible that some other underdeveloped countries could do the same (cf. Chirot, 1986:256–261).

SUMMARY

1. Worldwide differences in levels of economic and social development have long been a crucial concern of many social scientists. Underdeveloped nations are those that have the lowest levels of technological and economic development within the capitalist world-economy. They should not be confused with undeveloped societies, which are truly preindustrial and precapitalist. Developed nations are those advanced industrial countries that have attained the highest levels of technological development and economic prosperity within the world-economy.

2. Underdevelopment is perhaps best assessed in terms of a society's level of GNP, but there are numerous other indicators of underdevelopment. These include marked levels of economic inequality, high rates of population growth, poor standards of nutrition and health, and a high percentage of the population still employed in agriculture.

3. The modernization approach to underdevelopment is an older approach still favored by most social scientists, at least those in the developed world. It postulates that underdevelopment occurs because a society has certain internal deficiencies preventing it from transcending economic and social traditionalism. These deficiencies include insufficient capital formation, outdated techniques of business practice, and a value system oriented to the past.

4. Rostow's theory is perhaps the leading example of modernization theory. Rostow postulates that societies pass through a definite series of stages on their way to becoming developed—traditionalism, preconditions for takeoff, economic takeoff, sustained growth, and drive to maturity. Underdeveloped nations have remained stuck in the stage of traditionalism. Reactive nationalism is a major stimulus for a society to advance beyond this stage and attain self-perpetuating economic growth.

5. In general, the modernization theorists believe that intellectuals and business and government leaders in the developed world can help promote development in the Third World by assisting Third World nations to overcome their fundamental deficiencies.

6. In the late 1960s and early 1970s dependency theory began to emerge as an alternative to modernization theory. This theory is a version of the Marxian theory of capitalism applied to a world level. It holds that underdevelopment results from the economic dependency on foreign economies into which some nations have fallen. Frank has suggested that the advanced capitalist countries have dominated and exploited the poorer regions in order to attain their high levels of prosperity. Amin suggests that the domination of one nation by another produces an economic disarticulation that inhibits economic development.

7. Two different versions of dependency theory can be identified. A strong version, associated with Frank and Amin, sees economic dependency as always leading to the development of underdevelopment. In this version, development cannot occur so long as dependency continues, and the only real hope for underdeveloped countries is therefore to withdraw from the capitalist system through socialist revolution. A weaker version of dependency theory holds that economic dependency is the basic root cause of historical patterns of underdevelopment, but that development is possible under certain recent forms of dependency. This version of dependency theory is preferable to the stronger version, but the versions are more similar than different and both are highly preferable to modernization theory. The results of recent empirical research, as well as various historical analyses, confirm this.

8. Wallerstein's world-system theory is very similar to the weaker version of dependency theory. Wallerstein claims that contemporary underdeveloped nations have become what they are as the result of centuries of domination by the capitalist core. Most of these countries are continuing to fall father and farther behind the core, not only relatively but absolutely. However, a few of these countries may be able to improve their position in the world-economy by seizing upon opportunities available at certain historical junctures in the development of capitalism.

9. In light of the conclusions of dependency and world-system theories, it is difficult to be optimistic about the future of the underdeveloped world. Optimism is made even more difficult by the extremely high population growth rates of many of these countries. These rates constitute not only a major obstacle to development, but suggest the possibility of economic catastrophe in the decades ahead. On the other hand, despair is hardly called for since it is difficult to know how valid current demographic projections for the Third World really are.

SPECIAL TOPIC: EAST ASIA AND THEORIES OF UNDERDEVELOPMENT

Since about the mid-1950s a startling degree of economic development has occurred in the East Asian societies of Taiwan, South Korea, Hong Kong, and Singapore. Before 1950 these societies were very poor members of the capitalist periphery, but they are now among the most prosperous societies outside the capitalist core. Taiwan and South Korea have per capita GNPs that approach $3000 per year (see Table 9.1, pp. 188–189), and Hong Kong's and Singapore's levels of per capita economic productivity are more than double that figure. All of these societies have extremely low infant mortality rates for non-core nations, as well as rates of population growth more similar to core than to non-core societies (Table 9.1). Moreover, at least in Taiwan and South

Korea, this development has occurred without producing the extremely sharp income inequalities so characteristic of other rapidly growing less-developed countries. These countries today have income distributions that resemble those of core nations.

Collectively, these four East Asian countries are frequently known as the "Newly Industrializing Countries," or NICs. It has frequently been asserted that the economic development of the NICs is a fatal blow to dependency theory (Barrett and Whyte, 1982; Berger, 1986). Certainly if we are talking about the strong version of dependency theory, it is impossible to deny that assertion (Bienefeld, 1981). However, this East Asian development may not be inconsistent with the weak dependency theory or with world-system theory. Indeed, it would seem that world-system theory is extremely well suited to explain what has been happening in recent decades in the NICs. In order to show that this is so, I shall confine myself to Taiwan and South Korea. Hong Kong and Singapore are really city-states rather than countries, and they have only a tiny agricultural sector. Because of their unique nature, they are not good test cases for any theory of underdevelopment.

Taiwan and South Korea seem to be exceptionally good examples of what Wallerstein has called "development by invitation" (Bienefeld, 1981; Cumings, 1984), and their accomplishments result from a unique combination of five circumstances. Some of these circumstances involve internal characteristics of the societies themselves, while others involve the larger world-economy and their relationship to it (Bienefeld, 1981; Cumings, 1984; Crane, 1982; Koo, 1987; Evans, 1987).

First, it is true that both Taiwan and South Korea have a history of economic dependency, but the dependency they experienced has been unique. Around the turn of the twentieth century Taiwan (then known as Formosa) and Korea (which, of course, had not yet been divided into South Korea and North Korea) became colonies of Japan. But Japan was no ordinary colonizer, for it engaged in practices not found among European colonizers. The Japanese built up in these colonies a large infrastructure of transportation and communication, and even established heavy industries, especially in steel, chemicals, and hydroelectric power. Thus, even though Taiwan and Korea became dependent, they nonetheless acquired certain technological and economic resources generally absent in other dependent countries. These resources helped establish a foundation for developmental efforts once Japanese colonialism ended.

Second, both Taiwan and South Korea undertook major land reforms after World War II. These reforms produced a much more egalitarian distribution of land. It is well known that land-reform efforts have failed, or not really even been attempted, in most other less-developed countries. In most of these countries land is enormously concentrated in the hands of a handful of rich landowners, and this uneven distribution is a major obstacle to development. But land reform in Taiwan and South Korea led to major increases in agricultural output, and industrialization efforts could therefore begin to succeed.

However, as important as these conditions were, they could never have led to significant economic development if Taiwan and South Korea had not been favored by two features of the external environment. First, there was the unique geopolitical situation these countries were in. During the 1950s the United States became the world's leading economic power, and it began to perceive a severe threat to its economic position from the Soviet Union and China, the latter having just had a revolution (in 1949) and become part of the socialist world. There was great fear that both Taiwan and

Seoul, South Korea. This nation has undergone remarkable economic development since the 1950s. What does this economic success tell us about theories of development and underdevelopment?

South Korea would become part of this world, and so the United States began to pump huge amounts of money, in the form of both aid and loans, into both countries. Although the United States has given aid and loans to many other countries, the amounts going into Taiwan and South Korea were unparalleled. There is no doubt that this economic assistance played a crucial role in helping launch these countries' developmental efforts.

All of this was happening during a period in which the world-economy was undergoing major expansion. Thus, the increase in world economic demand made "room" or "space" available for some countries to improve their position. Moreover, the United States directly encouraged the upward mobility of Taiwan and South Korea by opening their own domestic markets to the products of these countries. This occurred primarily after 1960. In the 1950s the industrialization of Taiwan and South Korea was oriented mainly to producing for their domestic markets, but after 1960 it shifted toward an emphasis on selling competitively in the world market. This kind of industrialization, known generally as *export-led industrialization,* is a common developmental strategy of less-developed countries. Whether it works or not is another question. That it has worked so well for these two countries depended significantly on the protected markets that the United States carved out for them in its own territory.

Finally, it cannot be overlooked that the biggest single investor and the biggest director of economic growth in both countries was the state. This, too, was the legacy of Japanese colonialism. Both Taiwan and South Korea had formulated their state apparatuses on the Japanese model and had developed the kind of highly efficient state that could, in the context of the other four conditions, lead them into significant economic development. Specifically, the state in these two countries played a major role in keeping the wages of workers down, something that is essential for export-led industrialization because it makes products cheaper and thus more competitive on the world market. It also built up military-style discipline in the factories, thus contributing to high productivity.

Because of the success of Taiwan and South Korea, the question has naturally arisen as to whether they constitute models for economic development that other countries could imitate. Some social scientists who are especially enthusiastic about East Asian development believe that they do (cf. Berger, 1986). Yet this is a very dubious notion. As Bruce Cumings has said, "The developmental 'successes' of Taiwan and Korea are historically and regionally specific, and therefore provide no readily adaptable models for other developing countries interested in emulation" (1984:38). Indeed, it is not even clear the extent to which Taiwan and South Korea are genuine successes and whether they can sustain their development in the decades ahead. South Korea has, in fact, encountered a number of serious economic problems. Its economic growth has slowed considerably since 1980, and it has now accumulated a huge foreign debt. It has moved from the periphery into the lower reaches of the semiperiphery, but there are signs that it may not be able to go much further. Taiwan continues on a smoother course, but historical precedent suggests great caution in expecting too much of it (Cumings, 1984).

In summary, some important things have been happening in East Asia since the end of the Second World War, but these events do not suggest a fundamental flaw in radical theories of underdevelopment, especially world-system theory. East Asian development is not only compatible with world-system theory, but can only be properly understood in terms of it.

FOR FURTHER READING

Amin, Samir. *Accumulation on a World Scale*. New York: Monthly Review Press, 1974. A detailed statement of Amin's version of dependency theory.

Bornshier, Volker, and Christopher Chase-Dunn. *Transnational Corporations and Underdevelopment*. New York: Praeger, 1985. An excellent empirical exploration of the leading assumptions of dependency and world-system theories of underdevelopment.

Chirot, Daniel. *Social Change in the Modern Era*. Orlando: Harcourt Brace Jovanovich, 1986. An exploration of the development and contemporary character of the capitalist world-economy that takes up many aspects of the social, economic, and political situation of Third World nations. Focuses closely on the relationship between the Third World countries and the capitalist core. (The reader is reminded that the 1977 version of this book is still worth consulting.)

Evans, Peter B. *Dependent Development: The Alliance of Multinational, State, and Local Capital in*

Brazil. Princeton: Princeton University Press, 1979. An excellent case study of dependent development in Brazil. Focuses on the shaping of Brazilian economic development by three groups: foreign capitalists, local capitalists, and the Brazilian state.

Frank, Andre Gunder. *Dependent Accumulation and Underdevelopment.* New York: Monthly Review Press, 1979. A major statement of dependency theory by one of its chief formulators.

Fröbel, Folker, Jürgen Heinrichs, and Otto Kreye. *The New International Division of Labour.* Cambridge: Cambridge University Press, 1980. Postulates that a "new international division of labor" is being created through the relocation by core capitalists of many segments of their operations in the capitalist periphery. Contains detailed case studies of this phenomenon.

Hoogvelt, Ankie M. M. *The Third World in Global Development.* London: Macmillan, 1982. One of the better introductions to current issues and theoretical debates in the study of underdevelopment.

Hoselitz, Bert F. *Sociological Aspects of Economic Growth.* New York: Free Press, 1960. Another famous example of modernization theory. This one attempts to explain development and underdevelopment by drawing explicitly on Parsonian functionalist evolutionary theory, particularly Parsons's concept of the "pattern variables."

Moulder, Frances V. *Japan, China and the Modern World Economy.* New York: Cambridge University Press, 1977. An impressive attempt to explain the historical divergence of China and Japan as the result of their relationship to the capitalist world-economy.

Roxborough, Ian. *Theories of Underdevelopment.* London: Macmillan, 1979. Another good introduction to underdevelopment theories.

Wolf, Eric. *Europe and the People Without History.* Berkeley: University of California Press, 1982. Written from a world-system perspective, this book contains much useful information regarding the historical impact of expanding European capitalism upon many precapitalist societies.

CHAPTER 10

Social Stratification in Industrial Societies

This chapter continues the discussion of social stratification begun in Chapter 6. Its focus is a close comparative analysis of the stratification systems of the major industrial societies, both capitalist and state socialist. An effort is made to ascertain to what extent the contemporary state socialist societies have fulfilled Marx's prediction about a "classless society" resulting from the collectivization of the means of production. In addition, the major sociological theories of stratification within contemporary capitalist societies—particularly those of Karl Marx and Max Weber—are explored and assessed.

THE TRANSITION TO INDUSTRIAL SOCIETY: A REDUCTION OF STRATIFICATION?

As Chapter 6 showed, there is a striking trend in the evolution of forms of stratified life throughout human history. The movement of societies from the hunting and gathering to the agrarian stage is closely associated with the development of increasingly complex and extreme forms of stratification. However, as Lenski (1966) argues, with the passage from agrarian to industrial societies, a reversal of this trend seems to have taken place. Lenski believes that basic inequalities in power and privilege are actually less severe in modern industrial societies than they were in agrarian societies of the past.

Lenski attempts to support his argument by contending that the share of total wealth claimed by the dominant class is considerably less in industrial than in agrarian societies. He estimates that the dominant class of agrarian societies typically claimed about 50 percent of the total social wealth, but that the dominant classes of industrial societies have probably claimed no more than half this amount, and oftentimes considerably less. He therefore believes that industrial societies are characterized by a reduction of the extremes of economic inequality and a greater diffusion of economic resources throughout the population.

Lenski has proposed a number of factors to explain this development, but one of these he sees as especially important: the rise and spread of democratic political ideologies. With the rise of democratic ideologies, Lenski argues, the possibility arose for the many to combine politically against the few. This has had dramatic consequences for the general reduction of economic inequalities.

Lenski's argument that the economic elite in industrial societies claims a smaller share of the total social wealth than the elites of agrarian societies seems well taken, and the available evidence does appear to support his overall point. Yet several major problems with his line of theorizing come to mind. One of these is that the main thrust of his analysis of industrial stratification is phrased in terms of a broad contrast with the past. As such, it tends to obscure the extent to which major economic inequalities continue to prevail within industrial societies. The inequalities of contemporary industrial societies seem to be sharp enough and significant enough to permit analysis on their own terms, not just in terms of a general comparison with earlier agrarian societies (Rossides, 1976).

Another problem involves Lenski's explanation of the greater diffusion of economic resources throughout industrial populations. The causal factor he relies on most heavily, that of the rise of democratic ideologies, is inadequate. In fact, Lenski's own evidence strongly refutes his argument. As he notes, economic inequalities appear to be less severe in the Soviet Union than in the United States. Since the former is governed by a monolithic totalitarian state and the latter by a liberal democracy, it is extremely difficult to support the view that democratic ideology is *the* primary factor responsible for a reduction in economic inequalities. Clearly other factors must be at work. Moreover, this difference between the Soviet Union and the United States suggests that the general category of "industrial society" is too broad for a proper understanding of the evolution of social stratification. That is, one must distinguish between the major economic forms of industrial society in order to understand contemporary stratification systems.

Finally, in concentrating on the difference between agrarian and industrial societies, Lenski ignores the entire world-system context in which industrial societies arose. The transition to industrial society was first and foremost a transition to a capitalist world-economy, and industrialization occurred earliest and most extensively in the richest and most economically advanced capitalist societies. Furthermore, as the last chapter has shown, the economic and industrial development of some societies has meant the corresponding underdevelopment of others, and these underdeveloped societies have exhibited extreme social and economic inequalities. In fact, contemporary underdeveloped nations may well display a level of economic inequality and human misery and suffering on a grander scale than exhibited by most agrarian societies of the past (cf. Wallerstein, 1984a). Thus, while industrial societies may be less extensively stratified than agrarian societies of the past, the extent of economic inequality *at a world level* seems actually to have *increased* with the rise of capitalism and industrialism (cf. Bornschier and Chase-Dunn, 1985). This fact must be a central one in any assessment of the nature and meaning of broad evolutionary trends in social stratification.

SOCIAL STRATIFICATION IN INDUSTRIAL CAPITALIST SOCIETIES

The Distribution of Income and Wealth: The United States and Britain

Data collected under the auspices of the U.S. government (U.S. Bureau of the Census, 1984) show that, for 1982, the highest-paid 5 percent of Americans received 16.0 percent of the total national income (Table 10.1). When the data are divided into income quintiles (fifths) of the population, they show the following: The top income quintile received 42.7 percent of the total national income; the next quintile received 24.3 percent; the middle quintile received 17.1 percent; the next-to-lowest quintile received 11.2 percent; and the bottom quintile received a mere 4.7 percent of the total.

These data demonstrate a highly unequal

Table 10.1 INCOME DISTRIBUTION IN THE UNITED STATES, 1947–1982

	Income at selected positions (dollars)[a]					Percentage distribution of aggregate income					
Year	Lowest	Second	Middle	Fourth	Top 5%	Lowest fifth	Second fifth	Middle fifth	Fourth fifth	Highest fifth	Top 5%
1982	11,200	19,354	27,750	39,992	64,000	4.7	11.2	17.1	24.3	42.7	16.0
1977	7,903	13,273	18,800	26,000	40,493	5.2	11.6	17.5	24.2	41.5	15.7
1972	5,612	9,300	12,855	17,760	27,836	5.4	11.9	17.5	23.9	41.4	15.9
1967	4,097	6,700	9,000	12,270	19,025	5.5	12.4	17.9	23.9	40.4	15.2
1962	3,000	5,000	6,800	9,500	14,900	5.0	12.1	17.6	24.0	41.3	15.7
1957	2,488	4,234	5,594	7,505	11,494	5.1	12.7	18.1	23.8	40.4	15.6
1952	2,053	3,321	4,493	6,077	9,455	4.9	12.3	17.4	23.4	41.9	17.4
1947	1,584	2,556	3,466	4,918	8,072	5.0	11.9	17.0	23.1	43.0	17.5

[a]Upper limit of each fifth.

Source: U.S. Bureau of the Census, *Current Population Reports, Series P-60, No. 142. Money Income of Households, Families and Persons in the United States: 1982.* Washington, D.C.: U.S. Government Printing Office, 1984, Table 17. The figures are based on all families and unrelated individuals. Dollar figures are given in current dollars.

distribution of income in American society. They show that the most prosperous 5 percent of the population received nearly four times the income of the least prosperous 20 percent. Looked at another way, they show that the top 20 percent received a greater total income than the bottom 60 percent combined. In addition, the figures reveal virtually no change at all in the income distribution over the past 35 years.

Such data, however, do not fully reveal the actual extent of income disparities. A more adequate picture of overall income distribution is obtained when income deciles (tenths), rather than quintiles, are used in the analysis. Gabriel Kolko (1962) has calculated the distribution of income in the United States from 1910 to 1959 using income deciles. The data he presents reveal a radically unequal distribution of income that has not changed in any major way during this entire period. For example, in 1910 the top income decile received 33.9 percent of the total income, while the bottom decile received only 3.4 percent of the total. By 1959 the income share going to the top tenth had declined slightly, to 28.9 percent, but so had the share going to the bottom tenth, to 1.1 percent. The bottom 50 percent of the population received only 27 percent of the national personal income in 1910, and by 1959 the share of this poorer half had even declined slightly, to 23 percent. Thus, for both 1910 and 1959 the top 10 percent of the population received a greater total income than the bottom 50 percent. Throughout the entire period the only income groups to experience significant increases in income shares were the second- and third-richest income deciles, which experienced modest increases. These groups, however, were hardly among those in serious need of a greater share of the national income (Kolko, 1962).

These data support two major conclusions: There are vast inequalities in the distribution of income in the United States, and this pattern of unequal distribution has shown no significant trend toward greater equalization over a 50-year period. While there have been major increases in the standard of living for a large part of the American population during the twentieth century, such increases should not be confused, as they often are, with any trend toward income equalization.

It is likely, however, that even these figures understate the real extent of income inequality in American society, for there are forms of income that go unreflected in the figures. Many persons receive considerable amounts of "income in kind" rather than in direct cash payments, and such income is quite disproportionately concentrated among the already wealthy. Income in kind is especially prominent among the top income tenth, and especially among the top 5 percent (Kolko, 1962). It takes the form of expense accounts and many other types of executive benefits, and such benefits have long been an acknowledged form of

Despite their affluence, industrial capitalist societies are still plagued with substantial segments of their populations living in poverty.

the remuneration of many corporate executives (Kolko, 1962). Large-scale and often unlimited expense accounts are now commonly extended to persons employed in or near the upper reaches of the corporate world. The top corporate elite also commonly receive such material benefits as a company car, a gas credit card, country club memberships, and even such luxuries as the use of yachts and private planes and company-paid jaunts to private retreats and exotic watering places (Kolko, 1962). While all these benefits do not count as forms of reportable personal income, they constitute just as real forms of material privilege nonetheless.

The existing income distribution figures also fail to reflect income that goes unreported and dividend income from stock ownership that remains undisbursed to stock owners. Kolko believes that this unreported income, mainly in the form of dividends, interest, and so on, is largely confined to persons in the upper-income brackets. Not reporting such income is, of course, illegal, but it is apparently a widespread practice nevertheless. Were such income to be included in the income distribution figures, the pattern of income inequality would be even more extreme than it already is. In addition to such practices, there are legal ways in which actual income can go unreported. As Kolko notes, corporations often vote to retain dividend earnings on stock so that their wealthy stock-owning directors will not be personally liable to pay taxes on the dividend income. The upshot of this practice is that "the corporations represent vast income reserves for the economic elite" (Kolko, 1962:23).

It is widely believed that taxation, through the allegedly "progressive" income tax, has served to reduce income inequalities and bring about a redistribution of income from wealthier to poorer individuals. This belief, however, is largely unjustified. Available studies show that taxation produces no notable equalization of income (Rossides, 1976). Actual rates of taxation of the American public indicate a huge gap between theory and practice in the tax structure. While the federal income tax is, in principle, progressive, the rich have built so many loopholes and safeguards into the tax laws that they are able to avoid any major redistribution of their huge incomes. Indeed, the rich have become so skilled at tax avoidance that they have placed the actual burden of taxation onto the shoulders of low- and middle-income groups (Kolko, 1962).

The distribution of total wealth (i.e., total assets minus liabilities) in the United States reveals much greater extremes than the distribution of income. Indeed, wealth is enormously concentrated at the top. Data collected by the federal government (Office of Management and the Budget, 1973) show the following pattern of distribution for 1962: The wealthiest quintile of the population owned 76 percent of the total wealth; the next quintile owned 15.5 percent; the middle quintile owned 6.2 percent; the next-to-poorest quintile possessed but 2.1 percent; and the poorest fifth could claim only 0.2 percent. Such figures reveal an enormous concentration of property, demonstrating that the wealthiest 20 percent of the population possesses more than three times the total wealth available to the remaining 80 percent.

Additional data on the concentration of wealth show essentially the same pattern. In 1972 the top 1 percent of the population held 56.5 percent of the total corporate stock, 60 percent of all bonds, and 89.9 percent of all trusts (U.S. Bureau of the Census, 1982). Closer scrutiny reveals that most of these assets are actually concentrated within the top 0.5 percent of the population. For the same year the top 0.5 percent owned 49.3 percent of the corporate stock, 52.2 percent of the bonds, and 80.8 percent of the trusts (U.S. Bureau of the Census, 1982).

Britain displays strikingly similar inequalities in the distribution of income and wealth. Estimates show that in 1979 the top income tenth in the United Kingdom commanded 26.1

percent of the total income, while the bottom 30 percent received only 10.4 percent (Atkinson, 1983:63). This pattern has changed little since 1954, when the top income tenth received 30.1 percent of the income and the bottom 30 percent received 10.3 percent (Atkinson, 1983:63). These are pretax figures, but calculations show that, for the United Kingdom just as for the United States, taxation has affected the income distribution only in the very slightest way (Atkinson, 1983:63).

Regarding the distribution of wealth, Westergaard and Resler (1975) show that, in 1954, the richest 5 percent of the population owned 48 percent of all cash and bank deposits, 71 percent of all government and municipal securities, and 96 percent of corporate stock. More recent data for all wealth categories show that the richest 5 percent possessed 45 percent of the wealth in 1979 (Atkinson, 1983:161). Although the distribution of wealth is somewhat less unequal now than it was 40 years ago (Atkinson, 1983:168), the concentration of wealth is still enormous. Britain remains, like the United States and all modern capitalist societies, a society permeated by deep economic inequalities (Westergaard and Resler, 1975).

The Class Structure of Industrial Capitalist Societies

There is currently no broad consensus among sociologists about how to characterize the class structure of contemporary capitalism or, for that matter, about how to define the concept of **class** itself. Instead, two distinct approaches to the definition of class and the identification of the major classes within contemporary capitalism exist: the conventional approach and the Marxian approach. The *conventional approach* designates occupation as the principal criterion for distinguishing classes from each other. This approach conceives of classes as broad groupings of persons who share similar levels of privilege and prestige on the basis of their roles within the occupational structure. The *Marxian approach* identifies ownership or nonownership of the crucial forces of production (in this case, capital) as the distinguishing feature of a social class. It thus conceives of classes as social groups organized around forms of property ownership. However, the Marxian approach is not a singular one, for Marxists disagree with each other in important ways about the class structure of contemporary capitalism.

The Conventional Approach A good illustration of the conventional approach is found in Daniel Rossides's (1990) analysis of the class structure of contemporary American society. Rossides identifies five major social classes in the contemporary United States: the upper

Vincent Astor walking his dog in Marblehead, Massachusetts, during the yachting season. To what social class did Astor belong?

class, the upper-middle class, the lower-middle class, the working class, and the lower class.

The upper class, no more than about one or two percent of the population, consists of those families possessing great wealth and power, much of which is derived from inheritance. The members of this class occupy the key positions in corporations, banks, insurance companies, and so on. They enjoy very high prestige and are often strongly oriented toward the consumption of elite symbolic culture (e.g., fine art, music). In short, this class is an extraordinarily privileged, powerful, and prestigious segment of the American social structure.

The upper-middle class is composed primarily of successful business managers, members of the learned professions (e.g., law, medicine, architecture), and well-placed civil and military officials. It includes approximately 10 percent of the population. Its members generally earn high incomes and accumulate substantial wealth through savings and investment, and they typically enjoy high social prestige. The lower-middle class, consisting of approximately 30 percent of the population, includes mainly small businessmen, lower-level professionals (e.g., public school teachers, social workers, nurses), and sales and clerical workers. Most persons in this class receive moderate incomes and have but small amounts of savings and other personal wealth. Only fairly modest levels of prestige are accorded the members of this class.

The working class in American society comprises roughly 40 percent of the population. The members of this class are employed as skilled, semiskilled, or unskilled manual and service workers. The class as a whole is subject to fairly high rates of unemployment, and its members frequently suffer under the burdens of no savings or investments and low social prestige. The incomes received by persons in this class are relatively low, on average, when compared to the incomes received by members of higher classes.

The lower class, roughly 20 percent of the American population, consists of those persons who may be regarded as living under conditions of poverty. Included in this class are "the chronically unemployed, underemployed, and underpaid, abandoned mothers, and the poor who are sick, disabled, or old" (Rossides, 1976:28). The members of this class suffer from greater or lesser degrees of acute economic distress, and have extremely low social prestige. Indeed, they are often regarded as lazy and worthless persons who constitute drains on society's resources.

Marxian sociologists have generally been quite critical of this conventional approach to the problem of class. As Erik Olin Wright and his associates have written (Wright, Hachen, Costello, and Sprague, 1982:718–719):

> Most sociological discussions of class either explicitly or implicitly view classes as essentially aggregations of occupational categories. Even where they disagree on the conceptual content of the concept of class, they agree that operationally classes can be identified as groups of occupations.
>
> Marxists generally reject this conceptual conflation of class and occupation and insist that these two concepts designate qualitatively distinct dimensions of the social organization of work. Occupation broadly designates the technical content of jobs; class designates the social relations of domination and appropriation within which those technical activities are performed. . . . A carpenter, for example, could easily be a worker, a semiautonomous employee, a manager or a petty bourgeois artisan. In each of these cases the technical content of the job remains largely the same (transforming lumber into buildings or whatever), but the social relational content changes.

How, then, do contemporary Marxists conceptualize class and arrange the class structure of modern capitalism?

A Marxian Approach Karl Marx defined social classes as groups organized around property relations. He identified two major classes in the early industrial capitalist society of his time: the bourgeoisie, or capitalists, the owners of capital; and the proletariat, or workers, those who were propertyless and thus had to sell their labor power to the capitalists in order to make a living. Marx recognized the existence of other minor social classes, but he saw the nature of capitalist society as revolving mainly around the relationship between capitalists and workers.

Capitalism has changed a great deal since Marx's day. The major change most relevant to our discussion here is the rapid growth of numerous classes located somewhere between the traditional bourgeoisie and the traditional proletariat, classes that are hard to identify and categorize unambiguously. It has been extremely difficult for modern Marxists to identify these classes within an orthodox Marxian framework that claims that classes are organized purely around modes of property ownership. Therefore, most modern Marxists have modified and updated the Marxian conception of class. They have generally done so by arguing that contemporary classes rest not only on forms of property ownership, but also on modes of domination and control—that is, ways in which some persons direct the activities of others within the work process (Parkin, 1979).

Members of the capitalist working class: coal miners in Kentucky.

One of the most impressive efforts to develop a Marxist conception of classes under contemporary capitalism is that of Erik Wright (1979; Wright et al., 1982). Wright stresses that classes in modern capitalism cannot be thought of simply as different levels or gradations of privilege and prestige, as the conventional approach tends to assume; rather, they must be conceptualized as groups whose members occupy positions within the social relations of economic production. These relations involve differential property ownership and differential levels of domination and control. Wright thus stresses that social classes are *relational*, rather than *gradational*, categories.

In order to capture the complexity of the contemporary capitalist class structure, Wright distinguishes between what he calls basic class locations and contradictory class locations. **Basic class locations** are positions in the social organization of production that are relatively unambiguous with regard to the nature of property ownership and domination and control. **Contradictory class locations** are positions within the productive process that are characterized by some of the elements of two different basic class locations. Contradictory class locations are therefore not consistent with regard to property and domination. For this reason it is more difficult to categorize social positions not belonging to basic class locations.

A diagrammatic representation of Wright's image of the contemporary capitalist class structure is given in Figure 10.1. Within his category of basic class locations, Wright identifies three basic social classes: the bourgeoisie, the proletariat, and the petty bourgeoisie. The *bourgeoisie* consists of the major owners of capital, that is, the leading members of corporations, banks, insurance companies, and so on. The economic basis of this class is property ownership pure and simple. The members of this class derive their income and wealth, in the classical Marxian formulation, from the exploitation of the working class: from the extraction of surplus labor and surplus value from workers. This class probably constitutes less than one or two percent of the population. Its members have ultimate power over all other positions within the productive apparatus of modern capitalism. The *proletariat* consists of workers in the classical Marxian sense. In Wright's formulation, it consists of those propertyless persons who sell their labor power to capitalists. Moreover, workers are at the bottom of the ladder in terms of domination and control within the workplace. They give orders to no one, but their own work is closely directed and supervised by others. Wright estimates that the proletariat consists of approximately 41 to 54 percent of the population of capitalist societies.

Capitalists and workers occupy the basic class locations within the capitalist mode of production. This mode is characterized by the extraction of surplus value from the labor of workers and the continuous accumulation of capital over time. As Wright notes, however, not all economic positions within modern capitalist society are within the pure capitalist mode of production. Some are in the *simple commodity mode of production*, a minor mode

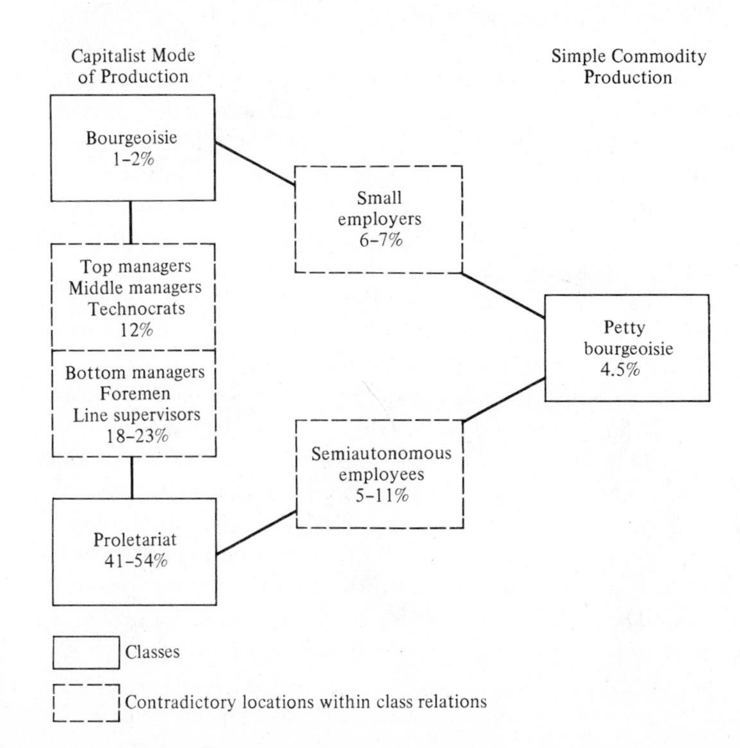

Figure 10.1 Wright's model of the contemporary capitalist class structure. (*Source:* Erik Olin Wright, *Class, Crisis and the State*. London: New Left Books, 1978, p. 63.)

that exists alongside the pure capitalist mode. In the simple commodity mode of production, profits do not result from extracting surplus value—from exploitation of labor—but from the individual producer's own efforts. Furthermore, these profits are usually so small that little if any accumulation can result. There is one basic social class within this simple commodity mode, the *petty bourgeoisie*. It constitutes less than five percent of the population in Wright's estimate. Members of this class are small businessmen and craftsmen who employ no workers, exploit no labor power, and dominate no one within an authority hierarchy. The income of this class's members comes from small-scale property ownership. This class is, in a sense, a holdover from an earlier phase of capitalism, and it is destined to disappear with the further evolution of the capitalist system.

Within the category of contradictory class locations Wright also identifies three classes: managers and supervisors, small employers, and semiautonomous employees. *Managers and supervisors* occupy a contradictory class location between the bourgeoisie and the proletariat. Persons in these positions own no property and must therefore sell their labor power and earn their livings through salaries or wages. This is a characteristic they share in common with the proletariat. Yet, although they must sell their labor power, they occupy a position within the hierarchy of production in which they dominate or control others, particularly the proletariat. Top and middle managers are closer to the bourgeoisie. They have considerable authority to organize production and the very top managers earn at least a portion of their incomes by sharing in the profits of the company. Lower-level managers, foremen, and other supervisors are, on the other hand, closer to the proletariat. In fact, Wright believes that some are so close that they might just as well be placed within it. These persons directly supervise the routine work of others but are themselves extensively controlled by top and middle managers. Wright estimates that managers and supervisors taken together make up about 30 percent of the population.

Small employers, about 6 or 7 percent of the population, occupy a contradictory position between the bourgeoisie and the petty bourgeoisie and thus share characteristics of both. Unlike the petty bourgeoisie, they employ at least one worker, and therefore at least part of their income is derived from the exploitation of labor power. Unlike the bourgeoisie proper, however, they exist on a relatively small scale and have much less opportunity to accumulate capital.

Semiautonomous employees are professional workers within bureaucratic organizations. They occupy a contradictory class location between the petty bourgeoisie and the proletariat. Probably no more than 10 percent of the population, these workers must sell their labor power to others and earn their incomes through salaries. But unlike other workers, they have considerable freedom in the direction of their work. Although subject to the authority of managers, their high level of specialized knowledge dictates that they be allowed much personal decision making in carrying out assignments. Lawyers in corporations, physicians in research organizations, professors in universities, and engineers in organizational settings are prime examples of semiautonomous employees.

Although Wright's scheme is not always easy to apply to concrete persons and positions within modern capitalism, in some respects it is an improvement on the conventional approach, which essentially equates class with occupation. In fact, Wright has compared his scheme with the conventional class-as-occupation approach in terms of their respective abilities to predict income inequality, and empirically his scheme has proved the better predictor (Wright, 1979). This is one reason for preferring it to the conventional approach.*

*In a more recent work, Wright (1985) has made some substantial modifications in his conceptualization of class

Social Mobility Within Modern Capitalism

A belief widespread among the members of modern capitalist societies is that one's class position need not be fixed at birth. It is thought that all individuals have good opportunities for moving up to a higher class—that is, for upward **social mobility.** This idea has taken a particularly strong hold in the United States, where it tends to dominate thinking about the nature of stratification. Most Americans appear to believe that the American class system is highly "open," permitting a high degree of upward movement for persons who have the necessary motivation to get ahead. To what extent is this belief in the opportunity structure of modern capitalism justified?

---

and in his class scheme. He has eliminated the category of semiautonomous employees and subdivided the managerial/supervisory class into numerous subclasses, largely according to the extent of possession of educational credentials. These changes stem from a questioning of the use of domination or authority relations as a dimension of class relations. Wright has attempted to move toward a reconceptualization of class that makes the concept of exploitation central. Since exploitation is a central Marxian notion in a way that domination is not, as a Marxist he undoubtedly feels that this is preferable. However, the results leave much to be desired. Wright ends up using the concept of exploitation in non-Marxist ways and stretches it beyond the breaking point. Moreover, his new class scheme contains 12 classes, making it rather unwieldy, and many of these classes are ill-defined. Thus one can raise serious questions about whether Wright's latest ideas are an intellectual advance. Indeed, Wright himself recognizes that his new formulations present a number of new problems.

Obviously the difficulties Wright is having suggest serious obstacles in the path of any effort to produce a coherent Marxian analysis of class relevant to the late twentieth century. To make a Marxian scheme applicable at all, ideas from different intellectual traditions—especially the Weberian tradition—have to be imported into it (Parkin, 1979). There is nothing wrong with that, except when these ideas are twisted out of shape in order to call them Marxian. Perhaps the most sensible thing to do is simply to confront them on their own terms, which is what I try to do later in the chapter.

For these reasons, and because Wright's new analysis is much too technical and abstract to be presented in an introductory textbook, I have retained his original position as probably the best illustration of a Marxian approach to class.

The best-known study of social mobility in American society is that of sociologists Peter Blau and O. D. Duncan (1967). Drawing upon a sample of more than 20,000 American men between the ages of 20 and 64 collected in 1962, Blau and Duncan came to the following general conclusions about mobility in the United States (summarized in Vanfossen, 1979): (1) Mobility has been a fairly widespread characteristic of American society. (2) Mobility is far more common over short, rather than long, distances. (3) Upward mobility is more common than downward mobility. (4) The expansion and contraction of certain occupational groupings accounts for some of the observed mobility. (5) Proprietorship represents a significant source of rigidity in the occupational structure; that is, independent professionals, proprietors, and farmers display the greatest occupational inheritance and self-recruitment. (6) The education received by a son is of considerable significance in determining his adult occupational position. And (7) rates of social mobility have increased very little, if at all, during the past 50 years.

While one of Blau and Duncan's major conclusions is that mobility is widespread in American society, this judgment must be carefully assessed in the context of their other findings and the nature of their data. As Vanfossen (1979) points out, the larger the number of occupational categories that are used in a study, the larger will be the measured rate of social mobility. Blau and Duncan used 17 occupational categories, a very large number and far more than usually employed. It is not surprising, then, that they found considerable movement within the occupational structure. In light of this, one of their other major conclusions must be taken very seriously: that most upward mobility is of short distance. In other words, while many men are upwardly mobile during their lifetimes, most do not move very far. In fact, a great deal of observed mobility consists of movement from lower to upper blue-collar (manual) positions, from upper blue-collar to

Clerical workers in a large modern organization. In the conventional approach to social class, to what class do these workers belong? To what class would they be assigned in the Marxian view?

lower white-collar (nonmanual) positions, or from lower white-collar to upper white-collar jobs. There is very little movement of persons from near the bottom to near the top of the class structure, and movement from the lower class into the upper-class elite is a rare phenomenon indeed. It therefore seems just as important to emphasize the rigidity, as opposed to the flexibility, inherent in the American class structure, for the direct familial inheritance of class position is a fundamental feature of life in all major capitalist societies.

A considerable amount of mobility is due to factors having nothing at all to do with an ideology of equal opportunity. As Blau and Duncan themselves note, the expansion and contraction of occupational groupings due to technological change is a significant factor promoting mobility. Throughout the twentieth century all major industrial societies have undergone major technological changes that have greatly expanded the number of white-collar jobs available. Many of these jobs could be filled only by recruiting persons from lower-status backgrounds. In addition, differential class fertility rates force a certain amount of upward mobility. Persons in higher-class positions tend to have fewer children than those in lower-class positions. This means that not all higher-class positions can be filled by children of persons from the same class. Therefore, some recruitment from subordinate classes is always necessary.

What conclusions are warranted regarding social mobility in the United States? There is a substantial amount of upward movement of individuals within the class structure; however, this fact by itself means very little, for most movement is over short distances. Most persons, therefore, end up in adulthood at or near where their parents were, and movement from the very bottom stratum to the very top is practically nonexistent. Furthermore, it is incorrect to ascribe all the mobility that does occur to America's alleged ideological commitment to equality of opportunity. While some persons do indeed improve their positions by exceptional motivation, hard work, or even luck, much mobility is an inherent feature of the structure of modern capitalism: of the constant technological and occupational change produced by that system. Above all, it is important not to exaggerate the extent of mobility in American society and thereby underemphasize the heavy inheritance of class position that does take place.

What has been said above regarding the United States also holds for the most part for industrial capitalist societies in general. Most current studies show that, while they do display some differences, industrial capitalist societies are strikingly alike in their mobility patterns and overall levels of fluidity. This is true even when the societies in question have differed appreciably in the extent to which they have tried to promote high levels of mobility, and it is also a pattern that has held over a considerable period of time (Kerckhoff, Campbell, and Winfield-Laird, 1985; Erikson, Goldthorpe, and Portocarero, 1982; Goldthorpe, 1980; Halsey, Heath, and Ridge, 1980).

PATTERNS OF STRATIFIED SOCIAL LIFE IN STATE SOCIALIST SOCIETIES

We now turn our attention to the question of the extent to which class distinctions are to be found in the contemporary state socialist societies.

Basic Class Structure and Inequalities of Privilege

Parkin (1971) has provided a useful historical overview of the changing nature of social stratification in the Soviet Union. As he notes, in the period immediately following the rise of the Communist party to power, there was a marked tendency toward the establishment of economic equality. Fundamental reforms were put into effect in order to equalize the distribution of incomes, and a drastic reduction of the wage differential between blue-collar and white-collar workers was achieved. (Similar income equalization policies were pursued as well after World War II in the other major Eastern European Communist nations.) In addition to these measures, established privilege was attacked via major educational reforms. These reforms were designed to bring large numbers of youth from subordinate classes into higher education.

Beginning in the early 1930s, however, this major egalitarian push was halted and even partially reversed through new policies established by Stalin. Stalin launched a major attack on all equalization programs, declaring himself steadfastly against *uravnilovka* ("equality-mongering"). It was argued that, in order to achieve full industrialization and the building of a modern society, greater material incentives had to be offered to persons engaged in more highly skilled forms of work. This policy was responsible for the re-establishment of sharp income differences between major occupational groups. Such new economic inequalities continued until approximately the mid-1950s. Around this time, a new attack on income inequality began and income differentials were reduced once again. Since the late 1980s, the program of economic reforms known as *perestroika* has included an attempt to increase income differentials. At this writing, it is difficult to know just how far this attempt will go (see the Special Topic on *perestroika* at the end of Chapter 8).

On the contemporary scene, it is clear that there are a number of social groupings that can be distinguished by different income levels and other forms of privilege. Whether or not these groups should be called "classes" is to some extent a matter of definition. Official Soviet ideology (at least prior to 1985 and the beginnings of *perestroika* and *glasnost*) has referred to them as "nonantagonistic strata," noting that the groups are not distinguished by the ownership of private property, which has been formally abolished in the Soviet Union. Thus so-called nonegalitarian classlessness has been said to prevail under state socialism. That is, there are different social groups possessing unequal amounts of material privilege, but these groups cannot be thought of as classes since their level of privilege does not depend on their possession or lack of property. Since private ownership of property is absent, one group does not gain by holding other groups down, and the social relations between such groups are therefore not antagonistic ones.

From a classical Marxian viewpoint, which equates class with property ownership, the official Soviet view is not unreasonable. But the Western Marxian conception of class has been substantially modified in recent years, and Western Marxists include the notion of domination or control as an essential component of their concept of class. Following this line of reasoning, it seems perfectly sensible to regard the major socioeconomic groups within state socialist society as classes, since they are in fact based on different levels of control over economic resources.

The class structure of state socialist society may be characterized in the following manner, listing the classes from highest to lowest (Parkin, 1971): (1) the white-collar intelligentsia, consisting mainly of workers in professional, managerial, and administrative positions; (2) skilled manual workers; (3) lower-level white-collar workers; and (4) unskilled workers.

The most privileged class within state socialism is the white-collar intelligentsia. Parkin suggests that the major class cleavage within state socialism is between this group and all the rest. The intelligentsia not only receives higher incomes than the rest, but its members also receive bonuses and special wage supplements, as well as other less measurable rewards: high-quality accommodations, opportunities to travel abroad, the use of official cars and state property, and others. Furthermore, the social distinction between the intelligentsia and other classes is magnified by the fact that its members are more likely to be party members. Party membership in itself confers additional benefits. These include the pulling of strings or the winning of favors, an opportunity to acquire the best theater tickets, or the ensuring of a place for one's children at good schools and universities.

Is the intelligentsia to be regarded as a ruling class in the Marxian sense? Some scholars have argued that at least a segment of it is. Milovan Djilas (1957), for example, has argued that a small section of the intelligentsia, consisting of full-time party administrative functionaries, constitutes a ruling elite that is broadly similar to the ruling classes of capitalist societies. Djilas sees this elite, which he refers to as a "new class," as a property-owning, highly privileged, and self-perpetuating class that dominates the rest of state socialist society.

Although Djilas's argument has considerable merit, it has received its share of criticism, and his thesis must be qualified in several ways. Anthony Giddens (1980), for example, while not disputing the existence of such an elite group, argues that it cannot be strictly compared to a capitalist ruling class. He observes that in state socialist society the dominant class enjoys rights only over the dispensation of collective property, and that this gives it a different character from capitalist classes, which have control over large supplies of private capital. In a similar vein, Parkin notes that, while all members of the intelligentsia are able to transmit a certain amount of privilege to their children, none of them can transmit privilege in the same way or to the same extent as can the members of a capitalist class; therefore, the intelligentsia is not a self-recruiting and self-perpetuating class in the same sense that a capitalist elite is.

Class Structuration Under State Socialism

The degree to which a class hierarchy has inherent rigidities such that the classes become relatively isolated from one another and hence impermeable to the exchange of members is known as **class structuration** (Giddens, 1980). The main indicators of the degree of class structuration in any society are its rate of social mobility and the extent to which its classes have become culturally distinctive groupings. A society with high class structuration will consist of classes that are sharply distinguishable culturally and are largely impermeable, self-recruiting groups. By contrast, low class structuration prevails when the rate of social mobility is high and when the cultural differences among classes are minimal. What is the overall level of class structuration in state socialist society?

There is widespread agreement that rates of social mobility in the major state socialist societies are relatively high, or at least that they have been in the recent past (Parkin, 1971; Giddens, 1980; Yanowitch, 1977). For instance, a 1963 study of Hungary showed that nearly 77 percent of white-collar intelligentsia positions were filled by persons from worker and peasant backgrounds (Parkin, 1971). In addition, the Yugoslavian census of 1960 indicates that 62 percent of persons in managerial and administrative positions came from manual backgrounds (Parkin, 1971). Furthermore, in the Soviet Union in the late 1960s the proportion of the intelligentsia recruited from manual and peasant families amounted to approximately 40 to 50 percent (Yanowitch, 1977). When recruitment to the intelligentsia from lower-level white-collar families is added to that supplied by manual and peasant families, a clear majority of the intelligentsia was recruited outside their own class (Yanowitch, 1977).

These data support the conclusion that there is a marked "openness" to state socialist class structures. Not only are rates of social mobility notably high, but a good deal of this mobility is of the "long-distance" sort. As Parkin has remarked in this connection (1971:157): "What, perhaps, gives mobility rates in socialist society their special significance is the fact that they indicate large-scale movements across the entire range of the reward hierarchy, not merely the interchange of personnel at the class margins."

The data on mobility indicate a relatively low degree of class structuration in state socialist society. What is known about the cultural distinctions among classes tends to support the same conclusion. Although Yanowitch stresses the fact that Soviet classes are distinguished by lifestyle and consumption habits, it does not appear that the differences are of major significance. Indeed, Parkin argues for a low degree of cultural distinctiveness of classes under state socialism. In support of his claim, he points out that negative or defensive value-orientations do not seem to have developed among the members of subordinate classes; that there appears to be no distinctive "working-class subculture" like that found in capitalist societies; and that members of the intelligentsia have failed to develop a highly distinctive culture, accent, and mode of dress similar to that typical of capitalist elites. These considerations compel Parkin to conclude (1971:158): "Those theorists who claim that socialist society is 'classless' because it lacks sharp [cultural distinctions among classes] have thus touched upon an important feature of this type of society."

SOCIAL STRATIFICATION IN INDUSTRIAL SOCIETIES: A COMPARATIVE ASSESSMENT

Capitalist and state socialist societies share both important similarities and differences in their stratification systems (Rossides, 1990:456–457). The main similarity is that both have very comparable divisions of labor and hence very similar occupational groupings. In both types of society people engage in much the same kinds of work, and in both systems economic rewards are closely tied to one's position in the system of production. In addition, both systems emphasize individual achievement, and both have high rates of social mobility when compared to agrarian societies of the past. A final similarity is that privileged classes have considerable success in transmitting advantages to their children, either in the form of direct privilege or by giving them opportunities to acquire privilege.

One important difference between the stratification systems is that the range of income inequality under state socialism appears to be considerably less extreme than under capitalism. David Lane (1971; citing Lenski, 1966) observes, for example, that top incomes in the Soviet Union may reach 300 times the minimum and 100 times the average income. Such differentials are substantially less than those found in the United States, where the highest incomes may reach 11,000 times the lowest and 7000 times the average income. Thus the state socialist nations have created notably greater economic equality than is characteristic of the capitalist West.

A second difference between the two types of society is that lower white-collar employees do not have the same relative social position under state socialism that they have within capitalist societies. Such workers within capitalism rank above all categories of manual laborers in terms of privilege and prestige, but in the socialist world they rank below skilled manual workers (although above unskilled workers). Throughout the state socialist world in the mid-1960s lower white-collar employees earned incomes that averaged around 85 to 95 percent of the incomes of all manual workers combined (Parkin, 1971). This seems to result from a general elevation of the value of skilled manual labor, a judgment that undoubtedly derives from the inclination within Marxism to view manual work as having a special "dignity."

A third major difference between capitalism and socialism concerns the nature and composition of the dominant classes that prevail under each. Within capitalist societies, the dominant class is an enormously wealthy elite whose privilege rests upon its possession of private capital. This class is heavily self-recruiting and self-perpetuating. By contrast, the dominant class under state socialism does not owe its special privilege to the possession of private property, but rather to its position within the hierarchy of political authority. Because it does not control private property, the state socialist dominant class is less able to transmit its privileges to its children. It therefore is more "open" and less self-perpetuating than a capitalist elite. Although it has enormous power over the masses and engages in totalitarian rule, it is not the same kind of ruling class as that formed by capitalist elites. David Lane explains further (1971:130):

> The incumbents of power positions (those with authority) do not form an ownership class which can be understood in classical Marxist terms. Assets are not disposed of through families in state-socialist societies. Government ministers and directors of factories do not pass on rights over ministries or factories to their sons as may capitalists in capitalist societies. Also, those with control over property giving them privileges in the distribution of rewards are not conscious of their property rights and therefore they do not form a ruling class as defined by Marx. This difference represents a break between the system of stratification in Western advanced capitalist societies and those of the Soviet type.

Another major difference between the two types of stratification systems involves the degree of class structuration. While capitalism produces a relatively high degree of class structuration, in the state socialist societies class structuration is fairly low. Classes are not culturally distinguishable to the same degree as within capitalist society, and rates of social mobility are much higher, especially in terms of movement over long distances in the class structure.* Thus, socialist society has a greater overall "openness," and classes there are not strictly comparable to those within capitalism.

Finally, capitalist and state socialist systems of stratification have not arisen from the same foundations and do not persist for quite the same reasons (cf. Parkin, 1971, 1979; Goldthorpe, 1966). Capitalist stratification systems arise through the operation of the economic market or, more specifically, through the activities of individuals and groups who structure and control the nature of market forces. State socialist societies, however, do not have market systems (or have only rudimentary aspects of market principles), and thus stratification cannot arise in the same way it does within capitalism. It seems to arise instead from the *political system*, from the actions of those who control the *state* (Goldthorpe, 1966). The party bureaucracy has the power to make policies that directly determine the nature and extent of economic inequalities. As we saw earlier in tracing the historical ebb and flow of state socialist inequalities since 1917, it has used its power to do just that. While those in power in state socialist society have brought about some significant reductions in economic inequality, they have nevertheless acted to set aside special privileges for themselves.

*This conclusion requires qualification with respect to the recent past. Some observers of the contemporary Soviet scene have suggested that a stagnating economy throughout the past two decades has led to declining educational opportunities and thus greater restrictions on upward mobility for many individuals (Lapidus, 1983). However, in the absence of any firm data on mobility rates for very recent years, it is not possible to determine the actual extent to which the class structure of the Soviet Union might be rigidifying.

THEORIES OF INDUSTRIAL STRATIFICATION SYSTEMS

Sociologists have proposed three main theories to explain the character of modern industrial stratification systems: the functionalist theory, the Marxian approach, and the major alternative to Marxism, the Weberian approach.

The Functionalist Theory

The functionalist theory of stratification is set forth by sociologists Kingsley Davis and Wilbert Moore (1945). This theory basically employs the same logic as Parsons's functionalist evolutionary theory discussed in Chapter 6, except that Davis and Moore focus on modern society. Their leading argument is that stratification arises from the basic functional requirements of organized social life and is therefore a fundamentally necessary and inevitable feature of human societies.

Davis and Moore reason that, in order to survive or function effectively, all societies face the fundamental problem of motivating a sufficient number of their members to fill the most "functionally important" social positions. They believe that a system of stratification—a system of unequal rewards—is the mechanism that societies settle upon to solve this crucial problem. Stratification therefore arises as an incentive system, as a means of motivating people to carry out vital social responsibilities. For those talented persons who are willing to work hard and make sacrifices in order to gain entry into certain crucial occupational positions, top rewards will be forthcoming. Likewise, untalented or unmotivated individuals will have to settle for less demanding roles accompanied by lower rewards.

Davis and Moore point out that the rank of a social position (i.e., the level of rewards accompanying it) in any society is determined by two principal factors. One of these is the position's alleged "functional importance," a concept that is crucial to Davis and Moore's argument. They note that not all social positions are "equally important" to societal functioning. Some are more important in that they make a greater contribution to the survival and well-being of society. The second factor said to determine positional rank is the scarcity of personnel available to fill the position. Other things being equal, a position for which available personnel are relatively scarce should have a high rank. Scarcity of personnel can result either from a lack of sufficient talent in the population or from the strong demands of training associated with some positions. In regard to the latter point, Davis and Moore observe that modern medicine is within the abilities of most persons, but that the training for medical careers is so demanding that many persons will ordinarily be reluctant to undertake it. Attaching high rewards to the role of physician is, therefore, a socially created device designed to eliminate scarcity of personnel qualified for the position.

The Davis-Moore theory has been extensively criticized and widely debated over the years (Tumin, 1953; Huaco, 1963; Anderson and Gibson, 1978; Chambliss and Ryther, 1975). Perhaps the most telling argument against it is that its concept of "functional importance" will not stand up to careful inspection. In what sense, for example, can the engineers of a factory be considered more important to that factory than the less rewarded manual workers (Tumin, 1953)? It is clear that both play necessary roles in such an organization. This line of reasoning can be extended indefinitely. By Davis and Moore's logic, garbage collectors should be extremely low in functional importance, since such positions receive very low rewards and are widely regarded as undesirable. Yet without garbage collection, severe sanitation and health problems would soon develop in our major cities, problems such as New York and Paris witnessed in the 1960s. Many other social positions that are poorly rewarded in many societies can be shown to have considerable functional importance for those societies. There appear, then, to be serious difficulties with the functional importance concept, a concept that is vital to the entire functionalist explanation.

Other important objections can also be raised against the theory (Tumin, 1953). For instance, Davis and Moore's assumption that the stratification system promotes efficient use of a society's supply of talent is highly questionable. The more rigid a stratification system is, the less a society can discover just how much talent it has, since social rewards will be largely determined by inheritance rather than by effort. Moreover, stratification not only impedes a society's discovery of its range of talent, but also blocks its full use of available talent.

Additionally, it is conceivable that rewards other than economic privilege and prestige may be effective motivators of people. For instance, such rewards as "joy in work" and "social duty" might serve as important inducements for people to perform important social roles (Tumin, 1953). Finally, stratification systems clearly seem to have many negative social consequences. For example, they unequally distribute favorable and unfavorable self-images; they encourage hostility, suspicion, and distrust among individuals and groups; and they unequally distribute the sense of membership and identification that people feel with society (Tumin, 1953).

The functionalist theory thus seems inadequate as an explanation of stratification in industrial societies. In fact, some sociologists regard it as little more than a rationalization and ideological justification for prevailing social and economic inequalities (Anderson and Gibson,

1978; Rossides, 1976). What, then, would a more acceptable theory of industrial stratification systems look like?

The Marxian Approach

Classical Marxism regards stratification as arising from the continuous struggle between and among individuals and groups for access to scarce resources, the most important of which is economic property. Groups that gain control of property—the crucial forces of production—are able to use this control to exploit others and reap rewards for themselves. Their superior position with regard to property gives them power over others, and this superior privilege and power are translated into superior prestige. Dominant groups, in addition, commonly develop ideologies designed to justify their superior power and privilege, to make them seem right and honorable. For instance, modern capitalists justify their superior wealth by asserting that it is their just reward for risk taking in investment. Moreover, they claim that their entrepreneurial activities lead to a general improvement in the total social wealth and therefore benefit everyone. They utter statements like "What is good for General Motors is good for the country." Contemporary Marxists would argue that this statement is an aspect of a self-serving ideology, and that, moreover, it is basically false. They would claim instead that what is good for General Motors (i.e., the top owners and managers of that company) may very well be bad in several respects for much of the rest of the country.

Erik Wright (1979) has carried out a valuable study that attempts to test the overall merits of the Marxian approach to stratification. He uses his class scheme as a predictor of income inequality in the contemporary United States. (Wright's scheme, of course, departs notably from the classical Marxian formulation of class as based on property.) Wright begins by specifying the basis for income in each of his classes. The bourgeoisie receives its income from the exploitation of workers, which it carries out by paying them less than the full value of the goods and services they produce. The proletariat receives its income in the form of wages paid by capitalists. The level of these wages is determined by the market for labor. Capitalists generally attempt to hold these wages down as low as possible, for in the classical Marxian formulation their profits are determined by the level of wages they pay. The wages paid to workers derive from the respective bargaining strengths of capitalists and workers, and these strengths are determined by numerous historical, social, and economic factors (e.g., level of unionization, relative demand for labor power, and so on).

Members of the petty bourgeoisie employ no workers and therefore cannot rely on the exploitation of labor for their income. Instead, they must rely on their own efforts. The harder they are willing to work, the more income they stand to receive.

Managers and supervisors derive their income from salaries (or wages) paid them by the capitalist class. Their income levels will vary closely in accordance with their position in the hierarchy of authority within their organization. Top managers perform activities crucial to the making of profit by the company, and therefore they must be paid high salaries as inducements for them to carry out their functions well.* As Wright notes (1979:89), "Large income differentials between hierarchical levels are essential for underwriting the legitimacy of authority."

Small employers derive their income both from their own efforts and from their exploitation of labor. The closer they are to the bourgeoisie, the more their income is derived from

*Is this, perhaps, an instance of the small kernel of truth that most of us recognize within the functionalist theory?

such exploitation. Some small employers, such as lawyers and physicians engaged in self-employed private practices, derive their income not from exploiting labor power but from their control over prices (fees). Their income comes from their capacity to manipulate market forces to their advantage. Semiautonomous employees derive their incomes from paid salaries. These incomes are usually fairly high because income level must serve as an inducement for them to perform well in tasks demanding creativity and responsibility.

Most of Wright's predictions about the income levels of different classes were well supported by his empirical results. He found a significant income gap between managers/supervisors and workers. Moreover, the income of managers and supervisors was, as expected, closely tied to position within the managerial hierarchy. The data also showed that small employers had a higher income level than all other classes except the bourgeoisie. Wright summarizes the results of his study in the following manner (1979:223–224):

> It may seem ironic that in a Marxist study of the relationship of income inequality to class relations, there has been virtually no empirical analysis of the principal class antagonism within capitalist society: the capital-labor relationship. Although we have been able to analyze in some detail the contradictory class position between the petty bourgeoisie and the capitalist class (small employers), we have not been able to analyze proper capitalists. And we certainly have not touched on anything that could legitimately be called the "ruling class" within advanced capitalist society. Ultimately it is important to investigate income determination in the capitalist class itself, but this is simply impossible using survey data.
>
> Nevertheless, in spite of the partial nature of the analysis of property relations, the results clearly demonstrate that even small property ownership is consequential. The mean income of small employers is over twice that of workers. . . . Furthermore, the income gap between employers and workers is much greater than between workers and managers. . . .
>
> Income, of course, is only one of the ways of empirically demonstrating the reality of class divisions. If data were available, it would be easy to demonstrate that classes, defined by social relations of production, are even more decisively differentiated in terms of wealth and political power. Real economic control over the means of production . . . remains the essential basis of distributive relations, and any investigation of inequality needs to take these relations of production into systematic consideration.
>
> For over a generation theorists . . . have argued that authority and/or knowledge stratification has superseded property stratification as the organizing principle of inequality in contemporary society. Our results indicate that even when a simple juridical criterion is used to define property relations (self-employed employers), and even when the sample necessarily excludes the wealthiest segments of the capitalist class, the division between those who own property and those who do not is substantial, and that it is considerably greater than the differences between "knowledge classes" or "authority classes."

In more recent research based on a modified and expanded version of his class categories, Wright (1985) has obtained slightly different results. His data for the United States show that "expert managers"—managers with advanced educational credentials—earn somewhat more than small employers. The data for Sweden are even more striking. They show that four categories of managers and supervisors, including even those with moderate educational credentials, earn more than small employers. Overall, the American and the Swedish data show that educational credentials and organizational authority are major determinants of income level. Although Wright tries to interpret these findings in Marxian terms, he ties himself in theoretical knots in doing so. After all, educational credentials and organizational authority are phenomena that are alien to a Marxian approach to stratification. What his findings really suggest are the limitations of Marxism and the relevance of certain Weberian ideas to understanding contemporary stratification patterns.

The Weberian Alternative to Marxism

Max Weber (1978; orig. 1923) agreed with Marx that the concept of class was a central one for the analysis of stratification in capitalist societies. But Weber saw Marx's analysis of stratification as limited to the discussion of class and therefore as too narrow. Weber believed that there were two other types of stratified groups that played important roles in any society's stratification system: status groups and parties. **Status groups** were identified by Weber as groups whose members share common lifestyles and levels of social honor or prestige. A **party** is a political association whose members share in the exercise of a certain amount of social power.

Thus Weber identified three aspects of stratification—property, honor and lifestyle, and power—and three types of stratified groups corresponding to these criteria. He also went on to point out that property, honor, and power may operate somewhat independently of one another. That is, a group that possesses property may not rank high in terms of status and power; likewise, a group that has a high status might not be a property-owning group. But Weber also stressed that although the three criteria are logically independent, they tend to be closely associated. Thus, property ownership generally does confer considerable status and power.

Weber's concepts of class, status group, and party are abstract analytical categories and can be difficult to apply in clear and distinct ways to concrete social groups. A given social group might be characterized as both a class and a status group, for instance. Using Weber's criteria, we would have to identify the nobility of the European Middle Ages as both a class and a status group: its economic position was rooted in the ownership of land, but it lived a lifestyle emphasizing the pursuit of warfare as an occupation, chivalrous conduct, and disdain for commercial activity.

A Weberian analysis of contemporary capitalism recognizes the existence of a powerful, property-owning bourgeoisie that has great impact on the functioning of modern society. But it also acknowledges the existence of other groups whose social position is not tied to property ownership. Members of the learned professions, for instance, possess considerable privilege and high social status, but not as property owners. These groups are best thought of, therefore, as status groups rather than as classes. What accounts for their superior privilege and status?

Weber used another concept in his analysis of stratification that is at least as important as, if not more important than, the concepts of class, status group, and party: the concept of **social closure** (Weber, 1978; orig. 1923; cf. Parkin, 1979; Murphy, 1988). Weber used this concept to indicate the strong tendency for social groups to seize upon certain social criteria as marks of distinction, as means by which to set themselves apart from outsiders. These criteria include such things as sex, race, cultural background (nationality), educational level, and common occupation. By using some criterion to close themselves off from others, the members of a social group attempt to monopolize resources that will bring them economic success and social esteem.

Weber's concept of social closure is an important supplement to the Marxian analysis of modern stratification systems. It may in fact be the case that the Marxian stress on property ownership can be subsumed under the concept of social closure (Parkin, 1979). That is, property ownership may be viewed as simply one form (although an especially important form) of social closure. Members of the capitalist class, for instance, use their ownership of huge supplies of capital as a means for creating and main-

Frank Parkin. For many years Parkin was a fellow of Magdalen College, Oxford University; he now lives in Spain. Parkin has written some hilarious novels that are biting satires of modern society, but he is best known as a serious Weberian conflict analyst of stratification.

taining their extremely high privilege and prestige.

But other criteria may be used by other groups. Parkin notes that in modern society educational credentials seem to have emerged as one of the most important means of social closure. By achieving a certain level of education (which means the possession of a certain type of diploma), the members of a group hope to establish a minimum credential for entry into certain occupations with high payoffs in terms of privilege and prestige. As Ivar Berg has noted in this connection (1971:185; cited in Parkin, 1979:59):

> Educational credentials have become the new property in America. That nation, which has attempted to make the transmission of real and personal property difficult, has contrived to replace it with an inheritable set of values concerning degrees and diplomas which will most certainly reinforce the formidable class barriers that remain, even without the right within families to pass benefices from parents to their children.

Recall also that in recent research on the United States and Sweden Erik Wright (1985) has shown that educational credentials are a major determinant of income level. In both countries, managerial personnel with advanced educational credentials earn approximately twice the income of managers without such credentials.

If educational credentials are a major means of social closure in modern industrial societies, they are not the only ones. The learned professions rely to some extent on these credentials as criteria for setting themselves apart, but they also use two other means that have been crucial to their economic success: the manipulation of symbolic culture, and the development of powerful forms of political organization (Weber's "party"). Law and medicine, for example, are in most industrial societies, and especially in the United States, highly lucrative professions that bring great social prestige to their members. Lawyers and physicians have long understood how to achieve high levels of economic and social success. They monopolize specialized forms of knowledge that are crucial to their clients' and patients' well-being. In order to display their monopolization of an esoteric body of knowledge, they have developed elaborate terminological systems that are derived from Latin and that only they adequately understand. These systems are designed, at least in part, to impress those they serve. This makes it easier for the members of such professions to claim that they are uniquely deserving of the high economic rewards they receive.

The monopolization of a body of specialized knowledge is necessary to the success of the learned professions, but by itself is not sufficient. There must be a form of political organization designed to protect and promote privilege and prestige. Physicians have such an organization in the American Medical Association, lawyers in the American Bar Association. The AMA has been called the second most powerful political lobby in the United States (the first is the oil corporation lobby). For decades it has restricted admissions to medical schools, thereby keeping the supply of doctors low relative to the demand (Freeman, 1976). This artificial manipulation of the market helps to insure much higher incomes than would otherwise be possible (Freeman, 1976). In addition, for many years the AMA has vigorously opposed even the hint of socialized medicine in the United States. It has lobbied in the federal government to preserve the "free enterprise" system of health care, and has successfully prevented the development of any major form of nationalized health care. It seems worthy of note that in those modern industrial societies that have health care systems closely regulated by the government, the income level and social status of physicians relative to the rest of the population is notably lower than in the United States (cf. Starr, 1982:6).

To accept much of what the Weberian approach to stratification has to offer does not mean that the Marxian approach must be abandoned. On the contrary, the Weberian and Marxian approaches may usefully be regarded as complementary rather than contradictory. Yet there is at least one sense in which the Weberian approach is clearly superior, and that is in the analysis of state socialist societies. Since these societies do not have private forms of property ownership, classical Marxian theory is really helpless to explain why they are highly stratified. But the stratification systems of these societies can be accounted for by employing a Weberian perspective. The Soviet bureaucratic elite and other members of the intelligentsia use educational credentials and party membership as means of social closure. As Parkin has commented (1979:53):

> There is no need to become entangled in semantic debates over whether or not workers in socialist states are "really" exploited. The relevant question is not whether surplus extraction occurs, but whether the state confers rights upon a limited circle of eligibles to deny access to the "means of life and labor" to the rest of the community. If such exclusionary powers are legally guaranteed and enforced, an exploitative relationship prevails as a matter of definition. It is not of overriding importance to know whether these exclusionary powers are exercised by the formal owners of property or by their appointed agents, since the social consequences of exclusion are not demonstrably different in the two cases.

THE FUTURE OF SOCIAL STRATIFICATION

This chapter and Chapter 6 delineate the existence of a variety of forms and degrees of stratification from about the intensive horticultural stage onward. Despite important differences, what all these systems have in common is structured social conflict: the struggle among groups for control over valuable resources, particularly wealth and power. Indeed, it makes very good sense to view structured conflict as both a basic cause and a prime outcome of all systems of stratified social life, whether they be African horticultural systems, agrarian feudal orders, or capitalist and socialist industrial class systems.

In view of the failure of state socialism to eradicate class stratification despite its collectivization of the forces of production, a crucial question concerns whether optimism is warranted regarding the creation of some future society that lacks stratification. Many sociologists, Marxists in particular, continue to believe that such optimism is a quite rational guide to thought about the future. Orthodox Marxists anticipate a future society in which structured conflict can be eliminated, and thus stratification with it.

Table 10.2 THEORIES OF STRATIFICATION IN INDUSTRIAL SOCIETIES

Theory	Characteristics	Evaluation
Functionalist theory	Argues that stratification is a universal and inevitable feature of human societies because it makes a crucial contribution to any society's survival and well-being. In particular, unequal rewards function as an incentive to motivate people to take on a society's most functionally important roles and thus get the important work of society effectively done. An individual's level of economic and social reward is commensurate with his or her contribution to societal functioning.	Has numerous serious weaknesses, and is more an ideological justification for stratification than an explanation of it. Rejected in this book.
Marxian theories	Emphasize private ownership of property as the key determinant of the structure of stratification. The main axis of stratification in capitalist societies is the struggle between the bourgeoisie and the proletariat. Individuals command privilege and prestige in proportion to their level of property ownership.	Identify a critical dimension of stratification in capitalist societies, but have difficulty explaining the high rewards of persons who are not property owners, such as learned professionals and many business managers. Also have difficulty explaining the stratification patterns of state socialist societies.
Weberian theories	Emphasize the importance of dimensions of stratification not rooted in property relations. Focus on the various ways in which groups attempt to monopolize resources in order to acquire high levels of privilege and prestige. Thus, individuals' levels of social and economic reward are proportional to their control over important resources.	Are extremely useful supplements to Marxism in that they seem able to explain aspects of stratification inadequately dealt with by Marxian theories. Also seem to have a higher level of realism about the likelihood of abolishing stratification in future societies.

The major alternative to the Marxian view of stratification is that of Weber. Although both Marx and Weber were conflict theorists, unlike Marx, Weber was pessimistic about the future of modern society. He saw little possibility of a classless society, even in a thoroughly socialist world. Old forms of domination would disappear only to give way to new forms. As Frank Parkin (1979), a contemporary Weberian sociologist, has put it, stratification systems represent forms of "permanent tension." He does not mean that the same stratification structures persist forever, but that social tension or struggle over numerous kinds of scarce resources is a basic, and probably ineradicable, fact of human social life.

It is difficult to choose absolutely between these competing viewpoints, for both seem to have their strengths and weaknesses. On the one hand the Marxian viewpoint seems in many ways more a declaration of faith than a scientific assessment of the facts. Compared to it, the Weberian perspective seems more in touch with the hard realities of the human situation. On the other hand, the history of the state socialist societies does indicate that significant reductions in social and economic inequalities are indeed possible. Although this book is more sympathetic to the Weberian position on this score, this fact permits at least some hope that this position may be too pessimistic.

SUMMARY

1. Although modern industrial societies in one sense are less stratified than agrarian societies of the past, considerable caution is required when assessing recent evolutionary trends in stratification. In the world-system as a whole the level of stratification has been increasing rather than decreasing. Modern industrial societies are themselves still characterized by extreme stratification.

2. Income is very unequally distributed in industrial capitalist societies, and there has been no major change in this distribution in the twentieth century. Wealth is much more unevenly distributed than income. In the United States, for example, half or more of the corporate stocks, bonds, and trusts is owned by only 0.5 percent of the population.

3. Sociologists have not been able to agree on just what a social class is or what the class structure of modern capitalism looks like. Traditional sociologists define class in terms of occupation and generally identify an upper class, an upper-middle class, a lower-middle class, a working class, and a lower class. Marxian sociologists conceptualize class in terms of relations of property ownership and workplace authority. The Marxian sociologist Erik Wright identifies six basic classes within contemporary capitalism: the bourgeoisie, the proletariat, the petty bourgeoisie, managers and supervisors, small employers, and semiautonomous employees. Both traditional and Marxian approaches have strengths and weaknesses.

4. Considerable mobility occurs within modern capitalist societies, although its extent is usually exaggerated. Most changes of class position are over short distances, and movement from near the bottom to near the top of the class structure is rare. Much mobility in industrial capitalism is due to technological and occupational change.

5. State socialist societies currently are stratified into groups with different levels of control over economic resources. Party membership and educational credentials are the keys to economic and social success. The basic classes are the white-collar intelligentsia, skilled manual workers, lower white-collar workers, and unskilled workers. The party bureaucracy, the highest echelon within the white-collar intelligentsia, constitutes a ruling class; this ruling class, though, is not strictly comparable to a capitalist bourgeoisie.

6. Capitalist and state socialist societies are similar in their divisions of labor, the kinds of work people do, and their emphasis on individual achievement. The main differences between these societies' stratification systems are (a) the range of income inequality is much less under state socialism; (b) lower white-collar workers are less highly regarded under state socialism; (c) the dominant class under state socialism is less wealthy and less hereditary in character; (d) state socialist societies have class groupings that are less culturally distinctive, and the rate of mobility from one class to another is notably greater; (e) state socialist stratification derives from political decisions rather than property ownership and market forces.

7. There is still much disagreement among sociologists about how to explain stratification systems in industrial societies. The three major theories that have been developed are the functionalist, Marxian, and Weberian theories. These theories are summarized and assessed in Table 10.2.

SPECIAL TOPIC: THE SOCIAL DEMOCRATIC EXPERIMENT

The Scandinavian countries have become well known in recent decades for the prominence they give to political parties espousing a "socialist" view of the world. As Frank Parkin (1971) observes, the Swedish Social Democratic party has held a virtual monopoly of political power since the early 1930s. The Labour party in Norway has been in office rather continuously for approximately half a century. In Denmark the Social Democratic party became that country's largest party in 1924, and the Social Democrats have been the leading political force for most of the time since. Such parties were originally elected to office to bring about a fundamental redistribution of income and wealth from the privileged to the less privileged, to direct their respective societies toward economic equality. Such equality was to be effected largely in political terms, that is, by leaving relatively unaltered the basically capitalist character of the economy. Thus social democracy in Scandinavia has been an experiment in creating economic equality within the very confines of capitalism itself.

Numerous scholars have argued against the possibility of success of any such experiment (cf. Parkin, 1971). Many functionalists have claimed that all modern industrial societies need a minimal level of economic inequality; since inequalities serve important social functions in recruiting persons to different social positions, any attempt to impose equality by political means is bound to fail. Marxists have also been quite critical of the soundness of the social democratic experiment, though obviously for entirely different reasons. From the Marxian standpoint, "Labour governments cannot radically improve the position of the subordinate class because they are tolerated in power only in so far as they refrain from making serious inroads into the privileges of the dominant class" (Parkin, 1971:105). For Marxists, equality cannot feasibly coexist with capitalism, for this type of economic system is inherently premised upon the existence of economic inequality; equality can only result when capitalism is genuinely dissolved into economic socialism. Against both of the above views Parkin points out (1971:105):

> *Social Democrats claim that left-wing governments have consistently introduced legislation designed to improve the lot of the less privileged. By initiating reforms in taxation and education, by the expansion of health and welfare programmes, full employment policies and the like, the position of the working class and the poor has been significantly improved under Labour regimes. Even when the means of production are largely in private hands, and where the economy is still organized along market principles, a government with a democratic socialist ideology, it is suggested, is still able to some extent to shift the balance of advantages in an egalitarian direction.*

One of the best-known analyses of the social democratic experiment is that of Parkin (1971), who believes that the social democrats have done essentially nothing to shift their societies toward greater economic equality. To support this viewpoint, Parkin draws upon data regarding comparative income inequalities in several advanced industrial countries. These data show, for instance, that in 1956 higher administrative and professional workers in Norway earned 2.2 times the income of unskilled laborers; in 1964 they were earning 2.4 times as much. Similarly, Swedish professionals and higher administrators earned 2.0 times the income of unskilled workers in 1953; by 1963 the figure had climbed to 3.1 times as much. Such data, of course, indicate actual *increases* in income inequality. Moreover, the recent extent of income inequality in Scandinavia parallels closely what prevails in the major capitalist nations. Parkin's data demonstrate the following facts about the early 1960s: Norway's range of income inequality between unskilled workers and professionals was about equal to that of the United States, and greater than that of West Germany; Sweden had a greater range of income inequality than either the United States or West Germany; and Denmark had a greater range than the United Kingdom, the United States, and West Germany. The data on which these conclusions are based are crude and somewhat limited in that they do not reveal the full income distribution for any of the societies considered. Nonetheless, they do show that, much like the other capitalist nations, the Scandinavian societies remain highly class-divided. This fact leads Parkin to conclude (1971:121):

> *All this must raise serious doubts [about] claims concerning the ability of parties or governments based on the underclass to redistribute material rewards in an egalitarian manner. . . . This does not offer much support to the view that socialist governments in capitalist societies can combat the pressures of the market more effectively than can their opponents.*

Parkin's pessimistic conclusions regarding the social democratic experiment are strongly echoed by Paul Stevenson (1974) in regard to Sweden. From a review of several studies, Stevenson concludes that economic inequalities in Sweden are not notably different from those in other capitalist nations, and that they seem to have widened in recent years. Stevenson has even attempted to estimate the extent to which poverty remains a significant feature of Swedish society: "Jarnek considers those who receive less than 14,500 kroner a year in 1966 as 'extremely low paid.' About 15 percent of the employed earn less than this amount. . . . Some 76.1 percent of single Swedish taxpayers earned less than $3,846 (20,000 kroner) in 1967 while 25.9 percent of married taxpayers fell under this income level" (1974:49).

In more recent research comparing income distributions in a number of Western capitalist societies, Stevenson (1982) has shown that, as of the early 1970s, Sweden had the most unequal distribution before taxation but the most equal distribution after taxes. This suggests a more positive view of social democracy. However, considerable restraint in adopting such a view is still called for (Stevenson, 1982). The fact remains that the after-tax income distribution in Sweden is still very similar to that in many other Western capitalist societies. Moreover, the other Scandinavian countries have not been any more successful than, or perhaps not even as successful as, Sweden in redistributing income. In the final analysis, if the really important question is how the achievements of social democratic countries compare to those of countries that have not adopted social democratic practices, then the achievements of social democracy seem meager indeed.

Since their initial rise to power in the 1930s, social democratic parties appear to have undergone strong ideological changes. These changes have generally been in the direction of a definition of equality as "equality of opportunity" and away from a concern with the direct redistribution of material benefits. As Parkin puts it, the socialist labor parties have attempted to move toward a form of "meritocratic socialism." They have done this primarily by expanding the access of working-class youth to higher education. This transformation should not come as a major surprise. For the social democratic governments of Scandinavia have been erected within the framework of basically capitalist economies, economies organized around and dominated by a capitalist class concerned with protecting its privileges. The social democratic parties have had to contend with this major fact, and in order to govern successfully they have undoubtedly had to accommodate themselves to it. This accommodation has taken the form of a strong capitulation to the interests of the economic elite, and thus of major compromises of their own philosophical principles (cf. Szymanski, 1978). All of this suggests a basic sensibility to the Marxian claim that genuine equality can only come about through major economic, and not just political, transformations.

The failure of the social democratic experiment to produce a significantly more egalitarian society does not necessarily mean that it has been a complete failure. Socialist democracy has perhaps made some limited accomplishments (cf. Castles, 1978; Stephens, 1980; Steinmo, 1988; Davis and Scase, 1985). Although the Scandinavian countries do not seem to have abolished poverty, perhaps they have done more than have other capitalist societies to reduce its extent and to cushion its blow (cf. Steinmo, 1988). Furthermore, the highly nationalized systems of health care in Scandinavia appear to have given members of subordinate classes a better chance at high-quality health care than their counterparts have in the rest of the capitalist world. Finally, it might be argued that the Scandinavian nations have done more to protect workers against the worst effects of unemployment, inasmuch as social democratic governments give considerable aid to unemployed workers in finding new jobs. Of course, all of these consequences, such as they may be, are still far short of the original aims of the Scandinavian socialist parties. This fact must be given center stage in any careful assessment of the experiment in democratic socialism.

FOR FURTHER READING

Davis, Howard, and Richard Scase. *Western Capitalism and State Socialism: An Introduction*. Oxford: Blackwell, 1985. Useful material on stratification patterns in industrial capitalist and state socialist societies.

Giddens, Anthony. *The Class Structure of the Advanced Societies*. Second edition. London: Hutchinson, 1980. A valuable theoretically informed analysis of many of the issues involved in studying classes in modern industrial societies. Useful discussions of Marx and Weber on capitalist society and of the nature of classes under contemporary state socialism.

Giddens, Anthony, and David Held (eds.). *Classes, Power, and Conflict: Classical and Contemporary Debates*. Berkeley: University of California Press, 1982. An excellent collection of essays on numerous aspects of stratification in industrial societies.

Goldthorpe, John H. *Social Mobility and Class Structure in Modern Britain*. Oxford: Clarendon Press, 1980. A major study of social mobility in contemporary Britain. Shows that, despite the egalitarian efforts of Labour governments over several decades, Britain remains a deeply class-divided society in which the rate of mobility has changed little.

Lane, David. *The End of Social Inequality? Class, Status, and Power Under State Socialism*. London: Allen and Unwin, 1982. A worthwhile examination of many features of stratification within state socialist societies by a well-known student of the subject.

Matthews, Mervyn. *Privilege in the Soviet Union*. London: Allen and Unwin, 1978. One of the best and most detailed studies of the social and economic privileges of the Soviet elite.

Murphy, Raymond. *Social Closure: The Theory of Monopolization and Exclusion*. Oxford: Clarendon Press, 1988. A valuable assessment and extension of the neo-Weberian closure theories of Frank Parkin and Randall Collins.

Parkin, Frank. *Marxism and Class Theory: A Bourgeois Critique.* New York: Columbia University Press, 1979. A very provocative critique of the Marxian approach to classes in industrial societies. Parkin suggests that a Weberian approach provides the best alternative to Marxism.

Szymanski, Albert. *Class Structure: A Critical Perspective.* New York: Praeger, 1983. Despite Szymanski's predictable Marxian excesses, as well as a tendency to view state socialism unrealistically, contains useful discussions of many features of stratification within industrial capitalism.

Westergaard, John, and Henrietta Resler. *Class in a Capitalist Society: A Study of Contemporary Britain.* New York: Basic Books, 1975. An analysis of the class structure of modern Britain from a Marxian standpoint.

Wright, Erik Olin. *Class Structure and Income Determination.* New York: Academic Press, 1979. One of the most impressive attempts by a Marxist to conceptualize the contemporary capitalist class structure and to show how such a conceptualization is a good predictor of economic inequality. (Readers interested in this book should be sure to consult Wright's *Classes* [London: Verso, 1985], a work in which Wright significantly modifies some of his thinking.)

CHAPTER 11

Political Evolution and the Origin of the State

In this chapter and the next we explore the evolution of political organization. As we shall see, forms of polity are closely tied to the nature of economic organization and social stratification. The chapter examines four major stages in political evolution widely recognized by social scientists: bands, tribes, chiefdoms, and states. Particular emphasis is given to the key differences between societies organized into states and prestate societies. Some well-known theories of the origin of the state in human history are also examined. In the following chapter, the crucial problem of the evolution of the state since the emergence of modern capitalism is considered.

THE NATURE OF POLITICAL ORGANIZATION

Broadly conceived, the **polity** is the aspect of society that serves to maintain law and order within a society and to regulate the external relations between or among societies. The political system establishes a means of social control or regulation designed to keep the behavior of individuals and groups within certain bounds and to make and implement decisions in behalf of the entire society or certain segments of it. The polity is universally found in human societies since all societies have some established means of social control and decision making. The specific nature of political control and decision making, however, varies greatly from one society to another. Different kinds of societies will have different mechanisms for keeping things under control and insuring that decisions and plans can be successfully implemented. It is useful to think of three such political mechanisms: influence, power, and authority.

Influence is *the likelihood that the behavior, decisions, or advice of one or more persons will be followed or copied by others.* Influence is a strictly informal process of social control occurring as a regular result of constant and close social interaction. This form of control predominates in societies that are small, relatively simple in structure, and characterized by the regular face-to-face interaction of most of their members. While influence is not necessarily the only mechanism of political control in such societies, it is overwhelmingly the predominant mechanism. What is most characteristic of influence is that it lacks "teeth." It cannot guarantee that decisions or advice will be followed, but can only make it more or less likely that they will be. A political leader possessing only influence, then, has no capacity to force others to do his bidding; he may only suggest or implore and hope to be effective.

A distinctively different mechanism for bringing about social control is **power,** a central feature of most political systems. Paraphrasing the classic definition given by Max Weber (1978; orig. 1923), power may be defined as *the capacity to control the behavior of others even against their resistance.* Power contains precisely the element that is lacking in the case of influence, namely, the capacity to overcome resistance and insure that the will of the powerholder prevails. Behind power, then, lurks the constant threat of *coercion* or *force* should orders or decisions not be willingly complied with. Given these considerations, power requires a certain level of organizational development. Therefore it usually begins to appear as a prominent feature of social life only with the transition to intensive horticultural societies possessing social stratification. It is at this stage of sociocultural evolution that the administrative machinery that power requires can be created.

The strength of power is that it is backed by the capacity to use force. Paradoxically, this is also its weakness, for that force may not always be sufficient to prevail against the will of those persons and groups subjected to it. The weakness of force is that it is an *external* means of getting people to comply; it does not require their psychological commitment to rules and orders, but demands only that such rules and orders be obeyed. Yet because power requires no psychological allegiance to commands, those commands may go unheeded when the threat of force is inadequate. The holders of power throughout human history have clearly understood this fact; and for this reason they have generally been eager to gain not only obedience to commands, but psychological commitment to them. Such psychological identification with the ruling powers naturally increases the likelihood of obedience. When such psychological identification has been created, the use of power has been *legitimized*—that is, justified or rationalized as morally right and proper—by the people themselves. When this occurs, power gives way to **authority,** the political form that Weber identified as *rule by the consent of the governed.*

Sociologists have generally made much of the notions of authority and **legitimacy,** arguing that most political regimes have rested on authority rather than on raw force—that the people have committed their hearts and minds to their own subordination. Some sociologists, though, have suggested that this picture of political systems is not a realistic one. Immanuel Wallerstein (1974a) and Pierre van den Berghe (1978), for instance, insist that the consent of the governed has been largely absent from most political regimes. They believe that most complex political systems have been to one extent or another outright tyrannies resting on a solid foundation of physical force.

Wallerstein and van den Berghe have a significant point to make. Social scientists have undoubtedly exaggerated the extent to which genuine legitimacy has prevailed within political systems. Numerous peasant and slave rebellions throughout human history, for example, bear witness to the frequent withholding of legitimacy. Yet it seems that the view of Wallerstein and van den Berghe goes too far in the other direction. Indeed, a number of political systems have been vigorously supported by the masses. The contemporary U.S. government, for instance, undoubtedly enjoys an enormous level of legitimacy, and perhaps even the contemporary Soviet state does as well. In any event, the question of the extent to which polities receive legitimation is an empirical one that will have to be settled by the concrete examination of particular cases.

THE GENERAL PATTERN OF POLITICAL EVOLUTION

Like the study of sociocultural evolution in general, the investigation of political evolution initially requires a typology of stages. The best-known and most widely adopted typology of political stages is that developed by Elman Service (1971b), who distinguishes four major stages in political evolution: band, tribe, chiefdom, and state. His typology is the basis for the discussion of the major evolutionary transformations within political society. The typology is outlined in Table 11.1.

Bands

The most rudimentary form of political society is the **band,** a form of polity typically associated with hunting and gathering societies. As Service (1971b) points out, all band-level political structures are found within hunting and gathering societies, even though not all hunter-gatherers are politically organized at the band level; and such societies as have developed beyond the band level have had some infrastructural features unusual for hunter-gatherers.

Morton Fried (1967) has provided a valuable description of the nature of political leadership in band-level society. As he points out, it rests on influence and typically lacks any sort of real power. In addition, leadership tends to be displayed in transient fashion, frequently shifting from one person to another. These shifts in leadership appear to be associated more with the nature of social situations than with the nature of persons. Fried also notes that the nature of leadership bears a close relation to variations in ecology and demography. More extensive leadership (and greater power underlying leadership) is associated with denser populations and more productive subsistence patterns.

The political structure of band-level societies is thus a rather loosely organized pattern of frequently shifting, informal leadership. This leadership is typically invested in a person known as a *headman,* although he is often not the only person who exercises influence or leadership. Some band-level societies are so loosely organized that they appear to lack any sort of

Table 11.1 STAGES IN THE EVOLUTION OF POLITICAL ORGANIZATION

Stage	Characteristics	Mode of subsistence technology
Band	Primary political role is that of headman, with informal leadership capacity and no power over others.	Hunting and gathering
Tribe	Political leaders generally acquire leadership through their roles as economic redistributors. Leaders have high prestige but little or no power. Leadership typically limited to local village level. Villages are largely autonomous political segments; i.e., there is no unification of villages into a common political framework.	Simple horticulturalists and some pastoralists
Chiefdom	A centralized polity organized into a hierarchy of powerful chiefs and subchiefs. Individual villages lose their political autonomy and are subordinated to centralized authority.	Intensive horticulturalists, a few hunter-gatherers, and many pastoralists
State	A political system having great concentration of power in a few hands, monopolization of the means of violence, expropriation of surplus production, and a legitimizing ideology.	Agrarian, some intensive horticultural, and all modern industrial societies.

leadership structure altogether. The Eskimos are an excellent example of this most rudimentary of all known political structures. As Fried has said of them (1967:86–87):

> We pick up the Eskimos once again as the leading illustration of a society with minimal regular leadership. . . . Steenhoven says that, in the large European-influenced summer camp at Eskimo Point, there was absolutely no trace of leadership in the conduct of hunting or movements away from camp. Inland, away from alien influence, a partial and intermittent leadership was found with regard to hunting.

Perhaps more typical of band-level society are the !Kung, who have a somewhat more regular structure of leadership (Fried, 1967). Even here, however, leadership is quite loosely and informally organized. !Kung leaders direct migration and subsistence activities and perform certain ceremonies, but the position they hold contains no power, honors, or rewards. Fried appears to catch the essence of political organization at the band level when he says (1967:83):

> It is difficult, in ethnographies of simple egalitarian societies [i.e., band-level societies], to find cases in which one individual tells one or more others, "Do this!" or some command equivalent. The literature is replete with examples of individuals saying the equivalent of "If this is done, it will be good," possibly or possibly not followed by somebody else doing it. More usually the person who initiates the idea also performs the activity. . . . The leader is unable to compel any of the others to carry out his wish.

Tribes

Perhaps the clearest and most consistent usage of the term **tribe** has been provided by Elman Service (1971b) and Marshall Sahlins (1963, 1968; cf. Fried, 1967). Both Service and Sahlins conceive of a tribal society as one in which a larger unit, typically identified in cultural and linguistic terms, is divided into a number of smaller, relatively unintegrated villages. These smaller village units, while culturally identified with the tribe as a whole, are characteristically economically self-sufficient and politically autonomous. The tribe therefore has a *segmentary* character. The individual village units of the tribe maintain a high degree of autonomy, and there is no unification of the villages into a single political unit. To seek the nature of the political organization of tribal society, then, one must look within the villages themselves rather than at the tribal unit as a whole.

The tribe is typically associated with simple horticultural and some pastoral societies. Marshall Sahlins (1963) has described the basic features of one type of tribal politics through reference to the famous Melanesian big-man systems of leadership. As the primary political leaders of tribal society, big men are individuals whose public actions are designed to make invidious comparisons with others. Big men, however, do not come to office in the sense that they acquire a hereditary position by birthright. Rather, they must achieve the position by their own actions, and the status of big man is therefore personally acquired. Qualities necessary to the attainment of big-man status generally include ability as an organizer of economic production and a redistributor of wealth, skill in oratory, magical powers, and perhaps bravery in war. Success in competitive feasting is, as noted earlier, an especially important quality necessary to the attainment of top leadership. Tribal politics is therefore personal politics; the status of big man is not a title to be conferred, but a position to be earned through skill and hard work. Although the status is not easily won, it can be easily lost should laziness creep in and important skills deteriorate.

The status of big man confers great prestige and renown on the person who achieves it. However, this status confers no real power or authority to command the actions of others. Big men advise, suggest, and cajole, and more often than not their wishes will be followed. But they lack any real power since they lack the capacity to force others to do their bidding. The political nature of big-man leadership, therefore, rests on influence. Lacking the capacity to command others, big men are successful leaders only to the extent that they serve the public good. In a real sense they are *servants* of the people, servants who depend on the good graces of their followers to retain high status. The status of big man is symbiotic with society at large; in exchange for prestige and renown, big men must serve long-range societal interests, or else they will not continue to be big men. Failure to serve the public good ends in demotion from big-man status.

Nuer leopard-skin chief. Although he is an important political leader, he lacks genuine power or authority over others.

The Nuer are also a society in which a tribal form of politics prevails. The Nuer are pastoralists who inhabit a part of the Sudan in eastern Africa. Among them a number of positions of informal leadership exists, but none confers any real power or authority. One of the most important positions of leadership among the Nuer is that of "leopard-skin chief." The leopard-skin chief is charged with special responsibilities in regard to the ending of feuds, but this should "not imply that he has any right to command obedience. The right to wear a leopard-skin cloak is the privilege and the symbol of his position" (Mair, 1964:41). Lucy Mair summarizes the tribal character of politics among the Nuer (1964:63):

> Among them certain persons are leaders in the sense that they are respected, and people will wait to see what they do and then follow suit; others have ritual powers that are not shared by all members of the community, and certain ceremonies can be performed only by these men. But none of these persons can claim to give orders, nor do they even announce decisions which have been taken collectively.

Law and Order in Band and Tribal Societies

Band and tribal societies lack any specialized kind of legal or political machinery. They have no political officials with the power or authority to make decisions and implement them. The question therefore arises as to how such societies maintain law and order, or an acceptable level of internal peace and harmony. They obviously do, since social breakdown or anarchy are no more characteristic of band and tribal societies than of any other type of society.

Numerous mechanisms exist to maintain internal peace in societies lacking formalized political and legal authorities. Mention may be made here of only two. Among the Eskimos, a well-known mechanism for settling conflict and restoring order is the "song duel." The song duel is a social ritual in which individuals who are engaged in a difficult dispute attempt to settle it by "outsinging" each other. One person begins by singing aloud his grievances against the other, and the other person is given his chance to sing a reply. In their songs, the disputants attempt to shame each other. The winner of this contest is decided by community agreement. Once the community has decided upon the winner, the loser usually accepts the decision and the dispute is put to an end.

A more widespread mechanism for keeping the peace is found in the beliefs and fears that many band and tribal societies have about the practice of witchcraft. Many anthropologists have suggested that the fear of witchcraft, or of being accused of practicing witchcraft, serves as an important mechanism of social control when formalized political controls are absent. Beatrice Whiting (1950) and Guy Swanson (1960) have attempted to test this idea empirically. In a study of 26 small-scale societies, Whiting found that of 16 societies in which beliefs and fears about witchcraft were important, 15 (94 percent) lacked political officials with the legitimate right to levy punishments for offenses. By contrast, in the 10 societies that had no significant concerns about the practice of witchcraft, only 2 (20 percent) lacked such political officials. Similar results were obtained in Guy Swanson's study. In his study of 28 societies, he found (Wallace, 1966:182) that "witchcraft is highly prevalent—indeed, occurs almost exclusively—in those societies where social roles are not subject to effective control by secular authority."

Anthony Wallace (1966) suggests that when people fear having witchcraft used against them, or fear being accused of practicing witchcraft, they will be especially careful to "toe the line" so as to avoid offending others. Under such circumstances, people become convinced of how important it is not to be taken for perpetrators of evil, and this generally makes them more cooperative (Harris, 1971).

Since band and tribal societies typically lack social class divisions, conflict does not arise between and among social groups with differential access to the most valued economic resources, but rather tends to be highly personal and individualized. In societies where disputes are primarily of this personal sort, maintaining an effective social peace is not especially difficult, and elaborate political institutions are not required. However, specialized and elaborate forms of political machinery *are* required in more highly complex societies where structured class conflict becomes a significant feature of social life.

Chiefdoms

The next major evolutionary stage beyond the tribal level of political society is the **chiefdom,** a form of political organization strikingly different in several basic respects from the tribal polity. Chiefdoms are most characteristically found among intensive horticultural and pastoral societies. What distinctively separates chiefdoms from tribes is that the former achieve a political unification and centralization conspicuously lacking in the latter. The chiefdom is marked by the integration of many separate villages into a centrally coordinated complex whole governed from the top down. Marshall Sahlins (1963) again offers a classic description.

Sahlins's analysis of this form of political society is based upon the classical chiefdoms of Polynesia as they existed prior to European contact in the late eighteenth century (cf. Kirch, 1984). The most advanced of the Polynesian chiefdoms were found on the islands of Tonga, Tahiti, and Hawaii. Here were sovereignties that included as many as tens of thousands of persons spread over areas as extensive as hundreds of square miles. The classical Polynesian chiefdom was a pyramidal arrangement of higher and lower chiefs. These chiefs were regular and official holders of offices and titles, and they claimed authority over permanently established groups of followers. Authority resided in the office itself, and not merely in the person holding the position. Chiefs gained access to their positions through a line of hereditary succession.

Polynesian chiefs had rights of call on the labor and agricultural produce within their domain, which gave them considerable economic leverage over a large number of people. Through extraction of economic surplus, they established and controlled large storehouses that were used for such things as the lavish entertainment of the people and visiting chiefs, the subsidizing of craft production and technical construction works such as irrigation systems, and the organization and conduct of military campaigns. While a portion of the storehouses was redistributed to the people, a substantial part of it was used to support a permanent administrative apparatus created to carry out a variety of political functions. Such administrative officials as supervisors of the stores, talking chiefs, ceremonial attendants, and high priests, as well as specialized warrior corps, were supported from this chiefly surplus.

The pastoral Basseri are also politically organized as a chiefdom. The central leader is a chief who is granted considerable authority to command the actions of others. As Barth (1961) notes, power is conceived as emanating from him, not delegated to him by his followers. The chief plays a major political role in settling disputes that the contending parties have been unable to settle informally. In this regard, Barth comments that the chief (1961:77)

> constitutes the only "court" in the tribal system. The chief is not bound by custom or precedent in his decision—the cases that are brought before him are precisely such as cannot be mediated within the framework of tradition, for reasons of their subject, or the personalities involved. . . . Quite explicitly, he is expected to make the decision which he feels is "best for the tribe"—he is expected to exercise his privileged arbitrary authority within a very wide area of free grace, unhampered by considerations of individual justice as derived from rules. Only in disputes over the division of inheritance does he restrict his autocratic power—such cases he frequently refers for decision to a religious judge in a sedentary community.

It is clear that a significant evolutionary gulf separates tribal leaders of all sorts from genuine chiefs. Indeed, the chiefdom marks the beginning of the institutionalization of political power and authority in social life. Polynesian chiefs (and other genuine chiefs as well) developed the powers of government to the point where they no longer had to depend upon the voluntary compliance of their followers in order to make and implement decisions. As Sahlins has pointed out, their followers were now dependent *on them*, a complete reversal of the political arrangements of tribal society. The real beginnings of power and authority emerge with the chiefdom because it is there that the necessary administrative machinery needed to compel compliance is created. Polynesian chiefs could not only issue commands, but could back them up as well. When that is possible, genuine power has become a significant social force.

Yet there are definite limitations placed upon the power of chiefs. Chiefs are still related to the common people through kinship ties, and they are expected to be generous and benevolent and to serve the common good. The Basseri, for example, clearly anticipate that a chief will show his followers the utmost consideration. There is much concern that he be hospitable by providing such gifts as weapons and horses to his most prominent followers (Barth, 1961).

Chief and elders of the village of Adaklu-Tokor in Ghana being consulted by members of a British health team, which is attempting to gain permission to carry out survey work and DDT spraying. In genuine chiefdoms, chiefs carry much authority and responsibility.

Chiefs who fail to meet these expectations frequently find themselves in the midst of a popular, and more than likely successful, revolt. In ancient Polynesia, for instance, many a chief who "ate the powers of government too much" was dethroned and put to death (Sahlins, 1963). Thus, while chiefdoms have been able to institutionalize genuine power and authority, there are clear restraints on their coercive capacities. Lacking a genuine monopoly of force, and tied to the people through kinship and expectations of generosity, primitive chiefs have not been allowed to become true tyrants.

States

The chiefdom, containing only a limited capacity for compulsion, is inadequately backed by the administrative machinery necessary to overcome the most severe forms of resistance. When this administrative machinery is finally created, that form of political society known as the **state** has evolved.

The state not only continues the general evolutionary process of the increasing concentration of power; it establishes a *monopoly of force* necessary to back that power up and insure that the will of the power holders shall prevail. Indeed, this capture of a monopoly of force is essential to the very definition of a state.* As Morton Fried notes (1967:230):

*Some social scientists have challenged this notion. Anthony Giddens (1985) and Robert Carneiro (1981), for instance, point out that many societies that are almost universally considered to be states have lacked a true (i.e., complete) monopoly over the means of violence. Some

> Of great importance is the claim of the state to paramountcy in the application of naked force to social problems. Frequently this means that warfare and killing become monopolies of the state and may only be carried out at times, in places, and under the specific conditions set by the state.
>
> In the final analysis the power of a state can be manifested in a real physical force, an army, a militia, a police force, a constabulary, with specialized weaponry, drill, conscription, a hierarchy of command, and the other paraphernalia of structured control.

While holding a monopoly of force is crucial to the nature of the state, other characteristics of state-level polity are also significant. One is that the state emerges under conditions in which the significance of kinship ties is reduced. Kinship ties, such as those of chiefdoms, serve to mitigate the development of coercive power. With the transition to the state, these ties between ruler and ruled are generally eliminated. Therefore, state-level rulers no longer subjugate their kinsmen, but dominate a great mass of unrelated individuals.

States have two additional characteristics worth noting (van den Berghe, 1978). One is the extent to which they promote elaborate legitimizing ideologies. The naked use of force alone may be insufficient to guarantee compliance with the state's wishes, and rulers therefore commonly attempt to convince the people of their moral right to rule. The greater the psychological commitment of the people to the state, the less the likelihood of rebellion against it. Legitimizing ideologies have taken a variety of forms, but a very common tactic has been for state rulers to justify their rule in religious terms: to claim supernatural sanction of their role in society. Finally, states, unlike chiefdoms, have generally not been redistributive centers. The flow of the surplus to the state has been a one-way flow, and such surplus expropriation has resulted in substantial—indeed, often enormous—enrichment of the ruling powers.

As a stage in political evolution, the state typically emerges within agrarian societies, and most states throughout history have therefore been *agrarian states*. While these states have shared certain basic characteristics, there have been several different forms of the agrarian state (see the Special Topic at the end of this chapter). Not all states, however, have been confined to the agrarian level. There have been a few instances of *primitive states*, those formed within essentially primitive, intensive horticultural societies. Most notable are some of the intensive horticultural states that flourished in the nineteenth century in western and southern Africa, such as the west African Ashanti state and the south African Zulu state. George Peter Murdock (1959) has called such states *African despotisms*. He lists as among their prominent features such attributes as monarchical absolutism, conceptions of divine kingship, ritual isolation of kings, insignia of office, royal courts, territorial bureaucracy, and ministers of state. The intensive horticultural chiefdoms of Polynesia also appear to have evolved into short-lived primitive states immediately after European contact (Service, 1975).

Of course, with the rise of capitalism and industrialism, states were by no means eliminated from the scene, and all industrial societies are organized into powerful and extensive state systems; we may thus speak of *modern states*. There have been two major forms of the state in modern industrial societies. In the West, the principal form of the state is a parliamentary democracy. Here the all-powerful and despotic nature of the state has been significantly tempered with the introduction of certain basic freedoms and at least some semblance of control by the people of the basic apparatus of

---

individuals and groups outside the state, they claim, sometimes possess a certain capacity to use various means of violence. While this is undoubtedly true, the fact remains that in these societies the state's capacity for overcoming organized resistance to its rule is still enormous, and this is the key idea implied by usage of the word *monopoly*.

government. Even though the parliamentary democracies have not actually created a genuine democratic order, at least they have eliminated some of the worst and most despotic forms of state power. The other major kind of modern industrial state, the totalitarian state, has arisen in the non-Western state socialist societies. Here, despite some pretense of democracy, the state operates in its more typical despotic fashion, except in this case with an awesome monopoly of force made possible by an industrial level of technology. (Western parliamentary democracies and non-Western totalitarian states are discussed in detail in the next chapter.)

Thus the state in one form or another represents the outcome of a long process of political evolution in which democracy and equality were increasingly undermined and replaced with the domination of the many by the few. Although the evolution of the state was achieved in gradual rather than sudden fashion, its actual emergence represents a great watershed in human history. For it was here that powerful leaders no longer needed to promise to be generous to their followers. They could and did promise their followers little or nothing, save continuous subjugation and constant toil, and they had a sufficient monopoly of force to back up their rule. What were some of the earliest states like, and how and why did they come into existence?

THE ORIGIN OF THE STATE

Pristine Versus Secondary States

In order to analyze the rise of the state in human society, it is useful to follow Morton Fried's (1967) distinction between **pristine** and **secondary** states. According to Fried, secondary states are those that have arisen as the result of the presence of one or more pre-existing states. Contact between a nonstate society and one or more state-level societies may create conditions in which the former is rapidly turned into a state. Many, if not most, of the primitive states in Polynesia and Africa arose in this manner. Secondary states, however, need not form through intersocietal contact. When new forms of the state gradually or suddenly replace old states within the same sociocultural system, then we can also speak of the new state as a secondary state. According to this conception of a secondary state, the overwhelming majority of states in human history have been secondary in nature.

On the other hand, the very first states arose under conditions in which there was no pre-existing state. These are the states that Fried has termed *pristine*. As he says, "When a pristine state emerges it does so in a political vacuum. That is, there is no other more highly developed state present that might help it toward stateship" (Fried, 1967:231–232).

Obviously there have been only a handful of pristine states in human history. Pristine states arose in four regions of the Old World and two regions of the New World. The earliest of the Old World states evolved in Mesopotamia (what is now mainly Iraq) and Egypt approximately 6000–5000 B.P. The first state arose in China with the creation of the Shang Dynasty in approximately 3750 B.P. In India, state-level society was evolving around 4500 B.P. All of these Old World states emerged in geographical regions dominated by major rivers. Thus the earliest Mesopotamian states arose in the fertile area between the Tigris and Euphrates rivers, the state in China evolved along the Yellow River in northern China, and the earliest Indian state emerged along the Indus River.

In the New World, pristine states evolved somewhat later. The two regions of New World state formation were Mesoamerica (mostly what is now Guatemala and Mexico) and Peru. In the Mesoamerican lowlands, the first states to emerge were those created by the Olmec and Maya cultures. The Olmec state flourished between 3200 and 2800 B.P. The Mayan state achieved its peak between approximately A.D. 300 and 900. In the Mesoamerican highlands, just north of what is now Mexico City, the first state was formed around the city of Teotihuacan in approximately 2000 B.P. The most powerful of the Mesoamerican highland states, though, was established by the Aztecs, whose capital city was known as Tenochtitlán. The Aztecs reached the apex of their development in the early sixteenth century. Sometime around 2000 B.P. in Peru, a series of wars and conquests led to the formation of more complex and extensive political units. These eventually reached imperial scope and culminated in the establishment of the Inca Empire, which reached its zenith in the fifteenth and sixteenth centuries (Harris, 1975).

The Emergence of Pristine States

A study that presents a clear picture of the main features of pristine state formation has been carried out by Robert Adams (1966). Adams's study is devoted to a comparative analysis of pristine state formation in one Old World case—Mesopotamia—and one New World case—central Mexico. A major conclusion concerns the striking similarities in state formation in each instance. His analysis therefore offers considerable insight into state formation as a classic process of parallel evolution. It is highly probable that the processes involved in state formation in Mesopotamia and Mexico were broadly similar to those involved in the emergence of the other pristine states.

Basic to the emergence of the state in these two cases was the development of social stratification. Adams characterizes Early Dynastic Mesopotamia as being highly stratified. At the pinnacle of Mesopotamian society stood princely families who, during late Early Dynastic and Akkadian times, were increasingly extending their control of land. These ruling families apparently headed manorial estates. A significant proportion of the labor force employed on these estates consisted of slaves.

At the top of the Aztec social hierarchy were royal households that in due time evolved into an endogamous (in-marrying) nobility sharply distinguished from the rest of the population by wealth, education, diet, and dress. Great estates were at the king's disposal; large amounts of surplus production were generated by these estates, the surplus flowing as tribute from commoners to the ruling class. At an intermediate level in the social hierarchy were groups of warriors and merchants. Below them were localized kin groups that were internally stratified and held corporate (collective) title to land. Below these, in turn, were persons who cultivated the private lands of the nobility and who have been likened to medieval serfs. At the very bottom of the social order stood slaves.

In both Mesopotamia and Mexico we find a general pattern of political evolution characterized by the emergence of theocratic polities and their eventual transformation into militaristic and, ultimately, conquest states. The early formation of the state in both cases was marked by a decidedly religious focus, with much emphasis on temple building and governance by priesthoods. The dominance of religious groups, however, soon gave way to the rise to power of militaristic groups. Political power came to be increasingly concentrated in dynastic institutions at the expense of earlier communal and religious bodies. Archaeological evidence demonstrates the existence of palaces containing private apartments for the ruling family and the families of top-ranking administrative officials and personal servants. In Mesopotamia there is good evidence for the existence of an array of political functionaries such as gatekeepers, cooks, servants, messengers, and slaves. Clearly the palace structure associated with both states indicates the development of highly stratified societies in which the power

A depiction of the pharaoh Khufu (Cheops) overseeing the construction of his great pyramid at Giza. The role of the pyramids in Egyptian civilization was more symbolic than practical: they were conceived by their originators as physical representations of the power of the state and the presumed greatness of it leaders.

and complexity of governing bodies had been erected on a major scale. Both societies had parallel conceptions of kingship, and both ultimately evolved into major conquest states that extended their territorial control over wide regions. This increasing conquest of neighboring lands and peoples brought greater demands for tribute, increasing stratification, and yet further intensification of the autocratic features of the state.

Theories of the Origin of the State

A variety of theories attempting to explain the general process of pristine state formation have been proposed by social scientists. The most important of these are (1) *functionalist* theories, which stress the role of the state as a societal integrator and see it arising as a necessary organizational structure to coordinate complex sociocultural systems; (2) *Marxian* theories, which give priority to the importance of class struggle in explaining the rise of the state; and (3) *ecological* theories, which place emphasis on the role of population pressure and environment in the formation of the state.

A Functionalist Theory A well-known functionalist theory of the state is found in the work of Elman Service (1975, 1978). Rather than conceiving of the state as an oppressive and exploitative institution, Service thinks of it as a form of centralized leadership that organizes and coordinates society for the mutual benefit of its various individuals and groups. When the state arises, therefore, the principal distinction within society is not between wealthy and poor or oppressors and oppressed, but between governing and governed groups. The state originates in order to serve more effectively the needs of the governed.

Service sees three principal types of benefits arising from the creation of the state. The first concerns economic redistribution. The state is an organ that mobilizes natural resources and persons for important production and consumption functions. More diversified ecological zones are said to be exploited through state-level organization. The products of skilled workers and diverse ecological zones are seen as being brought together for the benefit of the court, the bureaucracy, the priesthood, the army, and also for the citizenry at large. A second major benefit conceived by Service is that provided by new forms of war organization. Intensified warfare is said to be an integrative feature of society in that it brings in increasing wealth in the form of booty, captives, and tribute and thus enhances the "national pride." A third major benefit allegedly produced by the state is that of public works. The state oversees the construction of temples, tombs, pyramids, walls, roads, irrigation systems, and many other public projects.

Great skepticism appears warranted with respect to this theory. It seems unduly optimistic in the extreme to argue that the rise of the state produced positive benefits for the members of society collectively. Of course, the rise of the state did produce certain crucial benefits, yet not for society as a whole. On the contrary, these benefits largely accrued to the ruling class. Service suggests that the waging of war was a benefit, again for society as a whole. Yet the spoils of war were primarily claimed by the most privileged members of society, especially the ruling class. Service also claims that the building of temples, tombs, pyramids, and other public works was a great social benefit. Yet the vast majority of the citizenry did not have their lives improved by such public works. In fact, many persons suffered much additional hardship because of these construction projects, since they were the ones who contributed the labor necessary to their realization.

The Marxian Theory The alternative to a functionalist interpretation of the origin of the state is some type of conflict theory, one version of which is the Marxian theory. The classical Marxian view of the state holds that the state, in Marx's own words, is "the executive committee of the ruling class." That is, the state is a political body that exists primarily as a means of protecting the economic interests of the dominant social class within a stratified society. With the division of society into classes, the state becomes a virtual necessity from the standpoint of the dominant class. Friedrich Engels summarizes this view quite well (1970:232,235; orig. 1884):

> At a definite stage of economic development, which necessarily involved the cleavage of society into classes, the state became a necessity because of this cleavage. . . .
> The central link in civilized society is the state, which in all typical periods is without exception the state of the ruling class and in all cases continues to be essentially a machine for holding down the oppressed, exploited class.

Morton Fried (1967, 1978) is a vigorous contemporary defender of this view of the origin of the state. For Fried, once a society has developed a system of social stratification, the emergence of the state is all but assured. The appearance of differential access to resources means the emergence of privileged and disprivileged groups, and those holding a privileged position must secure and protect it against the threats of the disprivileged to take it away. Indeed, Fried's conception of "state" and of "stratified society" are fundamentally the same (1967:225–226):

> The state forms in embryo in the stratified society, which, by this reasoning, must be one of the least stable models of organization that has ever existed. The stratified society is torn between two possibilities: It builds within itself great pressures for its own dissolution and for a return to a simpler kind of organization. . . . On the other side, the stratified community, to maintain itself, must evolve more powerful institutions of political control than ever were called upon to maintain a system of differential ranking. . . . Usually that bolstering involves the appearance of agents who function to maintain the economic and political system and whose position in that system has nothing to do with kinship.

One difficulty with Fried's version of the Marxian argument concerns his claim that there are no known societies that are stratified and that also lack a state. Actually, there have been a number of stratified societies that lacked true state-level polities. Classical chiefdoms, such as those of Polynesia, were certainly stratified, since there was a division of those societies into social groups having unequal control over productive resources. But the classical Polynesian chiefdoms were by definition not states, since they lacked a sufficient monopoly of force to override the will of their members consistently.

Nevertheless, with appropriate modification Fried's general point holds up well: Societies with especially elaborate and intense stratification systems do have states, and in these societies there is a very close connection between the ruling economic class and the state. And, although the question is still an open one, considerable evidence suggests that elaborate stratification systems with their ruling classes historically came first and then were followed by the emergence of the state (Fried, 1978:46; Haas, 1982). All of this points to considerable merit on the part of the Marxian theory, or at least suggests that it is moving us in a more fruitful direction than Service's functionalist theory.

However, the issue cannot be settled so easily, for there is a different conflict theory that we have yet to consider—Carneiro's famous circumscription theory—that seems at least as compelling as the Marxian interpretation.

The Circumscription Theory Many scholars have called attention to the role of demographic and ecological factors in the rise of the state (cf. Kirch, 1984; Johnson and Earle, 1987), but the best-known theory of this type is Robert Carneiro's (1970, 1981, 1987) *circumscription theory.* This theory is in fact more than just a theory of the origin of the state; it is a theory of the entire course of political evolution.

Carneiro notes that a factor common to all major areas of the world where pristine states arose was what he has called *environmental circumscription.* This exists when areas of rich agricultural land are surrounded either by areas of very poor or unusable land or by natural barriers, such as major mountain ranges. The potential operation of this factor can be seen in such areas of pristine state formation as the

Middle East, where fertile river valleys were surrounded by vast expanses of arid land deficient in rainfall, and in Peru, where fertile valleys were blockaded by major mountain ranges.

In order to show the likely consequences of circumscribed environments, Carneiro begins with an illustration of a completely different kind of ecological situation, the Amazon Basin of South America. Here was a vast area of tropical forest in which nothing even approaching indigenous state formation occurred. This region of the world has probably long been occupied by numerous horticultural villages. An abundance of land was available for horticulture, population density was typically quite low, and hence there was little if any problem of population pressure. Warfare, while common in many horticultural societies of the region, was not fought directly over land itself. With an abundance of land suitable for horticulture, defeat in warfare meant that the defeated group could simply move away and re-establish itself on new land. Under such circumstances, we would expect that individual societies would be able to maintain their autonomy and preserve their existing sociopolitical adaptation to the environment.

The situation is different where environmental circumscription is present. As Carneiro notes, where there are sharp limits on the availability of productive land, population growth soon leads to growth in the number of villages occupying the land, with the result that all arable land is eventually under cultivation. This puts pressure on individual villages for the intensification of production in order to feed the expanding population. With continuing population growth, population pressure becomes a severe problem, leading, most likely, to the intensification of warfare in order to capture additional land. Under such circumstances, the consequences of warfare for the defeated group cannot be dispersal to a new region, since there is no suitable place to go. The conquered group will therefore likely be politically subordinated to the victorious group, leading to the establishment of complex political systems at the chiefdom level. With further population growth and increased militarism over the struggle for land, chiefdoms will ultimately evolve into yet more complex, state-level polities. The ultimate outcome of such an evolutionary process might well be the formation of vast political empires, such as those that prevailed in such circumscribed areas as Peru and the Middle East.

Two wrinkles that Carneiro has added to this basic theory involve the concepts of *social circumscription* and *resource concentration*. Social circumscription occurs when the barriers to human movements are other societies rather than features of the geographical environment. This can operate as a factor in political evolution apart from, or in addition to, physical circumscription. Resource concentration exists when

Robert L. Carneiro. Carneiro is Curator of South American Indians at the American Museum of Natural History in New York. His circumscription theory is a major contribution to our understanding of long-term political evolution.

an environment is especially abundant in plant and animal resources. This abundance tends to attract people to the area and stimulate population growth. Population pressure is a likely result, but movement out of the area may be impeded by the presence of other groups—by social circumscription. Warfare and political conquest, and thus political evolution, are expected outcomes. Carneiro (1987) suggests that it is this kind of process that has produced substantial political evolution in uncircumscribed environments, such as some regions of Amazonia.

The circumscription theory is perhaps the most impressive theory of political evolution we have, and it has stood the test of time remarkably well (Graber and Roscoe, 1988). It has been extensively tested through archaeological and anthropological research, and the results have been much more on the positive than on the negative side (Kirch, 1984, 1988; Schacht, 1988; Carneiro, 1988). It is likely that Carneiro has come very close to identifying some of the key elements in long-term political evolution. However, one nagging difficulty concerns Carneiro's strong emphasis on warfare and his relative neglect of economic processes in political evolution. As Patrick Kirch (1988) and Robert Schacht (1988) have pointed out, there is a very close correlation between agricultural intensification and political evolution, and both of these are closely related to population pressure and environmental circumscription. Could it be that chiefdoms and states are political responses to the growth of the stratification systems that are associated with agricultural intensification, as the Marxian theory is basically suggesting? Could such economic changes be more important than, or at least as important as, warfare? More research is clearly needed to establish solid answers to these crucial questions, and so in the meantime it is difficult to make a clear choice between the circumscription theory and the Marxian theory—assuming, of course, that such a choice needs to be made.

Secondary State Formation

Pristine states perished long ago, but once they evolved they created the conditions for both the intensification of state power and the formation of many more states over larger parts of the globe. The states that developed in response to the prior existence of one or more earlier states are those we call secondary. Most of the states that have ever existed have been secondary in nature. The conditions that give rise to secondary states are not the same as those that have led to pristine state formation.

As Marvin Harris (1977) has argued, a number of secondary states have formed in order to defend themselves against the encroachment of other state-organized societies. Some developed in order to acquire control over strategic trade routes, and yet others emerged among nomadic peoples when they attempted to plunder the wealth of state-level societies living on their borders. In this regard, Harris (1977:81) notes that

> low-density pastoralist peoples—Turks, Mongols, Huns, Manchus, and Arabs—have repeatedly developed states but only by preying upon the preexisting Chinese, Hindu, Roman, and Byzantine empires. In West Africa secondary states developed as a result of Moslem and European attempts to control the slave, gold, and ivory trades, while in southern Africa the Zulu developed a state in the nineteenth century to meet the military threat posed by Dutch colonists invading their homeland.

It seems that secondary state formation is generally a conscious or intentional process. People are aware that they are creating a state and fully intend to bring it about. In all probability, pristine state formation was very different. As Morton Fried suggests, "No individual choices in the matter were ever presented in any significant sense" (1967:226). What is critical to see, as Harris (1977:81) notes, is that pristine states

Table 11.2 THEORIES OF POLITICAL EVOLUTION

Theory	Characteristics	Evaluation
Functionalist theory	Long-term political evolution produces increasingly well-adapted political structures, the best-adapted of which is the state. The earliest states more adequately served societal needs than did previous political structures. Early states functioned as important economic redistributors, as superior war machines, and as administrative units devoted to the construction of important public monuments.	A very dubious theory that greatly overrates the beneficial consequences of chiefdoms and states for society as a whole, and greatly undervalues the narrow self-interest of elites in generating and sustaining chiefdoms and states.
Marxian theory	More powerful and advanced political systems accompany the rise and evolution of social stratification. The state comes into play in order to protect and enhance the interests of the economically dominant class in a situation in which it is threatened by subordinate classes.	Far superior to the functionalist argument, but by itself not a fully adequate or complete explanation.
Circumscription theory	Political evolution occurs most rapidly and extensively in environments posing physical or social barriers to territorial expansion. When population pressure reaches high levels in such regions, people can no longer avoid its negative consequences by migrating to new regions. The result is increasing social conflict culminating in higher and higher levels of political conquest. The state ultimately emerges from this process.	An extremely impressive theory that undoubtedly captures many of the most important dimensions of political evolution. May be complementary to the Marxian theory.

occurred as the result of an unconscious process: The participants in this enormous transformation seem not to have known what they were creating. By imperceptible shifts in the redistributive balance from one generation to the next, the human species bound itself over into a form of social life in which the many debased themselves on behalf of the exaltation of the few.

SUMMARY

1. Political systems are the means whereby societies maintain internal law and order and manage intersocietal relations. In many societies political leaders have acquired power and authority over others. Power involves the capacity to compel the actions of others, whereas authority gives moral legitimacy to political rule. In the simplest societies only social influence prevails. This is an informal means of political control lacking any features of compulsion.

2. The band is the simplest level of political organization. Bands are characteristic of hunter-gatherers. Power and authority are absent, and leadership tends to be highly informal. Tribes are also political structures in which power and authority are not present. Tribes have often been described as segmentary forms of political organization. Different villages within a larger cultural unit are highly autonomous and there is no overarching structure of the whole.

3. Band and tribal forms of political organization have no formalized means of political control, but they are anything but anarchic. Numerous informal mechanisms, such as witchcraft accusations and song duels, exist to maintain law and order.

4. A third stage of political evolution is the chiefdom, which marks the beginnings of power and authority in social life. Chiefs have considerable control over their followers, including the capacity to use force. Chiefdoms are unified, integrated political systems in which villages lose their autonomy and are subordinated to the whole. They have been found among many intensive horticulturalists and pastoralists.

5. A crucial watershed in political evolution was the origin of the state. The key characteristic of the state is its monopolization of the means of violence within a territory. This means that the state has a highly developed capacity to overcome numerous forms of resistance to it.

6. The first states arose some 5000 to 6000 years ago in Mesopotamia and Egypt, and slightly later in China and India. States first arose in the New World around 3000 B.P. in Mesoamerica and some time after 2000 B.P in Peru. These first states are generally known as pristine states. Once pristine states formed in these regions of the world, they created the conditions for the formation of many other states, which are known as secondary states. The process of pristine state formation is a classic instance of parallel evolution. Explaining this process is one of the crucial problems of modern macrosociology.

7. The most important theories of political evolution in general, and the evolution of the state in particular, are the functionalist, Marxian, and circumscription theories. The basic features of these theories, and an evaluation of them, are found in Table 11.2.

SPECIAL TOPIC: FEUDALISM AND ORIENTAL DESPOTISM

All agrarian societies are highly stratified, state-organized societies. However, just as agrarian societies have differed in their modes of economic and social organization, so have they differed in their state structures. Two types of agrarian states have been of persistent interest to social scientists: **feudal states** and what might be termed **agrobureaucratic states.**

In feudal societies landownership is private, and the landowning nobility subjects a class of peasants beneath them; over this class they exercise political rule and legal jurisdiction. However, such landownership is not unconditional or absolute, acquired once and for all and without strings. Rather, land is acquired in the form of a **fief.** A fief is a grant of land given by a superior lord to a lesser lord or vassal in return for the performance of certain obligations, especially military service and personal protection. The vassal granted a fief acquires with it the legal jurisdiction over the peasantry who are associated with it. Ownership and control of land are thus intimately connected with the political institution known as **vassalage.** Vassalage is the personal tie between unequally ranked landlords. It takes the form of a contract binding the parties into mutual obligations, and it is symbolized by personal oaths of loyalty. Through this institution, a complex hierarchy of lords is established, extending from the lowest-ranking vassal at the bottom all the way to the king or monarch at the top. In principle, the monarch may be the owner of all land, but in actuality this land is granted out as fiefs to a whole series of lords of different rank. Each lord exercises jurisdiction only over those lands that have been granted him.

Vassalage and the fief therefore establish a particular kind of political system characterized by its *decentralization,* by what Perry Anderson (1974a) calls the "parcellization of sovereignty" among a hierarchy of lords. Rather than investing power in a centrally coordinated state, the feudal polity spreads it out among a host of lords, each of whom has strictly circumscribed jurisdiction over a limited geographical region and a limited number of persons. Because of the decentralized nature of the feudal polity, the residence of lords is in the countryside (i.e., in their castles), and an ideology exalting the virtues of rural life typically accompanies this practice.

True feudal systems fitting the above description have by no means typified agrarian societies. Indeed, only two major examples of feudal societies are generally agreed on by historians. The prototype of feudalism prevailed in western Europe from about the ninth to the fifteenth century. In addition, historians are generally agreed that a type of feudalism existed in Japan from about the fourteenth to the nineteenth century. Despite their local differences, the European and the Japanese feudal systems were strikingly similar. In both cases we find the essential features of feudalism (P. Anderson, 1974b:413):

The court of the emperor of China. For most of the last two thousand years of its existence as a genuinely agrarian civilization, China was characterized by a massive centralized governmental apparatus.

> *The links between military service, conditional landownership and seigneurial jurisdiction. . . . The graded hierarchy between lord, vassal, and rear-vassal, to form a chain of suzerainty and dependence. . . . An aristocracy of mounted knights formed a hereditary ruling class.*

What accounts for feudal regimes? Most students of this problem have suggested that feudal forms of government arise as responses to the new military needs encountered after the breakdown of large centralized empires. European feudalism, for example, was created in the aftermath of the fall of Rome. The collapse of Roman political authority left communities vulnerable to attack by marauding Germanic tribes that preyed upon much of what was formerly the Roman Empire. It was therefore necessary to fuse political rule with military specialization as a means of protection against these attacks.

While many agrarian societies have been called feudal, most have developed political systems that contrast sharply with the decentralized character of feudal regimes. Indeed, the general tendency in agrarian societies has been for the *centralization,* rather than the fragmentation, of power. Many agrarian civilizations have been marked by highly centralized, bureaucratic, and intensely powerful states in which the masses were highly subordinated to a tiny elite.

The kind of state that we have called an agrobureaucratic state is one having essentially the following characteristics: Massive amounts of power are concentrated in the hands of a tiny group of persons or, indeed, in the hands of a single ruler standing at the apex of society; private ownership of land may exist to some extent, but land is primarily owned by the state itself; the state involves itself intensively in directing various forms of public works affecting the entire society; and the state rules the mass of people in despotic fashion, severely punishing any activity perceived as a threat to its existence. Such states have been found in many of the great agrarian civilizations, such as China, India, and ancient Mesopotamia and Egypt. No doubt other agrarian societies have had similar state systems. These states stand quite far removed from the vassalage and fief systems of feudal regimes. They are all-powerful, despotic states severely repressing their subjects (Harris, 1977:157):

> *Despite the development of philosophies and religions advocating justice and mercy, the rulers of these vast realms frequently had to rely on intimidation, force, and naked terror to maintain law and order. Total submissiveness was demanded of underlings, the supreme symbol of which was the obligation to prostrate oneself and grovel in the presence of the mighty. . . . In all of these ancient empires there were ruthless systems for routing out and punishing disobedient persons. Spies kept the rulers informed about potential troublemakers. Punishments ranged from beatings to death by torture. . . . In ancient India the magistrates condemned disobedient subjects to eighteen different kinds of torture, including beatings on the soles of the feet, suspension upside down, and burning of finger joints. . . . In China the emperor punished those who expressed incautious opinions by having them castrated in a darkened cell.*

The modern notion of despotic agrobureaucratic states is based upon Marx's famous idea that many non-European societies were typified by a peculiar **Asiatic mode of production.** Marx argued that such great Asian societies as India and China were strikingly different from European feudalism. He held that the Asiatic mode of production was especially characterized by an absence of private ownership of land and by the presence of a centralized state that regulated complex irrigation systems throughout vast territories. He thought that large-scale hydraulic agriculture, necessitated by arid climates, was the technological basis for the lack of private landownership and for the centralizing and despotic character of the state.

The most prominent modern scholar to elaborate upon the notion of an Asiatic mode of production is Karl Wittfogel. Wittfogel (1957) has argued the case for a particular type of society—what he has most frequently called **Oriental despotism**—typified by state ownership of land; the presence of large-scale irrigation works necessary for hydraulic agriculture; and the existence of a cruel, despotic state claiming total power over its subjects. Like Marx, Wittfogel claims that the basis for such a despotic state is the need for hydraulic agriculture in arid climates. Wittfogel believes that the centralized powers of government were required to create and maintain a vast network of irrigation works. The larger these works became, the greater became the centralized and despotic character of the state. Wittfogel, however, has gone at least one major step beyond Marx. He has extended the idea of Oriental despotism to include non-Asian societies with small-scale waterworks (such as Hawaii) as well as non-Asian societies having no irrigation systems at all (such as Russia). In the latter case, Wittfogel has argued that once an Oriental despotism developed, it could be carried by diffusion to other societies. Ultimately Wittfogel has come to view many quite diverse societies in many parts of the world as examples of Oriental despotism.

Wittfogel ultimately carries the notion of despotic hydraulic civilizations too far. He has been sharply criticized for mixing into a common type many highly diverse societies (P. Anderson, 1974b). This criticism seems justified when Wittfogel offers as examples of hydraulic civilizations such primitive and stateless societies as aboriginal Hawaii and the horticultural Hopi Indians of the southwestern United States. He has also been criticized on the grounds that a number of societies had developed the centralizing features of government before complex irrigation systems were found within them. Yet Wittfogel's theory is not one of the origin of the state, but of the emergence of a *particular kind* of unusually despotic state (Harris, 1977). And in this respect Wittfogel has vigorous defenders. Harris (1977), for example, argues that the record of archaeological discoveries generally reveals step-by-step increases in the despotic power of the state that parallel respective increases in the size and complexity of irrigation works.

Although there can be no doubt that in certain respects Wittfogel has carried his theory beyond its feasible limits, the real point is whether there is a basic core of truth in Wittfogel's principal claims. Such civilizations as China and India most certainly were despotic, centralized, agrobureaucratic states. But whether or not hydraulic agriculture was the technological basis for such despotisms is still an unsettled question.

FOR FURTHER READING

American Behavioral Scientist. The March 1988 issue (Volume 31, Number 4) of this journal is entirely devoted to articles evaluating Carneiro's circumscription theory. Contains a reply by Carneiro.

Fried, Morton H. *The Evolution of Political Society.* New York: Random House, 1967. An important work developing Fried's conception of the major stages in the evolution of political organization. Of particular significance is Fried's analysis of the emergence of social stratification and the state.

Haas, Jonathan. *The Evolution of the Prehistoric State.* New York: Columbia University Press, 1982. A discussion of archaeological evidence regarding the origin of the state with a particular focus on the opposition between functionalist and conflict theories of state origins. Comes down basically on the conflict side.

Harris, Marvin. *Cannibals and Kings: The Origins of Cultures.* New York: Random House, 1977. Several chapters of this engaging work deal with the emergence of various forms of state-organized society. Material, especially ecological, factors are given primary emphasis in Harris's theoretical analyses.

Johnson, Allen W., and Timothy Earle. *The Evolution of Human Societies.* Stanford, Calif.: Stanford University Press, 1987. A valuable treatment of general social evolution with a particular emphasis on political evolution. The theoretical perspective is materialist, with a strong role being given to population pressure.

Kirch, Patrick Vinton. *The Evolution of the Polynesian Chiefdoms.* New York: Cambridge University Press, 1984. An extremely thorough archaeological analysis of social and political evolution in Polynesia by a recognized expert. The most comprehensive evolutionary analysis of this important region of the world to date.

Mair, Lucy. *Primitive Government.* Baltimore: Penguin Books, 1964. A well-known discussion of various types of political systems among primitive societies, from bands to states. The ethnographic examples are drawn from Africa, the region in which Mair specializes.

Sahlins, Marshall. "Poor Man, Rich Man, Big Man, Chief: Political Types in Melanesia and Polynesia." *Comparative Studies in Society and History* 5:285–303, 1963. A fascinating discussion of the contrast between the tribal and chiefdom stages of political organization using Melanesian and Polynesian societies as case studies.

Service, Elman. *Primitive Social Organization: An Evolutionary Perspective.* Second edition. New York: Random House, 1971. The development of Service's conception of the major stages in political evolution: band, tribe, chiefdom, and state.

Service, Elman. *Origins of the State and Civilization.* New York: Norton, 1975. A valuable discussion of some well-known primitive states and of the rise of pristine states in both the Old and New Worlds. Contains much useful descriptive material as well as Service's functionalist explanation of the origin of pristine states.

Wenke, Robert J. *Patterns in Prehistory: Mankind's First Three Million Years.* Second edition. New York: Oxford University Press, 1984. Extensive discussion of the origin of the state in all the major centers of pristine state formation.

Wittfogel, Karl. *Oriental Despotism.* New Haven: Yale University Press, 1957. A classic study of those despotic agrarian states that Wittfogel believes arose through the establishment of large-scale hydraulic agriculture. Despite some serious drawbacks, the book is a major contribution to the study of agrarian political systems and may still be regarded as fundamental reading.

CHAPTER 12

The State Since the Evolution of Capitalism

This chapter continues the discussion of political evolution begun in Chapter 11. Its focus is on the development of the state since the rise of modern capitalism. The chapter begins by looking at the development of the early modern state: the transformation of weak feudal states into the strong centralized bureaucratic states of early modern Europe. Attention then shifts to the capitalist origins of parliamentary democracy in the West, followed by a close look at the character and functions of the state in modern capitalist society. The state in modern state socialist societies is also examined, particularly in terms of why an authoritarian mode of government has accompanied the socialist organization of the economy.

THE EARLY MODERN STATE

Our discussion of the feudal state pointed to decentralization as one of its principal features. This fragmented form of political organization, however, lasted only a few centuries. With the crisis of the feudal mode of production and the emergence of a capitalist economy in Europe, feudal states were fairly rapidly turned into massive centralized structures far different from their predecessors. From approximately the sixteenth to the eighteenth century, much of Europe was marked by the rise of what has been variously called the **early modern state** or **absolutist monarchy.** Absolutism centralized the powers of government in the hands of a powerful monarch and a large bureaucracy that supported his rule. The state now intervened in directing the affairs of society and its various segments in a much more intensive way than under the old feudal regimes. One of the most important characteristics of this new type of state was its role as a war machine; large standing military units became prominent. Accompanying this centralization of monarchical power was the famous legitimizing ideology of the absolute monarchies: the "divine right of kings."

Such absolute monarchies were characteristic of western Europe, but they also arose in eastern Europe, especially in Russia where an extremely strong absolutism emerged. The earliest of the monarchical states arose in Spain. Here, beginning in the late fifteenth century, the Hapsburg Dynasty came to power with the marriage of Ferdinand and Isabella. The Hapsburgs concentrated their attention on plundering the wealth of the New World through the establishment of colonies in the Americas. The treasure controlled by the Hapsburgs was greatly swelled by the precious metals shipped back to Spain from its overseas colonies. Absolutism in France was the result of a gradual development dating as far back as the fourteenth century (P. Anderson, 1974b). But it was in the late seventeenth century, under the reign of Louis XIV, that French absolutism achieved the zenith of its power. Louis XIV was the supreme symbol of absolute rule throughout all of Europe. He is reputed to have said *l'État, c'est moi* (I am the state). While he may never have uttered those precise words, such language clearly expresses his view of his own power (Burns, 1973). The weakest and most short-lived of all the western European absolutisms was formed in England. Absolutism began there in the late fifteenth century with the rise to power of the Tudors, who were eventually replaced by the Stuarts at the beginning of the seventeenth century. English absolutism was not to survive past the end of the seventeenth century.

The rise of European absolute monarchies coincided with the collapse of feudalism and the emergence of the capitalist world-economy. This major economic transformation undoubtedly lay behind the major political changes that were taking place. What is not yet settled, though, is the question of the specific role played by the early modern states within the framework of greatly changing economic conditions. From a Marxian standpoint, the role of the absolutist state during this transitional period has been conceptualized in two very different ways. On the one hand, the absolutist state has been viewed as a force mediating the interests of the old feudal nobility and the rising capitalist class (Engels, 1970 [orig. 1884]; Wallerstein, 1974a). On the other hand, the new centralized states have been seen as serving to protect and shore up the declining interests of the old nobility against the advances of the bourgeoisie (C. Hill, 1953; Kiernan, 1965; P. Anderson, 1974b; cf. Kiernan, 1980).

Louis XIV, the "Sun King."

The view that absolute monarchies mediated the interests of nobles and capitalists was originally held by Engels, who saw absolutism as a balancing mechanism attempting to achieve an equilibrium between these two classes (cf. P. Anderson, 1974b). Wallerstein (1974a) appears to take a similar view. He informs us (1974a:355) that

> within the framework of a capitalist world-economy . . . a strong state is the best choice between difficult alternatives for the two groups that are strongest in political, economic, and military terms: the emergent capitalist strata, and the old aristocratic hierarchies.
>
> For the former, the strong state in the form of the "absolute monarchies" was a prime customer, a guardian against local and international

> brigandage, a mode of social legitimation, a preemptive protection against the creation of strong state barriers elsewhere. For the latter, the strong state represented a brake on these same capitalist strata, an upholder of status conventions, a maintainer of order, a promoter of luxury.

Perry Anderson (1974b) is the best-known representative of the alternative position: that absolutism served to bolster the interests of the nobility in an age of great economic change. One important way in which Anderson's position differs from Wallerstein's is that Anderson does not regard absolutist Europe as yet having a capitalist economy. Rather, he sees the age of absolutism as governed by "a complex combination of feudal and capitalist modes of production." Furthermore, he argues that the disappearance of legal serfdom did not mean the end of feudal exploitation of the peasantry. Instead, with the traditional bond between lord and serf broken, the nobility looked to a strong centralized state to enforce its continued domination and exploitation of the peasants. Absolutism was thus a new form of the power of the noble class in an era when its traditional power over the peasantry had been destroyed by rising capitalism (P. Anderson, 1974b:18):

> Absolutism was essentially just this: *a redeployed and recharged apparatus of feudal domination,* designed to clamp the peasant masses back into their traditional social position—despite and against the gains they had won by the widespread commutation of dues. In other words, the Absolutist State was never an arbiter between the aristocracy and the bourgeoisie, still less an instrument of the nascent bourgeoisie against the aristocracy: it was the new political carapace of a threatened nobility.

The present state of our understanding of this problem does not permit any definite resolution of the disagreement between Wallerstein and Anderson. Nonetheless, Michael Hechter and William Brustein (1980) have carried out an analysis of the early modern state that suggests that both Wallerstein and Anderson have captured significant portions of the truth. They propose that because of the growing threat the bourgeoisie was posing for the landlords, "the first modern states in western Europe were set up at the behest of the landed aristocracy" (1980:1085). However (1980:1086):

> Once the state gained power at the expense of its constituents it was free to pursue its own interests, subject, as always, to existing constraints. At first the modern state enacted policies on behalf of the landed aristocracy. . . . But gradually thereafter, modern western European history tells the story of how the state slowly deprived the landed aristocracy of its prerogatives, biting the very hands that had once fashioned its existence.

In other words, although the early modern state arose because of the special economic needs of the aristocracy, this state eventually gained a strong measure of freedom from that class. Indeed, in due time it increasingly came to serve economic interests directly opposed to those of the aristocracy: the interests of the expanding capitalist class. This state was becoming more and more a capitalist state.

THE EMERGENCE OF MODERN STATES

In the contemporary world we find two major forms of the state. In the West the state takes the form of a **parliamentary democracy.** Such a state is characteristic of the major industrial capitalist societies of Western Europe and North America, although it prevails elsewhere as well. In general, where we find highly developed capitalist societies, we find parliamentary democracy as the dominant form of polity.

It is necessary to indicate briefly what is meant here by the term *democratic,* since this concept is subject to important variations in meaning. In its literal sense, democracy means "government by and for the people." This meaning implies the absence of a ruling elite that makes governmental decisions independently of the wishes of the populace as a whole. It would be a grave distortion to restrict the concept to this literal meaning, since it is doubtful that any such form of government exists anywhere in the world above the tribal level of society. Rather, democracy for our purposes has three principal features: (1) Governmental officials are elected to office and presumed to be representatives acting in the interests of the people. (2) Some sort of parliamentary or congressional structure exists as a power base at least partially independent of the power of presidents or prime ministers. (3) Individual rights and freedoms are accorded to the people and are generally honored more often than not.

The other major form of the state in modern society is a **totalitarian dictatorship.** This form of the state prevails in the Soviet Union and its satellites in Eastern Europe; that is, it prevails where socialism is the economic form. A totalitarian dictatorship is typified by the marked absence of those principal features characteristic of parliamentary democracy. Power is massively concentrated in a central agency that directs the affairs of society, individual liberties do not exist, free elections are not held, and no opposition to the government is permitted, either ideologically or in actual practice. In short, a general state of political repression prevails.

Why have such divergent political outcomes been associated with major industrial societies? Why did parliamentary democracy arise in England, France, and the United States, while totalitarianism arose in Russia and Eastern Europe?

THE ORIGIN OF WESTERN PARLIAMENTARY DEMOCRACIES

A famous study devoted to precisely these questions is Barrington Moore's *Social Origins of Dictatorship and Democracy* (1966). Moore proposes five general factors that he believes were heavily responsible for the gradual emergence of parliamentary democracy in England and France: (1) the development of a balance to avoid too strong a monarchy or too independent a landed nobility; (2) an economic evolution toward commercial or capitalist agriculture; (3) the eventual weakening of the power and economic significance of the nobility; (4) the prevention of a noble-capitalist coalition against the peasants and workers; (5) a revolutionary break with the past. Of these factors, Moore gives greatest emphasis to the second: the turn toward commercial agriculture.

In England the path was set for the triumph of parliamentary democracy with the outcome of the English Civil War of the mid-seventeenth century. This outcome was one that increased the political significance of parliament at the expense of the king. The outcome of the Civil War was also a victory for the forces of capitalism—for the interests of the commercially minded members of the landed upper classes. As Moore states (1966:19): "The outcome of the struggle was an enormous if still incomplete victory for an alliance between parliamentary democracy and capitalism." Moreover (1966:20):

> Both the capitalist principle and that of parliamentary democracy are directly antithetical to the ones they superseded and in large measure overcame during the Civil War: divinely supported authority in politics, and production for use rather than for individual profit in economics.

In brief, the beginning of the turn toward democracy in England was closely associated with the triumph of the economic interests of capitalist farmers.

Democracy made its entrance in France through the French Revolution of the last decade of the eighteenth century. As Moore notes, the Revolution destroyed the entire complex of aristocratic privilege—monarchy and landed nobility—and did so in the name of private property and the legal equality of the citizenry. This set the stage for the rise to economic power of the bourgeoisie and the triumph of democracy. Moore sees as crucial to the rise of democracy in France the destruction of the dominance of the landed nobility. This class did not turn toward commercial agriculture as many nobles did in England, and it was hostile to liberal democracy. It therefore had to be gotten out of the way in order for capitalist democracy to emerge in France. The French Revolution was the great upheaval that made such consequences possible.

As in England and France, a major parliamentary democracy emerged on American soil. Albert Szymanski (1978) has analyzed the growth of American democracy in terms of its foundations in the spread of capitalism to the United States. Szymanski notes that the wealthy upper classes emerged in a dominant position at the end of the Revolutionary War. These capitalist forces could therefore begin asserting their influence on the future development of the American polity. Following Charles Beard's (1962; orig. 1913) classic economic interpretation of the American Constitution, Szymanski argues that the constitutional structure of American democracy was built directly around dominant capitalist interests. He argues that the Constitution, rather than an expression of the will of the people, was a class document. It was written to protect the privileges of private property and to limit the genuine influence of the people on the policy formulations of the government.

The American Civil War and its outcome are a further indication of the capitalist basis of American democracy. Until the war, the American state was under the control of a coalition of wealthy Northern merchants and Southern slaveowners. By 1860 the growing antagonism between these two groups had become severe. While the Southern slave system was an integral part of the American capitalist system (indeed, of the world-economy, since huge amounts of cotton were exported to England), by 1860 the system of slave labor had become a hindrance to the further expansion of the economic interests of the Northern industrial merchants. The Civil War was an expression of the conflict between these two systems (B. Moore, 1966; Szymanski, 1978). The outcome of the war, of course, spelled victory for the Northern industrialists. With this result, the United States was able to embark on a massive expansion of its industrial capitalist system. The political outcome of all this was the increasing domination of the American state by industrial capital.

The overall picture that emerges from the foregoing is that the rise of parliamentary democracy in the West was made possible by the rise of the capitalist market economy. The question arises, of course, as to why the growth of capitalism should ordinarily be accompanied by democratic forms of government. The answer appears to lie in the fundamental need of the capitalist class for a democratic state. Capitalism involves the private pursuit of profit in a market. In order to maximize the accumulation of capital, capitalists need to neutralize the interference of government with their operations. Such neutralization is best achieved when the state is a democratic one that protects the free play of the forces of private property. Rather than an "idea" somehow implanting itself in people's minds, parliamentary democracy was a real political force driven to dominance by the real economic forces that had need for it.

POWER, POLITICS, AND THE STATE IN MODERN INDUSTRIAL DEMOCRACIES

Given this historical origin of the major parliamentary democracies, what are they like now? Has a true system of democracy, one in which the diverse interests of many individuals and groups are adequately represented by the state, succeeded in taking root? We may attempt to answer these questions by examining the three major views of the nature of the state in contemporary democracies: the liberal view, power elite and Marxian views, and the Weberian view.

The Liberal Theory of the State

The **liberal theory** of modern politics holds that the state in parliamentary democracies is the impartial servant of society as a whole. This view disclaims that the state "takes sides"—that it is aligned with one or more groups against others. The state is said not to favor capital over labor, men over women, whites over blacks, or one ethnic group over any other. On the contrary, the nature of the state is such that it attempts to resolve the disputes or conflicts that arise between these various groups in a way that is in everyone's best interests. This is the theory of the state that is overwhelmingly endorsed by the vast majority of citizens in the Western world, regardless of the specific content of their political philosophies. The great majority of political officials claim to believe in it as well. Despite some of their specific differences, Edward Kennedy and George Bush both heartily endorse the liberal view.

The most important version of the liberal theory is the **pluralist** conception of modern democracy (Galbraith, 1952; Riesman, 1950; Dahl, 1961).* The distinguishing feature of pluralism is its rejection of the idea that any single group is capable of gaining so much power that it dominates all important forms of political decision making. The pluralists believe that many different groups have power in modern democracies and that when these groups do battle in the political arena they neutralize each other so that no single one gains prominence over the others. Sometimes one group wins, sometimes another, but no group wins consistently. Citizens thus hold power because they are represented by interest groups capable of advancing their concerns in a successful manner. Thus, pluralists would hold that power resides in such diverse groups as the American Medical Association, the oil corporation lobbies, the United Auto Workers, the American Association of University Professors, the Daughters of the American Revolution, antiabortionists, the Congress of Racial Equality, the National Organization for Women, and so on.

*Elman Service's functionalist theory of the origin of the state, discussed in Chapter 11, is another variant of the liberal theory applied to an earlier era.

Power Elite and Marxian Views of Modern Democracy

Many scholars have flatly rejected these pluralist claims, arguing instead for a **power elite** conception of modern democracy. This view essentially began with C. Wright Mills's classic *The Power Elite* (1956), and has been perpetuated by such scholars as G. William Domhoff (1970, 1978, 1983) and Michael Useem (1984). However, Mills's work is still the purest example of this line of thinking, and therefore I shall focus my attention on it.

In *The Power Elite* Mills argues that the power to control and direct the major activities of American society is concentrated in the hands of a relatively small number of persons. These persons constitute a homogeneous and unified elite standing at the very apex of society. Members of the elite are drawn from three principal arenas of American life: the executive branch of government, the leadership of the top corporations, and the top brass of the military. Such an elite has been dubbed by many scholars since Mills's day "the military-industrial complex." Far from seeing the various members of this elite as having diverging and often conflicting interests, Mills sees them as holding a fundamental unity of interests. This basic commonality of interests creates psychological unity within the group, with the result that its ideological outlook—its basic social, political, and economic world-view—is of a singular sort.

While Mills sees all three branches of the power elite as highly significant, he points to the top corporations as the keystone of power in American society. Below this power elite, Mills finds an intermediate layer of power that consists primarily of the Congress and the various interest groups that lobby it. Finally, at the very bottom of the power structure stands the great mass of ordinary citizens who are relatively powerless in the face of pervasive control at the top.

It is quite clear that Mills views the notion that genuine democracy prevails in the United States as nothing more than a myth (he actually refers to it as a sort of "fairy tale"). Rather than the people controlling the government for their own interests, the government is strongly controlled by corporate and military leaders who are primarily concerned with advancing *their* interests.

The Marxian view of power in contemporary democracies is similar to the Millsian view, but with at least one important difference: Marxists stress that power is not really in the hands of three parts of a unified power elite, but is overwhelmingly monopolized by the capitalist class. The interests of even the military brass and the executive branch of the government are subordinate to the needs of the top capitalists.

The Marxian view of contemporary democracy is that the parliamentary democratic state is a *capitalist state*. That is, the state is actively aligned with the capitalist class and undertakes activities to serve its interests. As some Marxists have put it, the state "governs," but the capitalist class "rules." Contemporary Marxists have generally stressed three primary functions of the capitalist state (cf. Miliband, 1977): legitimation, repression, and accumulation.

When the capitalist state engages in **legitimation,** it is attempting to foster a consensus among the citizenry regarding the basic economic soundness and moral integrity of capitalist society—to get the people to commit their hearts and minds to it, and to believe it is superior to other forms of society. It may attempt to do this in numerous ways. For instance, it generally attempts to insure that what is taught in state-supported schools actively encourages support for the political and economic status quo (cf. Bowles and Gintis, 1976). By requiring all students in secondary schools to take courses in civics or citizenship, and by presenting an exclusively (or largely) favorable image of capitalism and modern democracy in those courses, the educational system is helping to foster a basic consensus.

Repression occurs when legitimation fails. Repression involves preventing people from taking actions that would harm the state and the capitalist system in major ways. Repression need not involve violence or force, although it frequently involves such measures. Denying visas to foreign intellectuals who have views unfavorable to the capitalist system, and who may wish to enter a particular society to promote those views, is a very real form of nonviolent repression.

The capitalist state, in the Marxian view, also has a third extremely important function, that of **accumulation.** This function involves establishing policies that assist the capitalist class in its accumulation of capital. Accumulation activities on the part of the state are numerous in modern capitalist societies. When the U.S. government recently provided large loan guarantees to Chrysler Motor Company to keep it afloat, it was exercising its accumulation function. In a similar vein, when the government establishes laws that create major tax loopholes for the rich and shift the burden of taxation onto ordinary citizens, it is assisting in the capital accumulation process. Likewise, when a government like that of the United States actively opposes Third World governments that are hostile to the interests of American capitalism, it is attempting to maintain a favorable political climate for capital accumulation. Furthermore, as James O'Connor (1973) has suggested, the state has increasingly been called upon in recent decades to assist in the accumulation process in all major capitalist societies. In O'Connor's view, the increase in state spending this has entailed has finally led to what he calls a "fiscal crisis of the state." This is a crisis in revenue collection on the part of the state that necessitates drastic cutbacks in many government services to noncapitalist groups.

In recent years there has been a tendency among Marxists to regard the state in capitalist societies as having a "relative autonomy." That is, even though the state primarily serves the interests of the capitalist class, it is not rigidly tied to this class as if by an umbilical cord. Indeed, it may serve interests other than those of capitalists. The British Marxist Ralph Miliband (1977) has, in fact, suggested that the contemporary state must have a certain amount of autonomy if it is to serve the capitalist class well. As Miliband notes (1977:87–88):

> Its relative independence makes it *possible* for the state to play its class role in an appropriately flexible manner. If it really was the simple "instrument" of the "ruling class," it would be fatally inhibited in the performance of its role. Its agents absolutely need a measure of freedom in deciding how best to serve the existing social order.
>
> This . . . has the major advantage of helping to explain a crucial attribute of the state in capitalist society, namely its capacity to act as an agency of reform.
>
> Reform has been a major characteristic of capitalist regimes. . . .
>
> But to act as the organizers of reform, powerholders have needed some elbow room, an area of political maneuver in which *statecraft* in its literal sense could be exercised. What to concede and when to concede—the two being closely related—are matters of some delicacy, which a ruling class, with its eyes fixed on immediate interests and demands, cannot be expected to handle properly.

A major example of what Miliband is talking about occurred in the United States in the 1930s. President Roosevelt undertook major economic and social reforms designed to lift the United States out of the Depression and restore economic growth. Yet Roosevelt was hated by the capitalist class, and his efforts at reform were widely decried by its members. However, as many observers, both Marxist and non-Marxist alike, have pointed out, through these major reforms Roosevelt actually "saved the capitalist system" (Szymanski, 1978; cf. Piven and Cloward, 1971).

If the most important function of the state in capitalist society is furthering capital accumulation for the capitalist class, how does it do this? Through what processes does the state actually become a capitalist state? Szymanski (1978) has suggested several mechanisms, which he divides into two main categories: direct and indirect.

The direct mechanisms of capitalist class control of the state primarily involve *the selection of state personnel* and *lobbying*. Szymanski notes that much of the top personnel of the state is actually made up of persons drawn from the capitalist class itself. Many U.S. presidents have come from the capitalist class, and a great many cabinet posts in the U.S. government have been occupied by prominent members of this class. Beth Mintz (1975) conducted a study of the social and economic backgrounds of cabinet members throughout the twentieth century and found that 78 percent belonged to the economic elite (cf. Szymanski, 1978:219). Moreover, extremely important government councils, such as the Council on Foreign Relations and the Committee for Economic Development, are largely made up of top capitalists.

Lobbying is also a major means by which the capitalist class controls the state. Lobbies attempt, usually with great success, to influence state policy in a variety of ways: by financing much of the electoral campaigns of members of Congress; by promising good jobs to legislators after they leave government service; by providing legislators with careful studies that offer persuasive arguments for the lobby's special viewpoint; and by "wining and dining" state officials in order to bring them around to certain viewpoints.

Two indirect mechanisms discussed by Szymanski are *ideological manipulation* and *structural determination of state policies*. Ideological manipulation involves efforts by institutions like the mass media and the schools to indoctrinate individuals with the values of the capitalist system. (This point was made earlier in discussing the legitimizing role of the state.) By structural determination of state policies Szymanski means that in a modern capitalist society the state officials usually have no real choice but to support policies that serve the capitalist class. If they are to function and be effective in making state policy at all, that policy must predominantly serve top capitalists. As Szymanski explains (1978:268–270):

Robert McMamara (*right*) engaged in a discussion with then–President of the United States Lyndon B. Johnson in 1964. McMamara left a top position as a director of a giant American corporation to become Secretary of Defense in the Kennedy administration in 1961. What do such actions suggest about the role of the state in modern capitalism?

> The state nevertheless will act in the interests of the capitalist class in capitalist society, because the structure of its environment requires it to perform its functions for capital. This is true whether the occupants of the state office and the majority in the legislatures are conservatives, fascists, liberals, Social Democrats, Socialists, or even Communists, just as long as the basic mode of production in the economy remains capitalist.
>
> . . .
>
> Social Democratic governments in France in the 1930s and the post–World War II period, the government of the Social Democrats in Germany in the post–World War I period and in the 1960s and 1970s, and the Social Democrats in Scandinavia followed basic policies only slightly different from those of the Gaullists in France, the Christian Democrats in Italy or Germany, or for that matter the policies of any of the non-Social Democratic regimes in the advanced capitalist countries. . . .
>
> Socialist governments that have attempted to do more than just implement the policies dictated by the logic of capitalism have found themselves in very serious crises from which they have not been able to extricate themselves. . . .
>
> Even the presence of Communists . . . in governments in capitalist society makes very little difference.
>
> . . .
>
> The personal chances of success of politicians thus is closely linked with the successful performance of the functions of the capitalist state. Consequently, it is not a matter of good or bad intentions, or the desire to realize the popular will or serve the narrow interests of the rich, but rather a matter of the imperatives of the system being exerted through the state officials.

The Weberian View of the State

The Weberian conception of the state is more closely aligned with the Marxian view than with the liberal view. Weberians concede that the state in capitalist society does have important connections with the capitalist class and does to some extent serve its interests. Yet they stress that the state is to a very considerable degree an autonomous body with interests all its own. The Weberians thus see politics as in no sense reducible to class or economics, but as a substantially independent and self-contained sphere (cf. Evans, Rueschemeyer, and Skocpol, 1985;

Giddens, 1985; Mann, 1988). In other words, they carry the Marxian idea of "relative autonomy" to a much greater extreme. As Theda Skocpol comments in summarizing this view of the state (1979:29–30):

> The state properly conceived is no mere arena in which socioeconomic struggles are fought out. It is, rather, a set of administrative, policing, and military organizations headed, and more or less well coordinated by, an executive authority. Any state first and fundamentally extracts resources from society and deploys these to create and support coercive and administrative organizations. . . .
>
> Where they exist, these fundamental state organizations are at least potentially autonomous from direct dominant-class control. The extent to which they *actually* are autonomous, and to what effect, varies from case to case. . . .
>
> State organizations necessarily compete to some extent with the dominant class(es) in appropriating resources from the economy and society. And the objectives to which the resources, once appropriated, are devoted may very well be at variance with existing dominant-class interests. . . . Indeed, attempts of state rulers merely to perform the state's "own" functions may create conflicts of interest with the dominant class. . . . The state has its own distinct interests vis-à-vis subordinate classes. . . . The state's own fundamental interest in maintaining sheer physical order and political peace may lead it—especially in periods of crisis—to enforce concessions to subordinate-class demands. These concessions may be at the expense of the interests of the dominant class, but not contrary to the state's own interests in controlling the population and collecting taxes and military recruits.

A major application of Weberian state theory in recent years has been to the development of welfare systems and various forms of public social spending in industrial societies. Theda Skocpol and several of her colleagues have been the intellectual leaders, at least in the United States, of this line of theory and research (Skocpol, 1980; Skocpol and Ikenberry, 1983; Orloff and Skocpol, 1984). They have insisted, for example, that New Deal legislation in the United States cannot be understood in terms of the socioeconomic characteristics of American society alone. Rather, the particular facets of U.S. government (and politics more broadly) have to be brought into the equation to make sense of this development. They have also suggested that Britain's much more extensive public spending for health and welfare programs compared to that of the United States in the early part of the twentieth century cannot be explained apart from important political differences between the two societies. Specifically, they believe that these differences involve Britain's possession of a civil service and the legacy of a centralized welfare administration, and, on the other hand, the lack of an established civil bureaucracy in the United States. Such differences meant that Britain had the means to develop extensive social programs, but that in the United States "modern social-spending programs were neither governmentally feasible nor politically acceptable" (Orloff and Skocpol, 1984:739).

Of the various theories of the state reviewed here, the liberal theory is the least persuasive. While groups other than the capitalist class do have some capacity to advance their own interests, they are seldom able to do so when the satisfaction of these interests would conflict in a major way with capitalist interests. Thus, the power elite and Marxian theories are the most impressive, and the advocates of these theories have assembled much data in their support, only some of which could be mentioned here. Yet the Weberian view of the state cannot be easily overlooked. It is still a very open question just how much autonomy the modern democratic state has, but that it has a reasonable amount cannot be seriously denied. Politicians always have their own interests, and these may sometimes clash with those of the dominant class in major ways.

Table 12.1 THEORIES OF THE STATE IN MODERN DEMOCRACIES

Theory	Characteristics	Evaluation
Liberal theory	The democratic state is a neutral arbiter of the competing and conflicting interests of diverse social groups. The democratic arena allows groups to "neutralize" each other in the sense that no group is consistently able to dominate the others.	Markedly underrates the extent to which genuine power is concentrated in the hands of a few, who are able to effect political decisions promoting their own interests.
Power elite theory	In its classic Millsian version, real power is concentrated in the hands of a three-way elite consisting of top corporate leaders, the executive branch of the government, and the top leaders of the military.	Highly preferable to the liberal theory, but may undervalue the role of the logic of capitalism in shaping power and decision making.
Marxian theory	The democratic state is a capitalist state. It is controlled by a capitalist economic logic that dictates that most important political decisions will be favorable to the interests of capitalists. The state may have a "relative autonomy," but it functions on behalf of the capitalist class in the long run. The most important functions the state performs for the capitalist class are repression of system-threatening dissent, ideological legitimation of the capitalist system, and direct and indirect assistance in the accumulation of capital.	Probably the best of all the theories, but the state may be more autonomous than even its most flexible theorists allow for.
Weberian theory	The democratic state is neither a neutral arbiter of conflicting interests nor a simple agent of the capitalist ruling class. It is a significant force in its own right, with its own interests and aims. The major aim of the state is in using power and extending the scope of its power. The state frequently serves capitalists' interests, but often opposes them as well.	No doubt a useful counterpart to the Marxian theory. It may also be very useful in explaining politics in modern noncapitalist societies.

THE STATE IN THE CONTEXT OF THE CAPITALIST WORLD-SYSTEM

So far our discussion has not explicitly considered the world-system context in which modern capitalist states exist. Just as problems of economic organization in the modern world cannot be understood apart from the existence of a capitalist world-economy, the nature of states throughout the world cannot be properly understood without recognition of their role in a worldwide system of political order. The world-system perspective, then, adds an important dimension to an understanding of modern capitalist states (cf. Chirot, 1977; Bollen, 1983).

The Interstate System

A fundamental characteristic of the capitalist world-system ever since the beginning of its existence is its politically decentralized character. The capitalist system has always consisted of a multitude of competing and conflicting states, a form of political organization known as the **interstate system** (Wallerstein, 1974a,b; Chase-Dunn, 1989a). No single state has ever succeeded in achieving such a level of political control over all of the others that a world-empire would have resulted. There have been several efforts at such world-empire creation—most notably by the Hapsburgs in the sixteenth and seventeenth centuries, by Napoleonic France in the early eighteenth century, and by Germany in the twentieth century (Chase-Dunn, 1989a)—but each of these efforts failed. It would seem that the very logic of capitalism as an economic system makes it extremely difficult for a world-empire to emerge. As soon as any state begins to follow a path that it hopes will lead to world political domination, the other states start to gang up on it so as to prevent such an occurrence. Thus capitalist economics and the interstate system go hand in hand. Indeed, had the capitalist world-system ever succumbed to world-imperial domination, it is doubtless the case that its essentially capitalist nature would have disintegrated (Wallerstein, 1974a,b; Chase-Dunn, 1989a).

Much controversy has arisen over whether the capitalist world-economy and the interstate system are fused together as part of a single reality, or whether the interstate system is a substantially autonomous reality in its own right. Contemporary Weberians see the interstate system as largely autonomous (Skocpol, 1977; Zolberg, 1981). They believe that capitalism and the interstate system are intertwined, but that the world political system must be studied as a reality in its own right. States are actors in a world political order in which political and military objectives cannot be understood

Heads of state of several Western capitalist nations conferring at the NATO summit meeting held in Brussels in May of 1989. The interstate system and the capitalist world-economy are inextricably intertwined.

simply in terms of capitalist economic interests. There is no doubt a good deal of truth in this assertion, but the position adopted in this book is that the political and military objectives of capitalist states cannot seriously depart from the capitalist economic interests that form the context in which these states operate. In Christopher Chase-Dunn's (1989a) words, there is only "one logic" within the capitalist world-system, a single logic in which economics and politics are essentially inseparable. The driving force behind this logic is, of course, that of incessant capital accumulation.

World-System Status and the Form of the State

We must now consider the crucial question of how a nation-state's position within the capitalist world-system determines the particular type of state structure that it evolves. Looking first at the capitalist core, we find that in this zone highly stable democratic forms of the state are found. It was in the core that parliamentary democracy first arose, and today every single core state is democratic. We have already seen why this should be the case. Core capitalist societies have strongly developed capitalist classes with a strong need to minimize the interfering role of the state in their entrepreneurial activities (even though they try to use the state to interfere in economic activity when this is to their advantage). Moreover, core societies have large and highly educated middle classes that strongly expect—indeed, demand—that general rights and liberties be upheld (Chirot, 1977). By and large, the tradition of democratic government has become so strongly entrenched in the advanced capitalist societies that it has come to a certain extent to constitute an independent force in its own right. Democratic philosophies pervade the whole fabric of life in these societies.

However, it should by no means be assumed that democracy can be taken for granted in the core nations. These nations are vulnerable to antidemocratic movements of all sorts. Some have actually experienced periods of the suspension of democracy, and others may see such political developments in the future. For example, Germany from 1933 to 1945 suffered through an intense period of *fascism*. Germany's fascist regime—the Nazis—suspended civil liberties and engaged in a general political repression of the population. It also used violence and terror against many segments of the population, most notably the Jews. Fascist regimes tend to arise in capitalist societies caught in the midst of severe economic crisis, and fascism is actually an attempt to bring the nation out of the crisis. Fascist destructions of democracy may well occur in core nations in the future if they experience marked declines in their economic fortunes. Daniel Chirot (1977), for instance, has suggested that fascism may be a significant threat in the United States in the near future if its current economic problems worsen significantly.

In the capitalist periphery, democracy is very much the exception. Peripheral capitalist societies typically have one form or another of nondemocratic regime. Regimes based on military dictatorship, for instance, are widespread throughout the peripheral capitalist world. These dictatorships serve to enforce ruling class domination in societies where economic inequalities often reach grotesque proportions. Democracy is not possible in societies where exploitation and abject human misery and suffering reach such levels. It is, in one way of putting it, a "luxury" that peripheral capitalist societies (or, more accurately, their ruling classes) cannot "afford."

In the modern capitalist semiperiphery democracy is also seldom found. The reason is in part the same as in the case of the periphery. Many semiperipheral societies have levels of exploitation and misery too high to permit the widespread granting of rights and liberties.

Ferdinand Marcos, former president of the Philippines. After Marcos was driven from office, the extraordinary extent of the wealth he had accumulated became widely known. Many observers of the Filipino political scene had long been aware of Marcos's brutality as a political dictator. The accumulation of wealth and the abuse of power by a political leader are both relatively common situations in the Third World

Discontent is simply too high, and political repression is necessary to keep a minimum of order. But world-system theorists have also stressed that the development of strong authoritarian states can be a real advantage to semiperipheral societies seeking to improve their status in the world-economy. (South Korea since the early 1950s and Brazil from the mid-1960s to the mid-1970s are especially good illustrations of this point.) As Chirot has suggested, these types of states help to promote the economic aims of semiperipheral societies by holding down consumption in order to free more funds for investment, as well as by a variety of other economic measures. Such states may become important forces to contend with politically and militarily in the international arena, especially if they are strategically placed so as to be important to the interests of the major core powers.

In recent years there has been much talk about a "redemocratization" process occurring in parts of the periphery and semiperiphery, especially in Latin America. What has been happening is that some Latin American countries—Brazil, for example—have replaced military governments with civilian ones that have come to power through an electoral process. Some observers view this as perhaps the beginning of a movement away from authoritarian and repressive states and toward genuine democracy (Cammack, 1986)—or at least think that the possibilities are there for the creation of a much more democratic order. Others are more pessimistic, or at least more cautious. Fernando Henrique Cardoso (1986) suggests that we should take the new democratizing trends with a grain of salt. As he says, "At the level of society, they exist and are universal; however, at the level of the state, they encounter resistance, and in some societies this resistance is successful" (1986:30). Herman and Petras (1985) take an even stronger view, noting that military power has not been eroded despite the adoption of a formal democratic apparatus. Indeed, to the extent that it is not actually continuing, the use of state terror through "death squads" continually lurks in the background (Petras, 1987). Moreover, a sense of historical perspective also gives us reason to be more than just a little cautious about strong claims for the significance of the redemocratization trends. Throughout this century, politics in many Latin American countries has shown something of a cyclical alternation between more and less repressive regimes (Skidmore and Smith, 1989; E. Stephens, 1989). Given this pattern, the prediction of a directional trend toward democracy seems highly premature.

But even if the kind of democracy that is occurring in Latin America is more outer shell than real substance, what accounts for it? Bruce Cumings (1989) suggests both economic and political reasons. On the economic side, "democratization was a political corollary to very strong demands for markets in developing countries to be opened up to American goods, especially service industries like banks and insurance, but also tobacco, grain and meat" (1989:30). Thus core, especially American, economic interests can create external pressures on Third World governments to adopt democratic arrangements. On the political side, the move toward democracy (or at least its outer shell) is a way of managing and defusing system-threatening discontent. Cumings believes that this is what explains recent democratization efforts in South Korea (1989:32):

> Korean democratization owes more to a controlled process of opening channels and valves for the voicing of excluded interest (or the blowing off of steam), than to a consolidation of stable pluralist representation. . . . It is the result of conflict and negotiation amongst the state, military and business elite, cushioned and succoured by the United States, with the goal of demobilizing the volatile popular sector. Events in South Korea in the past three years are remarkably similar to those of the Figueiredo regime in Brazil after 1979: opening the system to the moderate opposition, tolerating strikes, freeing up the press, and allowing exiled anti-regime opponents to return.

HISTORICAL SOURCES OF TOTALITARIAN DICTATORSHIPS

Modern totalitarian dictatorships are best represented by the Communist states of the Soviet bloc. The Communist state emerged in Russia following the Bolshevik revolution of 1917. While this state is a twentieth-century phenomenon, the forces giving rise to it are to be found well back in Russia's past. It is therefore necessary to consider the economic and political conditions that prevailed in Russia in prerevolutionary times.

As L. S. Stavrianos (1975) has commented, Muscovite civilization in the fifteenth century was strikingly different from what prevailed in western Europe at the same time. It notably lacked the commercialism that was coming to characterize the West and was to give the West a dynamic motor for great capitalist and industrial development. Moreover, while serfdom was being abolished in western Europe, it was being institutionalized and intensified in Russia (P. Anderson, 1974b). A particularly oppressive form of serfdom came to be characteristic of Russian economic life from this time until the twentieth century. The economic system was held in place by a powerful absolutist monarchy—the Tsarist state—that held sway for some 300 years. These particularly oppressive and exploitative conditions gave rise to a large number of unsuccessful peasant rebellions throughout the centuries. Stavrianos (1975) reports, for instance, the occurrence of more than 500 peasant disturbances between 1825 and 1855. Ultimately legal serfdom was abolished in Russia in 1861, but this did not lead to any significant improvement in the economic conditions of the peasantry, for it still bore an extremely heavy tax load (Stavrianos, 1975). Peasant unrest therefore continued throughout the remainder of the nineteenth and into the twentieth century.

Despite some degree of commercialistic penetration of agriculture during the last half of the nineteenth century, the Russian agricultural system at the beginning of the twentieth century was still predominantly characterized by highly exploitative feudal economic relations (P. Anderson, 1974b). At the same time, a significant degree of industrial capitalist production was beginning to characterize the towns. Industrialization brought with it generally the same conditions it had earlier created in western Europe: the severe exploitation of a class of urban factory workers. The combination of these two factors—a large oppressed peasantry and a sizable urban proletariat—created a highly explosive situation in the early twentieth century. The ultimate outcome of this situation was, of course, the Bolshevik revolution, a revolution against the Tsarist state made by both peasant and proletarian forces.

It is important to see that the revolution was made not against a capitalist state but against a despotic absolute monarchy that supported a large landed nobility (P. Anderson, 1974b). The Bolshevik revolution, like the French Revolution before it, succeeded in sweeping this nobility away. Yet unlike the French Revolution, the Bolshevik revolution did not bring to dominance a capitalist class that would pave the way for parliamentary democracy. Rather, the Bolshevik revolution was a socialist revolution whose ultimate consequences were to be quite different from some of its major aims. Instead of destroying the despotic power of the state and bringing about general social and political democracy, the revolution led to a new kind of despotic state: a totalitarian industrial state resting on the state's monopolization of the economy (Djilas, 1957; Wittfogel, 1957).

If there is any single factor that appears crucial in directing postrevolutionary Russia away from democracy, it would seem to be the absence of a strong indigenous capitalism there at the time of the revolution. Milovan Djilas explains (1957:19–20):

> All so-called *bourgeois* [i.e., capitalist] revolutions . . . had to end up in political democracy. That is understandable. Their task was chiefly to destroy the old despotic political system, and to permit the establishment of political relationships which would be adequate for already existing economic and other needs, particularly those concerning the free production of goods.
>
> The case is entirely different with contemporary Communist revolutions. These revolutions did not occur because new, let us say socialist, relationships were already existing in the economy, or because capitalism was "overdeveloped." On the contrary. They did occur because capitalism was not fully developed and because it was not able to carry out the industrial transformation of the country.
>
> In France capitalism had already prevailed in the economy, in social relationships, and even in the public conscience prior to inception of the revolution. The case is hardly comparable with socialism in Russia, China, or Yugoslavia.

THE MODERN TOTALITARIAN STATE

A classic description of the contemporary Communist state has been provided by Milovan Djilas in his book *The New Class* (1957). Djilas is a former vice president of Yugoslavia who was expelled from the Communist party in 1954 after appealing for democratic reforms. In 1956 he was sentenced to a 10-year prison term for expressing the ideas contained in *The New Class.* Although released in 1961, he was reimprisoned in 1962 after the publication of his *Conversations with Stalin.*

As Djilas notes, "Everything happened differently in the U.S.S.R. and other Communist countries from what the leaders—even such prominent ones as Lenin, Stalin, Trotsky, and Bukharin—anticipated. They expected that the state would rapidly wither away, that democracy would be strengthened. The reverse happened" (1957:37). Djilas explains that the postrevolutionary Communist party had an extraordinarily high degree of ideological and organizational centralization. Remaining on the political scene long after victory, the party began strengthening and consolidating its power over the rest of society. It maintained an atmosphere of constant political vigilance; ideological unity within the party was demanded and great attention was paid to routing out both real and potential opposition. Terrorist and oppressive methods were needed to achieve these goals. The result was the creation, in Djilas's words, of "a class whose power over men is the most complete known to history"—the Communist bureaucratic elite.

Lenin's Tomb in Red Square, Moscow.

Until very recently, this bureaucratic elite had maintained an administrative monopoly over the entire social order, including complete control over virtually all economic activity; had tolerated no ideological deviation from the party line and swiftly used force to punish those who did deviate; and had tyrannized the mind by suppressing all intellectual and artistic discoveries and creations that contradicted official party dogma. It is little wonder that Djilas has called the power of this class the "most complete known to history."

However, since the mid-1980s, with the coming to power of Mikhail Gorbachev, the Soviet Union has inaugurated the policy of *glasnost*, which is essentially devoted to greater "openness" in political and social life. The mass media are given more freedom to report events accurately and thoroughly; there is more toleration of intellectual and artistic freedom of expression; some elections of public officials are being held; and some political prisoners have been released. Does *glasnost* signify, as Jeffrey Goldfarb (1989) has asked, a "withering away of totalitarianism"? There are many optimistic observers in the West who think that this is precisely what is happening in the Soviet Union. Goldfarb himself, however, suggests that much caution is in order. *Glasnost* cannot be understood as simply some sort of philosophical or intellectual sea change that is based on a sudden awareness of the humanistic implications of democracy. On the contrary, *glasnost* is a political strategy with a definite economic end: that of facilitating the success of *perestroika*. Moreover, it appears to be geared toward co-opting the oppositional elements within Soviet society by giving them more of the rhetoric of democracy than its genuine substance. Even if *glasnost* is successful at all—that is, if it does not collapse entirely—the result may only be what Goldfarb calls "neototalitarianism": a less pernicious and more open form of totalitarianism, but a form of totalitarianism nonetheless.

Recent events in Eastern Europe, however, suggest that Goldfarb's caution may be excessive. In the fall of 1989 Poland, East Germany, Czechoslovakia, and Romania experienced major transformations in their totalitarian regimes. The political monopoly of the Communist party was broken and significant steps were taken in the direction of much greater democracy and openness. Dramatic political developments are also occurring in the Soviet Union. As Alec Nove (1989) has made abundantly clear, *glasnost* is for real. There is a level of openness and frank reexamination now going on within the Soviet Union that would have been considered unthinkable just a few short years ago. Moreover, in early 1990 the Soviet Union began to take serious steps toward creating a multiparty political system.

Glasnost and *perestroika* are obviously intimately related, as Gorbachev and other contemporary Soviet leaders have made abundantly clear. And just as *perestroika* represents the movement of the Soviet Union toward full reintegration into the capitalist world-economy, so *glasnost* is the political expression of that economic shift. The shift toward greater participation in the world market requires a much greater degree of political openness than has previously been the case. The political upheavals in Eastern Europe show us just how this is so. The movements toward democracy in Eastern Europe are not some sort of "people's revolutions" designed to introduce democracy for its own sake. On the contrary, to the degree that they can be called revolutions at all, they are what some social scientists call "revolutions from above"—revolutions initiated by one segment of the political elite against another. These revolutions have occurred both because of the shifting economic (and hence political) interests and outlook of an elite segment, and because the Soviet Union has greatly relaxed its military and political domination of Eastern Europe.

A realistic prediction, I think, is that the

A conference of the Soviet Communist party in Moscow, June 1988. Since the time this picture was taken, the Communist party has lost its political monopoly and the Soviet Union has moved toward a multiparty political system. How far this democratization of Soviet political life will be carried is still very uncertain.

Soviet Union and Eastern Europe will continue along their current path toward greater democracy and openness. But be that as it may, we must still explain why these societies have had totalitarian regimes. In the case of Eastern Europe, of course, these regimes were originally imposed, and to a large extent maintained, from the outside by the Soviet Union (Yugoslavia being an exception). But what is the reason for the totalitarian character of the Soviet Union itself? This character offers little comfort to those who hold to the classical Marxian view of the state. Marx thought that with the coming of socialism the state would ultimately "wither away." Since the state was called into existence in order to protect and enhance the interests of an economically dominant class, it would no longer be needed in a socialist and classless society. The massive intensification of state power in all contemporary state socialist societies obviously gives the lie to this notion. Immanuel Wallerstein has tried to save the Marxian view by arguing, first, that the Soviet Union is not really socialist and, second, that totalitarianism has resulted from the severe threat it has experienced, both economically and militarily, from the Western capitalist world (cf. Chase-Dunn, 1982). In a genuine socialist society—the socialist world-government that will ultimately replace the capitalist world-economy—this threat will disappear, and the repressive state will then wither away (Wallerstein, 1984b).

Although this argument initially appears to contain a strong air of special pleading, it actually has much to recommend it. From about the late 1920s until sometime during the 1950s, the Soviet Union withdrew greatly from the world capitalist system and followed an economic policy devoted to catching up with Western capitalism. It was precisely during this time that totalitarianism—indeed, Stalinist terrorism—was at its height (Nove, 1989). This terrorism substantially ceased after the death of Stalin in 1953, and with the shift to the new regime of Nikita Khrushchev a bit of openness first started to appear (Nove, 1989). And, indeed, it was during the Khrushchev period that the Soviet Union starting showing signs of moving back toward greater participation in the world-economy. The fact that the current Soviet regime, with its strong orientation toward the world market, has made such a dent in the totalitarian state strongly suggests that totalitarianism is a political strategy closely associated with closure to a hostile world-economy.

However, this may not be the whole story. A well-known competing explanation is at hand in the Weberian view of the state. Weber thought that socialism would necessarily lead to extensive bureaucratic centralization of power in the hands of a ruling minority. Such centralization would be necessary as a means of managing the affairs of a socialist economy. Thus, socialism would inevitably end up being much less democratic than capitalism. Bureaucracy encourages the concentration of power, and once such power has developed it becomes self-perpetuating and its stranglehold is extremely difficult to break.

At this moment it is difficult to tell which of these two explanations, the world-system or the Weberian explanation, is the better. The coming decade may provide a natural experiment that will help us make a choice. If the Soviet Union and Eastern Europe move significantly farther along the road to democracy, then the world-system explanation will appear to be vindicated. However, if they appear unable to go as far as it now appears they might, then Weber's argument about the self-perpetuating character of bureaucratic power will seem a potent one.

CONCLUSION: LIBERTY, THE STATE, AND HUMAN SERVITUDE

The only true democracies that have ever prevailed in the world are found among band and tribal societies. In these societies, no socioeconomic class of persons standing apart from the rest gains control over society's resources, and hence no political institution based on the application of force is necessary. With the rise of social classes, all this changes, and privileged groups begin to call forth coercive political regimes to protect their privilege. When there exists a sufficient monopoly of force to suppress the dissent of the masses against the prevailing social order, the state has come into existence. With but a handful of modest exceptions, its existence has meant the elimination of human freedom and the plunging of the great majority of individuals into various degrees of servitude. It seems appropriate to concur with the judgment of Marvin Harris (1977:69–70):

> For the past five or six millennia, nine-tenths of all the people who ever lived did so as peasants or as members of some other servile caste or class. With the rise of the state, ordinary men seeking to use nature's bounty had to get someone else's permission and had to pay for it with taxes, tribute, or extra labor. The weapons and techniques of war and organized aggression were taken away from them and turned over to specialist-soldiers and policemen controlled by military, religious, and civil bureaucrats. For the first time there appeared on earth kings, dictators, high priests, emperors, prime ministers, presidents, governors, mayors, generals, admirals, police chiefs, judges, lawyers, and jailers, along with dungeons, jails, penitentiaries, and concentration camps. Under the tutelage of the state, human beings learned for the first time how to bow, grovel, kneel, and kowtow. In many ways the rise of the state was the descent of the world from freedom to slavery.

Of course, the state has taken rather different forms in different kinds of societies, and some states have been considerably more oppressive than others. At the more oppressive end of the spectrum are the Oriental and industrial despotisms; at the less oppressive end, the parliamentary democracies of modern times. Even in the case of the latter, however, plenty of coercion is available if needed. Furthermore, even limited historical perspective clearly indicates that parliamentary democracy has not been a typical outcome in political evolution, and even here no true system of democratic order prevails. The political results that followed the Russian Revolution have been, alas, much more typical of the major political transformations occurring within the past 6000 years of human history: an old tyranny has been replaced by a new one.

As for what the future holds, some students of political evolution have predicted the evolution of a single world-state overseeing a single world-economy. Robert Carneiro (1978) has gone further and actually attempted to estimate the time at which such a state could be expected to occur. As Carneiro notes, a basic trend in political evolution is a decrease in the number of political units found on the earth and an increase in the size of each unit. Extrapolating from this trend and making certain mathematical measurements of it, he predicts that the political unification of the world will occur by no later than A.D. 2300.

Given the likelihood of the formation of a world state in the not-too-distant future, the crucial question obviously concerns what its character would be like. Would it be more on the democratic or on the repressive side? Would it be a true vehicle for the creation of a more just and egalitarian world order, or would it bring in its wake a more severe form of human misery and injustice than anything seen to date? At the end of Chapter 20 I will return to these questions.

SUMMARY

1. Between the sixteenth and the eighteenth centuries the highly decentralized feudal states of western Europe were converted to strong centralized bureaucratic structures.

Some scholars have seen the new absolutist states as mediating the economic interests of the bourgeoisie and the aristocracy, while others have viewed them as being efforts to bolster the declining interests of the old aristocracy.

2. Parliamentary democracy is a form of government characterized by election of political leaders, separation of the various branches of government into relatively independent power blocs, and accordance of rights and liberties to the citizenry. The earliest beginnings of parliamentary democracy are associated with the advent of Western capitalism.

3. Although the rise of parliamentary democracy is often interpreted in idealist terms as the independent development of a political philosophy, it is more appropriately seen as a political force serving definite economic interests. Democracy was largely a product of the rise of the bourgeoisie, who found this form of government most compatible with the economic freedom they desired.

4. There are currently three different views of the nature and role of the state in modern capitalist society. The liberal view holds that the state is a neutral agent attempting to serve all individuals and groups impartially. Power elite and Marxian views stress the role of the state as a servant of the interests of only a few, particularly the capitalist class. The Weberian view of the state stresses that it is not merely the servant of the capitalist class, but has an independent role of its own to play. The agents of the state have their own interests, and these may conflict with the interests of the capitalist class.

5. Marxists suggest that the state in capitalist society has three functions: legitimation, repression, and accumulation. They also suggest a number of ways in which the state under capitalism serves the interests of the capitalist class. First, state personnel are disproportionately made up of individuals drawn from the capitalist class. In addition, powerful capitalist interests exert enormous lobbying pressure on the state. Finally, there occurs what has been called the structural determination of state policies: if the personnel of the state wish to stay in power, they must make the economy work effectively, and in a capitalist economy that means administering it along lines favorable to capitalists.

6. The world-system perspective on modern states has many insights to offer. There is an interstate system of competing and conflicting nation-states that is deeply intertwined with the capitalist world-economy. Within this interstate system, core states generally have parliamentary democracies, although they are vulnerable to various types of antidemocratic movements. Peripheral states seldom enjoy democracy. The absence of democracy in peripheral societies is understandable given their high levels of social and economic inequality. Semiperipheral societies, also seldom democratic, often develop authoritarian states in order to improve their status in the world-system.

7. Modern totalitarian forms of government have been characteristic of the Soviet Union and Eastern Europe. Totalitarianism is characterized by an absence of individual rights and liberties and severe repression of the entire population. In recent years totalitarian regimes have been challenged and undercut throughout Eastern Europe, and in the Soviet Union the liberalization policy known as *glasnost* has opened up that society quite substantially. These political changes are best interpreted as political manifestations of the reincorporation of state socialist societies into the capitalist world-economy.

8. World-system theory suggests that totalitarianism has been associated with an economic policy of closure from the world-economy. It has been produced by a need for socialist states to protect themselves economically and militarily from the hostile world capitalist system. An alternative explanation, based on Weber, holds that socialism leads naturally to a massive enlargement of the functions of the state, and thus to an enormous concentration of power in the hands of a state bureaucracy. Once in existence, this bureaucracy may be difficult to dislodge. Both of these explanations may contain significant insights.

9. Our knowledge of political evolution suggests that a single state is likely to unify the world within the next several centuries. Many crucial questions remain concerning the particular character of this state and the kind of economic system that it would represent and administer.

SPECIAL TOPIC: THE PUZZLE OF NATIONALISM

One of the most persistent intellectual problems in modern social science is that of *nationalism*. Nationalism in the modern world involves the strong identification of individuals with their nation-states, indeed, the celebration by state leaders and ordinary individuals alike of the uncommon virtues that these nation-states are thought to contain. Who can deny the extraordinary significance that nationalism has in our time? Modern sports provide an extremely good indicator of the pervasiveness of the phenomenon. Before the start of baseball games in the United States, "The Star-Spangled Banner" is always sung. The same thing happens before hockey games, except that "O Canada" is sung as well since the majority of the players are Canadian. International soccer matches in Europe and Latin America frequently involve violence pitting the fans of one nation against the fans of another. And when the Olympic Games are held, the nationalistic sentiments of fans and sports announcers clearly overshadow the athletic contributions of individuals.

Why is nationalism such an important feature of the modern world? There have been numerous theories attempting to explain it (cf. Breuilly, 1985:18–35), and it would be too much to try to review them all here. Anthony Smith (1986), however, has suggested a dichotomy that offers a useful way of thinking about how various scholars have tackled this problem. Smith distinguishes between *modernists* and *primordialists*. Modernists hold that nationalism is a unique product of the modern world having no true parallels in past societies. It arose no earlier than the fifteenth or sixteenth centuries, and did not really become well developed and crystallized until the eighteenth. As would be expected, modernists have some fundamental disagreements with each other about precisely what accounts for modern nationalism. The Marxists represent one wing of the modernist camp. Marx himself generally held that nationalism was an outgrowth of capitalism. It emerged as an ideology that was useful to the capitalist class in controlling workers, because it gave legitimacy to the capitalist system of which they were a part. In time, he thought, workers would recognize nationalistic affiliations for what they were—forms of "false consciousness"—and shed them in favor of international class alliances ("Workers of the world, unite") designed to overthrow capitalism.

This interpretation fares badly in face of the fact that nationalism has not weakened in the time since Marx lived, and especially in view of the extreme nationalism that is associated with state socialist societies like the Soviet Union. There is another line of Marxian argument, though, that attempts to deal with these uncomfortable facts: Wallerstein's world-system argument. For Wallerstein, capitalism has always been a global and international phenomenon, and from the beginning it was associated with nation-states as the principal economic actors. Nationalism has therefore been a natural ideological accompaniment of the form of organization of the capitalist world-economy. Like Marx, Wallerstein expects nationalism ultimately to disappear, although he believes this will take much longer and will only occur with the worldwide transition from capitalism to socialism a century or two from now.

A very different type of modernist interpretation is found in the work of Ernest Gellner (1983). Gellner proposes what is essentially a type of functionalist explanation. He claims that industrialization and modernization have uprooted traditional communities and the sentiments and ties that have held people together. People have been thrown into increasingly anonymous urban environments in which they have been required to do entirely different kinds of work. Under these circumstances, a need has arisen for a new unifying or integrating ideology, and nationalism is this ideology. Nationalism mobilizes the commitment of the population to the state, helping it to concentrate the resources necessary for continuing industrialization and modernization.

In contrast to these diverse kinds of modernist argument, the primordialists argue that nationalistic sentiments are rooted in a fundamental tendency for people to create and identify with communities based on race, religion, ethnicity, territory, language, or some combination of these. Modern nationalism is therefore simply one version of a human tendency that has always been, and will always be, manifested in history.

A May Day parade in the Soviet Union. Nationalism, often of a very intense sort, is an ideology that is highly characteristic of all nation-states within the modern interstate system.

One problem with this position is that most primordialists have offered little clue as to the specific origin of the tendency that they see underlying nationalistic sentiments (A.D. Smith, 1986; van den Berghe, 1981). They see this tendency as "natural," but it is not really clear what that is supposed to mean. In recent years, though, another kind of primordialist argument has been presented that attempts to identify the locus of the natural human tendency toward ethnic and nationalistic affiliations: sociobiology. Pierre van den Berghe (1981), for example, has suggested that ethnic ties are basically extensions of kin selection, and thus that they are firmly rooted in the human biogram. Of course, nationalism is not strictly equatable with ethnic affiliation, but the two are closely related and seem very closely tied to something we have already established as a human universal: ethnocentrism. A popular sociobiological argument in recent years is that the tendency toward ethnocentrism was implanted in the human biogram long ago (Reynolds, Falger, and Vine, 1986). Under the conditions of life that the earliest hominids faced, fierce loyalty to a local community would have been highly adaptive, and thus would have been favored by natural selection. Once implanted in the human biogram, it has continued to survive in modern humans, but now under circumstances in which it is probably more maladaptive than adaptive.

Although a lot of caution needs to be exercised in its evaluation, this argument is difficult to discount. One cannot help being impressed by the true universality of ethnocentrism, although its scope and intensity vary from time to time, place to place, and individual to individual. And one cannot help but be struck by the enormous staying power of ethnic and nationalistic ties, especially in the face of circumstances in which their demise has been predicted. Modern nationalism is, of course, more than just a particular form of ethnocentrism. But it has at its core a strongly ethnocentric character.

However, I want to avoid drawing any especially strong conclusions about the sources of modern nationalism. As Anthony Smith has noted, the modernists are at least partly right in recognizing that nationalism in our day has features that have never been found previously in world history. The nation-state is a creation of the modern world, and the interstate system that accompanies the capitalist world-economy has no true historical parallel. Yet the explanations of nationalism by various wings of the modernist camp leave much to be desired. We are thus pushed in the direction of the primordialists, whose claims deserve serious consideration. In the end, though, it would be foolish to say that we really understand what nationalism is all about. It remains one of the most persistent puzzles in modern social science.

FOR FURTHER READING

Anderson, Perry. *Lineages of the Absolutist State.* London: New Left Books, 1974. A well-known attempt at a Marxian explanation of the rise of the absolute monarchies in western and eastern Europe.

Carnoy, Martin. *The State and Political Theory.* Princeton: Princeton University Press, 1984. An excellent (and truly unsurpassed) overview of theories of the modern state, with a particular stress on classical and contemporary Marxian theories.

Domhoff, G. William. *Who Rules America Now?* New York: Simon and Schuster, 1983. An important attempt to show the influence of the capitalist class on political decision making in the contemporary United States. Takes a theoretical position that draws on both power elite and Marxian assumptions.

Evans, Peter B., Dietrich Rueschemeyer, and Theda Skocpol (eds.). *Bringing the State Back In.* New York: Cambridge University Press, 1985. A fine collection of articles calling for more attention to the state as a quasi-independent social force.

Giddens, Anthony. *The Nation-State and Violence.* Berkeley: University of California Press, 1985. A major work on the state that inclines more toward the Weberian perspective than toward any other.

Kennedy, Paul. *The Rise and Fall of the Great Powers.* New York: Random House (Vintage), 1987. A detailed analysis of the rivalry among capitalist states from the sixteenth century to the present. Focuses in particular on the reasons for the ascent and decline of states within the interstate system.

Mann, Michael. *The Sources of Social Power. Volume 1: A History of Power from the Beginning to* A.D. *1760.* Cambridge: Cambridge University Press, 1986. Several chapters treat the development of the modern state from a basically Weberian perspective.

Miliband, Ralph. *Marxism and Politics.* Oxford: Oxford University Press, 1977. One of the better discussions of the Marxian approach to the problem of the state.

Moore, Barrington, Jr. *Social Origins of Dictatorship and Democracy.* Boston: Beacon Press, 1966. An excellent and widely praised sociological analysis of the historical forces giving rise to divergent political outcomes in the modern world. Moore seeks the basic causes for the emergence of Western parliamentary democracy, fascism, and Asian communism.

Smith, Anthony D. *The Ethnic Origins of Nations.* Oxford: Blackwell, 1986. An exceptionally learned treatment of both the unique features of modern nationalism and its commonalities with similar attachments throughout human history.

Szymanski, Albert. *The Capitalist State and the Politics of Class.* Cambridge, Mass.: Winthrop, 1978. An excellent general treatment from a Marxian perspective of the role of the state in modern capitalism.

Tilly, Charles (ed.). *The Formation of National States in Western Europe.* Princeton: Princeton University Press, 1975. A well-known collection of essays on the development of centralized bureaucratic states during the transition from feudalism to capitalism.

CHAPTER 13

Comparative Patterns of Racial and Ethnic Stratification

The concepts of **race** and **ethnic group** have long been an important part of the terminological repertoire of sociologists and other social scientists. This is so because for at least the past several hundred years race and ethnicity have been factors extremely basic to the construction of numerous systems of stratification. This chapter discusses the various forms of stratified social life that have been erected along the lines of racial and ethnic distinctions. The discussion turns on how these systems originated and underwent various transformations, and special attention will be given to the underlying causes of such origins and transformations.

Until recently, the study of the relations between racial and ethnic groups suffered from a number of very serious impediments. Older approaches tended to be ahistorical and to lack any comparative foundation; most studies focused on contemporary American society. Great emphasis was given to the study of prejudice—an attitude of ill will of the members of one racial or ethnic group toward another—and this phenomenon was seen as being largely the result of certain personality configurations. Larger social forces, especially economic ones, were either excluded from consideration or treated as being of secondary significance. Racial and ethnic antagonism was frequently seen as the result of irrational or perverse psychological motives or needs on the part of some individuals; the "cure" for this antagonism was seen to lie in the removal of such unhealthy motives and needs. This kind of approach was bound to run into an intellectual dead end, and it did.

Sometime during the late 1960s, many social scientists began to see the limitations of these older approaches. Many stopped talking about "prejudiced personalities" and started talking about the larger social and economic forces that generated racial and ethnic divisions and inequalities and made some people prejudiced in the first place. In addition, interest in the study of slavery, both in the U.S. South and elsewhere, was greatly revived. Gradually the attention of many social scientists has shifted toward a more historical and comparative approach in which racial and ethnic stratification is seen as simply a special case of the more general phenomenon of stratified social life (van den Berghe, 1967). Much attention is now being given to how racial and ethnic stratification result from large-scale economic forces generating opposition between groups, and how these forces have served to maintain or destroy certain patterns of racial and ethnic stratification. This more recent kind of approach has already yielded much greater insights than did older ones.

THE CONCEPTS OF RACE AND ETHNICITY

The concept of race has for many years been a rather difficult one for social scientists to define. For a long time physical anthropologists approached this concept by conceiving it in strictly biological terms, races being viewed as groups of persons separated by constellations of distinctive genetic characteristics. Various classifications of racial "stocks" and "substocks" were proposed. But these anthropologists could not agree among themselves on the number of stocks and substocks that were to be identified, nor could they agree on precisely how one stock or substock was to be distinguished from another (van den Berghe, 1967). In time it came to be recognized that there was no such thing as a distinct or "pure" race, and that racial distinctions represented an almost infinite range of gradations and variations. Because of these problems, physical anthropologists have recently restricted the term race to refer to a "breeding population," a group of persons sharing a common genetic heritage and within which the rate of inbreeding is very high. Since breeding populations frequently overlap in complex ways, constellations of genetic traits form a continuous series of small gradations rather than a set of discrete, clear-cut groups.

Racial groups, however, represent more than simply physically distinguishable categories of persons. They also represent important *social* categories, groups of persons who identify themselves, and are generally identified by others, as distinctive and as occupying a particular social location with regard to other groups. An excellent illustration of this point is afforded by the contrasting systems of racial classification of the United States and Brazil. Historically, the United States has recognized only two racial groups (whites and blacks) and has classified persons into one group or the other according to what Marvin Harris (1964) has called the **rule of hypo-descent.** According to this rule, any person known to have any black ancestry, no matter how remote, is classified as black. The United States has not recognized any intermediate categories of racial identity. By contrast, Brazil has never applied such a rigid descent rule to the classification of racial identity. In Brazil, as Marvin Harris points out (1964:57–58):

> Over a dozen racial categories may be recognized in conformity with the combinations of hair color, hair texture, eye color and skin color which actually occur. These types grade into each other like the colors of the spectrum and no one category stands significantly isolated from all the rest. . . .
>
> It was found, in addition, that a given Brazilian might be called by as many as thirteen different terms by other members of his community. These terms are spread out across practically the entire spectrum of theoretical racial types. A further consequence of the absence of a descent rule is that Brazilians apparently not only disagree about the racial identity of specific individuals, but they also seem to be in disagreement about the abstract meaning of the racial terms as defined by words and phrases.

Harris goes on to note that the Brazilian system makes it possible for people to change their racial identity in their lifetime. This change can be accomplished through the achievement of economic success or the attainment of advanced education. Brazilians have a saying that "money whitens the skin," which means that the greater the wealth a person acquires, the lighter will be the racial category to which he or she is assigned.

If we combine the sociologist's notion of race as involving social definitions with the physical anthropologist's conception of race as a biological category, we end up with essentially the following definition: a race is *a group or category of persons who identify themselves, and are identified by others, as having a socially meaningful distinctiveness that rests on physical or biological criteria.*

In contrast to the term race, the term ethnic group shall be used to refer to *a social group or category whose distinctiveness rests on cultural, rather than biological, criteria.* In reality, racial and ethnic groups often overlap: a group whose distinctiveness rests primarily on biological criteria may also have a cultural distinctiveness. Despite their frequent intermingling in reality, however, the concepts of race and ethnicity are analytically separate. Usage of the terms in this chapter reflects this analytical distinction.

TWO TYPES OF RACE AND ETHNIC RELATIONS

A useful typology presenting two fundamentally different forms of racial and ethnic stratification has been developed by Pierre van den Berghe (1967) (Table 13.1). What is most useful about this typology is that it relates a society's particular form of racial/ethnic stratification to its material infrastructure and to the broader aspects of its social structure. In addition, as van den Berghe has stressed, the typology permits systematic comparative study of those societies that have been prominently stratified along racial and ethnic lines. It also allows an examination of the historical evolution of racial/ethnic stratification patterns and of the forces directing such evolutionary changes. The typology will

Table 13.1 VAN DEN BERGHE'S PATERNALISTIC AND COMPETITIVE TYPES OF RACE RELATIONS

	Paternalistic	Competitive
	Factors determining the prevailing type of race relations	
1. Economy	Nonmanufacturing, agricultural, pastoral, handicraft. Mercantile capitalism. Plantation economy.	Typically manufacturing, but not necessarily so. Large-scale industrial capitalism.
2. Division of labor	Simple ("primitive") or intermediate (as in preindustrial large-scale societies). Division of labor along racial lines. Wide income gap between racial groups.	Complex (manufacturing) according to "rational" universalistic criteria. Narrow gap in wages, no longer strictly racial.
3. Mobility	Little mobility either vertically or horizontally (slaves, servants, or serfs "attached" in space).	Much mobility both vertical and horizontal (required by industrial economy).
4. Social stratification	Caste system with horizontal color bar. Aristocracy versus servile caste with wide gap in living standards (as indexed by income, education, death and birth rates). Homogeneous upper caste.	Caste system but with tendency for color bar to "tilt" to vertical position. Complex stratification into classes within castes. Narrower gaps between castes and greater range within castes.
5. Numerical ratio	Dominant group a small minority.	Dominant group a majority.
6. Value conflict	Integrated value system. No ideological conflict.	Conflict, at least in Western "Christian," "democratic," "liberal" type of society.

(*continued*)

Table 13.1 (continued)

	Paternalistic	Competitive
	Aspects or components of the racial situation	
1. Race relations	Accommodation. Everyone "in his place" and "knows it." Paternalism. Benevolent despotism.	Antagonism. Suspicion, hatred. Competitiveness (real or imaginary).
2. Roles and statuses	Sharply defined roles and statuses based on ascription (birth). Unequal status unthreatened.	Ill defined and based on achievement. Unequal status threatened.
3. Etiquette	Elaborate and definite.	Simple and indefinite.
4. Forms of aggression	Generally from lower caste: slave rebellions; nationalistic, revivalistic, or messianistic movements. Not directly racial.	Both from upper and lower caste. More frequent and directly racial: riots, lynchings, pogroms; passive resistance, sabotage, organized mass protests.
5. Miscegenation (interbreeding)	Condoned and frequent between upper-caste males and lower-caste females. Institutionalized concubinage.	Severely condemned and infrequent.
6. Segregation	Little of it. Status gap allows close but unequal contact.	Much of it. Narrowing of status gap makes for increase of spatial gap.
7. Psychological syndrome	Internalized subservient status. No personality "need" for prejudice. "Pseudotolerance."	"Need" for prejudice. Linked with sexuality, sadism, frustration. Scapegoating.
8. Stereotypes of lower caste	Childish, immature, exuberant, uninhibited, lazy, impulsive, fun-loving, good humored. Inferior but lovable.	Aggressive, uppity, insolent, oversexed, dirty. Inferior, despicable and dangerous.
9. Intensity of prejudice	Fairly constant.	Variable and sensitive to provocative situations.

Source: Pierre L. van den Berghe, *Race and Racism: A Comparative Perspective*. New York: Wiley, 1967, pp. 31–32; slightly modified.

therefore serve as the conceptual foundation for much of what follows in the rest of the chapter.

Van den Berghe distinguishes between **paternalistic** and **competitive race relations.** Paternalistic race relations are characteristic of complex preindustrial societies based on large-scale agricultural production, particularly plantation agriculture. The most prominent societies resting on paternalistic race relations are the preabolition regimes of Brazil, the southern United States, and South Africa. Under a paternalistic system, the society is rigidly stratified into racial groups having a "castelike" nature, and many social scientists have referred to these racially distinctive groups as "castes." There exists a tremendous gulf between these castes in status, wealth, occupation, education, health, and general lifestyle patterns. No mobility between racial castes is allowed. Race becomes the major criterion determining the division of labor. A highly developed ideology of racial superiority and inferiority exists. The dominant group views itself as inherently superior, either on biological or cultural grounds or both, to the subordinate group. The subordinate group is seen as childish, immature, irresponsible, fun-loving, and happy-go-lucky—as inherently inferior, but nevertheless as lovable when "in their place." The system is therefore construed along the lines of a strict master-servant model. The superordinate group dominates the economy (it owns the bulk of the land, labor, and other natural resources), and this economic dominance gives it firm control over the political system and the law. Thus, as van den Berghe is quick to point out, paternalistic race relations are extreme examples of the exploitation of, and the tyranny over, the many by the few. Corresponding to this master-servant system is a mode of social life marked by low physical distance (i.e., little physical segregation), but high social distance. An elaborate system of social etiquette governs the interaction between dominant and subordinate groups. Since subordinate group members are highly structured inferiors, they may be permitted close physical contact with members of the dominant group without this serving as a threat to the status of dominant group members.

The competitive type of race relations is in many ways the polar opposite of the paternalistic type. It is characteristic of industrial societies with a complex division of labor and with the system of production based on manufacturing. The dominant racial group is a numerical majority or a fairly sizable minority. The contemporary United States, South Africa, and Britain are among the more prominent societies displaying competitive race relations. Under this type of racial stratification system, class differences become more important than differences based on racial caste distinctions, and race is no longer the primary criterion for the recruitment of persons to occupational positions. The political system is often what van den Berghe calls a **Herrenvolk democracy,** that is, one in which parliamentary democracy is limited in its application to the dominant racial group. The master-servant model collapses and is replaced by severe competition between the subordinate racial group and the working class of the dominant group. Physical segregation becomes extensive in order to preserve the dominant group's privileged position. The dominant group's image of the subordinate group is transformed from one of irresponsible and childish yet lovable inferiors to one of aggressive, "uppity," dishonest competitors for scarce resources and challengers to the status quo. The condescending benevolence characteristic of paternalistic race relations largely disappears and is replaced by hostility and outright hatred by many members of the dominant group for the subordinate group. Conflict between the dominant and subordinate groups becomes a frequent occurrence, taking the form of lynchings, race riots, and mass movements of political opposition. What is most characteristic of competitive race relations is that many members of the dominant racial group are thrown into open competition with members of the subordinate group in the search for jobs (hence the name "competitive"). This contrasts markedly with the paternalistic situation where the two groups are rigidly separated in the occupational structure, where one group is overwhelmingly the structured inferior of the other, and where the dominant group holds the other down through a benevolent despotism (hence the name "paternalistic").

All of the systems of plantation slavery that arose in the New World with the advent of modern capitalism have exhibited to one extent or another versions of the paternalistic type of race relations. Furthermore, several of these paternalistic systems evolved into competitive systems with abolition and increasing industrialization.

SYSTEMS OF PLANTATION SLAVERY IN THE NEW WORLD

The Capitalist World-Economy and the Origins of New World Slavery

Slavery is *a mode of labor organization and control in which some people are legally owned for life as a form of human property, are compelled to work by those who own them, and are* *generally deprived of all or most political liberties or rights*. Slavery of one sort or another has existed in many different societies at many points in history. It was, for example, the principal form of labor organization in ancient Greece and Rome. There, however, slavery was unconnected with race. The kind of slavery we are concerned with here, on the other hand, was intimately connected with race, for the great majority of the slaves were black men and women drawn from Africa. We may call this kind of slavery *plantation slavery*, for the slaves were put to work on large-scale plantations producing cash crops for a world economic market.

It is no accident that systems of plantation slavery arose in conjunction with the early development of the capitalist world-economy. As Immanuel Wallerstein (1974a:88) has pointed out, slavery "is preeminently a capitalist institution, geared to the early preindustrial stages of a capitalist world-economy." New World plantation slavery arose as a fundamental means of labor organization oriented to the production of goods that could be sold in a world economic market for profit. Slavery was fundamentally an economic institution from the very beginning. While it was also a social and political institution—a whole way of life for both masters and slaves—it was originally and primarily brought into existence for economic reasons. But why slavery as basic to certain sectors of the early capitalist economy? Why not some other system of labor, such as serfdom or wage-labor? Wallerstein (1974a) argues that slavery was a highly profitable system of labor control under conditions of large-scale plantation agriculture in which major cash crops were being produced for an extensive market. Hence slavery was a rational labor choice for early capitalist entrepreneurs who were pursuing large-scale agricultural production for profit in faraway lands.

Major systems of plantation slavery developed in several areas of the New World. It is currently estimated that approximately 9.5 million Africans were imported as slaves into the New World via the Atlantic slave trade (Fogel and Engerman, 1974). The biggest consumer in the slave trade was Brazil, which took 38 percent of the total. The British Caribbean, the French Caribbean, and Spanish America took 17 percent each, and the United States and the Dutch, Danish, and Swedish Caribbean took another 6 percent each (Fogel and Engerman, 1974).

Many European nations were involved in the slave trade and the establishment of plantation societies in the New World. Portugal established Brazil as a major slave society. Spain established slavery in Mexico and various parts of South America and, after a lapse, established a substantial slave society in Cuba in the nineteenth century. England had the British West Indies (mainly Barbados and Jamaica) and, of course, the United States until its independence. France had the French West Indies, consisting mainly of St. Domingue (now Haiti) and Martinique. Even Holland and Denmark were involved, with the Dutch establishing a small slave society in Dutch Guiana (now Surinam) and the Danes another small one on the island of St. Croix.

By far the biggest cash crop produced by the New World slave systems was sugar, an item greatly in demand by Europeans for sweetening their coffee. Brazil, the British and French West Indies, and Cuba were the biggest producers of sugar. A number of other products were generated for the market by plantation slavery, among them coffee, cocoa, tobacco, indigo, hemp, and rice (Fogel and Engerman, 1974). Cotton, of course, was the major product of slavery in the United States, but it did not become significant until after the beginning of the nineteenth century.

It should also be mentioned that not all slaves were put to work in plantation agriculture; in addition to those who worked as household servants, many were used in mining operations, particularly in Spanish America and Brazil.

A slave ship. Slave trading was an integral part of the capitalist world-economy until well into the nineteenth century.

Slavery in the U.S. South

Although slavery began in the U.S. South toward the end of the seventeenth century, the U.S. South did not emerge as a major slave society until the beginning of the nineteenth century. After this time, its principal commodity was, of course, cotton, the bulk of which was exported to England to feed its flourishing textile mills. By the middle of the nineteenth century slavery had expanded from its beginnings in Maryland and Virginia to encompass much of the Deep South, and it had spread as far west as Texas.

Blacks always constituted a numerical minority in the slave system of the United States. In the Southern colonies in 1650 they made up only 3 percent of the total population, while by 1770 their percentage had risen to 40 percent (Fogel and Engerman, 1974). These figures are in striking contrast to what prevailed in many other plantation systems, where blacks were often a very large numerical majority. Furthermore, the average plantation size in the United States was considerably smaller than that in the prime sugar-producing societies. The average size of a slave holding in Virginia and Maryland at the end of the eighteenth century was less than 13 slaves (Fogel and Engerman, 1974). In the antebellum period (1800–1860), only the great planters had plantations with as many as 100 to 200 slaves, and the majority of plantations contained 30 or fewer slaves. These figures are quite small when we consider that many sugar plantations in the West Indies and Brazil had as many as 500 slaves.

The U.S. Southern slave system was dominated by a wealthy and powerful planter class, a slavocracy that consisted of only a small minority of all slaveholders. This planter class controlled the economy through its ownership of land and people, dominated the political system, and created the laws of the slave South to serve its own ends. Many historians have thought of the great planters as essentially an aristocratic class with an ideology that was antagonistic to the calculative outlook of capitalist entrepreneurs (Genovese, 1965, 1969). However, in their famous study of the economics of Southern slavery, *Time on the Cross* (1974), Robert Fogel and Stanley Engerman demonstrate convincingly that the planters were "shrewd capitalistic businessmen" with a highly rational and calculative outlook. Actually, given the larger economic system of which they were part, how could they have been otherwise? Since they were producing for a world economic market, it is inconceivable that they could have turned a deaf ear to questions of profit and loss and still have survived.

In the southern United States the relations between masters and slaves were governed by a pervasive social structure and ideology of paternalism. The plantation was a largely self-contained world where masters and slaves lived in close and continuous contact with one another. Social interaction between the races was regulated by a highly developed etiquette. Slaves were supposed to behave submissively toward their masters through the use of terms of respect as well as gestures and speech signifying their own inferiority, but masters addressed slaves by their first names. While sexual activity between black men and white women was severely condemned, white masters frequently had sexual relations with their black slave women. Young white boys often had their first sexual experience with slave girls, and it was a fairly common practice for masters to keep several slave women as concubines. In the ideological realm, whites held an elaborate set of stereotypes regarding the inferiority of blacks. Blacks were generally regarded as irresponsible grown-up children. Masters treated slaves much as a stern but loving father would treat his small children (van den Berghe, 1967).

Slavery in Brazil

One of the largest and most significant of all the New World plantation systems was developed by the Portuguese in Brazil. The first slaves were introduced into Brazil from Africa around the middle of the sixteenth century, and by the seventeenth century a well-developed slave system was in operation. The great majority of Brazilian slaves worked on sugar, coffee, cotton, and cacao plantations. Sugar dominated Brazilian slavery during the seventeenth century. A minimum of about 80 slaves seemed to be required for the operation of a successful sugar plantation, and some of the plantations employed several hundred slaves (van den Berghe, 1967). When the economic significance of sugar waned, Brazil shifted to the large-scale development of coffee plantations, and coffee was the dominant cash crop in the eighteenth and nineteenth centuries.

Brazil had an intense reliance on the Atlantic slave trade, taking, as previously noted, 38 percent of the total number of slaves imported into all of the New World. Brazilian slavery was based on large-scale operations, and black slaves came to outnumber whites throughout Brazil's slavery period. In 1789, out of a total population of 2.3 million, 1.5 million were African slaves. In 1872 whites still represented only 38 percent of the total population (van den Berghe, 1967). In contrast to the U.S. South, Brazil had a slave labor force that did not reproduce itself. Because of the continual influx of slaves, little attention was given to the reproductive powers of slave women, and they produced few offspring. Slaves were worked to the limit and replaced by new ones when they died.

The Brazilian slave system was highly paternalistic and bore many striking resemblances to the slave society of the southern United States. Van den Berghe provides an informative description of Brazilian plantation life (1967:65–66):

> It is clear that the *fazenda* [sugar-cane plantation] was a classic example of paternalistic race relations. It was a self-sufficient microcosm with its own food supply, repair shops, chapel, resident priest-tutor, cemetery, hospital, and school. . . .
>
> Residentially, the big house *(casa grande)*, inhabited by the owner's family and by domestic slaves, dominated the nearby slave quarters *(senzala)* that housed the field hands and skilled craftsmen. Relations between masters and house slaves were intimate, that is, both spatially and emotionally close, though socially very distant. White children were raised by Negro wet-nurses *(amas)* and given a slave of their age and sex as play companions. When a white boy reached sexual maturity, he was sexually initiated with one of his father's slaves and continued to engage in promiscuous concubinage with female slaves throughout his sexually active lifetime. Interracial concubinage with female slaves was completely accepted for white men, and, according to the dual standard of sexual morality, marriage was not considered an impediment to the maintenance of a slave harem. Even the Catholic clergy interbred extensively with women of color. . . .

Brazilian slaves washing for diamonds.

> The division of labor along racial lines was quite clear-cut. The Portuguese aristocracy was a leisure class *par excellence,* engaged almost solely in war and love making. . . .
>
> Social distance between masters and slaves was maintained through a punctilious etiquette of subservience and dominance. Sumptuary regulations, forms of address, and symbolic gestures regulated social intercourse between people of vastly different status who were in constant and intimate contact with each other. For example, masters were carried about in litters and were accompanied by a retinue of slaves arranged in a well-regulated procession when going to public places. . . .
>
> Many stereotypes about the Negro developed during the slavery period and are still part of the Brazilian folklore. The Afro-Brazilian was regarded as a lascivious, physically unattractive, happy-go-lucky grownup child.

With only a slight change in wording here and there, van den Berghe's description of Brazilian paternalism could equally well serve as a description of plantation life in the southern United States.

Slavery in the West Indies and Cuba

The British West Indies were composed of several small islands in the Caribbean, the most notable of which were Barbados and Jamaica. These islands were given over to extensive plantation slavery during the seventeenth and eighteenth centuries, and sugar was by far the largest cash crop. An increasing number of slaves were imported after the middle of the seventeenth century to work rapidly developing sugar plantations. By the eighteenth century the British West Indies had become totally dependent on sugar production (Foner, 1975). The economy and polity were dominated by a small planter class, the most important segment of which consisted of absentee owners. These owners lived in splendor off their great profits in England and left their plantations under the care of overseers (Foner, 1975). Philip Foner (1975) describes British West Indian slavery as especially harsh and cruel.

The French West Indies consisted of the islands of Guadeloupe, Martinique, and, most importantly, St. Domingue (Haiti). Great profits were made from the sugar plantations of St. Domingue in the eighteenth century. Like most sugar plantations elsewhere, those of the French West Indies were very large in scale. Black slaves, therefore, greatly outnumbered whites. In St. Domingue in 1790 there were 32,000 resident whites, 24,000 freedmen, and 48,000 slaves (Foner, 1975). The French planter class, like its British counterpart, consisted largely of absentee owners. French West Indian slavery was also characterized by great brutality (Foner, 1975).

The Danish West Indies consisted mainly of the small island of St. Croix. The Danes were mainly absentee owners on sugar plantations.

The Dutch West Indies principally involved the country of Surinam on the northern coast of South America. Like most of the other West Indian planters, the Dutch were absentee owners. Surinam contained large sugar, coffee, cotton, and lumber plantations, on which the black slaves overwhelmingly outnumbered the whites. The Dutch were renowned for their atrocious treatment of slaves (Genovese, 1969).

Under the direction of Spain, Cuba became a major sugar-producing slave society in the nineteenth century when St. Domingue collapsed from a successful slave insurrection. Foner describes nineteenth-century Cuban slavery as extremely brutal and exploitative, and he further notes that the level of brutality increased proportionately with the intensification of sugar production.

The different slave systems of the West Indies shared many features in common. In all of them sugar production was the key to the economy. All were dominated by planter classes whose members consisted mainly of absentee owners. And all were exceptionally brutal. Under these kinds of conditions, the paternalism so characteristic of the U.S. South and Brazil undoubtedly could not fully develop (Genovese, 1969).

Recapitulation: Slavery and the Capitalist World-Economy

In examining the plantation slave systems of the New World, one can look at them from two different, yet equally significant, points of view. One can look at their internal dynamics, at the nature of their master and slave classes and the relations between these classes. One can then get some insight into how the systems functioned and what consequences they had for those persons and groups who lived within them. One can also, however, look at these slave societies from a larger perspective, from the point of view of their involvement in a capitalist world-economy. From this perspective, it is possible to get a clearer idea of the fundamental forces that generated, sustained, and ultimately destroyed New World slave societies. So far, we have been looking at slavery from both points of view, but we have said less than we can about the relationship of individual slave societies to the capitalist world-economy.

An insightful study of the role played by slavery—particularly British West Indian slavery—in the development of British capitalism has been carried out by Eric Williams in his book *Capitalism and Slavery* (1966; orig. 1944). Williams's main argument is that slavery played a vital role in generating the profits that led to the great expansion of British capitalism and the financing of the Industrial Revolution.

Williams places great emphasis on the role of the *triangular trade* in the development of British capitalism. The triangular trade linked Africa, the British West Indies, and Britain together into a vast network of economic interdependence. Ships would sail from Britain with a supply of manufactured goods. These would be exchanged at a profit for Negroes in Africa. The African slaves were in turn traded on the plantations at another profit in exchange for plantation produce to be taken back to Britain.

The triangular trade stimulated a host of industries. Shipbuilding was one of the more prominent of these, for specific types of vessels were manufactured for the slave trade. The shipbuilding industry led to the development of the great British seaport towns of Bristol, Liverpool, and Glasgow. The manufacture of woolen and cotton goods also received a great boost, for these items were of considerable importance for the purchase of slaves. Another industry that grew in response to the triangular trade was sugar refining, and the prosperity of cities like Bristol and Glasgow rested heavily on their sugar-refining industries. Since rum could be distilled as a by-product of sugar production, the rum-distillation industry also became important. The metallurgical industries expanded: chains and padlocks were manufactured for confining slaves; guns were shipped to Africa in exchange for slaves; and sugar stoves, rollers, wrought iron, and nails were manufactured for the plantations. Banking was directly stimulated, for shipbuilders and slave traders were instrumental in establishing the first banks. Insurance companies also got started, since slave traders felt a need to insure their human cargoes against loss.

The British West Indian plantations therefore played a crucial role in the economy of the British Empire in the eighteenth century. They were a key link in a vast economic network that led to the massive expansion of British capitalism. During this time the British North American colonies played a very secondary role in British economic life. But following the American Revolution the role of the British West Indies declined and that of the United States greatly accelerated. During the first half of the nineteenth century, U.S. slavery played a major role in the advance of British capitalism. The great industry in Britain during this time was, of course, textile manufacturing, and Britain's demand for raw cotton increased enormously. By the middle of the nineteenth century the United States was providing the bulk of this cotton: "The United States supplied less than one-hundredth part of British cotton imports in the five years 1786–1790, three-quarters in the years 1826–1830, four-fifths in 1846–1850" (Williams, 1966:128). British capitalism was thus enormously responsible for the great expansion of the cotton kingdom of the U.S. slave South during the nineteenth century.

It is clear that plantation slavery was intimately involved in the whole process of Western capitalist development, particularly in Britain. Capitalism found slavery extremely useful in achieving its economic ends. Eventually, however, capitalism found slavery an impediment to its further development. When that time arrived, powerful capitalist entrepreneurs were instrumental in destroying those very slave systems that had originally nourished them.

INDUSTRIAL CAPITALISM AND THE DEVELOPMENT OF COMPETITIVE RACE AND ETHNIC RELATIONS

As capitalism generated the Industrial Revolution, and as industrialization intensified and spread, the New World systems of plantation slavery were all destroyed. Blacks ceased to be slaves, but for the most part they did not cease to be oppressed and exploited members of racially divided societies. As the old paternalistic systems came apart, they were quickly replaced by racially stratified societies in which a new type of race relations—the competitive type—rose to prominence. In these societies, blacks were nominally free, but they still had to struggle against forces that sought to keep them at the bottom of the social order.

The Abolition of the Slave Trade and Slavery

Britain abolished its role in the slave trade in 1807. Although some illegal slave trading activities did continue after this date, Britain had nevertheless officially declared that its participation in slave trading had come to an end. The abolition of slavery itself came some years later: Britain abolished it throughout its empire in 1833, the United States put an end to it in 1863, and in 1888 it came to a halt in Brazil. What were the driving forces leading up to these events? As for the abolition of Britain's involvement in the slave trade, Immanuel Wallerstein (1979a) offers a plausible explanation. He suggests two reasons Britain wanted an end to the slave trade. First, by the beginning of the nineteenth century Britain was starting to make colonial intrusions into Africa in order to make use of it as a crop-producing area; therefore, Africans were becoming more valuable to Britain as colonized workers in their homelands than as slaves in distant lands. Second, Britain wished to deny its European competitors access to slaves. Wallerstein therefore sees Britain's abolition of the slave trade as having been guided by rational economic motives.

As for the abolition of slavery itself, generations of scholars have called attention to the role of humanitarian sentiments, arguing that these played a critical role in bringing slavery to a halt. There were, of course, many individuals—in Britain, the United States, and elsewhere—throughout the eighteenth and nineteenth centuries who called for an end to slavery on so-called humanitarian grounds. But, as Eric Williams (1966) has noted, the "humanitarian" motives of these persons have been widely misunderstood. Williams believes that the humanitarian sentiments expressed by many Englishmen who called for an end to slavery were essentially nothing more than a cover for underlying economic motives. While many influen-

This illustration appeared on the front page of the antislavery newspaper *Emancipator* in 1839. Many people opposed slavery for moral and humanitarian reasons, but there is no reason to believe that moral appeals actually contributed to slavery's ultimate demise.

tial individuals condemned slavery on moral grounds, they actually had firm economic motives for wanting it ended. Williams notes, for example, that while many of the abolitionists were condemning West Indian slavery, they tolerated—indeed, encouraged—slavery in Brazil, Cuba, and the United States. This was during a time when the West Indies had become economically burdensome to Britain at the same time that Britain continued to have a vital economic interest in the perpetuation of slavery in Brazil, Cuba, and the United States. Williams explains further (1966:190–191):

> The abolitionists were boycotting the slave-grown produce of the British West Indies, dyed with the Negro's blood. But the very existence of British capitalism depended upon the slave-grown cotton of the United States, equally connected with slavery and polluted with blood. The West Indian could legitimately ask whether "slavery was only reprehensible in countries to which [*sic*] those members do not trade, and where their connections do not reside." . . . The boycotters of West Indian sugar sat upon chairs of Cuban mahogany, before desks of Brazilian rosewood, and used inkstands of slave-cut ebony. . . .
>
> Was Brazilian sugar necessary? The capitalists said yes; it was necessary to keep British capitalism going. The abolitionists took the side of the capitalists.

Barrington Moore (1966) has also downplayed the role of moral or humanitarian considerations, and emphasized the role of economic forces, in attempting to explain the Civil War and the abolition of slavery in the United States. Moore's argument is that the Southern slave system had eventually become incompatible with the economic interests of Northern industrial capitalists. Southern slaveholders and Northern industrialists, he claims, were locked in a bitter struggle over who was going to control the lands of the Western frontier, and it took a war to settle this struggle.

Wallerstein (1979a) has approached this problem from the point of view of the capitalist world-economy as a whole. He argues that slavery had to be abolished because it was becoming too economically costly to a world-economy that had lost its major slave-producing region (Africa).

The explanations of Williams, Moore, and Wallerstein are slightly different, but all focus upon the economic rationality that lay behind the abolitionist movement. While the precise forces that brought all slave systems to an end are not yet clear, it is reasonably certain that the general forces were of an economic nature. Capitalism created slavery when and where it was economically profitable, and destroyed it when it became too costly.

The Development of Competitive Race Relations in the United States

Pierre van den Berghe (1967) has provided a valuable discussion of the emergence and development of competitive race relations in the United States. As he notes, the end of slavery marked the beginning of a whole new phase in the relations between blacks and whites. The black man ceased to be seen as a "happy, singing slave" and increasingly came to be viewed as "uppity" and "pushy," as not knowing "his place," as an economic competitor with whites, and as a rapist of white women.

Economically, slavery gave way to a system of sharecropping and debt peonage. Many freedmen found that they had to stay on the land in order to eke out a living. The plantation owners divided their land into small plots that could be farmed by individual tenants. Freedmen were lent food, seeds, tools, and other necessary items in order to farm their share of the land. The plantation owners arranged things so that the black tenants could never repay these debts, and blacks therefore fell into a system of debt peonage in which they were as securely tied to the land and their landlords as they had been under slavery.

By the last quarter of the nineteenth century, lower-class whites found themselves in increasing contact and competition with millions of freed blacks. Whites and blacks were "forced by economic conditions to confront one another, bump shoulders, and compete on a wide scale for the same jobs" (W. Wilson, 1978:56). The increasing economic threat that blacks posed to whites gave rise to political disfranchisement and the development of an elaborate system of "Jim Crow" segregation. In the South at least, segregation began to penetrate into virtually every sphere of social life: "It became a punishable offense against the laws or the mores for whites and Negroes to travel, eat, defecate, wait, be buried, make love, play, relax, and even speak together, except in the stereotyped context of master and servant interaction" (van den Berghe, 1967:89–90).

In addition to disfranchisement and segregation, there also arose another tactic designed to remove or neutralize the economic threat posed by blacks: terrorism. The Ku Klux Klan emerged and made extensive use of intimidation, brutality, and murder against blacks. Vigilante groups were also formed and these too engaged in acts of terrorism in order to keep the Negro "in his place." Lynching became a significant feature of social life as a device for maintaining white supremacy.

Around World War I blacks began to migrate to the North in search of jobs in an expanding northern industrial economy. Here blacks competed severely with whites for jobs. During this time blacks were frequently used by white businessmen as strikebreakers. The increasing influx of blacks created housing shortages in northern cities, and competition also arose between whites and blacks over access to facilities for recreation and relaxation, such as playgrounds and public beaches. These occur-

Scene from a Chicago race riot of 1919. Race riots broke out in a number of major northern American cities at approximately this time, which can be largely attributed to the fact that the migration of blacks from the South was posing an increasing economic threat to whites.

rences created great hostility between whites and blacks, and this hostility erupted into a number of race riots, among the more serious of which occurred in East St. Louis in 1917 and in Chicago in 1919. As William Wilson (1978:76) notes, "In the final analysis, the rioting served to underscore the effect of economic changes on the interracial arena, as all of the major interracial riots had either a direct or indirect connection with industrial strife."

By the 1930s the major cities of the North had sizable concentrations of blacks, and the black ghetto was well on its way to being consolidated. Most northern blacks were concentrated in these ghettoes. By the end of World War II, according to Wilson (1978), another new era of American race relations was beginning, an era in which the social and economic fortunes of blacks were coming to be more determined by class than by racial factors.

Racial and Ethnic Stratification in South Africa

Van den Berghe (1967) has provided a perceptive analysis of the development of racial stratification in South Africa.

What is now the Republic of South Africa was originally colonized by the Dutch, who began to settle there in 1652. By the end of the seventeenth century, a rigid system of racial stratification existed. In 1658 the Dutch began the importation of slaves. The form of slavery that came to be established was one based on medium-sized farms engaged in diversified agriculture rather than on large plantations. Nevertheless, South African slavery did develop a paternalistic character. The white farmer lived on an autonomous estate surrounded by his black slaves. The division of labor was clearly established along racial lines, with whites regarding manual work as degrading. An unequal status system was maintained through an elaborate racial etiquette.

Some of the Dutch were not slaveowners, but seminomads who were constantly expanding into the frontier regions. These, known as the Boers, colonized native Hottentot pastoralists, whom they reduced to the status of serfs. Boer expansion was greatly slowed in the 1770s when the Boers encountered the Bantu tribes, but it began again in 1836 with the Great Trek, which lasted for a decade.

The era of competitive race relations in South Africa began toward the end of the nineteenth century. With the discovery of gold in 1886, South Africa began to industrialize, with the gold-mining industry leading the way. This industry was dominated by British colonists, who had begun to settle in South Africa around the turn of the nineteenth century. British mine owners had an enormous need for unskilled mine workers and set their sights on the many African tribesmen who lived throughout the region. Through a variety of coercive methods, many of these tribesmen were drawn into the gold-mining industry, where they eventually came to constitute a severe economic threat to white mine workers. The extreme economic competition between white and African mine workers led, particularly in the period 1910–1924, to the early formation of what is today the practice of *apartheid*, or a strict policy of racial segregation and exclusion directed against Africans. Apartheid did not become an official government policy until 1948 with the coming to power of the Afrikaner Nationalist Party, but its essential foundations had been established by 1924 (Ndabezitha and Sanderson, 1988).

Today South Africa is undoubtedly the most conflict-ridden, racially divided society in the world. It is divided into four main racial groups: (1) the Europeans, or whites, totaling about 18 percent of the population; (2) East Indians, who amount to about 3 percent of the population; (3) the Coloureds—persons of mixed European and native Hottentot ancestry—numbering about 10 percent of the total; and (4) Africans, who constitute the bulk of the population, with 70 percent of the total (this group consists of various African tribesmen who have been incorporated into the South African state at different intervals). The last three groups are collectively known as "nonwhites," and a rigid caste line separates them from the Europeans.

The system of apartheid that governs the relations between whites and nonwhites in South Africa is a vast social phenomenon that contains important social, economic, and political dimensions. More narrowly, it refers to a policy of strict separation between the races that applies to virtually every aspect of social life. Strict apartheid laws apply to housing, schools, transportation, hospitals, cemeteries, toilets, sports facilities, and churches, as well as many other things. However, the economic and political dimensions of apartheid are more important in the sense that they have greater significance for the quality of life for the vast majority of the population.

The whites in South Africa hold a massive monopoly over power and wealth. Whites own the bulk of the land, and the English own the bulk of the mining and manufacturing industries and control a great deal of South Africa's banking, finance, and commerce. Since 1948 the Afrikaners (descendants of the Dutch, who speak a modified form of Dutch known as Afrikaans) have monopolized political power. The army, navy, judiciary, and all the higher positions in the civil service are dominated by whites. Whites control nearly all the more attractive jobs, and nonwhites are overwhelmingly concentrated in the lower-paying, low-prestige jobs. In 1960 the average family income of whites was approximately 14 times that of Africans and 5 times that of Coloureds and Indians. (The ratio of white to African income had declined slightly by 1975, but was still very great: about 10:1 [Nattrass, 1981:288]).

A repressive political regime has characterized South Africa for many years. Although the nation is technically a parliamentary democracy, its democratic procedures apply only to whites, and there is no pretense of democracy for nonwhites. It is a classic example of a *Herrenvolk* democracy. Africans have no right to vote. They must carry identification cards with them everywhere and present these to the police upon demand. More than a million Africans are arrested each year, most of these on technical and minor violations of apartheid laws. Africans spend their lives under the constant shadow of police surveillance, intimidation, and brutality.

In the past decade or two the extreme racial divisions within South Africa have become even more apparent, and have been brought to world attention. Many forms of violence between Africans and whites have erupted, and government repression of Africans has substantially intensified. It is obvious that the level of African resentment of whites is extreme, and that the society has become so polarized that whites have felt that the only way to maintain their superior economic and social position is to resort to severe repressive measures. This clearly

Apartheid: a segregated bathing beach in South Africa.

means that the current South African situation is an especially precarious one whose future is very uncertain.

Competitive Race Relations in Contemporary Britain

Race relations in Britain have historically displayed a number of striking contrasts with race relations in the United States and South Africa. Most obviously, Britain has never had a slave economy within the British Isles, and thus until very recently few blacks have ever been resident there. In the early part of the twentieth century there were perhaps only a few thousand blacks living in all of Britain (Fryer, 1984).

Nonetheless, the situation has changed very significantly since the end of World War II. Because of labor shortages in Britain in the immediate postwar years, a number of people from some of Britain's former colonies—mainly the West Indies, India, and Pakistan—began to be attracted to the British Isles. Many British employers, in fact, actively recruited workers from these areas (Layton-Henry, 1984). Immigration from these regions increased substantially throughout the 1950s and into the early 1960s. In 1953 some 2,000 immigrants poured into Britain, by 1957 the annual number had increased to over 42,000, and by 1961 the number had swelled to more than 136,000 (Layton-Henry, 1984). Today about 4 percent of Britain's population consists of West Indian, Indian, or Pakistani ethnic minorities (Fryer, 1984).

In the early postwar years, when only a small number of immigrants were coming, there was much resistance on the part of most Britons to the acceptance of the immigrants as equals, but there was little overt ethnic hostility. However, the situation was soon to change. By the late 1950s, race riots had broken out all over Britain, especially in the bigger industrial cities. Cries increasingly went up for immigration control, and in 1962 a governmental policy restricting immigration was established in the form of the Commonwealth Immigrants Act. Since this provided only a mild measure of immigration control, however, opponents of immigration continued to press their case (Layton-Henry, 1984). New immigration restrictions were passed into law in 1968 and 1971 (Fryer, 1984), and the campaigns that produced these laws were increasingly accompanied by overtly racist rhetoric. Outbreaks of racial violence continued to occur sporadically throughout the 1960s, 1970s, and even into the early 1980s. These included physical assaults and killings of members of ethnic minorities by whites, as well as a riotous counterattacks by the ethnic minorities themselves (Layton-Henry, 1984; Fryer, 1984).

Throughout the 1980s there has been a subsidence of racial violence and other forms of overt racial hostility, but Britain has become a racially antagonistic society in which West Indian, Indian, and Pakistani ethnic minorities are disproportionately concentrated at the bottom rungs of the economic ladder. They do many of the jobs no one else wants. Moreover, the threat of overt violence is still highly present, and it is likely to erupt again in the very near future.

Theories of Competitive Race Relations

A variety of theories have been proposed to explain the existence of racial antagonisms during the era of competitive race relations. The most valuable of these theories emphasize racial antagonism as an outcome of economic forces and class struggle. But even these economic theories present somewhat contrasting and conflicting interpretations of the basic causes of racial antagonism.

The *orthodox Marxian* interpretation argues that racial antagonism is a direct product of the conflict between capital and labor (Cox, 1948; Szymanski, 1976; Reich, 1977). Capitalists desire the cheapest labor possible and act in ways deliberately designed to keep the cost of labor down. Capitalists make use of racial distinctions to further their own economic interests. They consciously promote racial antagonism between white and black workers, thereby dividing the working class against itself. This prevents the working class from achieving a high degree of solidarity and making full use of its organizational potential, thus limiting its ability to push for higher wages.

Edna Bonacich (1972, 1979) has suggested that this interpretation is a considerable oversimplification of the dynamics of racial antagonism. She argues instead for a *split labor market theory.* The central assumption of this theory is that racial antagonism first develops in a labor market that is split along racial lines. For a labor market to be split, it "must contain at least two groups of workers whose price of labor differs for the same work, or would differ if they did the same work" (1972:549). The split labor market theory holds that, rather than being the result of a simple conflict between capitalists and workers, racial antagonism is the outcome of the relationships among three economic groups: capitalists, higher-paid labor, and cheaper labor. Capitalists have as their main aim the acquisition of as cheap and docile a labor force as possible. When labor costs are too high, capitalists will, if possible, turn to the use of cheaper labor. The main interest of higher-paid labor is to keep its wages up and prevent other groups of workers from undermining its economic security. It therefore fears competition from cheaper labor and will do what it can to remove it as a threat. Cheaper labor, naturally, wishes to maximize its economic interests and this frequently brings it into competition with higher-paid labor. Capitalists may attempt to use cheaper labor as strikebreakers and undercutters.

Edna Bonacich. Bonacich is a professor of sociology at the University of California, Riverside. She developed, and in numerous publications has substantially elaborated on, the split labor market theory of ethnic antagonism.

Racial or ethnic antagonism develops when higher-paid labor and cheaper labor are of different racial or ethnic groups. This antagonism may take one or the other of two principal forms, depending upon the underlying conditions: exclusion movements or caste systems.

Exclusion movements typically arise when the cheaper labor group lives outside a given territory but wishes to immigrate into it. With the movement of cheaper labor into a labor market previously controlled by higher-paid labor, higher-paid labor experiences a direct economic threat and begins making demands that the cheaper labor group be excluded from the labor market altogether. Bonacich argues that this is what happened when cheaper labor groups of Chinese and Japanese immigrated to the United States in the late nineteenth century. As Chinese and Japanese immigration increased, higher-paid labor perceived a direct threat to its economic well-being and began voicing demands that the Asian workers be prevented from immigrating; these demands were, in fact, acted upon by the U.S. government (cf. Boswell, 1986).

Caste systems rather than exclusion movements result when cheaper labor is already present in the labor market and cannot be excluded. Under this arrangement, higher-paid labor gains monopolistic control over the better, higher-paying jobs and consigns cheaper labor to poorer-paying jobs, thereby removing them as an undercutting threat. Bonacich argues that such caste systems have been most prominently represented by the racial stratification systems of the United States and South Africa (cf. Bonacich, 1972, 1981).

In contrast to orthodox Marxian theory, which sees racial antagonism as resulting simply from the conscious actions of capitalist entrepreneurs, Bonacich's split labor market theory sees racial antagonism as primarily the result of the conflict that arises between different segments of the working class. She therefore implicates higher-paid workers in the formation of racial antagonism in a way that is ignored by the orthodox Marxian interpretation. Although both theories emphasize economic conflict as the basis for racial/ethnic antagonism, they do so in distinctively different ways.

William Wilson (1978) believes that both the orthodox Marxian and split labor market interpretations have validity, but that they must be applied to different historical circumstances. Wilson divides the history of the United States into three different historical periods according to the pattern of race relations prevailing in each: the preindustrial, industrial, and modern industrial periods of race relations. The preindustrial period was characterized by the system of plantation slavery. Wilson argues that the orthodox Marxian theory satisfactorily explains the racial stratification system prevailing during this time. White slaveowners constituted the dominant economic class and consciously turned blacks into slaves in order to advance their own economic interests.

With the end of slavery, the industrial period of American race relations began, lasting until about the end of World War II. This period was characterized by continual strife between white and black workers as freed blacks directly competed with whites for jobs. Wilson holds that the patterns of race relations prevailing during this period cannot be accounted for by the orthodox Marxian theory; rather, the split labor market theory is said to do a much better job of explaining the kinds of racial conflict that emerged. The evidence presented by Wilson seems to bear out this contention. Again and again we find capitalists interested in, and to a large extent succeeding in, employing cheaper black workers in large numbers. Yet white workers who were economically threatened by such actions were highly successful in trying to establish racial caste arrangements to protect their more privileged economic position.

Finally, the modern industrial period of race relations is said to characterize the United States from the end of World War II to the present. Wilson believes that neither theory can adequately explain the structure of racial stratification during this period (see the Special Topic at the end of this chapter).

Wilson's claim regarding the complementarity of the orthodox Marxian and split labor market theories also seems to apply to the history of racial antagonism in South Africa. The orthodox Marxian theory seems to apply to the preindustrial period in South Africa, but from the beginnings of South African industrialization the split labor market theory seems a much more adequate interpretation (Bonacich, 1981; Ndabezitha and Sanderson, 1988). As noted earlier, the era of competitive race relations in South Africa began with the development of large-scale gold mining in 1886. White mine owners used numerous coercive methods to attract Africans to the mines to work for wages. For a variety of reasons Africans could be employed at a markedly lower wage rate, and thus there was a split labor market present in South Africa right from the beginning of its competitive race relations era. Capitalist mine owners

Chinese and American workers constructing the last mile of the Central Pacific Railway in 1869. During the second half of the nineteenth century, Chinese workers were brought to the West Coast of the United States in increasing numbers because of the cheapness of their labor. Can you predict the consequences for interethnic relations with whites?

tried to employ Africans in larger and larger numbers because of the cheapness of their labor, and this meant that they became an increasing economic threat to white mine workers. As a result, numerous forms of conflict broke out between white and African workers, and white workers vigorously attempted to prevent mine owners from gaining access to Africans. By 1924 white workers had succeeded in electing a government highly sensitive to their demands to exclude African workers from competition with them, and thus by this time the foundations of the modern system of apartheid had been established (Fredrickson, 1981). The exceptional repressiveness of the apartheid system today no doubt reflects the desperate efforts of a privileged white numerical minority to protect itself against the tremendous economic threat posed by roughly two-thirds of the population.

Turning our attention to Britain, it would appear to be almost a perfect case for the application of split labor market theory. There is a striking correlation between the post–World War II increase of immigration into Britain from the West Indies and the Indian subcontinent and the emergence of racial antagonism. Britons harbored considerable racial and ethnic intolerance before the war (Fryer, 1984), but in the early years of the postwar immigration there was relative acceptance of the immigrants (Layton-Henry, 1984), probably because they as yet constituted no significant economic threat (indeed, due to the immediate postwar labor shortage, many Britons welcomed them). But as their numbers grew, they began to pose a serious undercutting threat to native Britons. As Zig Layton-Henry has pointed out (1984:50):

> There were efforts by local branches in the transport industry to exclude black workers, but concern about immigration was more widespread than this. . . . In 1956 when tension rose Jack Jones, Midlands organiser of the Transport and General Workers' Union, suggested that coloured workers "can form a pool of cheap labour which can be used to depress wage standards and fight the trade unions" (*Birmingham Mail,* 5 June 1956). In May 1955 the biennial conference of the Transport and General Workers' Union had called for the strictest control over all forms of immigration and in 1957 a motion calling for the government to exercise strict control over the number of coloured workers who were allowed to enter Britain was passed with executive support. . . . The new General Secretary, Frank Cousins, said in his winding-up speech, "We cannot afford that these people should be allowed unrestricted entry into this country as a basis for the reduction of our bargaining powers" (*Manchester Guardian,* 11 July 1957).

It seems clear that the critical element in contemporary British race relations has been the concern over immigration. White workers have formed themselves into various exclusion movements, and in the 1960s they were supported in their efforts by their chief political representative, the Labour party. This was so even though the Labour party was philosophically opposed to immigration restriction (Layton-Henry, 1984).

THE ORIGIN AND EVOLUTION OF RACISM

The phenomenon known as **racism** has been of great concern to social scientists for some time. Most modern social scientists use the term *racism* to mean *an elaborate ideology holding that one race is by nature superior and that all others are by nature inferior to it.* The term "by nature" is of critical importance, for it implies that the superiority of one race and the inferiority of others is a result of their genetic characteristics. Racist doctrines therefore assume that the social, economic, and political achievements of the members of one race are the result of their superior genetic endowment; likewise, the "failures" of the members of other races are said to be due to genetically linked deficiencies. These alleged deficiencies are usually believed to lie in the realm of intelligence and character, but racist doctrines frequently extend themselves to include other traits as well. When racism exists, it is not a personal belief system characteristic of individuals, but a significant part of the whole ideological superstructure of a society (Noel, 1972a; See and Wilson, 1988).

The notion of racism has frequently been confused with the concepts of ethnocentrism, prejudice, and discrimination. But as Donald Noel (1972a) points out, these concepts do not refer to the same thing and it is of considerable importance to distinguish among them. **Ethnocentrism** refers to the beliefs held by the members of a culture that their way of life is superior to the lifeways of the members of other cultures (see Chapter 2). Racism differs from ethnocentrism in two principal ways. First, ethnocentrism is a belief system based upon notions of cultural, rather than biological, superiority. Second, ethnocentrism is a genuinely universal feature of human social life, while racism has been characteristic of only some societies for the past several hundred years. Racism is therefore a much more culturally and historically restricted phenomenon than is ethnocentrism.

Prejudice is an attitude of dislike or hostility of a member of one racial or ethnic group toward the members of some other racial or ethnic group. Ordinarily, this attitude is applied categorically, that is, toward the members of a racial or ethnic group collectively. Whereas racism is a belief system, prejudice is an emotional response or feeling. And whereas racism is a component of a society's ideological superstructure, prejudice is a property of an individual person (Noel, 1972a). It is perfectly possible for a society to be a racist one and yet at the same time for many of its members to be relatively unprejudiced. This situation prevailed in the antebellum U.S. South, for example; white slaveowners held racist conceptions of blacks, yet they frequently found them to be "lovable creatures." By the same token, it is possible for persons to be prejudiced without harboring racist beliefs.

Finally, the concept of **discrimination** refers to the unequal and unfair treatment of one racial or ethnic group at the hands of another group. While discrimination is frequently associated with racist beliefs and prejudiced feelings, it does not have to be and sometimes is not.

With a handful of possible (and probably minor) exceptions, racism arose only with the advent of modern capitalism and the European colonization of the world. Oliver Cox (1948) has argued that racism did not exist in any of the great early civilizations, such as the Egyptian, Babylonian, and Persian Empires. He also notes that even the ancient Greeks and Romans, who made such extensive use of slavery, developed no ideologies that might be labeled racist. The civilizations of classical antiquity used culture and language, but not race, as a basis for making distinctions of superiority and inferiority. Cox concludes that it was not until the beginning of the capitalist exploitation of non-Western peoples that racism began. Noel (1972a) argues that racism began to crystallize in the Western world in the eighteenth century and did not reach its peak until the nineteenth century. Both Fredrickson (1971) and van den Berghe (1967) view racism as primarily a nineteenth-century Western phenomenon. Van den Berghe (1967:15) has asserted that "it came of age in the third or fourth decade of the nineteenth century, achieved its golden age approximately between 1880 and 1920, and has since entered its period of decline."

The following conclusions are probably warranted regarding the emergence and development of racism: (1) It either did not exist or was relatively insignificant prior to the development and expansion of European capitalism. (2) It arose in a general and somewhat rudimentary fashion in conjunction with European colonialism and the establishment of New World plantation slavery; it therefore formed a significant part of the ideological superstructures of plantation slave societies. (3) It did not reach its peak until well into the nineteenth century; during this time, it came to be greatly elaborated and intensified, and by the early part of the twentieth century it had penetrated into almost every nook and cranny of Western social life.

Some scholars believe that negative beliefs about and attitudes toward blacks preceded the existence of slavery and actually helped to give rise to it. Winthrop Jordan (1974), for example, makes much of the fact that Englishmen in the early sixteenth century held a number of negative conceptions of Africans, regarding them as "lustful," as "heathens," and even as "beasts." He believes that these early conceptions played at least some role in turning Africans into slaves in the North American colonies. But the conceptions that Jordan refers to were not components of a genuine racist ideology; rather, they no doubt represented the ethnocentric reaction of Europeans to people who differed radically from them in cultural terms. Englishmen of the early sixteenth century were highly ethnocentric, but they were undoubtedly not yet accustomed to racist thinking. And it scarcely seems plausible to argue that ethnocentrism gave rise to the necessity for slavery.

In a similar vein, Carl Degler (1972) has claimed that North American slavery was molded to a considerable extent by the prior existence of racial prejudice among the colonists. Degler is ultimately trying to show that slavery as a politico-economic and social system was heavily conditioned by the mental conceptions of those who established and maintained it. But, as Noel (1972b) remarks, Degler ends up blurring the distinction between racism, prejudice, ethnocentrism, and discrimination, and his argument only produces confusion. His preoccupation with the colonists' mental conceptions of blacks, furthermore, leads him to ignore the immense role of economic forces in the creation of slavery (Noel, 1972b).

It would seem that scholars such as Jordan and Degler have been looking at things from the wrong end: instead of examining how slavery may have been a result of certain mental conceptions, it would seem much more fruitful to examine how the establishment of slave systems led to the transformation of the slaveholders' ideological conceptions about the people they were enslaving. When we pose the question in this fashion, we may begin to understand how and why racism as an ideology came into being.

There is now a high degree of consensus among modern social scientists that racism emerged in order to justify and rationalize the brutal oppression and exploitation to which millions of people were subjected under the conditions of plantation slavery (Cox, 1948; Williams, 1966; Foner, 1975). Philip Foner indicates that racism was first applied by the Spanish to the enslavement of the Indians of the New World. But he goes on to remark (1975:89) that "racism's real development came with the importation of the more permanent slaves—the Africans—and it was the English who made the leading contribution toward this development." By indicating that racism arose as a rationalization and justification for slavery, it is not being suggested that those who harbored racist thoughts did not really believe in them—that they were merely trying to convince others of the moral propriety of what they were doing. On the contrary, those who harbored racist conceptions of blacks no doubt were deeply convinced of the basic correctness of their beliefs. And in being so convinced that what they were doing was justified by the inherent inferiority of blacks, they could continue to do it without feeling so guilty about it.

Noel (1972a) notes that the development of slavery coincided with the emergence of democratic political principles in the Western world. Since slavery was obviously so incompatible with those democratic ideals, it would have required special justification to avoid a massive contradiction. Racist ideologies, arguing that the natural inferiority of black Africans suited them only for a condition of servitude, provided such a justification.

It is still necessary to account for the tremendous intensification that racist thought underwent in the nineteenth century. This might be explained, paradoxically, in terms of the abolition of slavery itself. Abolition meant that millions of blacks were turned loose to compete in the labor market with whites, thus posing a severe economic threat. One way of meeting this threat would be to attempt to exclude blacks from many economic positions by virtue of their race alone. An elaborate racist ideology could be an extremely effective tool in this regard; it could be used as an ideological weapon to justify, under altered economic circumstances, the restriction of blacks to the lowest-paying jobs. This argument is strengthened by the fact that racism in the United States was at its peak when blacks posed the greatest economic threat to working-class whites, that is, from about 1890 to 1930 (W. Wilson, 1978). As Wilson observes (1973:42):

> When the system of racial stratification is challenged both by subordinates seeking to share the dominant group's rights and privileges and by other individuals and groups opposed to race exploitation, the need for a more explicit and forceful justification of racial domination emerges. This is when dominant-group spokesmen with vested interests begin to denounce the subordinate racial group publicly.

In other words, when the system of racial stratification is under attack, an intensification of racism can be anticipated.

TYPES AND VARIETIES OF MINORITY GROUPS

Much of what we have been discussing in this chapter can be examined through the use of the concept of a **minority group.** A minority is a social group having a number of principal characteristics: it exists within the confines of a larger state society; its members are either physically or culturally distinguishable from the members of other groups within the same society; and it suffers to one degree or another from unequal and unfair treatment at the hands of these other groups. These other groups that dispense unequal treatment to minority groups are usually called **majority groups.** As sociologists use it, the term *minority* always refers to the fact that such a group occupies an inferior social, economic, and political position within a larger society, and it should not be taken to refer to the numerical size of the group. Although most minorities are small in numbers compared to majority groups, this is not always the case. Africans in the Republic of South Africa, for example, are an extremely oppressed minority, yet they make up more than two-thirds of the South African population.

Sociologists commonly distinguish three major kinds of minority groups: racial, ethnic, and religious minorities. Racial minorities are those that are distinguishable largely or exclusively in terms of their biological characteristics. Blacks in the United States and Africans and Coloureds in South Africa are good examples of racial minorities. Ethnic minorities are distinguishable by their cultural heritage rather than by their biological makeup. A great many modern nations contain ethnic minorities within their boundaries, for such minorities are formed either through the constant shifting of political boundaries or through systematic immigration. Irish and Italians in the United States, East Indians in South Africa, and Chinese in Malaysia are only a few of the dozens of ethnic minorities that exist around the world. Religious minorities are, of course, those that are primarily distinguishable by their religious tradition. Jews in the United States are usually said to constitute such a minority—although they are distinguishable along ethnic lines as well. In actuality, of course, these types of minorities frequently overlap. Racial minorities may also have culturally distinctive traits and thus be an ethnic minority too, and ethnic minorities often have distinctive religious traditions that set them apart.

Genuine minority groups did not exist until the rise of the state in human history (Wagley and Harris, 1958). When this occurred, state-level societies began a never-ending process of political conquest of other societies. This process has resulted in a continuous redrawing of political boundaries over the past several thousand years, and as this has happened, many formerly autonomous groups have become incorporated as minorities within larger societies. But if political conquest is a major factor that has led to the formation of minorities, it has not been the only factor. Different types of minority groups have also been created through immigration, whether forced or voluntary. Through these processes of political conquest and forced and voluntary immigration, minority groups of various types exist in virtually all modern complex societies. Indeed, as Anthony Smith has commented (1981:9–10):

> The fact is that very few of the world's states are ethnically homogeneous, and many of them are distinctly polyethnic in composition. According to Walker Connor, of 132 independent states in 1971, only 12 were ethnically homogeneous, representing 9.1 percent of the total, while another 25 (or 18.9 percent) have a single ethnic community comprising over 90 percent of the state's population. A further 25 have a single ethnic community comprising 75–90 percent of the population, and 31 have an ethnic community representing 50–74 percent of the state's population. On the other side, in 39 states (or 29.5 percent), the largest ethnic group comprised less than 50 percent of the population; while in 53 states (40.2 percent), the population is divided into more than five significant groups.

Colonized and Immigrant Minorities

The experiences of some minority groups have been radically different from those of others. In this connection, Robert Blauner (1972) has made a distinction between two types of minorities according to the manner in which each was created: colonized and immigrant minorities. Blauner identifies as **colonized minorities** those that have been formed when a stronger group colonizes a weaker group for the purpose of exploiting its labor or acquiring its land. By contrast, **immigrant minorities** are those that have been created through the voluntary immigration of a group to another political society.

Blauner applies this distinction to understanding the fate of different minority groups in the United States. He classifies blacks, Chicanos (Mexican-Americans), and Native Americans (the remnants of North American Indian tribes) as colonized minorities, while identifying the main European ethnic immigrants as immigrant minorities. He notes that the fate of the colonized minorities has been distinctly different from that of the immigrant minorities. The colonized minorities remain highly visible groups concentrated disproportionately at the bottom of the socioeconomic and political system, but the main immigrant minorities have become rapidly assimilated into American culture, have lost much of their social visibility, and have been highly successful in penetrating into the middle (and occasionally upper) levels of the socioeconomic structure. Blauner believes that the much greater success of the immigrant minorities is largely a result of their much more favorable starting position. They came to the United States voluntarily; they shared a number of broad cultural characteristics in common with Americans when they arrived; a great many of them possessed useful occupational skills that were in high demand; and they never had to bear the burden of racist stigmas (even though they were subjected for a while to ethnocentric attitudes and stereotypes).

By contrast, blacks came as slaves and served in that capacity for more than 200 years, had no education and few occupational skills when they were freed, and became a severe economic threat to working-class whites from the end of the Civil War on. Chicanos became U.S. citizens when the United States forcibly annexed major sections of Mexican territory. These new Mexican-Americans were mostly illiterate and exploited peasants when they were incorporated into the United States. The story of the Native Americans is well known. Hundreds of thousands of North American Indian tribesmen were killed through the colonization of North America and the expansion into the Western frontier. Those Indians who remained alive were herded onto reservations under white control; their indigenous cultures were destroyed, and the lives of most were shattered.

It should not be difficult, therefore, to understand why blacks, Chicanos, and Native Americans have lagged greatly behind the European ethnic immigrants in their quest for a fair share of the American social, economic, and political pie. As Blauner's discussion makes clear, the starting points of these colonized minorities heaped severe handicaps upon them that even hundreds of years of struggle have not been able to overcome.

Middleman Minorities

Some minorities have neither remained at the bottom of the class structure nor become heavily assimilated into the dominant culture. They have retained their cultural heritage and worked themselves into a unique position in the middle range of the socioeconomic structure. Such specialized minorities have been termed **middleman minorities** (Blalock, 1967; Bonacich, 1973; Turner and Bonacich, 1980).

Middleman minorities have essentially the following characteristics: rather than being concentrated in lower-level socioeconomic positions, they tend to occupy an intermediate position in the class structure; they tend to be concentrated in occupations involving trade and commerce, and they are also frequently employed as agents, labor contractors, rent collectors, money lenders, and brokers; and they usually have very high levels of ethnic solidarity and consciousness, commonly setting themselves apart and resisting assimilation into the dominant culture. Prominent middleman minorities include such groups as the Jews in Europe, the Chinese in Southeast Asia, Asians in East Africa, Parsis in India, and Japanese and Greeks in the United States. It is interesting to note that some groups, such as Chinese, East Indians, and Jews, have become middlemen wherever they have gone.

An interesting theory of middleman minorities has been presented by Bonacich (1973; cf. Turner and Bonacich, 1980). Bonacich believes that these minorities have arisen from the following sequence of events: Some groups left their homelands in search of economic opportunities elsewhere. However, they immigrated for the purpose of quick economic gain rather than to settle permanently in a new land. This motivation has had two main consequences: it has meant that such groups have greatly resisted absorption into the new culture, since they have had every intention of returning to their homeland after the achievement of economic success, and it has meant that they have attempted to concentrate themselves in occupations where economic success could be quickly realized. This latter fact explains, then, why such groups have been heavily concentrated in "middleman" occupations: These occupations do not tie up capital, and they tend to serve as good sources of easily liquidated wealth. Of course, many members of these ethnic groups have never been able to realize their goal of returning to their homeland, and those who have stayed in the host country have come to constitute permanent middleman minorities.

Bonacich has placed special emphasis on the fact that middleman minorities have frequently been subjected to high levels of hostility from various members of the host country. Middleman groups have been accused of being clannish and alien, of holding themselves aloof and believing they are superior to members of the host country, of being disloyal to the host country, and of being parasites who drain the host country of its economic resources. In addition to these negative stereotypes, middleman minorities have suffered from "efforts to cut off their means of livelihood, riots and pogroms, exclusion movements and expulsion, removal to concentration camps, and 'final solutions'" (Bonacich, 1973:589). Bonacich argues that this hostility has not been the result of abstract ethnocentric attitudes or prejudices; rather, she believes that it has resulted from the economic

A Jewish ghetto in Poland earlier in this century. The Jews have been one of the world's most prominent middleman minorities.

threat (or perception thereof) that middleman groups have posed for members of the host society. This threat is a result of the entrenched monopolies that middleman groups have developed over some occupations. As Bonacich puts it (1973:592): "The difficulty of breaking entrenched middleman monopolies, the difficulty of controlling the growth and extension of their economic power, pushes host countries to ever more extreme reactions. One finds increasingly harsh measures, piled on one another, until, when all else fails, final solutions are enacted."

Consociational Democracy

All of the types of ethnic relations discussed thus far are ones in which social conflict and antagonism are prominent. Indeed, it seems that such conflict is a common feature of ethnic relations the world over. But must ethnic relations always be conflict-ridden? Can multiethnic societies exist without significant conflict among the different ethnic groups?

The existence of what has been called **consociational democracy** permits an affirmative answer to the last question (Lijphart, 1977; van den Berghe, 1981). Consociational democracy prevails when distinct ethnic groups within a single state coexist in a remarkably harmonious manner. There is no hierarchical ordering of the groups, and thus no group dominates or exploits any other. There is a sharing of political power, and all the ethnic groups are proportionately represented in the class structure. As van den Berghe (1981) has suggested, consociationalism is a highly fragile situation, and several important factors must operate together to make it work. He argues that a successful consociational democracy is most likely when several ethnic groups territorially, genetically, and functionally interpenetrate, that is, when ethnic groups are extensively geographically mixed; when there is a high rate of intermarriage among the groups; and when they share common economic, religious, linguistic, or cultural institutions.

Several states have been nominated for the status of consociational democracies, among them Canada, Belgium, and Switzerland—and even rancorous Lebanon! However, the only genuinely successful instance of consociationalism appears to be Switzerland. This country is composed of four main ethnic groups, identified by their linguistic affiliation. Germans constitute 75 percent of the population; the French make up 20 percent; the Italians are only 4 percent; and the Romansh speakers are just 1 percent. Religiously, Switzerland is nearly equally divided between Protestants and Catholics, and religious distinctions cut across language groups. Socioeconomic differences crosscut ethnic differences.

Van den Berghe has suggested that Switzerland represents a rare combination of circumstances favorable to ethnic harmony. It is highly unusual in that it did not arise through either conquest or the breakdown of a multinational empire. Its exceptional terrain made it almost impossible to invade, and it developed an economy built around providing specialized goods and services to its neighbors (e.g., cannon, watches, special banks). It actually evolved as a "loose confederation of hill tribes." Switzerland has perhaps been so unique that, as van den Berghe has wittily remarked, "if it had not existed, it would have had to be invented" (1981:194).

ETHNICITY IN EVOLUTIONARY PERSPECTIVE

Until recently, the dominant view of the future of ethnicity has been a functionalist one. The functionalist theory has argued that ethnic affiliations are primordial attachments characteristic of preindustrial societies, attachments destined to disappear with the full maturation of industrial society (cf. Hraba, 1979; A. D. Smith, 1981; Hechter, 1975, 1976). In the modern industrial world, ethnic ties are highly maladaptive and are thus increasingly dissolved. Modern industrial societies emphasize achievement and universalistic values incompatible with the particularism of ethnicity. Ethnic sentiments and ties are highly dysfunctional to the rational organization of labor systems basic to industrialism. Moreover, the expansion of international trade, transportation, and communication brings culturally diverse people into greater contact with one another and helps to erase ethnic differences.

The events of the twentieth century, and particularly of the past 30 or 40 years, have clearly shown that the functionalist theory of ethnic change is a failure (A. D. Smith, 1981; Hechter, 1976). Rather than becoming less significant, ethnic ties have actually become considerably more significant as the twentieth century has progressed. As Anthony Smith points out (1981:10, 12):

> For the crucial fact is that interethnic conflict has become more intense and endemic in the twentieth century than at any time in history. Few countries have been able to avoid serious ethnic conflicts.
>
> . . .
>
> In every continent and practically every state, ethnicity has reappeared as a vital social and political force. The plural composition of most states; their policies of cultural integration; the increasing frequency and intensity of ethnic rivalries and conflicts; and the proliferation of ethnic movements: these are the main trends and phenomena which testify to the growing role of ethnicity in the modern world.

In the context of these remarks, Smith goes on to list several dozen examples of recent ethnic conflicts or ethnic movements, among them ethnic riots in Malaysia, Japanese hostility to

Burakumin, the Muslim-Hindu conflict that divided Pakistan from India, civil war in Lebanon, the Palestinian conflict in the Middle East, racial conflict in South Africa, conflict between Hausa and Ibo in Nigeria, the Québecois movement in Canada, the black revolt in the United States, the conflict in Northern Ireland, conflict between Flemings and Walloons in Belgium, and the Russian persecution of several ethnic minorities in the Soviet Union. Undoubtedly Smith's list, a much longer one than the one above, could be extended considerably.

Basically, there are two reasonable alternatives to the functionalist theory. One is an economic conflict theory. This theory suggests that the revival of ethnicity is the historical legacy of generations (or even centuries) of economic domination of some ethnic groups by others. Contemporary ethnic conflict is thus the ghost of historically subjugated minorities coming back to haunt dominant ethnic groups and force them to pay for their sins. This kind of theory has already been used in this chapter to explain several examples of ethnic and racial conflict, but it also seems to apply very well to many other cases. Two instances stand out in particular. The French Canadian Québecois movement for separation in Canada is a good example. Even in Quebec, where they substantially outnumber English speakers, French Canadians are a highly dominated ethnic minority. The economy is disproportionately controlled by English Canadians, and French Canadians are in general much worse off economically than English Canadians. Their situation is not totally unlike that of blacks in the United States, and in Canada one commonly hears utterances of prejudice toward the French similar to those heard in the United States toward blacks.

The situation in Northern Ireland is even more clearly one in which economic conflict plays a major role. The conflict between Protestants and Catholics there is often interpreted as a battle over religion, but it is more appropriately viewed as a conflict in the socioeconomic sector. As Michael Hechter (1975) has shown, the roots of the present Irish conflict must be understood in terms of the history of British colonialism in Ireland. Ireland was for several centuries in a peripheral relationship to England. It was turned into a raw-material-producing and -exporting region for England's benefit, and came to be an "internal colony." English colonization of Ireland was accompanied by extreme ethnic hostility. English landlords in Ireland were Protestants who despised the traditional culture and religion of their Catholic peasant subordinates.

The situation in Northern Ireland today appears as the historical legacy of this economic situation. Catholics are disproportionately concentrated at the bottom of the socioeconomic ladder. They are subjected to economic discrimination and looked down upon by the Protestant majority. While it is undoubtedly the case that the conflict between Protestants and Catholics is about more than socioeconomic differences, these are at the root of the conflict.

The other kind of theory that might help to explain the current persistence of ethnicity (if not its strong revival) is sometimes called **primordialism** (cf. van den Berghe, 1981; A.D. Smith, 1981, 1986). Primordialism holds that ethnic ties are fundamental, indeed irreducible, kinds of human attachments that can be softened but never entirely eliminated. Unlike the functionalist theory, this view holds that ethnic ties are fundamental to the basic character of human relations, including those in industrial societies (refer back to the Special Topic at the end of Chapter 12).

The biggest problem with most primordialist arguments, as noted earlier, is that they posit ethnic affiliation as a "natural" human tendency without actually telling us why this should be so. As van den Berghe has remarked (1981:17): "As a theoretical underpinning, the primordialists had nothing better to fall back on than the nebulous, romantic, indeed sometimes racist ideologies of nationalists to which the primordialists pointed as illustrations of their contention. What kind of mysterious and suspicious force was this 'voice of the blood' that moved people to tribalism, racism and ethnic intolerance?"

The sociobiological version of primordialism, however, overcomes this difficulty by suggesting that the tendency toward ethnic attachment is rooted in the human biogram (cf. van den Berghe, 1981; Reynolds, Falger, and Vine, 1986). Among ancient hominids strong group loyalties would have been highly adaptive as mechanisms for individual survival, and thus would have been favored by natural selection. As suggested earlier, this argument cannot be comfortably ignored, and it may be entirely complementary with explanations of ethnic attachment that emphasize economic conflict. Ethnic attachments are obviously greatly affected by a range of sociocultural conditions, especially economic ones. But, since they have a remarkable persistence throughout human space and time (cf. A. D. Smith, 1986), it is difficult to believe that they are simply at the mercy of sociocultural forces. Sociobiological arguments cannot contribute much toward explaining most of the dimensions of racial and ethnic stratification that we have explored in this chapter, but they may be relevant to explaining why at least some tendency toward ethnic affiliation and identity is a constant in human societies.

SUMMARY

1. Sociologists generally define racial groups as physically distinguishable populations accorded social significance. Ethnic groups are populations that are culturally, rather than physically, distinguishable. In reality, however, racial and ethnic groups often extensively overlap.

2. Two major types of race relations may be distinguished: paternalistic and competitive. Paternalistic race relations are characteristic of preindustrial societies based on plantation agriculture and slavery. Castelike divisions between a dominant racial group and a subordinate group emerge, and an elaborate racial etiquette regulates the relations between them. Competitive race relations are associated with industrial capitalist societies with a manufacturing economy and wage labor. The paternalism and racial etiquette of former times give way to severe conflict between racial groups over access to economic positions.

3. The slave trade and slavery were a vital part of expanding capitalism in the New World. Slavery was found in peripheral capitalist societies and seemed to be the most profitable way of organizing a labor force under the particular economic arrangements of those societies. There was a close link between the slave economies and the development of capitalism in the core nations.

4. Slavery in the U.S. South achieved its peak in the period 1800–1860, when it was largely given over to the production of cotton. A classical paternalistic system of race relations emerged from it. Slavery in Brazil differed from slavery in the U.S. South in a number of ways; nevertheless, Brazilian slavery generated a paternalistic pattern of race relations that was strikingly similar to U.S. Southern racial paternalism. Slavery also existed in the West Indies. Here it seemed to take an especially cruel and despotic form, and racial paternalism was seemingly largely absent, doubtless because most West Indian planters were absentee owners and because of the overwhelming demographic dominance of the slaves.

5. The argument that slavery was abolished for moral and humanitarian reasons is highly dubious. It seems instead that economic factors were crucial. Slavery had outlived its economic usefulness and was increasingly incompatible with the rapidly expanding system of industrial capitalism.

6. The end of slavery ushered in the era of competitive race relations. In the United States severe forms of economic and social conflict between whites and blacks began in the late nineteenth century and have continued throughout much of the twentieth. Whites have used segregation, terrorism, and a range of exclusionary practices as various means of counteracting the economic threat posed by blacks. The most extreme version of competitive race relations anywhere in the world has been found in South Africa for the past century. South Africa is dominated by a white numerical minority that holds an enormous monopoly over power and wealth. A rigid system of apartheid governs the relations between whites and nonwhites. In recent years racial conflict has grown and has taken increasingly violent forms. Contemporary Britain is also characterized by a competitive form of race relations. This has developed after World War II as a result of extensive immigration into Britain from its former colonies in the West Indies and the Indian subcontinent.

7. Two major theories of competitive race relations are the orthodox Marxian theory and the split labor market theory. The Marxian theory argues that capitalists attempt to stir up racial conflict so as to divide the working class and make it more exploitable. The split labor market theory views racial antagonism as emerging from a more complex situation in which higher-paid workers of the racial or ethnic majority attempt to prevent lower-paid workers of minority groups from economically competing with them on equal terms. This effort may result in exclusion movements or caste systems.

8. Racism is an ideology holding some racial groups to be biologically inferior to others. It must not be confused with prejudice, ethnocentrism, or discrimination. Racism seems to have arisen in the West as a means of giving moral justification to slavery, and its intensification after the end of slavery can be understood as the result of the enormous economic threat posed by blacks.

9. Numerous racial, ethnic, and religious minorities exist in complex societies all over the world, and ethnically heterogeneous societies are far more common than ethnically homogeneous ones. Ethnic complexity has arisen from such factors as colonialism, political conquest, and immigration. Ethnic diversity is usually associated with stratification and conflict, but there are occasional societies, such as contemporary Switzerland, in which ethnic diversity is largely associated with equality and harmony.

10. The functionalist evolutionary theory of ethnicity asserts that with the maturation of industrial societies ethnic distinctions will increasingly disappear. In the twentieth century, though, ethnic distinctions have in many ways become more meaningful, and ethnic conflict has increased. Ethnic divisions are deeply intertwined with the economic organization of society and its conflicts, and are not simply symbolic expressions of traditional group attachments. It is also possible that a basic tendency toward ethnic affiliation has roots in the human biogram, as a number of sociobiologists have recently suggested.

SPECIAL TOPIC: THE QUESTION OF BLACK PROGRESS

In the past decade or so a crucial question for many social scientists has been the extent to which blacks in the United States have made progress in achieving equality with whites. As these social scientists note, the civil rights movement of the 1960s was specifically devoted to the accomplishment of this aim. So now, some 30 years after the beginning of that movement, what has been the level of its success?

Reynolds Farley (1984) has described three different views that have been taken on the question of black progress. The *optimistic view* holds that blacks have generally been making progress over the past decades; the *pessimistic view* claims that black progress has been illusory, or at least far more limited than generally believed; and the *polarization thesis* claims that, while some blacks have indeed been progressing significantly, a larger number have been experiencing a worsening of their life chances and have been falling further and further behind whites.

Perhaps the best representative of the optimistic view is Farley himself. Farley acknowledges that in some areas blacks still lag as much behind whites as they did three decades ago. For example, black unemployment is still about twice as high as white unemployment, residential segregation between whites and blacks is still marked, and little progress has been made toward the integration of schools in the nation's largest cities. However, Farley claims that in other respects blacks have progressed significantly. Racial differences in educational attainment have declined, blacks are far more likely to hold prestigious and high-paying jobs, and the earnings of employed blacks have increased notably. Farley concludes that, on balance, black gains have been both substantial and widespread.

The pessimistic view has been embraced most vehemently by Alphonso Pinkney (1984). Pinkney does not claim that blacks have made no progress at all in recent years, but he does assert that the extent of this progress has been greatly exaggerated by both white and black social scientists. He focuses most heavily on what he believes is the strong persistence of racism, prejudice, and discrimination. He is convinced that the United States is still a thoroughly racist society, despite the decline of some of the more blatant forms of racism. This racism has allegedly become an autonomous and self-perpetuating ideology that is responsible for continuing racial discrimination and subordination. As a result, blacks have made only very limited gains in upgrading their occupations and income levels and in being treated as equal partners with whites.

Opposed to both of these views is the polarization thesis, which to my mind is the most sensible of the three. Undoubtedly the most important representative of this view is William Julius Wilson, a leading black sociologist. Wilson's view is a complex and subtle one that has been developed in two books written a decade apart. In *The Declining Significance of Race* (1978), Wilson argues that the United States has experienced three distinct historical periods of race relations: the preindustrial, industrial, and modern industrial periods. As noted in the main text, Wilson has argued that the orthodox Marxian theory seems to explain the pattern of race relations in the preindustrial period, while the split labor market theory does a much better job of explaining racial antagonism during the industrial period. But after the end of World War II the United States entered the modern industrial period of race relations, a period to which, Wilson believes, neither the orthodox Marxian nor the split labor market theory adequately applies. Indeed, he advances an entirely new thesis to account for the pattern of race relations during this period. He claims that the modern industrial period has witnessed the "declining significance of race" and, correspondingly, the increasing significance of class. That is, he argues that the economic fortunes of blacks are now determined more by the forces of *class* than by those of *race*.

Wilson rests the burden of his argument on an analysis of the changing shape of the black class structure over the past several decades. He notes that a black middle class began to form in the first quarter of the twentieth century. Until after World War II this class constituted only a very small proportion of the total black population. However, beginning around 1950 it began to expand considerably. It grew from 16 percent of the black population in 1950 to 24 percent in 1960 and approximately 35 percent in 1970.

(Wilson's definition of "middle class" for the black population includes working-class blacks with stable incomes.) Wilson traces this increase primarily to a general expansion of the corporate and governmental sectors of the economy, arguing that such an expansion greatly increased the availability of white-collar job opportunities for the more talented and better-educated blacks.

This growth of a black middle class has been accompanied by the continued concentration of many blacks at the lowest rungs of the socioeconomic ladder, resulting in an income distribution among blacks now more unequal than among whites. Thus, despite the substantial upward mobility achieved by blacks in recent decades, a large black underclass of ghetto poor remains; furthermore, the economic situation of this underclass has been worsening significantly in recent years. These black poor, Wilson argues, represent the legacy of many decades of previous discrimination against blacks. But he also goes on to point out that, at the present time, their economic fortunes are determined more by the class position they share with lower-class whites than by their race. Put another way, Wilson is saying that a large black underclass *came to be formed* through decades of systematic racial discrimination, but that its *persistence* owes more to its identity as a class than to continued racial discrimination.

In terms of the question of black progress, then, Wilson's argument is that over the past four or five decades the black community has become increasingly bifurcated into a small middle class and a large underclass. In *The Truly Disadvantaged* (1987) he concentrates specifically on the situation of the black underclass. As he notes, just from the time he wrote his previous book this underclass has become increasingly impoverished, demoralized, and isolated. Its members have suffered from increasing joblessness, family breakdown, and welfare dependency, and have turned more and more to

William Julius Wilson. Wilson is chairperson of the Department of Sociology at the University of Chicago. His contributions to an understanding of the historical evolution of relations between blacks and whites in the United States, as well as the current plight of many blacks in this country, have been outstanding.

violent crime and other extralegal activities in order to cope with their deteriorating situation. Wilson invokes a number of factors to explain this continued deterioration. Although the black underclass was formed as a result of many decades of extreme racial discrimination, it is not discrimination that accounts for its worsening condition, but primarily a particular combination of economic, demographic, and social conditions. Many industries have left the central cities where the black underclass is concentrated, withdrawing with them a large number of the jobs for which poorly educated blacks can most qualify. There has also been a major increase in the number of black youth, thus adding to the problem of joblessness. At the same time, the expansion of corporate and governmental sectors of the economy has, as already noted, permitted the more talented and better-educated blacks to move increasingly into stable white-collar jobs. As they have done so, these middle-class blacks have moved out of black neighborhoods, where they once lived with lower-class blacks, into formerly all-white working-class and middle-class neighborhoods. This has dealt an extremely serious blow to the social integration of black communities and contributed even further to the economic plight of lower-class blacks. As Wilson explains (1987:56–57):

> *The exodus of middle- and working-class families from many ghetto neighborhoods removes an important "social buffer" that could deflect the full impact of the kind of prolonged and increasing joblessness that plagued inner-city neighborhoods in the 1970s and early 1980s. . . . This argument is based on the assumption that even if the truly disadvantaged segments of an inner-city area experience a significant increase in long-term spells of joblessness, the basic institutions in that area (churches, schools, stores, recreational facilities, etc.) would remain viable if much of the base of their support comes from the more economically stable and secure families. Moreover, the very presence of these families during such periods provides mainstream role models that help keep alive the perception that education is meaningful, that steady employment is a viable alternative to welfare, and that family stability is the norm, not the exception.*
>
> . . .
>
> *Thus, in a neighborhood with a paucity of regularly employed families and with the overwhelming majority of families having spells of long-term joblessness, people experience a social isolation that excludes them from the job network system that permeates other neighborhoods and that is so important in learning about or being recommended for jobs that become available in various parts of the city. And as the prospects for employment diminish, other alternatives such as welfare and the underground economy are not only increasingly relied on, they come to be seen as a way of life.*

How can this increasingly desperate situation be turned around? As Wilson argues convincingly, it cannot be done simply by so-called race-specific policies, such as affirmative action programs. Such programs are really only effective in opening up opportunities for the better-off blacks who need them the least. What is called for is nothing less than a fundamental government-led program of economic reform that would create many new jobs specifically obtainable by the black underclass. It remains to be seen whether such a program will be forthcoming in the near future.

FOR FURTHER READING

Bonacich, Edna. "The Past, Present, and Future of Split Labor Market Theory." In Cora B. Marrett and Cheryl Leggon (eds.), *Research in Race and Ethnic Relations*, Volume 1. Greenwich, Conn.: JAI Press, 1979. An excellent survey by its originator of what the split labor market theory of racial antagonism has accomplished, of currently ongoing research generated by it, and of some of its weaknesses that need to be addressed in the future.

Fogel, Robert William, and Stanley L. Engerman. *Time on the Cross: The Economics of American Negro Slavery.* Volume 1. Boston: Little, Brown, 1974. A detailed study of the economic aspects of slavery in the United States. Provides great insight into such crucial questions as the efficiency and profitability of slavery and the material conditions of slave life.

Frederickson, George M. *White Supremacy: A Comparative Study in American and South African History.* New York: Oxford University Press, 1981. A well-known comparative treatment of the history of race relations in the United States and South Africa.

Harris, Marvin. *Patterns of Race in the Americas.* New York: Norton, 1964. An illuminating comparative study of paternalistic systems of labor organization and control in Latin America. Explains why the Spaniards developed a debt-peonage system in their New World colonies rather than the system of slavery that the Portuguese established in Brazil. Many useful insights regarding Brazil's slave system are provided.

Hechter, Michael. *Internal Colonialism: The Celtic Fringe in British National Development, 1536–1966.* Berkeley: University of California Press, 1975. A valuable study of the historical subjugation of the Celtic ethnic minorities in Britain from an essentially world-system perspective.

Layton-Henry, Zig. *The Politics of Race in Britain.* London: Allen and Unwin, 1984. An excellent depiction of the emergence of competitive race relations in Britain since the end of the Second World War.

Rex, John, and David Mason (eds.). *Theories of Race and Ethnic Relations.* Cambridge: Cambridge University Press, 1986. A particularly good collection of essays dealing with a wide range of theoretical issues in the contemporary study of race and ethnicity.

Smith, Anthony D. *The Ethnic Revival.* Cambridge: Cambridge University Press, 1981. Although the author presents an unpersuasive theory of the revival of ethnic sentiments in the twentieth-century world, he does make some reasonable arguments concerning the limitations of materialist theories of ethnicity.

van den Berghe, Pierre L. *Race and Racism: A Comparative Perspective.* New York: Wiley, 1967. The presentation and illustration of van den Berghe's paternalistic-competitive typology of race relations through an historical and comparative analysis of four different societies. Must reading for the serious student of racial and ethnic stratification.

van den Berghe, Pierre L. *The Ethnic Phenomenon.* New York: Elsevier, 1981. The presentation of a wealth of comparative data on various types of racial and ethnic stratification. A typical van den Berghe book in being meaty, provocative, and well written.

Williams, Eric. *Capitalism and Slavery.* New York: Putnam, 1966. (Originally published 1944.) A classic study of the contribution of British West Indian slavery to the expansion of British capitalism and the Industrial Revolution.

Wilson, William Julius. *The Truly Disadvantaged: The Inner City, the Underclass, and Public Policy.* Chicago: University of Chicago Press, 1987. A seminal contribution to the worsening plight of the black underclass in the United States. Should be read in conjunction with the author's *The Declining Significance of Race* (University of Chicago Press, 1978).

CHAPTER 14

The Sexual Division of Labor and Sexual Inequality

All human societies use sex as a major criterion for assigning individuals to tasks within the social division of labor. While all societies usually have a number of roles that can be suitably performed by either sex, they prescribe some roles as distinctly masculine and others as distinctly feminine. Indeed, no society anywhere in the world is either casual or random in the sex-typing of many of its tasks. Furthermore, not only do all societies have a sexual division of labor, but all have as well corresponding ideological conceptions of the nature and significance of masculinity and femininity, including evaluative notions of the relative status of the sexes. Thus no society is either casual or random in evaluating the social standing of each sex or the differential contribution made by each sex to that society's overall functioning. In short, all societies have a sexual division of labor, structured forms of **sexual inequality,** and ideological conceptions of masculinity and femininity. This chapter attempts to describe and explain numerous aspects of these universal social phenomena.

THE SEXUAL DIVISION OF LABOR AND SEXUAL INEQUALITY: THE OVERALL PATTERN

There is considerable variation across societies in the assignment of people to sex-typed occupational roles. Some activities—such as pottery making, weaving, or horticulture—that are assigned to women in some societies are assigned to men in others. But despite these variations, there are a number of occupations that are consistently assigned to men and others that are consistently assigned to women in the great majority of the world's societies.

Using a sample of 185 societies, Murdock and Provost (1973) have attempted to identify the most consistently "masculine" and "feminine" occupations found throughout the world. They identify as the most consistently masculine occupations the following: hunting large game animals; metalworking; smelting ores; lumbering; woodworking; making musical instruments; trapping; boatbuilding; stonework; working in bone, horn, and shell; mining; quarrying; and bonesetting. The most consistently feminine occupations are those involving fuel gathering, preparing drinks, gathering and preparing wild plant foods, dairy production, laundering, water fetching, and cooking. Women are also extensively involved throughout the world in rearing children and performing general domestic activities.

In general, those activities that are consistently assigned to men tend to be ones requiring greater physical strength, higher levels of risk and danger, more frequent travel from home, higher levels of group cooperation, longer periods of technical training, and higher skill levels (Parker and Parker, 1979). By contrast, consistently feminine occupations involve relatively less danger, tend to be more repetitive, do not require intense concentration, are more easily interruptible, and require less training and fewer skills (Parker and Parker, 1979).

Of greater concern in this chapter is the relative status of the sexes: the degree to which the sexes are unequally placed and valued, as well as the degree to which human societies are male- or female-centered. William Divale and Marvin Harris (1976) have identified the existence of a widespread material, social, and ideological complex of male supremacy in band and tribal societies. They note that male supremacist institutions in these societies are expressed in numerous ways. Marriage and kinship practices, for instance, reveal marked sexual asymmetry in their organization. Patrilocality and virilocality—forms of postmarital residence organized through males—are approximately eight times as frequently found as matrilocality and uxorilocality—forms of postmarital residence organized through females.* Furthermore, patriliny—the tracing of descent through males—is approximately five times as common as matriliny—the tracing of descent through females. Moreover, even matrilineal societies invest authority over the domestic group's affairs in the hands of males rather than females. Marked sexual asymmetry is also revealed in marriage practices, inasmuch as polygyny—the marriage of one man to several wives—is found 141 times as often as polyandry—the marriage of one woman to several husbands.

Pervasive sexual asymmetry is also highly characteristic of band and tribal political institutions. Headmanship is characteristic of hunting and gathering societies, but there is no such thing as "headwomanship." Likewise, bigmanship is widely found among horticulturalists, but its logical counterpart, "bigwomanship," has never been reported to exist. Male monopoly over political leadership is also expressed in the fact that men completely monopolize the weapons of war and the hunt, even to the extent that women are often forbidden to touch or handle these weapons.

Sexual asymmetry is particularly characteristic of the ideological sector in band and tribal societies. Divale and Harris note here the existence of widespread beliefs emphasizing the inferiority of females. Women are widely believed in many societies to be sources of evil and pollution, and many taboos exist in order to restrict their activities, particularly during menstruation. Furthermore, male gods generally outnumber female gods, and legendary heroes outnumber legendary heroines. In many societies, men menace women with masks, bull roarers, and other sacred paraphernalia. Sexual asymmetry in the ideological sector is also revealed by the widespread cultural preference for male children, a preference that is often embodied in the rule that the firstborn must be a male.

Many other examples of the male-centeredness of band and tribal social institutions can be added to the list provided by Divale and Harris. Male ritualistic activity is generally far more frequent and elaborate than the ritualistic activity associated with females; male secret soci-

*See Chapter 15 for fuller discussions of these and related terms.

eties have no strict female counterpart; men dominate the prestige spheres of economic activity; the labor performed by women is generally accorded lower status than that performed by men; and women are often subjected to forms of serious physical abuse (gang rape, for instance), whereas this is seldom if ever the case for men.

Sexually asymmetrical institutions are by no means confined to band and tribal societies, however. On the contrary, societies at more advanced evolutionary levels reveal new, and often more intensive, forms of female subordination. In agrarian societies, economic and political affairs are tightly organized under male control, and women are shunted off into the seclusion of a private, domestic world. In most such societies, the activities of women are very tightly controlled, and there is often special concern with women's sexuality. In short, the status of women in agrarian societies is generally so low that they are treated like dependent minors. The agrarian world is an almost completely male-centered and male-dominated world.

Industrial societies are also characterized by significant inequalities between the sexes, although not to the extreme found in the agrarian world. Males typically dominate positions of high status in all industrial societies, and industrial state systems are heavily under the control of males. Women are heavily confined either to lower-status, lower-paying jobs or to the domestic sector and its functions (or to both). Women are still widely regarded, both by men and by themselves, as holding a status that is secondary to men's. Sexual equality is characteristic of no industrial society found in the world today.

The picture that strikingly emerges from the foregoing is one of widespread, indeed universal, female subordination. Of course, in some societies the overall status of females is fairly high, but there is no known society in which females achieve complete equality with males in all of the relevant sectors of social life. In each and every society about which we have reliable information, the social standing of men is higher than that of women. This is true even in the most sexually egalitarian of all societies, hunters and gatherers. Here men monopolize positions of leadership; and hunting, a male monopoly, is defined as more prestigious than gathering, a female monopoly.

Despite an occasional dissenting voice (e.g., Leacock, 1978), a widespread consensus exists among social scientists concerning the universality of male dominance and female subordination. Certainly few take seriously the speculative claims of some nineteenth-century anthropologists about the original existence of primitive matriarchies, societies in which women dominated men. No matriarchy has ever been discovered, and it seems exceedingly unlikely that one ever will be. By the same token, few contemporary social scientists claim that there is any society anywhere in which complete sexual equality can be found. The view of Michelle Rosaldo and Louise Lamphere (1974:3; cited in Giele, 1977) may be taken as representative of modern social-scientific opinion:

> Everywhere we find that women are excluded from certain crucial economic or political activities, that their roles as wives and mothers are associated with fewer powers and prerogatives than are the roles of men. It seems fair to say, then, that all contemporary societies are to some extent male-dominated, and although the degree and expression of female subordination vary greatly, sexual asymmetry is presently a universal fact of human social life.

THE SEXUAL DIVISION OF LABOR AND SEXUAL INEQUALITY IN EVOLUTIONARY PERSPECTIVE

As Rosaldo and Lamphere have noted in the quote above, despite certain universal features of the relations between the sexes, these relations vary markedly from one society to another. These variations are just as worthy of social-scientific study as are the universals. The best way to examine such variations is to explore the association between sex-role patterns and a society's technological adaptation.

Hunting and Gathering Societies

The principal economic roles in hunting and gathering societies are strongly sex-typed. Hunting is overwhelmingly the province of males, while gathering is basically a female task. While women may occasionally hunt small game and do some fishing, large-game hunting and deep-sea fishing are universally monopolized by men. Likewise, while men may sometimes participate in gathering activities, gathering is mostly the concern of females. Hunting and gathering societies vary in the proportion of subsistence provided by either meat or plant food. Among some hunters and gatherers, such as the Eskimo, hunting accounts for nearly all of the total subsistence needs. Among most hunting and gathering societies, however, the foods provided by gathering account for well over half of the total subsistence. This fact underlines the tremendous importance of gathering for most foragers, and indicates that women generally play a prominent productive role in such societies.

In assessing the relative status of the sexes among hunter-gatherers, Ernestine Friedl (1975) has noted that men generally have greater opportunities than women have for the achievement of recognition and prestige, and that these greater opportunities stem primarily from their roles as hunters. Hunting gives men the opportunity for the extradomestic exchange of meat, the most prestigious food among foragers. Where men provide most of the food supply through meat, as among the Eskimo, their status is much higher than that of women. By the same token, where men do little hunting and where the contribution of women to subsistence is high, the status of men and women is more nearly equivalent.

The male contribution to subsistence through hunting also appears to give them an opportunity for control over women. Where men engage in little hunting or where the male monopoly over meat is low, men exercise little control over women. Polygyny, for instance, is rare in societies of this type. But where male hunting provides the great bulk of the food supply, male aggression toward women is prominent and a pattern of strong male dominance exists. Among the Eskimo, for example, a generalized pattern of male dominance and female subordination is found. Women are treated as sex objects and have little control over their own destiny. Friedl thus concludes that male dominance is greatest where men monopolize economic production, and that sexual equality is most nearly approached in foraging societies in which men and women work together to provide subsistence.

Generalizing about sex roles in hunting and gathering societies is no easy task, given the variable patterns that have been found. Among some foragers, such as the Eskimo or various Australian groups, male dominance is distinctly present and a virtual male supremacy complex exists. Among other groups, such as the !Kung, sexual equality is closely approximated. Beyond these variable patterns, it appears that the following generalizations can be established: (1) Males tend to monopolize political decision making and to have at least somewhat higher status in all hunting and gathering groups. (2) In most, but by no means all, groups, women enjoy a high degree of autonomy and relatively high status. (3) Sexual equality is more nearly attained among foragers than among all other societal types.

Horticultural Societies

In their major study of the relations between the sexes, Kay Martin and Barbara Voorhies (1975) analyze women's position in horticultural

!Kung women digging bulbs. Among the !Kung, women make a major economic contribution, as they do in most hunting and gathering societies.

societies. They do not separate simple and intensive horticulturalists.

Women generally continue their important role in economic production among horticulturalists. In analyzing a sample of 515 horticultural societies drawn from the *Ethnographic Atlas* (Murdock, 1967), Martin and Voorhies note that women dominate cultivation in 41 percent of these societies; men dominate cultivation in 22 percent; and in 37 percent men and women share in the performance of cultivative tasks. Furthermore, the greater the importance of crops in the total diet, the more likely males are to be involved in cultivation.

The status of women among horticulturalists cannot be analyzed independently of kinship patterns, since these bear a strong relationship to the nature of women's activities. Using a sample of 104 horticultural societies, Martin and Voorhies found that 56 percent had patrilineal descent and another 24 percent had matrilineal descent. In general, the status of women is higher among those horticulturalists practicing matrilineal descent. Among matrilineal horticulturalists, women are the focus of the entire social structure, and this elevates their overall social standing. Kinship links are traced through women, and men trace their genealogical connections through their mothers and sisters rather than through their fathers. In such societies, females are central to the conduct of economic activity. Land is owned matrilineally and women cultivate it on behalf of their own matrilineages, which means that women often wield considerable influence over political affairs. However, politics in matrilineal horticultural societies is still in the hands of men, except in this case men exercise authority in their roles as brothers of women rather than as husbands. Thus, although matrilineal societies generally hold women in fairly high regard, women are still politically subordinated to men, and their general status ranks below that of men. Matriliny reduces, but does not eliminate, male dominance.

Since patrilineal societies trace descent through males, males become the focus of the social structure among patrilineal horticulturalists. Land is owned and inherited through males, and females hold a more peripheral relationship to economic resources than is the case in matrilineal horticultural societies. Women among patrilineal horticulturalists are economic producers for kin groups organized through and dominated by their husbands. It therefore follows that the status of women in these societies is generally quite low, and certainly lower than among horticulturalists organized matrilineally. In patrilineal societies husbands acquire rights in a woman as a childbearer, and any offspring belong to the father and his kin group. Women represent investments for the patrilineages of their husbands or fathers. In her father's patrilineage, a young girl performs valuable labor services, and upon her marriage she becomes valuable for both her labor and her reproductive services in the patrilineage of her husband. Women frequently transfer their kin group membership at marriage from their father's to their husband's patrilineage, and when this occurs marriage means that women enter a world of strangers. Women ordinarily hold very low status in this new world. They typically do not achieve respect and influence until they reach old age, and even then they do so only through their connections with sons or other male relatives.

A great range of variation in the status of women is found among horticulturalists. At one extreme we find groups like the Iroquois, a North American Indian society in which women had unusually high status and influence (J. Brown, 1975). At the other extreme we find societies like the Yanomamo, where female subordination is intense and where social life is overwhelmingly male-centered (Chagnon, 1983). Among horticulturalists, the Iroquois come much closer than do the Yanomamo to being the exception, for women on balance tend to have a very low status. Certainly it seems reasonable to say that horticultural women generally hold lower status than their counterparts among hunter-gatherers. But it is in agrarian societies that female status reaches its depths.

Agrarian Societies

In the transition from horticultural to agrarian societies, profound changes took place in technology and economic life. These changes had major consequences for the nature of the relations between the sexes (Martin and Voorhies, 1975). With the shift to intensive forms of agrarian cultivation, women were largely cast out of an economically productive role, and economic production came to be strongly dominated by men. As men took control of production, women were assigned to the household and the domestic activity connected with it. There thus developed what Martin and Voorhies have called the "inside-outside dichotomy," or what others have termed the "public-domestic" distinction. This involves the partitioning of social life into two largely separate and distinct realms. On the one hand, there is the "public" sphere of activities that take place outside the domicile. This sphere includes economics, politics, religious life, education, and so on. It is a sphere monopolized by and for men. On the other hand, there is the "inside" or domestic sphere of household activity, a realm principally concerned with cooking, cleaning, laundering, and nursing and rearing children. This sphere came to be considered distinctly feminine in nature.

It appears that the inside-outside dichotomy did not emerge in fully identifiable form until the rise of agrarian societies, for most societies below the agrarian level either do not recognize such a distinction or have developed it only minimally. With the emergence of this distinction, men and women came to live in markedly different social worlds, and there developed an elaborate ideology celebrating the "natural" superiority of males and emphasizing the "natural" inferiority of females. The rise of the inside-outside dichotomy was associated with the descent of woman to the lowest point of her structured inferiority.

A widespread feature of life in most agrarian societies has been the seclusion of women and the restriction of many of their activities (Martin and Voorhies, 1975; cf. Mandelbaum, 1988). Women have been forbidden to own property, to engage in politics, to pursue education, or to engage in virtually any activity outside the walls of their domicile. In many agrarian societies, women have been legal minors and dependent wards of men. Their seclusion from men has been symbolized, especially in the Islamic world, by the wearing of clothing to conceal all body parts but the eyes. Agrarian societies have typically exercised very tight controls over female sexuality. Many agrarian societies demand premarital virginity on the part of girls, and both illicit premarital and extramarital sexual activity has been severely punished, even including the killing of the offending woman by her husband or other kinsmen. By contrast, agrarian societies have permitted and even encouraged nonmarital sexual activity for males. Women are also usually forbidden to initiate divorce, normally an exclusive male prerogative.

Agrarian societies generally think of males as ideally suited for those tasks that demand intelligence, strength, and emotional fitness. Women, by contrast, are deemed most suitable for roles that are menial, repetitive, and uncreative. By and large, women are social appendages of fathers and husbands and are in general completely economically dependent upon them. Women are viewed as dependent, immature, and in need of male protection and supervision; and these conceptions have been deeply imbedded in agrarian religion, morality, and law (Martin and Voorhies, 1975).

While intensive male dominance is a widespread occurrence in many horticultural and some hunting and gathering societies, agrarian societies have been the most consistently, thoroughly, and intensively male supremacist. In the material, social, and ideological sectors of agrarian life, women have typically been assigned a highly inferior status. This fact is in all probability closely related to the nature of agrarian economic production.

Industrial Societies

Industrial Capitalist Societies Capitalism and industrialism have been responsible for bringing women back into the sphere of economic production. Nevertheless, many aspects of the old agrarian sex-role pattern remain. Women still do the bulk of the domestic labor and men still dominate politics, the most prestigious and highly paid jobs, and other extradomestic spheres of social life. Women are still mainly confined to poorly paid, low-prestige jobs, for example, clerical, secretarial, and service work. Women also dominate jobs that have a strong nurturant component, such as elementary school teachers and nurses. Only small inroads have been made by women into the top managerial and executive positions in corporate life, and men still monopolize the high-status professions, such as architecture, law, medicine, engineering, and university teaching. In situations in which men and women hold the same or similar jobs, women are usually paid significantly less. Currently, the median income of American women in full-time jobs is only about 62 percent of that of men (U.S. Bureau of the Census, 1985).

Many social scientists, Marxists in particular, have portrayed capitalism as actually having negative consequences for the social position of women (Thomas, 1988). Yet despite their generally subordinate status in many spheres of social life, women have in many respects been emancipated since the advent of capitalism. They have, for instance, achieved virtual political and legal equality with men, and women are no longer regarded merely as legal minors and dependent wards of men. Compared to women in nearly all agrarian and Third World societies, as well as to women in many horticultural and pastoral societies, women under capitalism have achieved a dramatic improvement in their status and in their capacity to control their own lives free from male tyranny.

Edward Shorter (1976) has suggested that this improvement may have begun at least as early as the eighteenth century. Many women became integrated into the capitalist market economy through employment in cottage industries and early forms of factory work, and this newfound economic role improved women's overall power, autonomy, and status with regard to men. As Shorter notes (1976:520):

> In the capitalist market economy, unlike the traditional moral economy, women's work brought in resources from outside. . . . Therewith the woman's contribution to the household economy became obvious and quantifiable. The weekly wage packet turned into a weapon in the struggle for domestic power.

Since the end of World War II, Western industrial societies have witnessed major changes regarding the role of women in the work force.

Shorter stresses that these changes in women's status were confined to peasants and workers, and that for the middle and upper classes the situation was perhaps different. In these more prosperous groups the status of women may actually have declined in the early phases of capitalism as women's economic dependence on their husbands grew. But as Shorter points out, peasant and working-class women constituted the great bulk of the population in these times.

The substantial improvement in the status of women in much more recent times can be linked to their rapid movement into the labor force in the twentieth century. Women are now a substantial portion of the labor force in all industrial capitalist societies (Table 14.1). In the late nineteenth century women were greatly in demand as secretaries and clerical workers. However, the vast majority of working women before World War II were single, widowed, or divorced. Most married women, especially those with dependent children, stayed in the home. For example, in the United States in 1930 only 11.7 percent of married women worked outside the home, compared to 50.5 percent of single women and 34.4 percent of women who were widowed or divorced (U.S. Department of Commerce, 1975). Since World War II, though, the increase in the labor force participation of married women, even those

Table 14.1 WOMEN'S LABOR FORCE PARTICIPATION IN SELECTED INDUSTRIAL COUNTRIES, 1960–1986

	% of women in labor force[a]				Women as % of labor force		
Country	1960	1970	1980	1986	1970	1980	1986
United States	42.6	50.4	61.3	66.5	36.7	41.9	43.8
Canada	33.7	41.1	57.8	64.3	32.2	40.0	42.9
France	45.4	47.5	52.5	57.2	36.6	40.1	42.7
West Germany	49.2	48.1	50.0	51.4	35.9	37.8	39.0
Japan	60.1	55.4	54.9	57.4	39.3	38.7	39.8
Sweden	50.1	60.6	75.7	80.5	39.5	45.2	47.3
United Kingdom	46.1	53.5	61.7	63.5	36.2	40.3	42.0

[a] Labor force of all ages as a percentage of the population 15 to 64 years old.

Sources: U.S. Bureau of the Census, *Statistical Abstract of the United States.* Washington, D.C.: U.S. Government Printing Office, 1985 (Table 1492) and 1988 (Table 1402).

with young children, has been remarkable. In the United States in 1948, for instance, only 10.8 percent of married women with children under six years of age were in the labor force (U.S. Department of Commerce, 1975); however, by 1984 51.8 percent of women in the same category were in the labor force (U.S. Bureau of the Census, 1985).

Over the past few decades women have also made significant inroads into the learned professions. In the United States in 1960 women made up only 5.5 percent of physicians, 0.8 percent of dentists, 2.5 percent of lawyers, and 0.4 percent of engineers. But by 1982 they constituted 25 percent of physicians, 15.4 percent of dentists, 33.4 percent of lawyers, and 10.8 percent of engineers (U.S. Bureau of the Census, 1985). Although women have hardly achieved equality with men in their access to these professions, the situation has improved dramatically nonetheless.

State Socialist Societies In the Soviet Union women are now half the labor force, and they are found at all levels of the Soviet work force. The high representation of women in the Soviet labor force is due in large part to the great manpower shortage that resulted from the Soviet Union's participation in World War II. Following the war, women began to enter a great many occupations in very large numbers. Today Soviet women are highly represented at all levels of the occupational structure, including the professions. It is particularly interesting to note the participation of women in the professional fields. As Bernice Rosenthal (1975) notes, women constitute 72 percent of the doctors; 35 percent of the lawyers; 47 percent of the judges and associate judges; 90 percent of the dentists, medics, and nurses; 58 percent of agricultural specialists with advanced degrees; 76 percent of the accountants, statisticians, and planners; 38 percent of all scientists; and 33 percent of engineers.

These figures seem to suggest an enormous stride by Soviet women toward equality in the economic sector. However, the figures are seriously misleading, as Rosenthal explains (1975:444–446):

> The position of a Soviet doctor cannot be compared to an American one. Medicine is notoriously ill-paid. . . . Within the medical profession, men head the hospitals and departments; they are the surgeons, the highest-paid specialty, and women are the general practitioners, midwives, nurses, and ward attendants. . . . Law is not a particularly lucrative profession either and within it the "advocats" (the best paid specialty) are usually men. Women judges and associate judges (the official figures lump the

two together) are concentrated in the lower courts.

. . .

Within the research hierarchy, only 2 percent of the Full Members of the prestigious Soviet Academy of Science are women and only 2.5 percent of the Corresponding Members. No woman has ever been President, Vice-President, Chief Scientific Secretary, or member of the Presidium of the Soviet Academy of Science.

. . .

In Soviet society, power, money, and prestige go to top executives in factories and collective farms. Women are extremely rare in positions of authority where they have to give orders to men. In factories, women are 6 percent of the directors, 16 percent of the chief engineers, and 12 percent of the department heads. . . . Women executives are most prominent in routine jobs; they do not set policy. Secondary-level positions such as bookkeepers, "rate-setters," and technicians are predominantly female.

. . .

Not only are the top levels of Soviet society less accessible to women than to men, but women are overly represented at the lowest levels of the Soviet economic spectrum. Though women constitute half the labor force, their total wages are only one quarter of all wages earned. . . . Well over half of Soviet women earn less than the average Soviet wage of 103 rubles/month. Furthermore, many women are paid at piece rates; their wages often fall below the official Soviet minimum wage of 60 rubles/month.

From Rosenthal's comments, it is clear that Soviet women hold a very secondary status in the Soviet economic structure, a status that, in fact, closely resembles that of women in the occupational structures of the capitalist societies. Women are also severely underrepresented in Soviet politics. The political participation of women in Soviet society is heavily confined to positions in the lower reaches of government; they are seldom found in top political positions (Rosenthal, 1975).

While women play a major role in the Soviet economy, this has not excused them from do-

Soviet women designing clothing. Does socialism liberate women?

mestic work. Household labor in the Soviet Union is still viewed as work that is distinctly "feminine," and men contribute little or nothing to domestic work. This has given Soviet women a double burden: the responsibility for employment in the workplace combined with virtually full responsibility for domestic tasks. As Rosenthal comments (1975:429): "The 'dual burden' of home and work poses a formidable barrier to equality which is yet to be surmounted."

It thus seems clear that the Soviet Union has scarcely made any greater progress toward sexual equality than have the major industrial capitalist societies. In both capitalism and state socialism, basic sexual inequalities remain a very significant part of social life. To this point in human history, neither industrialization nor political ideology has been successful in putting an end to male dominance and the subordination of women. This fact can hardly be ignored in any explanation of the fundamental causes of sexual inequality.*

The Third World

In many ways the status of women in the contemporary underdeveloped world closely resembles that found in agrarian societies of the past (Ward, 1985). In the peasant agricultural sector men tend to dominate agricultural work, and this economic control gives them control over the other major institutional sectors of social life. Thus, strongly patriarchal relations between the sexes are a pervasive feature of peasant life in the Third World, with the old agrarian inside-outside dichotomy remaining firmly in place.

Outside the agricultural sector, work roles are of course very different, but the status of women still appears to be very low. Women tend to be heavily concentrated in the lowest-paying jobs with the lowest social prestige. They are notably underrepresented in professional and managerial positions and overrepresented in service work, especially in such domestic service jobs as housekeepers, cooks, wet nurses, governesses, and servants. Women are also heavily overrepresented in such traditional craft jobs as those involving pottery making, dressmaking, basket and mat making, and weaving (cf. Chinchilla, 1977; Arizpe, 1977).

Recent changes in the organization of the world capitalist system have had significant implications for women's work and status in the Third World (cf. Ward, 1985). In the past two decades there has emerged a tendency toward a "new international division of labor" (Fröbel et al., 1980). Developed capitalist countries have been relocating many of their industries in the underdeveloped world as a means of using cheaper labor and thus cutting production costs. The industry most frequently the subject of this industrial relocation is the textile industry, and countries such as Singapore, Hong Kong, South Korea, Taiwan, Jamaica, the Dominican Republic, and El Salvador are some of the leading countries in which this relocation is occurring (Safa, 1981). The Third World workers involved are overwhelmingly women, especially young, single women.

What are the implications of these major economic changes for Third World women? One basically positive result is that their new employment gives many women a new economic autonomy and loosens the control of their families, especially their fathers, over them. Yet as Helen Safa (1981) has pointed out, this new economic autonomy seems to be accompanied by a severe form of economic exploitation. The jobs that women perform in these new industries require very little skill and pay very little. For the most part the work is very tedious and often requires long periods of intense concentration. In electronics industries, where workers have to spend most of their time looking

*A somewhat more positive assessment of the position of women in state socialist societies in general has been presented by Molyneux (1982).

An Iranian woman wearing concealing garments. Few societies subordinate women more than does contemporary Iran.

through microscopes, they often suffer from impaired vision after only a few years on the job (Safa, 1981). Moreover, not only is the pay extremely low, but fringe benefits are generally nonexistent, as are opportunities for worker unionization or other forms of worker organization that might improve conditions. In many Third World countries with these new industries, the governments have taken extreme measures to prevent workers from organizing, including the violent suppression of worker protest (Safa, 1981).

Firm generalizations about the status of women in the Third World are difficult to make, for there are some notable variations from country to country. By and large, though, women occupy a highly inferior status in the Third World, and it is doubtful that their position has improved with some of the most recent economic changes. The plight of the Third World today is a very serious one, and women clearly bear the burden of this plight more than men.

THEORIES OF SEXUAL INEQUALITY

A variety of theories have been proposed to account for the nature of the sexual division of labor and sexual inequality. Some of these theories focus primarily on explaining the universal pattern, while others are more concerned with accounting for variations in sex roles. *Sociobiological* theories attempt to explain the universality of male dominance by reference to fundamental biological differences between the sexes. These theories assume that, regardless of the degree of social elaboration of sexual inequality, sex-role differences are erected in accordance with certain basic features of human biology. *Materialist* theories attempt to explain sex-role patterns as products of the infrastructural arrangements of a society. They concentrate more on the variations in sex-role systems, and generally assume that it is the nature of technology, economic production, and ecology, rather than biological necessity, that principally determines how the sexes relate to each other. *Political* theories also attempt to explain variations in sex-role patterns. The most prominent of these theories emphasize variations in the prevalence of warfare as the key determinant of variations in sex roles. Finally, *feminist* theories suggest the widespread existence of a patriarchal ideology of male domination as the basis for sexual inequality. Since these major types of theories endeavor to explain different aspects of sexual inequality (that is, universality versus variation), they may be complementary rather than contradictory.

Sociobiological Theories

Well-known sociobiological interpretations of sex roles have been presented by Pierre van den Berghe (1973) and Lionel Tiger and Robin Fox (1971). Van den Berghe presents a bioevolutionary theory based upon evidence from primate studies and a speculative reconstruction of hominid evolution. His main argument is that all contemporary sex-role arrangements reflect the basic "biogram" that modern humans inherited from their primate and hominid ancestors. This biogram is one that predisposes men to hunt, to make war, and to protect the group, and women to nurture children. It is said to underlie the universal pattern of male political dominance over females.

It is important to realize that van den Berghe offers this sociobiological theory only to account for the universality of male dominance. Variations in the form or intensity of male dominance, he says, are not due to biology, but to the various cultural elaborations on the human biogram. Thus there is nothing in this particular theory that is designed to explain the basic differences in sex-role arrangements from one society to another. Van den Berghe's theory is "biosocial" in that it proposes that both biological and sociocultural factors are necessary to account for all of the aspects of sex-role behavior.

Essentially the same line of reasoning is pursued by Tiger and Fox. They assume males to be politically dominant in all societies by virtue of their innate biological predispositions, holding that males naturally tend to form close social bonds with one another as a strategy for group defense. The ancient hominid biogram lives on in contemporary humans, directing the sexes toward fundamentally different kinds of activities. As they put it (1971:97, 99–100, 101):

> It would be difficult to avoid the conclusion that at least some differences between the sexes—both physiological and behavioral—are biologically based. Consequently, if some universal form of human activity appears to be dominated by one or the other sex, there is at least a prima facie case for looking at this dominance as a sex-linked characteristic. Men universally dominate the political arena.
>
> . . .
>
> We have seen how sexual differentiation is rooted in primate political-breeding processes: the dominant males are the focus of attention and hence cohesion; they dominate by overt strength and by ritualized threat and display; they protect and keep order; they compete in a never-ceasing test of their ability to dominate; but they also combine in coalitions to exercise more effective dominance or to forage and explore.
>
> . . .
>
> To make women equal participants in the political process, we will have to change the very

process itself, which means changing a pattern bred into our behavior over the millennia. It may well be possible, but it will not be easy.

A good deal of evidence has now accumulated to suggest a number of biological foundations to human sex-role patterns. Much of this evidence is reviewed by Parker and Parker (1979). Evidence from observations of infrahuman primate behavior, cross-cultural studies of sex differences, and studies of sex differences in human development all point toward the conclusion that human biology is a significant component in differential behavior of the sexes.

Parker and Parker note that aggression is a behavioral difference between the sexes that is extremely widespread in the animal world. Among mammals males generally exhibit higher levels of aggression, and among the nonhuman primates males are generally reported to be substantially more prone to rough-and-tumble play and threat and dominance behaviors. Moreover, these differences seem to begin in early childhood and last throughout the organisms' lifetimes, just as they tend to do in humans.

Parker and Parker also review evidence that suggests that the male sex hormone testosterone is significantly linked to aggressive behavior. Studies using rhesus monkeys have shown that animals with higher levels of blood plasma testosterone are more inclined toward aggressive and dominance behavior and less inclined toward "maternal" forms of behavior.

Finally, the Parkers examine data on human development highly suggestive of differential biological propensities of the sexes (cf. Money and Ehrhardt, 1972). Longitudinal studies of females who prenatally had higher than normal levels of the male sex hormone androgen show that such females develop differently from other females. They exhibit higher levels of aggression and energy expenditure, are more likely to select males rather than females as their companions, show less interest in doll play or other forms of feminine play associated with maternal behavior, show greater interest in nondomestic careers, and are more frequently described as tomboys.

On the basis of their detailed review of the above and other findings, Parker and Parker conclude that "there is a neat and logical fit between biopsychological sex differences and uniformities in the sexual division of labor" (1979:299).

In addition to the foregoing, we cannot overlook some of the more obvious biological differences between the sexes: that men are physically larger and stronger and that women bear and nurse children. These biological facts no doubt play a crucial role in shaping certain aspects of the sexual division of labor. It is clearly advantageous for societies to make men the hunters, for pregnant and lactating women would undoubtedly be less adept at hunting than men. Men are not burdened with these responsibilities, and they are as well swifter and stronger, facts that make males the logical choice as the sex to hunt wild game (especially big game).

Moreover, men's greater strength is certainly one reason they monopolize the more strenuous and demanding tasks in all societies. Women, for example, usually take a major part in cultivation in horticultural societies, and this type of cultivation does not require great physical strength. Men, however, monopolize economic production under intensive agriculture, and labor under such conditions requires high levels of strength and energy expenditure. In addition, it is not difficult to see why all societies tend to associate women with child-rearing functions, since it is the women who must bear and nurse children. There is also a sound reason why the world's societies tend to assign women jobs that are lower in skill level and more easily interruptible. Since child care responsibilities require unpredictable and frequent interruptions of any other simultaneous task, lower-skilled jobs requiring lower levels of concentration are more suited to the sex with primary child care duties (cf. Blumberg, 1978).

Women's childbearing and child-rearing responsibilities also seem to be pertinent to explaining the overall participation of women in economic production, especially why they lost so much of their productive role in the transition to agrarian societies. As just noted, men's greater physical strength and stamina have undoubtedly played an important role in their dominance of agrarian economic production. Yet women's responsibilities for producing and rearing children may have been just as important if not more important. Women tend to have more children in agrarian societies than in any other type, thus increasing their child care obligations. It becomes very difficult for women with such duties to participate heavily in economic activities that would take them away from their children for long periods of time. It is also difficult for mothers to take their children into the fields with them, because agrarian activities like plowing often spell serious danger for young children (cf. Ember, 1983; Blumberg, 1978).

Workers in an Israeli kibbutz. The kibbutzim have fallen far short of their original goal of eliminating the sexual division of labor and sexual inequality.

Human biology may also be implicated in the major transformation in sex roles that has occurred within the Israeli kibbutzim (Tiger and Shepher, 1975; Spiro, 1979). The kibbutzim (singular: kibbutz) are communal settlements established in Israel by Eastern European Jews in the early part of the present century. Many of these settlements remain today and continue to thrive. The kibbutzim were established according to strong ideological principles of economic and sexual egalitarianism. In the beginning men and women worked alongside one another in agricultural tasks, women were actively involved in political administration, children were reared in communal nurseries, and both men and women took responsibility for such service work as cooking, laundering, and child-rearing.

From this initial position of near sexual equality, the kibbutzim have changed within one or two generations into societies marked by sharp sex-role differences. Men now monopolize agricultural work, and women have taken primary responsibility for cooking, laundering, and attending to children in the nurseries. In addition, men have come to be highly overrepresented in political administration. Tiger and Shepher (1975) report that women have voluntarily removed themselves from agricultural production and from politics. They have also made increasingly vocal demands over the years for the opportunity to spend more time individually with their own children. Tiger and Shepher interpret these changes as arising from the natural biological propensities of the sexes: the natural inclination of men to perform strenuous labor and dominate politics, and the inclination of women toward service-related and child-rearing roles.*

*Even if biology has played a role in the kibbutz sex-role changes, it is clear that other factors have been involved as well. Blumberg (1976) has suggested what some of these other factors may have been.

Materialist Theories

Marxist Theories A Marxian interpretation of the subordination of women has been given by Frederick Engels in his famous book *The Origin of the Family, Private Property, and the State* (1970; orig. 1884). Engels drew his inspiration for this book both from Marx's own ideas and from the work of the nineteenth-century evolutionary anthropologist Lewis Henry Morgan. According to Engels, early forms of human society were characterized by production-for-use economies. The household was communal in nature, and all work was done for the household as a whole. Women were equal participants in the affairs of the group and made important contributions to economic production.

With the development of private property, all this was swept away. Men came to be the owners of property and production-for-exchange replaced production-for-use. As the owners of private property, men rose to political dominance. Women began to produce for their husbands rather than for the group as a whole. Thus, according to Engels, it was the development of private property and its subsequent control by men that was the basic cause of the subordination of women.

This interpretation is at best only partially correct. Engels thought that societies lacking private property and social classes gave equal standing to women. But as we have clearly seen, this is not the case. Not only is some degree of male dominance universal, but many prestate and preclass societies are characterized by intensive forms of female subordination. It certainly cannot be the case, then, that private property and social classes were *the* fundamental causes of woman's subordination. Nonetheless, these factors have in fact been associated with a precipitous overall *decline* in the status of women. Engels has therefore generated a significant insight even though his theory is not acceptable as a general theory of the subordination of women.

Karen Sacks (1975, 1979) has presented a Marxian elaboration of Engels's argument. She argues that in sociocultural evolution the general decline in women's status has been significantly correlated with the development of production-for-exchange and private property. This has occurred because of its advantages for ruling classes. Men are selected for the production of goods of value to the ruling class because, not having to nurse and rear children, they can be more intensively exploited than women. Women therefore come to be shunted off into domestic work. Once the division is made between women's domestic work and men's work in the larger productive arena, the conditions are created that allow women to be defined as less than full adults and as dependent wards of men.

Sacks's overall effort to link women's status to the nature of a society's mode of production has much to commend it (cf. Hendrix and Hossain, 1988), but there is one aspect of her theory that is highly dubious: her proposal that males control economic production in class-divided societies because of the desires of ruling classes. It is unlikely that ruling classes have much to do with it. Even without the actions of a ruling class, males would still take charge of economic production in societies where production requires intensive labor inputs and where women's reproductive responsibilities interfere with a heavy participation in production.

Marxian theories focusing specifically on the subordination of women in modern capitalist societies have also been prominent in recent years (cf. Morton, 1971; Vogel, 1983). These theories link sexual divisions to the need of capitalists for an exploitable labor force. They suggest that the dominance of men over women is an outcome of the dominance of capitalists over workers. Women play a crucial role in the reproduction of labor power that men cannot play. That is, since women are the childbearers they must produce and continue to produce more offspring as future workers for capitalists.

This requires their concentration in domestic work, which helps to insure the dominance of their husbands over them.

The notion that it is woman's special role as a childbearer that contributes to her subordinate position is an important idea. The concentration of women in domestic labor and their corresponding removal from the workforce deprives them of valuable resources that can be used in their struggle for equality with men. However, the problem with the Marxian analysis on this score is that it insists on seeing this as a class phenomenon. How then can we explain the inferior position of women who do not belong to the subordinate class? The difficulty Marxists have in answering this question with any theoretical consistency suggests that there is more to the subordination of women than they propose.

Non-Marxian Materialist Theories An important non-Marxian materialist theory of sex roles has been developed by Martin and Voorhies (1975). They claim that sex roles should be viewed largely as adaptive consequences of particular ecological, technological, and economic arrangements.

That men hunt and women gather in hunter-gatherer societies is viewed as highly adaptive within the framework of that mode of production. Since women's gathering activities mean that they contribute heavily to subsistence, men are unable to monopolize economic resources and to use such monopolization to create strong forms of female subordination. Since women contribute in a major way to subsistence, they command resources of their own and are able to turn this resource control into relatively high status.

The status of women in horticultural societies is linked to the material conditions that determine their control over resources. In horticultural societies lacking severe pressure against natural resources, matrilineal descent is common. This generally gives women fairly high status because women become the focus of the entire social structure; land is owned and inherited by matrilineal kin groups, and women's productive labor is undertaken for the benefit of their own matrilineages. In horticultural societies where there is severe pressure against resources, patrilineal descent typically develops. Women's labor is performed for the benefit of their husbands' or fathers' patrilineages, and women come to be viewed as resources to be used for the benefit of males. Under such conditions, the status of women is relatively low.

Male domination of production in agrarian societies is viewed by Martin and Voorhies as highly adaptive. Men are much better suited than women to perform activities requiring intensive labor, since women must assume responsibility for bearing and nursing children. Male control over economic resources allows them to gain control over the entire extradomestic sphere of social life, and as they do so women's status drops to an extremely low point.

Industrial societies have historically perpetuated much of the old inside-outside dichotomy of agrarian societies largely because men have continued to dominate production. However, the advance of industrial technology has done much to alter many aspects of traditional sex roles. Increasingly sophisticated technology has now made it possible for women to perform quite ably a great many extradomestic roles. As they have begun to do this, their overall status has improved markedly.

A similar theory has been developed by Rae Lesser Blumberg (1984). Blumberg argues that the key factor determining the status of women in the world's societies is their *level of economic power.* Where women's economic power is high, women are able to translate this power into relatively high status; conversely, where the economic power of women is low, their overall social status is almost invariably low.

Blumberg proposes three factors that determine women's level of economic power. One of these is the strategic indispensability of women's labor. This factor includes such things as the extent to which women contribute to total household subsistence needs, the control women workers may have over technical expertise, the degree to which women workers have freedom from male supervision, and the size and cohesiveness of female work groups. A second factor is the organization of the kinship system. Where matrilocality and matriliny prevail, women's economic power is higher because of their greater involvement in property ownership and management. A final factor is the overall character of the stratification system. Blumberg argues that women fare less well in societies with well-developed stratification systems because intensive stratification tends to reduce the overall level of economic power that women possess.

Blumberg stresses that the possession of economic power by women means more than simply the capacity to translate this power into high status—into a positive regard and respect for them on the part of men. It means as well an overall capacity to manage their own lives in ways relatively free from male control. As Blumberg puts it, economic power gives women substantial "life options." These options include the ability to control such things as reproduction, sexuality, marriage, divorce, household affairs, freedom of movement, and access to education.

Rae Lesser Blumberg. Blumberg is a professor of sociology at the University of California, San Diego. Her comparatively based materialist theory of sexual inequality is a major contribution to this area of macrosociology.

The interpretations offered by Martin and Voorhies and by Blumberg appear to overcome the main limitations of a Marxian approach. These theorists convincingly demonstrate that sex roles are closely related to underlying infrastructural arrangements. They therefore make sense out of the entire range of variation presented by sex-role systems. Where women take a major part in production, they control resources, which they then convert into relatively high status and control over their own lives. By contrast, where women are largely excluded from production they command few resources; male control over economic resources translates into the opportunity to control and subordinate women in all of the major spheres of social life, and men are quick to take advantage of this opportunity to advance their own interests.

Political Theories

Divale and Harris (1976) have proposed an ingenious theory to explain the predominance of male supremacist social institutions in band and tribal societies. According to this theory, male supremacist institutions in band and tribal societies arise as a by-product of warfare. Warfare, in turn, emerges as a means of regulating population pressure against scarce resources. Warfare reduces population pressure by dispersing populations and creating a more favorable ratio between population and the food supply, especially the supply of animal protein. The practice of female infanticide is also implicated as a factor that serves to regulate population pressure. By selectively killing off a certain proportion of female infants, band and village societies are able to stabilize their populations and prevent severe deterioration in their standards of living.

There thus arises what Divale and Harris call the "warfare–female infanticide–male supremacy complex," a functionally related pattern of traits. Both warfare and female infanticide contribute to the maintenance of male supremacist institutions. The superiority of men in using hand-held weapons means that they will become the warriors, and warfare makes it necessary to train males to become aggressive and militant. Likewise, females are trained to become passive because they become rewards for male success in battle (through the practice of polygyny). Female infanticide also has consequences for the creation of male supremacist institutions, because an ideology of male supremacy can be used as a justification for killing female babies.

Divale and Harris have tested their theory using data from 112 band and village societies, and they claim that the theory is supported by the data. Furthermore, Harris (1977) points to the intensive pattern of warfare, female infanticide, and male supremacy among the Yanomamo as an ethnographic case that illustrates and supports the theory. The Yanomamo are one of the world's most militant societies. Yanomamo men are well known for their extreme levels of aggression, both against other men and against women. Intravillage male violence is commonplace, and intervillage warfare and preparation for warfare are chronic features of Yanomamo life. And it would be difficult to find a society more thoroughly imbued with male supremacist institutions. Men thoroughly control the economic and political sectors of life, and kinship is strongly male-centered. Men dominate religious life, and only they are permitted to use the hallucinogenic drug *ebene*, an important part of Yanomamo religious activity. Men regularly engage in various sorts of violent acts against women: striking them with axes, shooting them with arrows, holding glowing sticks against their flesh, pulling at their earrings until their earlobes are loosened from the head. Ideologically, Yanomamo men consider women to be thoroughly inferior second-class citizens who deserve the position they have in life. Yanomamo women seem more or less resigned to their fate, and young girls learn from an early age that their world will be an almost completely male-centered one.

Another social scientist to stress warfare as the key to understanding male domination is Randall Collins (1975, 1985b). However, Collins's theory, more general than Divale and Harris's, applies across the full range of (at least preindustrial) societies. Collins suggests that in situations in which there is little military threat and weapons are not well developed, there is not much reason for males to organize into military groups. Under such circumstances, relatively egalitarian relations between men and women prevail. On the other hand, the need for well-developed military organization favors an emphasis on male physical and aggressive characteristics, and this tends to produce high levels of male domination.

These political theories are carefully reasoned and there is considerable evidence that militarism and male domination are linked. However, it seems implausible to regard such theories as constituting an acceptable general interpretation of male supremacist institutions, for it is unlikely that warfare is among the principal causes of male domination. There are too many examples of societies without warfare but with strong male domination, or with warfare but with considerable importance given to women. Nonetheless, it may well be that warfare is an important variable leading to the *intensification* of a pre-existing state of male dominance. Among societies like the Yanomamo, for instance, male supremacist institutions are carried to an exaggerated extreme and are found in

Yanomamo warriors. It would be difficult to find a people whose social life and consciousness are more thoroughly masculinized.

close connection with chronic warfare (cf. Chagnon, 1983). But this fact does not elevate warfare to the status of the primary determinant of male domination.

Feminist Theories

In the past two decades another line of theorizing has emerged as an influential perspective regarding the position of women in social life: *feminist* theory (Firestone, 1970; Kuhn and Wolpe, 1978; Hartmann, 1979; cf. Hamilton, 1978; cf. Eisenstein, 1979). The feminist perspective generally assumes that the economic structure of society is an important determinant of women's status, but it holds that there is another factor that is perhaps even more important. This is *patriarchy,* a complex set of behavioral and ideological traits leading men to assert dominance over women. Patriarchy is assumed to be a widespread tendency in human societies and to have a substantial independence from the economic and class structure of society.

One of the earliest and most prominent representatives of this viewpoint is Shulamith Firestone (1970). Firestone has declared that the subordination of women results primarily from a "power psychology" that men use against women. She believes that this phenomenon is rooted in the most fundamental biological difference between the sexes: the fact that women get pregnant and carry children. For Firestone, this fact imposes a biological burden on women that men seize upon for their own benefit.

The feminist perspective makes an important contribution in forcing recognition that the subordination of women cannot be understood simply by understanding their position in the economy. The male-female cleavage in social life does indeed seem to have a dimension all its own. Nonetheless, feminist theories typically fail to advance very far beyond this general notion. The central concept of the feminist perspective, patriarchy, has been a slippery one that has been inconsistently defined by feminists (cf. Vogel, 1983). Many feminists seem to mean by it simply a kind of psychology of male domination, whereas others appear to have in mind a more materialist (apparently biological) notion. Feminists are also either vague or inconsistent in locating the roots of patriarchy (some actually seem to suggest that the concept is self-explanatory [cf. R. Collins, 1986]). Some, like Firestone, root it in the reproductive differences between the sexes, prompting criticism by other feminists (cf. Eisenstein, 1979). Others seem largely to avoid the hard question of exactly what patriarchal relations between the sexes stem from.*

Theories of Sexual Inequality: Some Conclusions

What may be concluded about the causes of the sexual division of labor and sexual inequality in human societies? In view of the considerable evidence reviewed, the following conclusions seem appropriate: marked and cross-culturally consistent asymmetries in the sexual division of labor, as well as the universal pattern of at least some degree of male dominance, are to be explained as results of the basic biological differences between the sexes; major cross-cultural variations in the sexual division of labor and in the intensity of male dominance are to be explained primarily by reference to ecological, technological, and economic arrangements; in some societies, warfare may strongly intensify patterns of male dominance.

As the preceding suggests, there is no single factor or set of factors capable of completely explaining the relations between the sexes. Different factors have to be introduced to explain different aspects of sex-role arrangements. It also seems inappropriate to conceptualize sexual hierarchies in exactly the same fashion as we conceive of hierarchies based on class and race. Class and racial hierarchies have nothing to do with biological differences among individuals or groups, but are consequences of particular systems of economic production. Hierarchies based on sex are also strongly conditioned by productive arrangements, but the matter does not appear to stop there. The evidence suggests that sexual hierarchies, at least in terms of their minimal universal features, are also erected upon the basic human biogram.

MALE AND FEMALE IN THE FUTURE

We may agree with Martin and Voorhies when they assert that "the major trend for men and women in the future, as we see it, is that gender roles will become increasingly unimportant" (1975:406). Capitalism and industrialism have already brought women back into the productive process, and it can be anticipated that future technological and economic changes will continue this trend. As women participate more and more vigorously in more and more aspects of the productive process, their status rises; they come to be thought of less as domestic wards of men and more as independent persons in their own right.

However, to assert that sex roles will become increasingly unimportant is not to say they will disappear altogether. For this to occur, technology would have to advance to the point of assuming women's reproductive function. Even then it is highly doubtful that sex roles would evaporate entirely. This assertion rests on a

*Care should be taken to avoid confusing feminist *theory* and feminism *as a political position* that works for social, economic, and political equality for women. Criticism of the former certainly implies no judgment against the latter. Feminism as a social and political movement is an important and vital phenomenon.

Table 14.2 THEORIES OF SEXUAL INEQUALITY

Theory	Characteristics	Evaluation
Sociobiological theories	Focus on the universal features of sexual inequality. Suggest that male monopolization of politics, warfare, and a society's high-status positions is rooted in genes developed millions of years ago by our ancestors. Women's inclinations toward nurturant roles are also considered to be biologically rooted.	Much evidence has now accumulated to suggest some basic validity to many sociobiological claims. However, these theories are only relevant to explaining universal (or at least very widespread) features of sexual inequality. They cannot explain important variations in patterns of sexual inequality.
Marxian theories	Emphasize class divisions and patterns of economic exploitation as basic to understanding the subordination of women. Long-term evolutionary versions stress the evolutionary decline in the status of women and see it as resulting from the growth of private property, production-for-exchange, and class stratification. Versions focusing only on modern capitalism see women's subordination as stemming from capitalism's need for an exploitable labor force.	Are on the right track in seeing a general connection between the mode of economic production and the status of women, but go awry in tying the specific explanation of female subordination to stratification and class struggle.
Non-Marxian materialist theories	Link the relations between the sexes to specific technological, economic, demographic, and ecological conditions. Where these conditions favor the heavy participation of women in economic production and a high level of economic power for women, women will tend to have a relatively high status. Otherwise, they tend to be strongly subordinated to men.	Achieve the best explanations of historical and cross-cultural variations in patterns of sexual inequality. Superior to Marxian theories in showing how class stratification and sexual inequality are largely independent phenomena.
Political theories	View male domination as a by-product of warfare and militarism. Where warfare and military organization are prominent features of social life, a premium is placed on training men to be highly aggressive, and this leads to an exaggerated emphasis on masculinity and a corresponding demeaning of women.	Are not adequate as a general explanation of patterns of sexual inequality, but may usefully supplement materialist theories in that they may help explain some features of extreme forms of male domination.
Feminist theories	Assert that a universal condition of patriarchy underlies the subordination of women in the world's societies.	Are unhelpful. It is unclear just what the concept of patriarchy is supposed to mean, and the roots of this so-called patriarchy are seldom consistently or intelligibly identified.

view of the importance of biological differences between the sexes, differences that only further biological evolution, and not sophisticated technology, can eliminate. Since no such biological evolution of the human species can be anticipated in the near (or even the distant) future, such differences will remain with us. And if these differences help to shape the nature of human sex roles, as the evidence currently suggests they do, then sex roles will continue to play at least some part in future sociocultural systems.*

SUMMARY

1. All human societies have a sexual division of labor and sexual inequality. Men tend to be assigned work that involves greater physical strength and danger, more technical training, and more frequent absences from home. Women tend to be assigned roles that are more repetitive and require less concentration. Sexual inequality universally favors the male sex. This is evident in societies' political and familial institutions, in their ideological superstructures, and in numerous other aspects of the daily interaction of men and women.

2. The variations in sex-role patterns among societies are also of crucial significance. Hunter-gatherer societies, more than any other type of society, approximate a condition of sexual equality. Women often have considerable authority and autonomy in these societies, and strong beliefs in female inferiority are generally absent.

3. Horticulturalists vary markedly in the status given to women. In some horticultural groups, such as the Iroquois, women have very high status and great authority. In others, such as the Yanomamo, women are intensively subordinated and subjected to a wide range of physical abuses. Variations in horticultural sex-role patterns have much to do with kinship structures.

4. It is in agrarian societies that the status of women is lowest. These societies are notable for their strong inside-outside dichotomies. Men tend to dominate all activities outside the household, while women are largely confined to life oriented around the household. In most agrarian societies women are regarded as dependent wards of men. Powerful beliefs in the inherent inferiority of the female sex are found in these societies.

5. Capitalism and industrialism have in many ways liberated women from the extreme subordination they suffered in the agrarian era. Women now have much greater autonomy and are held in much higher regard. In recent decades women have come to occupy increasingly prominent positions in the work world, and they are even gaining greater access to the learned professions. Important dimensions of sexual inequality remain, however. The high position of women in state socialist societies has been exaggerated. In some ways the position of women in such societies is actually less favorable than their position within industrial capitalism.

6. It is difficult to generalize about the status of women in Third World countries, but in general women seem to have a very low status. Moreover, they are more severely affected than men by the economic burdens of life in such societies.

7. Social scientists have proposed many theories of sexual inequality. The most important of these are sociobiological, materialist, political, and feminist theories. They are described and evaluated in Table 14.2.

*It needs to be stressed that the argument that human biology plays a role in the relations between the sexes should never be used as a justification for any prevailing pattern of sexual inequality. There is a huge difference between a scientific analysis of the conditions giving rise to a human situation and a moral endorsement of that situation. Furthermore, even to the extent that biology is significantly implicated in some aspects of sex-role patterns, as many social scientists have pointed out, "anatomy is not destiny."

SPECIAL TOPIC: THE RISE OF MODERN FEMINISM

A striking feature of life in industrial capitalist societies in the past century has been the rise of feminism. There have actually been two waves of feminist activity. The first began around the middle of the nineteenth century and occurred off and on until around 1920. Women became very active in the antislavery movement, and they also led numerous crusades against vice, particularly alcohol consumption and prostitution. Probably the best-known of these movements was the Women's Christian Temperance Union (R. Collins, 1985b). Around the turn of the twentieth century, women in many industrial societies were pushing vigorously for the right to vote. The first country to give women voting rights was New Zealand in 1893; Australia, Sweden, Norway, and Finland soon followed New Zealand's example. England extended suffrage to women in 1918, the United States in 1920, and France not until the late 1940s (R. Collins, 1985b).

Feminism was basically dead in the major industrial capitalist societies from about 1920 until the early 1960s. Since that time a second major wave of feminism has occurred. Women have demanded equality with men in the major spheres of social life, and have made enormous inroads into the labor force. A new feminist consciousness has emerged: women see themselves as the equals of men and as deserving of the same basic social rewards that men have traditionally received. In addition, many women have sought an autonomy and a separate identity heretofore denied them. They have come to view themselves as having an existence apart from their roles as wives and mothers, and have insisted that men acknowledge this separate identity. These phenomena are well illustrated by the increasing frequency with which women retain their maiden names upon marriage (or hyphenate their maiden names with their husbands'), by a rise in the number of marriage postponements, and by declining rates of marriage and childbearing.

The second wave of feminism has also witnessed a vigorous development of organizations designed to promote women's interests. Undoubtedly the most important of these has been the National Organization of Women (NOW), which was founded in the United States in 1966. The most important driving force behind this organization was Betty Friedan, who became its first president. Friedan had authored just three years earlier the book that some have seen as the intellectual catalyst of the modern feminist movement, *The Feminine Mystique* (1963), a book strongly condemning the subordination of women in contemporary society. NOW is today a major organization that lobbies for women's rights at a national level and opposes conditions that hinder women's efforts to achieve equality with men in all areas of social life. For instance, it vigorously pushes for women's rights to control their own childbearing and for strict legal equality between men and women. But it was an effective organization even in its early years, as Joan Mandle points out (1979:171):

> *The year 1970 was a major watershed for NOW as an organization and for the women's movement as a whole. In August, NOW sponsored a highly successful Women's Strike for Equality, the largest demonstration concerning women ever held in the United States. The strike was particularly important for the women's movement because it involved close cooperation between NOW and many other women's groups, all of which supported the action, and also because NOW's local chapters expanded rapidly in the aftermath of the massive publicity given to the strike.*

The two waves of feminist activity have been closely associated with significant changes in the character of Western capitalism, particularly as these changes have affected the position of women in the labor force. The first wave of feminism coincided with the movement of women in large numbers into various types of white-collar secretarial and clerical jobs in the expanding corporate sector of the economy (R. Collins, 1985b). The most recent wave of feminism has closely corresponded to the rapid entry of married women with small children into many sectors of the work force. According to Marvin Harris (1981), the labor of these women has been increasingly sought by capitalists to fill the rapidly growing number of service and information jobs in the economy. Harris believes that this increased participation of women in the labor force eventually encouraged in them a feminist consciousness. As they worked alongside men more closely, and as they came to see how much less they were being paid for essentially the same work men were doing, women came to be more acutely aware of the powerful forces of economic discrimination that were working against them. This understanding helped to promote a broader consciousness regarding the overall social position of women.

Thus Harris believes that modern feminism—both as an ideology and as an organized social movement—is ultimately traceable to major economic changes in which women have been increasingly incorporated into the work world outside the home. Given that further changes along these lines are likely in the decades ahead, the social power and feminist consciousness of an increasing number of women will continue to grow. As they do, women will advance still farther along the road toward genuine equality with men.

FOR FURTHER READING

Blumberg, Rae Lesser. "A General Theory of Gender Stratification." In Randall Collins (ed.), *Sociological Theory 1984*. San Francisco: Jossey-Bass, 1984. An important theory of sexual inequality by a sociologist sensitive to the necessity of a historical and comparative perspective for intelligent theorizing.

Chafetz, Janet Saltzman. *Sex and Advantage: A Comparative, Macro-Structural Theory of Sex Stratification*. Totowa, N.J.: Rowman and Allanheld, 1984. A perspective on sexual inequality much like that of Martin and Voorhies and of Blumberg.

Friedl, Ernestine. *Women and Men: An Anthropologist's View*. New York: Holt, Rinehart and Winston, 1975. A short but informative book that examines the relations between the sexes in hunting and gathering and horticultural societies.

Leacock, Eleanor B., and Helen Safa (eds.). *Women's Work: Development and the Division of Labor by Gender*. South Hadley, Mass.: Bergin and Garvey, 1986. Essays and case studies focusing on the impact upon women of expanding capitalism in the Third World.

Martin, M. Kay, and Barbara Voorhies. *Female of the Species*. New York: Columbia University Press, 1975. A detailed evolutionary analysis of sex roles throughout the entire spectrum of human societies. Argues that sex roles are mainly adaptive consequences of ecological, technological, and economic forces.

Rossi, Alice S. "Gender and Parenthood." *American Sociological Review* 49:1–19, 1984. A persuasive argument for the social importance of biological differences between the sexes, especially in regard to parenting. Originally delivered as the Presidential Address before the 1983 annual meetings of the American Sociological Association.

Sokoloff, Natalie J. *Between Love and Money: The Dialectics of Women's Home and Market Work*. New York: Praeger, 1980. A valuable overview of recent Marxian and feminist theories of women's subordination.

Thomas, Janet. "Women and Capitalism: Oppression or Emancipation?" *Comparative Studies in Society and History* 30:534–549, 1988. An overview of contrasting theoretical viewpoints regarding the impact of early capitalism and industrialism on the status of women.

Tilly, Louise A., and Joan W. Scott. *Women, Work, and Family.* New York: Holt, Rinehart and Winston, 1978. An important study of the impact of industrialization on women's work in England and France.

van den Berghe, Pierre L. *Age and Sex in Human Societies: A Biosocial Perspective.* Belmont, Calif.: Wadsworth, 1973. Discusses sexual differentiation among primates, the human biology of sex, and the nature of sex-role differentiation across a wide range of human societies. Suggests that human sex-role patterns are rooted in biology but are elaborated in diverse ways by culture.

Vogel, Lise. *Marxism and the Oppression of Women: Toward a Unitary Theory.* New Brunswick, N.J.: Rutgers University Press, 1983. An interesting historical treatment of the various strands of thinking by Marxists on "the woman question," from Marx and Engels to contemporary Marxists. Also presents a Marxian theory of women's subordination under contemporary capitalism.

CHAPTER 15

Marriage, Family, and Kinship in Comparative and Evolutionary Perspective

Systems of marriage, family, and kinship are the institutionalized means whereby human societies organize and carry out important activities involving mating and reproduction. Among other things, familial institutions provide for legitimate rights to sexual access, the procreation and training of children, the organization of domestic work groups in accord with a sexual division of labor, and the transmission of property and other forms of inheritance. Familial institutions establish networks of social bonds between individuals based on **affinity** (i.e., marriage) and **consanguinity** (i.e., "blood" or genetic relatedness); these networks are devoted to the performance of crucial social functions.

Marriage, family, and kinship institutions are universally found in human societies. Nevertheless, the nature of these institutions differs markedly from one society to another. In modern industrial societies, family systems assume a role secondary to that of the economy and polity in organizing and integrating the society, and a great many social relationships in industrial societies lie outside the framework of family life. In preindustrial—and especially in primitive—societies, however, family assumes a predominant significance as a mode of organization of many spheres of social activity. In the primitive world, activities that are themselves principally economic, political, religious, and so on are carried out in the context of kinship groups. In primitive society, kinship is *dominant,* so much so that many social scientists have referred to primitive societies as *kinship-based societies.* But while kinship may be dominant in the primitive world, it is not *determinant.* That is, while kinship may be the context in which such activities as economics and politics are carried out, kinship itself does not shape the nature of those activities. On the contrary, the preponderance of evidence suggests that family and kinship systems are largely determined by the material conditions of social life. It is a principal goal of the following two chapters to demonstrate the way in which family and kinship systems are responsive to material forces and thereby to show how changes in underlying material conditions lead to corresponding changes in modes of marriage, kinship, and family life.

The present chapter takes a very broad comparative and evolutionary look at family and kinship. It ignores many of the subtle details of family life, concentrating instead on the general types of family and kinship systems and their adaptive significance for individuals in various types of human societies. The next chapter takes a somewhat closer look at family life in one particular civilization: Western capitalism. It is principally concerned with understanding the past 300 years of family evolution in the West and the reasons that Western family patterns have changed so substantially in this period of time.

THE NATURE OF KIN GROUPS

When all the many details are taken into consideration, there is a dazzling array of kinship groups found throughout the world. Yet when minor variations are ignored, there are only a few basic types of kinship groupings among the world's societies. It is convenient to think of three such types: nuclear families, extended families, and corporate descent groups. While not exhaustive, these three types include most of the fundamental kinship groupings found throughout the world.

The **nuclear family** is a kinship unit consisting of the married spouses and their immediate offspring who maintain a common household and act together as a social unit. It is widespread in human societies; indeed, it is found almost universally. Despite its widespread occurrence, however, the nuclear family is the principal kinship unit only in some societies. A great many hunting and gathering societies emphasize the nuclear family as the predominant kin group. Furthermore, the nuclear family is the principal familial unit in all industrial societies (the only possible exception is Japan, which places considerable emphasis on larger groups of kin). As the smallest and simplest unit of kinship, the nuclear family therefore is mainly limited in its significance to the extremes of the evolutionary spectrum. Among societies closer to the middle of the evolutionary spectrum—that is, among horticultural and agrarian societies—the nuclear family generally pales in significance and is subsumed within larger kinship groups. These larger kinship units may be either extended families or corporate descent groups.

The **extended family** is a kinship group consisting of a number of related nuclear families bound together and acting as a unit. Such a group, which may or may not share a common household, gets its name from the fact that it *extends* the range of kinship beyond the narrow boundaries of the nuclear family. Extended families are generally of much greater significance in preindustrial societies of all types than they are in industrial societies. Logically, however, some kind of extended family unit exists in all societies since the tracing of relatives obviously does not stop at the boundaries of the nuclear family. Even in industrial societies, the extended family is a unit of at least some social significance: extended kinspeople often give financial and other forms of aid to one another, and holidays and other special occasions are frequently times at which the extended family convenes and acts as a unit.

Extended families usually consist of reasonably small networks of kin. In many societies, however, kinship ties can be extended even further to include a great many individuals within one's sphere of kinship. When this happens, **corporate descent groups** are frequently formed. These groups are networks of individuals who trace descent, or genealogical connection, from a common ancestor. Corporate descent groups, which may include hundreds or even thousands of persons, function as single, discrete units of kinship. They are the largest and most complex type of kin group found in human societies. Corporate descent groups are entirely nonexistent in industrial societies, and they are infrequently found among hunters and gatherers. Among horticulturalists and agriculturalists, however, they are extensively found; indeed, they are the predominant type of kinship unit in most horticultural societies.

SYSTEMS OF RESIDENCE AND DESCENT

Local Groups and Descent Groups

Two of the most important characteristics of kinship systems are **rules of residence** and **rules of descent.** All societies use these criteria for organizing individuals into various types of kinship groups. Rules of residence determine who goes to live with whom upon marriage. They establish *local groups,* or groups of kinspeople who cooperate in the performance of domestic and extradomestic activities. The primary rules of residence in use by the world's societies are depicted in Table 15.1.

As Table 15.3 (page 361) clearly reveals, **patrilocality** is overwhelmingly the preferred residence rule in the world's cultures, accounting for slightly more than two-thirds of the residential practices in a sample of 857 societies. Under this residential system, husbands bring wives home to live with them in their father's households. Far less common is **matrilocality,** which accounts for only 13 percent of the residential practices of the sample of 857 cultures. With matrilocality, wives bring their husbands home to live with them in their extended family households. Rarer yet is the interesting practice of **avunculocality.** In this system, residence occurs with the husband's mother's brother. While this practice may seem rather bizarre at first glance, it actually can be shown to make perfectly good sense when the conditions under which it is found are revealed.

Some societies do not restrict marital residence exclusively to either the wife's or husband's kin groups. Thus arises the practice of **bilocality,** a system under which the married couple alternates its residence between the husband's and wife's kin groups. **Ambilocality** occurs when the married couple has a choice of living with either the husband's or wife's group. A rare, but quite fascinating, residence practice is **natolocality.** In this arrangement, husband and wife do not live together, but rather remain in their natal households (i.e., the households of their birth). Finally, there is the residence system that is most familiar to the members of Western industrial societies: **neolocality.** Under this system, the married couple establishes a new, independent household of its own. While neolocal residence is sometimes found in preindustrial societies, it is most frequently found in societies of the industrial type. Indeed, neolocality is the standard residence practice in virtually all industrial societies. Neolocal residence is highly adaptive in societies emphasizing the small nuclear family, such as our own.

In contrast with rules of residence, rules of descent establish broad networks of genealogically related individuals, many of whom frequently do not live together. Whereas local groups consist of individuals who reside to-

Table 15.1 RULES OF POSTMARITAL RESIDENCE IN THE WORLD'S SOCIETIES

Patrilocality:	The married couple resides in the household of the husband's father.
Matrilocality:	The married couple resides in the household of the wife's mother.
Avunculocality:	The married couple resides in the household of the husband's mother's brother.
Bilocality:	The married couple alternates its residence between the husband's and wife's kinship groups.
Ambilocality:	The married couple may choose to take up residence either with the husband's or with the wife's kinship group.
Natolocality:	Husband and wife do not live together; each stays in the household into which he or she was born.
Neolocality:	The married couple establishes an independent residence of its own.

gether, descent groups include all individuals who maintain common genealogical ties, regardless of whether they live together. The distinction between local groups and descent groups is therefore one between *common residence* and a *sense of common identity.*

While all societies have descent rules, the nature of the kinship groups or categories formed by these rules differs significantly from one society to another. In the majority of the world's societies, the descent rule is combined with a kinship system resting on **ancestor-focus** (Fox, 1967). This situation creates what we have already termed corporate descent groups. These are groups of individuals who trace descent from a common ancestor (real or mythical) who is believed to have been the founder of the group. Membership in a corporate descent group defines for individuals the rights and obligations they have in regard to the other members of their group. Corporate descent groups generally have the following characteristics (W. Stephens, 1963):

1. ***Corporateness.*** The group possesses a unity in the sense that the entire group may act as a single legal individual in behalf of any of its members.
2. ***A name.*** Since the group has corporateness, it is natural for it to have a name to signify its identity. The names of corporate descent groups are frequently taken from plants, animals, or other natural phenomena.
3. ***Exogamy.*** Most corporate descent groups forbid the marriage of their members to any other member of the group, thus forcing them to select marriage partners from among other descent groups.
4. ***Common religious observances.*** The members of a corporate descent group frequently symbolize their identity through the enactment of common ritual and ceremony.
5. ***Corporate property ownership.*** The members of a corporate descent group commonly hold collective title to land and other property. Individuals may therefore own land only as members of the group. This is perhaps the most crucial characteristic of a corporate descent group.
6. ***Obligations of mutual aid and hospitality.*** Members of a corporate descent group are frequently called upon to render assistance to one another in times of need.

Corporate descent groups vary greatly in terms of size and complexity. They range from as small as a dozen or so members in some cases to as large as a million members in others (the latter, for example, in the case of the traditional Chinese clan). On average, they probably contain from a few dozen to a few hundred members. Such groups also vary in terms of the degree of certainty that members have of their relatedness. A corporate descent group whose members can precisely identify their genealogical connections to one another is commonly known as a **lineage.** When the members of a corporate descent group can only assume, rather than precisely identify, their genealogical connections, the group is generally known as a **clan.** Clans are therefore typically larger than lineages, and several lineages may be grouped together to form a clan.

Societies having corporate descent groups, as indicated earlier, base their kinship systems on ancestor-focus. A number of societies, however, use **ego-focus** as a basis for forming kin groups. When this occurs, kinship is traced from the point of view of *any given living individual,* rather than from some putative common ancestor (Fox, 1967). Ego-focus gives rise to small-scale personal kin groups known as **kindreds.** These groups are not corporate and maintain few of the functions of corporate descent groups. Kindreds are typically inactive much of the time, and are activated only on special occasions, for example, during times of festival or ritual or when the need arises for the group to aid one of its members. Kindreds are of greatest significance in societies that emphasize the nuclear family as the primary kinship group, that is, in industrial and in many hunting and gathering societies.

The primary rules of descent found in human societies are shown in Table 15.2.

Patrilineal Descent

Patrilineal descent is the most common of all the major types of descent groupings, accounting for nearly half of the world's descent systems (Table 15.3). Patrilineal descent systems are those in which descent is traced through males. This means that a young man, for example, would trace his primary kin ties through his father, his father's father, his father's father's father, and so on. This same young man would therefore belong to a descent group consisting of his father (and father's father, etc.), his father's brothers, his own brothers, and his own sons. His mother may or may not be a member of his patrilineal group (this varies from one patrilineal society to another), but certainly his

Table 15.2 DESCENT SYSTEMS IN THE WORLD'S SOCIETIES

I. Unilineal descent:	Descent traced through a single line only, either through males or through females.
A. Patrilineal descent:	Descent traced only through males (i.e., through one's father, father's father, father's father's father, etc.).
B. Matrilineal descent:	Descent traced only through females (i.e., through one's mother, mother's mother, mother's mother's mother, etc.).
C. Double descent:	A descent system in which both patrilineal and matrilineal descent exist side by side in the same society.
II. Cognatic descent:	A system in which both males and females are used in the establishment of descent groupings.
A. Ambilineal descent:	Descent in which corporate descent groups are formed by tracing relationships through either males or females.
B. Bilateral descent:	Descent in which personal kindreds are formed by tracing relationships through both males and females simultaneously.

Table 15.3 FREQUENCY OF OCCURRENCE OF RESIDENCE AND DESCENT SYSTEMS

	Rule of descent									
	Patrilineal		Matrilineal		Double		Bilateral		Total	
Rule of residence	N	%	N	%	N	%	N	%	N	%
Patrilocal	384	96.2	18	14.8	25	92.6	161	52.0	588	68.6
Matrilocal	0	0.0	44	36.0	0	0.0	67	21.7	111	13.0
Avunculocal	0	0.0	36	29.5	1	3.7	0	0.0	37	4.3
Bilocal	5	1.3	14	11.5	1	3.7	53	17.2	73	8.5
Neolocal	6	1.5	6	4.9	0	0.0	28	9.1	40	4.7
Duolocal	4	1.0	4	3.3	0	0.0	0	0.0	8	0.9
Total	399	100.0	122	100.0	27	100.0	309	100.0	857	100.0
Percent of grand total		46.5		14.2		3.2		36.1		100.0

Source: Slightly modified from Pierre L. van den Berghe, *Human Family Systems: An Evolutionary View.* New York: Elsevier, 1979, p. 111, Table 11.

mother's primary relatives (e.g., his mother's father, mother's mother, mother's brothers and sisters) will not be members of his group.

Patrilineal societies vary in terms of the placement of wives in descent groups. A girl, of course, is born into the patrilineal group of her father. But what happens to her upon marriage cannot be predicted in the abstract. In many patrilineal societies, a woman remains a member for life of her father's patrilineage, and therefore upon marriage she is still something of an outsider in the patrilineal group of her husband. In other patrilineal societies, a woman is absorbed upon marriage into the patrilineal group of her husband. In this latter case, she may still retain some ties with her father's group despite the fact that her ties are now primarily to her husband's group.

The primary kinship tie in patrilineal societies is between father and son. The inheritance of land and other forms of property, for example, passes from father to son. Women are usually deemed important mainly as procreators; the continuity of the group, however, is established through males, since children are generally regarded as belonging primarily to their father rather than to their mother.

Of course, any individual has many more relatives in a patrilineal group than those listed here, since we have concentrated only on identifying primary kinspeople. The important point is that **patriliny** links people on the basis of their descent through the male line. A person's patrilineal relatives are therefore those who are related in the father's line, rather than in the mother's. By using the principle of descent in the male line only, patrilineal societies are able to organize their members into neat, mutually exclusive, nonoverlapping kin groups of a corporate nature.

Matrilineal Descent

While **matrilineal descent** is not nearly as common as the patrilineal variety, it does occur in approximately 14 percent of the world's societies and is therefore by no means rare (Table 15.3). This type of descent system has some very interesting features, and it is not simply the mirror opposite of patriliny (Fox, 1967).

Matrilineal descent traces kinship ties through females. A young man recognizes descent through his mother, mother's mother, mother's mother's mother, and so on. Any person is a member of a group constituted by his mother (and mother's mother, etc.), his sisters, his brothers, and his mother's sisters and brothers. A person's father, however, is never a member of his own matrilineal group. Thus, a woman's children belong to her matrilineal group, but a man's children do not belong to his. It is clear that husbands and wives do not share the same matrilineal group. Unlike some patrilineal societies, individuals in matrilineal societies never transfer their descent group membership upon marriage. One is born and remains for life in the same matrilineal descent group. Again, it is not advisable here to attempt to trace all potential relatives in a matrilineal system. The principle that matrilineal descent rests upon is that basic kinship ties run through females; thus women, and not men, are the perpetuators of matrilineal groups.

Matrilineal societies are different in several crucial respects from those based on patriliny. Indeed, matrilineal groups encounter one very special problem: while **matriliny** traces descent through females, it nevertheless leaves males in control of the affairs of descent groups. However, while men in patrilineal societies control their groups as fathers and husbands, men in matrilineal societies exercise control *as brothers and uncles.* A man in a matrilineal society actually has two primary social roles to play. On the one hand, he will be the husband of a woman in another matrilineage; on the other hand, he will be performing as a brother in his own matrilineage (i.e., that of his sister and mother). It is a man's role as a brother in his own matrilineage that is of greater social significance, for he has a special tie to his sister's children, especially her sons. He has a heavy responsibility for the training of these sons, and inheritance will pass from him (as a maternal uncle) to these nephews.

This fact gives rise to two basic kinds of "fatherhood" in matrilineal societies: "biological fatherhood" and "sociological fatherhood." A man will be a biological father to his own sons (who belong to the matrilineage of their mother) and a sociological father (as a maternal uncle) to his sister's sons (his maternal nephews) in his own matrilineage. This produces a strain in matrilineal societies that is not found under patriliny. In patrilineal societies, a man is only a biological father to his own sons in his own patrilineage, but a man under matriliny is both a "father" and a "maternal uncle." Maternal uncles have primary responsibility for the rearing of young boys, but biological fathers often intrude upon the rights of these maternal uncles in attempting to assume responsibility for their own sons.

Because matrilineal societies trace descent through females but keep males in charge of the domestic group's affairs, they encounter some special problems that are absent with patrilineal descent. Since patriliny and matriliny are not simply mirror opposites of each other, it is desirable to summarize their principal differences (Zelditch, 1964; Schneider, 1961):

1. Under patriliny, females can be severed from membership in their natal descent group and fully absorbed into the descent group of their husband. But under matriliny, no such severance can take place, and both men and women remain members of their natal descent group for life.
2. With patriliny the roles of husband and father are of crucial importance. But with matriliny such roles are not even necessary to the maintenance of the group.
3. The establishment of strong husband-wife bonds is not compatible with matrilineal descent. With patrilineal descent, however, such bonds are both compatible and desirable.
4. In patrilineal systems, no special mechanisms are needed to deal with in-marrying affines. But in matrilineal systems, in-marrying affines are a threat to the descent group and special mechanisms are needed to deal with such threats.
5. In matrilineal societies, the bonds that may develop between child and biological father tend to be in direct competition with the bond between that child and his mother's brother (his maternal uncle). In patrilineal societies, no such problem arises.

Unilineal Descent and the Principle of Complementary Filiation

The existence of **unilineal descent groups** within a society should not be construed to mean that individuals have kinship ties only with other individuals who are related strictly through males or strictly through females. In other words, it is not the case that in patrilineal societies all of a person's relatives are traced through males, nor is it the case that in matrilineal societies all of a person's relatives are traced through females. What the principle of unilineal descent establishes is a set of *primary* kinship ties. In all societies, individuals are obviously related to others through both their mother and their father, but unilineal descent makes one line the basis for the formation of corporate groups.

The existence of secondary relationships through one's mother in a patrilineal society, as well as secondary relationships through one's father in a matrilineal society, is generally known as **complementary filiation** (Fox, 1967). It is interesting to note how these secondary relationships are usually structured. In patrilineal societies one's patrilineal relatives are generally regarded in stern and formal ways, while relationships through one's mother are often warm and relaxed; conversely, in matrilineal societies it is the matrilineal relatives who are frequently treated in stern and formal ways, while relationships through one's father are those that are warm and easygoing.

Bilateral Descent

Bilateral descent involves the tracing of genealogical relatedness through both males and females simultaneously. This does not result in the formation of corporate descent groups (it logically cannot result in such groups being formed); rather, small-scale, personalized, ego-focused groups known as *kindreds* are produced. Kindreds are in actuality only special-purpose extended kin groups that may long remain dormant and may only be activated on special occasions. Kindreds extensively overlap (father and son, for example, have overlapping, yet different, kindreds), and because of this they can never be corporate groups. Such groups are most common in many hunting and gathering and virtually all industrial societies. In our own society, for example, when a person makes reference to all the members of his extended family unit, he is referring to a bilateral kindred.

Forms of Residence Under Patriliny

As Table 15.3 reveals, patrilineal societies are overwhelmingly patrilocal. The great majority of patrilineal societies therefore neatly combine both residence and descent in the hands of males. The following examples will serve to illustrate the actual operation of patriliny and patrilocality (Fox, 1967).

In traditional China, descent was organized in terms of exogamous patrilineages. A lineage was divided into sublineages, and these were often dispersed throughout several villages. Residence was patrilocal. Upon marriage, a woman transferred her descent group membership from that of her father to that of her husband; she became completely severed from her natal patrilineage and was absorbed completely into her husband's group.

A patrilineal system of a somewhat different nature exists among the Tallensi of northern Ghana. Residence among the Tallensi, who raise cattle as well as cultivate fields, is patrilocal. Descent groups exist in the form of patriclans, which are further divided into patrilineages. The rule of exogamy applies to the clan as well as the lineage. While women move in with their husbands, they never move far away, and therefore it is easy for them to retain close ties with their natal patrilineage. In this regard, the Tallensi contrast strikingly with traditional China. Whereas in China women were completely lost to their natal patrilineages, among the Tallensi women continue to play an important role in the descent group of their fathers and brothers.

Forms of Residence Under Matriliny

Since most patrilineal societies are patrilocal, descent and residence are neatly tied together. Things are not nearly so neat among matrilineal peoples. Matrilineal societies display a wide range of residence rules (Table 15.3). The most common residence rule associated with matriliny is matrilocality, but still only slightly more than a third of matrilineal societies have adopted it. One such matrilocal-matrilineal society is that of the Hopi Indians of the American Southwest (Keesing, 1975). The major descent groups among the Hopi are exogamous matriclans, and these are landowning corporate groups. Hopi matriclans are further subdivided into unnamed matrilineages. An adult man takes up residence with his wife's household, where he is, of course, an outsider. Despite the fact that the men disperse upon marriage, they never move far away from their natal households, and thus it is relatively easy for them to continue to carry out important activities in their own matrilineal groups.

Matrilineal societies are almost as likely to adopt avunculocality as matrilocality (Table 15.3). A well-known matrilineal society practicing avunculocal residence is the Trobriand Islanders (Keesing, 1975). Among these people, women go with their husbands to live in the household of the husband's mother's brother. During adolescence, a boy will move away from his parents' household and return to the village of his own matrilineal group. The boy's sisters will remain in their father's household until the time of their marriage; at this time, of course, they will move to the households of their husbands' mothers' brothers.

Forms of Residence Under Bilateral Descent

When bilateral descent is found among hunters and gatherers, it is very frequently associated with patrilocal residence. Matrilocality and bilocality, however, are also found to some extent in these societies. Among bilaterally organized industrial societies, residence is normally neolocal.

THE CAUSES OF RESIDENCE AND DESCENT SYSTEMS

As Robin Fox (1967) has pointed out, many scholars have talked about residence and descent systems as if they simply dropped from the sky upon the peoples practicing them. Such a view is scarcely likely to provide much illumination about the causal dynamics of these systems. A better approach would be to examine residence and descent systems as adaptive consequences of the practical conditions of social life (Keesing, 1975; Harris, 1979; Goody, 1976).

An essential first premise holds that *residence systems are logically prior to descent systems.* This means that the members of a society must first organize themselves in workable household arrangements before they organize their descent patterns. From this point of view, descent systems largely reflect and serve to validate the kinds of household arrangements already established. To complete the causal chain, the problem is then one of determining the conditions likely to produce one residential pattern versus another. This approach yields some solid results. However, it must be borne in mind that, once in existence, descent patterns may have causal significance in their own right. It may sometimes be the case that some residential patterns actually result from the prior establishment of a particular kind of descent system. Such logic, for example, seems necessary in order to understand the otherwise puzzling phenomenon of avunculocality.

The Causes of Patrilocality and Patriliny

While the reasons for the overwhelming popularity of patrilocality and patriliny are still not fully understood, a number of factors have been proposed as important causal mechanisms. These include population pressure, limited land and resources, frequent warfare with neighboring groups, and the presence of concentrated forms of wealth (Harris, 1975; Martin and Voorhies, 1975). Under these kinds of conditions, keeping fathers, sons, and brothers physically together so they can pursue their common interests in land and people is a highly adaptive social arrangement (Harris, 1975).

Male-centered kinship practices are commonly found among widely differing societies. This suggests that patrilocality and patriliny are adaptive under a wide range of material conditions, and thus appear to have considerable adaptive flexibility. Hunting and gathering societies, for example, are quite frequently patrilocal. This probably reflects the need to keep male kinsmen together for crucial hunting purposes. Hunters and gatherers, however, tend more toward bilaterality than toward patriliny; but this seems to result from the need for such societies to maintain highly flexible and loosely structured kin groups, groups that are highly

The Nuer. These East African pastoralists, like most pastoralists everywhere, are a strongly patrilineal people.

adaptive to the hunting and gathering mode of subsistence. The kinship systems of horticultural societies also tend strongly toward patrilocality and patriliny, and the factors proposed by Harris and by Martin and Voorhies may well be crucial determinants of male-centered kinship among such peoples. Agrarian societies likewise frequently opt for patrilocality and patriliny. Since men overwhelmingly dominate economic production in such societies, there is a strong need to keep male kinsmen together to form cooperative work teams, and patriliny can easily result from such household arrangements.

The Causes of Matrilocality and Matriliny

Since patrilocality and patriliny are so common, and since they are found under such variable conditions, there is an especially critical need to identify the factors that cause some societies to adopt matrilocal and matrilineal institutions. It seems that the origin of matriliny is almost always to be found in a prior condition of matrilocal residence. The problem, then, is to determine the factors that make matrilocality highly adaptive.

The most widely accepted explanation of matrilocality at present is that offered by Melvin and Carol Ember (1971). They argue that when societies engage in at least some degree of internal warfare (i.e., warfare with neighboring societies close to home), patrilocal residence is the typical result. However, when societies engage in purely external warfare (i.e., warfare at long distances from home), and when this warfare forces women to be heavily involved in economic production, then matrilocality is the typical outcome. Thus, when men are gone from their home territories for long periods of time, and when this results in a heavy female contribution to subsistence, there is a strong need to keep the women of kin groups together. The available evidence tends to support Ember and Ember's conclusions. A classic instance of a society with matrilocal and matrilineal institutions is that of the Iroquois of western New York state. These people engaged in extensive warfare with societies hundreds of miles away. Men were frequently gone from home for extended periods on warfare and hunting expeditions. In addition, women took a predominant role in subsistence activities. The Iroquois thus fit Ember and Ember's conclusions, as do many other societies.

The argument developed by the Embers can be generalized to suggest that *any activity* that produces long-term absence of males from home base puts pressure on a society to become matrilocal (Harris, 1975, 1979). For instance, among the Navaho of the American Southwest (a matrilocal and matrilineal people) the women tended sheep close to their own households, but the men raised horses and worked for wages, activities that required long-term absences from home. For another example, among the matrilineal (but avunculocal) Trobriand Islanders men were frequently absent from home on long-distance trading expeditions.

Even if the preceding arguments about the origins of matrilocality and matriliny are correct, we must still explain why almost as many matrilineal societies are avunculocal as are matrilocal. In this regard, it is necessary to abandon the assumption that residence is prior to descent, for avunculocality distinctly appears to be a result of the prior existence of matrilineal descent. As Fox (1967) has pointed out, matrilo-

The Trobriand Islanders, the world's best-known matrilineal and avunculocal society.

cal residence works best in those matrilineal societies where households are not highly dispersed and where concentrations of wealth are not large. If households were to become highly dispersed, or if large concentrations of wealth were to begin to form, then matrilocality would begin to present a problem. If the men were highly dispersed from their own matrilineal groups, it would be difficult for them to participate in the regular functions of such groups. Furthermore, with growing concentrations of wealth, men would have difficulty managing and controlling that wealth. Therefore, when a matrilineal society begins to grow in scale, complexity, and wealth concentration, there is considerable pressure placed upon it to shift away from matrilocality. The residence solution to which such a society is apt to shift is avunculocality, for this residence system once again physically unites the male directors of matrilineal corporate groups, allowing them to participate efficiently in the management of their groups' affairs. Avunculocality therefore appears to be an adaptive solution to problems encountered in the evolutionary growth of matrilineal systems.

The Causes of Bilateral Descent

The causes of bilateral systems are well known. These systems occur principally in hunting and gathering and industrial societies. Both types of societies, despite their overwhelming differences in most respects, share one crucial characteristic: a technoeconomic system requiring a great deal of geographical mobility. Hunters and gatherers must be mobile because of their constant need to search for food. The members of industrial societies are frequently mobile because they are searching for jobs, getting transferred in their jobs, and so on. Under such conditions, a small-scale, loosely structured, and highly flexible family system is most adaptive. Bilateral kin groups provide just such a system.

MARRIAGE IN COMPARATIVE PERSPECTIVE

There are three basic forms of marriage found in the world's societies: monogamy, polygyny, and polyandry. (Some scholars have proposed a form of "group marriage," but there is no good evidence that this has ever existed.) **Monogamy** refers to the marriage of one man to one woman. While this is the marriage form familiar to the members of Western industrial societies, it is clearly in the minority as a preferred marriage practice throughout the world. Only about 20 percent of all societies actually prefer this form and institutionalize it as the required practice. It is the required form of marriage in all contemporary industrial societies, and many agrarian societies have adopted it as the standard (or even required) practice. Monogamy seems to occur as the exclusive marriage form in societies where having more than one wife is economically too costly.

By far the most preferred marriage practice in human societies is **polygyny,** which involves the marriage of one man to two or more women. Approximately 80 percent of the world's societies prefer this form of marriage. Despite the overwhelming preference for polygyny, however, the practice is greatly limited in those societies in which it does occur. In fact, the majority of persons in polygynous societies end up marrying monogamously. It is not hard to see why this is the case. With an approximately evenly balanced sex ratio, it would be logically impossible for all men to engage in polygynous marriage. Thus, only a minority of men actually have multiple wives in polygynous societies, and these are usually men of highest social rank.

Two main kinds of polygynous systems must be distinguished: *harem polygyny* and *hut polygyny* (van den Berghe, 1973). Harem polygyny occurs in agrarian societies and in some intensive horticultural societies. It results in a political ruler's having a very large number of wives (a harem) at his command. Far more common, however, is hut polygyny. Under this form of polygyny, a man typically has no more than three or four wives. The wives often have independent households, and the husband takes turns sleeping with all of them. Wives are often graded into senior and junior wives, and there are usually mechanisms available to deal with whatever jealousy might arise between co-wives.

Polygyny is most common in horticultural societies and is also widely found in hunting and gathering and agrarian societies (however, in the last it is generally limited to elites, the overwhelming majority of peasants being strictly monogamous). It is considerably more common in patrilineal than in matrilineal societies. What accounts for the widespread preference for polygynous marriage? Some social scientists suggest a sociobiological explanation, arguing that it is a natural result of the male's reproductive strategy (van den Berghe, 1979; Hartung, 1982). Men's desire to marry many women stems from an unconscious biological strategy of attempting to maximize the representation of their genes in the society's total gene pool. An alternative explanation focuses on the economic benefits to men of having sev-

The senior wife of the King of Akure in Nigeria is greeted by some of his additional 155 wives. Polygynous marriage, especially the harem type of polygyny depicted here, generally involves a hierarchical arrangement among co-wives.

eral wives (cf. White and Burton, 1988). When women have important roles in economic production, having multiple wives means that a man can accumulate more wealth than would otherwise be the case; hence, multiple wives can be a great economic asset. The sociobiological and economic explanations may be complementary rather than competing (van den Berghe, 1979). The conscious desire to increase wealth may be rooted in the same portion of the human biogram that guides the unconscious aim of enhancing inclusive fitness.

Polyandry is a marriage form involving the marriage of one woman to two or more men. It is quite rare, occurring in only about 0.5 percent of all societies. When polyandry occurs, it is often *fraternal*, which means that a woman marries a group of brothers. Societies having polyandry usually also have polygyny and monogamy. Since polyandry is so rare, the conditions for its occurrence are quite special. It is usually associated with a situation of **hypergyny,** that is, women systematically marrying men of higher social rank, which leads to the development of polygyny at the top of the society and a serious shortage of women at the bottom. In such a situation, unless lower-status men wish to remain celibate, polyandry is their only real option. The rarity of polyandry, especially when placed alongside the widespread preference for polygyny, suggests that biological factors are at work (van den Berghe, 1979). Polyandry minimizes, rather than maximizes, the male's inclusive fitness, and this may be the basic reason it is so uncommon around the world.

INCEST AVOIDANCE, EXOGAMY, AND ENDOGAMY

The Nature of Incest Avoidance

Many sociologists and anthropologists lump the concepts of incest avoidance and exogamy together and treat rules of exogamy as merely extensions of the incest prohibitions applied to the nuclear family. However, as van den Berghe (1979, 1980) has pointed out, the two concepts do not refer to the same thing. While they have a superficial similarity, it is crucial to identify them as separate phenomena. **Incest avoidance** refers to the avoidance of sexual intercourse with close kin, especially the other members of one's nuclear family. This phenomenon is a universal feature of human societies. By contrast, **exogamy** involves a rule against marriage with other members of one's own corporate kin group (van den Berghe, 1979, 1980). While widespread, exogamy is not a universal phenomenon. Without this distinction, it is difficult to understand not only the nature of these phenomena, but also the reasons they exist in human societies.

It is also important to distinguish between incest *avoidance* and incest *taboos* (Fox, 1967; van den Berghe, 1979, 1980). Incest avoidance means that incest is simply not engaged in, while the **incest taboo** refers to a society's strong sanctions against its commission. While incest avoidance is universal, incest taboos are not. A number of societies feel horror and revulsion about the commission of incest, but many others merely find it incredible and laughable that anyone would think of engaging in it.

Incest does indeed occur to some extent in many societies. When it does, it is most frequently of the father-daughter variety; brother-sister incest seems much less common, and mother-son incest is rare (Fox, 1967; Shepher, 1983). Furthermore, some societies have institutionalized incestuous matings within their ruling classes, a phenomenon known as **royal incest.** This occurred, for example, among the ancient Egyptians, Hawaiians, and Incas, as well as in a number of state-level African societies (van den Berghe and Mesher, 1980).

Explanations for Incest Avoidance

Although many theories of incest avoidance have been presented, virtually all of these fall into one or the other of two basic types: sociocultural and biological theories. Well-known sociocultural explanations have been advanced by Malinowski (1927), Parsons (1954), and Lévi-Strauss (1969). Malinowski argues that sexual relations among nuclear family members would turn the nuclear family into a seething cauldron of jealousies and conflicts, thus threatening to destroy its basic organization. Incest therefore came to be prohibited in order to preserve the unity and integrity of the nuclear family as a basic social unit. A similar argument has been advanced by Parsons. He argues that incest would disrupt the stability of the nuclear family by leading to massive role confusion and consequent difficulties in the socialization of children. One of the most famous of all theories is that developed by Claude Lévi-Strauss. Lévi-Strauss's argument is that the incest taboo signaled the passage of humankind from nature to culture. By prohibiting sex and marriage with close kin, human societies forced people to seek mates outside their own families. This in turn led to the formation of bonds or "alliances" among various human groups, thus allowing people to live at peace with one another. As van den Berghe (1980) comments, this theory is not so much wrong as simply misplaced, for it is really a theory of exogamy and not of incest avoidance (although Lévi-Strauss makes no real distinction between the two).

Biological theories of incest often take as their point of departure the contention that incestuous mating leads to an unacceptably large number of genetically defective offspring. It is sometimes held that high rates of inbreeding in human populations would ultimately lead to their extinction through the accumulation of a host of genetic defects. Evidence has now accumulated to indicate that inbreeding does indeed lead to the production of a larger number of genetic deficiencies than would occur from the mating of genetically unrelated individuals (Shepher, 1983). However, as Frank Livingstone (1969) has shown, this need not produce any deleterious long-range genetic consequences for human populations. Populations can be highly inbred for long periods of time and still survive quite well. On the basis of these facts, then, it is difficult to argue that incest avoidance is a biologically evolved survival mechanism in the human species. Nonetheless, since outbreeding increases heterozygosity (i.e., genetic variability), it may well have biologically adaptive significance, and therefore it could be wired into human biology (van den Berghe, 1979; Shepher, 1983).

A much-maligned biological theory of incest avoidance was produced in the late nineteenth century by Edward Westermarck (1891). Westermarck's theory might be labeled the "familiarity breeds indifference" theory of incest avoidance. Westermarck argued that a natural sexual indifference emerged between individuals who were reared together early in life. He believed that people who were reared together in early childhood simply were not interested in sexual relations with each other. Such indifference was not held to be dependent on a genetic relatedness of the individuals involved. Genetically unrelated persons reared together would develop this indifference, while brothers and sisters reared apart would not develop feelings of sexual disinterest.

Although Westermarck's theory has been heavily criticized over many decades, it is currently undergoing a revival resulting from the discovery of some very interesting data. One source of information comes from Joseph Shepher's (1971) study of marriage patterns in an Israeli kibbutz. In analyzing 2769 marriages between kibbutz members, Shepher found that only 14 marriages were undertaken between children who were reared together. These kibbutz youth, then, showed an absolutely overwhelming preference to marry outside of their own childhood groups. This occurred in spite of the fact that there was no norm against marrying childhood associates; in fact, youth were often encouraged to marry those with whom they had been closely associated. When Shepher queried these kibbutz youth about their failure to marry childhood associates, they responded with such statements as "we feel like siblings" or "we have no attraction toward each other." Thus these kibbutz marriage patterns seem to offer strong support for the operation of a "Westermarck principle."

Another source of data highly consistent with Westermarck's theory comes from Arthur Wolf's (1970) investigation of Taiwanese marriage practices. Wolf found the existence in the recent past of two principal marriage patterns in Taiwan: "major marriages" and "minor marriages." In a major marriage, the bride and groom are individuals who were not familiar with each other in childhood; often the couple does not even meet until the day of the wedding. In the minor marriages (known locally as *sim-pua* marriages), the bride is a woman who was adopted into her husband's household as an infant or young girl and reared in close association with her future husband. Thus, in the minor marriages the bride and groom are persons who were reared together virtually as brother and sister from infancy or early childhood. On the basis of Westermarck's theory, Wolf predicted that persons marrying in *sim-pua* fashion would show much higher levels of marital dissatisfaction than persons marrying in the major fashion. This is exactly what he found. His data showed the following: (1) 24 percent of the minor marriages ended in divorce or separation, compared to only 1 percent of the major marriages; (2) 33 percent of the women engaged in minor marriages had been involved in adultery, compared to only 11 percent of the women in the major marriages; and (3) minor marriages produced substantially fewer offspring than did major marriages, strongly suggesting that sexual intercourse was considerably less frequent in the minor marriages.

A very similar situation has been found in Lebanon (McCabe, 1983). In some Lebanese groups a form of marriage involving cousins who were close childhood associates is common. Marriages between these cousins lead to the same apparent sexual disinterest that Wolf found in the Taiwanese *sim-pua* marriages. More than four times as many cousin marriages as all others end in divorce, and the cousin marriages produce about 23 percent fewer children than all the other marriages.

When all the evidence is taken into consideration, a biological interpretation of incest avoidance seems most acceptable. In regard to the sociocultural interpretations of incest avoidance, there is no reliable evidence to suggest that incestuous activity would necessarily lead to the destruction of the nuclear family. It seems highly unlikely that nuclear family members do not have sex with each other because they see that it would destroy their family unit; more likely, they do not have sex with each other because they do not want to have sex with each other. The data assembled in support of Westermarck's theory seem very impressive indeed. It is therefore hard to resist the idea that incest avoidance is a basic part of our biological programming. Incest avoidance probably arose in biological evolution as a mechanism for maintaining heterozygosity, and thereby enhancing adaptive capacity. This interpretation is strengthened by the fact that incest avoidance appears to be widespread among the higher infrahuman animals, and thus of biologically adaptive significance for them as well (Parker, 1976; Bischof, 1975).

Critics of the above line of reasoning—those who still prefer a sociocultural interpretation of incest avoidance—will no doubt wish to point at this time to the existence of institutionalized forms of royal incest. How can such incestuous practices exist, they will say, if we are biologically programmed to avoid incest altogether? There are two parts to the answer to this question. The first is that incest avoidance is no doubt a generalized biological tendency, not a fixed, immutable instinct. The second part is that there are numerous instances of human behavior that indicate that culture can override what we otherwise have a natural tendency to do. (We come naturally equipped with sex urges, for example, yet there are many religious orders that maintain vows of celibacy.) We should regard royal incest as a highly specialized cultural practice that has the capacity to override, for a special purpose, natural inclinations. If the brothers and sisters who mated with each other under such systems were separated during early childhood, there should be no problem regarding their indifference to each other; under such conditions, culture could override biology with no difficulty. But why did royal incest itself develop? It probably arose among the ruling classes that practiced it as a mechanism for keeping wealth and power confined to a select circle of ruling kinspeople.

Exogamy and Marital Exchange

As indicated earlier, exogamy refers to the cultural rule that prohibits marriage within one's own corporate descent group. Exogamy differs from incest avoidance in two principal ways: it applies primarily to marriage rather than to sex, and it is applied to much larger groupings of kin (whole descent groups rather than nuclear families). Rules of exogamy are widespread in human societies, but they are most commonly found in horticultural societies, where we find the widespread occurrence of corporate unilineal descent groups. The vast majority of those societies having unilineal descent groups have exogamous practices. Since marriage is prohibited in one's own descent group, all persons must seek mates among other groups.

In many societies, exogamy implies only a *negative rule* of marriage. This means that marriage is prohibited within one's own group, but there is no specification with regard to marrying into any other particular group. Societies having only this negative rule have *complex* marriage systems (Lévi-Strauss, 1969; Fox, 1967). Most societies having exogamous descent groups are characterized by such systems. In some societies, however, there is both a negative rule and a *positive rule* of marriage. This means that there is an additional specification as to the group or groups into which a person is permitted to marry. Societies having both a negative and a positive marriage rule have *elementary* marriage systems (Lévi-Strauss, 1969; Fox, 1967). Elementary marriage systems are premised upon the structured exchange of women between or among descent groups. Descent groups develop ties with one another whereby they agree to exchange women as marriage partners in some specified fashion. The systems that develop are frequently known as **systems of marital exchange** (see the Special Topic at the end of this chapter).

In accounting for the widespread prevalence of exogamous rules that frequently lead to elaborate systems of marital exchange, the theory most widely accepted by social scientists is Lévi-Strauss's *alliance theory.* According to this theory, rules of exogamy lead to the formation of widespread ties or "alliances" between and among different kin groups. These alliances serve to integrate the society and prevent or minimize destructive conflict among groups. By marrying each other's daughters and sisters, descent groups come to depend intimately on one another, and this dependence forces such groups to live in at least relative peace. Exogamy therefore serves as an important mechanism of political integration in societies lacking advanced governmental institutions. It is noteworthy that when advanced state-level institutions begin to emerge in human societies, exogamous unilineal kin groups frequently begin to decay.

Endogamy

Unlike exogamy, **endogamy** is not so much a rule as a statistical tendency. This phenomenon reflects the preference of individuals to marry within their own groups. Endogamy has been widely practiced in many societies, and it has been found to apply to many different types of groups. Castes in India, for example, are prescriptively endogamous. There is great pressure for persons to marry within their own subcaste, and severe sanctions for failure to do so. In medieval Europe, royalty married other royalty. In fact, ruling classes in all state-level societies have had enormous endogamous preferences. In the contemporary United States, blacks overwhelmingly marry other blacks, whites overwhelmingly marry other whites, and Jews express a very strong preference for marriage with other Jews. These examples could be multiplied almost indefinitely. From the examples given, it is clear that endogamy is practiced most frequently by such groups as castes, classes, and racial, ethnic, and religious groups.

While exogamy is most frequently found among horticultural societies with unilineal descent groups, endogamy is most often a product of complex, state-level societies. Hence, it is of greatest moment in agrarian and industrial societies. It occurs primarily as a means of preserving a group's economic and political resources or its cultural identity.

BRIDEWEALTH AND DOWRY

In many societies, the transfer of women in marriage is associated with the payment of various forms of wealth to the kin group of the bride. This is often said to compensate her group for the loss of her economic and reproductive services. Such payment is known as **bridewealth.** Bridewealth is especially prevalent in patrilineal societies and is much less common in societies having matrilineal, double, or bilateral descent. Van den Berghe (1979) reports that 71 percent of patrilineal societies make use of bridewealth, compared to only 37 percent of matrilineal societies and only 32 percent of societies with double or bilateral descent. It is not at all difficult to see why bridewealth should be much less frequently found among matrilineal societies; here, of course, women's economic and reproductive services are never lost to their own kin groups. What is somewhat surprising is why bridewealth exists at all in matrilineal societies.

Far less common is **dowry,** a system whereby a woman takes property with her into a marriage. While dowry seems to mean the opposite of bridewealth, this is not quite the case. For dowry actually means that a woman receives an early inheritance from her parents, and she is able to use this inheritance to contract a marriage (van den Berghe, 1979; Goody, 1976). This practice is almost exclusively restricted to complex agrarian societies characterized by intensive social stratification. Its function appears to be to allow a woman to obtain a husband of equal or higher status (van den Berghe, 1979); thus it serves to preserve the social and economic standing of whole families.

Valuable studies of bridewealth and dowry have been carried out by Jack Goody (1976) and by Alice Schlegel and Rohn Eloul (1988). Goody found that bridewealth was the principal mode of contracting marriage in Africa, while dowry was widespread throughout European and Asian agrarian societies. In attempting to explain these observations, Goody relied heavily on the fact that the African societies practiced horticulture, while in Europe and Asia plow agriculture predominated. The African societies were less stratified and had lower population densities and more available land. By contrast, the Eurasian agrarian societies had intensive social stratification, high population densities, and a scarcity of land. These divergent features of the two regions make bridewealth adaptive in the one, but dowry much more adaptive in the other. Marvin Harris explains why this would be the case (1979:106–107):

> As Goody suggests, we can begin to lift the veil on puzzles such as why bride price is the char-

A woman in Jeddah, Saudi Arabia, wearing a *hijazi* veil, an important form of dowry.

acteristic mode of legitimizing marriages in Africa, whereas across preindustrial Europe and Asia, dowry was and is the predominant form of marital exchange. Given the greater extent of economic differentiation in the plow regions, marriage alliances functioned to consolidate property holdings within classes, estates, castes, and descent groups. As Goody explains, dowry is used to prevent property from passing out of privileged strata into less privileged strata. Bride price, on the other hand, expresses a greater willingness to share privileges compatible with a situation in which population density is relatively low, land is cheap, and the social distance between rulers and commoners is not very great.

. . . African elites use the bride price to establish and consolidate alliances. As wife-givers, they receive wealth from, rather than give wealth to, each son-in-law. And they pay out for each son's wife. This system is predicated upon a much greater degree of equality between the sexes than in the dowry system. Dowry is unintelligible unless it is seen as an attempt to compensate husbands for the responsibility of supporting women whose productive and reproductive potentials are held in small esteem. . . . Dowry, in other words, is a symptom of acute reproductive pressure; while bride price is a symptom of the ability of the infrastructure to absorb more labor.

Schlegel and Eloul reach similar conclusions on the basis of their worldwide study of bridewealth and dowry (1988:301):

We suggest that bridewealth is most likely to occur in food-producing societies where the economic value of women is high, directly through their labor or indirectly through their reproduction of sons. Where there is patrilocal residence, which is usually the case, it serves to circulate women so that no household ends up with fewer women than it produced, thus ensuring that the economic investment that mothers and fathers make in daughters is not lost but is paid off through daughters-in-law. . . .

The effect on households of dowry is very different, concentrating rather than circulating them. . . . Women take property into marriage. By doing so, they balance the economic claims they make on their new households, where female labor does not have the same high value it does in bridewealth societies, with the property they bring in. The result is that where there is patrilocal residence, the woman's claim on houseroom is, in essence, "paid for" by the dowry she contributes.

The existence of bridewealth and dowry demonstrates that marriage quite frequently reflects the larger interests of entire groups of kinspeople. (Many other aspects of human marriage systems, such as exogamy, also reveal the same thing.) The spatial and social distribution of systems of bridewealth and dowry also reveals that, like so many other features of human social behavior, marriage practices are highly responsive to underlying material conditions.

MARRIAGE, FAMILY, AND KINSHIP IN EVOLUTIONARY PERSPECTIVE

Unlike the evolution of such phenomena as technology, economy, and political organization, the evolution of family and kinship systems reveals no overall linear direction. On the contrary, the evolution of family systems reveals a *curvilinear* pattern (Blumberg and Winch, 1977); small-scale nuclear families coupled with bilateral descent predominate at the hunting and gathering and industrial ends of the evolutionary spectrum, while more elaborate unilineal corporate descent groupings are concentrated in societies found closer to the middle ranges of the spectrum (i.e., in horticultural and many agrarian societies). Furthermore, it is not possible to view different forms of unilocal residence and unilineal descent as representing different "stages" in sociocultural evolution. Patrilocality and matrilocality, for example, as well as patriliny and matriliny, are different adaptations to different underlying conditions; none of these can be placed as "lower" or "higher" (or as "earlier" or "later") developments in sociocultural evolution (i.e., they are forms of specific rather than general evolution [cf. Aberle, 1961]). Nevertheless, marriage, family, and kinship systems are general evolutionary phenomena, for they display regular variations along the entire course of evolutionary transformation.

Based on a sample of 90 hunter-gatherer societies, Martin and Voorhies (1975) found that 62 percent were bilateral, 26 percent were patrilineal, and only 12 percent had either double or matrilineal descent. Residence is typically patrilocal or bilocal, and the nuclear family unit is given great emphasis. Hunting and gathering societies therefore tend to have very flexible family systems that are highly adaptive under the migratory conditions of a foraging existence. Despite the similarity of hunting and gathering family patterns to those found in industrial societies, there is a crucial difference. Among hunter-gatherers, kinship represents the whole fabric of social life, and virtually everyone is a kinsman. Thus kinship dominates the social lives of hunter-gatherers to an extent that would be inconceivable to the members of industrial societies.

Marriage in hunting and gathering societies is frequently polygynous, but polygyny occurs less often here than among horticulturalists. Marriage is sometimes legitimated with bridewealth, but, again, this occurs far more infrequently than in horticultural societies. Exogamy rules are invariably applied to the nuclear family, and quite often they are extended to larger categories of kin. Occasionally they apply to the entire band.

Horticultural societies are overwhelmingly characterized by the existence of corporate descent groups, generally of the unilineal variety. Patriliny is the most frequent descent type, but matriliny occurs in a fair proportion of cases. Martin and Voorhies (1975), using a sample of 104 horticultural societies, report that patriliny occurs in 56 percent of them, matriliny occurs in 24 percent, double descent in 3 percent, and bilateral descent in 16 percent. In most such societies, the nuclear family becomes highly subordinate to these larger groups of kin. Such large-scale kin groups dominate the fabric of social life, and they define for each individual his or her proper place in the world. Individuals relate to one another on the basis of their membership in these corporate groups—as members of the same or different groups and as particular kinds of relatives in the same group. All social activities are carried out within the framework of kinship.

Such groups become so prominent at this stage of sociocultural evolution because they arise to regulate the access of individuals to land and the products of that land. Unilineal descent has the great advantage of allowing the formation of discrete, mutually exclusive, nonoverlapping groups of kinspeople. This permits each person to be a member of one and only one distinct group. Membership in such a group defines one's rights in land and other property and, additionally, establishes a distinct set of relatives who may provide aid and assistance when required.

Corporate descent groups play vital roles in the regulation of marriage. They are typically exogamous, and this forces persons to seek mates among groups other than their own. Marriage in horticultural societies is frequently polygynous, and the vast majority of horticulturalists clearly prefer this form of plural marriage. The payment of bridewealth very of-

Members of an extended family in eastern Poland on their way to church. Where peasants still survive, as in the contemporary underdeveloped world or in sizable parts of Eastern Europe, extended families are generally the norm because they are highly adaptive in the context of the economic conditions peasants face.

ten accompanies marital transactions, especially in patrilineal societies.

With the rise of intensive social stratification and the state in agrarian societies, kin groups begin to decline in significance. Classes, castes, and estates become key elements in social organization and begin to displace some of the former functions of kinship groups. The state replaces kinship as the prime integrator of society. While kinship remains of durable significance in the lives of most individuals, its structure changes. Unilineal descent declines in favor of a rise in bilateral descent, and both descent types are about equally represented in agrarian societies. A sample of 53 agrarian societies shows 45 percent of them to be patrilineal, another 45 percent to be bilateral, and only 9 percent to be matrilineal (Martin and Voorhies, 1975). Thus, while many agrarian societies continue to have corporate descent groups, almost as many have large bilateral extended families.

Although many agrarian societies have institutionalized polygyny, monogamy is overwhelmingly the marriage practice of most people. This expresses the increased costs associated with supporting more than one wife. Furthermore, endogamy is probably more important than exogamy as a marriage principle in most agrarian societies. Marriage becomes highly restricted to the members of one's own class, caste, or ethnic group. Bridewealth payments virtually disappear in favor of dowry.

Industrial societies are integrated by complex economies and states, not by kinship. Kinship and family life come to be greatly reduced in significance. The nuclear family emerges as the predominant family unit, and bilaterally extended kin networks, though still in existence, play a much smaller role in social life. The family in industrial societies is a much less functional unit than in preindustrial societies, many of its former functions having been usurped by other institutions. It is, for example, no longer a unit of economic production, but is relegated to a consumptive role in the economy.

Marriage in industrial societies is universally monogamous, with polygamy legally prohibited. In addition, it is strongly regulated by endogamous considerations. People tend to marry within their own social class and racial, ethnic, and religious groupings. Within this context, marriage is largely a matter of mutual free choice unconstrained by the larger interests of kin groups.

SUMMARY

1. The most basic types of kin group in human societies are nuclear families, extended families, and corporate descent groups. Nuclear families consist of a husband, a wife, and their offspring living together and maintaining a common household. Extended families are larger networks of related nuclear families. Corporate descent groups are especially large extended family groupings found in many preindustrial societies.

2. All societies have means for organizing residence and descent groups. Residence groups are groups of kinspeople who maintain a common household. They may be patrilocal, matrilocal, avunculocal, bilocal, ambilocal, natolocal, or neolocal. Descent groups are groups of individuals who organize themselves according to certain principles of kinship connection. These principles may be patrilineal, matrilineal, double, ambilineal, or bilateral in nature.

3. Patrilineal descent is the most common descent type in the world's societies. It traces descent through the father, and descent groups are formed around the relationship between father and son. Patrilineal groups are almost always patrilocal. Matrilineal descent is a less common type that traces descent through the mother's line. The core of a matrilineal descent group consists of a set of sisters and their brothers who are managers of the group's affairs. Matrilineal descent systems are unique in their establishment of "sociological fatherhood," an arrangement in which children are reared primarily by their maternal uncles rather than by their biological fathers. Matrilineal descent groups are most commonly matrilocal or avunculocal, but they also employ other residence arrangements.

4. Most social scientists believe that residence systems are established first and give rise to descent arrangements. Patrilocality and patriliny seem to be found under a wide range of infrastructural and structural conditions, but especially where there is high population pressure, frequent warfare with neighboring societies, and the concentration of wealth. The most generally accepted theory of matrilocality is that it arises from conditions requiring men frequently to be absent from their home territories for long periods of time. Warfare conducted at long distances from home seems to be the most common reason for such absence. Once matrilocality has developed, matriliny seems to arise naturally from it. Some matrilocal and matrilineal societies tend to evolve in the direction of preserving their matrilineal institutions but adopting avunculocality, possibly due to the need to reunite male kinsmen to manage new forms of wealth.

5. The three basic forms of marriage throughout the world are monogamy, polygyny, and polyandry. Polygyny is the preferred marriage form in most of the world's societies, but most people end up marrying monogamously. Polyandry is a rare practice.

6. Incest avoidance is a universal feature of human societies. Many societies actually establish very strong sanctions against incest. There is little consensus among social scientists about the causes of incest avoidance. Arguments suggesting that incest has been prohibited because it would threaten the stability of the group have been the most common. Others believe that incest avoidance may arise from natural biological inclinations. Some recent evidence supports this view. Incest avoidance should not be confused with exogamy, which is a prohibition of marriage within corporate descent groups. Exogamy is widespread in primitive societies, and seems to play a crucial role in establishing alliances among kinship groups so as to minimize destructive social conflict. Endogamy is a widespread practice in complex stratified societies. It is the tendency for people to marry within their own class, race, etc.

7. In many primitive societies bridewealth is commonly paid by the kinship group of the groom to the kinship group of the bride, allegedly to compensate the wife's group for the loss of her productive and reproductive services. In agrarian societies dowry replaces bridewealth. Dowry is a fund of valuables a woman accumulates in order to contract a marriage in the first place.

8. Marriage, family, and kinship are evolutionary phenomena, although not in any simple way. The relationship between kinship and a society's technological stage of development is curvilinear. Bilateral descent and emphasis on the nuclear family tend to be found at the least and most advanced ends of the evolutionary spectrum, that is, among hunter-gatherers and industrialists. Horticultural societies commonly have unilineal corporate descent groups. These groups play important roles in the management of land. Agrarian societies also tend to emphasize unilineal corporate descent groups, although not so strikingly as horticultural societies.

SPECIAL TOPIC: SOLIDARITY AND POLITICAL ECONOMY IN MARITAL EXCHANGE

One of the more fascinating features of primitive societies concerns certain aspects of their marriage practices. In many band and tribal societies women are often exchanged in marriage between and among exogamous descent groups according to very definite criteria.

In numerous societies the form of marital exchange is what Claude Lévi-Strauss (1969; orig. 1949) has called **restricted exchange,** or what is often known as **bilateral cross-cousin marriage.** In this situation, women are mutually exchanged by descent groups in each generation. Thus if the women of Group A marry into Group B, then the women of Group B marry into Group A. A descent group will generally have exchange relations with more than one other descent group, in which case any group to whom it gives women will give it women in return, and in the very same generation. What restricted exchange really amounts to is an agreement among the men of different descent groups to exchange women mutually as marriage partners generation after generation.

A cross-cousin is the offspring of one's father's sister or one's mother's brother (offspring of the father's brother or mother's sister are known as parallel cousins). In restricted exchange the system is actually structured so that a young boy will marry a girl who is simultaneously his father's sister's daughter and his mother's brother's daughter. She is thus a double, or bilateral, cross-cousin.

The other major type of marital exchange that Lévi-Strauss speaks of is called generalized exchange, which has two subtypes. **Short-cycle generalized exchange,** also known as **patrilateral cross-cousin marriage,** occurs when the descent groups doing the exchanging skip a generation in returning women to other groups. Thus if Group A gave women to Group B in one generation, then B would not give women to A until the following generation. Both A and B are mutually exchanging women, but unlike restricted exchange the relationship alternates between generations. This form of exchange is called patrilateral cross-cousin marriage because it logically results in a young boy marrying his father's sister's daughter.

Long-cycle generalized exchange (or **matrilateral cross-cousin marriage**) involves highly asymmetrical exchange relations between descent groups. In this form of exchange, groups stand in permanent wife-giving or wife-taking relations with other groups. Thus if Group C gives to Group D, then it never takes back from D. Likewise D may give wives to F, but if so it never receives wives in return from F. This marriage arrangement results in young boys marrying their mother's brother's daughter: hence the name matrilateral cross-cousin marriage.

As we noted in the main body of the text, Lévi-Strauss's theory of marital exchange is that it results from the attempt of kinship groups to form alliances with one another so as to achieve an acceptable level of societal integration. Exchanging women is thus a form of reciprocity, and this reciprocity helps to prevent or minimize destructive social conflict. Lévi-Strauss believes this is the case in all three types of exchange. He notes, though, that in regard to generalized exchange, matrilateral marriage is much more common than the patrilateral variety. He argues that this is so because matrilateral marriage ties more groups together and produces a higher level of social solidarity.

Marvin Harris has strongly questioned this interpretation of generalized exchange.

Harris concedes that bilateral marriage can be explained as an attempt to generate solidarity. Bilateral marriage, though, is characteristic of highly egalitarian societies, whereas generalized exchange tends to be found in societies on the verge of, or already in the early stages of, social stratification. Harris suggests that generalized exchange is an important aspect of the stratification systems of these societies, and that it must be understood as a social device designed not to promote social solidarity but to serve the interests of superordinate groups.

Since matrilateral marriage is far more common than patrilateral marriage, Harris devotes special attention to trying to explain it. He suggests that where matrilateral marriage prevails the wife-giving groups are superordinate and their giving of wives to subordinate groups is the principal means whereby they create and maintain their domination. In giving women to other groups they receive in return certain highly valued forms of material compensation. For example, among the Kachin of Burma, a tribal society with perhaps the best-studied system of matrilateral marriage (cf. Leach, 1954), the dominant descent groups give women to subordinate groups and receive cattle and labor services in return. Thus, for Harris matrilateral marriage is not an instrument of social solidarity, but rather one of political economy. As he remarks (1979:183–184):

> *Matrilateral marriage, far from promoting solidarity, reflects a breakdown in reciprocity, and a movement toward differential control over production and reproduction by hierarchized descent groups. . . . Matrilateral marriage divides a community up into descent groups that stand to each other as wife-givers to wife-takers. To be compensated for the "gift" of their sisters and daughters, the wife-givers do not wait upon the completion of the cycle A→B→C→A. Rather, they almost always demand immediate compensation in the form of bride price or bride service or a combination of both. This means that any group managing to raise and marry off more daughters than another group is in a position to concentrate wealth and labor power to a greater extent than other groups.*
>
> *On the average, the larger the descent group, the larger the number of daughters. The more daughters, the greater the concentration of dependent labor power and wealth in the form of sons-in-law and bride price. Large prosperous groups have no difficulty in meeting their obligations both as wife-givers and wife-takers. Smaller and less prosperous groups, however, soon become in effect dependents of the larger ones, and as their fortunes decline, their married men may even take up residence among the dominant wife-givers . . . as permanent second-class citizens.*

FOR FURTHER READING

Fox, Robin. *Kinship and Marriage*. Baltimore: Penguin Books, 1967. An extremely well-written and highly informative introduction to the comparative study of marriage and kinship systems. Excellent chapters on incest avoidance, residence, descent, and marital exchange systems.

Goody, Jack. *Production and Reproduction: A Comparative Study of the Domestic Domain*. New York: Cambridge University Press, 1976. A valuable discussion of how the organization of economic production shapes many features of family structure. Focuses upon the ways in which Eurasian agrarian family systems diverge from those found in African horticultural societies.

Keesing, Roger M. *Kin Groups and Social Structure*. New York: Holt, Rinehart and Winston,

1975. A good brief introduction to the major features of kinship systems in primitive societies. The varieties of kinship organization are nicely illustrated with numerous ethnographic case studies.

Paige, Karen Ericksen, and Jeffery M. Paige. *The Politics of Reproductive Ritual.* Berkeley: University of California Press, 1981. A provocative attempt to interpret widespread social rituals, such as female puberty rites, male circumcision rituals, and segregation of menstruating women, as mechanisms for generating political solidarity in preindustrial societies.

Schneider, David M., and Kathleen Gough (eds.). *Matrilineal Kinship.* Berkeley: University of California Press, 1961. The most comprehensive source available on matrilineal descent systems. Detailed case studies of different matrilineal societies in addition to discussions of the general features of matrilineal kinship.

Shepher, Joseph. *Incest: A Biosocial View.* Orlando: Academic Press, 1983. A recent and highly comprehensive review of evidence favoring a sociobiological interpretation of incest avoidance.

van den Berghe, Pierre L. *Human Family Systems: An Evolutionary View.* New York: Elsevier, 1979. Contains many useful discussions of a wide range of kinship phenomena and attempts to show how both biological and sociocultural factors are intertwined in shaping these behavioral patterns.

Winch, Robert F. *Familial Organization.* New York: Free Press, 1977. A valuable collection of essays by Winch and his associates on a variety of topics, such as family organization in evolutionary perspective and the material forces underlying family systems.

CHAPTER 16

The Development of the Modern Western Family

Most readers of this book live in a society whose family system is based on the strong affection and close companionship of the spouses, and in which the basis of marriage is romantic love rather than economics or family lineage. Young people expect to choose a spouse free from family dictates and to have a close companionate and sexual relationship with that person. Yet this mode of family and marital life is a unique creation of the modern world. Nowhere before about the seventeenth or eighteenth century in the West was family and marital life organized in this fashion.

This chapter tells the story of the evolution of the modern Western family system. It examines family life in preindustrial Europe and North America and the profound changes it began to undergo some centuries ago. It explores several aspects of family life in the contemporary era, particularly racial and social class variations in family patterns; the current upheaval in relations between husband and wife reflected in skyrocketing divorce rates and increased preference for cohabitation in the absence of marriage; and the current crisis in the relations between parents and their adolescent children. The chapter concludes with some thoughts about the possible future of the family.

HOUSEHOLD COMPOSITION IN THE PREINDUSTRIAL WEST

In all modern industrial societies the nuclear family is overwhelmingly dominant. The close relationship between the industrial mode of social life and the nuclear family once led sociologists to argue that industrialization caused the emergence of the nuclear family. It was thought that prior to industrialization people throughout western Europe and North America lived basically in large extended families. In the last 20 years or so, however, new research by sociologists and social historians interested in the history of the Western family has shown that this older view is incorrect, or at least that it must be strictly qualified.

Two of the earliest sociologists to challenge the traditional wisdom were Sidney Greenfield (1961) and Frank Furstenburg (1966). Both Greenfield and Furstenburg claimed that the nuclear family was commonly found in Colonial America and western Europe long before industrialization, and that the effects of industrialization on family structure had been exaggerated. But perhaps the most important research on this issue has been carried out by the British historical sociologist Peter Laslett and his colleagues (Laslett, 1977; Laslett and Wall, 1972). Detailed empirical studies have convinced Laslett that most people in Colonial America and in England, France, and Germany during the seventeenth and eighteenth centuries lived in nuclear family households whose average size was about five or six members. Moreover, Laslett argues that predominance of the nuclear family was unique to western Europe and North America; in eastern Europe and non-Western civilizations, the familiar extended family pattern was much more characteristic.

It is interesting that family patterns in preindustrial Europe bore a close relationship to the spread of capitalism (Table 16.1). Those areas where core capitalism had penetrated most significantly were overwhelmingly characterized by nuclear family arrangements. Other areas of western Europe, such as southern France and parts of Germany and Austria, tended to have a type of extended family known as the **stem family** as the dominant type (Shorter, 1975). In the stem family, the farmer and his wife passed their farm to one of their sons. The son and his wife took over farming the land and lived with the son's parents until their death. With the birth of the son's children, there would for a time be three generations living together in extended family style. In eastern Europe an even more elaborate extended family system was the norm. In Yugoslavia the main family unit was known as the *zadruga* (Shorter, 1975). The *zadruga* was a household of perhaps three or four nuclear families who submitted to the authority of a patriarch and who constituted a single economic unit. The average *zadruga* con-

Table 16.1 HOUSEHOLD COMPOSITION IN SELECTED PREINDUSTRIAL COUNTRIES

Country	Community/region	Date	% simple family households	% complex family households
1. Colonial America	Rhode Island	1689	97	3
2. Belgium	Lampernisse	1814	69	20
3. Belgium	Lisswege	1739	85	12
4. Northern France	Villages around Valenciennes	1693	86	11
5. Northern France	Brueil-en-Vexin	1625	84	7
6. England	30 reliably recorded villages	1622–1821	72	15
7. Russia	Kurland (Spahren estate)	1797	43	51
8. Russia	Mishino estate	1814	8	85
9. Serbia	Belgrade	1733	55	32
10. Estonia	Vandra	1683	45	52
11. Hungary	Alsónyék	1792	44	54
12. Italy	Molise, Isernia	1753	63	37
13. Italy	Fiesole, Tuscany	1790	40	51
14. Southern France	Montplaisant	1644	51	37
15. Southern France	Mirabeau	1745	51	42
16. Austria	Heidenreichstein manor	1763	—	25
17. Germany	Grossenmeer	1785	68	30

Note: Simple family households consist of a married couple, or a married couple (or widow) with children. Complex family households are extended families of one type or another.

Sources: 1. Laslett (1977); 2. Danhieux (1983); 3. Laslett (1977); 4. Flandrin (1979); 5. Lions and Lachiver (1967); 6. Laslett (1977); 7. Plakans (1982); 8. Czap (1983); 9. Laslett (1977); 10. Palli (1974); 11. Andorka and Farago (1983); 12. Douglass (1980); 13. Laslett (1977); 14. Biraben (1970); 15. Flandrin (1979); 16. Berkner (1972); 17. Laslett (1983).

tained anywhere from 10 to 30 members. In parts of Russia a similar type of extended family called the *Gesind* prevailed. This was a household averaging about 14 members (Shorter, 1975).

It thus seems that the rise of the nuclear family in the West was more closely linked to the development of capitalism than to industrialization. In fact, as the above clearly suggests, and as Table 16.1 indicates even more dramatically, there seems to have been a very close relationship between European household patterns and the hierarchical structuring of the capitalist world-economy during its early stages (Alderson and Sanderson, 1989). Not only was it in the capitalist core that the nuclear family household first became established as the norm, but the more economically dissimilar a region was to the core the less likely was it to contain nuclear family households. Thus, household patterns were more likely to be complex in semiperipheral regions than in the core, but peripheral regions were even more likely to have complex households (and, when they had them, to have complex households of greater size and elaborateness).

The reason for this association between household structure and types of capitalist production has to do with the way in which households respond to labor needs (Alderson and Sanderson, 1989). In the core, the nuclear family household was economically adaptive for the capitalist farmers who were increasingly coming to characterize this zone. The existence of a capitalist labor market made it more efficient for farmers to hire agricultural workers than to produce them themselves. The economic demands faced by semiperipheral sharecroppers and peripheral peasants, however, were very different. Such workers were under strong pressures to keep their levels of economic production very high, for they were producing for some type of overlord, and not just for themselves. This created a need for extensive labor teams, and such teams had to be created largely by relying on family members. In the case of peripheral peasants, the absence of a capitalist labor market offered no choice in the matter. Semiperipheral sharecroppers often could draw on a capitalist labor market to hire some of the labor they needed, and sometimes did so. However, this strategy was usually too economically costly and thus tended to be avoided (Berkner and Shaffer, 1978).

What then remains of the thesis that industrialization has caused the nuclear family? Although the thesis must obviously be highly qualified, it need not be abandoned entirely. Clearly industrialization has accelerated the move toward the nuclear family even in those regions where such a family form preceded industrialization. Moreover, in those parts of the world where the nuclear family was not the dominant form before industrialization, industrialization has produced a marked movement toward the dominance of the nuclear family (Goode, 1970). In Japan from the seventeenth to the middle of the nineteenth century, for example, the extended family was widespread (Laslett, 1977). Yet in modern Japan the nuclear family is clearly the norm (Kumagai, 1986). Because of the demands for geographic mobility produced by a modern industrial economy, the extended family would be a major encumbrance in the lives of most individuals, and thus the nuclear family is really the only suitable type.

In addition, once the extended family is no longer economically adaptive, the emphasis on the nuclear family may well be encouraged by the desire of individuals in the West for greater freedom from control by the older generation. This notion is suggested by a comparison of the West with Japan. In Japan the emphasis on the nuclear family has not gone as far as it has in the West (Kumagai, 1986), and Japan is notable for its antagonism to Western-style individualism and freedom. (The significance of this emphasis on freedom in the shaping of the modern family will be explored more fully at a later point in the chapter.)

THE EVOLUTION OF THE MODERN FAMILY SYSTEM

The story of the emergence of the modern family is a fascinating one, and has been told especially well by two contemporary social historians, Edward Shorter in his book *The Making of the Modern Family* (1975) and Lawrence Stone in *The Family, Sex and Marriage in England, 1500–1800* (1979). Shorter's study concentrates on France, but he believes his analysis to be applicable to most of western Europe. He believes that the transition to the modern family in most of western Europe began around the middle of the eighteenth century. Stone's book deals with England, and he dates the beginning of the transition toward modernism there about a century earlier. Both writers are basically agreed that this family transition began in the middle and upper classes and diffused later to the lower classes.

The Traditional European Family

The premodern European family bears little resemblance to the modern family in terms of the whole tone and texture of familial relationships. There is, first of all, little evidence that the relationship between husband and wife was typically one based upon strong mutual affection and a sense of companionship. Although romantic love as we know it today existed, it was uncommon and was not considered an appropriate basis for marriage. Marriages were arranged by the families of the respective spouses, and economic considerations determined the choice of a spouse, or even the decision to marry at all. Clearly marital unions were fundamentally economic rather than affective relationships. As Shorter has noted in this connection (1975:57):

> The prospect of death seemed to arouse no deep sentiments between spouses. Among rustics to the east of Paris (Seine-et-Marne), special testamentary provisions were seldom made for spouses in a will. And so much more firmly did economics rather than emotion bind together the peasant couple that when the wife fell ill, her husband commonly spared the expense of a doctor, though prepared to "cascade gold" upon the veterinarian who came to attend a sick cow or bull. That was because, in the last analysis, a cow was worth much more than a wife.

Of course a wife was valuable—and precisely in economic terms. Her domestic labor was essential, and she played a crucial role as a producer of offspring. Yet her value to her husband went little beyond this, and social and economic conditions in premodern Europe really did not permit the development of strong affection within the marital relationship.

The premodern parent-child relationship was also vastly different from its modern counterpart. There seems to have been little in the way of sentimental ties between parents and their children. Mothers infrequently nursed their own children. Children were commonly fostered out right after birth to paid wet-nurses who cared for them for perhaps a year or more. Moreover, children were frequently treated in ways that today would be regarded as extreme forms of child abuse. They were left unattended for long periods of time, often were hung by their clothing on hooks to keep them out of the way, and, as Shorter has remarked, were frequently left to "stew in their own excrement" for long hours. In addition, they were commonly subjected to all manner of violence from which they frequently died or suffered great injury. There is also the fact that children in the same family were often given the same first name. A newborn infant might be given the name of an older sibling who had recently died, or two living children might have the very same name. This suggests no conception of the child as a unique individual with whom a parent can have a special relationship.

The reason for this indifferent or even callous attitude toward children must be sought in the difficult economic and social conditions of the day. As Stone has pointed out, the rate of infant death was so high in premodern Europe that it would have been unthinkable for a mother to invest considerable emotion in her children. To become emotionally attached to them, then watch them die in such high proportions, would be too traumatic an experience to bear. The basic lack of parental affection, then, was not something parents voluntarily chose, but rather something that was imposed on them by external conditions. Parental indifference was a predictable (and psychologically adaptive) response to debilitating economic conditions and a high rate of infant and child death.

A final characteristic of the traditional family was its fundamental lack of privacy or "separateness" from the rest of society. The family form that most of us live in today—a private social unit relatively isolated from the rest of society—scarcely existed. As Shorter has remarked, the traditional family was "pierced full of holes." Outsiders interacted freely with members of the household, and the relations between family members and outsiders were just as close as those among the family members themselves. There was, in other words, no real boundary between the family and the rest of society.

The Rise of the Modern Family

The traditional family was basically an economic subsystem of the larger society, "much more a productive and reproductive unit than an emotional unit" (Shorter, 1975:5). It was most vitally concerned with transmitting property between the generations and with reproducing the species. Its crucial role as a transmitter of property explains the powerful role of family elders in the arrangement of marriage. But in the seventeenth and eighteenth centuries this mode of family life began to decay and give way to the kind of family unit familiar to us in the late twentieth century. Lawrence Stone has suggested that the rise of the modern family involved the emergence of four fundamental characteristics: increasing ties of affection between family members; a growing concern with the right to individual freedom and happiness in marriage; growing concern with sexual pleasure and an increasing tendency to separate it from sin and guilt; and a growing desire for a private family life.

One of the most important aspects of the transition to the modern family was the emergence of romantic love as the basis for marriage. Romantic love has no doubt existed since the earliest human societies, but in no society before the seventeenth or eighteenth century has it played a significant role in the selection of marriage partners. The rise of romantic love as the basis for marriage was an extraordinarily revolutionary phenomenon.

There were really two aspects of this phenomenon. First, young people began to reject parental interference in the choice of marriage partners and increasingly demanded the right to choose for themselves. Second, the marriage itself came increasingly to be seen as an affective rather than an economic unit, one held together by the sentimental attachment of the spouses rather than by considerations of property ownership. The tie between the spouses thus shifted from an emotionally weak or indifferent one to one in which affection was of paramount significance. They were becoming companions sharing a long life together. Spouses (and courting couples) began to idealize one another and to prefer each other's company to that of everyone else. They spent countless hours with each other, called each other by special names of endearment, and expressed their attachment in poetry, literature, and song.

One of the most interesting features of eighteenth- and nineteenth-century literature, for instance, is the rise of the romantic novel, a magnificent symbolic expression of the great family change that was occurring.

The sentimental revolution in the family also transformed the relations between parents and their children; a growing concern of parents (mothers in particular) for the welfare of their children became manifest. Mothers began to breast-feed their children rather than send them out to wet-nurses, and to concern themselves with child-rearing practices that would produce healthy personalities. There was a dramatic decline in the neglect and physical abuse of children, and methods of punishment were progressively liberalized. An era of permissiveness in child rearing was clearly dawning.

Sexual behavior also began to change in major ways. In premodern Europe there was, of course, a sexual urge present in both sexes, and both men and women sought out sex for pleasure to some extent. Yet marital and nonmarital sex were both infrequent and relatively insignificant by modern standards. The relations between the sexes were, as Shorter has suggested, "resolutely unerotic." It is likely that premarital sexual behavior was uncommon, especially for women, and extramarital affairs were in all probability very infrequent (for women they must have been extremely rare). There is also little evidence of much autoerotic behavior.

The seventeenth and eighteenth centuries witnessed a major change in these traditional sexual patterns. A great increase in premarital sex seems to have occurred in these times, for we see a marked rise in rates of illegitimacy. Marital sex also seemed to become more common and to be given more erotic significance. Social life was becoming, at least relative to the past, highly eroticized, and the idea of sexual pleasure as an end in itself was becoming significant.

Hardly less important than these changes was the corresponding change in relations between the family and the outside world, what Shorter has called "the rise of domesticity." The modern family was becoming more and more private, and the boundaries between it and the rest of society more and more closely drawn. In the premodern family the relations between family members and outsiders were as close as those among the members of the family itself, but in the seventeenth, eighteenth, and nineteenth centuries all that changed. By the middle of the nineteenth century the family had become a unit insisting upon its private existence and its separation (or even isolation) from the outside world. Shorter provides a clear understanding of what the rise of domesticity was really all about (1975:227–228):

> Domesticity, or the family's awareness of itself as a precious emotional unit that must be protected with privacy and isolation from outside intrusion, was the third great spearhead of the great onrush of sentiment in modern times. Romantic love detached the couple from communal sexual supervision and turned them towards affection. Maternal love created a sentimental nest within which the modern family would ensconce itself, and it removed many women from involvement with community life. Domesticity, beyond that, sealed off the family as a whole from its traditional interaction with the surrounding world. The members of the family came to feel far more solidarity with one another than they did with their various age and sex peer groups. We know in practical terms when domesticity is present if, like the French, people begin removing their names from the front doors to insure that no one will knock; if, as in Germany, long Sunday walks through the woods begin to tear Papa from his card games; and if, as happens everywhere, people begin spending greater proportions of their time at home.

Victorianism and the Twentieth Century

The nineteenth century represented a sort of reversal of the sexual liberalization process. Between about 1800 and 1870 western Europe and North America were caught in the throes of increasing sexual repression. Strong norms evolved against premarital sexual behavior for both sexes, and even marital sex came to be strongly associated with sin and guilt. This was the era that in retrospect we have come to know as the Victorian age. It was an age in which sex became an unfit topic of discussion between members of the opposite sex, and the human body itself came to be thought of as basically evil. Sex became, as never before, a negatively charged and tabooed realm of human behavior and discourse.

An especially provocative interpretation of Victorianism is that it was a strategy used by women to improve their status at a time when family life, sex roles, and sex itself were undergoing rapid transformation (R. Collins, 1985b; D. Smith, 1974; cf. Cott, 1978). This theory claims that women were attempting to overthrow the sexual double standard because of its adverse effects on them. By establishing a single standard of sexual conduct for both men and women, and thereby restricting sex within the bounds of marriage, women hoped to improve their chances in the new marriage market in which romantic love rather than economic suitability was the basis for marriage.

Whatever the reasons for the Victorian age, it is clear that it was a transitory phenomenon. By the last quarter of the nineteenth century the trend in sexuality that had begun to emerge in the seventeenth and eighteenth centuries clearly reasserted itself, and the twentieth century has by and large witnessed continued sexual liberalization. In fact, beginning in the early 1960s a "second sexual revolution" occurred (Shorter, 1975). There has been a dramatic increase in premarital and extramarital sexuality and a tremendous upsurge of interest in things erotic.

The trends toward romantic love and family privacy have also increased substantially. There has also been an intense increase in concern for children and their development. This, though, has been accompanied by a commitment on the part of some couples not to have children at all. There seems to have developed little in the way of a middle-ground position, especially among the middle and upper-middle classes: either couples decide to have children and invest enormously in them, or they decide to forego them altogether. Although these trends seem logically contradictory, they can be seen as simply two different facets of a single general phenomenon: the intense egoism and individualism that has steadily increased over the centuries since the rise of modern capitalism. People either vicariously live through their children, which is one type of self-absorption, or their self-absorption is so profound that children only constitute obstacles to the satisfaction of their personal needs and wants.

The structure of late-twentieth-century Western families contrasts markedly with that of this Victorian family. Why the changes?

Explaining the Transition to the Modern Family

The evolution of the modern family was largely a product of the vast changes that were taking place during these centuries toward a highly commercialized capitalist civilization (Shorter, 1975; Stone, 1979; Zaretsky, 1976; Lasch, 1977). Shorter links the rise of capitalism to the modern family revolution through the rise of economic individualism (1975:258–259):

> Laissez-faire marketplace organization, capitalist production, and the beginnings of proletarianization among the work force were more important than any other factors in the spread of sentiment.
>
> . . . How did capitalism help cause that powerful thrust of sentiment among the unmarried that I have called the romance revolution? . . . The logic of the marketplace positively demands individualism: the system will succeed only if each participant ruthlessly pursues his own self-interest, buying cheap, selling dear, and enhancing his own interests at the cost of his competitors (i.e., his fellow citizens). Only if this variety of economic egoism is internalized will the free market come up to the high expectations of its apologists, for if people let humanitarian or communitarian considerations influence their economic behavior, the market becomes inefficient; the weak cease to be weeded out. Thus, the free market engraves upon all who are caught up in it the attitude: "Look out for number one."
>
> . . . Egoism that was learned in the marketplace became transferred to community obligations and standards, to ties to the family and lineage—in short, to the whole domain of cultural rules that regulated familial and sexual behavior.
>
> . . . So capitalism exerted its impact upon romantic love through involvement in the market labor force: economic individualism leads to cultural egoism; private gratification becomes more important than fitting into the common weal; the wish to be free produces the illegitimacy explosion.

Exactly what kind of explanation is this? Many scholars have seen it as essentially an idealist rather than a materialist one because of Shorter's emphasis on changing modes of thinking and feeling (M. Anderson, 1980; C. Tilly, 1984). However, it is clear that Shorter's argument cannot be any sort of genuine idealism. Genuine idealist arguments see ideas as self-generating and self-perpetuating, thus ignoring the material or social context in which they originate and persist. This is clearly not what Shorter is doing. On the contrary, he is emphasizing the way in which new modes of thinking and feeling were rooted in changing economic circumstances. If his explanation of family change is not a form of materialism, then it comes very close to it.

This is even more strikingly the case in Shorter's explanation of the emergence of greater parental involvement in children, a phenomenon he links to the rising standard of living. Maternal indifference in premodern Europe was the unfortunate consequence of the low standard of living and the high childhood mortality rate. But with a notable improvement in the standard of living in the eighteenth and nineteenth centuries and a consequent reduction of infant and child death rates, mothers could begin to invest emotionally in their children.

What about the rise of domesticity, the increasing seclusion of the family from the outside world? Christopher Lasch (1977) has suggested that the private family of the eighteenth and nineteenth centuries emerged as a kind of shelter into which people could escape from the increasingly harsh realities of the outside world. The family became, in Lasch's memorable phrase, a "haven in a heartless world." The heartless world that Lasch has in mind is the competitive capitalist marketplace. The intensely competitive character of the work environment created the need for a refuge in which people could recover from the slings and arrows of the work world so as to be able to enter it again. As Lasch (1977:xix) has put it: "As business, politics, and diplomacy grow more savage and warlike, men seek a haven in private life, in personal relations, above all in the family—the last refuge of love and decency."

RACE AND CLASS CONTEXTS OF THE MODERN AMERICAN FAMILY

Working-Class Versus Middle-Class Families

In all modern industrial societies family patterns differ substantially according to social class. Some rather striking differences are found, for example, between working-class and middle-class families in the contemporary United States (Rubin, 1976; Collins, 1985b).

In the working class, marriage usually occurs at a fairly early age, perhaps as early as 17 or 18 for females and slightly later for males. In the middle class, by contrast, marriage is often delayed until well into the twenties for both males and females. These patterns basically reflect the differences in social and economic opportunities for working-class and middle-class youth. A major reason for delaying marriage among middle-class youth is college attendance. As Collins points out, most working-class youth do not go on to college and thus lack any particular motive for delaying marriage. Moreover, youth from the working class are usually eager to emancipate themselves from their parents.

There are also strong differences between the working and middle classes in styles of family interaction and sociability. There is much more sexual segregation of family activities in the working class. Men generally prefer the company of other men and often socialize with them in bars and other local hangouts. Women organize their activities around the domestic sphere, where they spend most of their time socializing with female friends and relatives. By and large, the working class is more family oriented. Working-class families seldom invite others to dinner parties, whereas for the middle class the dinner party is a major means of entertainment. Working-class families often feel more isolated from the outside world, and they tend to confine their sociability to family members (including extended kin) much more than is the case in the middle class.

The working-class family is generally more hierarchical in structure. Relations between husbands and wives and between parents and children are notably less democratic in the working class than in the middle class. Working-class families tend to be strongly dominated by the husband, who makes the major family decisions. He generally expects his wife to take care of the children and manage household affairs, even if she is working outside the home.

Working-class parents tend to use different styles of punishment than middle-class parents do and to have different expectations for their children's behavior. Working-class parents typically expect strict obedience from their children and conformity to dominant cultural values and norms. Punishment for infractions is often physical. Middle-class parents, on the other hand, generally value individuality and independence in their children much more than is typical in the working class. They tend to use psychological rather than physical forms of punishment (withdrawal of love, shame, etc.). These class differences are largely reflections of differences in work patterns. Working-class parents spend their lives taking orders and socialize their children to do the same. Middle-class parents, on the other hand, work at jobs where independence and creativity are more essential traits. They naturally wish to impart to their children the kinds of traits that are most highly valued in the middle-class world of work.

Black and Lower-Class Families

It has long been recognized that family patterns among blacks in the United States have exhibited some significant differences from the family patterns typically found among whites. Black family life is characterized by higher rates of marital desertion, a higher proportion of female-headed households, and a greater num-

Two American families: a middle-class family (*top*) and a working-class family (*bottom*). What influence does social class have on family life in modern Western societies?

ber of births out of wedlock. Moreover, the gap between white and black female-headed households has widened over the past quarter-century. In 1960, 6 percent of white households with dependent children were female-headed, whereas 21 percent of black households were female-headed (U.S. Bureau of the Census, 1985). By 1983 the number of white female-headed households with dependent children had increased substantially, to 14 percent; however, the number of black households headed by women had increased even more dramatically, to a full 48 percent (U.S. Bureau of the Census, 1985). Thus, today virtually half of all black families are female-headed.

Families in which the husband (or lover) deserts his wife (or lover) and leaves her to manage the household are generally known as **matrifocal families.** Matrifocal families are often three-generation extended households in which a grandmother and her daughter earn the living and bring up the children. Although the term *matriarchal* has sometimes been used to identify these units, this term is highly misleading, since it implies that the woman is the power broker within the family. The term *matrifocal* is clearly preferred, because it indicates that the family unit is focused around the mother (and possibly the grandmother as well) in the absence of a husband-father.

One explanation for the much higher proportion of matrifocality in American black families has been given by Daniel Patrick Moynihan (1965), a sociologist who became an advisor to President Nixon and later a U.S. senator from the state of New York. Moynihan argued that the black family was a disorganized, highly crippled structure that had created a "tangle of pathology" amidst black social life. Although such family disorganization was said to be originally traceable to the historical discrimination against blacks in American society, Moynihan argued that, once in existence, the disorganized black family was a self-reinforcing and self-perpetuating institution. As such, it lay at the root of the contemporary plight of blacks in the United States. In order to improve the social and economic status of blacks, Moynihan believed that the "tangle of pathology" had to be eradicated and replaced with a more stable family structure typical of white middle-class Americans.

What Moynihan was really arguing was that the black family was a cultural institution that had become independent of its origins in the American political economy. This assumption immediately engendered a wave of criticism. For example, Andrew Billingsley, one of Moynihan's most outspoken critics, has claimed (1968:199; emphasis added):

> Perhaps the greatest symbol of this kind of distortion in recent years is the widely read and even more widely discussed Moynihan Report. . . . While his own data showed quite the contrary, Moynihan concluded that "at the heart of the deterioration of the fabric of Negro society is the deterioration of the Negro family. It is the fundamental source of the weakness of the Negro community at the present time."
>
> A major distortion was his singling out instability in the Negro family as the causal factor for the difficulties Negroes face in the white society. *It is quite the other way round.*

In other words, Billingsley is arguing that the structure of black family life should be viewed not as a separate and self-perpetuating pattern but as a fundamental response to the social and economic plight of blacks in the United States.

The matrifocal family is by no means limited to the United States. Very similar family patterns have been discovered among the lower-class members of several societies in and around the Caribbean, especially in Barbados, Guyana, and Trinidad (Blumberg and Garcia, 1977). A valuable study of family life among lower-class blacks in Trinidad has been carried out by Hyman Rodman (1971). Rodman observed the familiar matrifocal pattern among these economically marginal Trinidadians: marginality of husband-fathers to their families, a casual attitude between spouses and frequent marital dissolution, a high rate of cohabitation in place of marriage, and a very high rate of illegitimacy. Rodman has been quick to see that this family pattern arose from the socio-economic position of the persons involved. The situation of the Trinidadian lower-class male was one involving poorly paid jobs and high rates of unemployment and underemployment. Because of their highly marginal and insecure economic situation, men were frequently unable to be adequate providers for their families. As Rodman comments, this fact "is so all-pervasive that it has ramifications for the entire system of family and kinship organization" (1971:178). All of the aspects of Trinidadian lower-class family life therefore make perfectly good sense as adaptations to a situation in which men can frequently expect to fail in making adequate economic provision for their families.

We cannot hope to explain the comparable situation of black family life in the United States by invoking the concept of a self-perpetuating "tangle of pathology," a concept that divorces family life from the economic roots that nurture it. Nor can we hope to explain it, as did an earlier generation of scholars, by seeing it as part of a continuing heritage of female-headed households that existed during slavery (Herzog, 1969). Recent research suggests that the image of the female-dominated slave family is largely mythical. Slaves for the most part lived in stable nuclear families with both parents present (Fogel and Engerman, 1974; Gutman, 1976). Indeed, we should be urged to remove the "black" in our terminology and see such families for what they really are: *lower-class* families. As numerous scholars have pointed out, there is nothing particularly distinctive about black families when they are compared to white families of the same socioeconomic level (Herzog, 1969; Blumberg and Garcia, 1977; van den Berghe, 1979). Pierre van den Berghe, for example, notes that "the more economically and socially successful blacks usually have stable, monogamous, nuclear families with few children, much like their white middle-class counterparts" (1979:185–186). And Elizabeth Herzog comments (1969:209): "Descriptions of white families at the very low income levels read very much like current descriptions of poor Negro families, with high incidence of broken homes, 'mother dominance,' births out of wedlock, educational deficit, crowded living, three-generation households, and failure to observe the norms of middle-class behavior." What we are faced with explaining, therefore, is a pattern of family life that frequently occurs among the lower classes of both advanced and peripheral capitalist societies. And such a pattern appears to be a direct response to an economic situation that frequently renders stable, monogamous unions very difficult to maintain.

This conclusion is strongly reinforced by a consideration of recent trends in the proportion of black families in the United States that are female-headed. As already noted, in the past few decades there has been an alarming increase in the number of black families that are headed by women. William Wilson (1987) has studied this trend for the years 1960–1980. He has constructed an index that he calls the "male marriageable pool index" (MMPI), which is the number of employed men per 100 women. The index is based on the logical assumption that to be a suitable candidate for marriage a man must hold a reliable job. For all regions of the United States except the West, Wilson found a close association between the rate of increase of female-headed families among blacks and the rate of decline of the MMPI, leading him to conclude that "in the three regions in which more than 90 percent of the nation's blacks reside, the MMPI remains a powerful predictor of the phenomenal rise of black female-headed families" (1987:100). Deteriorating family arrangements among blacks, then, are closely tied to deteriorating economic conditions.

A lower-class black family (*top*) and a middle-class black family (*bottom*). Black American families are essentially the same as their white counterparts at the same social class level.

THE CONTEMPORARY FAMILY REVOLUTION

Lasch's thesis, noted earlier, is that the modern private family emerged as a haven from the pressures of modern capitalist civilization. Lasch has also suggested, though, that in the past several decades the family itself has been under so much stress that it no longer is able to fulfill its role as a refuge. Whether actually true or not, the Western family since the early 1960s has suffered from enormous strains and has undergone profound changes. These involve both the relations between husbands and wives and those between parents and their adolescent children.

Recent Changes in Marital Relationships

One of the more widely discussed changes in family life since the early 1960s has been the marked increase in cohabitation—couples living together without marriage. Increased cohabitation has been a notable occurrence in all Western industrial societies, although it has been considerably more common in some than in others. In the United States, for instance, there was a doubling of the number of cohabiting couples during the 1970s, and from 1977 to 1979 alone there was a 40 percent increase in the cohabitation rate (Cherlin, 1981). Living together has also become common in France. A 1977 survey found that 31 percent of married couples between 18 and 29 years of age had lived together before they were married (Cherlin, 1981). In Sweden cohabitation has become virtually a universal practice, as 99 percent of Swedish couples live together before marriage (Cherlin, 1981).

The current high rate of cohabitation does not appear to pose a significant threat to marriage. As Andrew Cherlin (1981) suggests, cohabitation seems to be more a preparatory stage for marriage than a permanent substitute for it. That cohabitation has become so common, however, surely suggests that marital and family life has become decidedly different in the past quarter-century, and that people have very different expectations of it.

Another major change in family life in the past quarter-century has been the marked decline in fertility, or women's childbearing activities. The fertility rate rose significantly after World War II, and women whose prime childbearing years came in the mid- to late 1950s were producing an average of 3.2 children apiece (these were, of course, the years of the famous "baby boom"). But since the early 1960s the fertility rate has declined markedly, all the way to 1.9 children per woman for women whose prime childbearing years came in the 1970s. Since the middle of the 1970s the fertility rate seems to have leveled off at this current all-time low (U.S. Bureau of the Census, 1985).

Last, but hardly least, is the trend in divorce. As Figure 16.1 shows, the divorce rate has in general been rising since the mid-nineteenth century. It took a sudden spurt during World War II (because of the disruptive effects of the war upon married life), then returned to its prewar level and remained stable from the late 1940s until the early 1960s. Since then it has increased very sharply, from about 9 divorces per 1000 married women in 1960 to 22 divorces per 1000 married women in 1978. The current rate at which marriages are dissolving is very high. As Cherlin notes (1981:24–25), "If the annual divorce rates stay the same in the 1980s and 1990s as they were in 1977, 48 percent of those who married in 1970 will eventually divorce."

These recent trends in marital relationships are exemplified most strikingly by Sweden (Popenoe, 1988). At the present time Sweden has the lowest marriage rate of any industrial society and one of the highest average ages of first marriage. Since about 1960 marriage has been increasingly replaced by nonmarital cohabitation. For example, in 1960 only about 1

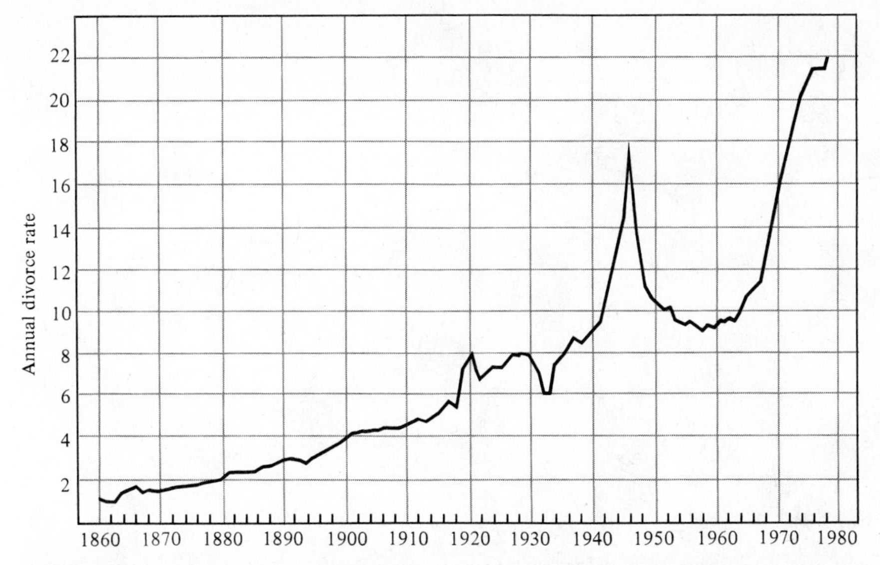

Figure 16.1 Divorce rates in the United States, 1860–1978. The divorce rate shown here is the number of divorces per 1000 married women aged 15 and over (1920–1978), or the number of divorces per 1000 existing marriages (1860–1920). (*Source:* Andrew J. Cherlin, *Marriage, Divorce, Remarriage.* Cambridge: Harvard University Press, 1981, p. 22, Figure 1-4.)

percent of all couples residing together were unmarried, but the number escalated to about 21 percent by 1983 (Popenoe, 1988). Sweden also leads the industrialized world in the percentage of families that are headed by a single parent and in the percentage of all households that are single-person households. In addition, it has the smallest average household size of any industrial society.

Explaining the Recent Family Changes

What accounts for the current upheaval in marital relationships? Why are young people living together frequently before marriage, having fewer children, and divorcing at alarming rates? It has often been said that the current family changes are attributable to changing values and attitudes in regard to family life. This explanation, though, has little to commend it. Even if true, it would be trivial, for we would still be faced with the problem of explaining why attitudes and values in regard to marriage and family life have changed. But the explanation does not even appear to be true. Recent survey and opinion-poll evidence suggests that familial attitudes and values did not begin to change until the late 1960s or early 1970s, whereas the recent behavioral changes in question really began during the early 1960s. It thus seems that changes in values and attitudes have actually followed rather than generated behavioral changes (Cherlin, 1981).

Cherlin's survey of the available evidence suggests to him that these recent trends are due to fundamental economic changes involving the participation of women in the labor force. These trends correspond very closely to the dramatic increase in the proportion of married women with dependent children who work full-time outside the household. As women have entered the labor force in much larger numbers, their economic power has been substantially amplified, and this has reduced their dependence on their husbands. They are therefore much less

Swedish couples. Contemporary trends in familial relationships have gone further in Sweden than in any other Western industrial society.

likely to stay in an unpleasant marriage. In the past women often felt they had little chance to end an unsatisfactory marriage because they would have had great difficulty supporting themselves and their children on their own. But this has now changed dramatically, and with these changes in the balance of power women's expectations of marriage have changed. They expect much more from it and are likely to end it quickly when it does not live up to their hopes. Men's expectations have changed correspondingly, and with both men and women now heavily involved in their careers it is difficult for children to be as important as they once were. Hence young couples are having fewer of them. Finally, cohabitation is a logical response to a higher rate of marital failure. Because they understand how risky marriage has become, young people want to go into it with the feeling that they have a good chance of making theirs work. Cohabitation, then, becomes a kind of trial period for a possible marriage.

Recent Changes in Parent-Child Relations

The current family revolution involves not only a change in marital relations, but just as important a change in the whole character of relations between parents and their children, especially adolescent children. These relations have been changing for a very long time, but in the past two or three decades the changes have accelerated markedly. The changes are in the direction of an increasing loss of parental control over children and an increasing separation of parents and children into two distinct worlds. As Shorter (1975) suggests, children are now caught up in an elaborate youth subculture that has at least as much role in shaping their basic values as do the teachings of their parents. Parents seem to be increasingly irrelevant as educators and teachers of the young, and many youth seem to view their parents (and members of the older generation generally) as having little of value to transmit to them. According to Shorter (1975:276–277), we are witnessing

> a fundamental shift in the willingness of adolescents to learn from their parents. In the 1960s, relations between the generations started to undergo the same evolution that kinship had earlier undertaken: from function to friendship. In the heyday of the modern nuclear family, the prime burden of transmitting values and attitudes to teenage children fell upon the parents, and the rules of the game were learned in the cloistered intimacy of countless evenings about the hearth. But as the post-modern family rushes down upon us, parents are losing their role as educators. The task passes instead to the peers, and with its transfer passes as well a sense of the family as an institution continuing over time, a chain of links across the generations. The parents become friends (an affective relationship), not representatives of the lineage (a functional relationship). If this is so, we are dealing with an unprecedented pattern.

As Shorter has himself noted, this revolution in parent-child relations seems to be a kind of "push-pull" phenomenon. The children have been pulled away by the massive development of an independent youth culture, but they also seem to have been pushed out of the family as a result of the fundamental changes it has undergone. Putting it baldly, parents simply do not have the time for their children that they once did. Given that the dual-career family has become a significant form of family life, it is difficult for either parent to have the time that was once available for intensive socialization and upbringing. Hence the closeness between parents and their children so characteristic of days gone by is more and more missing now, and that makes the pull of the adolescent subculture all the more enticing.

The Current Crisis of the Family

Despite the increased rate of cohabitation and divorce, people still want to marry. At least 90 percent of people are still opting for marriage, and the rate of remarriage after divorce is very high (Cherlin, 1981). So the family is not falling apart as an institution, even though it is very different from what it once was.

Perhaps the real crisis of the family is not that people are living together more without marriage or getting divorced more. Perhaps the real crisis is the increasing inability of the family to function, in Lasch's terms, as a haven or refuge, a development that Shorter refers to as the "destruction of the nest." The family seems to be increasingly losing its capacity to shelter the young and the men from the extreme pressures of competition in an advanced capitalist civilization, and it is exposing the women more and more to these pressures. Surely this has major implications for the psychological well-being of individuals in modern society, as well as for the whole tone and character of social life.*

*This assessment of the crisis of the family obviously conceives the family as a crucial social institution and views its weakening negatively. Although such a positive view of the family seems justified, the negative features of family life cannot be overlooked. As feminist social scientists stress, the family can be an important source of the subordination of women (cf. Thorne and Yalom, 1982; Vogel, 1983; L. Tilly, 1978). Moreover, as we have unfortunately learned in recent years through growing reports of the frequency of spouse abuse and child abuse, it can be a source of actual physical violence as well. Thus, the sexual and generational conflicts that are obviously a significant part of family life have to be weighed in the balance when assessing the overall role of the family in modern social life (Zinn and Eitzen, 1987).

THE FUTURE OF THE FAMILY

Everyone is interested in whether the family has a future. In regard to the immediate years ahead, Shorter sees it as a surviving, but profoundly altered, unit. He anticipates the virtual collapse of the nuclear family as we have known it. Emerging in its place will be the "free-floating couple, a marital dyad subject to dramatic fissions and fusions, and without the orbiting satellites of pubertal children" (Shorter, 1975:280).

While Shorter sees the family surviving even if in substantially different form, many other social observers have predicted the eventual death of the family, at least at some point in the future. Aldous Huxley's famous futuristic novel *Brave New World* and the science-fiction film *Logan's Run,* for instance, both depict a future society in which advanced technology has rendered the family superfluous. In *Logan's Run* few constraints are placed on sexual activity, marital and family units do not exist, and children have no knowledge of who their parents are. Other proponents of the "death of the family" thesis commonly present a message consistent with the theme of family absence found in *Logan's Run:* that advanced technology will eliminate the need for any sort of organized family life and that the family will disappear. Families will not even be necessary for reproduction, for this will take place via "test-tube babies."

Those who predict the long-term death of the family, or even those who see the family as a largely childless unit in the more immediate years ahead, are probably wrong. The existence of universally significant ties of marriage and kinship suggests that, as the sociobiologists insist, kin selection is wired into our basic biological structure. Kin selection involves the biological desire for close attachments between mates, as well as the desire for the production of offspring. Sociobiology can predict little, if anything, about how mating and reproduction will be structured in any particular society, but it can perhaps explain why they will exist *in some form* in all societies. Naturally, the universal existence of a behavioral pattern does not prove that it is biologically rooted, but such a fact is highly suggestive. Kinship not only exists in all societies, it is *important* in all societies.

A recent bit of evidence lends support to the above interpretation. This evidence comes from investigations of patterns of family life in Israeli kibbutzim (Tiger and Shepher, 1975; van den Berghe, 1979). These groups were founded in the early part of the present century on the basis of principles dedicated to sexual, economic, and political equality. The early kibbutzniks attempted to eliminate the separate existence of the family and established communal forms of child rearing. Although the kibbutzim have been highly successful in maintaining an approximate economic and political equality, they have been much less successful in regard to changing the character of family life. Despite their efforts, and in direct violation of kibbutz ideology, the family has emerged as a significant social unit. As Pierre van den Berghe comments (1979:72):

> While unmarried couples are allowed to live together without stigma, the vast majority of kibbutz adults get married and stay married. Kibbutzim now even go as far as financing the wedding party!
>
> Everybody in the kibbutz is, of course, well aware of marital and kin ties between members, and in some of the older kibbutzim which now have many second- and third-generation members, there are even extended families linking dozens of members and forming patterns of political alliances. Meals are taken in a common dining hall, but family groups reconstitute themselves at separate tables, especially for the more leisurely evening meal. Kin selection is obviously at work, and everyone recognizes it, indeed, by now, accepts it as inevitable.

While these findings certainly cannot be regarded as definitive, they do suggest the presence of strong biological propensities in *Homo sapiens* not only to mate, but also to maintain strong ties with close kin.

In conclusion, it would appear that the family is not merely a cultural creation that will be dispensed with when the level of technology so permits. At the same time that the family is a sociocultural phenomenon that varies according to underlying social and cultural conditions, it is also a unit that is probably premised upon the biological propensities and desires of its members. It is thus reasonable to expect some form of it to be found in future societies. While it might not *have* to exist, it is very likely that it *will* exist.

SUMMARY

1. Social scientists have revised their earlier view that industrialization created the modern nuclear family. Recent evidence shows that the nuclear family preceded industrialization in western Europe and North America. The nuclear family arose first in those regions most deeply penetrated by core capitalism.

2. The traditional European family was basically an economic rather than a sentimental institution. Affection was not a significant part of the marital tie, and most parents invested little emotion in their children. In many ways the relations between nonfamily members were as close as those between members of the same family.

3. In the seventeenth and eighteenth centuries the Western family began to evolve in the direction of greater sentimentality. Relations between spouses came to be based increasingly on affection, and romantic love became a common basis for marriage. Parental indifference toward children declined sharply, and parents began to pay much more attention to the personality development of their children. The family was also becoming an increasingly private group sealed off from the outside world.

4. These marked changes in family behavior occurred earliest and most extensively in England and France. They clearly were associated with the rise of modern capitalism. The economic individualism so basic to capitalism seemed to spill over into the organization of marriage and family life, as people grew increasingly concerned with their own individual needs in regard to sex and love. The increasing separation of the family from the outside world, though, seems to be an adaptation to the extreme competitiveness of the capitalist marketplace. The family was becoming a refuge from this competition.

5. In modern industrial societies family patterns differ appreciably in terms of social class and racial distinctions. The working classes are more familistic than the middle classes, and working-class young people marry earlier. Sexual separation in sociable activities is also stronger among the working classes. Working-class parents tend to be less democratic in rearing their children, and working-class families are more likely to be strongly male-dominated.

6. Black families in the United States have high levels of instability. Males frequently desert their wives and children, leaving women in charge of the family. The proportion of black households that are female-headed has increased alarmingly in the past quarter-century. The matrifocal character of the black family seems clearly to result from the economic marginality of black males, and not from any peculiar family value system among blacks. Black matrifocal families are mostly lower-class, and middle-class blacks, like their white counterparts, generally have stable nuclear families.

7. In the past three decades there has been a revolution in family life in modern industrial societies. The divorce rate has skyrocketed, and people live together more frequently without benefit of marriage. Women are also tending to have fewer children and to delay their first pregnancy. These changes seem to be most closely linked to the dramatic increase in the rate at which married women with young children have been entering the labor force. Parent-child relations have also been changing markedly, and in the direction of decreasing parental control over their children.

8. The family is a basic institution likely to survive current and future onslaughts against it. Perhaps kin selection is operative in humans as in other animals. If so, family ties are built on an almost ineradicable biological foundation.

SPECIAL TOPIC: EXTENDED KINSHIP IN INDUSTRIAL SOCIETIES

Although the nuclear family is the basic kinship unit in industrial societies, it is important not to lose sight of the fact that contemporary nuclear families are commonly imbedded in larger networks of extended kinship. Although greatly reduced in significance, extended kin networks are still important social units in industrial societies. Numerous studies of several industrial societies bring out the importance of kinship quite clearly. For example, Edward Shorter (1975) notes that in modern England one witnesses a "stunning intensity of kin contacts." He goes on to remark (1975:237–238):

> *We may offer a mass of evidence indicating the overwhelming importance of mothers and fathers, uncles and aunts, nieces and nephews, brothers and sisters, and in-laws in the life of the average twentieth-century Englishman. . . .*
>
> *The key to the network of relatives seems to be the close tie between mother and daughter, as newlyweds make a considerable effort to locate near the wife's family. But links between the married son and his parents are also strong, as are those that embrace brothers and sisters. . . . Over half of the old people (with married children) interviewed in London's middle-class suburb of Woodford and in London's working-class quarter, Bethnal Green, had seen at least one of their offspring the previous day, and an additional quarter had done so the previous week. On and on roll these studies, documenting how important the larger kin group is in the life of the British nuclear family in the postwar world.*

Numerous studies of the role of extended kin ties in the United States show precisely the same pattern. In summarizing the results of many of these studies, Sussman and Burchinal (1962) suggest the following general conclusions about extended familism: (1) Disintegration of extended family networks in urban areas because of a lack of contact is not a frequent occurrence, and very often just the opposite has happened. (2) Extended family social activities dominate the leisure-time pursuits of urban working-class couples. (3) Visiting of extended kinspeople is a primary activity of urban dwellers, outranking visitation with friends, neighbors, and co-workers. (4) The members of urban middle classes express an almost universal desire to have interaction with extended kin. Sussman and Burchinal also note that extended kin networks can be highly functional for their members. They frequently provide services (such as child care, advice and counseling, and household task assistance) and help (to family members on the move, to those in need of financial assistance, etc.) not easily, conveniently, or economically available from other sources. Sussman and Burchinal conclude that the American nuclear family is not an isolated unit, but rather is highly involved in important networks of extended kinship.

Winch and Kitson (1977) have conducted a more recent study of extended familism in the United States. They found that the great majority of the persons they studied were significantly involved in larger kin networks. On the basis of this finding, Winch and Kitson posit the existence of two somewhat different types of American family structures. The first is an *isolated nuclear family,* a nuclear family unit lacking the presence of extended kin in its own local community; Winch and Kitson estimate that about 13 percent of American families are of this type. The second was identified as an *embedded nuclear family,* or a nuclear family highly involved in a network of extended kin; this type of family structure was estimated to account for about three-fourths of American families.

Winch and Kitson also attempted to specify the conditions under which extended familism was most likely to develop. They suggested several kinds of conditions under which the sharing of resources among extended kin would be highly functional for individual family members. These include marked resource scarcity, such as among the poor; various forms of discrimination against families from racial and ethnic minorities; and the incompleteness of the family, such as in single-parent households. Extended familism is also likely to be important in families at the opposite end of the economic spectrum from poor and minority families. Among the very rich, extended family connections are obviously important in protecting and perhaps enhancing family wealth.

According to recent studies, then, it is clearly advisable not to overemphasize the separateness of the nuclear family in modern industrial societies. Significant ties to larger kin networks persist even in the face of the physical separateness of neolocal nuclear families.

FOR FURTHER READING

Anderson, Michael. *Approaches to the History of the Western Family, 1500–1914.* London: Macmillan, 1980. A brief and illuminating introduction to three contrasting theoretical approaches to the study of European family history since the sixteenth century.

Berger, Brigitte, and Peter L. Berger. *The War over the Family: Capturing the Middle Ground.* Garden City, N.Y.: Doubleday (Anchor Books), 1983. A defense of the family as a crucial social institution and a plea for its strengthening in the face of the tremendous recent pressures undermining its effectiveness.

Cherlin, Andrew J. *Marriage, Divorce, Remarriage.* Cambridge, Mass.: Harvard University Press, 1981. One of the best recent studies of the contemporary upheaval in marital and family relationships. Contains much useful statistical information and pays considerable attention to various theoretical interpretations of recent family trends.

Collins, Randall. *Sociology of Marriage and the Family: Gender, Love, and Property.* Second edition. Chicago: Nelson-Hall, 1988. Perhaps the best textbook on the sociology of the family in several decades. Unusually comparative and historical for family texts. Provocative reading on a range of historical and contemporary issues.

Gutman, Herbert G. *The Black Family in Slavery and Freedom, 1750–1925.* New York: Pantheon Books, 1976. One of the best in a wave of recent studies of the history of the black American family. Examines the black family from the last days of slavery to the early decades of the twentieth century and reveals that the prevalence of female-dominated households among blacks is a relatively recent phenomenon.

Popenoe, David. *Disturbing the Nest: Family Change and Decline in Modern Societies.* New York: Aldine de Gruyter, 1988. A study of the contemporary family revolution with an emphasis on Sweden. Claims that the family in modern industrial societies is in a state of serious decline.

Shorter, Edward. *The Making of the Modern Family.*

New York: Basic Books, 1975. Shows that a "sentimental revolution" occurred in western European family relations in the eighteenth and nineteenth centuries and attempts to identify its causes. Makes an important contribution to our understanding of the development of the Western family despite something of a tendency to romanticize the modern nuclear family.

Stone, Lawrence. *The Family, Sex and Marriage in England, 1500–1800.* Abridged edition. New York: Harper & Row, 1979. Another first-rate historical study of the western European family revolution of the seventeenth through the nineteenth centuries. The arguments are much the same as Shorter's, although with considerably more attention to historical detail.

Thorne, Barrie, and Marilyn Yalom (eds.). *Rethinking the Family.* New York: Longman, 1982. Some important essays on the contemporary family from a feminist perspective. Focuses on the family as a source of the oppression of women.

Tilly, Louise A. "The Family and Change." *Theory and Society* 5:421–434, 1978. A sharp critique of Shorter's *The Making of the Modern Family.* Suggests, no doubt with some justification, that Shorter has too negative a view of the premodern family, that he idealizes and romanticizes the contemporary family, and that he underplays the sexual and generational conflicts of family life.

Zaretsky, Eli. *Capitalism, the Family, and Personal Life.* New York: Harper & Row, 1976. A well-known look at the historical development of the family under modern capitalism from a Marxian perspective.

Zelizer, Viviana A. *Pricing the Priceless Child: The Changing Social Value of Children.* New York: Basic Books, 1985. A provocative work tracing the influence of industrialization in changing the social role of the child from that of economic asset to priceless object of parental affection.

CHAPTER 17

Educational Systems in Sociological Perspective

This chapter discusses education as a social phenomenon. **Education** is any sort of formalized or semiformalized system of cultural or intellectual instruction. While in this sense education is a universal feature of human societies, the concern here is primarily with those highly formalized systems of education characteristic of the Western world in the past century or two. The discussion will be concerned largely with the American educational system since it has been the focus of the best descriptive and theoretical work. Nonetheless, a worldwide perspective will be employed to some extent. In the last part of the chapter recent educational developments in other industrial societies and in the Third World will be examined.

THE NATURE AND TYPES OF EDUCATIONAL SYSTEMS

Education in Comparative and Historical Perspective

Education is a cultural universal, but its specific nature differs sharply from one society to another. Randall Collins (1977) has pointed to three basic types of education found throughout the world's societies: education in practical skills, education for status-group membership, and bureaucratic education.

Practical-skill education is designed to impart certain technical skills and capacities deemed to be important in performing occupational or other activities. It is typically based on a master-apprentice form of teaching. This kind of education is essentially the only kind of education in primitive societies. It is also found in agrarian societies (where, for example, craftsmen teach their skills to new recruits) and, to some extent, in modern industrial societies.

In primitive societies important crafts like metalworking and important social roles like that of the shaman are generally learned by apprenticeship. In agrarian civilizations, apprenticeship has also been the basis for transmitting the content of such occupational roles as physician, construction engineer, and architect. One of the most important skills to be taught formally has been literacy. Formal literacy training began in ancient Mesopotamia and Egypt, where specialized schools were established to train children for careers as scribes (R. Collins, 1977).

Practical-skill education is notable for its lack of the sorts of ritual accompaniments so characteristic of status-group and bureaucratic education. There are no attendance, examination, grade, or degree requirements since the only feasible test of the effectiveness of this type of education is its success in practice (R. Collins, 1977).

Status-group education is conducted for the purpose of symbolizing and reinforcing the prestige and privilege of elite groups in highly stratified societies. It is generally designed to be impractical in any technical sense and is often given over to the learning and discussion of esoteric bodies of knowledge. It has been widely found in agrarian and industrial societies. As Collins comments (1977:9–11):

> In historical perspective, education has been used more often for organizing status groups than for other purposes. Since the defining locus of status-group activity is leisure and consumption, status-group education has been sharply distinguished from practical education by the exclusion of materially productive skills. Because status groups have used a common culture as a mark of group membership, status-group education has taken the form of a club and has included much ceremony to demonstrate group solidarity and to publicly distinguish members from nonmembers. This club aspect characterized the activities of Chinese gentlemen who met for genteel conversation and poetry writing, as well as the periodic festivals put on for the Greek public by students, an elite sector of the population.
>
> Status-group education, then, has been ceremonial, aesthetic, and detached from practical activities. Its rituals rarely have dramatized rankings within the group; formal grades, competitive examinations, and degrees usually have been absent. . . . The main distinctions have been between insiders and outsiders, not among members of the group. Frequently, there have been no formal attendance requirements, and the absence of formal degrees has reflected the fact that acquisition of the status group's culture is the object of education. . . .
>
> . . . In China, the first educated men were diviners or sages, who read oracles for the court and probably passed their skills along through apprenticeship. . . . [In later eras the] leisure pursuits of Chinese gentlemen . . . centered on poetry writing and painting; the prestigious form of sociability was the "literary gathering" where literature was read and discussed. . . .
>
> . . . In India, from the beginnings of literacy, education was closely associated with status-group prestige. Brahmin priests monopolized knowledge of the Vedic traditions and thereby helped not only to close off entry to their caste but also to legitimate the caste system. . . .
>
> Similarly, in the Heian court of early Japanese civilization (A.D. 1000), men and women courtiers developed an elaborate culture of poetry writing and art appreciation and even produced the first great Japanese works of prose fiction, largely through informal family education. In the Islamic world, education developed from religious training in the holy scriptures and laws to a form of culture that, in the cosmopolitan cities of prosperous periods, provided entertainment and status for the wealthy. . . .
>
> In Europe, informal education as the basis of status emulation was most prominent during the Renaissance, especially in the wealthy commercial cities of Italy, but also in Germany, the Netherlands, France, and England. Poetry writing and allusions to the classics were marks of prestige in everyday social life.

Bureaucratic education is created by governments to serve either or both of two purposes: as a selection device for recruiting persons to governmental or other positions, or as a means of socializing and disciplining the masses in order to win their political compliance. This type of education has generally placed great emphasis on examinations, attendance requirements, grades, and degrees. It has been common in several of the great historic civilizations, especially in those with centralized bureaucratic states. In classical China, for instance, an elaborate form of bureaucratic education existed. The core of this educational system was its examination system. Rigorous examinations had to be passed in order for individuals to gain entry into the important positions in the gov-

Magdalen College, Oxford University, founded in 1458: status-group education *par excellence*.

ernment bureaucracy. The higher the position, the more elaborate the series of examinations a candidate had to pass. Usually only a tiny fraction of degree candidates was allowed to pass each examination (R. Collins, 1977).

Bureaucratic education has also been characteristic of more contemporary societies. As Collins notes (1977:19):

> The development of modern school systems resulted from the consolidation of strong European bureaucratic states that were independent of the Catholic church. These secular school systems taught in the national language rather than the pan-European language of church Latin. The militarily expansive and rigidly bureaucratized Prussian state led the way in the seventeenth and eighteenth centuries in building a public school system at the elementary and university levels and in drawing state officials from among holders of university degrees.

These different types of education are frequently combined in the same society. Agrarian societies, for example, often combined all three types, although one might very well have been given emphasis over the others. Modern industrial societies have educational systems that are primarily combinations of status-group and bureaucratic education, with the bureaucratic element taking priority. Although such systems also engage in the teaching of practical skills, this aspect is distinctly subordinate to the others.

The Emergence of Modern Educational Systems

Modern industrial educational systems arose mainly during the nineteenth century. Two somewhat different types emerged. Throughout most of western Europe there developed **sponsored-mobility educational systems.** Sponsored-mobility systems place students into one or the other of two educational channels early in their educational careers. Some students (a minority) are placed into the channel that leads to a university education and the occupational opportunities it affords. Others (a majority) are placed into the channel that terminates with a vocational education. By contrast, there arose in the United States (and perhaps to some extent in the Soviet Union and Japan) a **contest-mobility educational system.** This kind of system does no official channeling (although a subtle, informal kind of channeling or "tracking" exists), and a more open competition for the pursuit of advanced education occurs.

All modern educational systems have undergone substantial growth and expansion in the past century or so. However, the American educational system has expanded on a far greater scale than the rest. Indeed, the United States has had for some time by far the most massive educational system in the world (Table 17.1).

Table 17.1 EDUCATIONAL ENROLLMENTS FOR SELECTED NATIONS[a]

Nation	Primary education	Secondary education	Higher education
Developed nations			
United Kingdom	101	89	22
Netherlands	95	102	31
France	114	96	30
West Germany	96	74	30
Denmark	98	103	29
Sweden	98	83	38
Canada	105	103	55
United States	101	99	57
Australia	106	95	28
Japan	102	96	30
Soviet Union	106	99	21
Czechoslovakia	97	39	16
East Germany	101	79	31
Hungary	98	72	15
Poland	101	78	17
Yugoslavia	96	82	20
Underdeveloped nations			
Ethiopia	36	12	1
Nepal	79	25	5
Zaire	98	57	2
Tanzania	72	3	0
India	92	35	—
China	124	39	2
Ghana	66	39	2
Senegal	55	13	2
Indonesia	118	39	7
Nigeria	92	29	3
Egypt	85	62	23
Thailand	97	30	20
Peru	122	65	24
Turkey	116	42	9
Colombia	117	50	13
Chile	109	69	16
Brazil	104	35	11
Mexico	115	55	16
Argentina	108	70	36
South Korea	96	94	32
Trinidad and Tobago	95	76	4

[a] The figures shown represent the percentage of the relevant age group enrolled at each educational level for the year 1985. Some percentages exceed 100 because of a tendency to overestimate primary (and occasionally, secondary) enrollments.

Source: World Bank, *World Development Report 1988*. New York: Oxford University Press, 1988, pp. 280–281, Table 30.

Virtually all youth go on to a secondary education, and more than half of all high school graduates now attend college. The United States easily has the largest number of colleges and universities of any country in the world. An approximate picture of the current size and historical expansion of the American educational system can be obtained by examining Table 17.2. This table clearly shows "the rising importance of education in people's lives" (R. Collins, 1979:4).

Education in the United States has grown approximately as follows. In the early nineteenth century there was very little formal education. A handful of students attended the few (largely elite) colleges that existed, but many of these did not get degrees. There was no public system of primary or secondary education. About the middle of the nineteenth century, the first public primary schools were established, and primary education grew rapidly throughout the century. Public secondary education was established in the second half of the century, although it was mainly designed to serve a college-preparatory function, and very few students were enrolled in it. The early twentieth century witnessed the conversion of the secondary school from a college-preparatory to a mass institution, and enrollments soared. New educational philosophies and techniques were introduced to deal with the new kind of high school that was emerging. Another major change in American education occurred after World War II. During this period, college enrollments increased dramatically; in 1940, only 16 percent of high school graduates were going on to college, but by 1980 approximately 57 percent were doing so.

Table 17.2 EDUCATIONAL ATTAINMENT IN THE UNITED STATES, 1870–1980

Year	High school students/ population 14–17 years old (%)	High school graduates/ population 17 years old (%)	College students/population 18–21 years old (%)	B.A.'s or first/professional degree/population 21 years old (%)	M.A.'s or second/professional degree/population 25 years old (%)	Ph.D.'s/population 30 years old (%)	Median years of school completed/population 25 years and older (%)
1870	2.1	2.0	1.7				
1880	2.4	2.5	2.7				
1890	3.6	3.5	3.0				
1900	7.9	6.4	4.0	1.7	0.12	0.03	
1910	11.4	8.8	5.1	1.9	0.13	0.02	
1920	26.4	16.8	8.9	2.3	0.24	0.03	
1930	44.3	29.0	12.4	4.9	0.78	0.12	
1940	62.4	50.8	15.6	7.0	1.24	0.15	8.6
1950	66.0	59.0	29.6	14.8 (1949)	2.43	0.27	9.3
1960	87.8	65.1	34.9	14.3	3.25	0.42	10.5
1970	92.9	76.5	52.8	21.1	7.83	1.04	12.2
1980	—	87.6	57.1*	28.6	—	—	12.9

Sources: The data for 1870–1970 come from Table 1.1 of Randall Collins, *The Credential Society: An Historical Sociology of Education and Stratification*, New York: Academic Press, 1979. With one exception, the data for 1980 are estimates based on the educational expansion depicted in Table 213 of U.S. Bureau of the Census, *Statistical Abstract of the United States*. Washington, D.C.: U.S. Government Printing Office, 1985. These estimates are probably slightly inflated. The data marked with an asterisk come from Table 3.2 of UNESCO, *Statistical Yearbook*. Paris: UNESCO, 1983.

THEORETICAL INTERPRETATIONS OF THE AMERICAN EDUCATIONAL SYSTEM

The Functionalist Theory

The functionalist theory has until recently dominated American sociological thinking about education. It attempts to explain the nature of education and its expansion over the past century or so as a consequence of the functional requirements of an industrial society, particularly the requirements arising from technological and economic change. Education is seen as having taken its particular form because of the positive contributions it makes to the proper functioning of industrial society. The main principles of the theory are summarized by Collins (1979) as follows:

1. The educational requirements of jobs in industrial society are constantly increasing as a result of technological change. There are two aspects of this:
   a. The proportion of jobs requiring low skill declines while the proportion requiring high skill increases.
   b. The same jobs are continuously upgraded in their skill requirements.
2. Formal education provides the training necessary for persons to undertake the more highly skilled jobs.
3. As a result of the above, educational requirements for employment continuously rise, and more and more people are required to spend longer and longer periods in school.

Collins (1979) argues that the available evidence strongly contradicts this interpretation of education and educational change. Regarding proposition 1.a—that educational requirements increase because of a decrease in the proportion of jobs requiring low skill and an increase in the proportion requiring high skill—he suggests that such a process accounts for only a small amount of educational upgrading. For instance, one well-known study has found that only 15 percent of educational increase during the twentieth century could be attributed to shifts in the occupational structure (Folger and Nam, 1964). Propositions 1.b and 2—that educational requirements rise because the same jobs are upgraded in skill requirements, and that formal education provides necessary job skills—are also held to be contradicted by available evidence. Collins approaches a test of these propositions by asking, "Are better-educated employees more productive than less-educated ones?" and "Are vocational skills learned in school or elsewhere?" His answer to the first question is "no"; to the second, "elsewhere." Regarding the first question, he points to a major study (Berg, 1971) that shows that better-educated employees are typically not more productive than less educated ones, and in some cases are even less productive. In terms of the second question, he sets forth evidence indicating that students learn few or no vocationally relevant skills in school, and that most such skills are acquired rather quickly and easily on the job.

Collins makes a convincing case against the functionalist theory. He proposes his own theory of educational expansion, one that is a particular type of conflict theory. Before examining his theory, however, it is necessary first to look at a different kind of conflict theory.

A Marxian Conflict Theory: Bowles and Gintis

A Marxian-oriented conflict theory of American education has been presented by Samuel Bowles and Herbert Gintis in their book *Schooling in Capitalist America* (1976). Bowles and Gintis are less concerned with the reasons for educational expansion than they are with the whole quality and texture of American educational life. They clearly do not like it, believing it has been distorted by the capitalist economy that underlies it.

Bowles and Gintis believe that education in the contemporary United States is a deformed version of what education ideally should be. They hold that the proper purpose of education is to promote open intellectual inquiry, creativity, and positive human growth. The right kind of educational system is one that leads to personal satisfaction and intellectual and emotional fulfillment. But education in America does not lead to these consequences, they say. On the contrary, it produces widespread dissatisfaction and alienation. Furthermore, rather than promoting open intellectual inquiry, it actively attempts to instill ideological conformity to dominant beliefs and values, as well as behavioral conformity to dominant social relationships. It is like this, Bowles and Gintis say, because it has been fundamentally shaped by the underlying capitalist economy and the class inequality that is part and parcel of that economy. Rather than an agent for positive human development, education has been a tool used by capitalists to accomplish two primary purposes: to justify class inequality and to discipline the work force by instilling in students proper forms of worker consciousness. As Bowles and Gintis express it (1976:101):

> The struggle between working people and capital in the economy has its counterpart in educational conflict. . . . Employers and other social elites have sought to use the schools for the legitimation of inequality through an ostensibly meritocratic and rational mechanism for allocating individuals to economic positions; they have sought to use the schools for the reproduction of profitable types of worker consciousness and behavior through a correspondence between the social relationships of education and those of economic life.

One way in which Bowles and Gintis attempt to demonstrate their argument is by examining the meritocratic claims widely promoted by the educational system. These claims generally hold that economic success is largely the result of individual merit. Economic success is said to be due mainly to superior intellectual capacities, while failure results from the absence of such capacities. It is not hard to see how such a notion can serve as a powerful justification for class inequality. Bowles and Gintis assert, though, that the claim that the United States is basically a meritocracy is not valid, and they present some very impressive evidence to support their assertion. They show that economic success bears a very close relationship to the class level into which a person is born, but very little relationship to IQ and cognitive test scores.

Bowles and Gintis also attempt to support their interpretation of American education through employing what they call the *correspondence principle*. The main burden of their argument rests on this idea, by which they mean that the social relationships characteristic of the realm of education are reflections of the social relationships that prevail in the economy and the workplace. This is so because education is shaped by the economy and designed to serve it. In this regard, Bowles and Gintis present research findings that show that the personality traits most highly valued and rewarded in the classroom are the same ones most highly valued in the workplace. Furthermore, they show that social relationships at different levels of the educational world reflect social relationships at different levels of the work world. As they explain it (1976:132):

> Different levels of education feed workers into different levels within the occupational structure and, correspondingly, tend toward an internal organization comparable to levels in the hierarchical division of labor. . . . The lowest levels in the hierarchy of the enterprise emphasize rule-following, middle levels, dependability, and the capacity to operate without direct and continuous supervision while the higher levels stress the internalization of the norms of the enterprise.

> Similarly, in education, lower levels (junior and senior high school) tend to severely limit and channel the activities of students. Somewhat higher up the educational ladder, teacher and community colleges allow for more independent activity and less overall supervision. At the top, the elite four-year colleges emphasize social relationships conformable with the higher levels in the production hierarchy.

In other words, students are differentially socialized at different levels of the educational system. Schools that expect their students to end up at lower levels of the occupational structure socialize them for rule-following and dependability; in contrast, schools that anticipate that their students will end up at the higher reaches of the work world socialize them more for independence, creativity, and commitment to the organization. Schools thus socialize their students into the values most important for them to have in order to function properly in the world of work.

As a final step in their overall argument, Bowles and Gintis attempt to show how their theory makes sense of the historical evolution of American education. They note that the rise of mass public education in the middle of the nineteenth century corresponded to the beginnings of industrialization and the emergence of the factory system. They interpret the introduction of mass public education as a response on the part of capitalists to the increased need for socializing and disciplining a new kind of working population. They claim that capitalists were the strongest proponents of a system of public education, and that schools most frequently arose in those areas with the largest concentrations of factory workers. The conversion of the high school from an elite to a mass institution corresponded closely to the rise of corporate monopoly capitalism. By this time a very large proportion of the work force consisted of factory wage laborers, and many of these were recent immigrants. Bowles and Gintis argue that the expansion of the educational system to a new level was required as a stronger means of disciplining a larger, more ethnically varied, and more recalcitrant labor force.

Bowles and Gintis see the major expansion of higher education since World War II as a result of factors such as the greatly increased demand on the part of employers for technical, clerical, and other white-collar skills and the increased demand by minority and working-class youth for access to higher education. But other major changes in higher education have occurred as well in recent years. These have mainly involved increasing diversification and vocationalization. One of the most prominent of the recent changes is the massive growth of community colleges, schools that are strongly vocational in nature and that draw a large proportion of their students from working-class backgrounds. Bowles and Gintis see the rise of community colleges as a way of facilitating the increased demand for higher education without posing a threat to the status of the more elite colleges and universities.

Bowles and Gintis's theory has been extensively discussed in the years since it first appeared. The initial reaction to the theory on the part of many sociologists was enthusiastic and positive. However, in recent years the theory has fallen on hard times. It has come increasingly under fire, and even some Marxists and Marxist sympathizers have become dissatisfied with it. There is even some question about the extent to which Bowles and Gintis themselves would continue to defend it vigorously.

The most serious flaws in the theory can be identified basically as follows. First, their argument about the historical association between the onset of mass schooling and industrialization is open to serious question. In many western European countries and in Japan, as well as in the United States, mass education began to appear before the beginnings of industrialization (Boli, Ramirez, and Meyer, 1985). In the United States it appears that mass schooling began first as a rural phenomenon, and thus was hardly prompted by capitalist industrialization (Meyer, Tyack, Nagel, and Gordon, 1979).

Another difficulty concerns Bowles and Gintis's strong tendency to blame the educational system for the alienation and boredom of students. Even to the extent that this is true, it is a crass oversimplification, and several other factors have to be taken into account. For example, much of the negativism that American students at all educational levels feel toward schools and schooling is undoubtedly rooted in the anti-intellectual character of American culture. Moreover, how students respond to the whole process of schooling depends greatly on their family backgrounds and the extent to which their parents and preschool environments have prepared them to deal with academic matters (Postman, 1979).

A third problem with Bowles and Gintis's argument involves the very logic of their correspondence principle. They claim that the hierarchical structure of schools replicates the hierarchical structure of the workplace because the educational system is directly constrained by the capitalist economy—because capitalists have the power to command the organization of the educational system. However, they present no conclusive evidence to show this to be the case. An extremely plausible alternative explanation is that schools have developed hierarchical structures as a result of their own internal organizational dynamics (Murphy, 1988).

Consider also Bowles and Gintis's assertion that schooling is something that has been imposed on workers. Actually, a clear reading of the evidence shows that the working class has struggled vigorously for schooling (Collins, 1979). This has been the case in all Western capitalist countries, but it has been especially so in the United States. And not only has the American working class demanded access to education, but its actions have had considerable success in helping build an unusually open and democratic educational system (Rubinson, 1986).

Finally, extreme doubt seems in order regarding Bowles and Gintis's suggestion that in a socialist society a genuinely nonindoctrinational educational system would emerge. While the notion of a nonindoctrinational educational system is a noble ideal, is it realistic to assume that a socialist society would do any better on this score than a capitalist one? The actually existing socialist societies of the world certainly have not. Indeed, one might go further and ask whether a nonindoctrinational educational system would ever be a realistic possibility in any type of society. Don't senior generations as a matter of course desire to transmit their most cherished values and ideals to junior generations, and isn't a society's educational system one of the primary means of doing this?

Bowles and Gintis's theory obviously leaves a lot to be desired. However, although many of the specific formulations of this theory must be rejected, Bowles and Gintis's more general argument has much to recommend it. The educational system and the capitalist economy are closely associated. Capitalist culture does penetrate significantly into the workings of the educational system, especially at the level of higher education. In his *The Higher Learning in America* (1965; orig. 1918), the eminent social scientist Thorstein Veblen noted long ago the domination of American universities by businessmen. In the three-quarters of a century since Veblen wrote, American universities have become far more dominated by businessmen and their ethos. Indeed, these universities increasingly resemble business organizations in their overall character and functioning. Education has become increasingly characterized by the advancing commodification that is such an important trend in the evolution of capitalism.

A Weberian Conflict Theory: Randall Collins

A distinct alternative to the particularities of Bowles and Gintis's Marxian theory that retains a conflict theoretical focus is the neo-Weberian argument of Randall Collins (1979). Collins's theory is set out along the lines of the general conception of social stratification developed by Max Weber. In developing his theory, Collins makes particular use of Weber's concept of status group, and he sees status groups as being more important than classes in shaping the American educational system. Collins believes that the most important status groups in American society are ethnic groups.

Collins views the character of American education and its dramatic expansion throughout the past century primarily as results of the great ethnic diversity of American society. Such diversity has resulted in major struggles among ethnic groups for privilege and prestige. These struggles began mainly in the late nineteenth century and continued well into the twentieth. Education, Collins holds, became the major weapon used in such struggles. Dominant groups used the educational system as a means of maintaining their cultural and economic dominance. For them it was a mechanism for transmitting their dominant cultural values to new immigrant groups of workers, as well as a resource to be used to reinforce their economic dominance. But subordinate groups also saw it as a resource they could use in their attempts to improve their economic status. The possession of a certain amount of education came to be viewed as establishing a set of *credentials* that would provide access to certain desired occupational positions. Education thus became a primary arena in which different groups struggled for economic success. As these struggles progressed, education began to increase in size and importance.

Randall Collins. A leading American sociological theorist, Collins is currently chair of the Department of Sociology at the University of California, Riverside. He is a Weberian conflict theorist who has done much to develop that perspective.

As more and more persons began to obtain educational credentials, however, these credentials declined in value. Drawing an analogy to monetary inflation, Collins calls this process **credential inflation.** In the educational sphere credential inflation means that the same amount of education no longer "purchases" what it once did. One must acquire more of it just to keep even in the struggle for economic success. Collins argues that this is exactly what has been happening in the American educational system over the past century. The struggle over education has caused continuous educational inflation, resulting in the massive expansion of the educational system (and educational requirements for jobs) over time. Since it now takes a college degree to "purchase" a job that could have been obtained with a high school diploma 30 years ago, a greater number of young people are going to college. Most of them go not because of a desire for learning, Collins insists, but because they seek credentials that they hope will pay off in economic success.*

*The massive expansion of education has had essentially no effect on economic inequality, a fact pointed out both by Collins and by Bowles and Gintis. In view of Collins's argument, this should not be surprising. Educational credentials have expanded at all levels, and therefore status groups that had an educational head start many years ago have been able to maintain their lead. As some groups moved over time from high school completion to college completion, others simply moved from getting college degrees to doing postgraduate work, and so on.

Collins also makes special note of the fact that, as American education expanded, educational institutions were forced to make major changes in their curricula and in their overall character in order to appeal to an increasingly mass clientele. The most prominent changes involved the watering down of the classical liberal arts curriculum and the introduction of a host of extracurricular activities. The transformation of the high school into a mass institution, for instance, was accompanied by the so-called progressive movement in education. Two of progressivism's major innovations were the introduction of athletics and other extracurricular activities and the attempt "to substitute a rather vague 'life-adjustment' training for the classical curriculum" (R. Collins, 1979:115–116). Similar changes occurred when colleges and universities started to be attended by a larger clientele, most of whom were seeking educational credentials rather than intellectual stimulation. As Collins points out (1979:124–125):

> The main appeal of the revitalized university for large groups of students was not the training it offered but the social experience of attending it. The older elite was being perpetuated in a new, more easy-going form. . . . Through football games colleges for the first time became prominent in the public eye, and alumni and state legislators found renewed loyalty to their schools. At the same time, fraternities and sororities became widespread, and with them came college traditions of drinking, parties, parades, dances, and "school spirit." It is little exaggeration to say that the replacement of the pious, unreformed college by the sociable culture of the university was crucial in the growth of enrollments, or that football rather than science was the salvation of American higher education.
>
> . . . The rise of the undergraduate culture indicates first of all that college education had come to be treated as consumption by the new industrial upper classes, although it also attracted growing numbers of the intellectually oriented and those seeking careers in teaching. College attendance had become an interlude of fun in the lives of upper-class and upper-middle-class young Americans. . . .
>
> . . . [An attempt] to put training back as the central function of the college was a failure. Students did not want to disturb the rituals of freshman and sophomore class rivalries, junior dances, and senior privileges. . . . Most students found the essence of college education to be the enjoyable and status-conferring rituals and social life of college rather than the content of classroom learning.

Although Bowles and Gintis limit themselves to the United States, Collins (1977) has brought forth some comparative data to bolster his argument. As he notes, there are significant differences among the educational systems of industrial societies. England, Germany, and France, for instance, have very small educational systems of the sponsored-mobility type, while industrial societies such as the United States and the Soviet Union have large systems of the contest-mobility type. Educational inflation is considerably more characteristic of contest-mobility systems. Collins argues that the Bowles and Gintis labor-discipline argument cannot explain such differences, since all industrial societies have essentially the same need for labor discipline. But Collins holds that his theory can effectively explain the differences among industrial educational systems. He believes that less inflationary sponsored-mobility systems develop in societies where the level of class segregation is high. The class-segregated character of the educational system reflects, in other words, the class-segregated character of the larger society. By contrast, highly inflationary contest-mobility systems tend to emerge in societies in which the level of class segregation is low and "where class conflict has been submerged within a single market for cultural respectability" (Collins, 1977:26).

Collins's theory is a major improvement on the Marxian interpretation of Bowles and Gintis. However, there are two basic difficulties with the theory that should not escape attention. In the first place, Collins's argument that it is ethnic diversity that is the root cause of educational expansion is contradicted by empirical research (Boli, Ramirez, and Meyer, 1985). Indeed, even casual observation would suggest extreme skepticism on this count. For example, the world's most ethnically heterogeneous society, the Soviet Union, has undergone less educational expansion than the world's most ethnically homogeneous society, Japan. As we shall see later, there is a simpler and much more empirically accurate way of explaining educational expansion than by invoking the factor of ethnic heterogeneity.

However, once we remove this element from Collins's theory, we are left with no plausible account of why it is the educational system that becomes the focus of struggles for economic success and social mobility (Boli, Ramirez, and Meyer, 1985). This is the second difficulty with the theory. In order to see how this difficulty might be overcome, we need to consider yet a fourth type of theory of the emergence and expansion of mass education. This theory applies not merely to the American educational system, but to the emergence and expansion of mass schooling in all Western societies over the past two centuries.

Education as Nation-Building

The most recent theory of mass educational systems is one developed primarily by John Meyer and his colleagues (Meyer, Ramirez, Rubinson, and Boli-Bennett, 1977; Meyer, Tyack, Nagel, and Gordon, 1979; Boli, Ramirez, and Meyer, 1985). For lack of a better name, I will call this theory the *theory of education as nation-building*. The authors of this theory generally reject the main assumptions of all of the preceding theories, arguing in particular that none of these theories can satisfactorily explain the specific features of modern mass educational systems. These features, they claim, are primarily the following: (1) Mass educational systems are intended to be universal, standardized, and highly rationalized. In other words, they apply to everyone in the same basic fashion, cutting across the various lines of cleavage in a society (i.e., class, ethnicity, religion, race, gender, etc.). (2) Modern mass educational systems are highly institutionalized at a world level. They are extraordinarily similar in very different societies throughout the world, and have become increasingly similar through time. (3) Mass educational systems are specifically directed toward the socialization of the individual as the primary social unit. This is seen, for example, in the extent to which educational rituals celebrate individual choice and responsibility rather than the imbeddedness of individuals in such corporate groups as social classes, castes, or extended families.

The theory of education as nation-building proposes that mass educational systems arose in the modern world specifically as devices for the intensive socialization of the individual into the values and aspirations of the modern, rational nation-state. As John Boli, Francisco Ramirez, and John Meyer put it (1985:158), "In the broadest sense, mass education arises as a purposive project to construct the modern polity, reconstructing individuals in accordance with collective religious, political, and economic goods and purposes."

John Meyer, David Tyack, Joane Nagel, and Audri Gordon (1979) have applied this line of thinking to understand the development of American education from about 1870 to about 1930. Contrary to Bowles and Gintis, they stress that mass education during this time was not primarily an urban, industrial phenomenon. They claim that it was at least as characteristic of rural as of urban areas, and quite likely was even more prominent in the former. As such, it was motivated by the desire of important segments of American society to socialize their children into the new national culture that was emerging. This culture was capitalistic, rationalistic, and highly individualistic. As the authors explain (1979:601):

> One critical factor to understand in this whole process is the role of the American *farmer,* an important carrier of capitalistic culture, involved in rational calculations in a world market, and eager to maintain free action in a free society. . . .
>
> A political economy or moral polity based upon free individuals—freed from both traditional forms of community and from an old-world statism—requires great effort and constant vigilance: to educate these individuals (freedom from ignorance), to reform their souls (freedom from sin), to save them from political subordination (freedom from aristocracy), and to save them from sloth (freedom from old-world customs). To liberate such individuals and to link them by education and salvation to a millennial America seemed within the reach of a responsible citizenry. . . .
>
> The major educational agents of this individualistic political culture of capitalism—rational and universalistic in premises but almost stateless in structure—were actors whose authority was more moral than official. They combined in associations that look to 20th-century eyes like social movements—religious and other voluntary groups rather than organizations clothed with the authority of a bureaucratic state. . . . These groups acted not simply to protect the status of their own children but to build a millennial society for all children. Their modes of thought and action were at once political, economic, and religious. That these school promoters were often in fact ethnocentric and served their own religious, political, and economic interests is quite clear; but they were doing so in a very broad way by constructing an enlarged national society.

To my mind, this theory has much to recommend it and seems to make very good sense of those specific features of modern educational systems that Meyer and his colleagues see as most crucial. It can certainly help us understand not only the origins of mass education, but the reasons why primary education, and to some extent secondary education, has become so prominent in so many societies around the world. It also helps us see how an educational system can become the focus for struggles for individual economic success. Once in place for other reasons, an educational system can be quickly seen as offering resources that can be extremely useful in promoting the upward mobility of the individual. However, the theory seems inadequate as a means of understanding many of the developments in higher education, especially why it has expanded so rapidly and so substantially in some societies. Moreover, it may not be fully adequate even in explaining a good deal of the expansion of secondary education. To explain these things I think we have to fall back on the credential inflation argument of Collins—but with an altered conception of the particular mechanism that produces inflation.

THE WORLD EDUCATIONAL EXPLOSION

World Educational Expansion Since 1950

One of the more striking features of education in recent decades is its major expansion on a worldwide scale. As Table 17.3 reveals, more and more young people are enrolled in education almost everywhere. This is the case both in the advanced industrial and in the underdeveloped countries, and it is so for all levels of education (primary, secondary, higher). John Meyer, Francisco Ramirez, Richard Rubinson, and John Boli-Bennett (1977) have attempted to explain this remarkable expansion. They examined a host of variables that were hypothesized to be closely related to such expansion. Among these were level of urbanization, political modernization, state centralization, and economic dependence. None of these social variables was found to be a satisfactory predictor of educa-

American high school seniors signing yearbooks. The United States began moving toward mass public secondary education early in this century and has subsequently gone on to develop the world's largest and most comprehensive educational system. What makes it unique?

tional growth.* It seems especially noteworthy that even a nation's level of economic development, which has been widely proposed by many theories as the major determinant of educational growth, was found to be only weakly related to it.

Meyer et al. then developed an alternative model of educational expansion. This model holds that worldwide educational expansion in recent decades has occurred mainly as a result of certain aspects of demography and educational organization. That is, "education has expanded everywhere as a function of the available population to be educated and of the level of education existing in 1950" (Meyer et al., 1977:255). They report that a preliminary empirical test of this alternative model provided support for it.

There are two different ways of looking at Meyer et al.'s model. One is that it is really rooted in their more general model of education as nation-building. From this perspective, they

*Meyer et al. note that even though these variables may not at the present time satisfactorily predict educational growth, this does not mean that they were unimportant in earlier eras.

Table 17.3 WORLD EDUCATIONAL ENROLLMENT, 1950–1980

Educational level/ type of country	Percentages				Number of countries	
	1950	1960	1970	1980	1950–1970	1980
Primary students						
All countries	58	71	83	90	117	117
Richer countries	90	98	102	101	51	55
Poorer countries	37	53	72	80	56	62
Secondary students						
All countries	12.7	21.5	30.5	45.4	102	116
Richer countries	21.3	35.8	46.4	66.8	49	55
Poorer countries	5.3	9.4	17.0	26.2	46	61
Students in higher education						
All countries	1.4	2.8	5.3	12.1	109	116
Richer countries	2.6	5.2	9.2	18.6	46	59
Poorer countries	0.6	1.2	2.6	5.3	55	57

Sources: The data for 1950–1970 come from Table 1 of John W. Meyer, Francisco O. Ramirez, Richard Rubinson, and John Boli-Bennett, "The World Educational Revolution, 1950–1970," *Sociology of Education* 50:242–258, 1977. The data for 1980 come from UNESCO, *Statistical Yearbook*, Paris: UNESCO, 1983, Table 3.2. The figures represent the percentage of students in the relevant age category enrolled at a given educational level. Some figures exceed 100 percent because of a tendency to overestimate primary enrollments. Richer countries are defined as those above the median in per capita GNP, poorer countries as those below the median.

are "arguing that world-level cultural and organizational directives for economic development, citizenship, and 'progress' through the transformation of individuals press all countries toward expanding educational systems" (Fiala and Lanford, 1987:315). Meyer et al. do argue this, and to a certain extent they are probably correct (Fiala and Lanford, 1987). On the other hand, their emphasis on the "self-generating" process of worldwide educational expansion suggests that, whether they intend so or not, their conclusions dovetail nicely with Collins's conception of educational expansion as credential inflation. In fact, in a provocative book Ronald Dore (1976) has suggested that this process is what lies behind the recent worldwide growth of educational enrollments. Dore calls this process **qualificationism,** and he suggests that it is a significant phenomenon in all or most major industrial societies. Moreover, the underdeveloped nations appear to be involved in imitating the educational patterns of the industrial countries and thus building strong elements of qualificationism into their own educational systems. All (or at least most) contemporary nations have thus become infected with what Dore calls "the diploma disease."

Qualificationism at a World Level

Although qualificationism is perhaps a more prominent characteristic of the United States than of any other advanced industrial society, it has certainly become a significant feature of the educational systems of other industrial societies in the twentieth century. England and Japan, for instance, have experienced very significant growth of qualificationism throughout this century.

Historic changes in the career preparation of engineers and librarians are excellent indicators of the rise of qualificationism in the English educational system (Dore, 1976). In the late nineteenth century, civil engineers took no formal examinations and gained entry into their profession by an apprenticeship system. By the middle of the twentieth century this had changed markedly, so that educational certificates had become very important for entry into the profession. Furthermore, by 1970 formal educational preparation had become an absolute necessity. Librarians have followed a similar course. At the beginning of the twentieth century, no formal degrees were necessary for librarianship. Yet by the 1930s an educational certificate was becoming very useful; by 1950 it had become a minimal requirement; and by 1970 the length of formal educational preparation minimally necessary for librarianship had been lengthened. Moreover, the prospects were clearly in sight for lengthening it even more.

Qualificationism came to Japan at a much earlier stage in its economic development. As Dore remarks, almost from the very beginning of its industrialization it was building qualificationism into its career preparation. Even as early as 1910 many Japanese business firms were attempting to recruit only university graduates. University degrees were also becoming increasingly necessary at this time for entry into the technical professions and government administrative positions. Thus there was rapid growth in the number of universities throughout the twentieth century. In 1918 private colleges were given the right to call themselves universities. Two decades later 26 such universities existed. At the same time there were also 19 state universities and 2 municipal universities. Great expansion continued over the next four decades, so that by 1982 Japan had a total of 455 universities and an additional 526 junior colleges (*Statesman's Year-Book 1984–85*, 1984).

Many underdeveloped countries in recent decades seem to be experiencing a particularly acute form of qualificationism. They are victims of what Dore calls the "late-development effect": The later development starts, the more rapidly school enrollments increase. In such countries, educational certificates have been made necessary requirements for individuals to gain entry into modern-sector jobs (e.g., civil service posts, office jobs). These jobs are highly attractive because they promise a level of eco-

A *juku* ("cram") high school in Tokyo specializing in preparing students for university examinations. Japan has developed one of the world's most credentialized educational systems.

nomic reward far beyond that experienced by the average person. Therefore, the demand for them is very high, producing a substantial qualification inflation. In Kenya, for instance (Dore, 1976:67–68):

> Primary school enrollments increased from 780,000 in 1960 to over a million in 1965 and 1.4 million in 1970; secondary and university enrollments at an even faster rate. Predictably, the growth in school outputs has outstripped the growth in desirable modern-sector jobs.
>
> In 1960, probably about 13 percent of each age group was getting to the end of Standard 7 in primary school and over half of them were staying the extra year for Standard 8. They had good prospects of a job in a factory, office or government department. But soon, as their numbers increased without much increase in the number of job openings, the school-leaver employment problem became a major concern.
>
> . . .
>
> Now, the only worthwhile focus of ambition was on getting to secondary school. Hence, not unnaturally, all parental political pressures were concentrated on the expansion of secondary school opportunities. If the government would not build a secondary school in the district, the parents built one themselves, hoping that their *fait accompli* would eventually force the government to incorporate it into the subsidized system. The Harambee self-help secondary school movement spread throughout the country.

There are a number of serious consequences of the growth of qualificationism. Among these, two seem perhaps most important. One is the "overeducation" problem. As an increasing number of persons hold educational certificates of a certain level, and as the number of jobs requiring that educational level does not increase, many of the certificate holders are unable to gain employment at that level. They either end up taking jobs for which they have more education than necessary, or they go on to gain more education, hoping that this extra amount of education will secure for them the kinds of jobs they desire. Thus the overeducation problem is both the result of qualificationism and a cause of accelerated qualificationism.

A second serious consequence of the growth of qualificationism involves the quality of education itself. As Dore has remarked, when qualificationism gains the upper hand in an educational system, examinations begin to dominate the curriculum; learning becomes ritualized; curiosity and creativity are de-emphasized; and students not only fail to develop an interest in what they are learning, they even lose concern for its relevance. Education comes to be oriented around passing examinations and receiving chits, rather than around the expansion of the mind and the stimulation and satisfaction of intellectual curiosity. Classrooms become sterile places characterized by a kind of ritualized boredom. When students begin to grow aware of the real nature and functions of the educational system, and when credential inflation has reached very high levels, a "credential crisis" may occur. Collins believes that this has happened within the past two decades in the United States. As he remarks (1979:191–192):

> As of the 1960s, the credential system went into a state of explicit crisis. . . . There was tremendous pressure from subordinated ethnic groups, especially blacks and Latin Americans, for integration into the dominant educational and occupational institutions. The result has been a multifaceted crisis in confidence in the system and a variety of reactions and criticisms.
>
> . . . [Students began] to demand revision of traditional curricular requirements. Such demands were usually put in the form of a shift to greater "relevance," or toward the cultures of the ethnic minorities themselves. But in fact, the alternatives lacked substance; their principal appeal was negative, a reaction against the traditional requirements that were now recognized as purely procedural formalities of the process of gaining a credential. More recently, the idealistic rhetoric of curricular alternatives has been replaced by a manipulative cynicism. Students electing to remain within the system have

adopted the goal of high grades, irrespective of content and by any means whatsoever, producing an inflation in college grades, while at the same time achievement levels have been steadily dropping.

Although qualificationism produces these negative effects in both the developed and the underdeveloped countries, the effects seem to be worse in the underdeveloped world. Unemployment of credential holders has reached very high levels in some underdeveloped nations, producing tremendous frustrations for these persons. Moreover, as Dore remarks (1976:81):

> In the later developers the birth of a school system and the development of a qualification-based occupational system are likely to be simultaneous. The very concept of "school" and of formal education entered the society in recent times as part of the package of "modernity" brought by the imperialist powers. By contrast, most of the older industrial countries have formal pedagogical traditions (and some educational institutes) dating back to pre-industrial times *before* educational certificates acquired bread-and-butter value—dating back, in other words, to the time when learning was thought to be about getting *knowledge* or wisdom, to make a man respected or holy or righteous or rich. These older traditions still persist in the older countries. They serve to maintain the fiction that education is about moral and intellectual uplift and enrichment. And such fictions *are* important. What men define as real is real in its consequences. The fictions *do* serve as a countervailing force to weaken tendencies towards qualification-orientation, particularly when they are boldly reasserted by rebellious students demanding the end of examinations, and urging that universities should stop prostituting themselves by subserviently acting as graders of human material for the capitalist system (even if

A Burmese fourth-grade class. Primary education has expanded on a major scale in Third World countries during the past several decades. Is such educational expansion an unmixed blessing?

they do falter and fall into confusion when any university teacher offers to take them at their word and abolish all degree *certificates* as well as examinations). In later-developing societies, where all except the very first generation of purely soul-saving mission schools (and even some of those) had selection/credentialling functions, these useful countervailing fictions, having no roots in any local past, are harder to establish and sustain. The pursuit of certificates can be even more naked and unashamed.

Explaining the Worldwide Growth of Qualificationism

In accounting for this worldwide expansion of qualification-oriented education, it is necessary, as already noted, to abandon Collins's notion of ethnic group competition. What, then, is the alternative? Such educational expansion can most likely be explained as resulting from a combination of two factors. First, education has been a tool used by elites to help maintain social stability and preserve the basic character of the society. Such a strategy has been especially characteristic of the United States and, more recently, England and the Scandinavian countries. England has undergone a great deal of university-level expansion since the early 1960s, as have the Scandinavian countries beginning at a somewhat earlier date. In these societies greater numbers of working-class youth have been admitted to universities over the years. This is perhaps the simplest way for these societies to try to alter their reward structure: they try to create more "equality of opportunity" without actually changing the nature of the stratification system. This can be a very effective device for draining away potential hostility to the existence of deep economic inequalities. It is not hard to see, then, why well-placed groups would favor the continued expansion of education.

The second factor involved in producing educational expansion is the simple one of supply and demand; the logic of the "market" for educational credentials causes continuous qualification expansion. As more people gain credentials, their worth lessens in terms of the kinds of jobs they can lead to. Therefore, unless people are willing to lower their occupational aspirations, they must stay in school longer in order to achieve a higher credential. Moreover, educational certificates that were once merely desirable as a basis for acquiring a certain job eventually end up becoming minimal requirements. As Dore explains (1976:5):

> The way the qualification-escalation ratchet works is roughly like this. A bus company may "normally" require a junior secondary leaving certificate for £5-a-week bus conductors and a senior secondary leaving certificate for its £7-a-week clerks. But as the number of senior certificate leavers grows far larger than the number of clerkships that are available, some of them decide that £5 a week as a bus conductor is better than nothing at all. The bus company gives them preference. Soon all the available conductor slots are filled by senior certificate holders: a senior certificate has become a necessary qualification for the job.
>
> It is not entirely clear why employers allow qualifications to escalate in this way. The chief reason seems to be that they are simply unquestioning victims of the widespread myth that education "improves" people, and that they are therefore getting more for their money if they get a senior certificate for £5 a week rather than a junior certificate. . . . Or it might just be that, faced with fifty applicants for five bus conducting jobs, all of whom could do the job equally well, it just simplifies the whole process to consider only the ten people with senior certificates—and provides a clear objective and legitimate reason for saying no to the other forty. . . .
>
> Whatever the reason, it happens. Senior certificates get the bus conducting jobs: BAs preempt the clerkships. The pressure to get on higher up the school ladder is intensified: so is the pressure on the government to build more schools to *allow* more children to get higher up. And it is hard to see a limit to the process.

Table 17.4 THEORIES OF MODERN EDUCATIONAL SYSTEMS

Theory	Characteristics	Evaluation
Functionalist theory	Modern educational systems have originated and expanded as a result of the changing functional needs accompanying industrialization. Industrialization has increased the skill level of work, and education has had to expand in order to provide people with the training they need to function effectively in the occupational realm.	Although a widely accepted theory, it is contradicted by some important facts. Most of what people learn in school has little relationship to specific job skills, and most of these skills can be (and are) learned rather quickly on the job.
Marxian theory	In the famous version of Bowles and Gintis, modern educational systems arose as systems of labor discipline for the emerging working class, as well as legitimizing ideologies for the class inequalities of capitalist society. The needs of the capitalist class have shaped the content and character of education, and educational systems have expanded in conjunction with the evolution of industrial capitalism.	Although capitalism penetrates modern educational systems in various ways, the specific arguments of Bowles and Gintis and most other Marxian theorists falter in the face of considerable evidence. The onset of mass schooling and industrialization often do not correspond; the alienation of students from schools has strong roots outside the school system itself; the hierarchical structure of schools is not necessarily rooted in capitalism; and a nonindoctrinational educational system is not likely in any type of society.
Credential inflation theory	As developed by Collins and Dore, proposes that education is a highly valued commodity sought by individuals as a means of economic success and upward mobility. The educational system becomes a focus of struggle for diplomas and degrees. Once set in motion, this struggle undergoes a type of inflationary spiral, and thus education expands at all levels as individuals run faster educationally just to keep even in the struggle for success.	Identifies a crucial aspect of the process of educational expansion in the modern world. However, it is weak in accounting for the origin of mass education, as well as in explaining why educational systems become a major focus of economic struggles.
Education as nation-building	Modern mass educational systems originate and expand in order to provide the intensive socialization individuals need to become proper citizens in modern, rationalistic, technologically advanced industrial (or industrializing) societies. Education becomes a vast tool tying individuals to the aims of modern political systems in promoting economic development and overall societal modernization.	Seems to identify some of the critical forces underlying the birth of modern mass education, and also may successfully explain why modern educational systems are so broadly similar. But cannot explain much of the expansion that educational systems have undergone, especially at the level of higher education.

SUMMARY

1. Three major types of educational systems are found in the world's societies. Practical-skill education functions to transmit socially useful knowledge and skills to members of the younger generation. Status-group educational systems serve to signify the social status of high-ranking groups. They are generally highly impractical and are devoted to the transmission and discussion of esoteric bodies of knowledge. Bureaucratic educational systems function primarily to recruit personnel to jobs. They stress attendance requirements, grades, and diplomas.

2. Educational systems in modern industrial societies are combinations of status-group and bureaucratic education, but have been evolving increasingly in the bureaucratic direction in the past several decades. In some industrial societies sponsored-mobility systems prevail, in which case considerable educational tracking at an early age exists. In other industrial societies contest-mobility systems are found. These systems are more openly competitive and are not formally based on a tracking mechanism.

3. The United States has a contest-mobility educational system. It also has the world's largest educational system in terms of the number of students who go on to higher education. The U.S. educational system has undergone vast expansion in the twentieth century, an expansion greater than that experienced by any other industrial society. Currently nearly 60 percent of age-eligible students go on to attend college.

4. Four major theories of modern educational systems have been developed by sociologists. These are the functionalist theory, the Marxian theory, the theory of credential inflation, and the theory of education as nation-building. The main dimensions of these theories are laid out and critically evaluated in Table 17.4.

5. Since about 1950 a dramatic expansion of educational systems has occurred all over the world, even in some of the poorest nations. This process seems to be a major result of credential inflation. Credential inflation increasingly intensifies what Dore has called qualificationism: the development of educational systems as occupational recruitment devices rather than as knowledge-transmitting systems. Two negative consequences of qualificationism are the "over-education" problem and a general decline in the intellectual quality of education. These consequences are probably more severe in the underdeveloped countries.

SPECIAL TOPIC: THE EMERGENCE OF AN OVEREDUCATED SOCIETY

Beginning approximately in 1970, the United States started to become what some have termed an overeducated society. An overeducated society is not one whose members have become too knowledgeable or learned. Rather, it is one that has generated more students with educational credentials than can be absorbed into jobs that the credential-holders themselves generally deem satisfactory.

In his book *The Overeducated American* (1976), Richard Freeman points to two basic indicators of the United States's transition to an overeducated society. One of these is a decline in the salary levels of college-educated persons relative to those with only high school educations (Freeman, 1976:11–12):

> *Evidence that the salaries or income of college-trained workers, particularly those just beginning their careers, underwent a major and unprecedented*

downturn in the 1970s is impressive. By all relevant indicators, the income position of young graduates deteriorated sharply relative to that of other workers. . . . Whereas in the 1960s new college graduates obtained large gains in real salaries, generally above those of the other workers, they experienced a striking real and relative decline in the 1970s. From 1961 to 1969 humanities and social science graduates, for example, enjoyed a sizable increase in real pay, 2.7 percent a year, exceeding the rate of gain in average hourly earnings (2.6 percent), in annual full-time earnings (2.1 percent), and in other wage series in the economy. Then, from 1969 to 1975, their pay dropped precipitously—from $608 per month (in 1967 dollars) to just $470 per month—below the level obtained by similar graduates 15 years earlier. This sharp downward alteration in the salaries of new graduates in the 1970s was a major break with past economic developments.

. . . The drop in real income clearly produced a situation in which many graduates—who had opted for college during the booming 1960s—were severely disappointed with their economic status.

The other major indicator of the transition to an overeducated society that Freeman discusses is a dramatic increase in the difficulty college graduates began to experience in finding jobs commensurate with their education—or even any jobs at all. For example, in late 1972 the unemployment rate for the graduates of the class of 1972 was 11.7 percent. This figure exceeded the average for all workers, which was 5.1 percent, and the average for high school graduates of the same age, which was 7.7 percent. Graduates who had majored in the social sciences or humanities fared especially badly: their unemployment rate was approximately 16 percent.

Moreover, the following scenarios give ample testimony to the labor market difficulties of college graduates in the early 1970s (Freeman, 1976:28): Six months after their graduation, nearly one-fifth of the 1973 liberal arts graduates of a major university were unemployed, and another 15 percent of these graduates were working as janitors, factory workers, clerks, and receptionists; in the spring of 1975 students at the University of Illinois slept overnight in front of the placement office so they could sign up for job interviews; in the same year about twice the number of Harvard University students as time slots available lined up outside the career services office for interviews with banks; in replying to a questionnaire sent to them, only about one-sixth of Montclair State College graduates reported that their jobs were appropriate to their level of education.

There have been numerous and profound responses to these changes by both students and educational institutions. One early response by many students was simply not to go on to college. Whereas about 53 percent of 18- to 21-year-olds were attending college in 1970, the number had dropped to around 47 percent by 1973. It appears, though, that this decline in college attendance has been only temporary, for by 1980 the number of 18- to 21-year-olds attending college had increased again, to about 57 percent. More stable have been other reactions by students. In the past 15 years students have shifted their educational focus dramatically. Gone is the social and political consciousness so characteristic of the 1960s. Few students today have the kind of interest in social and political questions that were uppermost in the minds of many students in the 1960s. Most students today seem to be thoroughly bored with these concerns. Indeed, radicalism on the campuses of the 1980s seemed as dead as the dodo.

Students have also changed the focus of their majors in great numbers. There has been a precipitous decline in the number of students majoring in the social sciences and humanities; and fields like history, English literature, foreign languages, and philosophy are now starving for students. Students clearly feel that these more strictly intellectual subjects are luxuries they cannot afford. They have turned their attention instead to more practical fields, such as business administration and computer science, which they feel provide greater prospects for jobs. Even many of the most intellectually oriented students are turning toward these more practical fields, whereas in a good job market they would in most cases be engaged in the more intellectually abstract fields that really interest them.

Colleges and universities have responded to the changing orientations of students by shifting the focus of their curricula. In most American institutions of higher education administrators seem only too happy to develop more practical programs of study. This means introducing entirely new programs as well as shifting more traditional liberal arts fields toward a greater emphasis on the practical. Sociology and anthropology departments, for instance, have begun to give great emphasis to "applied sociology" and "applied anthropology" in order to cope with declining student interest in these fields.

As the United States has become an overeducated society the whole character of its educational system has begun to change, and in ways that many observers deem highly undesirable. Students feel more and more pressure to do well so they can be highly competitive in the job market upon graduation, and high grades have become almost an obsession. Moreover, the increasing emphasis on practicality has meant a corresponding erosion in emphasis on the liberal arts, the traditional core of higher education. Traditional educators feel increasingly uncomfortable with this erosion, believing that it leads to a terrible neglect of those areas of knowledge that truly mark an educated person. Thus, overeducation is itself a profound paradox, because overeducation in one sense actually seems to lead to "undereducation" in another.

FOR FURTHER READING

Aronowitz, Stanley, and Henry A. Giroux. *Education Under Siege: The Conservative, Liberal, and Radical Debate over Schooling*. South Hadley, Mass.: Bergin and Garvey, 1985. A valuable overview of the diversity of theoretical and political perspectives on contemporary education, along with the authors' own critical reactions to these perspectives.

Boli, John, Francisco O. Ramirez, and John W. Meyer. "Explaining the Origins and Expansion of Mass Education." *Comparative Education Review* 29:145–170, 1985. An approach to modern educational systems emphasizing the role of mass education in the building of modern rational states.

Bourdieu, Pierre, and Jean-Claude Passeron. *Reproduction: In Education, Society, and Culture*. Beverly Hills, Calif.: Sage, 1977. A famous book by two French social scientists that develops an argument about the social role of education similar to that of Bowles and Gintis.

Bowles, Samuel, and Herbert Gintis. *Schooling in Capitalist America*. New York: Basic Books, 1976. An argument for the shaping of American education by the capitalist economy. Despite its drawbacks, still essential reading in the sociological study of education.

Collins, Randall. "Some Comparative Principles of

Educational Stratification." *Harvard Educational Review* 47:1–27, 1977. A look at the major types of education in human societies. Emphasis is given to developing a theory of divergent educational systems in industrial societies. Provides an excellent comparative and historical baseline for understanding the nature of education in the United States and other contemporary industrial societies.

Collins, Randall. *The Credential Society: An Historical Sociology of Education and Stratification.* New York: Academic Press, 1979. A very insightful analysis of the American educational system and its monumental expansion over the past century. Should be required reading for all sociologists, educators, and policymakers.

Dore, Ronald. *The Diploma Disease: Education, Qualification, and Development.* Berkeley: University of California Press, 1976. A provocative analysis of the growth of qualification-oriented education on a worldwide basis throughout the twentieth century, with special attention to the growth of qualificationism in the Third World. This too should be essential reading, especially for educators and educational policymakers.

Halsey, A. H., A. F. Heath, and J. M. Ridge. *Origins and Destinations: Family, Class, and Education in Modern Britain.* Oxford: Clarendon Press, 1980. A major study of the role of education in the class structure of contemporary Britain.

Karabel, Jerome, and A. H. Halsey. *Power and Ideology in Education.* New York: Oxford University Press, 1977. An excellent collection of articles on various aspects of the sociology of education from a variety of theoretical perspectives.

Parkin, Frank. *The Mind and Body Shop.* New York: Atheneum, 1987. A wickedly hilarious novel by a well-known British sociologist that satirizes the growing commercialization and vocationalization of the British educational system.

CHAPTER 18

The Forms and Functions of Religious Belief and Action

The truth of religion comes from its symbolic rendering of man's moral experience; it proceeds intuitively and imaginatively. Its falsehood comes from its attempt to substitute itself for science and to pretend that its poetic statements are information about reality.

EUGENE GENOVESE

Religion is a universal feature of human social life in the sense that all societies have modes of thought and patterns of behavior that qualify to be labeled "religious." Much of what goes under the heading of religion belongs to the superstructure: it consists of specific types of symbols, images, beliefs, and values whereby human beings interpret their existence. However, since religion also embodies a ritualistic component, a part of religion belongs as well to the social structure. In this chapter we will explore how the structural and superstructural features of human religious life emerge in conjunction with the material infrastructure and other aspects of the social structure. As in other chapters, concern lies in both the sociocultural similarities and differences revealed by the phenomenon in question.

Our concern is necessarily of a scientific nature. We wish to determine what religion is, what various forms it has taken across time and space, and how it varies in accordance with material and social arrangements. Questions regarding the empirical reality of supernatural phenomena (whether or not God or other supernatural beings or forces actually exist) lie outside the bounds of scientific discourse. We shall therefore leave it to philosophers and theologians to speculate about the existence and possible nature of supernatural powers. But whether or not supernatural powers really exist, they become socially real and sociologically meaningful when people believe in them and act accordingly. It is the social reality of these beliefs and actions that is under investigation in this chapter.

Of course, many people will still insist that a scientific approach to the study of religious phenomena is inappropriate, if not logically impossible; they will claim that such an approach can yield no valid insights and can only serve to distort the proper spiritual meaning of such phenomena. However, social scientists have been systematically studying religious phenomena for approximately a century, and the results have been profoundly revealing.

THE NATURE OF RELIGION

Social scientists have had considerable difficulty in defining religion with any degree of precision. The main problem in arriving at a good definition has been to determine where the boundaries of the phenomenon should be placed. As Roland Robertson (1970) points out, two main kinds of definitions of religion have been proposed by social scientists: *inclusive* and *exclusive*. Inclusive definitions define religion in the broadest possible terms, conceiving of it as any system of belief and ritual that is imbued with "sacredness" or is oriented to "ultimate human concerns." Those who favor the inclusive view generally regard as religions not only theistic systems organized around the concept of a supernatural power or powers, but also various nontheistic belief systems such as Communism, nationalism, or humanism. By contrast, exclusive definitions restrict the term *religion* to those belief systems that postulate the existence of supernatural beings, powers, or forces. Nontheistic belief systems such as Communism or humanism, since they do not involve a supernatural realm, are automatically excluded, even though it may be granted that such nontheistic belief systems may share elements in common with religious systems. The following are good examples of inclusive definitions of religion:

> A religion is a unified system of beliefs and practices relative to sacred things, that is to say, things set apart and forbidden—beliefs and practices which unite into one single moral community called a Church, all those who adhere to them (Durkheim, 1965:62; orig. 1912).

> Let me define religion as a set of symbolic forms and acts which relate man to the ultimate conditions of his existence (Bellah, 1964:359).

> Religion, then, can be defined as a system of beliefs and practices by means of which a group of people struggles with these ultimate problems of human life (Yinger, 1970:7).

The first definition given above is very famous and has been cited repeatedly throughout the years by a host of sociologists. For Durkheim, the crucial characteristic of religion was that it was oriented toward a realm defined by human beings as *sacred*, that is, the object of special reverence, respect, and even awe. This realm stood in sharp contrast to the realm of the *profane*, or the world of ordinary, everyday existence. The second and third definitions cited above emphasize that religion is, above all else, oriented toward the "ultimate concerns" of humankind. What are these ultimate concerns? According to Yinger (1970), whose own definition makes them the essence of religion, they have to do with the fact of death; the need to cope with frustration, suffering, and tragedy; the need to bring hostility and egocentrism under control; and the need to "deal with the forces that press in upon us, endangering our livelihood, our health, and the survival and smooth operation of the groups in which we live—forces that our empirical knowledge cannot handle adequately" (Yinger, 1970:6).

At first sight, these definitions seem quite unobjectionable. Religion is, after all, generally associated with a realm postulated by human beings to be of sacred significance. Furthermore, it is generally the case that religious belief and action have a special concern for the ultimate problems of human existence given emphasis by Bellah and Yinger. Yet these definitions of religion are inadequate. The problem lies not in what they say, but rather in what they fail to say. In none of these definitions is religion restricted to systems of human thought and action that postulate the existence of supernatural powers or forces. All of the inclusive definitions allow anything to be called religion so long as it identifies a realm of sacred concern or relates to questions of ultimate meaning. Indeed, Yinger himself has stated that "some nontheistic systems of belief and action share so much in common with theistic ones that we do well to call them religions" (1970:13). Granted that some nontheistic systems share important elements in common with theistic ones, it is still an intellectual distortion to lump theistic and nontheistic systems together as if they were essentially the same kind of thing. It is of crucial significance whether or not a belief system postulates the existence of a supernatural realm.

It is clear that this book adopts an exclusive definition of religion. Others also prefer such restriction. Roland Robertson stresses the importance of an exclusive definition and holds that religion "is that set of beliefs and symbols (and values deriving directly therefrom) pertaining to a distinction between an empirical and a superempirical, transcendent reality; the affairs of the empirical being subordinated in significance to the non-empirical" (1970:47). Similarly, Anthony Wallace has defined religion as "that kind of behavior which can be classified as belief and ritual concerned with supernatural beings, powers, and forces" (1966:5). Along these same lines, we shall define **religion** as *an organized system of beliefs and practices, resting on unproved faith, that postulates the existence of supernatural beings, powers, or forces that act upon the physical and social world.*

There are three main elements in this definition. First, religion always involves both a set of rituals or practices and a set of beliefs; and these beliefs and rituals are socially organized and enacted by the members of a society or some segment of a society. The private thoughts of some individual do not constitute religion so long as they remain personal and unincorporated into some larger body of doctrine and ritual (i.e., these thoughts may be *religious* in nature, but by themselves they do not constitute *a religion*). Second, the beliefs in question are taken to be true on the basis of faith alone, there generally being no felt need to validate them in any empirical sense. Religious beliefs therefore lie outside the realm of scientific validation, and many of them as well lie outside the realm of scientific invalidation. In short, the criterion for the acceptance of religious beliefs has nothing to do with the standards of scientific evidence and proof or disproof. Finally, and most important, religion always involves the concept of a supernatural realm of existence that lies above and beyond the everyday, knowable, natural world. In the definition presented here, a system of belief and practice may be called religious only if it meets all three of the criteria stated above.

In addition to specifying what religion is, it is also desirable to indicate what it is not. In the first place, religion should not be seen as equivalent to a belief in a god or gods. While many religious systems postulate the existence of a god or gods who rule over humankind and to whom respect or reverence is due, many do not. Throughout Melanesia and Polynesia, for example, a central religious concept is that of *mana*. There is nothing godlike about *mana;* rather, *mana* is an abstract supernatural force that floats around and instills itself into people and things. People who have especially good fortune are said to be filled with *mana,* while those with bad fortune are said to have lost their *mana. Mana* can be controlled and used for beneficial consequences, but it is only an impersonal force, not a godlike or spiritlike being.

In addition, it is inappropriate to equate religion with a system of morality. Religious systems are often closely connected with systems of secular morality, but the two are hardly the same. There are many societies in which the religious system and the system of secular morality are quite independent of each other.

Many scholars have drawn a sharp distinction between religion and magic. The distinction usually made is that religion is based on "supplication," while magic depends on "manipulation"; that is, in religion human beings request, beg, or beseech things of the supernatural powers, who are free to deny such requests, while in magic human beings attempt to compel the supernatural forces to serve their ends (Malefijt, 1968). Some modern anthropologists, however, do not accept such a distinction, arguing that religion and magic are often intimately intertwined and that the distinction between them often gets lost in practice (R. Robertson, 1970).

A few words should be said about the differences between religion and science and about their relationship. Religion deals with the supernatural or "supraempirical" and bases its claims about the existence and nature of this realm on faith, divine revelation, or intuitive or imaginative experience. Science, by contrast, confines its claims to the natural or empirical world and demands that its claims be subject to agreed-upon standards of evidence and proof and disproof. There is a huge gulf separating these two modes of knowledge and understanding; they are based on radically different, indeed incommensurable, conceptions of what constitutes knowledge and truth. This means that there is a conflict between religion and science that is logically inevitable. Furthermore, where the claims that religion might make about empirical reality come into conflict with established principles of scientific knowledge, the claims of religion must give way to those of science, since the latter is a demonstrably superior mode of acquiring knowledge about the empirical world. Indeed, it has historically been the case that science has won out over religion where their claims about empirical reality have clashed. However, this does not mean that science can or should replace religion as a mode of understanding all aspects of human existence. So long as religion confines itself to the supernatural or supraempirical realm, it ceases to conflict with scientific principles, since no scientist can ever formulate tests to determine the nature or existence of such a realm. Religion therefore retains, and is likely to retain indefinitely, exclusive control over a realm of human understanding that is totally unapproachable by science.

THE EVOLUTION OF RELIGION

Scholarly work on the evolution of religion has lagged behind work on the evolution of many other features of sociocultural life. Nonetheless, some valuable schemes of religious evolution have been presented, and a few studies have been conducted that throw light on this important problem.

Bellah's Evolutionary Scheme

One well-known attempt to identify a series of stages of religious evolution is that of Robert Bellah (1964). Bellah lists five stages in the evolution of religion: primitive, archaic, historic, early modern, and modern. *Primitive* religion is said to be filled with myth and with a host of spiritual beings. Bellah comments on the "very high degree to which the mythical world is related to the detailed features of the actual world. Not only is every clan and local group defined in terms of the ancestral progenitors and the mythical events of settlement, but virtually every mountain, rock, and tree is explained in terms of the actions of mythical beings" (1964:362–363). But these spiritual beings are not gods for "they do not control the world and are not worshipped" (1964:362). Bellah also points out that primitive religion places great emphasis on ritual, and that in ritual performances the participants come to be identified with the mythical beings they represent. Primitive religion is notable for its lack of specialization: there are no priests, no congregation, and no spectators; and religion and society become fused as one.

In his category of *archaic* religion, Bellah places many of the religious systems of Africa, Polynesia, and the New World, along with the earliest religions of the ancient Middle East, India, and China. Archaic religions are characterized by the emergence of gods, priests, worship, sacrifice, and, very frequently, conceptions of divine kingship. The mythical or spiritual beings characteristic of primitive religion are transformed into gods: objectified beings who control the world and who are due reverence and worship. As such, "the distinction between men as subjects and gods as objects is much more definite than in primitive religion" (1964:365). Since archaic religions are generally found in societies possessing social stratification, religion comes to be closely intertwined with the stratification system. Upper-status groups usually claim superior religious status, frequently claiming to be of divine descent. Archaic religions are notable for their specialized priesthoods and for their legitimation of political leadership in religious terms.

The *historic* religions are those great world religions that emerged sometime during or after the first millennium B.C. The principal characteristic of these religions is their *otherworldliness*—their rejection of the value of the secular world and their establishment of another realm of existence (the afterlife) that is superior in value to the secular world. The prime goal of the historic religions is salvation, and the most important religious action is that which prepares the way for salvation. The historic religions therefore place great stress on the basically evil nature of the secular world and emphasize the necessity for a religious withdrawal from it. Bellah notes that the phenomenon of world rejection was virtually absent from primitive and archaic religions.

Early modern religion emerged with the Protestant Reformation. It continued the historic religions' distinction between the secular world and the other world, as well as its strong concern for salvation, but transformed the way in which salvation was to be achieved. Rather than through a withdrawal from the world, salvation came to be gained through a direct involvement in the affairs of the world. Early modern religion therefore marked a turning away from the world rejection theme of the historic religions.

Bellah believes that the twentieth century is witnessing the gradual emergence of *modern* religion. His conception of a modern stage of religious evolution is the most highly speculative and least clearly defined of all his stages. By modern religion, he means a form of religious life in which traditional religious concepts and rituals are at least partially supplanted by humanistic ethical concerns of a secular variety. At this stage of religious evolution, questions of ultimate human concern are answered increasingly in nontheistic terms. It is clear that Bellah can continue to call such an emergent phenomenon an aspect of religion only because he takes an inclusive view of religion. From the point of view of my exclusive definition of religion, what Bellah is describing, if it is occurring in the way he suggests, is not a new form of religion; rather, it is the gradual erosion of religion and its replacement by nonreligious belief systems.

Wallace's Evolutionary Scheme

Bellah's evolutionary scheme has its uses, and it is instructive in a general sort of way. His emphasis on the increasing objectification of supernatural powers or beings in the early stages of religious evolution, as well as his stress on the evolution of the world-rejection theme with the emergence of the historic religions, are important insights. Yet his tendency to see all primitive religions as of a single type distorts our understanding of religious life in primitive societies. This problem is overcome in Anthony Wallace's (1966) evolutionary classification of religious systems. Wallace not only distinguishes more carefully among various primitive religious systems, but also brings out some additional characteristics of religious evolution worth noting. An understanding of his scheme therefore complements Bellah's insights.

Wallace considers the religion of any society to be a conglomeration of **cult institutions.** A cult institution is "a set of rituals all having the same general goal, all explicitly rationalized by a set of similar or related beliefs, and all supported by the same social group" (1966:75). Four main types of cult institutions are identified by Wallace. **Individualistic cult institutions** exist when there are no shamans, priests, or other religious specialists available to perform rituals; rather, each person acts as his or her own specialist, performing specific rituals as the need arises. In **shamanic cult institutions** there exists a part-time religious specialist—a shaman—deemed to have special religious qualifications and powers. For a fee, shamans intervene with the supernatural powers on behalf of their clients. In contrast to individualistic cult institutions, shamanic cult institutions maintain a religious division of labor in which there is a distinction between religious specialists possessing special skills and powers and laymen who lack such special attributes. A third level of cult institution is the communal. **Communal cult institutions** are characterized by groups of laymen who "are responsible for calendrical or occasional performance of rituals of importance to various social groups ranging in scope from the members of special categories—such as age grades, the sexes, members of secret societies, particular kinship groups, and sufferers from particular diseases—to the whole community" (1966:86–87). Communal cult institutions include the agricultural rituals of the Iroquois, the ancestor ceremonies of the Chinese and some African tribes, and totemic and puberty rituals among the Australian aborigines. While communal cult institutions are characterized by a specific type of religious specialization, there is no full-time priesthood or extensive religious hierarchy. The latter are found, however, among **ecclesiastical cult institutions.** These cult institutions are based upon the existence of professional priesthoods organized in bureaucratic fashion. Members of the priesthood are full-time religious specialists elected or appointed to permanent religious offices. A sharp demarcation exists between priests and religious laymen; the former monopolize religious knowledge and the direction of religious rituals, while the latter are typically passive recipients of knowledge and ritual.

Wallace identifies four evolutionary types of religion based on combinations of cult institutions: (1) **shamanic religions,** which contain only individualistic and shamanic cult institutions; (2) **communal religions,** which contain communal, shamanic, and individualistic cult institutions; (3) **Olympian religions,** which contain individualistic, shamanic, and communal cult institutions, as well as ecclesiastical cult institutions organized around polytheistic pantheons of high gods; and (4) **monotheistic religions,** which contain individualistic, shamanic, and communal cult institutions, along with ecclesiastical cult institutions organized around the concept of a single high god.

Wallace believes that shamanic religions prevail primarily among hunting and gathering societies. The Eskimos have a shamanic religion. They populate the world with a variety of greater and lesser spirits, the most important of which is Sedna the Keeper of the Sea Animals. A major cult institution is the Shamanic Cult. The most important activity performed by the shaman is his annual trip to the bottom of the sea, a trip in which he attempts to persuade Sedna the Keeper of the Sea Animals to release the game she controls in order that the Eskimos can live through another year. Eskimo shamans are also frequently called upon for the diagnosis of illness. The Eskimos also maintain two individualistic cults, the Spirit Helper Cult and the Game Animal Cult. Religious activity in these cults involves the individual enactment of certain ritual performances as well as the individual avoidance of certain taboos.

Communal religions are most characteristic of horticultural societies. Wallace indicates that such religions have been found among many North American Indian societies, among African societies (excepting Muslim North Africa and the centralized African kingdoms), and among a number of Melanesian and Polynesian peoples. The Trobriand Islanders of Melanesia are organized along the lines of a communal religion. The major cult institution is what Wallace terms the Technological Magic Cult. In this cult, public magicians preside over communal rituals involving garden magic, canoe magic, and fishing magic. These rituals are calendrical in nature, being tied to the cycle of the seasons. In addition to this communal cult, the Trobriand Islanders have one other communal cult, shamanic services, and engage in a variety of individualistic religious practices.

Ecclesiastical religion: Temple of the Warriors at Chichén Itzá, Mexico, an important Mayan ceremonial center later taken over by the Toltecs.

Olympian religions are most commonly found among intensive horticultural and early agrarian societies. Olympian religions have been found among the early civilizations of the New World, such as the Mayas, Aztecs, and Incas; among many of the centralized chiefdoms or kingdoms of Africa; among East Asian societies on the edges of China and India, such as the kingdoms of Burma, Indonesia, and Korea; and among the ancient Greeks and Romans. The African kingdom of Dahomey possesses an Olympian religion. In addition to individualistic, shamanic, and communal cults, the Dahomeans have a Great Gods Cult. This cult has many of the features of an established church, as it actively supports and legitimizes the Dahomean ruling class. This cult possesses a priesthood and many temples. The pantheon of gods is divided into four subpantheons, and each of these is associated with a separate religious order. Each religious order contains its own priesthood, temples, and rituals. As is typically the case in Olympian religions, each deity is associated with a particular aspect of nature over which it exercises control.

The great world religions, such as Judaism, Christianity, Islam, and Hinduism, are, of course, monotheistic religions. Such religions arose in the context of complex agrarian societies and have continued right into the modern industrial era. Although there are a number of fundamental differences among these great monotheistic religions, all share in common the conception of a single high god to whom great reverence and obedience is due.

Studies of the Evolution of Religion

Wallace limits his conception of montheistic religion to the historic world religions that

Table 18.1 RELIGION IN SOCIOCULTURAL EVOLUTION

Type of religion (Wallace's scheme)	Typical technological level of society	Example
Shamanic: only individualistic and shamanic cult institutions present	Hunting and gathering	Eskimos, !Kung, Mbuti of central Africa
Communal: individualistic, shamanic, and communal cult institutions present	Simple horticultural	Trobriand Islanders, many North American Indian tribes
Olympian: individualistic, shamanic, communal, and polytheistic ecclesiastical cult institutions present	Intensive horticultural and early agrarian	Mayas, Aztecs, Incas, ancient Greeks and Romans, African kingdoms
Monotheistic: individualistic, shamanic, communal and monotheistic ecclesiastical cult institutions present	Complex agrarian and contemporary industrial	Ancient China and India, medieval Europe, contemporary Western capitalism, contemporary Japan

emerged during or after the first millennium B.C. Yet as Guy Swanson (1960) has pointed out, a number of primitive and ancient societies worshiped a deity believed to have been the sole creator of the world. Swanson identifies such a form of religious practice as the worship of "high gods," and through a study of 50 primitive and ancient societies he has attempted to specify the social conditions under which the belief in a high god emerges.

One important finding to emerge from Swanson's investigation was that the belief in a high god was strongly related to the presence within a society of a number of sovereign groups arranged in hierarchical order (a sovereign group is one that exercises an independent jurisdiction over some sphere of social life). Societies having only one or two sovereign groups seldom held to a belief in a high god, while the great majority of those societies possessing three or more hierarchically ordered sovereign groups had such a belief. These findings demonstrate that the belief in a high god is only likely to be found in societies beyond a certain level of social and political complexity.

Swanson also produced other findings directly relevant to an understanding of the evolution of religion. He notes that in many societies the supernatural powers are felt to take no active interest in the everyday moral behavior of individuals. Yet in many other societies the supernatural powers are actively interested in everyday morality, and supernatural sanctions are invoked in order to help ensure conformity to moral rules. Swanson's results show that supernatural sanctions for moral behavior are most likely to be present in societies possessing one or more of the following features: considerable debt relations, social classes, individually owned property, and primogeniture. The factor most strongly correlated with supernatural sanctions for morality was the presence of social classes. This finding demonstrates how the functions of religion are transformed in accordance with other sociocultural transformations. With the emergence of social stratification, a particularly important need arises for privileged social strata to defend their high social, economic, and political position. Religion becomes a prime means of such defense. Superior wealth, power, and status can be legitimized in religious terms—as being in accordance with divine or supernatural will—and the threat of supernatural penalties can be invoked as a means of ensuring the conformity of the disprivileged to the rules set forth by the privileged.

Another study dealing with the evolution of religion is that of Ralph Underhill (1975). Like Swanson, Underhill sought to determine the specific social conditions responsible for the presence within some societies of a belief in a high god. Using a very large sample of primitive and ancient societies, Underhill found that the presence of a high god was strongly correlated with a society's degree of economic and political complexity. In general, the more economically and politically complex a society, the more likely it was to possess belief in a high god. Furthermore, Underhill claims that, while both economic complexity and political complexity were strongly related to the presence of a high god, economic complexity was somewhat more strongly related. Underhill interprets his findings in Marxian terms (1975:860):

> My overall interpretation is that the nature of the economic system is of ultimate importance. Economic complexity has myriad social and ideological effects, including effects on . . . religious beliefs. . . .
>
> As far as the data have taken us, Marx and Engels have been supported. They saw the importance of economic realities lying beneath religious beliefs, yet also recognized the complexities of social organization and ideology in the "superstructure."
>
> God, I suggest, is a "representative of the forces of history." He is a reflection of existing economic and social relationships. His concern is to preside, at the ultimate level, over economic and political complexities.

RELIGION AND POLITICS

The specific ways in which religion and politics have been associated in various societies have long been subject to commentary by social scientists. Many social scientists have taken the view that religion has primarily served as a means of legitimizing and protecting the interests of established political systems and the ruling classes served by these political systems. In this view, religion is an inherently conservative force, actively promoting the maintenance of the established political and social order and neutralizing any significant attempts to change that order. Yet it has also been pointed out that religion has frequently served as a rallying call for attempts to make major changes in established institutions. This second view holds that religion is not necessarily conservative in nature and, in fact, is often a radical force.

The Marxian View

The classic statement of religion's role in the protection of established social arrangements is that of Marx. Marx wrote very little about religion, but what he did have to say was especially poignant. His most famous comments on religion were made in an early essay written in 1843. In this essay he described religion's social role in the following terms (Marx, 1963:43–44; orig. 1843):

> Religion is the general theory of this world, . . . its logic in popular form . . . , its moral sanction, its solemn complement, its general basis of consolation and justification. It is *the fantastic realization* of the human being inasmuch as the *human being* possesses no true reality. The struggle against religion is, therefore, indirectly a struggle against *that world* whose spiritual *aroma* is religion.
>
> Religious suffering is at the same time an *expression* of real suffering and a *protest* against real suffering. Religion is the sigh of the oppressed creature, the sentiment of a heartless world, and the soul of soulless conditions. It is the *opium* of the people.

In this passage, Marx declares religion to be an expression of oppression and suffering, as well as a means of rationalizing and justifying the prevailing social order. Most importantly, Marx refers to religion as the "opium of the people." By this he means that religion acts upon people in a druglike fashion: it alleviates suffering, but it does not eliminate the conditions that produce that suffering. Therefore it merely placates people, allowing them to accept the social conditions under which they live in the hope of an afterlife in which all suffering and misery will be forever banished. Since religion merely soothes human suffering but does not eliminate its basis, it allows people to continue to accept the world as it is and not try to change it. Thus Marx saw religion as an inherently conservative force since it mutes the possibility of people acquiring a revolutionary consciousness through which the world itself can be changed.

Weber's Contribution

Max Weber (1978; orig. 1923) shared some of Marx's views regarding the political and social functions of religion. Weber saw religion performing distinctly different functions for different social strata in societies possessing social stratification. For privileged social strata, he argued, religion serves primarily as a means of legitimizing or justifying their superior social position and class privileges. For disprivileged strata, on the other hand, religion is primarily important as a means of dealing with oppression, suffering, and injustice: as a means of compensating in another life for the failures and inadequacies of the present life. As Weber puts it (1978:491–492):

> Since every need for salvation is an expression of some distress, social and economic oppression is an effective source of salvation beliefs, though by no means the exclusive source. Other things being equal, strata with high social and economic privilege will scarcely be prone to evolve the idea of salvation. Rather, they assign to religion the primary function of *legitimizing* their own life pattern and situation in the world. . . . What the privileged classes require of religion, if anything at all, is this legitimation.
>
> . . .
>
> Correspondingly different is the situation of the disprivileged. Their particular need is for release from suffering. . . . Their need for religious salvation, where it exists, may assume diverse forms. Most important, it may be conjoined with a need for just compensation, envisaged in various ways but always involving reward for one's own good deeds and punishment for the unrighteousness of others. This hope for and expectation of just compensation, a fairly calculating attitude, is, next to magic (indeed, not unconnected with it), the most widely diffused form of mass religion all over the world.

From this it follows that religion's role in the social order tends strongly in a conservative direction. As a legitimator of the social position of dominant groups, religion announces that the established social, economic, and political order is an expression and embodiment of supernatural will, and therefore should be accepted just as it is. Even though many may suffer under the existing social arrangements, this suffering is only temporary and will be relieved in a better world to come.

Evidence in Support of Marx and Weber

The evidence in support of the claims of Marx and Weber is strong. Some of this evidence has already been touched upon. As we have seen, religion is transformed in close accordance with the evolution of economic and political systems. In societies lacking social stratification, the supernatural powers are infrequently concerned with the everyday moral doings of human beings. But with the emergence of stratification the supernatural powers develop a significant concern with secular morality and are commonly invoked as a means of regulating earthly social arrangements. Furthermore, the evolution of powerful centralized political systems—chiefdoms and states—is highly correlated with the evolution of powerful priesthoods and ecclesiastical religious institutions. Priests typically share heavily in the exercise of political power. Early chiefdoms or kingdoms, in fact, tended to be theocracies, forms of government carried out by religious functionaries. As chiefdoms evolved into states, government came to be lodged primarily in the hands of secular political officials rather than priest-chiefs or priest-kings; nevertheless, these secular officials still retained close ties with priests and actively used the priesthood as a means of bolstering their own power. Most chiefs and kings throughout history have justified their rule in religious terms, either claiming direct descent from the gods or to be God's principal representative on Earth.

The evolution of the great historic religions, with their theme of world rejection and belief in the fundamentally evil character of the world, also demonstrates a close connection between religion and established political arrangements. All these religions evolved in complex, highly stratified societies in which the oppression and exploitation of the masses had reached intolerable proportions. The world came to be seen as an evil place from which escape was necessary. Strong themes of escape from the world, of religious withdrawal, are profoundly conservative. Since they lead people to search for solace only in another life to come, they actively block the development of a revolutionary consciousness whereby the secular world itself can be changed.

There is also another kind of evidence that strongly indicates the role of religion in actively promoting and maintaining established social and political arrangements. This evidence comes from recent surveys conducted by sociologists regarding the way in which religious and political beliefs tend to be combined in individuals' minds. All the evidence to be discussed comes from studies of the religious and political beliefs of the members of contemporary Western societies.

Charles Glock and Rodney Stark (1965) sought to determine the connection between religion and radical politics. One part of their study focused on the relationship between religion and political party affiliation in France. They placed the French political parties on a continuum ranging from the most radical to the most conservative. From the political left to the political right, they ranked the parties as follows: Communist, Socialist, Radical, Poujadist, Gaullist, and Peasant and Independent. They then examined the religious beliefs and practices of the members of these various parties. What they found, in short, was a very strong connection between political conservatism and orthodox religious belief and practice, and a corresponding antagonism between orthodox religion and radical politics. Some of their specific findings are worthy of note. They found that only 7 percent of the Communists were currently engaged in the practice of their religious faith, while 67 percent of the Gaullists and 68 percent of the members of the Peasant and Independent party were so engaged. When they examined party members' beliefs in the existence of God, they obtained even more remarkable results. Only 9 percent of the Communists were certain of the existence of God, while 75 percent of the Gaullists and 77 percent of the Peasant and Independent party members were certain of God's existence. In addition, they found that the members of the more radical parties were much more likely than the members of the conservative parties to harbor specific forms of hostility toward the Church. In general, Glock and Stark found that the more radical the political party, the more likely it was for its members to disavow traditional religious belief and practice. Glock and Stark also examined the relationship between religion and politics in the Netherlands, and their results bear out the findings they obtained in the case of France. Glock and Stark conclude from these results that religion and radical politics tend to be mutually corrosive: involvement in radical politics is highly associated with the rejection of orthodox religion, while conservative political activity is closely linked with traditional religious belief and involvement in organized religion.

Another study that shows much the same thing was conducted by Gary Marx (1967). Marx sought to discover whether religion among black Americans served as an "opiate" or as an inspiration for militant action in the struggle for civil rights. He found that religion generally served as an opiate. For example, only 26 percent of the persons he studied who could be classified as "very religious" held a militant stance regarding the struggle for civil rights, while 70 percent of the persons classified as "not at all religious" expressed a militant position. Marx's findings, that religious involvement dampens enthusiasm for radical political activity, are also borne out in many other studies of the connection between religious and political beliefs (cf. Sanderson, 1973). In one large-scale study of the religious and political orientations of American college students, orthodox and fundamentalist religious beliefs were found to be highly correlated with attitudes of political conservatism; conversely, people who rejected traditional religious beliefs and practices also strongly tended to reject a variety of conservative political positions (Sanderson, 1973).

Thus, a variety of evidence offers strong support for Marx's claim that religion is an "opium of the people." Yet to leave matters here would be to give a markedly distorted picture of the role of religion in human society, for there is another side to the connection between religion and politics that has not yet been examined. There are numerous instances in which religion has served as an important catalyst for attempts to change the world. At many points in history and in a great many places, people have formed themselves into religiously inspired movements devoted to basic alterations in the established social order.

REVITALIZATION AND MILLENARIAN MOVEMENTS

The socioreligious movements just referred to have most commonly been called **revitalization** or **millenarian movements.** The term *revitalization* implies an attempt to create a new or "revitalized" mode of existence that would be highly preferable to the current state of affairs. The term *millenarian* is most frequently applied to socioreligious movements that anticipate the coming of a millennium—a new age of peace, harmony, and prosperity, a literal paradise on Earth—and that are often led by charismatic leaders held to be messiahs.

Revitalization or millenarian movements typically occur under conditions of extreme social stress or crisis: in periods of rapid social change when people are uprooted and disoriented from their traditional patterns of life; when native cultures are severely altered by colonialism, warfare, or the invasion of an alien culture; or when oppression and exploitation have reached intolerable limits. Under such conditions, millenarian movements are likely when people are confused or befuddled as to what is really happening to them, and when more strictly secular means of dealing with this stress are unavailable (Harris, 1974). Virtually all millenarian movements contain both religious and political elements in their ideologies and in their strategies for change; however, the particular mixture of the religious and the political varies widely from one movement to another. Some movements are highly political and militantly radical, expecting and pushing for immediate social change. Others stand more toward the religious end of the spectrum, with otherworldly religious themes substantially overshadowing secular political themes. Yet others mix in nearly equal portions of other-worldly religion and secular politics. But, in all cases, revitalization or millenarian movements are premised upon a refusal to accept things as they are. The members of all of them hope and expect some type of meaningful change to occur in their lives.

These socioreligious movements have occurred at many points in history and virtually throughout the world. They have been found in classical antiquity, medieval and modern Europe, Melanesia, Polynesia, Africa, South America, North America, and Indonesia, among other places. Many are still found today, even in the industrialized West. Most of these movements have ended in failure, but a few have been successful to one degree or another. Christianity, for example, was originally the outgrowth of Jewish millenarianism. The best-known revitalization and millenarian movements (in addition to the early Jewish ones) are those that have occurred in Melanesia and medieval Europe, and among the Indians of North America.

Jewish Military Messianism and the Origins of Christianity

Marvin Harris (1974) has provided a provocative analysis of Jewish military messianism as it existed around the time of Christ. In addition, he has attempted to demonstrate the way in which it gave birth to Christianity.

The ancient nation of Palestine had long been subject to colonial rule by a host of powerful empires. Under Roman rule, which prevailed for many years both before and after the life of Jesus, most of the Jews who inhabited Palestine were subject to enormous oppression and exploitation. As Harris has pointed out, Palestine was a victim of extreme colonial misrule. The vast majority of the population consisted of landless peasants, poorly paid artisans, servants, and slaves. Apart from them were tiny elites of priests, landowners, and merchants who lived in magnificent luxury. Peasants were subject to especially heavy taxes and various forms of labor conscription by absentee landlords. Administrative corruption and inflation in the economy were rampant. The result of all this was an intense hatred on the part of the Galilean peasants for the Jerusalem aristocrats.

It was during the period of Roman rule that the tradition of Jewish military messianism developed into a potent religious and political force. Many men came forward and claimed to be messiahs who would deliver Palestine from the clutches of Roman oppression and establish the Kingdom of God on Earth. These would-be messiahs were neither strictly religious nor strictly political in their words and deeds. Rather, they fused the religious and the political inextricably together. In addition to enunciating religious proclamations about the coming of the Kingdom of God, they were actively engaged in military operations designed to bring it about. Many messiahs organized armies and fought against the Roman legions. At least two major wars were fought against the Roman armies, one in A.D. 68–73 and the other in A.D. 132–136, but these were only the most prominent of the military activities directed by the Jewish forces against Rome.

Jesus was one of many Jewish messiahs who arose in Palestine to fight against Roman oppression and exploitation. It is widely believed—indeed, it is a cardinal principle of Christianity—that Jesus's teachings were strictly of a peaceful nature, that he was opposed to violence and vengeance. Harris sharply disputes this image of Jesus as the "Prince of Peace" and claims that Jesus's activities were actually highly consistent with the whole tradition of Jewish military messianism (Harris, 1974:187–188):

> Jesus and his disciples did nothing that would have distinguished them from the members of

Services at a Jewish temple in San Francisco. The origins of Christianity must be sought in the political and economic relations between the early Jews and ancient Rome.

an incipient military-messianic movement. They even provoked at least one violent confrontation. They stormed into the courtyard of the great temple and physically attacked the licensed businessmen who changed currencies so that foreign pilgrims could purchase sacrificial animals. Jesus himself used a whip during this incident.

. . .

Even his most intimate disciples were clearly not prepared to "turn the other cheek." At least two of them had sobriquets which suggest that they were linked with militant activists. One was Simon, called "The Zealot," and the other was Judas, called "Iscariot." There is an uncanny resemblance between Iscariot and *sicarii,* the word used by Josephus to identify the knife-wielding homicidal dagger men. . . .

Two other disciples had warlike nicknames—James and John, the sons of Zebedee. They were called "Boanerges," which Mark translates from Aramaic as "Sons of Thunder" and which could also mean "the fierce, wrathful ones." . . .

The gospels also indicate that some of the

> disciples carried swords and were prepared to resist arrest. . . .
>
> All four gospels record the fact that the disciples put up armed resistance at the moment of Jesus's capture.

But if Jesus was a typical Jewish military messiah, why have his teachings and actions come to be thought of as purely peaceful in nature? Harris argues that this has occurred because of a highly selective reinterpretation of Jesus's actual thought and conduct. Harris believes that it was after the Jewish forces were defeated in the messianic war of A.D. 68–73 that Jewish Christians began the selective reinterpretation of Jesus's messiahship. This reinterpretation, he believes, was a necessary response to the failure of their messianic war against Rome (Harris, 1974:195, 202):

> In the aftermath of the unsuccessful messianic war, it quickly became a practical necessity for Christians to deny that their cult had arisen out of the Jewish belief in a messiah who was going to topple the Roman Empire.
>
> . . .
>
> Jewish Christians now readily joined with gentile converts to convince the Romans that *their* messiah was different from the zealot-bandit messiahs who had caused the war and who were continuing to make trouble: Christians, unlike Jews, were harmless pacifists with no secular ambitions.

Millenarian Movements in Medieval Europe

Just as Christianity arose out of millenarian activity, new forms of millenarian activity were soon to arise out of Christianity, at least after it became a highly established institutionalized religion. By the later Middle Ages, millenarian movements directed against the ruling religious, economic, and political powers were becoming quite common; from the eleventh to the sixteenth centuries, a great variety of millenarian movements arose throughout many areas of Europe. An outstanding study of these movements has been conducted by Norman Cohn in his book *The Pursuit of the Millennium* (1970). As Cohn notes, the great majority of these movements were guided by eschatological fantasies: by doctrines espousing that the end of the world was near at hand and that a messiah was coming to install a heavenly paradise on Earth. Decade after decade, century after century, and place after place, men arose claiming to be messiahs returned to Earth to establish the millennium. These messiahs preached eschatological doctrines to those who would listen, organized bands of followers around themselves, and instructed their followers in the actions necessary for bringing the millennium into existence. In many cases, these messiahs advocated and actually carried out militant actions against both secular and religious authorities. A European millenarian movement that was especially militant was the Anabaptist movement.

Most Anabaptists were disoriented and alienated peasants and artisans. They believed in the communal holding of property, regarded the state with suspicion, and tended to reject society at large. Many of them were obsessed by the belief in the coming of a day of reckoning in which the mighty would be cast down and Christ would return to establish a millennium on Earth. In the early 1530s they took over the town of Münster in Germany and proclaimed it to be the New Jerusalem. Under their leader, Jan Matthys, they felt that they were inaugurating a social revolution. Matthys and a few lesser leaders began a propaganda campaign against the private ownership of property, and the followers of the movement were forced to turn all their money and possessions over to the group. Matthys soon established dictatorial control over his followers, but shortly after having done so, he died. His replacement was a man named Jan Bockelson. Bockelson established a new government in Münster, and this government was given authority over all public, private, spiritual, and material concerns. He also established a new moral code that was so strict that it made such things as quarreling and lying capital offenses. He made it a capital offense for any follower to disagree with him, and an executioner was even appointed to take care of those who would dare challenge his authority. Eventually, Bockelson declared himself to be a king—King of the New Jerusalem—and he began to dress in magnificent robes and to wear rings and chains made of the finest metal. At the same time, he imposed a life of severe austerity on his followers: they were forced to work without compensation; he dreamed up schemes to test their loyalty; and he threatened them with death for the slightest violation of his commands.

The Anabaptist occupation of Münster ended in complete disaster. Famine eventually hit the town, and it became so severe that people were actually forced to eat grass, moss, old shoes, the whitewash on walls, and even the bodies of the dead. At this point Bockelson told his followers that he would change the cobblestones into bread. Death from starvation became such a common occurrence that large communal graves had to be dug. When people tried to leave the town, Bockelson had them beheaded; often the body was quartered and its sections nailed up for public display as a warning to others. Such activities eventually became almost an everyday occurrence. Finally, the troops who had been besieging the town for some time overwhelmed it and brought the New Jerusalem to an end. Bockelson and the other leaders of the movement were executed.

The Anabaptist movement may seem like a particularly extreme occurrence, and in some ways it was. Nevertheless, medieval Europe was witness to many other millenarian movements in which extremes of behavior were typical. In the thirteenth and fourteenth centuries, for example, groups of flagellants engaged in religious rituals in which they beat themselves with spikes until chunks of flesh were torn from their bodies. Why were such groups given to these extreme forms of behavior? As Cohn has made clear, most of the followers of medieval millenarian movements consisted of uprooted peasants or chronically unemployed artisans. These people experienced acute social and economic stresses and lacked any real secular means of dealing with such stresses. Under such conditions, they became particularly vulnerable to the messianic claims of charismatic psychopaths who offered them some hope of escape from their suffering. Marx's claim that religion is the "sentiment of a heartless world" seems most appropriate in understanding the involvement of the most downtrodden members of medieval Europe in millenarian activities.

Cargo Cults and the Ghost Dance

Beginning around the end of the nineteenth century, many areas of Melanesia fell under European colonial domination, resulting in severe dislocations in the lives of native inhabitants of the region. Under these conditions, revitalization movements known as **cargo cults** developed. The most persistent ideological element in these cults is the belief that shiploads of modern Western industrial goods (cargo) will be arriving at any moment for the complete use and enjoyment of the natives. These goods are being sent and accompanied by the natives' dead ancestors, who have come back to life. When the goods arrive, a new age of joy and prosperity will commence. In earlier times, the cargo was believed to be arriving by ship, and the natives busied themselves building ports where the ships could dock. But with the arrival of the airplane, the cargo was said to be coming by plane; this prompted many cult members to build runways on which the planes could land. The cults have also perpetuated doctrines regarding the reorganization of native society.

Above all, the Europeans would be thrown out and native society returned to the control of the natives themselves.

Peter Worsley (1968) has described the nature of many of these cults. One such cult is the Vailala Madness, a movement that first developed in Papua New Guinea in 1919. The Vailala Madness was led by a prophet named Evara, a man filled with divine revelations. He prophesied the arrival of a steamer that would be bringing cargo and the spirits of the dead ancestors. This cargo—flour, rice, tobacco, rifles, and other items—was claimed rightfully to belong to the Papuans, not to the whites. In order to obtain the cargo for themselves, the Papuans had to drive out the whites. Many of the adherents to this cult referred to themselves as "Jesus Christ men," and some claimed to have visions of God or Christ and to have received messages from them. The movement also embodied as a central theme a belief in the ascent of the dead to Heaven.

Revitalization movements arose among a number of North American Indian tribes in the nineteenth century as a response to the encroachment of the whites and the destruction of traditional cultures. The most famous of these was the Ghost Dance, which appeared in two waves, the first in 1870 and the second in 1890 (Lanternari, 1963; cf. Thornton, 1981). The first wave of the Ghost Dance occurred among the Paviotsos, Indians living between Nevada and California. The Paviotsos were led by a prophet named Wodziwob, who founded the movement after receiving a vision in 1869. In his vision, Wodziwob saw a railroad train carrying the Indians' ancestors. He held that these travelers were going to announce their return to Earth with a great explosion: "Wodziwob's revelation occurred at the top of a mountain: the Great Spirit announced that a major cataclysm would soon shake the entire world, in the course of which the white man would vanish from the Indian land. The earth would open up to swallow the whites, while all their buildings, goods, and tools would remain for the use of the Indians" (Lanternari, 1963:132). Wodziwob's revelations began to spread in two different directions, and soon they had reached tribes all over the western part of the United States. The Ghost Dance of 1890 was started by a Paiute Indian named Wovoka. Wovoka preached a strict moral code to his people: They were not to fight, lie, steal, or drink whiskey, and they were to work hard and love one another. He prophesied that the whites would be blown away by high winds, but that all their possessions would be left to the Indians (Malefijt, 1968). Like the earlier version of the Ghost Dance, this one spread widely and rapidly to other tribes, among them the Shoshoni, Arapaho, Cheyenne, Kiowa, and Sioux.

A Contemporary Millenarian Movement*

Millenarian movements have by no means been limited in their occurrence to primitive, ancient, or medieval societies. On the contrary, they have continued to be found even in Western industrialized societies. One of the most recent examples of a millenarian movement is the People's Temple organized under the leadership of the Reverend Jim Jones. This cult flourished in the United States during the 1960s and 1970s. It bears a striking resemblance to many other millenarian movements of the past.

The Reverend Jim Jones founded the People's Temple in Indianapolis, Indiana, in 1956. In due time, his church grew and expanded. In the 1960s the organization was moved to California, eventually establishing itself in San Francisco. By this time, Jones was well on the way to thinking of himself as a messiah who had come to deliver his followers—most of whom consisted of poor, disoriented, and alienated

* This discussion is based on Axthelm et al. (1978) and Steele et al. (1978).

persons—from the wickedness of the world. He preached against corruption, racial bigotry, and other evils, and advocated a communitarian doctrine. He asked his followers to give all their money and worldly possessions to the Temple, and he imposed upon them a strict morality. In due course he ceased to think of himself as a mere messiah and began to suggest to his followers that he was actually God in the flesh. His followers were reproached for paying more attention to the Bible than to him. He claimed to be able to heal the sick of even the most dreaded diseases, and elaborate stunts were concocted to demonstrate such powers to his congregation. As an earthly God, he wielded total power over his recruits; punishments were meted out for even the slightest violations of his commands.

In 1974 Jones and several hundred members of the People's Temple established a communitarian settlement in the jungles of Guyana, a settlement that came to be called Jonestown. The People's Temple members who followed Jones to Guyana expected to find there a true paradise on Earth; what they found instead was a living hell. They were forced to work long hours in the fields under a hot sun; they were constantly harangued and subjected to lengthy "re-education meetings" when they were exhausted from working in the fields; ingenious techniques were dreamed up for terrorizing children who misbehaved; they were not allowed to receive mail from their families back home; violations of rules were met with beatings, and beatings were also administered to anyone caught attempting to leave the settlement; and "loyalty tests" were administered by asking cult members to consume drinks they were told were poisonous. Rather than a paradise on Earth, Jonestown was literally an armed camp whose members were tortured and terrorized.

In November of 1978 Congressman Leo Ryan of California visited Jonestown in order to investigate growing reports of abuses there. As Ryan was leaving Jonestown at the conclusion of his visit, taking with him several members of the cult who wished to leave, he and several members of his party were shot and killed by some of Jones's armed executioners. Following this event, Jones forced all the members of the Jonestown settlement—some 900 in all—to consume poisoned drinks in a ritual of mass suicide, while at the same time putting a bullet through his own head. The bodies lay bloated and rotting when U.S. officials arrived on the grisly scene.

One cannot fail to notice the stunning similarities between Jim Jones of the People's Temple and Jan Bockelson of the Anabaptists. Although separated by more than 400 years, these leaders engaged in strikingly similar activities. Both were charismatic psychopaths who led their followers into disastrous consequences. However, from a sociological point of view what is most interesting is not the personalities of these men but the fact that they could get so many people to believe in them and carry out their instructions. Even in the last moments of the Jonestown settlement, many of Jones's followers thought of him not as a dangerous psychopath but as a divine deliverer from the evils of the world; many, in fact, took their poisoned drinks quite willingly. Jones's seductive power over his followers, like that of Bockelson's, lay in the fact that these followers were disoriented and alienated people who were seeking a means of coping with a world they found to be corrupt and unjust.

Theoretical Recapitulation

Marx held religion to be both the "sentiment of a heartless world" and the "opium of the people." The appearance of revitalization movements at time after time and in place after place certainly lends credence to his claim that religion functions as the sentiment of a heartless world. Revitalization movements have been

Aftermath of the collective suicide of members of the People's Temple cult, Jonestown, Guyana, 1978.

limited in their occurrence to several specific conditions. They have typically arisen among the poorest, most disinherited, and most exploited and oppressed members of the social order. In addition, they have been quite common occurrences in many parts of the world where native cultures have been severely disrupted by invading colonial powers. This is not to suggest, of course, that religion always or only functions in this manner, for this is certainly not the case. As a universal social institution, religion performs many other important functions as well. But about religion's crucial role in injecting heart into heartless conditions there can be no serious doubt.

Marx's claim that religion functions as an "opiate" is much more problematic. In the last section, we saw that this is very frequently the case. However, the widespread existence of revitalization movements clearly demonstrates that religion is also a mechanism commonly designed to produce fundamental changes in established social arrangements. Jewish messiahs were attempting to topple the Roman Empire; Indians of North America used the Ghost Dance as an attempt to expel the invading whites; and the followers of Jim Jones were attempting to create a more satisfying lifestyle in a world that gave them little satisfaction. While it is probably true that religion is more often than not a force that leads people to accept the world as it is in the hope that the next one will be better, in some cases religion has precisely the opposite effect. In this sense, religion is a tool that may be used in two contradictory ways: as a means of preserving a social order intact, or as a means of producing radical changes in that order. Marx's statement that religion is the opium of the people is true, but it is a half-truth.

RELIGION AND THE MODERN WORLD

The Protestant Reformation*

During the time that Europe was experiencing the transition to a capitalist world-economy, a major transformation in the realm of religion was underway: the Protestant Reformation. The Reformation can be said to begin in 1517, for this was the year that Martin Luther nailed his famous 95 theses to the church door. Luther, of course, was the originator of reformationist ideas and the founder of that major branch of Protestantism known as Lutheranism. Luther's objections to Catholicism centered on what he perceived as widespread abuses and corruption within the Church, as well as on the whole Catholic doctrine of salvation through the absolution by priests of sins. Luther wanted to establish a religion that would return to the original spirit of Christianity as expressed in the Bible, and he declared a doctrine of salvation that was rooted in deep personal faith in God rather than in the actions of religious functionaries representing a religious bureaucracy (the Church).

Luther's ideas had an almost immediate popular appeal and spread quickly and widely. It was not long before they were adopted throughout several of the sovereign states that are now part of modern Germany, and they spread to the Scandinavian countries of Sweden and Denmark (Table 18.2). In England, a very similar form of Protestantism, Anglicanism, became established. Luther was soon followed by other

* This discussion is based on Spitz (1985) and Swanson (1967).

Table 18.2 PROTESTANT AND CATHOLIC STATES IN SIXTEENTH-CENTURY EUROPE

States Adopting Lutheranism or Anglicanism

- The German states of Prussia (1525), Württemberg (1535), Saxony (1539), Brandenburg (1539), and Hesse (1605)[a]
- Denmark (1536)
- Sweden (1536)
- England (1553)

States Adopting Zwinglianism or Calvinism

- The Swiss cantons of Geneva (1536), Basel (1528), Schaffhausen (1530), Bern (1528), Zurich (1525), Glarus (1531), and Appenzell (1523)
- The German states of Cleves (1569) and Mark (1569)
- Bohemia (1593)
- United Provinces (Netherlands) (1579)
- Hungary (1540)
- Transylvania (1557)
- Lowland Scotland (1560)

States Remaining Catholic

- The Italian states of Venice and Florence
- The Swiss cantons of Schwyz, Unterwalden, Uri, Zug, Fribourg, Lucerne, and Solothurn
- Poland
- France
- Austria
- The German states of Bavaria, Jülich, and Berg
- Portugal
- Spain
- Ireland
- Highland Scotland

[a] The dates in parentheses refer to the year in which a state formally adopted Protestantism or by which a majority of the citizens had become Protestant. The religious situation in a few of these states changed in later years, usually as a result of political conquest.

Source: Guy E. Swanson, *Religion and Regime: A Sociological Account of the Reformation*. Ann Arbor: University of Michigan Press, 1967.

Martin Luther, one of the two great theological leaders of the Protestant Reformation.

Protestant reformers, the most notable of whom were the Swiss Huldrych Zwingli and the Frenchman Jean Calvin (John Calvin). Calvin was clearly the more important. Although French, Calvin spent most of his time in Geneva, Switzerland, and thus that city became the birthplace of Calvinism. Calvin's ideas were similar to Luther's and he was obviously influenced by him. There were, of course, many different features to his theology. Perhaps the most important of these was his famous doctrine of predestination, which held that God had from all eternity predestined some persons for salvation and others for damnation. This was a modification of Luther's notion of salvation through faith, and of course a marked departure from the Catholic Church's approach to salvation. Like Lutheranism, Calvinism spread quickly and widely (Table 18.2). It was adopted in many Swiss cantons, in the Netherlands, in several German states, in Lowland Scotland, and even for a time in parts of Poland and Hungary.

Many areas of Europe were highly resistant to the Reformation (Table 18.2). In the leading countries of Mediterranean Europe—Italy, Spain, and Portugal—Protestant ideas had little influence, and Catholicism remained overwhelmingly dominant. The Catholic Church also remained secure in several Swiss cantons, in several sovereign German states, and in Austria, Ireland, Highland Scotland, and most of eastern Europe. France also remained Catholic, even though Protestant ideas spread quickly after their initial formulation. A significant minority of the French population did convert to Protestantism, but the Protestant movement in France was violently crushed and the number of persons still embracing Protestantism dwindled to a tiny few.

Explaining the Reformation

To understand the causes of the Reformation—why it began and why its ideas were adopted when and where they were—it is vital to understand the most important doctrinal differences between Catholicism and Protestantism. Max Weber (1958; orig. 1905) argued, and there is every reason to believe he was correct, that the most important doctrinal innovation of Protestantism lay in its conception of salvation. Protestantism eliminated the formal Church's role in granting salvation. Rather than gaining their salvation through the mediation of priests, individuals gained salvation by approaching God in a very direct and personal way. Luther's doctrine of salvation by faith and God's grace and Calvin's conception of salvation through predestination both connected God directly with each individual and eliminated the bureaucratic organization of the Church as an agent in salvation. As many sociologists have argued, this meant that, in contrast to Catholicism, Protestantism was a highly *individualistic* religion. This can be especially seen in the seventeenth-century elaboration of Calvinist doctrine. The rigid doctrine of predestination set forth by Calvin in the sixteenth century was gradually modified and made more flexible. It came to be argued by Calvinists that God did indeed predestine each person, but He had permitted a way for each individual to know, if not to change, His will. Individuals who had achieved worldly success through their own sacrifices and intense efforts could take this as a sign from God that they were among the saved. This was the famous Protestant ethic that figured so prominently in Weber's *The Protestant Ethic and the Spirit of Capitalism* (1958 [orig. 1905]; cf. Robertson, 1959).

It is a sad fact that sociologists have largely neglected the Reformation. This stems both from the ahistorical outlook of most sociologists, and from the still highly underdeveloped status of the sociology of religion. Even Weber's famous work linking Protestantism and capitalism was devoted only to explaining the rise of capitalism, and Weber offered no systematic explanation for the rise of Protestantism itself. One of the most thorough sociological analyses of the Reformation is that of Guy Swanson (1967), who sets forth a political theory. Swanson argues that the Reformation was adopted in those European states that had come to have an organization devoted to serving various kinds of external interests, such as bodies of merchants, artisans, or nobles. This idea is rooted in Swanson's more general claim that religion's basic importance is as a mechanism designed to symbolize and legitimize political structures. Swanson's analysis of 41 sovereign European states shows that there was, indeed, a striking correlation between the form of government (as conceptualized and categorized by Swanson) and the adoption or rejection of Protestantism. However, it is very likely that the correlations to which Swanson points actually disguise another factor that was at work. This factor was economic. To a great extent, the modes of government that Swanson sees as associated with the adoption of Protestantism *were governments in which capitalist economic interests and ideals played a major role.*

To the extent that they concern themselves with questions of causation at all, many theologians and historians are inclined to argue that the Reformation was primarily devoted to the correction of major abuses of the Church, or that it was a kind of logical working out of theological doctrines—a kind of internal development of the logic of religious ideas (cf. Lortz, 1972). There is no doubt that the leaders of the Reformation were concerned with many activities of the Church that they regarded as abuses, and that they were highly motivated to correct these problems. However, abuses had been going on for a very long time. Why did a major attempt to correct them arise at the particular time it did, and why was the effort successful in some places but not in others? Furthermore, if Protestantism involved simply the internal development of religious ideas, why did the ideas take the particular form they did? The answers to these questions, I believe, most properly center on the close historical relationship between the Reformation and the emergence of modern capitalism (cf. Engels, 1978 [orig. 1850]; Walker, 1972; Wuthnow, 1980b). Weber was right in pointing to a close historical connection between Protestantism and capitalism, but he had the causal relationship backwards. Protestantism emerged in, or spread to, largely those parts of Europe that were in the forefront of capitalist advance. This was because Protestant ideas greatly helped to legitimate and express the capitalist world-view, as well as because of certain practical economic benefits that Protestantism could convey. As Robert Wuthnow has written (1980b:63–64):

> The Protestant Reformation occurred in the context of rapid population growth, a long-term rise in grain prices, great expansion in the volume and circulation of money due to the importation of bullion from America, naval and military innovations, and an intensification and broadening of trade. This expansion greatly benefited the German and Polish nobility, the Swiss city magistrates, and the Dutch and English merchants, all of whom prospered from the expanding trade between the Baltic and the Mediterranean. It was [in these areas] that the Reformation first became institutionalized. The reformers' attacks against the Church implicitly desacralized the Hapsburg empire, whose legitimacy rested heavily in the defense of universal faith, and broadened access to legitimate authority. . . . [T]he Reformation prompted the secularization of church lands, giving elites revenues independent of church and other taxes, and encouraging land reform beneficial to commercial agriculture. . . . After the middle of the sixteenth century, owing significantly to the financial burdens which Spain incurred in combating the Protestant heresies, the core of the European economy shifted increasingly to the north, and with it the Reformation became firmly established.

In a more recent work, Wuthnow (1989) has suggested a more complex relationship between capitalism and the Reformation. In what is essentially a type of neo-Weberian argument, Wuthnow claims that capitalism was linked to the Reformation indirectly rather than directly. The spread of capitalism led to political support for the reformers' ideas when the state came to be freed from the control of the landed nobility. Under such circumstances, governments were enthusiastic about the religious reforms because of the many practical political benefits they could convey. On the other hand, where the landed nobility continued to control the state, the latter crushed efforts at religious reform. The nobility and the Church were closely linked, especially in terms of the strong social legitimation that the Church provided for the nobility's dominant position. Thus the nobility had every reason to resist all efforts at undermining the Church's authority and continued influence.

Wuthnow's theory has a certain appeal. It seems particularly relevant, for instance, in explaining the deviant case of France, the one core capitalist society in which Protestantism made little headway. As Wuthnow suggests, in France "the nobility were too much in control of the state for the Reformation to succeed" (1989:91). However, as suggestive as it is, Wuthnow's argument is by no means proven. His analysis is unbalanced in the sense that he considers only whether or not the state was controlled by the nobility. He does not consider the fact that, in those early capitalist areas in which the state had been freed from the nobility's control, the state had fallen under the control of other economic groups, namely merchants and capitalist landlords. Because he ignores the strategic importance of such groups,

Wuthnow is unable to prove that it was politics rather than economics that really counted. The role of economics is also strongly suggested by the fact that, as Wuthnow himself notes time and again, the reformers' ideas were most prominently taken up and promoted by urban classes—merchants and craftsmen—and were strongly resisted by rural classes—landlords and peasants.

Types of Religious Organization in Modern Industrial Societies

Substantially as a result of the Protestant Reformation, modern industrial societies are characterized by great religious diversity, containing within their boundaries a large number of different religious groups. Nevertheless, all of these diverse religious groups can be classified into a limited number of organizational types.

An early student who was concerned with the problem of types of religious organization was Ernst Troeltsch (1931). Troeltsch identified two polar types of religious organization, which he called **church** and **sect.** His conceptualization of the church identified it as a religious organization having the following characteristics: It was large, literally coextensive with society as a whole; individuals were born into it and baptized as infants; it had an official ecclesiastical structure in which priests were earthly extensions of God; it placed great emphasis on established doctrines and dogmas; and it accepted the secular world as it was, even identifying itself quite closely with the ruling secular powers. The Roman Catholic Church of the Middle Ages was held to be the example *par excellence* of this type of religious organization.

The sect stood at the opposite extreme from the church. It was small, membership in it being limited to a select number of individuals; individuals joined the group as adults; its members constituted a "community of believers" who thought of themselves as religiously distinct from the members of other religious groups; it had no official ecclesiastical structure, its ministry being lay; it placed great emphasis on "living the right kind of life"; and it was hostile toward the secular world, which it generally perceived to be corrupt and decadent.

Sociologists have generally found Troeltsch's concepts useful, but only as a starting point. Most have felt the need to distinguish an additional number of types in order to capture fully the variety of religious organization in industrial societies. J. Milton Yinger (1970) has distinguished five basic types of religious groups: ecclesias, denominations, established sects, sects, and cults.

Yinger identifies the **ecclesia** in terms quite similar to Troeltsch's conception of the church. However, he views the ecclesia as even more aligned with society's dominant segments than was the medieval Roman Catholic Church. Hence the ecclesia fails to serve the needs of many of its members, particularly those from lower social strata. For this reason, Yinger refers to the ecclesia as "a universal church in a state of rigidification." The Lutheran Church in Scandinavia and the Anglican Church in England are among the better examples of the ecclesia.

The **denomination** is a conventional and respectable type of religious organization that is in substantial harmony with the secular powers. Unlike Troeltsch's church or the ecclesia, however, the denomination is not coextensive with society as a whole; rather, it is limited by such boundaries as those of class, race, and region. Contemporary denominations are typically former established sects or sects that have evolved into more conventional and respectable organizations. In the United States, such groups as Presbyterians, Methodists, and Baptists are good examples of denominations.

The **established sect** is viewed by Yinger as a sect (in Troeltsch's sense) that has retained

The denomination is such a common form of religious organization in America that some sociologists have referred to the United States as a "denominational society."

many of its sectlike characteristics while at the same time having evolved some distance in the direction of conventionality and respectability. In this sense, established sects lie partway between denominations and sects, having some of the characteristics of each. Yinger cites the modern-day Quakers as an example of this type of religious group. Yinger's conception of the **sect** is essentially the same as Troeltsch's. (It should be pointed out that sects are quite akin to millenarian movements, and some sects actually are millenarian in nature.) However, he distinguishes among several different types of sects. *Acceptance sects* generally do not seek to change the world, and they live in harmony with it; their sectlike quality is based on their adherence to religious doctrines that are esoteric and mystical in nature. *Aggressive sects* reject the world and seek to alter it, often on the basis of eschatological fantasies. The Jehovah's Witnesses belong to this type of sect. A third type of sect is the *avoidance sect*. Such sects reject the secular world, but make no particular effort to alter its nature; rather, the members of such groups withdraw from the world and seek special religious knowledge and insight of a personal nature. Some of these groups, such as the Pentecostals, "seek trances, visions, and the 'gift of tongues'—temporary escapes into a world where their standards rule" (Yinger, 1970:277–278).

Cults are religious groups standing at the farthest extreme from the ecclesia. They are typically very small, short-lived, and built around a charismatic leader. Although similar to sects, they are more extreme in their religious doctrines, frequently representing a radical break with the dominant religious tradition or traditions of a society. As Yinger indicates, they are "religious mutants." Examples include the Church of Satan and the Krishna Consciousness organization in the United States.

These types of religious organization illustrate quite well how diverse religious forms are adapted to the needs of different individuals and groups within industrial societies. As Yinger has made clear, the ecclesia is almost wholly centered around the needs and interests of the dominant segments of society. Denominations are groups that embrace a wide variety of members, but they still tend to be oriented toward individuals and groups from particular social backgrounds. In American society, for example, upper-middle-class individuals tend to be Episcopalians, Congregationalists, or Presbyterians; likewise, Baptists tend to draw their members disproportionately from the lower socioeconomic strata. It is generally agreed that sectarian groups are responses to various kinds of deprivation. Most commonly it is economic deprivation that pushes people toward sects, but other kinds of deprivation may also be responsible for sect formation; various kinds of psychological deprivation are sometimes prime motives leading individuals to join particular sects. Cults typically arise under conditions of very rapid social change; such change leaves many people confused and befuddled about the nature of the world and predisposes them to seek solutions to their confusion in extremist religious groups. In the 1960s and 1970s, for example, many new cults sprang up in the United States. These cults were direct responses to the disorienting changes that were taking place during those years (cf. Glock and Bellah, 1976; Harris, 1981). Religion is a prime means of providing answers to the fundamental problems of human existence; as those problems differ, so will the kinds of religious responses called forth to deal with them.

SECULARIZATION AND THE FUTURE OF RELIGION

The Controversy over Secularization

The concept of **secularization** refers to the process by which religion's influence over many spheres of social life has been steadily reduced. Many sociologists have subscribed to the view that secularization has been a major trend in Western societies in the past few centuries, or at least since the onset of industrialization. They have held that the forces of scientific advance, industrialization, urbanization, and the overall rationalization and modernization of society have caused religion to recede more and more from the arenas of social life that it traditionally occupied. The stronger versions of this *secularization thesis* claim that the process of secularization is an inexorable force that will culminate in the extinction of organized religion. Weaker versions claim only that secularization has historically been a significant trend and do not necessarily postulate the ultimate end of institutionalized religious activity.

Jeffrey Hadden (1987) has claimed that the secularization thesis has been so widely embraced by sociologists that it has become virtually an unchallenged, taken-for-granted truth. Hadden's point is not likely far off the mark. In recent years, however, a variety of challenges to the secularization thesis have emerged. Hadden himself claims that the thesis is empirically false, and that it has been sustained more by sociologists' antagonism to organized religion than by any systematic examination of the evidence. Against the secularization thesis Hadden places the following lines of evidence: (1) Since the end of the Second World War there has been a general religious revival, at least in the United States. (2) In recent years there has been a major growth in the more conservative religious traditions, that is, the evangelicals and fundamentalists. (3) The beliefs and behaviors of American Catholics have been dramatically affected by the Second Vatican Council, with the result that the authority of the Church is now stronger than at any point in American history. (4) The overwhelming majority of Americans still report a belief in God. (5) Church membership statistics in the United States have fluctuated only slightly in the past 40 years, and even church attendance has remained remarkably stable. (6) Religious devotion (e.g., prayer) has also remained very stable in recent decades.

Timothy Crippen (1988) also attacks the secularization thesis. He pursues a line of thinking that has become common among many opponents of the thesis, arguing that religion in modern society is undergoing *transformation* but not *decline* (cf. Bellah, 1970; Glock and Bellah, 1976; Wuthnow, 1976; Stark and Bainbridge, 1985). "Traditional religions may be waning," he suggests, but "even so, religious consciousness remains powerful and manifests itself in new beliefs and rituals corresponding to modern organizational forms of dominance and exchange" (1988:325). Crippen holds that "new gods" are arising to replace the "old gods," and that these new gods have much to do with "new sacred beliefs and rituals that symbolize the sovereignty of the nation-state and the moral integrity of the individual" (1988:331). The new kind of "religion" that Crippen is talking about is what Robert Bellah (1967) once called "civil religion."

Crippen's position is untenable, in my view, because it relies entirely on a classically inclusivist definition of religion. Although Crippen explicitly favors such a definition, he readily concedes that from the exclusivist's viewpoint there has indeed been an extensive secularization of social life in recent centuries. What then of Hadden's argument? Although the religious trends he points to are more or less accurately identified, the problem is that his argument is lacking in both historical perspective and a comparative foundation. Hadden is really discussing only one society, the United States, and his analysis of it covers a very brief period of time. This obviously will not suffice. It is well known that the United States is in many respects the most religious of all contemporary Western industrial societies, and many sociologists have spoken of "American exceptionalism" (Zeitlin, 1984). One cannot legitimately use a single society, let alone a highly unusual one, to disprove a general theory that is intended to apply to many societies.

The counterarguments of Hadden and Crippen, and of those sociologists who largely agree with them, therefore do not do much damage to the secularization thesis, at least in its weaker form. A staunch defender of the thesis is the well-known British sociologist of religion Bryan Wilson (1982). Wilson points out that the secularization thesis depends on the notion that earlier forms of human society generally gave a marked social significance to religion. This is generally true, Wilson says, arguing that "simpler cultures, traditional societies, and past communities . . . appear to have been profoundly preoccupied with the supernatural" (1982:150). Compared to these past societies and communities, Wilson asserts (1982:149), contemporary industrial societies have experienced

> the sequestration by political powers of the property and facilities of religious agencies; the shift from religious to secular control of various of the erstwhile activities and functions of religion; the decline in the proportion of their time, energy, and resources which men devote to super-empirical concerns; the decay of religious institutions; the supplanting, in matters of behavior, of religious precepts by demands that accord with strictly technical criteria; and the gradual replacement of a specifically religious consciousness (which might range from dependence on charms, rites, spells, or prayers, to a broadly spiritually-inspired ethical concern) by an empirical, rational, instrumental orientation; the abandonment of mythical, poetic, and artistic interpretations of nature and society in favour of matter-of-fact description and, with it, the rigorous separation of evaluative and emotive dispositions from cognitive . . . orientations.

It is impossible to deny that Wilson's characterization of religious change is an accurate one, and there is thus every reason to sustain the secularization thesis as it concerns the recent past. However, we still need to evaluate the version of this thesis that applies to the future of religion.

The Future of Religion

Given the secularizing trends of recent centuries, what can reasonably be expected regarding the future of religion? Will secularization continue and intensify, to the point that religion eventually will be eliminated from sociocultural

Children opening presents on Christmas morning. The commercialization of Christmas is only one of many indicators of the extensive secularization Western capitalist societies have undergone.

life altogether? Or will some fundamental core of religious belief and activity remain, no matter how scientifically and technologically sophisticated human societies become? Social scientists are highly divided in the answers they give to such questions. Many hold that modern science and technology will eventually destroy religion as a social institution. Others maintain that, even though its significance may be reduced still further, religion will remain as a persistent and permanent feature of sociocultural systems. Anthony Wallace takes the former view, claiming that (1966:264–265)

> the evolutionary future of religion is extinction. Belief in supernatural beings and in supernatural forces that affect nature without obeying nature's laws will erode and become only an interesting historical memory. To be sure, this event is not likely to occur in the next generation;

> the process will very likely take several hundred years, and there will probably always remain individuals, or even occasional small cult groups, who respond to hallucination, trance, and obsession with a supernaturalist interpretation. But as a cultural trait, belief in supernatural powers is doomed to die out, all over the world, as a result of the increasing adequacy and diffusion of scientific knowledge and of the realization by secular faiths that supernatural belief is not necessary to the effective use of ritual. The question of whether such a denouement will be good or bad for humanity is irrelevant to the prediction; the process is inevitable.

An opposing view is held by J. Milton Yinger. Yinger conceives religion to be a "residual" institution, by which he means that it is "that which always remains." Religion is a means of providing answers to ultimate questions; since ultimate questions will always be with us, and since it is impossible for science to attempt answers to some of these questions, religion will always remain in order to reduce uncertainty. Yinger states his case as follows (1970:9):

> Is there no core of functions that seems likely to be a continuing source of religious activity? Or are science, philosophy, art, government, medicine, and the like chiseling away at religion so steadily that it has become a "suicidal institution," as Dunlap calls it? I myself find it difficult to envisage a society in which no major problems of the ultimate variety we have discussed remain unresolved. We reduce the amount of premature death only to discover the tragedies of senescence. We begin to conquer poverty only to realize that the knowledge behind that achievement is part of a larger knowledge that brought the hydrogen bomb. I suspect . . . that the belief that man can devise secular processes for performing the functions now served by religion is itself a "citadel of hope," and not an empirically validated proposition. . . .
>
> . . . What evidence we have inclines me toward the view that religion as I have defined it is a permanent aspect of human society, which is no more likely to disappear than the family (however much it may change) or government (despite the enormous range of variation).

Wallace's scenario has much to recommend it. Science has already eroded religious belief, and we know that when people acquire highly developed intellectual outlooks (especially scientific ones) their religious beliefs tend to dissipate (Glock and Stark, 1965). Hence, if future societies are permeated by the mass dissemination of advanced forms of learning (and it seems reasonable to expect that they will be), religion might well collapse or be greatly reduced in significance. On the other hand, Yinger's scenario also has its attractions. The most ultimate of all the ultimate questions is that regarding human finitude—the fact that humans die. All cultures everywhere have shown some degree of preoccupation with this question. Humans have never wanted to accept their own finitude and have repeatedly created conceptions of an afterlife in order to disavow that things must end. Religion has been the only institutionalized means whereby human beings have grappled with the question of finitude. The question is completely off limits for science; no matter how successful science becomes in explaining and controlling the empirical world, it is powerless in the face of a nonempirical concern like this one. On the basis of these considerations, there is good reason to believe that some essential core of religious belief and ritual will continue indefinitely. Although the scope of religion's influence will no doubt be increasingly reduced in the future, it may well be unwise to predict that its influence will disappear altogether.

SUMMARY

1. Two fundamentally different types of definitions of religion have been offered by social scientists. Inclusive definitions stress that religion is a system of beliefs and practices orga-

Religious fundamentalist Pat Robertson announcing his candidcay for the U.S. presidency in 1986. The tremendous popular appeal of such fundamentalist leaders in recent years suggests that predictions of the evolutionary death of religion must be treated with considerable skepticism.

nized around things said to be sacred, or oriented toward ultimate human concerns. Exclusive definitions are more restrictive and limit the notion of religion to beliefs and practices postulating supernatural forces that act in the world. This book favors an exclusive definition.

2. Religion is an evolutionary phenomenon in much the same sense that the other components of human societies are. Robert Bellah has proposed that religion has evolved through five basic stages: primitive, archaic, historic, early modern, and modern. An alternative scheme of religious evolution has been offered by Anthony Wallace, who distinguishes four stages: shamanic, communal, Olympian, and monotheistic religions.

3. Empirical studies suggest close correspondences between the evolution of religion and the evolution of political economy. A study by Swanson demonstrates that religions generally develop supernatural sanctions for morality when societies become stratified. Underhill has found that beliefs in a high god are highly correlated with economic and political complexity.

4. In calling religion the "opium of the people," Marx was suggesting that religion serves as a means of relieving the suffering produced by exploitation and oppression. He was also suggesting that religion is profoundly a politically conservative force. Max Weber made similar suggestions. He noted that religion functioned for privileged groups as a social legitimator, whereas for disprivileged groups it served as a means of compensating for the inadequacies of their situation. Considerable evidence of both a historical and sociological kind lends support to the basic claims of Marx and Weber.

5. In many ways, though, the Marxian opium-of-the-people thesis is a half-truth. Religion is sometimes a radical rather than a conservative force. This is clearly indicated by the prevalence of revitalization or millenarian movements all over the world and throughout much of human history. These are radical social movements that combine religious and political themes in an effort to change the world in fundamental ways. Although the prevalence of revitalization movements suggests a definite limitation to the Marxian view, in another sense they support it because these movements strongly confirm Marx's notion that religion is the "heart of a heartless world."

6. Revitalization movements are generally responses to various types of social stress and crisis, such as result from extreme exploitation and oppression, warfare, or the destruction of an indigenous culture by a foreign invader. Perhaps history's most famous revitalization movement was primitive Christianity, itself an outgrowth of Jewish militaristic messianism. Christianity has been one of the few successful revitalization movements. Revitalization movements also occurred throughout Europe in the later Middle Ages, in Melanesia, and in the late nineteenth century among various North American Indian tribes. A famous contemporary revitalization movement was the People's Temple led by the Reverend Jim Jones.

7. Modern forms of religious organization essentially began with the Protestant Reformation of the sixteenth century. This was a great religious transformation that challenged the authority of the Catholic Church and its doctrine of salvation. It corresponded historically with the beginnings of the capitalist world-economy, and it is likely that Protestantism was a religious manifestation of this great economic change.

8. Various types of religious organization exist in modern industrial societies. Yinger has identified five basic types of religious groups: ecclesias, denominations, established sects, sects, and cults. These types of religious organization closely correspond to such social groups as classes, racial and ethnic groups, and regional groupings. This indicates the adaptiveness of religion to a variety of human needs.

9. In recent centuries increasing economic rationalization, industrialization, urbanization, and scientific advance have led to the extensive secularization of modern industrial societies. However, the extent to which secularization will continue is very much an open question. Some social scientists suggest that the evolutionary future of religion is extinction, while others hold that, because of religion's function as a "residual" institution, some minimal core of religious belief and practice is likely to persist indefinitely.

SPECIAL TOPIC: RELIGION AS THE WORSHIP OF SOCIETY

One of the more provocative sociological analyses of religion was carried out by the eminent French sociologist Emile Durkheim in the early part of this century. In his book *The Elementary Forms of the Religious Life* (1965; orig. 1912), Durkheim attempted to understand the social role of religion by studying its simplest or most elementary forms. In this book he analyzed the totemic religious rituals of the Arunta, an Australian hunter-gatherer society about which considerable ethnographic knowledge already existed.

Durkheim's general sociological perspective was that social life constitutes a level of reality all its own that is not interpretable in terms of the characteristics of individuals. Sociologists, he claimed, study *social facts,* phenomena that exist apart from individuals and exert a controlling influence on them. Durkheim believed that social facts can only be explained in terms of other social facts, and he applied this sociological perspective in his study of religion. Religion is something eminently social, not psychological. It arises because humans live in society and thus develop certain basic needs as a result of their collective life. Religion exists because it fulfills certain crucial social functions that cannot be fulfilled without it. Its chief role, Durkheim thought, is that of a societal integrator. It binds people together by uniting them around a common set of beliefs, values, and social rituals. It thus helps to preserve society or the group as a moral community.

Durkheim noticed that among the Arunta ritual and ceremony were exceptionally important parts of social life. He derived a radical (and highly speculative) thesis from this. The fact that the Arunta worshiped supernatural powers was not what was most important about their activity. Whether they knew it or not, they were really worshiping the power of their own society, the power of society over each individual. Their religious ritual demonstrated and symbolized the need for individuals to submit themselves to the will of the group. In coming together in ritual, the Arunta publicly reaffirmed their commitment to one another and to society as a whole. Durkheim thought that this was not only what the Arunta did, but is what people in all religions do. He thus concluded that it is the ritualistic component of religion that is most important because it is through ritual that the binding power of the community is symbolized.

Durkheim himself was an atheist who thought that the concepts and ideas of religion were empirically false. Yet he approved of religion because of its socially integrating character. His favorable view of the role of religion in society led him to be concerned about what he saw as its gradual demise in the modern world under the influence of modern science and technology. Traditional religion, he thought, would eventually die out. Its disappearance would hold dire consequences for the integration of society unless an acceptable replacement were to emerge. In this regard Durkheim was optimistic. He saw a replacement emerging in the form of a new system of beliefs and rituals that worshiped society directly rather than indirectly—in the ideology of *nationalism.* People would come to see the power and importance of society and would worship it directly instead of through the mediating role of religious rituals. Nationalism would become the new religion of modern industrial society (there is no contradiction here when we recall that Durkheim adopted an inclusive definition of religion that defined it as concerned with objects that were socially identified as sacred).

Durkheim's analysis of religion has been enormously influential in twentieth-century sociology. His notion that religion plays a crucial role as an integrator of society contains much truth. Particularly in band and tribal societies does religion perform this role, but religion is an important social integrator in more complex societies as well. In fact, in this regard Durkheim and Marx are not far apart in their views, for Marx clearly understood that religion plays a major role in eliciting the commitment of individuals to the basic character of their social order. This was much the point of his "opium of the people" thesis. Yet Marx stressed what Durkheim largely overlooked: that religion can be a divisive force as well as an integrating one. One only has to cast a cursory glance over society and history to see how much this is so. Historical conflict between Muslims and Hindus in India that led to the creation of Pakistan, centuries of conflict between Catholics and Protestants in Ireland, and the contemporary volatile conflict between

Christians and Muslims in Lebanon are only a few instances of religion's socially divisive role. A Durkheimian perspective on the social nature of religion, then, has much value, but there is a one-sidedness to it that can only be counteracted by the adoption of a more conflict-oriented analysis.

FOR FURTHER READING

Cohn, Norman. *The Pursuit of the Millennium: Revolutionary Millenarians and Mystical Anarchists of the Middle Ages.* Revised edition. New York: Oxford University Press, 1970. A scintillating discussion of millenarian movements in medieval Europe.

Glock, Charles Y., and Rodney Stark. *Religion and Society in Tension.* Chicago: Rand McNally, 1965. A collection of valuable essays on various aspects of the sociology of religion, including the relationship between religion and politics and between religion and science.

Harris, Marvin. *Cows, Pigs, Wars, and Witches: The Riddles of Culture.* New York: Random House, 1974. Provocative discussions of Jewish military messianism, early Christianity, and the "great witch craze" of early modern Europe.

Lanternari, Vittorio. *The Religions of the Oppressed.* New York: Knopf, 1963. Millenarian movements in Africa, Native North America, Native South America, Melanesia, Polynesia, and Indonesia.

Spitz, Lewis W. *The Protestant Reformation, 1517–1559.* New York: Harper & Row, 1985. Although utterly lacking in theory, a useful contemporary exposition of the basic character of the Reformation.

Swanson, Guy. *The Birth of the Gods.* Ann Arbor: University of Michigan Press, 1960. A detailed study of 50 primitive and ancient societies that attempts to uncover the basic social conditions giving rise to various forms of religious belief.

Thomas, Keith. *Religion and the Decline of Magic.* New York: Scribners, 1971. A provocative study of widespread beliefs in such things as astrology, witchcraft, and magical healing in sixteenth- and seventeenth-century England and their ultimate decline.

Turner, Bryan S. *Religion and Social Theory: A Materialist Perspective.* London: Heinemann, 1983. One of the few recent efforts by a sociologist to develop a materialist (basically Marxian) analysis of religion.

Wallace, Anthony F. C. *Religion: An Anthropological View.* New York: Random House, 1966. The leading textbook on religion from an anthropological slant.

Wilson, Bryan. *Religion in Sociological Perspective.* New York: Oxford University Press, 1982. An overview of some major concerns in the sociology of religion by a noted British specialist.

Worsley, Peter. *The Trumpet Shall Sound: A Study of "Cargo" Cults in Melanesia.* Second edition. New York: Schocken Books, 1968. The best available study of Melanesian cargo cults. In addition to presenting information on a wide range of cults, offers a lengthy discussion of a number of theoretical issues involved in the study of these and other revitalization movements.

Wuthnow, Robert. *Communities of Discourse: Ideology and Social Structure in the Reformation, the Enlightenment, and European Socialism.* Cambridge, Mass.: Harvard University Press, 1989. The first major section is perhaps the best systematic sociological treatment of the Reformation to date.

Yinger, J. Milton. *The Scientific Study of Religion.* New York: Macmillan, 1970. The leading textbook on religion from a sociological slant.

CHAPTER 19

The Social Foundations of Science

This chapter presents a historical and sociological account of science as a social institution. By **science** we usually mean a mode of intellectual inquiry that seeks a coherent understanding of the world through reliance upon systematic observation of it. The ultimate intellectual aim of most scientific activity is the development of coherent theories that explain the greatest number of phenomena in the simplest possible way. In addition to being a mode of inquiry, science consists of an accumulated body of observations and theories; hence, science is both a mode of investigation and the accumulated results of that investigation.

Conceived in this way, science belongs principally to the superstructural component of human societies. Does this mean that science is primarily a result of underlying infrastructural and structural conditions? The answer to this question is both "yes" and "no." It is yes in terms of whether and to what extent any given society is involved in scientific undertakings. Infrastructural and structural factors are principal determinants of a society's level of scientific activity and its degree of respect for and nurturance of science. On the other hand, the answer is mainly no with regard to the *specific content* of scientific ideas themselves. Although infrastructural and structural forces are not irrelevant to the actual content of scientific thinking, such forces do not play a major role in shaping the theories produced by scientists. (This is especially the case in the natural sciences; in the social sciences, it is less true.) Compared to other aspects of the ideological superstructure, the content of science has a remarkable degree of independence from infrastructural and structural causation. Scientific thought is not merely subjective, but can legitimately lay claim to being a highly objective form of knowledge.

Nonetheless, the autonomy of scientific knowledge is only a partial autonomy, and social considerations do influence the nature of scientific thought. This is especially the case in regard to the generation of scientific ideas (as opposed to their validity or merit). Therefore, sociologists must examine the way in which social factors affect the inception of scientific notions. But even more important, the sociological study of science is concerned with specifying the conditions under which science emerges and becomes a significant force in human societies.

A BRIEF HISTORICAL SKETCH OF WESTERN SCIENCE

Science is both a mode of inquiry and a body of ideas resting upon systematic observation of the world. Science proceeds and progresses through the continuous interplay of theory and observation. Proposed theories require systematic testing against facts collected through observation. Theories that correspond to facts better than do other theories are provisionally regarded as superior and retained by the scientific community until better theories are available.

A common error involves confusing science with technology. Although obviously related, they must be defined separately. As noted in Chapter 3, technology consists of the tools, techniques, and accumulated knowledge relevant to a society's adaptation to its natural and social environment. Technology's goal is a practical one, and in this respect it differs from science. Science, while hardly irrelevant to practical considerations, is a more or less intellectual process, one often undertaken for its own sake. Science aims at developing theories that have great intellectual appeal; technology knows no such aim. While science frequently has utilitarian aims and consequences, much of it does not, and many people work at science only for the intellectual gratification it brings; technology, by contrast, is valued *purely* for its utilitarian results.

Although technology is a societal universal, it seems wrong to consider science one. It is true that all human societies rely upon systematic observations to produce some knowledge, but for most societies in human history these observations have been designed for technological rather than scientific ends. While all human societies have made at least some use of systematic observation, the majority of them have not been interested in building abstract intellectual theories out of these observations. Observation alone does not make activity scientific, for science requires that observation always be closely coupled with theoretical work. A society should be regarded as having science when at least some of its members are systematically engaged in observational efforts designed to produce theoretical accounts of certain phenomena, and when at least some of these intellectual workers have little or no concern for the practical application of their theories.

Science originated with the transition to civilization some 5000 to 6000 years ago. The first scientists were ancient Egyptians, Sumerians, and Babylonians who engaged in some rather sophisticated work in mathematics and astronomy. The transition to civilization in China and India was also marked by the emergence of some scientific activity, as was the origin of civilization in the New World. But the two greatest bursts of scientific activity occurred among the ancient Greeks (in the first few centuries B.C.) and in western Europe from the sixteenth century on. The Greek achievement in science was by far the greatest in history until the sixteenth century, when western Europe reacquired and revitalized the lost Greek accomplishments and used them as the basis for a set of much greater scientific achievements.

The Scientific Achievements of the Greeks*

Greek science was born with the emergence of the Ionian thinkers in the sixth century B.C. Many of the Ionians were broadly materialistic in their scientific outlook, attempting to explain phenomena by reference to naturalistic processes and without any appeal to schemes of divine intervention. Perhaps the most interesting Ionian materialist was Democritus, the original inventor of the atomic theory. Democritus conceived of the universe as being composed of innumerable small, indivisible

*This section and the next are based heavily on Bernal (1971).

particles—atoms—that moved about in the void of empty space. This idea, although considered heretical at the time, was the original basis for our modern understanding of atomic particles.

The next phase of Greek science, the Athenian (480–330 B.C.), was marked most significantly by the contributions of Aristotle. He made important contributions in the areas of logic, physics, and biology. Aristotle held that something was explained if its "nature" was identified, applying this idea to both the physical and biological worlds. Embodied in this notion is a doctrine of *final causes*, which holds that phenomena are endowed with purposes or goals that they are striving to reach.

Aristotle tutoring the young Alexander. The Greeks were not the first civilization to emphasize science, but their scientific contributions were outstanding and formed an important basis for the development of modern science after the sixteenth century.

The most important achievements of Greek science were produced during the Hellenistic stage (330 B.C. to second century A.D.). Hellenistic scientists made significant contributions in the areas of astronomy and mathematics. The most important of these scientists were Hipparchus, who constructed the first catalogue of the stars; Aristarchus of Samos, who placed the sun rather than the earth at the center of the universe; and Ptolemy, who "developed a predictive model to understand planetary motions and decode the message in the skies" (Sagan, 1980:51). The greatest contributions to Hellenistic mathematics were made by Euclid, whose formulations have been to the present day the basis for much of geometry. Important contributions were also made to the science of mechanics by Archimedes.

With the eventual collapse of Greek civilization and the coming of the Romans, science underwent a great decline. The Romans despised much of Greek culture and had little or no use for its science. By the time Roman society finally gave way to the Dark Ages and European feudalism, science had become a much less significant feature of social life than it had been during the heyday of the Greeks. While scientific work continued to be carried on during this time, European feudalism is scarcely known as a scientifically minded civilization.

The Scientific Revolution in Western Europe

With the rise of modern capitalism a gigantic new burst of scientific activity began. This burst, which occurred in the sixteenth and seventeenth centuries in Italy and various parts of western Europe, has been called the Scientific Revolution.

The Scientific Revolution essentially began with Copernicus's attack on the old Aristotelian view of a static, earth-centered universe, the orthodox view held throughout the Middle Ages. Copernicus took the bold step of insisting upon a heliocentric, or sun-centered, conception of the universe. This idea was a great inspiration to later scientists, who attempted to demonstrate it and improve upon it. The first to do so was Tycho Brahe, who collected many observations on the positions of stars and planets. Tycho's results led to further scientific progress when they were taken up and worked on by his assistant, Johannes Kepler. Kepler was mainly concerned with providing a representation of planetary motion. He succeeded in showing that the motion of Mars was elliptical rather than circular. On the basis of this he formulated a law of planetary motion, to which two other laws were eventually added.

Even greater achievements were made by Galileo. Galileo was extraordinarily fortunate in that he had the newly invented telescope available as a tool for astronomical observation. He immediately turned his telescope toward the heavens and what he saw had revolutionary implications. As Bernal has noted (1971:427), "In the first few nights of observation of the heavens he saw enough to shatter the whole of the Aristotelian picture of that serene element."

Clearly the greatest contributions of the Scientific Revolution were made by Isaac Newton, whose leading ideas were to provide the standard thinking in physics and astronomy for the next two centuries. He invented the infinitesimal calculus and discovered the inverse square law of gravitation. His great work, *De Philosophiae Naturalis Principia Mathematica*, published in 1686, remains today one of the greatest works in the entire history of science. The *Principia* was an exposition and mathematical demonstration of Newton's famous theory of gravitation.

By the end of the seventeenth century the Scientific Revolution was complete and science had become an institutionalized feature of western European society, at least in England and France. But scientific progress was barely getting started, for gigantic strides were made in the nineteenth and twentieth centuries. Perhaps the greatest accomplishment of the nineteenth century was Darwin's theory of evolution by natural selection. The outstanding contribution of the twentieth century was probably Einstein's theory of relativity, which overthrew much of Newtonianism and revolutionized physics and astronomy. Many of Einstein's ideas still provide the basis for work in these two fields.

Isaac Newton (1642–1727), one of the greatest contributors to the scientific revolution of the seventeenth century.

The social sciences got their start in the late eighteenth and early nineteenth centuries. Although these sciences have not yet achieved the level of maturity of the natural sciences, they have made considerable intellectual progress. There is no doubt that we know a great deal more about the workings of societies today than we did 200 years ago.

The pace of scientific growth over the past

Albert Einstein (1879–1955) at home in Princeton, New Jersey. No one before or since has had a greater appreciation of the role of parsimony in the building of scientific theories.

several hundred years has been enormous. As Derek de Solla Price (1963) has shown, science has been growing at an exponential rate for the past two or three centuries. At the present time, science is an enormous social force. It has grown from "little science" to "big science": from a situation in which a handful of individuals labored away in their private studies and laboratories to one in which thousands of scientists conduct their research within the confines of large, bureaucratized universities and research institutes (Price, 1963). Science is now a crucial feature of modern industrial societies, essential to the functioning of their economies and technologies.

What has been responsible for this enormous growth of science and for the Scientific Revolution that lay immediately behind it? What accounts for the flourishing of science in ancient Greece? In short, what are the conditions under which science develops and flourishes in a particular society?

EXPLANATIONS FOR THE EMERGENCE AND GROWTH OF SCIENCE

The Merton Thesis: Protestantism and Science

Perhaps the most famous attempt by a sociologist to explain the emergence of science is that of Robert Merton. In his well-known book *Science, Technology, and Society in Seventeenth Century England* (1970; orig. 1938), Merton attempted to account for that aspect of the Scientific Revolution that occurred in England in the seventeenth century. He modeled his work on Weber's account of the rise of Western capitalism in *The Protestant Ethic and the Spirit of Capitalism*. Just as Weber thought that Western capitalism originated through a complex set of economic forces and religious ideas, Merton held that Western science was also the product of both economic and religious factors. Interestingly, most sociologists seem to have forgotten Merton's emphasis on economic forces and to have paid almost exclusive attention to his account of the role played by religion in stimulating scientific advance.

Merton argued that Puritan religious values provided a favorable social and intellectual atmosphere for scientific activity. He believed that these values encouraged the rational and empirical study of nature as one means of glorifying God and His creations. To support his argument, Merton produced evidence suggesting that men of Protestant religious outlook played a crucial role in the leadership of the Royal Society of London in the middle of the seventeenth century. Merton pointed to Theodore Haak as a pronounced Calvinist; to Denis

Papin as a French Calvinist forced out of France because of religious persecution; to Thomas Sydenham as an ardent Puritan; to Sir William Petty as a man strongly influenced by Puritanism; and so on.

The Merton thesis seems fundamentally ill-conceived. It focuses excessively on the particular motives of a handful of prominent individuals, a very bad strategy for understanding a major historical event. The theory has been severely criticized and virtually exploded. One major argument against it has concentrated on challenging Merton's conception of a close link between Puritan values and a scientific outlook. One critic has commented that Calvinist teachings were just as compatible with mysticism as they were with science (Rabb, 1962). In a similar vein, it has been claimed that there was no particular streak of intellectual curiosity in most of the early Puritans, and that some of them were even critical of the scientific attitude because they saw it as a threat to Christianity (Greaves, 1969; cf. Becker, 1984). Along another line of attack, it has been shown that only a small percentage of the members of the Royal Society in the middle of the seventeenth century were in fact Puritans (Mulligan, 1973). Finally, and notably, science flourished in Catholic countries, and many of the early contributions to European scientific advance came from Catholic scientists (Rabb, 1965). Catholic Italy was in the forefront of the Scientific Revolution in the sixteenth century; furthermore, both France and Italy (Catholic countries) had a higher rate of scientific activity in the middle of the nineteenth century than did the Netherlands (a Protestant country) (see Figure 19.1).

There is no compelling logic to Merton's thesis, and the evidence seems to point squarely against it. Fortunately, better theories are available, one of which is even suggested by Merton himself.

Scientist at work on the Strategic Defense Initiative Weapons Project at Los Alamos National Laboratory, Los Alamos, New Mexico. Is this "little science" or "big science"?

Materialist Explanations

In addition to suggesting the possible role of Puritanism in the Scientific Revolution, Merton called attention to economic factors as important causes of the new scientific advance. As have other scholars, Merton placed special emphasis on a key technological problem confronted in early modern England: the problem of finding the longitude while at sea. As English commercial activity increased, and as more and more ships put out to sea, this problem became one of vital concern. As Merton notes, the various methods proposed for finding the longitude led directly to a number of scientific investigations: computation of lunar distances from the sun or from a fixed star; observations of the eclipses of Jupiter's satellites; observations of the moon's transit of the meridian; and the use of pendulum clocks and other chronometers at sea (Merton, 1957). In addition to navigational concerns, other pressing technological and economic problems were a major stimulus to scientific research. These problems mainly involved mining and military technology. Merton has even been able to estimate the extent to which scientific research was shaped by economic needs. His calculations show that, for the years 1661–1662 and 1686–1687, slightly more than half of the scientific problems worked on by members of the Royal Society were directly or indirectly related to economic concerns.

Perhaps the most vigorous proponent of a materialist understanding of scientific advance is J. D. Bernal (1971). He holds (1971:47) that "the track science has followed—from Egypt and Mesopotamia to Greece, from Islamic Spain to Renaissance Italy, thence to the Low Countries and France, and then to Scotland and England of the Industrial Revolution—is the same as that of commerce and industry." For Bernal, then, science flourishes when technological and economic conditions produce a need for its accomplishments. He sees, for example, the scientific achievements of the Hellenistic period of ancient Greece as stimulated by Alexander's conquests in Egypt. These conquests expanded Greek commercial activity and enhanced the role that science could play in economic production. Likewise, the Scientific Revolution of western Europe is seen as a direct result of the rise of capitalism. As one country after another rose to prominence in the capitalist economy, science quickly followed suit.

Obviously neither Merton nor Bernal is suggesting that economic influences upon scientific activity are due strictly to practical considerations. Science is not the same thing as technology, and many individual scientists have been entirely unconcerned with the practical implications of their research. Merton puts his finger precisely on the dual way in which economic and technical forces can stimulate scientific work (1957:609):

> It is important to distinguish the personal attitudes of individual men of science from the social role played by their research. Clearly, some scientists were sufficiently enamored of their subject to pursue it for its own sake, at times with little consideration of its practical bearings. Nor need we assume that *all* individual researches are directly linked to technical tasks. The relation between science and social needs is twofold: direct, in the sense that some research is advisedly and deliberately pursued for utilitarian purposes, and indirect, insofar as certain problems and materials for their solution come to the attention of scientists although they need not be cognizant of the practical exigencies from which they derive.

There can be little doubt that technological and economic factors have been the principal stimulus to scientific advance in human history. However, by themselves they do not appear to give the whole answer. Why, for example, did the Romans develop science so minimally? After all, Rome was as commercially minded as Greece, and would therefore appear to have had the same basic use for science. It seems there must be another key ingredient, something that was lacking in Rome but present in Greece.

Science and the Capitalist World-Economy

An intriguing theory of the rise of science in early modern Europe has been developed by Robert Wuthnow (1980a). Wuthnow's theory is rooted directly in Wallersteinian world-system theory. Although it is not strictly materialist, it is highly compatible with the materialist arguments just discussed. In addition, Wuthnow's analysis perhaps supplies the key ingredient missing in the materialist arguments, thereby supplementing and enhancing those arguments.

Wuthnow pays particular attention to the fact that Europe during the sixteenth and seventeenth centuries, while strongly integrated commercially by a capitalist economy, was politically decentralized (cf. Ben-David, 1965). He holds that this decentralization played a key role in stimulating scientific advance in at least three ways. First, political decentralization provided a certain degree of freedom for scientists to conduct their work. For instance, if scientists were confronted in their own country with a political atmosphere unfavorable to science, they could continue to pursue scientific work by escaping to a country where the atmosphere was more supportive. Considerable evidence points to the frequency with which many early European scientists left their homelands in order to have the freedom to pursue science. Second, the decentralized character of capitalist Europe meant that individual countries engaged in intense economic, political, and military competition with each other. Science played an important role in this competition. By promoting science and the practical results it could bring, governments hoped to enhance their capacity to compete on more favorable terms. Finally, decentralization meant that many different scientific communities existed throughout Europe, and these communities both competed with one another and communicated and shared information. The result of such activities was the enhancement of both the quantity and quality of scientific research.

Wuthnow also presents data that demonstrate that the economic position of a European country in the capitalist world-economy vitally influenced its level of scientific activity (Figure 19.1). These data show, among other things, the following: The sharp economic decline of Spain in the sixteenth century was accompanied by a corresponding decline in its number of scientists; the transition of Italy to semiperipheral status after about 1600 was accompanied by a general decline in scientific activity; scientific activity dropped off in the Netherlands after 1650, that is, at approximately the same time that its economic position deteriorated due to military defeats by England and France; by the beginning of the eighteenth century, England and France were clearly the great powers in the European capitalist economy, and they also had the largest number of scientists from this time on.

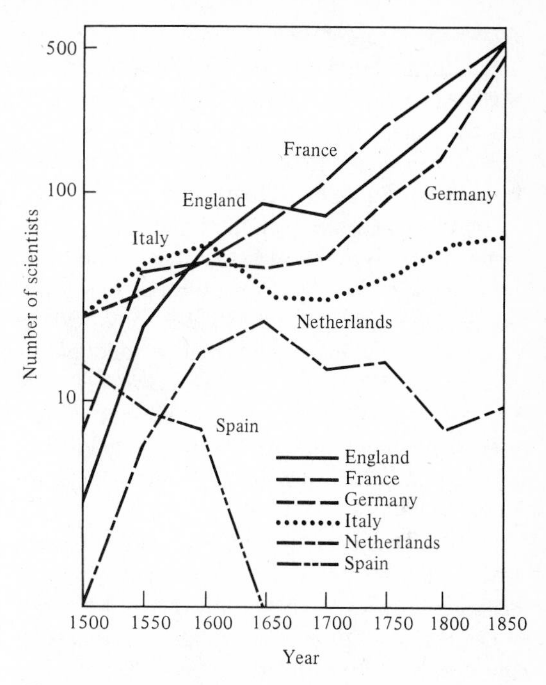

Figure 19.1 European scientific activity by country, 1500–1850. (*Source:* Robert Wuthnow, "The World-Economy and the Institutionalization of Science in Seventeenth Century Europe." In Albert Bergesen (ed.), *Studies of the Modern World-System,* New York: Academic Press, 1980, p. 48.)

In general, Wuthnow's data show a very close correspondence between the rise and fall of a country's economic activity and the rise and fall of its scientific activity. They are fully consistent with, and actually highly supportive of, a materialist explanation for the Scientific Revolution. But Wuthnow's emphasis on the importance of political decentralization seems to go one step beyond the materialist argument itself. Political decentralization may have been important not only in the case of early modern Europe; it may also have been important in stimulating the growth of science in other times and places. For instance, science blossomed in ancient Greece but took little hold in ancient Rome. Since these two civilizations were quite similar economically (both were agrarian slave-based civilizations with high degrees of commercial activity), economics alone cannot explain the attraction of the Greeks toward science. However, the political differences between these civilizations cannot be overlooked in terms of their implications for science. Rome had a massive empire, a form of political organization that tends to inhibit scientific growth because it stifles individual freedom and creativity. But Greece had a decentralized system of city-states, a political arrangement that may well have provided an important context for the free reign of intellectual curiosity. Furthermore, early European science really blossomed first in Italy, a region that was also politically organized along a city-state pattern.

Political decentralization therefore seems to bear an important relationship to the growth of science. However, decentralization by itself means very little; it cannot really be a cause of science, but only a supportive context in which science has the possibility of emerging (Wuthnow, 1980a). Feudal Europe, for example, was highly decentralized, yet science was little developed there. It seems that societies are most likely to get strong bursts of scientific advance when they have a combination of two elements: political decentralization and a level of commercial activity that gives science a strong practical significance. These elements were certainly present in ancient Greece, in Renaissance Italy, and in western Europe in general from the sixteenth century on. At least one of them was missing in ancient Rome and in feudal Europe. Moreover, both were clearly absent from traditional China, a civilization noteworthy for its comparatively low level of scientific development. As Joseph Needham has said by way of comparing the European and Chinese cases (1974:106), the Chinese centralized bureaucratic state

> at first favoured the growth of natural knowledge . . . while later on it inhibited the rise of modern capitalism and of modern science in contrast with the other form of feudalism in Europe which favoured it—I mean of course by decaying and generating the new mercantile order of society.

SOCIAL INFLUENCES ON THE CONTENT OF SCIENCE

To this point we have considered only the conditions that stimulate scientific activity in general. Clearly, whether science is practiced or not, and whether it is either strongly or weakly promoted, are matters that are overwhelmingly socially determined. Whether the actual *content* of science—the specific ideas that scientists set forth—is determined by underlying social conditions remains to be seen.

Western thinkers have traditionally viewed the content of science as entirely free from social determination. Most Western scholars have held that scientific ideas emerge and progress according to an internal logic of their own, irrespective of social influences. This position has generally been known as the *internalist* view of scientific thought (Rose and Rose, 1976; Hull, 1988). Most sociologists have strongly shared this perspective. As the noted sociologist of science Joseph Ben-David claims, for instance (1971:13–14): "The possibilities for . . . [a] sociology of the conceptual and theoretical contents of science are extremely limited."

By contrast, some thinkers have argued that scientific ideas are largely shaped by external social influences. Proponents of this view (most notably some Marxian social theorists, although not Marx himself) have claimed that science does not produce objective knowledge; rather, it only produces knowledge of a highly subjective and relative sort. This position is known as the *externalist* view of science (Rose and Rose, 1976; Hull, 1988). In recent years a number of sociologists have been persuaded by this view, claiming against the traditional view that the contents of science are socially rather than intellectually determined (Mulkay, 1979; H. Collins, 1981).

Both of these views are too extreme (the latter more than the former) and must be rejected. A middle-ground position is the only feasible one. Such a position views the content of science as somewhat conditioned by external social forces, but at the same time as having a substantial internal logic of its own.

Some Dubious Proposals

A strong argument that the acceptance of certain scientific theories largely involves social considerations can be found in the work of Theodore Brown (1970; cf. Laudan, 1977). Brown has attempted to explain the acceptance of a mechanistic approach to life by a number of eminent seventeenth-century British physicians and natural philosophers. He claims that the motivations of these thinkers in accepting mechanism were basically political rather than intellectual. They happened to be associated with an organization—the Royal College of Physicians—whose prestige and licensing monopoly were under attack from rivals, apparently because the College was associated with a physiological theory increasingly considered to be outdated. By adopting the newer mechanistic approach, the physicians could fend off the threat to their established political position by their rivals.

An even more extreme view of the social determination of scientific theory acceptance has been presented by a number of contemporary British sociologists, led by Harry Collins. This group, which advocates a position they call "relativism," holds that scientists' empirical analyses play little or no role in determining the theories they will accept. Instead, acceptance of certain theories is a matter of "social negotiation," of scientists spinning out an interpretation of data that they can agree on. The power, resources, and interests of different scientists determine their bargaining strength and the way in which the social processes of negotiation will proceed.

Collins and his associates have carried out numerous studies based on interviews of scientists as diverse as physicists and parapsychologists who were asked how they went about reaching theoretical consensus (H. Collins, 1981; Pickering, 1981; Collins and Pinch, 1978). Collins documents a number of instances in which advocates of one position attempt to discredit the findings of representatives of other positions on grounds that have little or nothing to do with the empirical suitability of the findings. Moreover, Collins shows that the power and prestige of certain scientists are important in determining the acceptability of their views. On the basis of these and similar considerations, Collins rushes toward the enormous conclusion that "the natural world in no way constrains what is believed to be" (1981:54).

On the whole, the arguments just reviewed are not very convincing. There can be no doubt that scientists, like other social actors, are influenced by considerations of power, prestige, and the like. After all, science, like other social institutions, is a social process, and individual scientists like all social actors are motivated to satisfy their own interests. But the fact that social and political factors enter into the process whereby scientists deliberate about theories scarcely compels the radical conclusion that these factors are the only ones relevant to the outcome. Indeed, as Laudan has pointed out, one fundamental interest that scientists have is a *cognitive* one: they have an overriding interest in producing good theories. Good theories are those that accord well with the data or make good empirical predictions. Although these data are frequently ambiguous, and although scientific controversies often develop over their interpretation, the fact remains that scientists often reach very high levels of theoretical consensus and are able to settle controversies in ways that are unimaginable to nonscientists. This suggests that the natural world does indeed act as a very powerful constraint on the beliefs of scientists.

Moreover, the Collins approach is badly flawed in a logical sense. Collins uses his empirical analyses of scientists' behavior to argue that empirical analyses are meaningless in the development of theories. This is a hopelessly self-defeating strategy (Laudan, 1982; cf. Hull, 1988). Collins cannot have it both ways. If he is going to study things empirically, then he cannot seriously maintain his strong relativist position without lapsing into contradiction.

Some Reasonable Proposals

To reject the more extreme proposals of Brown and Collins does not require rejection of the general notion that social factors play at least some role in shaping the content of scientific ideas. It is perhaps the case that social influences play a greater role in regard to the **logic of discovery**—the process whereby ideas are initiated by scientists—than they do in regard to the **logic of justification**—the means by which ideas are deemed to be worthy of acceptance. (Note that it is really the latter that Brown and Collins are concerned with.)

One of the best-known instances of the probable strong influence of social factors on the origin of a scientific theory is the case of Darwin's theory of evolution. It is generally agreed that Darwin arrived at his great idea after collecting detailed observations of plant and animal life, after paying close attention to the activities of animal breeders, and after reading some important intellectual works, especially those of the geologist Charles Lyell and the philosopher Thomas Robert Malthus. Malthus had a particularly strong influence on Darwin through the former's emphasis on the important role played by struggle and competition in social life. However, the influence of Malthus on Darwin may have been as strong as it was because of the exposure of both thinkers to much the same social environment. As Michael Mulkay argues (1979:107), "There are some grounds . . . for suggesting tentatively that the use of Malthusian doctrine by Darwin and his colleagues was made possible by their sharing a series of background assumptions about the nature of social life which were derived from dominant features of their own society."

The nature of the social milieu that both Darwin and Malthus shared was basically that of early industrial capitalism in England. Social and economic life at the time was extraordinarily grim, at least for the majority of the population who struggled to stay alive by laboring in the industrial sweatshops. Life appeared as a gigantic struggle for survival, and there were many who did not make it. It seems likely that this general social and economic climate influenced the development of Darwin's thinking about nature. In fact, Marx once observed that "it is remarkable how Darwin has discerned anew amongst beasts and plants his English society with its division of labor, competition, elucidation of new markets, 'discoveries' and the Malthusian 'struggle for existence.' . . . In Darwin the animal kingdom figures as bourgeois [capitalist] society" (Marx, 1979:157; orig. 1862).

Darwin's ideas, then, were probably at least partially conditioned by the general nature of the society in which he lived. It is surely no accident that the idea of evolution by natural selection was discovered when and where it was. Moreover, Alfred Russell Wallace, another Englishman, developed essentially the same idea at approximately the same time. In addition, some of the very first theories of social evolution arose at and shortly after this time, and two of the most prominent social evolutionists were Englishmen (the sociologist Herbert Spencer and the anthropologist E. B. Tylor). Clearly something must have been "in the air."

Another example may be drawn from the social sciences. Compared to the natural sciences, these sciences reveal a substantially greater conditioning by external social influences. Therefore it is not especially difficult to make a case for the role of external influences in social-scientific thinking. The collapse of functionalism and the rise of conflict theory in American sociology in the 1960s and 1970s is a case in point.

Functionalism was the dominant macrolevel sociological approach from about 1945 until around 1965. It was a strategy well suited to its times: a period of relative political calm and complacency in American life, one in which college students were swallowing goldfish and cramming into telephone booths rather than raising penetrating intellectual and political questions (cf. Huaco, 1986). By the late 1950s functionalism's intellectual merits were beginning to be questioned, and by the middle of the 1960s the attacks against it were of major significance. It was charged with being static and ahistorical as well as highly abstract and untestable; with substituting final causes for an understanding of the real workings of societies; and, most important, with ignoring or downplaying the importance of social conflict and change. On the political side, it was accused of being an inherently conservative approach to the study of social life. By 1970, functionalism was well on its way to being replaced by, among other things, conflict theories, which gave explicit attention to the importance of conflict and change in social life. The conflict approach was already based on certain Marxian formulations, but even more explicitly Marxian ideas were to follow within a few years.

These major intellectual changes to a large extent seem to have been the products of the major changes that occurred in American social life in the 1960s. Rather than a time of complacency and conservatism, the 1960s were a time of rebellion, both political and cultural. New lifestyles were adopted and major challenges were made to the political and economic status quo. Students protested against the Vietnam War, the poor against poverty, blacks against racism, women against sexism, and so on. None of these phenomena was predicted or adequately explained by functionalist analyses, and functionalism seemed more and more useless as conflict and discord mounted. It appeared increasingly obvious that what was needed was a theoretical approach that could account for the major upheavals that were taking place in American (and more broadly, Western) society. And so conflict-oriented analyses, Marxian approaches, and more historically oriented approaches rapidly came to the forefront.

It would not be difficult to add many other examples to the two given above. For instance, theories linking lower IQ scores among blacks to biological differences among the races were widespread among American biologists and social scientists in the first half of this century. This seems to have derived in good part from the racist character of the surrounding culture. In addition, the strong repudiation of Marxian economic theory among Western economists must be understood in part as resulting from the capitalist character of Western civilization. The list could go on and on.

Despite what has been argued above, however, two important points must be stressed. One is that social factors appear to play much the smaller role in the determination of scientific thought. The larger role is played by the rationality of scientific theory formulation and empirical testing that occurs apart from social and cultural considerations. The second point that needs to be established is that, even though scientific theories may find their origins to some extent in social influences, this is unrelated to the merits of those theories. Darwin's theory of evolution, for instance, is an especially well-corroborated theory and one of the great unifying ideas of modern biology and much of anthropology. Thus, it should not be thought that simply because social forces are implicated in the development of any particular scientific theory, this theory is therefore necessarily without any objective merits.

NORMS AND INTERESTS IN THE BEHAVIOR OF SCIENTISTS

An issue of persistent concern to sociologists of science has been the extent to which science is a normative activity. Several decades ago Robert Merton (1973; orig. 1942) argued a position that has come to be widely accepted among sociologists: that the behavior of scientists is guided by an explicit set of norms that are crucial to the success of science as a social institution.

Merton has suggested that the following norms are most basic to science. *Emotional neutrality* is the standard that says that scientists should not get emotionally attached to their ideas. They should remain dispassionate so as not to lose a sense of perspective and objectivity. *Universalism* prescribes that the acceptance or rejection of scientific claims should have nothing to do with the personal or social attributes of scientists, such as their race, social class, personality, or standing within the scientific community. *Communism* forbids the hoarding of scientific information and insists that scientific data and theories must be made thoroughly accessible to the community of scientists. *Disinterestedness* specifies that scientific self-interest must be subordinated by individual scientists to the good of the scientific community as a whole. Finally, *organized skepticism* insists that scientists adopt an attitude of critical doubt toward all ideas put forth, including their own.

Merton has more recently proposed the idea that the scientific community contains two opposing sets of norms—norms and counternorms—and that scientists are often ambivalent in regard to which set of norms to follow. Ian Mitroff (1974) has carried out an interesting study to test this idea. Mitroff's study involves detailed interviews with various scientists associated with the Apollo moon missions. Mitroff found what he believes is strong confirmation of Merton's view about the ambivalence of scientists. The scientists Mitroff talked to gave unambiguous evidence that emotional commitment is just as much a part of scientists' behavior as is emotional neutrality. The scientists spoke at length about how intensely personal scientific work was, and about how enormously involved many scientists got with their ideas. Moreover, Mitroff found unmistakable evidence of the widespread existence in science of organized dogmatism, secrecy in regard to data and theories, and particularism alongside universalism. Scientists spoke extensively about many of their colleagues who dogmatically defended views to the bitter end, who refused to make information public, and who often accepted certain ideas because of the fame or authority of the person proclaiming them.

It seemed clear to Mitroff that the Apollo scientists recognized the existence of two contrary sets of norms in science, and saw both sets as contributing in crucial ways to the good of science. In this regard, it should be noted that both Merton's and Mitroff's arguments are couched within a functionalist theoretical context. Norms and counternorms are seen as promoting the overall well-being of science, and that is why they exist in the first place.

Yet there are some good grounds for being highly skeptical of this functionalist claim. If one scrutinizes the comments Mitroff's scientists made to him, their remarks do not necessarily look like statements about norms. It is just as plausible to interpret them as statements about the *interests* of scientists and how these are expressed differently in different situations. As Michael Mulkay has argued (1976:645):

> One of the influences upon scientists' choice of one polarity rather than another [i.e., a norm or counternorm] is likely to be their interests or objectives. It can be assumed that, for a given group of scientists, these interests will vary from one social context to another. Thus . . . when researchers were frustrated by the apparent reluctance of others to make significant findings available to them, they tended to select principles favouring communality which justified their

Interviews conducted by sociologists with some of the scientists asssociated with the Apollo moon missions have shown that many of our commonsense views of science are actually highly idealized.

condemnation of the others' behavior and added weight to their own exhortations. In contrast, those scientists who had made the discovery were able to find principles in favour of personal ownership of results. It is worth noting that the principles actually implemented in this case were those proposed by the more powerful, that is, the scientists who had access to and control over the valued information.

Mulkay goes on to suggest that what Merton and Mitroff are calling norms and counternorms are more appropriately viewed as "vocabularies of justification": as statements whereby scientists justify and legitimize their actions to each other and to the larger community.

Combining Mulkay's argument about Mitroff's data with some of the findings of Harry Collins mentioned earlier, it appears that science is remarkably like other arenas of social behavior. Like individuals in other social contexts, scientists are hardly immune from considerations of power, prestige, and self-interest. Nor are they immune from the basic human tendency to clothe their self-interested actions in more socially acceptable terms. The noble image of the dispassionate, open-minded, and altruistic scientist, while containing considerable truth, is at best a half-truth. Yet this image is what scientists want nonscientists to believe about them.

What we have just stated are the rudiments of a conflict view of science, a view that seems much more realistic than the functionalist conception (see the Special Topic at the end of the chapter). A conflict view of science concentrates on the similarities between science and other social institutions. Nonetheless, this perspective should not be taken too far. There is still a sense in which science is unlike other institutions and other ways of knowing. This can be seen in the extent to which its concepts and theories are constrained by nature, and thus the degree to which they have a rationality and progressiveness about them. Science is indeed political, but it cannot be reduced to politics.

SUMMARY

1. Science is a mode of inquiry that attempts to develop theoretical concepts and principles through empirical study of the world. It is also the accumulated body of knowledge resulting from empirical investigation. Science is not a cultural universal. It first arose with the birth of civilization in both the Old and New Worlds.

2. The first great burst of scientific activity occurred among the ancient Greeks. The earliest Greek scientists were materialistic thinkers who attempted to explain phenomena as the result of naturalistic processes. Aristotle was a great Greek scientist who contributed significantly to physics and biology. The heyday of Greek science was its Hellenistic period. During this period, important contributions were made in the areas of astronomy, mathematics, and mechanics.

3. Science had little impact in medieval Europe. It began dramatically to expand once again in the sixteenth and seventeenth centuries in western Europe. Physics and astronomy led the way in the Scientific Revolution, and the greatest scientists of the period were Copernicus, Tycho Brahe, Kepler, Galileo, and Isaac Newton. By the end of the seventeenth century science had become an institutionalized feature of social life in western Europe. Great scientific strides were also made in the eighteenth, nineteenth, and twentieth centuries. During this time science has grown exponentially. Modern science is now "big science," and it is essential to the functioning of modern industrial societies.

4. Robert Merton has suggested that Protestantism played an important role in stimulating the Scientific Revolution in England. This theory, though, seems contradicted by considerable evidence, such as the fact that early Calvinist teachings were just as compatible with mysticism as with science, or the fact that science developed significantly in Catholic countries like Italy and France.

5. The main alternative to this explanation is the materialist view, which holds that science is stimulated when a society has an economic need and desire for the technological applications science can produce. Science seems to be most significantly stimulated when a society has a vibrant commercialism and a political atmosphere conducive to the intellectual freedom science requires. Ancient Greece and early modern Europe met both these criteria.

6. Traditionally, Western scholars have regarded scientific ideas as remarkably free from external social influences. This view—the internalist view—holds that scientific thought follows its own internal logic of development. The internalist view has been challenged in recent years by the externalists, who claim that science is not a unique form of human activity. In this view, scientific ideas are shaped largely by a range of social influences. A middle-ground position is preferable to either of these two extremes. Scientific ideas are clearly subject to various social influences, but they still retain a remarkable autonomy from such influences. In the long run science is unique in its capacity to achieve rationally produced objective knowledge.

7. The functionalist view of science suggests that such norms as emotional neutrality, universalism, communism, disinterestedness, and organized skepticism are crucial to scientific success. In more recent years functionalists have suggested that science may sometimes follow an opposite set of norms, and that these counternorms may also be essential to scientific success. Functionalist talk of norms and counternorms seems misplaced. It is more likely that, as a conflict view of science suggests, scientists follow different sets of individual and group interests that are often justified by appeal to the employment of norms or counternorms.

SPECIAL TOPIC: AN EVOLUTIONARY VIEW OF SCIENTIFIC CHANGE

It has long been axiomatic that science is a uniquely rational and progressive mode of acquiring knowledge. No other mode of intellectual inquiry, it has been claimed, has the capacity that science does for generating increasingly adequate concepts and theories about the world (cf. Popper, 1959; Toulmin, 1972; Laudan, 1977, 1984). However, there has remained much debate about just what it is about science that makes it uniquely progressive. In his recent book *Science as Process* (1988), David Hull proposes to resolve this debate by presenting a provocative evolutionary account of science. He considers the behavior of scientists to be essentially like that of organisms in the natural world, with the result that natural selection operates on scientific behavior to produce evolutionary transformations in scientific concepts and theories.

Hull's view of science is essentially Darwinian. Science is a struggle for survival involving extreme competition, and survival in this game does not go to the timid or the weak. The scientific game is normally played fairly brutally, and survival in science—which means getting one's ideas accepted by sizable segments of the scientific community—generally goes to those who most vigorously push their ideas and who can stand the heat of conflict and competition with other scientists. This means that the most successful scientists are often the most aggressive, or even nasty, individuals. Moreover, Hull stresses that science does not progress *in spite of* this fact, but actually *because of* it. As he notes (1988:31–32):

> *Some of the virtues which scientists fail to exemplify are not and never have been part of the ethos of science. Neither humility nor egalitarianism has ever characterized scientists, and no one has ever given any good reasons why they should. . . .*
>
> *I argue an even stronger thesis: some of the behavior that appears to be the most improper actually facilitates the manifest goals of science. . . . [T]he existence and ultimate rationality of science can be explained in terms of bias, jealousy, and irrationality. As it turns out, the least productive scientists tend to behave the most admirably, while those who make the greatest contributions just as frequently behave the most deplorably.*

Throughout *Science as a Process* Hull provides detailed evidence of the extent to which nasty and aggressive behavior is a commonplace in science. Scientists usually want to see such behavior as an exception, or as being limited to certain fields or to a handful of specific times and places, but Hull claims that it is the norm. And if it contributes to the advance of science, how does it do so? Hull argues that cooperation and competition are both absolutely basic to science. Scientists cooperate with each other for self-interested reasons. They collaborate with those scientists whose ideas and research skills help advance their own ideas, and they use—by discussing and citing—the work of others for the same reason. Pushing his evolutionary argument as far as possible, Hull sees in such behavior attempts on the part of scientists to maximize what he calls their *conceptual inclusive fitness.* Thus, the scientific cooperation that appears to be motivated by altruism—by a concern for the greater good of science as a whole—is really scientific self-interest in disguise. And if scientists are cooperating with their "conceptual kin," they must obviously pursue combative strategies against conceptually dissimilar scientists. Conceptual opponents must be defeated, and extremely strong strategies may need to be adopted to ensure this end.

But again, although the vigorous efforts that scientists employ to defeat their opponents are normally condemned, these efforts paradoxically turn out to be essential to scientific advance. Along with the empirical procedures on which scientists intimately depend, they give science a self-correcting mechanism that is the secret of its success. Aggressive and highly biased scientists are confronted, within the vast arena of science, by other equally aggressive and equally biased scientists, but whose biases are often profoundly different. As Hull has remarked (1988:321), "The self-correction so important in science does not depend on scientists presenting totally unbiased results but on other scientists, with different biases, checking them." As a result, prolonged battles ensue in which better concepts and theories gradually win out over poorer ones.

It is obvious that Hull's arguments have major implications for the debate between externalists and internalists. Hull's conception of science allows for—indeed, insists upon—the role of a range of external factors in science. If nothing else, scientists have strong career interests that may greatly determine their theoretical and conceptual allegiances. In the end, though, it is of secondary significance to know why particular scientists develop the allegiances that they do, just as it is of less importance to know why particular ideas are advocated at certain places and times. In the end all of these ideas, regardless of where they come from or who promotes them, will be submitted to rigorous tests of adequacy by those who bitterly oppose them. And this process of scientific natural selection is one that is largely, although not exclusively, internal to scientific communities themselves.

FOR FURTHER READING

Bernal, J. D. *Science in History.* 4 volumes. Cambridge, Mass.: MIT Press, 1971. An extraordinarily comprehensive treatment of the entire history of science by a well-known Marxian historian of science. Although largely descriptive, it also presents Bernal's materialist interpretation of scientific advance.

Collins, Randall, and Sal Restivo. "Development, Diversity, and Conflict in the Sociology of Science." *Sociological Quarterly* 24:185–200, 1983. A good overview of recent research, debates, and controversies in the sociology of science.

Hull, David L. *Science as a Process: An Evolutionary Account of the Social and Conceptual Development of Science.* Chicago: University of Chicago Press, 1988. Presents a theory holding that scientific advance is rooted in the struggle for survival among scientists and scientific ideas. A masterful work filled with rich detail about the often unpleasant behavior of scientists toward each other.

Kuhn, Thomas S. *The Structure of Scientific Revolu-*

tions. Second edition. Chicago: University of Chicago Press, 1970. Perhaps the most famous attempt in the past quarter-century to characterize the nature of science and scientific change.

Laudan, Larry. *Progress and Its Problems: Towards a Theory of Scientific Growth*. Berkeley: University of California Press, 1977. A major work by a prominent philosopher of science designed as a defense of the view that science is a largely rational and progressive endeavor.

Merton, Robert K. *Science, Technology, and Society in Seventeenth Century England*. New York: Howard Fertig, 1970. (Originally published 1938.) Merton's argument concerning the role of Puritan religious values and economic forces in the emergence of seventeenth-century English science.

Mitroff, Ian. "Norms and Counter-Norms in a Select Group of the Apollo Moon Scientists: A Case Study of the Ambivalence of Scientists." *American Sociological Review* 39:579–595, 1974. Despite the limitations of Mitroff's interpretation, shows the extent to which scientists violate Merton's proposed norms of science. Particularly illuminating are long quotes from the interviews with scientists.

Mulkay, Michael. *Science and the Sociology of Knowledge*. London: Allen and Unwin, 1979. A good example of how many British sociologists have recently viewed the nature of science. Contains a very useful discussion of how sociologists and philosophers have changed their views about the nature of science over the past quarter-century.

Wuthnow, Robert. "The World-Economy and the Institutionalization of Science in Seventeenth-Century Europe." In Albert Bergesen (ed.), *Studies of the Modern World-System*. New York: Academic Press, 1980. An interesting attempt to explain the Scientific Revolution from a world-system perspective. Presents some particularly valuable data on the relationship between capitalist economic activity and science.

Yearley, Steven. *Science, Technology, and Social Change*. London: Unwin Hyman, 1988. A good overview of some important issues in the sociology of science with a focus on the role of science in social and historical change.

CHAPTER 20

Whither Humankind? The Future of Sociocultural Evolution

In this final chapter we take a look into the future. We do this by first summarizing the broadest changes in human societies over the past 10,000 years and their significance for the human condition and the quality of human life. How societies have been changing, and the principles governing such changes, must be explored if there is to be much hope of making intelligent judgments about the future. The look at the future—a look that will concentrate on futuristic issues and themes not already examined in previous chapters—will be divided into two parts. The first deals with what the classical sociologists—Marx, Durkheim, and Weber—theorized about the drift of Western history in their time and about what such drift implied for the future. The second part considers the future as it is contemplated by several living thinkers, focusing in particular on the crucial issues of environmental deterioration and the likelihood of nuclear warfare. The chapter and the book conclude by briefly considering the importance of a general theory of world history as a reliable guide to thinking about the future.

THE PAST 10,000 YEARS: CULTURAL PROGRESS?

Before taking a look into the future, it may be helpful to recapitulate some of the major evolutionary trends over the past 10,000 years, particularly those that have most directly involved the overall quality of human life. These mainly concern the *standard of living*, the *quantity and quality of work*, *equality*, and *democracy and freedom*. To discuss these evolutionary trends in a meaningful way, an abstract concept known as the **average world citizen** is employed, and the implications of major evolutionary changes are judged from the perspective of this hypothetical individual. The average world citizen is the typical member of the typical type of human society prevailing in any given historical era. For example, 15,000 years ago all humans lived in hunting and gathering societies, and thus the average world citizen was a hunter-gatherer. By contrast, some 4,000 years ago the agrarian way of life had basically become the predominant form of social life on Earth, and thus the average world citizen was a peasant farmer. Since most of the world's population currently lives in the underdeveloped nations, today's average world citizen is a Third World peasant or urban worker. It must be remembered that the employment of the concept of the average world citizen is a purely methodological device designed to simplify the discussion about the nature and meaning of broad evolutionary trends. To talk about an average world citizen is to talk about how evolutionary trends affect the majority of the world's population, if not all individuals, groups, and societies.

The Standard of Living

To be able to talk at all about evolutionary trends in the standard of living, the highly subjective nature of this concept must be neutralized. Societies have different conceptions of the kinds of material things that are needed or desired. In the advanced industrial capitalist societies of today, for instance, people have come to depend on such things as fast cars, stereo systems, and microwave ovens, and they feel deprived if these things are taken away. Hunter-gatherers, on the other hand, have no need or desire for such material items, and they certainly do *not* feel deprived because they lack them. Since the desire for such things is an artificially derived rather than a basic human need, it is not meaningful to compare hunter-gatherers and modern industrialists (or the members of any other type of society) in terms of whether or not they possess such goods.

The only meaningful comparison of societies' standards of living is in terms of a universally desired good or state of affairs, something all humans need and desire and whose absence produces a feeling of deprivation. The *quality of the diet* is proposed as such a universal measure of the standard of living.

Using this measure, there has been an overall decline in the standard of living over the past 10,000 years, at least when judged from the perspective of our average world citizen. The most recent evidence suggests that ancient hunter-gatherers probably enjoyed diets that were abundant in calories, fully adequate in animal proteins, and highly nutritious. As argued in Chapter 4, hunter-gatherers probably constituted an "original affluent society"—a type of society in which people are able to satisfy all their basic needs with a minimum of effort.

The decline in the standard of living began with the transition to the first agricultural (horticultural) communities (see the Special Topic in Chapter 4). The real decline in the living standard, though, was brought about several thousand years later at about the time people were greatly intensifying their agricultural methods. By the time the average world citizen had become a peasant, the standard of living had dropped very sharply. The average peasant in the average agrarian society of the past had a diet markedly inferior to that of the average hunter-gatherer of earlier times. Peasant diets were notoriously deficient in calories, proteins, and nutrients, and they probably also had a stultifying monotony. As Lenski has noted in regard to medieval England (1966:270–271):

> The diet of the average peasant consisted of little more than the following: a hunk of bread and a mug of ale in the morning; a lump of cheese and bread with perhaps an onion or two to flavor it, and more ale at noon; a thick soup or pottage followed by bread and cheese at the main meal in the evening. Meat was rare, and the ale was usually thin.

Things were just as bad or worse outside Europe (at least in the past few centuries). As Fernand Braudel has remarked (1981:199):

> "In Japan," said a Spaniard (1609), "the only meat they eat is game which they kill by hunting." In India the population fortunately regarded meat with horror. . . .

> In China, meat was rare. There were hardly any animals for slaughter: just the household pig (fed at home on scraps and rice), poultry, game, and even dogs, which could be found in special butchers' shops or offered on doorsteps. . . . Except in Mongolia, where boiled mutton was common, meat was never served on its own. It was chopped into tiny pieces, the size of a mouthful, or even minced, as a contribution to the *ts'ai*—the many dishes combining meat and fish with vegetables, sauces and spices which were the traditional accompaniment to rice. . . . Even the rich mandarins, Father de las Cortes noted, "only nibble a few mouthfuls of pork or chicken or some other meat, as if to whet their appetites. . . . For however rich and mighty they are, they eat only tiny quantities of meat."

While the quality of the diet has improved today for those persons living in industrial societies,* these persons do not make up a majority of the world's population. Most people alive on Earth today live in the Third World and are poor peasants or urban workers. It is doubtful whether the average member of a contemporary Third World country is better off than the average peasant of past agrarian societies; in fact, it is arguable that contemporary Third World citizens may be worse off (cf. Wallerstein, 1984a). The extremely high infant mortality rates of Third World countries, for instance, suggest a very low health and nutritional status for many members of such countries.

If evolutionary trends in the standard of living were measured by the level of health and the incidence of disease, a similar picture would emerge. Hunter-gatherers were far healthier and freer from disease than commonly thought (Harris, 1977; Cohen and Armelagos, 1984; Cohen, 1989), and their life expectancies, though short, were comparable to those of peasants. Moreover, the great killer contagious diseases familiar to humankind were products of the high-density urban life of agrarian societies (McNeill, 1976). While modern medicine has made great strides in the advanced industrial countries, health care in the Third World countries today still leaves much to be desired. The members of many contemporary Third World countries have life expectancies much more like those of ancient agrarian peasants than like those of modern industrial workers.

There are two basic reasons for the overall decline in the standard of living. One of these is population growth. An increasing pressure of numbers compels people to adopt more intensive methods of production. Yet the adoption of such methods does not allow people to increase their living standard or even to maintain it, for the pressure of numbers drives the living standard ever downward. By intensifying their production methods, people are simply keeping their living standards from dropping to drastically low levels. The other basic cause of the decline in living standards is the rise of class stratification, itself due in part to the growth of population. As some individuals and groups gain control over productive resources, they are able to compel other individuals and groups to produce economic surpluses that the members of the dominant group may live off. In the preindustrial world this process reached its peak in agrarian societies and contributed very heavily to the low living standard of the peasantry. In modern capitalism, the world stratification system dominated by the core capitalists is the most important cause of the low living standard of Third World peoples.

The Quantity and Quality of Work

There is little doubt that the quantity of work has increased and its quality has deteriorated over the past 10,000 years. Hunter-gatherers seem to work less and enjoy more leisure time

*Or has it? The members of modern industrial societies notoriously suffer from obesity and such diet-related diseases as coronary artery disease, cancer, diabetes, and various intestinal disorders. These health conditions are generally unknown or uncommon in band and tribal societies (Burkitt, 1978).

than the members of all other types of societies. Evidence from contemporary hunter-gatherer societies indicates that they strongly resist advancing their technology because they realize this will bring increases in their work load. The members of horticultural societies do indeed appear to work somewhat harder and longer than people in hunting and gathering societies. But, as in the case of the standard of living, the truly marked change seems to be associated with the emergence of agrarian societies. The work load in agrarian societies is markedly greater than in all previous forms of preindustrial society. In the modern world, work levels are still very high in both the industrialized countries and the Third World nations. The average member of an industrial society may spend on the order of 60 hours a week in subsistence activities, if we add to the 40 hours per week spent earning a living the time spent shopping for food and preparing it, as well as the time spent maintaining a household. This is about three to four times the average weekly work load of many hunter-gatherers. The average Third World worker probably spends considerably more time than this in all subsistence activities.

A basic assumption of the preceding discussion is that people seem to obey what has been called a "Law of Least Effort" (Zipf, 1965; Harris, 1979). This law holds that, other things being equal, people prefer to accomplish activities with a minimum amount of energy expenditure. This seems to be a basic feature of human nature. Thus, increasing the work load is something people normally wish to avoid. Under what conditions will people work harder and longer than would otherwise be the case?

The Law of Least Effort at work.

There are perhaps three basic reasons why people will increase their energy expenditure: political compulsion, economic necessity, and psychological conditioning. People will work harder and longer when other people gain power over them and force them to increase their work load. They will also increase their work activities if compelled by a declining standard of living to intensify their productive efforts. Finally, people can be conditioned to believe that hard work is a moral virtue, laziness a moral defect (this idea has been basic to the Protestant work ethic of Western civilization in recent centuries). The first two of these have been the leading causes of the intensification of the work load over the past several millennia.

What, then, of the quality of work? Chapter 8 discussed the Marxian thesis that work is the primary means of human self-realization. Humans realize their humanity and achieve meaning in life when they manipulate the world according to their own purposes and designs. The primitive hunter and the agrarian craftsman were classic examples of self-fulfilled workers. To a large extent the same was true even of agrarian peasants. Despite their exploitation and low standard of living, they had considerable control over their work activities and worked in harmony with nature and the seasons. In precapitalist and preindustrial societies, then, work was not primarily alienated labor. The real emergence of alienated labor began with the transition to modern industrial capitalism. Here workers came to be reduced to instruments of production who performed routinized and fragmented tasks. They lost control over the means of production, had little control over their work activities, and had little sense of identification with the final product they produced. In the Third World, much work is also alienated labor, especially to the extent that capitalist methods of production and worker control have penetrated underdeveloped societies. Thus the trend in the quality of human work—one of the most basic of all human needs—has been negative.

Equality

There is no mistaking the overall trend in social and economic equality. It has been decidedly in the direction of greater *inequalities*, particularly those based on access to economic resources. Band and tribal societies are egalitarian societies in which the only real inequalities are those of status and influence. These inequalities are generally not socially inherited, and they are unrelated to control over economic resources or to political power. Influential and prestigious leaders in band and tribal societies have no greater wealth than others, nor do they have any capacity to compel the actions of others. In other words, in such societies class stratification does not exist.

Class stratification tends to emerge in more intensive horticultural societies, where population pressure has already reached significant levels. It is here that societies first come to be divided into groups possessing unequal levels of power and wealth, although the first forms of stratification usually do not impose severe economic penalties on the members of subordinate classes. But in high-density agrarian societies class stratification becomes so extreme that the members of subordinate classes generally suffer from marked economic deprivations. It is in such societies that a great social and economic gap between rich and poor emerges. Although contemporary industrial societies may have reduced some of the extremes of stratification compared to agrarian societies of the past, the economic inequalities among nations within the world-capitalist economy are probably greater today than ever before in human history.

The overall direction of the past 10,000 years of human history has been toward greater and greater exploitation in human affairs. Band and tribal societies display communal patterns of ownership, intensive cooperation and sharing, and a general absence of exploitation. With the growth of numbers and the emergence of scarcity in resources, people act more and more selfishly, and some groups begin to exploit others. More numbers produce more scarcity, more scarcity produces greater conflict over resources, and this in turn produces greater inequalities in power or control over resources. Furthermore, power begets power: Groups that end up on top want to stay there and even work to increase the favorableness of the view from the top. And thus stratification tends to feed on itself.

With the emergence of modern industrial capitalist and socialist societies, exploitation does not disappear but takes new forms that are more severe under capitalism. As capitalism has penetrated the globe, it has opened up huge economic gaps among the nations of the world. These gaps are growing rather than shrinking and have time and again led to explosive political conflict.

Democracy and Freedom

Although there is a strong tendency in Western capitalist society to use the concepts of democracy and freedom more or less interchangeably, the terms, though related, should really carry different meanings. Democracy is a process of self-government, one whereby people decide their own affairs through open discussion and debate and in the absence of any individuals or groups who can command their actions.

Given this definition, human societies over the past ten millennia have moved more and more away from democracy. Band and tribal societies are fundamentally democratic in that they lack elite groups capable of commanding the actions of others. Headmen and big men are leaders of some influence and respect, but they have no genuine power. People are under no obligation to obey their wishes, and such leaders have no possibility of imposing penalties on those who ignore their suggestions. Democracy is undermined at the same basic point in sociocultural evolution at which class stratification emerges. With the growth of large-scale agrarian societies and their elaborate stratification systems, democracy drops to a very low point. In such societies tiny elites rule the actions of others and have the capacity to impose severe penalties on them for disobedience.

In the modern world democracy is more an illusion than a reality. In the totalitarian socialist regimes, of course, it is not even an illusion. But even in the Western parliamentary democracies, genuine democracy really does not exist. If the arguments of Chapter 12 are correct, then modern Western parliamentary democracies are governed by elite groups whose actions are self-serving and to a very great extent beyond significant control by the masses.

But what of **freedom**? Assessing the evolutionary history of freedom depends crucially on what is meant by the concept, which has been subject to rather diverse definitions. In the Western tradition of thought, freedom has tended to be conceptualized as an absence of external constraints on the individual, who thus has the capacity to think, choose, and act according to his or her own standards of what is right and good. If freedom is given this meaning, then it has been increasing in the past 10,000 years of human history. Band and tribal societies are in this sense the least free in all of human history. In these societies, individual behavior is closely regulated by the basic standards of the community as a whole. Individuals are basically alike, and there is extremely strong group pressure to conform to the common standards of the group. Moreover, the penalties for failure to conform are often very severe, these being either death or banishment from the community.

It is doubtful that more advanced horticultural or agrarian societies are much different in this respect from simple band and tribal societies. Even in these more advanced societies, the power of custom and tradition is very great, there is tremendous pressure for social conformity, and the sanctions for nonconformity are severe. The real emergence of freedom is a product of the rise of modern capitalism, and especially of the rise of parliamentary democratic forms of government over the past two centuries or so. In modern capitalist societies tremendous freedoms are granted individuals. There is government protection for individual rights and liberties and strong encouragement of individual self-expression. The individualist conception of freedom pervades all of the basic social arrangements of modern Western capitalist societies (but not the non-Western capitalist society of Japan).

However, there is another conception of freedom, one that might be called freedom as *human species-realization*. This conception of freedom is associated with the Marxian tradition of thought (cf. Elster, 1985). Freedom in this sense involves the equal capacity of all individuals to realize their basic nature as human beings. For Marx, freedom existed when everyone had the full opportunity to achieve meaning and purpose in life, especially as this could be achieved through work. Marx thought that freedom could only be achieved in a classless society with a very advanced level of technology—in the future socialist society. He believed that modern Western capitalist societies, even though they granted certain political freedoms to individuals, failed to achieve true human freedom because most of the population was exploited by the capitalist class and had no genuine opportunity for the realization of their human nature. If we follow this tradition of conceptualizing freedom, freedom has not been increasing in human history, and in a sense has been decreasing inasmuch as the members of precapitalist societies generally do have considerable opportunity to realize themselves through their labor.

Associated with this conception of freedom is another important dimension. If freedom is human species-realization, and if humans are fundamentally social animals, then freedom can only be achieved in and through society. That is, people can only be considered free when they participate with their fellow humans in social relationships that are intrinsically enjoyable. This means that freedom is more likely in societies in which individuals place definite limitations on their own individual self-expression in favor of sharing a common set of values and standards with others. And since individual self-expression has become an increasingly common feature of Western societies, freedom in the Marxian sense is actually decreasing in such societies.

The Concept of Progress Revisited

The preceding discussion suggests once again what was asserted early in the book: that we must be extremely wary of using the concept of progress to characterize the major changes of the past 10,000 years. Indeed, it seems apparent that much of what has been happening over this period has actually been a form of cultural *regression*. How else are we to regard a general decline in the standard of living, an increase in the quantity and a deterioration in the quality of work, the emergence of marked social and economic inequalities, and the undermining of democracy? Of course, not all of these changes apply to all persons and groups in all societies. For some individuals and groups the standard of living has increased, work has become lighter, easier, and more gratifying, and the emergence of economic inequality and the undermining of democracy have actually been beneficial rather than detrimental. Yet for the majority of the world's population—for our average world citizen—things have been going downhill.

On the other hand, to suggest a general deterioration in the quality of life in some respects does not mean that improvements have not been occurring in other areas of social life. Humans have made enormous artistic, intellectual, literary, scientific, and technological achievements. Such achievements—those of Picasso, Mozart, Shakespeare, Einstein, da Vinci, et al.—cannot be swept aside as insignificant. It is possible to say, then, that humans have actually been making certain forms of progress over the past 10,000 years in spite of the very significant regressions that have been occurring.

A LOOK AT THE FUTURE: PERSPECTIVES FROM THE CLASSICAL SOCIOLOGISTS

We now turn away from what the past has produced to take a look into the future. We begin this examination of what the future may portend by analyzing the insights of the three greatest classical sociologists about the current and likely future drift of Western history.

Marx and Socialism

Marx was like many other nineteenth-century European social thinkers in having a progressivist theory of human history and an optimistic view of the future. In his evolutionary scheme, he saw humankind moving from primitive communism into various stages of society based on private property and social class divisions. Primitive communism, he thought, would have been idyllic if it had not been for the technological limitations that rendered life a grim and constant struggle for survival. (Marx wrote about primitive communism a good century or more before Sahlins formulated his notion of the "original affluent society.") With technological advance came the breakdown of communal economic relations and the growth of private property. Society passed through several stages of class-divided society in which oppression and exploitation were significant social phenomena: slavery, characterized by the ancient world of Greece and Rome; feudalism, characterized by the European Middle Ages; and capitalism, which evolved in the eighteenth century after several centuries of the breakdown of feudalism. Capitalism, Marx thought, contained the very seeds of its own destruction. It was an inherently unstable economic system that would ultimately destroy itself through the violent revolutionary overthrow of the capitalists by the workers.

The overthrow of capitalism would usher in the socialist society. Since capitalism was to be the final form of society based on antagonistic class relations, socialism would be a classless society. Private property would disappear and all property would be held by the state as the representative of the people. Production would take place for use and for the social good, not for profit. Work would be reorganized so as to lose its character as a commodity, and the alienated labor so characteristic of capitalism would disappear. Socialism would grant to all individuals the full opportunity to realize their nature as members of humanity, and thus it would promote real human freedom.

Marx never left more than a general sketch of what the future socialist society would be like, and he thought there were many alternatives open to people in building socialism. But to what extent have his predictions come true, or might they yet come to be realized in the future? The Soviet Union and the Eastern European societies have come closest of all existing societies to representing what Marx meant by socialism. Yet these societies depart markedly in several respects from the Marxian vision of the future socialist society. They are (or at least have long been) politically repressive, treat work and workers as commodities, and have levels of social and economic inequality that Marx would have considered highly unacceptable. It is likely that Marx would have been no more favorably disposed toward these societies than toward Western capitalism. Indeed, as we saw in Chapter 8, the state socialist societies have been increasingly adopting many of the overt features of capitalism.

It could still be argued that, despite the inadequacies of actually existing socialist societies, a future socialist society that does embody (or at least that comes much closer to embodying) Marx's ideals will yet emerge. Indeed, many Western Marxists anticipate such an occurrence. Immanuel Wallerstein (1984b), for instance, believes that within approximately 100 to 150 years the world-system of capitalism will collapse from the weight of its own internal strains and stresses and be replaced by a socialist world government that will very likely embrace many of Marx's philosophical ideals.

Although it is impossible to say whether Wallerstein's expectation is realistic, there is at least one form of evidence that lends credence to his argument. This involves the rise of anticore forces within the capitalist world-economy and the tendency of some peripheral capitalist countries to cut their ties to core capitalism and adopt socialist modes of organization. This is a growing phenomenon in the modern world. But whether this will actually lead to a shift in the balance of world forces toward socialism is very much an open question, leaving aside what the content of this form of socialism would actually be like.

Durkheim and Individualism

The French sociologist Emile Durkheim (1858–1917) had a perspective on the present and the future that contrasted sharply with Marx's. Durkheim saw Western civilization tending toward increasing **individualism.** By individualism Durkheim meant a moral doctrine and social philosophy that sanctified individuals, or treated them as the principal objects of moral concern. Individualism—or what Durkheim called the "cult of the individual"—gives great emphasis to individual rights and freedoms and to the needs and desires of individuals as distinct persons. It stresses the desirability of liberating individuals from irrational and unnecessary social constraints so that they are free to realize their ambitions and fulfill their potentialities. Durkheim saw individualism as growing with the advance of industrial society and being elaborated in the future as industrial society fully matured.

Moral individualism is a significant trend in Western society, and its roots go back well into the seventeenth and eighteenth centuries. The rise of individualism in the West can perhaps be most clearly seen in the emergence of the modern family. In seventeenth-century England and eighteenth-century France the family was changing into a much more affective unit that individuals looked to as a source of self-gratification, sexual and otherwise. As Lawrence Stone has noted, the family was becoming the focal point "for a new interest in the self, and for recognition of the uniqueness of the individual" (1979:153). There was emerging what Eli Zaretsky (1976) has called the *sphere of personal life*. This phenomenon, which seems to be directly linked to the individualizing tendencies of capitalism, had become especially significant by the second half of the nineteenth century (cf. Sennett, 1976).

Since Durkheim's death the sphere of personal life has expanded on a major scale, and individualism is now in many ways the guiding philosophy of interpersonal relations in Western societies. There are dozens of examples of this phenomenon. Our legal institutions are increasingly oriented toward the moral dignity of the individual. In the middle of the 1970s the United States Supreme Court declared that a woman has the right to control her own body and receive an abortion if she so desires. In Sweden in recent years laws have been passed making it illegal for parents to use corporal punishment in disciplining their children, signifying that children have rights of protection against such punishment (Popenoe, 1988). The so-called children's rights movement is emerging as a significant social force in other industrial societies as well.

Another major indicator of the growth of individualism is the so-called human potential movement. Various philosophies associated with this movement have swept the United States in the past two decades. These philosophies stress the desirability, indeed, the necessity, for individuals to engage in a range of experiences that allow them "personal growth." Not unrelated to the human potential movement is the rapid rise of a "drug culture." Recreational use of drugs for the achievement of pleasure and the "expansion of consciousness" is now a significant phenomenon in most Western societies.

The growth of individualism is also seen in the "sexual revolution" of the past two decades. From a rigidly puritanical outlook, Western society has moved in the direction of making sexual activity a moral and social necessity. To a considerable extent, people are meant to feel out of touch if they are not achieving their "sexual potential" in their social relationships.

Finally, increasing individualism is manifested in the growing antiauthoritarianism of Western societies, as expressed in the increasingly sharp reaction against the imposition of authority in social relationships. The traditional forms of authority associated with parents, bosses, religious and political leaders, teachers, and so on are being widely challenged today all over the West. It is often claimed that authority is inherently negative because it represses the natural tendencies and basic potentialities of the individual, which ought to be given free rein.

Many other examples of the growth of the "cult of the individual" could be added, but these should suffice to illustrate the point. The growth of individualism raises the crucial question of the extent to which it threatens the very fabric of society. Durkheim himself felt that it not only posed no real threat to the cohesion of society, but that it actually promoted such cohesion. It was a new moral doctrine so widely shared by the members of modern industrial societies that it promoted strong bonds among individuals. As Steven Lukes has commented (1972:166):

> Thus, far from the cult of the individual failing to constitute "a genuine social bond," he [Durkheim] came to see it as "the sole link which binds us one to another," the "only system of beliefs which can ensure the moral unity of the country"—a new religion which has "for its first dogma the autonomy of reason and for its first rite freedom of thought."

There are good reasons, though, to be skeptical of Durkheim's reasoning. In many ways what we seem to be witnessing in modern industrial societies is the growth of a new kind of selfishness and a lack of concern for others, or what Christopher Lasch (1979) has called a "culture of narcissism." American writer Tom Wolfe dubbed the 1970s the "Me Decade," and the tendency toward self-absorption seems to be a growing feature of Western society (Lasch, 1984). It appears that the growth of the cult of individual dignity has been carried so far that it no longer has the capacity to unite people, but rather drives wedges between them. It may well be that this moral philosophy is inevitably self-contradictory. That is, even though it is widely shared socially, its specific content works against any capacity it might have to unite individuals into a moral community. Instead, it promotes within them attitudes of selfishness that undermine the social fabric.

Weber and Rationalization

Max Weber did not share the generally optimistic views of the future held by Marx and Durkheim, but offered a fundamentally pessimistic interpretation of the fate of Western civilization. Weber believed that the overriding characteristic of Western society was its *rationality.* Over the past few centuries it had evolved toward a mode of social consciousness in which great emphasis was placed on the rational calculation of the most efficient ways to achieve desired goals. As this process—which Weber called **rationalization**—occurred, people relied less and less on customary or traditional modes of social interaction and came to orient their actions increasingly around deliberate calculation. Weber saw the growth of modern science and technology as an integral part of the rationalization process. It was the rise of the modern **bureaucratic** form of social organization, though, that he thought constituted the very paradigm of rationalization. He saw in modern bureaucracies, particularly those through which the state was administered, the epitome of a rationalized form of social consciousness and a rationalized set of social relationships.

Weber's overall attitude to modern bureaucracy was mixed. He saw bureaucracy as a more or less inevitable product of modern Western civilization because of its superior efficiency as an organizational form. Given the demands of modern society, no other form of organization could meet them as efficiently. Yet he also saw in the rise of bureaucracy tremendous potential for the depersonalization and dehumanization of social life. He thought this potential was already being realized and would be increasingly realized in the future. Weber thought that Western society was tending toward the imprisonment of the individual in an "iron cage" that could not be destroyed. Social relationships would become highly mechanical and impersonal and would lose their spontaneity. Social life would take on an increasingly drab, sterile, and "inhuman" character that individuals would have little possibility of changing.

Weber's predictions of three-quarters of a century ago have been substantially realized. More and more of the lives of individuals in Western industrial societies are now carried out in the context of large bureaucratic organizations. Most individuals work within them, pay taxes to them, receive their educations within them, and so on. More and more sectors of social life are subject to the bureaucratic form of organization, and these bureaucracies seem to be getting bigger and more complex all the time. Moreover, bureaucracies are especially vulnerable to a perverse type of irrationality that Robert Merton (1961) has called **goal displacement.** This occurs when the means that bureaucracies develop to reach their goals end up becoming the goals themselves. For example, in many modern universities, professors now complain of having to spend so much time working on committees and completing paperwork that they scarcely have time for the real goals of such educational institutions—teaching and research. In addition, one often hears older professors complaining of the increasing impersonality of relationships as their institutions have become larger and more bureaucratically structured.

Many other aspects of modern society tend to confirm Weber's view. Everywhere, even outside the context of bureaucracies, we find social relationships and consciousness being increasingly subject to the rationalization process. For instance, people seem less and less capable of performing sex with one another without the assistance of "sex manuals," now widely available in bookstores. These manuals, for the taste of many at least, make sex such a mechanical and scientific process that it begins to seem uninteresting. Here perhaps the most spontaneous of social relationships is reduced to a process of deliberate calculation that is reminiscent of a set of instructions for repairing a washing machine. The rationalization process is patently obvious in the recent rise in importance of the computer in modern society. In the past few years home computers have become widely available. It is interesting to observe the mesmerizing fascination these devices have for many people. The home computer is the mechanical embodiment of the rationalization process, promising as it does an enormous increase in the efficiency with which people can accomplish certain tasks.

Weber's view of the rationalization of modern society is a great insight; he thought that there was nothing that could effectively stop this process once it got started. This is perhaps true, given that no catastrophes beset humankind, catastrophes that would lead to a sharp reversal of the general direction of sociocultural evolution. At this point it may be wise to consider the possibility of such an occurrence.

A LOOK AT THE FUTURE: ENVIRONMENTAL DEPLETION

We now turn to a consideration of the future viewed from the perspective of living thinkers. The discussion is oriented around what I believe are the two most serious threats that the human species faces in the immediate years ahead: major ecological and demographic problems resulting from an extremely advanced technology and the serious world maldistribution of resources, and the possibility of world-annihilating war resulting from the extremely competitive interstate system of modern capitalism.

Ecological and Demographic Catastrophe? Robert Heilbroner's Pessimism

In his book *An Inquiry into the Human Prospect* (1980), Robert Heilbroner issues a deeply pessimistic judgment in regard to the future. As he puts it (1980:20):

> The outlook for man, I believe, is painful, difficult, perhaps desperate, and the hope that can be held out for his future prospect seems to be very slim indeed. . . . The answer to whether we can conceive of the future other than as a continuation of the darkness, cruelty, and disorder of the past seems to me to be no; and to the question of whether worse impends, yes.

Heilbroner sees three fundamental reasons the future looks so grim. One of these is the current rate of population growth on a world scale. He sums up the current world demographic situation as follows (1980:32–33):

> In general the demographic situation of virtually all of Southeast Asia, large portions of Latin America, and parts of Africa portends a grim Malthusian outcome. Southeast Asia, for example, is growing at a rate that will double its numbers in less than 30 years; the African continent as a whole every 27 years; Latin America every 24 years. Thus, whereas we can expect that the industrialized areas of the world will have to support roughly 1.4 to 1.7 billion people a century hence, the underdeveloped world, which today totals around 2.5 billion, will have to support something like 40 billion by that date if it continues to double its numbers approximately every quarter century.

One consequence of such a population glut would obviously be a marked deterioration in the economic conditions of the Third World countries. This deterioration would undoubtedly be accompanied by rising social disorder and the intensification of the dictatorial character of governments in order to control the disorder. As Heilbroner notes, "This condition could continue for a considerable period, effectively removing these areas from the concern of the rest of the world and consigning the billions of their inhabitants to a human state comparable to that which we now glimpse in the worst regions of India or Pakistan" (1980:38).

It is possible, of course, that some of the Third World countries will attempt to head off such problems before they become so severe. But this will require, Heilbroner argues, the emergence of "iron" governments devoted to establishing very strict birth control policies, such as are now in effect in China. Moreover, as Heilbroner points out, such governments are not likely to limit their authoritarian techniques to the regulation of the birth rate. They are likely to extend their power into many other sectors of social life as well, and thus the attempt to control population growth in many Third World countries will be accompanied by a general rise in political repression.

Heilbroner concludes his discussion of the likely effects of current population growth rates by arguing (1980:43–44):

> If current projections of population growth rates are even roughly accurate, and if the environmental limitations on the growth of output . . . begin to exert their negative influences within the next two generations, massive human deterioration in the backward areas can be avoided only by a redistribution of the world's output and energies on a scale immensely larger than anything that has hitherto been seriously contemplated. Under the best of circumstances such a redistribution would be exceedingly difficult to achieve. . . . Such an unprecedented international transfer seems impossible to imagine except under some kind of threat. The possibility must then be faced that the underdeveloped nations which have "nothing" to lose will point their nuclear pistols at the heads of the passengers in the first-class coaches who have everything to lose.

Heilbroner is also pessimistic about the future because of the current rate at which the industrial nations are using up natural resources. He believes we are now moving toward the finite limits of the earth's ability to support the industrial form of technology. In order to avoid an ecological catastrophe in the near future, the industrial countries must begin placing sharp limits on their rate of resource utilization. Heilbroner thinks this can only be accomplished through the rise of authoritarian governments, because private individuals and groups would not voluntarily restrict their rate of resource use. There is a definite prospect, then, for a very severe threat to, if not a collapse of, our basic democratic institutions: "For the majority of capitalist nations . . . I do not see how one can avoid the conclusion that the required transformation will be likely to exceed the capabilities of representative democracy" (Heilbroner, 1980:106). The prospect is also for a markedly reduced standard of living that would accompany reduced industrial activity.

There is yet a third possible threat to humankind looming in the future. This involves the heat generated as a by-product of industrial activity (Heilbroner, 1980:50):

> Even if we make the heroic assumption that all these difficulties will be overcome, so that another century of uninterrupted industrial growth, with its thousandfold increase in required inputs, will face no constraints from resource shortages, there remains one barrier that confronts us with all the force of an ultimatum from nature. It is that all industrial production, including, of course, the extraction of resources, requires the use of energy, and that all energy, including that generated from natural processes such as wind power or solar radiation, is inextricably involved with the emission of heat.
>
> The limit on industrial growth therefore depends in the end on the tolerance of the ecosphere for the absorption of heat. . . . The emission of man-made heat is . . . growing exponentially, as both cause and consequence of industrial growth.

Heilbroner believes that at the current rate of energy use we have perhaps a century or slightly more in which to solve the problem of "heat pollution." Failing that, the future is one of extinction of the human species.

A Critique of the Pessimistic View

The "gloom and doom" outlook on the future represented by Heilbroner has been severely criticized by the economist Julian Simon (1981).

Strip-mining in Arizona. Have we harmed ourselves beyond repair?

Simon argues strongly against the view that we are rapidly running out of crucial resources. He suggests that our natural resources are not even finite in any meaningful sense of that term, since technological breakthroughs are highly likely in the future, and these breakthroughs will probably head off any serious problems generated by resource depletion.

Simon believes that the doom-saying forecasters have gone wrong in a very fundamental methodological way: they have based their forecasts on the concept of "known reserves" of natural resources. As Simon argues, this concept is essentially worthless for making future predictions, since the "known reserves" of any natural resource are limited to how diligently scientists and engineers have searched for it. Simon claims that our natural resources probably exist in vastly greater abundance than the "known reserves" concept allows for. According to Simon, this kind of forecasting should be replaced with a method in which the price trends of resources are used to determine their scarcity. Price-trend data, he claims, clearly show that our resources are getting *less* rather than more scarce, since the historic trend of prices for these resources has been downward. In short, Simon believes there is no cause for alarm about the availability of crucial natural resources in either the near or the distant future.

Simon is also highly critical of those who predict dire social consequences for the future as the result of rapid population growth. He believes the historical record shows that population growth does not necessarily produce negative social consequences; indeed, he claims that in many instances population growth is actually beneficial rather than harmful. For instance, it is frequently a stimulus to technological advance. Thus there is no particular cause for worry about continuing population growth, either in the developed or the underdeveloped countries.

While it is difficult to evaluate Simon's (or Heilbroner's) claims about the availability of natural resources, there is good reason to be highly suspicious of his argument in regard to population. For instance, at one point he asserts the following (1981:185):

> In the 1960s demographers began to worry that fertility would not fall in poor countries even after mortality fell. Then, in the 1970s, evidence showed that fertility is indeed falling in at least some developing countries. So by now we can be reasonably sure that the European pattern of demographic transition will also appear in other parts of the world as mortality falls and income rises.

This is fallacious reasoning. While fertility rates have fallen in some poorer countries (China being the best example), they remain very high in the vast majority of the underdeveloped nations. It is illogical to assert, as Simon does, that there is reasonable certainty that the underdeveloped countries will soon be following the demographic path of the developed countries. In fact, nothing seems less certain. The underdeveloped countries are not following the historical demographic path of the developed countries any more than they are following their historical economic path.

To point out this fundamental logical flaw in Simon's argument, though, is not to suggest that he is clearly wrong and that Heilbroner and those who side with him are therefore correct. Rather, it is to suggest that Simon's strong dismissal of the kind of argument that Heilbroner is making is unwarranted. What might be regarded as an uncritically optimistic view of both the past and the future is very characteristic of Simon's book. He appears to have fallen victim to the view that humans have steadily been making progress over the millennia. For instance, he asserts that "the standard of living has risen along with the size of the world's population since the beginning of recorded time" (1981:345). This is simply untrue. As seen throughout this book, and as noted earlier in this chapter, from the Neolithic Revolution to the present, major technological changes seem to have been associated with declines in the standard of living for the majority of the world's population. Thus, although Simon continually argues that the doomsayers have not been learning the proper lessons from history, neither, it seems, has he.

As is fairly obvious, then, I am more sympathetic to the view of Heilbroner than to that of Simon. The attractive feature of Heilbroner's analysis is its hard-headed realism: its recognition of the genuinely excruciating problems now presented by several hundred years of the expansion of capitalism and industrialism. Yet Heilbroner's analysis, despite its merits, probably exaggerates the extent of the problem. Heilbroner is clearly an alarmist, but there is really no cause for concern in that. Alarmists reward us greatly if we heed their advice and they turn out to be right. The truly serious problem with Heilbroner's assessment of the future is not his alarmism; rather it is the near fatalism in his position. Although Heilbroner technically avoids stating fatalistic conclusions, he certainly seems to have one foot placed in that camp. Fatalism is unwarranted because of the tremendous limitations of our current level of knowledge. Who could have predicted the computer or the nuclear bomb from the vantage point of the sixteenth century? Who can really predict that we will be unable to make the kinds of gigantic technological leaps forward that we will need in order to make major strides in solving our most pressing ecological problems?

A LOOK AT THE FUTURE: WAR AND POLITICS

War and the Capitalist World-Economy

A number of scholars from several of the social sciences have noticed that over much of its history capitalism has been characterized by a highly regularized cyclical pattern of economic boom and bust (Goldstein, 1988; Wallerstein, 1984c). It has been observed that periods of economic upturn are invariably followed by periods of downturn, and that there is an amazingly regular rhythm to these oscillations. The first major scholar to identify this feature of capitalism was the Russian economist Nikolai Kondratieff (1984; orig. 1928), who identified economic cycles of approximately 50 years' duration. Once an upturn began it took about 25 years to reach its crest, and then a downturn began. The downturn itself lasted approximately 25 years, and after it reached bottom a new upturn would begin. The waves or cycles that Kondratieff identified have subsequently been named *Kondratieff waves*. However, since many other scholars have identified similar waves, these waves need not be associated exclusively with Kondratieff (Goldstein, 1988). For this reason I shall call them simply *long waves*.

Several scholars have also been struck by the association between long waves in the history of capitalism and in the incidence of war. In a recent major study of this problem, Joshua Goldstein (1988) has shown that long waves since 1495 have been remarkably correlated with the outbreak of major wars (Table 20.1). Goldstein identifies ten long waves since 1495 and finds that a major war between powerful states has almost always occurred in the latter half of the upturn phase of the cycle. The only exception to this striking regularity is World War II, which occurs at the beginning of an upturn. However, World War II may not be a genuine exception. Some social scientists regard World Wars I and II as really two phases of one great war, not as two separate wars. If this is a valid interpretation, then the pattern identified by Goldstein is perfect.

It needs to be stressed that Goldstein's data do not relate to the overall incidence of war (the frequency of war), nor to the duration of wars. Rather, they are concerned only with wars of great magnitude. The really big wars that have resulted in a large number of fatalities have always occurred near the end of an economic upswing. Although there are several possible ways of interpreting this empirical finding, Goldstein theorizes that powerful states fight truly major wars with each other only when they can bear the expense of doing so. Major wars occur near the end of an upswing, then, because it is only then that states are financially capable of undertaking such military efforts.

Implications for the Next Major War

On the basis of his findings, Goldstein goes on to predict the timing of the next major war. The world-economy has been in a downturn phase since about 1970, and thus the next upturn can be expected to begin around 1995. If it does,

Table 20.1 LONG WAVES AND MAJOR WARS IN THE HISTORY OF CAPITALISM, 1495–1975

Cycle	Starting date of war cycle	Peak war years	Length (years)	Ending date of corresponding long wave phase period
1	(1495)	1521–1529	(35)	1528
2	1530	1552–1556	28	1558
3	1558	1593–1604	47	1594
4	1605	1635–1648	44	1649
5	1649	1701–1713	65	1719
6	1714	1755–1763	50	1761
7	1764	1803–1815	52	1813
8	1816	1870–1871	56	1871
9	1872	1914–1918	47	1917
10	1919	1939–1945?	(27)	(1968/80?)

Cycle	Peak wars	Annual fatality rate at peak
1	First and Second Wars of Charles V; (Ottoman War vs. Hapsburgs)[a]	13,000
2	Fifth War of Charles V; (Ottoman War vs. Hapsburgs)[a]	22,000
3	War of the Armada; (Austro-Turkish War)[a]	11,000
4	Thirty Years' War: Swedish/French Phase	88,000
5	War of the Spanish Succession	107,000
6	Seven Years' War	124,000
7	Napoleonic Wars	156,000
8	Franco-Prussian War	90,000
9	World War I	1,934,000
10	World War II	2,158,000

[a] The dating of war peaks in cycles 1–3 is based primarily on intra-European wars rather than those against Turkey. Wars against Turkey are included in the statistics, however, and are shown above in parentheses.

Source: Joshua S. Goldstein, *Long Cycles: Prosperity and War in the Modern Age*. New Haven: Yale University Press, 1988, p. 241, Table 11.3.

this upturn will crest in approximately 2020, which would mean that the next major war can be expected during the decade between 2010 and 2020. Actually, Goldstein regards the entire period from 2000 to 2030 as a serious "danger period" for the outbreak of war, although he expects that the danger is greater later rather than earlier in the period.

Goldstein's predictions are contingent upon the validity of the assumption that the basic features of the world political system will not change appreciably in the years ahead. Some world-system theorists, however, think that this assumption is not likely to hold (Wallerstein, 1982; Arrighi, 1982; cf. Chase-Dunn and O'Reilly, 1989). They think that the presence of nuclear weapons changes everything. Since core states now have these weapons, war be-

A plutonium bomb. The modern interstate system makes the threat of nuclear devastation in the near future very real. Some social scientists think that a world state is our only real hope of avoiding such an eventuality.

comes unthinkable because it is recognized by all parties as unwinnable. But not all world-system theorists take such an optimistic position. Christopher Chase-Dunn and Kenneth O'Reilly (1989) have examined a number of factors that they believe strongly bear on the likelihood of a major war in the near future, what they call a "core war." These factors include the long wave, intensifying ecological problems, the declining position of the United States in the world-economy, efforts at nuclear disarmament, and the emergence of new international organizations designed to reduce the threat of war. They conclude that "developments that lower the probability of core war are not great enough to offset those factors that will increase the chance of war in the coming decades. The probability of serious war among core states over the next four decades may be as much as fifty-fifty" (1989:61).

Averting Catastrophic War: The Possibility of a Future World State

If a major core war were to break out early in the next century, it would not necessarily have to be a nuclear war, but in all probability nuclear weapons would be involved. There is therefore a distinct possibility in the near future of a war that would devastate civilization and perhaps threaten the very existence of human life. What might be done to avert such an unprecedented catastrophe? Chase-Dunn (1989b; Bornschier and Chase-Dunn, 1985) has argued that the answer lies in the creation of a *world state*. This would be an overarching political system that would centralize political and economic decision making on a world scale. It would eliminate the system of competing and conflicting nation-states—the interstate system—that has characterized the capitalist world-economy for approximately 500 years. As such, the threat of world-destroying war would be enormously reduced if not eliminated altogether. In addition, such a state could be an extremely effective tool in eliminating gross inequalities in the worldwide distribution of economic resources, and thus could do much toward rectifying the massive problems of economic underdevelopment in the Third World.

A session of the United Nations in progress. Some social scientists believe that the creation of a world state—a federation with considerably greater enforcing power than the United Nations currently has—will be necessary in the near future to avert a nuclear holocaust that could extinguish the entire human species.

Chase-Dunn suggests that a future world state ought to combine the best features of both capitalism and socialism. It should contain a centralized system of political and economic decision making, but at the same time be decentralized enough to allow for local and national differences in preferences and for important cultural differences. What Chase-Dunn really has in mind is a kind of federation that eliminates the worst and most dangerous forms of struggle between nation-states while simultaneously permitting them to retain a good deal of their identity. Thus, the world state is not a single political society, but an artificially imposed structure that oversees the political and economic functioning of various individual societies.

To his credit, Chase-Dunn recognizes that there are grave dangers inherent in the creation of a world state. The distinct possibility exists that such a state could become a kind of Orwellian monster, a state so powerful that it would constitute an extreme threat to individual freedoms of all sorts. He believes, however, that the risk is worth taking because the alternative risk—complete destruction of the human species—is just as great and so much more appalling. Moreover, if we know in advance the risks to freedom that a world state can pose, then we can take strong steps to try to avert this eventuality.

I am in strong agreement with Chase-Dunn's proposals, but serious questions can be raised about their workability, at least in the short term. If the next major war will be a nuclear war, and if it is no more than 20 to 40 years away, then very little time remains for the creation of the kind of political structure that Chase-Dunn has in mind. It is doubtful that the highly ethnocentric species known as *Homo sapiens sapiens* can exchange its intensely nationalistic ideologies for much more panhuman ones in such a short time. Over the longer term Chase-Dunn's proposals gain a much greater measure of realism. The big question is, though, will the longer term ever arrive?

CONCLUSIONS: THE FUTURE FROM THE PERSPECTIVE OF A GENERAL THEORY OF HISTORY

No one really knows what the future, even the very near future, has in store, and even the most brilliant social analysts have seldom been able to make reliable predictions about what is to come. But one thing is certain: If we do not have a good general theory of the past, then we have absolutely no hope of speculating intelligently about what is ahead. This book has offered a materialist and evolutionary perspective in order to understand the past, and it may be suggested that such a perspective is our most reliable guide to the future. I do not know whether the predictions of Heilbroner, Goldstein, and Chase-Dunn are good ones, but I do believe that, to some extent, they come to grips with the factors that are likely to be most centrally involved in shaping the future. Today we live in a capitalist world-economy that has been expanding and evolving for half a millennium. This world-economy is closely intertwined with an interstate system, and both of these interact with socialist states in major ways. The world-system of capitalism has created massive technological advance that now threatens our species, both in an ecological sense (through continuing environmental degradation) and in a political sense (through the threat of nuclear war). We are thus poised on the brink. It will do no good to put our heads in the sand and deny these realities. They exist, and they have a special kind of urgency about them. As intelligent citizens, we have an obligation to learn about them and to do whatever we can to avoid their leading us into the abyss. After all, what is the alternative?

SUMMARY

1. Over the past 10,000 years many of the fundamental changes in human social life seem to be more indicative of cultural regression than of progress. For most of the world's population the standard of living has declined, the quantity of work has increased and its quality has declined, inequalities in wealth and power have become increasingly prominent, and democracy has been steadily replaced by elite domination of the many by the few.

2. Karl Marx viewed the future as one in which a technologically sophisticated socialist society would emerge from the ruins of capitalism. This society would be based on the ownership of the means of production by the state, and economic production would take place for the general welfare rather than for private profit. Work would lose its character as a commodity and the alienation of the worker would disappear. Today's actually existing socialist societies depart markedly from Marx's conception of socialism. It is very much an open question whether capitalism will increasingly give way to socialism throughout the world and, if it does, whether this socialist world will be a substantial improvement on capitalism.

3. Emile Durkheim conceived the drift of Western history to be in the direction of an increasing regard for the individual person as a distinct object of moral concern. Numerous trends in the social organization of Western societies over the past century or so strongly suggest that Durkheim's insight is an important one.

4. Max Weber took a deeply pessimistic view of the future of Western civilization. For him rationalization was the master process of the past 500 years of human history. During this time human societies had become increasingly characterized by forms of social behavior given over to the rational calculation of the most efficient means to achieve certain ends. He thought that modern bureaucracy, science, and technology were the main features of modern existence. With their increasing growth, people will come to be imprisoned in an "iron cage" in which human relationships are more and more devoid of meaning. Many aspects of modern Western history suggest that Weber had a key insight in regard to the drift of modern history.

5. Robert Heilbroner is a modern thinker who also takes a deeply pessimistic view of the human prospect in the years ahead. He believes that world overpopulation and the overuse of natural resources spell potentially disastrous consequences for the quality of human life in both the short and the long run. The economist Julian Simon has been severely critical of this view, holding that the future is far rosier than doomsayers like Heilbroner believe.

6. War has been an extremely common activity throughout the history of capitalism, but the most severe wars have almost invariably occurred late in phases of economic upturn. Extrapolations from this historical trend suggest that the next major war is likely to break out sometime during the next 20 to 40 years. There is every reason to expect that such a war would involve the use of nuclear weapons. Alarmed by this horrible prospect, some social scientists have begun to propose the construction of a world state that could take major steps to prevent such an occurrence.

7. The general theory of human history presented throughout this book suggests that the future will be shaped most significantly by changes in the material conditions of social life. In order to understand the future we must pay closest attention to the world capitalist system and its international economic inequalities and political and military tensions. This world capitalist organization of production has both politico-military and ecological effects of vast significance.

SPECIAL TOPIC: THE RISE OF A POSTINDUSTRIAL SOCIETY?

One of the most influential sociological works of recent years is Daniel Bell's *The Coming of Post-Industrial Society* (1973). Since Bell's work was published, the phrase *postindustrial society* has appeared frequently and approvingly in numerous sociological textbooks and other works.

Bell foresees the emergence in the near future of a postindustrial society, a type of society that is already developing most noticeably in the United States but will also be evolving in other advanced industrial societies. The most fundamental feature of this emerging society is the emphasis on the production of services rather than goods, and especially certain types of services. Whereas the industrial society delivers services in such areas as transportation, utilities, and telecommunications, the postindustrial society emphasizes services involving health, science, and education.

The emergence of a postindustrial society thus involves a major transformation in the very basis of society. An industrial society, Bell argues, is based on property; a postindustrial society, on the other hand, rests on knowledge, particularly theoretical knowledge. As Bell puts it rather provocatively, the rise of a postindustrial society marks the transition from a labor theory of value to a "knowledge theory of value." This change in the very basis of social life is also marked by a change in the class structure. The new dominant social class is no longer a property-owning bourgeoisie, but a "social intelligentsia": a class of highly educated individuals whose social dominance rests upon their possession of advanced forms of theoretical knowledge. The most important members of this class are teachers, physicians, lawyers, scientists, and engineers, people for whom work has become a "game between people" rather than a game between people and things.

For Bell, then, the postindustrial society is one whose overall character is vastly different from industrial or "capitalist" society. The desire for profit is no longer the driving force of economic and social life. Life becomes oriented around the accumulation of knowledge and its use for human betterment. Corporations come to be subordinated to what Bell calls the "sociologizing mode." This means that their emphasis shifts toward providing extensive benefits for their employees as well as toward their "social responsibility." In addition to and in conjunction with these changes, the postindustrial society gives a new emphasis to leisure. People acquire advanced forms of education not only for their important social uses, but for enjoyment and intellectual uplift. In general, a postindustrial society is far better educated than an industrial one.

Although Bell's ideas have gained widespread acceptance among many contemporary sociologists, there is cause to be highly skeptical of most of them. The basic difficulties with Bell's analysis have been insightfully delineated by Stephen Berger (1974). Berger suggests that many of the developments discussed by Bell do not represent the emergence of a new type of society that is opposed to capitalism, but rather of a new phase in the very development of capitalism. The expansion of government services, for example, may be understood as a necessary step in the political management of an advanced capitalist society. Moreover, Berger argues, the original motivation behind technological forecasting was military in nature, and most of the recent expansion of science has been due to government involvement in defense and space exploration. Berger's central argument against Bell is best expressed as follows (1974:102):

> *I would argue that these changes, if they are real, represent only the continued operation of the logic of industry. That logic, as analyzed by . . . Karl Marx, included the continuous enlargement of the areas of human work which were dominated by commodity production and the continuous use of scientists and engineers to create machines, techniques, and modes of organization to replace and control workers. . . .*
>
> *. . . The shifts from goods to services and from manual to professional and technical workers make sense within an analysis of the dynamics of* capitalism.

To Berger's remarks several critical comments may be added. One concerns Bell's notion that a propertyless intelligentsia is emerging as the dominant class. A better interpretation, I believe, would hold that such a group, to the extent that it exists, lacks any real social power and is by and large in a service capacity to the capitalist system. After all, most teachers, scientists, and engineers are employed in large public bureaucracies. As Berger has noted, these public bureaucracies may be viewed from the perspective of the capitalist-induced expansion of government. A second comment involves Bell's treatment of the expansion of education. In this regard, Bell seems to confuse education with "schooling" (Berger, 1974). While it is certainly true that schooling has been expanding on a vast scale in the contemporary United States, this should not be construed, as Bell seems to do, as resulting from the greater need and desire for knowledge. A better interpretation is that schooling has been expanding as a result of the process of credential inflation so characteristic of American society.

FOR FURTHER READING

Bellah, Robert N., Richard Madsen, William N. Sullivan, Ann Swidler, and Steven M. Tipton. *Habits of the Heart: Individualism and Commitment in American Life.* Berkeley: University of California Press, 1985. A look at some of the most recent changes in American life and their implications, with a focus on American individualism.

Chase-Dunn, Christopher, and Kenneth O'Reilly. "Core Wars of the Future." In Robert K. Schaeffer (ed.), *War in the World-System.* Westport, Conn.: Greenwood Press, 1989. Some thoughts about the outbreak of the next major war between great powers.

Cohen, Mark N. *Health and the Rise of Civilization.* New Haven: Yale University Press, 1989. An extremely detailed analysis of health, nutrition, and disease among many different evolutionary types of society. Using extensive empirical data, Cohen makes a persuasive case for the relatively good health and nutrition of hunter-gatherer societies as compared to those that evolved later.

Diamond, Stanley. *In Search of the Primitive: A Critique of Civilization.* New Brunswick, N.J.: Transaction Books, 1974. Despite an excessive tendency to romanticize life in band and tribal societies, contains valuable insights into some of the disadvantages of more complex and technologically advanced forms of society.

Galtung, Johan, Tore Heiestad, and Erik Rudeng. "On the Decline and Fall of Empires: The Roman Empire and Western Imperialism Compared." *Review* 4:91–153, 1980. A comparison of the current state of the capitalist world-economy with the Roman Empire during the beginning of its decline. A provocative comparison, perhaps with considerable merit, but one that must be approached with caution.

Gendron, Bernard. *Technology and the Human Condition.* New York: St. Martin's Press, 1977. A good overview of various optimistic and pessimistic views regarding the future. Examines what the author calls the utopian, dystopian, and socialist views.

Goldstein, Joshua S. *Long Cycles: Prosperity and War in the Modern Age.* New Haven: Yale University Press, 1988. An exhaustive analysis of economic cycles of upturn and downturn in the history of capitalism, with a special application to war. Contains important predictions about the future.

Harvey, David. *The Condition of Postmodernity.* Oxford: Blackwell, 1989. An analysis of the emergence of a "postmodern" cultural sensibility since the early 1970s, especially as it is revealed in contemporary art, architecture, and intellectual life. Also sets forth an extremely provocative materialist interpretation of the postmodern condition, as well as a critique of it.

Heilbroner, Robert. *An Inquiry into the Human Prospect.* New York: Norton, 1980. One of the best-known of the recent spate of books taking a deeply pessimistic view of the human future.

Sennett, Richard. *The Fall of Public Man.* New York: Random House (Vintage Books), 1976. Despite some difficult and perplexing parts, offers some important insights into the individualizing tendencies of capitalism over the past two centuries.

Simon, Julian. *The Ultimate Resource.* Princeton, N.J.: Princeton University Press, 1981. A severe critique of the "gloom and doom" vision of the future and an argument for believing that there is every reason to anticipate a sunny future for humankind.

Stavrianos, L. S. *The Promise of the Coming Dark Age.* San Francisco: Freeman, 1976. Suggests hope for humankind despite the perils we currently face. Focuses on the "green grass growing" through the cracks in the concrete of the modern world.

Teich, Albert H. (ed.). *Technology and the Future.* Fourth edition. New York: St. Martin's Press, 1986. An excellent collection of essays on the role of advanced technology in shaping the human future. The essays represent highly diverse points of view.

Glossary

absolute immiseration, thesis of The view that the overall quality of human life in the capitalist periphery is deteriorating with the continuing evolution of the capitalist world-economy. Compare *relative immiseration.*

absolutist monarchy A type of state found in late medieval and early modern Europe in which a centralized bureaucracy developed around the king. This bureaucratic centralization was associated with the general intensification of state power.

accumulation The process whereby surplus value earned from capitalist activity is reinvested in that activity, thus causing an expansion of the overall scale of economic production and exchange.

accumulationist See *accumulation.*

adaptation Biologically, the process whereby organisms acquire the genetic materials that assist their survival in a particular environment. Socioculturally, the process whereby various features of social life develop because they meet certain needs and desires of particular individuals or social groups.

adaptive See *adaptation.*

affinity The existence of kinship ties based on marriage.

agrarian society A society whose members make a living by using the most intensive and advanced agricultural methods, such as plows and animal energy for plowing.

agriculture As distinguished from horticulture, a form of farming in which large plots of land (fields) are carefully prepared and then cultivated with the use of plows and traction animals.

agrobureaucratic state A type of agrarian state in which enormous power is concentrated in the hands of a ruler and the bureaucracy with which he or she is surrounded. Such a state centralizes its control over large territories and usually has extensive involvement in public works projects.

alienation In Marxian theory, that process under capitalism whereby the worker ceases to regard work as an intrinsically enjoyable activity, regarding it instead as stultifying and dehumanizing. In a more general sociological vein, a process by which people feel estranged from other people and the basic character of their society.

ambiliny The formation of corporate descent groups by tracing kinship connections through either males or females.

ambilocality Residence of the newly married couple with the husband's or the wife's kinship group.

ancestor-focus Tracing descent relationships from some real or mythical ancestor.

antagonistic cooperation Cooperative behavior resulting from people's attempts to serve their long-run selfish interests. Also known as *enlightened self-interest.*

anthropological linguistics The study of human languages, their relationship to sociocultural patterns, and their changes through time.

anthropology The study of humankind.

archaeology The study of the past through examination of artifacts left by earlier peoples. *Prehistoric archaeology* studies peoples who left no written records, while *historic archaeology* studies societies having developed writing.

articulated economy One whose multiple economic sectors are highly interconnected so that changes in one sector contribute significantly to changes in other sectors. Such an economy has balance and diversification.

Asiatic mode of production As conceived by Marx and earlier historians, a type of agrarian society characterized by an absence of private property in land and a highly oppressive centralized state brought into existence by a need to manage complex irrigation works.

authority The socially legitimated right to command the actions of others.

average world citizen A high-level abstraction referring to the typical member of the typical form of human society prevailing in any given historical era.

avunculocality Residence of the newly married couple in the household of the husband's mother's brother.

balanced reciprocity See *reciprocity.*

band A stage of political evolution in which the primary political leader is a headman who has no capacity to compel the actions of others. Also, the group in a hunter-gatherer society that forages and resides together.

basic class locations In Wright's Marxian class scheme, class positions that are consistent with respect to the dimensions of ownership and authority.

beliefs Ideas shared among the members of a group or society about what is true and what is false.

big men Men of considerable prestige and renown who perform important political and economic leadership roles in many horticultural societies, especially those of Melanesia.

bilateral cross-cousin marriage See *restricted exchange.*

bilateral descent The formation of personal kindreds by tracing one's relatives through both males and females simultaneously.

bilocality Alternating residence of the newly married couple between the husband's and wife's kinship groups.

binary oppositions Pairs of contrasting ideas claimed by some social theorists to be fundamental to human thinking and to underline the structure of society. Examples include male/female, up/down, black/white, and nature/culture.

biological evolution The genetic changes that occur over time within populations of organisms, most commonly as the result of the retention of favorable genetic mutations through environmental selection.

bourgeoisie In Marxian theory, the class owning capital.

bridewealth The payment of a sum of valuables by the husband's kin group to the wife's kin group upon marriage. Also called *brideprice.*

bureaucracy A form of social organization in which rationalization, or deliberate calculation of the most efficient ways to achieve goals, is a supreme characteristic. Bureaucracies generally have highly formalized modes of organization, elaborate hierarchies of command, and a strong reliance upon elaborate written forms of communication.

bureaucratic See *bureaucracy.*

bureaucratic education A type of educational system designed as a recruitment device for personnel to occupational positions, or as a means of socializing the masses in order to gain their political compliance.

capitalism An economic system devoted to the production and sale of commodities on a market, with the objective of earning the maximum profit and accumulating profit over time.

cargo cult A type of revitalization movement occurring in the twentieth century in parts of Melanesia in which native populations organize themselves for what they believe will be the future return of their dead ancestors bringing with them large supplies of Western goods.

caste A highly rigid stratification system, generally limited to South Asia, in which endogamous and highly impermeable social strata crystallize around distinct occupations.

chiefdom A centralized political system organized into a hierarchy of chiefs and subchiefs.

chiefly ownership A form of property rights characterized by the (at least theoretical) ownership of land by a ruling chief and his royal family.

church In Troeltsch's formulation, a type of religious organization coextensive with society as a whole, having an official ecclesiastical structure, placing great emphasis on established religious doctrines, and accepting the basic character of the secular world as it is.

clan A corporate descent group whose members cannot precisely identify their genealogical connections to one another but assume such connections nonetheless.

class See *social class.*

class structuration The degree of cultural distinctiveness of a social class and the level of impermeability among the classes in a class structure.

cognatic descent Descent in which both males and females are used to establish descent groupings.

colonized minority A minority group created through the colonization of a weaker racial or ethnic group by a stronger racial or ethnic group.

commodification The process whereby economic production is increasingly governed by considerations of exchange-value.

commodity An object produced by humans that contains both use-value and exchange-value.

communal cult institution One characterized by groups of laymen who perform religious rites that are important to such groups as age grades, secret societies, the sexes, and kinship groups.

communal religion One containing communal, shamanic, and individualistic cult institutions.

competitive race relations A form of race relations characteristic of industrial societies in which the members of historically dominant and subordinate racial groups engage in extreme competition and conflict over access to economic and other social positions.

complementary filiation The ties that individuals form with secondary relatives, i.e., with mother's relatives in patrilineal societies and with father's relatives in matrilineal societies.

conflict An opposition of interests between and among various individuals and social groups, which may or may not be overtly observable, and which may or may not break out into open dispute or physical violence. For example, the opposition of interests between capitalists and workers to which Marx pointed.

Conflict Principle The notion that social conflict is a fundamental feature of human relationships and a major determinant of the organization of society.

conflict theory A theoretical strategy that attempts to understand social phenomena as the result of the antagonistic interests and aims of individuals and social groups.

consanguinity The existence of kinship ties based on genetic relatedness.

consociational democracy A type of ethnic relations in which diverse ethnic groups share similar levels of wealth and social power and live in relative harmony with one another.

contest-mobility educational system One in which no official tracking or channeling of students exists, and in which students are in principle free to compete for as much education as their talents and inclinations allow.

contradictory class locations In Wright's Marxian class scheme, class positions that are inconsistent or ambiguous with respect to the dimensions of ownership and authority.

convergent evolution Changes in two or more originally dissimilar societies that make them increasingly alike.

core That dominant part of the capitalist world-economy that appropriates the bulk of the surplus produced throughout the system.

corporate descent group A network of kinspeople who trace descent from a common ancestor and who function as a single, discrete group.

corvée A system whereby the elite groups of highly stratified agrarian societies recruit large teams of laborers for special work projects.

cost/benefit analysis An analysis of human social and economic behavior that starts from the assumption that people will, within the constraints of their knowledge of their situation, take that course of action that maximizes their benefits and minimizes their costs.

cottage industry See *putting-out system.*

counterculture A smaller culture contained within a larger culture, but one that generally rejects much of the larger culture.

credential inflation A process whereby educational credentials (diplomas and degrees) decline in value over time because of the larger number of people who possess them. See also *qualificationism.*

cult A small and generally short-lived religious group whose doctrines and practices represent an extreme departure from the established religious traditions of a society.

cult institution A set of religious rituals having the same goal, rationalized by a set of similar beliefs, and supported by the same social group.

cultural anthropology The study of patterns of social life, with an emphasis on primitive and contemporary peasant societies.

cultural relativism The doctrine that cultural patterns can be evaluated only on their own terms, not in terms of any other patterns. Cultural relativism in the strict sense assumes that all cultural patterns are "equally valid," and that the culture itself makes anything right or wrong, good or bad, etc.

culture The total lifeways characteristic of the members of a society that are socially learned and shared and are not the direct result of human biology. Culture includes technology, knowledge, and organized patterns of action and thought.

demesne The "home-farm" of the feudal manor, or the land held directly by the landlord and cultivated exclusively for his own use.

demographic See *demography.*

demographic transition A process of demographic change associated with large-scale industrialization in which mortality and fertility rates drop sharply, family size declines, and the overall rate of population growth markedly slows.

demography Features of a human population, such as its size, density, and age and sex distributions.

denomination A conventional and respectable religious organization limited in its membership to individuals drawn from certain classes, races, or regions.

dependency theory An approach to the problem of economic underdevelopment that holds that underdevelopment results from the economic dependency to which many nations have been historically subjected. See *economic dependency.*

devolution Social change resulting in the emergence of characteristics typical of an earlier stage of sociocultural evolution.

dialectical materialism See *historical materialism.*

differential access to resources The existence of unequal levels of control over the means of production by different segments of a sociocultural system.

diffusion The spread of cultural elements from one society to another.

disarticulated economy One whose multiple sectors do not significantly interrelate such that growth in one sector contributes little or nothing to the growth of other sectors. Such an economy is characterized by a lack of diversification and by exaggerated specialization, typically of the raw-materials-production-for-export sector.

discrimination Unequal and unfair treatment of one social group (race, ethnic group, sex, etc.) by another.

distribution See *economic distribution.*

divergent evolution Changes in two or more originally similar societies that make them increasingly different.

double descent A descent system in which both patrilineal and matrilineal descent groups exist simultaneously in the same society.

dowry The property that a woman accumulates and takes with her into a marriage in order to contract the marriage in the first place.

ecclesia A religious organization similar to the church but less successfully meeting the needs of many of its members.

ecclesiastical cult institution One containing a specialized professional priesthood holding full-time bureaucratic offices.

eclecticism A viewpoint that holds that theoretical strategies must be used in combination in order to achieve acceptable explanations.

ecology The natural environment to which human societies must adjust, as well as the relationships between this environment and social patterns.

economic dependency A process whereby one society's economy falls under the domination of a foreign society.

economic distribution The set of social relationships through which people allocate the goods and services they produce.

economic exchange The social relationships through which people transfer valuables between and among one another.

economic production The set of social relationships through which people create valuables.

economic surplus A quantity of economic valuables above and beyond that necessary for the subsistence of the members who produce such valuables.

economy The set of social relationships through which people organize the production, distribution, and exchange of valuables.

education Any formalized or semiformalized system of cultural or intellectual instruction.

ego-focus Tracing descent relationships from the point of view of some living individual.

empirical Referring to the making of systematic observations and the collection of data in order to test the value of proposed ideas.

endogamy The tendency for persons to marry members of their own social group, especially their own race, ethnic group, religious group, or social class.

enlightened self-interest See *antagonistic cooperation.*

established sect A religious sect having evolved somewhat in the direction of conventionality and respectability.

ethnic group A social group or category having a socially meaningful distinctiveness that rests on cultural criteria.

ethnocentrism A universal social doctrine holding that one's own culture or society is superior to all others. Literally, "my group is the center."

ethnography A detailed written account of a culture by a foreign observer.

ethnomethodology A theoretical strategy in microsociology that resembles symbolic interactionism but is even more extreme in its emphasis on shared definitions of reality. Ethnomethodologists attempt to study, often in great detail, the ways in which people construct their definitions of social reality.

evolution See *biological evolution* and *sociocultural evolution.*

evolutionary theory A theoretical strategy that attempts to describe and explain directional sequences of long-term social change. *Functionalist evolutionary* theories tend to view long-term changes as increases in social complexity that produce increasingly well-adapted societies. *Materialist evolutionary* theories explain the major transformations that occur in human social life as responses to changing material conditions.

exchange See *economic exchange.*

exchange-value The value a good will fetch when it is exchanged for other goods.

exogamy The prohibition against marriage into one's own corporate descent group.

exploitation An economic process that occurs when one party compels another to give up more than it receives in return.

extended family A number of related nuclear families bound together and functioning as a definite social unit.

feudalism An economic and political system found in some agrarian societies in which a private landlord class holds land in the form of fiefs. See also *fief* and *vassalage.*

feudal state An agrarian state characterized by the fragmentation of power, that is, its dispersal among a range of political leaders, each of whom has control of a limited territory.

fief A grant of land given by an overlord to a vassal (lesser lord) in return for the performance of such obligations as military service and personal protection.

forced labor Any labor system in which workers are not free to negotiate the kind and amount of labor they will perform and their level of compensation.

formalism A perspective taken by students of precapitalist economies that holds that the principles of modern Western economic theory are valid for the study of precapitalist economies.

freedom In the Western individualist tradition, a relative absence of constraints on the individual's capacity to act and think according to his or her own personal standards. In the Marxian tradition, the full opportunity for persons to realize their basic nature as members of the human species.

functional analysis A viewpoint that assumes that social phenomena can be understood in terms of their usefulness in fulfilling the aims of individuals or groups. Not to be confused with *functionalism.*

functionalism A contemporary theoretical strategy that analyzes social phenomena in terms of the functions they perform in maintaining the existence or stability of society. Functionalists usually assume that societies have needs much as organisms do, and that they must develop particular structures to satisfy these needs.

generalized reciprocity See *reciprocity.*

geopolitics The intersection of politics and geography. Geopolitical considerations are those that involve the territorial and diplomatic relations among states, either regionally or worldwide. See *interstate system.*

goal displacement A phenomenon that occurs in modern bureaucracies when the means people develop to achieve certain goals end up becoming the goals themselves.

Herrenvolk democracy A parliamentary democracy that limits the application of its democratic principles to a dominant racial group.

historical materialism The original theoretical strategy of Marx and Engels, which was the first systematic form of sociological materialism. Also called *dialectical materialism.* See also *materialism.*

history The study of the past, both descriptively and theoretically.

horticulture A simple form of agriculture in which small plots of land (gardens) are crudely prepared and cultivated through the use of hand tools.

human nature Those psychological and biological qualities universally characteristic of the human species.

hunting and gathering society One whose members make a living primarily or exclusively through the hunting of wild animals and the collection of wild vegetable matter.

hypergyny The marriage of a woman to one or more men of higher social rank.

idealism In social science, the doctrine that the basic features of human social life result from the nature of human thought and ideas.

idealist See *idealism.*

ideological superstructure The organized set of beliefs, values, feelings, and symbols shared by the members of a sociocultural system.

immigrant minority A minority group created through the voluntary immigration of a racial or ethnic group to another society.

incest avoidance The strong tendency for persons in all societies to avoid sexual relations with close kin.

incest taboo The existence of strong sanctions against sexual relations between close kin.

inclusive fitness The sum total of an individual organism's own fitness and the fitness that organism has represented in the genes it shares with related organisms. Also known as *kin selection.*

individualism As conceived by the French sociologist Emile Durkheim, a social and moral doctrine that treats the individual person as the principal object of moral concern. Under this social philosophy the individual's rights, needs, aims, etc., are promoted through the very organization of society itself.

individualistic cult institution One in which each individual performs his or her own religious rites as the need arises.

industrial capitalism The form of economic activity that emerged in Europe with the Industrial Revolution and that today characterizes most of the societies of Western Europe, North America, Australia, and Japan. In Marx's formulation, it involves the making of profits through the exploitation of labor power in the very process of production itself.

industrialization The process by which a society comes to be characterized by an economic system and a mode of social life based around machinery and the factory system of manufacturing. See *mechanization.*

industrial society One having acquired a level of technology based upon the use of machines to replace hand labor and the widespread use of these machines in the process of economic production.

influence The process whereby the thoughts and actions of one party produce modifications in the thoughts and actions of other parties.

intensification of production An increase in the expenditure of energy involved in carrying out economic production. This may occur through greater work inputs, use of more natural resources, advancement of the level of technology, or any combination of these.

intensive horticultural society A horticultural society whose members have adopted more energy-intensive means of cultivation, such as shortening the fallow period of land or using more advanced tools and techniques of production.

interstate system The complex system of competing and conflicting nation-states that is closely intertwined with the capitalist world-economy.

kindred A small-scale personal kin group generally activated only at special times, such as ritual occasions or the need for assistance.

kin selection See *inclusive fitness.*

labor power In Marxian theory, the capacity of the worker to work.

Law of Least Effort The principle that, other things being equal, people prefer to carry out activities with a minimum amount of energy expenditure.

legitimacy See *legitimation.*

legitimation The process whereby certain social relationships are deemed to be morally right and proper.

liberal theory of the state A theory of modern politics holding that the state in contemporary capitalism is a neutral agent devoted to arbitrating the contending interests of various social groups. See also *pluralism.*

lineage A corporate descent group whose members can actually identify their genealogical connections to each other.

lineage ownership Communal ownership of land by large-scale kinship groups.

logic of discovery In science, the means by which ideas are originated by scientists.

logic of justification In science, the means by which ideas are demonstrated to be valid or intellectually worthwhile.

long-cycle generalized exchange A form of marital exchange in primitive societies in which corporate descent groups remain in permanent wife-giving or wife-receiving relationships with other groups, never giving wives to groups from which they receive them, and never receiving wives from groups to which they give them. Also known as *matrilateral cross-cousin marriage.*

macrosociology That type of sociology that studies large-scale forms of social organization, especially entire societies and the world network of societies. Macrosociology is in general comparatively and historically focused.

majority group A racial or ethnic group that treats another racial or ethnic group unequally or unfairly. See also *minority group.*

manor The lands and the labor force controlled by a feudal landlord.

market An economic institution that involves the buying and selling of goods and services in a socially organized manner.

market-dominated society A society having both markets and marketplaces and in which market principles govern economic activity.

marketless society A society having neither markets nor marketplaces.

marketplace A physical site where market activities occur.

material infrastructure The raw materials and social forms used by the members of a sociocultural system to meet their needs in regard to economic production and biological reproduction.

materialism In social science, the viewpoint that the basic features of human social life derive from the "material conditions of social life," such as the economy, the physical environment, and the level of technology.

materialist See *materialism.*

matrifocal family A family managed by an adult woman (or a woman and her mother), either because her husband has abandoned her or because she has never married.

matrilateral cross-cousin marriage See *long-cycle generalized exchange.*

matrilineal descent See *matriliny.*

matriliny Descent traced only through females.

matrilocality Residence of the newly married couple in the household of the wife's mother.

mechanization The process whereby machinery and other advanced forms of technology are increasingly applied to economic production. See *industrialization.*

mercantilism An economic practice in the seventeenth and early eighteenth centuries whereby governments granted monopolies to European trading companies so that these companies could make large profits from their trade with foreign colonies.

merchant capitalism In Marx's formulation, an early form of capitalism, prevailing approximately in the years 1450–1750, in which trading companies made profits throughout the world by capitalizing on favorable terms of trade.

microsociology That type of sociology that investigates patterns of social behavior that occur in small groups and face-to-face social relationships.

middleman minority A minority group whose members tend to occupy an intermediate position in the class structure, to be concentrated in occupations involving trade and commerce, and to have especially high levels of ethnic solidarity and consciousness.

millenarian movement See *revitalization movement.*

minority group A racial or ethnic group whose members suffer from unequal and unfair treatment at the hands of another racial or ethnic group. See also *majority group.*

modernization theory An approach to the problem of economic underdevelopment that postulates that contemporary underdeveloped nations remain in a "traditional" state because they contain certain internal deficiences that constitute obstacles to development.

mode of production A concept used by Marx and Engels to refer to a society's level of technological development combined with the overall organization of its economy (especially in terms of the ownership of property).

monogamy The marriage of one man to one woman.

monopoly capitalism That stage of capitalism, generally beginning in the last quarter of the nineteenth century, characterized by the rise of the giant corporation as the basic economic unit and the emergence of extensive foreign investment of core nations in the capitalist periphery.

monotheistic religion One containing individualistic, shamanic, and communal cult institutions in addition to ecclesiastical cult institutions organized around the concept of a single high god.

multinational corporation A company that has branches of production in several countries.

natolocality Residence of husband and wife in the separate households in which they resided before marriage.

natural selection The process whereby favorable genetic materials are retained because they have high survival value and unfavorable genetic materials are eliminated because they have low survival value. The retention and proliferation of new genetic materials amounts to *evolution*.

Neolithic Revolution That major technological transformation, beginning about 10,000 years ago, most importantly associated with the beginnings of agriculture.

neolocality Residence of the newly married couple in an independent household of its own.

norms Socially shared rules defining forms of behavior that are prohibited and forms that are desirable or essential.

nuclear family A kinship unit consisting of the married spouses and their immediate offspring who maintain a common household and act together as a distinct group.

Olympian religion One containing individualistic, shamanic, and communal cult institutions in addition to ecclesiastical cult institutions of the polytheistic type.

Oriental despotism As formulated by Karl Wittfogel, a type of agrarian state characterized by massive centralization of power, extensive involvement in public works projects, and brutal tyrannization of the mass of the subject population. See also *Asiatic mode of production*.

parallel evolution Changes in two or more societies that are similar in form and in the rate of change.

parliamentary democracy A type of government in which governmental officials are elected to office as presumed representatives of the people, a separation of powers of the branches of government exists, and constitutional liberties are generally accorded to the people.

partial redistribution See *redistribution*.

party A social group whose members aim to exert a certain degree and type of power in the political realm of society.

pastoralism See *pastoral society*.

pastoral society A society whose members survive primarily through the tending of animal herds.

paternalistic race relations A form of race relations characteristic of preindustrial societies in which the members of one racial group relegate members of another racial group to a subordinate social status, regarding them essentially as childlike beings needing the "fatherly" protection and guidance of the dominant racial group.

patrilateral cross-cousin marriage See *short-cycle generalized exchange*.

patrilineal descent See *patriliny*.

patriliny Descent traced only through males.

patrilocality Residence of the newly married couple in the household of the husband's father.

patrimonial ownership A form of seigneurial ownership in which land is privately owned by a landlord class and inherited in family lines.

peasant A farmer, ordinarily found in an agrarian or contemporary underdeveloped society, who typically exists in an economically and politically subordinate relationship to the principal owner or controller of the land from which he or she gains his or her subsistence.

peripheral market society A society having marketplaces, but in which market principles are not the primary organizers of economic life.

periphery The least economically developed part of the capitalist world-economy, extensively subjected to high levels of surplus expropriation by the core.

physical anthropology The study of human biological characteristics, especially as these involve the evolution of humankind over the past several million years.

pluralism A theoretical position holding that power in contemporary capitalist societies is dispersed among a wide range of contending groups so that no group consistently dominates the rest.

polity The socially organized means whereby a society maintains internal law and order and carries out relationships with other societies.

polyandry The marriage of one woman to two or more men.

polygyny The marriage of one man to two or more women.

population pressure A level of population density that, for any given society at a given level of technology, produces a deterioration in the economic standard of living.

potlatch An elaborate giveaway feast prominent among many of the Indian tribes of the Northwest Coast in recent centuries.

power The capacity of one party to compel the actions of other parties even against their will.

power elite A social group, or at least a loosely organized social network, whose members are devoted to controlling the key spheres of modern capitalist society. Also, the theory that postulates the existence of such a group.

practical-skill education A type of educational system primarily designed to teach certain technical skills.

prebendal ownership A form of seigneurial ownership in which land is owned by a powerful government that assigns officials to oversee its cultivation and make their living from it.

precapitalist economy See *precapitalist society.*

precapitalist society One existing before the emergence of modern capitalism, or not yet significantly characterized by capitalist economic features.

preindustrial society One existing prior to the Industrial Revolution, or not yet having acquired an industrial level of technology.

prejudice An attitude of dislike or hostility on the part of a member of one racial or ethnic group toward the members of some other racial or ethnic group.

prestige The social honor or respect accorded individuals or groups.

primitive communism A form of economic ownership in which all individuals and groups have equal access to the resources of nature that sustain life.

primitive society One that has not yet developed writing, has a relatively simple level of hunting-gathering, pastoral, or agricultural technology, and is strongly organized according to patterns of kinship.

primordialism In regard to the study of ethnicity, the view that ethnic identities are first-order human concerns that are difficult if not impossible to eradicate.

Principle of Infrastructural Determinism The notion that the material infrastructure has a logical priority in the creation of social life, and that the character of this component of society has a major influence on the character of the other societal components.

principle of parsimony A principle that holds that, other things being equal, those theories that explain the most with the least (i.e., that use the fewest and simplest assumptions, concepts, and principles) are to be preferred.

Principle of Sociocultural Adaptation The notion that the features of social life are created by people as rational responses to the basic problems they face and the needs and wants they have.

Principle of Sociocultural Integration The notion that the various components of society form together into an overall system.

pristine state A state that arises under conditions in which no pre-existing state is to be found.

private property The ownership and control of important productive resources by only a fraction of a group or society.

privilege The material benefits accruing to individuals or groups, or the opportunity to acquire such material benefits.

production See *economic production.*

production-for-exchange A type of economic production in which the aim of the producers is to create goods that will generate value when they are exchanged for other valuables, especially money.

production-for-use A type of economic production in which the aim of the producers is to create goods that have direct or indirect consumption value.

profit That portion of surplus value that remains once capitalists have met additional expenses of production, such as the payment of rent and taxes. See also *surplus value*.

progress A betterment or improvement in social life and its various features.

proletarianization The process whereby the contractual form of labor known as wage labor increasingly becomes the dominant form of labor organization. See *wage labor*.

proletariat In Marxian theory, the class that must sell its labor power to capitalists in order to earn a living.

protoculture The capacity of some infrahuman animals to engage in limited forms of tool use and limited symbol manipulation.

pure redistribution See *redistribution*.

putting-out system An early type of capitalist industry in which workers remained in their homes to produce goods destined to be sold by capitalist entrepreneurs. The entrepreneurs did not affect the production process except to advance raw materials and partial wages with their orders for goods. Also known as *cottage industry*.

qualificationism The process whereby an educational system comes to be oriented around the pursuit of education for its credential value rather than for its intrinsic merits. Also, the expansion of the credentializing character of an educational system over time. See also *credential inflation*.

race A category of persons who are identified by themselves and by others as having a socially meaningful distinctiveness that rests on biological criteria.

racism An elaborate ideology holding that one race is biologically superior and that all others are biologically inferior to it. This doctrine regards the unequal economic and social positions of different races as the outcome of their genetic differences.

rank society An unstratified society in which there is a limited number of high-status social positions for which individuals vigorously compete.

rational choice theory A microlevel theoretical strategy that assumes that humans are constructed so as to attempt to maximize their gains and minimize their losses, and that organized social life is the aggregate expression of the actions of individuals who are rationally calculating in this manner.

rationalization Weber's concept referring to the tendency of modern Western society to become increasingly subject to social relationships guided by the deliberate calculation of the most efficient ways to achieve stated goals.

reciprocity The obligation to repay others for what they have given to us, as well as the act of repayment itself. *Balanced reciprocity* occurs when the obligation to reciprocate is specific as to time and amount. *Generalized reciprocity* occurs when the obligation for repayment is vague and nonspecific.

redistribution A process of economic distribution in which goods are brought to a central source (person or group) and then returned in some manner to the points from which they originated. *Pure redistribution* occurs when all that is funneled in one direction is refunneled in the other. *Partial redistribution* occurs when only some of what is received is returned to the original parties.

relative immiseration, thesis of The view that the economic gap between core and periphery in the capitalist world-economy is widening, and thus that the overall quality of human life in the periphery is deteriorating relative to the core (rather than absolutely). Compare *absolute immiseration*.

religion An organized set of beliefs and practices resting on unproved faith and postulating the existence of supernatural beings, powers, or forces that act upon the physical and social world.

repression Any action by a state that forcefully prevents individuals from taking actions perceived as harmful to that state.

restricted exchange A form of marital exchange in primitive societies in which corporate descent groups mutually exchange women as marriage partners generation after generation. Also known as *bilateral cross-cousin marriage*.

revitalization movement A socioreligious movement in which people are attempting to bring about basic changes in the structure of society and establish a more meaningful and rewarding existence. Also known as *millenarian movement*.

royal incest Legitimated marriage between close kin who belong to a society's ruling class.

rule of hypo-descent A principle of racial classification, common especially in the United States, which assigns all offspring of racially heterogeneous parents to the socially subordinate racial group.

rules of descent The means by which the members of a society organize networks of kinspeople and specify the rights and duties of these kinspeople toward each other.

rules of residence The means by which the members of a society organize themselves into households or domestic residential groups.

scarcity An insufficient quantity of material resources relative to the technological level, the degree of population pressure, and the standard of living experienced by any group or society.

science A mode of intellectual inquiry seeking a coherent theoretical understanding of the world by reliance upon empirical procedures, that is, upon systematic observation and data collection. Also, the accumulated results of such intellectual activity.

scientific See *science.*

secondary state A state that has arisen as the result of the presence of one or more pre-existing states.

sect A small religious organization identifying itself as a community of select believers, having no official ecclesiastical structure, and generally maintaining a hostile stance toward the secular world as well as toward established religious organizations.

secularization The process whereby the influence of religion in social life is steadily reduced.

seigneurial ownership Ownership of land by a class of landlords having the power to impose severe penalties on other persons for the use of the land.

semiperiphery That segment of the capitalist world-economy that is neither as highly exploitative as the core nor as exploited as the periphery. This intermediate zone of the world-economy contains a mixture of core-like and periphery-like economic activities.

sexual inequality The presence of unequal levels of power and privilege between the sexes, including unequal evaluations of the sexes.

shamanic cult institution One in which part-time religious specialists known as shamans perform religious rites in return for a fee.

shamanic religion A type of religion containing only individualistic and shamanic cult institutions.

short-cycle generalized exchange A form of marital exchange in primitive societies in which corporate descent groups mutually exchange women as marriage partners. Groups that give wives in odd generations will take wives from those same groups in even generations. Also known as *patrilateral cross-cousin marriage.*

sign An element of animal communication whose meaning is determined by biological inheritance.

simple commodity production A precapitalist form of economic activity in which producers generate commodities designed to be exchanged for other commodities of equal value.

simple horticultural society One whose members earn a living through reliance upon the simplest agricultural techniques. Normally this involves long-fallow cultivation of small garden plots using hand tools.

slavery A form of labor organization in which some persons are legally owned as a form of human property, are compelled to work by their owners, and are deprived of most or all of their political rights.

social class In conventional sociology, a category of persons sharing a similar level of privilege and social status by virtue of their occupational roles. In Marxian sociology, a social group whose members share the same relationship to the ownership of productive resources, and who also share similar levels of control over their own or others' work. Compare *social stratum.*

social closure The tendency for social groups to use certain social criteria as marks of distinction whereby they can monopolize resources, such monopolization being thought essential to the acquisition of privilege and prestige.

social differentiation The increasing social complexity that frequently accompanies social change.

social inequality The existence of unequal levels of social influence or prestige among individual members of a society.

social influence See *influence.*

social institution Any part of a sociocultural system that involves established and regularized patterns of social behavior and consciousness, e.g., the economy, the polity, kinship, religion.

socialism In Marx's original works, a form of society in which private property and social classes do not exist, in which work is no longer treated as a commodity, and in which people have the genuine possibility of achieving human freedom. See also *state socialism.*

socialization The process whereby the members of a society transmit the content of their culture to new generations through various forms of child training and other instruction.

social mobility The upward or downward movement of individuals between positions in the class structure of a society.

social stratification The existence within a society (or world-system) of social groups that possess unequal levels of social power, privilege, and prestige.

social stratum A category of persons occupying the same approximate level of power, privilege, and prestige within a society. Compare *social class.*

social structure The organized patterns of social behavior common to the members of a sociocultural system.

societal needs A concept fundamental to functionalism that assumes that societies have basic requirements in much the same way that organisms or human individuals do.

sociobiology A theoretical strategy that attempts to explain various features of human social life as the result of certain universal biological characteristics of humankind.

sociocultural adaptation See *adaptation.*

sociocultural continuity The preservation of the basic features of a society over time.

sociocultural evolution Qualitative structural transformations within a sociocultural system (or one or more of its parts) that exhibit a directional pattern.

sociocultural extinction The elimination of a sociocultural system, either through the death of its members or through its absorption into another sociocultural system.

sociocultural system A social collectivity having organized its social life culturally.

sociology The scientific study of human social life in all its aspects.

sponsored-mobility educational system A type of educational system in which students are channeled into different educational tracks early in their careers based on their performance on standardized examinations.

state A political system claiming a monopoly over the use of the means of violence within a specified territory.

state socialism A form of economy in which the government is the principal owner and manager of the means of production.

state socialist See *state socialism.*

status group A social group whose members share a similar lifestyle or cultural outlook and a similar level of social status or prestige.

status-group education A type of educational system whose primary aim is to disseminate knowledge and styles of behavior, the possession of which serves to symbolize and reinforce the prestige and privilege of elite groups in highly stratified societies.

stem family A type of extended family in which an older couple live together with one of their sons and his wife and children.

structuralism An idealist theoretical strategy developed by the French anthropologist Claude Lévi-Strauss that holds that the features of society result from the tendency of the human mind to think in terms of pairs of opposing ideas.

subculture A smaller culture contained within a larger culture that generally accepts the broader patterns of the larger culture

substantivism A perspective taken by students of precapitalist economies that holds that the principles of modern economic theory cannot be applied to the analysis of precapitalist societies.

surplus expropriation The siphoning off of the economic surplus produced by one group into the hands of another group by means of one or another form of compulsion.

surplus value In Marxian theory, the increment in value that the capitalist generates over and above the original capital investment. See also *profit.*

symbol In communication, an element of speech that is arbitrary, or whose meaning is determined by social definition rather than by biological inheritance. Otherwise, any physical or social invention that signifies a socially shared meaning.

symbolic interactionism A major theoretical strategy in microsociology that stresses the definitional and subjective elements of social life. Symbolic interactionists place great emphasis on how people use symbols to construct shared definitions of reality and on how these shared definitions shape their social actions.

systems of marital exchange Organized social networks devoted to the giving and taking of women as marriage partners in primitive societies. See *long-cycle generalized exchange, restricted exchange,* and *short-cycle generalized exchange.*

technology The material means, which include tools, techniques, and knowledge, whereby humans meet their needs and desires.

theoretical strategy A highly generalized set of concepts, assumptions, and principles designed to explain phenomena in the broadest sense.

theory A statement (or interrelated set of statements) designed to explain some particular phenomenon or category of related phenomena.

theory of kin selection The basic premise of the sociobiological theoretical strategy that holds that many forms of human social behavior represent the efforts of individuals to maximize their inclusive fitness. See also *inclusive fitness* and *kin selection.*

theory of surplus value Marx's theory holding that capitalist profits derive from paying workers less than the full value of the commodities they produce. See also *surplus value.*

totalitarian dictatorship A type of government, generally associated with modern state socialist societies, in which all power is concentrated in the hands of a governmental elite that rules the people without regard to any concept of "popular sentiment" or individual rights and liberties.

tribe A network of bands or villages sharing a common culture and speaking the same language. Also, a level of political evolution characterized by the absence of centralized authority and political leaders with the power to compel the actions of others.

underdeveloped society One of the least technologically and economically advanced members of the capitalist world-economy.

undeveloped society A society outside the framework of a capitalist world-economy, which thus remains in a precapitalist and preindustrial state.

unilineal descent Descent traced only through a single line, that is, through males or through females.

unilineal descent groups See *unilineal descent.*

use-value The utilitarian value of a good, or the benefit it confers when it is consumed.

values Standards of worth held in common by the members of a society or any of its subgroups.

vassalage The personal tie between lords in a feudal society created by the granting of a fief from an overlord to a lesser lord (vassal), who in turn takes an oath to serve and protect his overlord. See also *fief.*

wage labor A labor relationship in which workers are legally free to bargain with employers for a specified rate of compensation for their work and the conditions under which they will perform that work.

world-economy A world-system lacking political centralization and that therefore contains within it a plurality of competing states. A world-economy is characterized by economic relations of production and exchange that serve to integrate it. See also *core, periphery,* and *semiperiphery.*

world-empire A world-system that is politically and militarily centralized or unified.

world-system Any relatively large social system having a high degree of autonomy, an extensive division of labor, and a plurality of cultural groups.

world-system theory A theoretical approach designed to explain many features of the evolution of capitalism since the sixteenth century. It holds that capitalism has evolved as a hierarchical arrangement of exploiting and exploited nations, each of which can be properly understood only as part of the entire system. As applied specifically to the underdeveloped nations of the contemporary world, it predicts that stagnation or deterioration will continue to be the lot of most. However, it does identify certain conditions that allow a few nations to improve their status at critical historical periods.

Bibliography

Aberle, David F. 1961. "Matrilineal descent in cross-cultural perspective." In David M. Schneider and Kathleen Gough (eds.), *Matrilineal Kinship*. Berkeley: University of California Press.

Abonyi, Arpad. 1982. "Eastern Europe's reintegration." In Christopher Chase-Dunn (ed.), *Socialist States in the World-System*. Beverly Hills, Calif.: Sage.

Abu-Lughod, Janet. 1988. "The shape of the world system in the thirteenth century." *Studies in Comparative International Development* 22(4): 3–24.

———. 1989. *Before European Hegemony: The World-System A.D. 1250–1350*. New York: Oxford University Press.

Adams, Robert McC. 1966. *The Evolution of Urban Society*. Chicago: Aldine.

———. 1972. "Demography and the 'Urban Revolution' in lowland Mesopotamia." In Brian Spooner (ed.), *Population Growth: Anthropological Implications*. Cambridge, Mass.: MIT Press.

Aganbegyan, Abel. 1988. "New directions in Soviet economics." *New Left Review* 169:87–93.

———. 1989. *Inside Perestroika: The Future of the Soviet Economy*. Translated by Helen Szamuely. New York: Harper & Row.

Ahluwalia, Montek S. 1974. "Income inequality: some dimensions of the problem." In Hollis Chenery (ed.), *Redistribution with Growth*. New York: Oxford University Press.

Alderson, Arthur S., and Stephen K. Sanderson. 1989. "Historic European household structures and the capitalist world-economy." Paper presented at the annual meetings of the American Sociological Association, San Francisco, August 10.

Alexander, Jeffrey C. 1982. *Theoretical Logic in Sociology, Volume 1: Positivism, Presuppositions, and Current Controversies*. Berkeley: University of California Press.

———. 1984. *Theoretical Logic in Sociology, Volume 4: The Modern Reconstruction of Classical Thought: Talcott Parsons*. Berkeley: University of California Press.

Alexander, Jeffrey C. (ed.). 1985. *Neofunctionalism*. Beverly Hills, Calif: Sage.

Alexander, Richard D. 1987. *The Biology of Moral Systems*. Hawthorne, N.Y.: Aldine de Gruyter.

Alland, Alexander, Jr. 1973. *Evolution and Human Behavior: An Introduction to Darwinian Anthropology*. Second edition. Garden City, N.Y.: Doubleday (Anchor Books).

Amin, Samir. 1974. *Accumulation on a World Scale*. New York: Monthly Review Press.

Anderson, Charles H. 1974. *The Political Economy of Social Class*. Englewood Cliffs, N.J.: Prentice-Hall.

Anderson, Charles H., and Jeffrey Gibson. 1978. *Toward a New Sociology*. Third edition. Homewood, Ill.: Dorsey Press.

Anderson, Michael. 1980. *Approaches to the History of the Western Family, 1500–1914*. London: Macmillan Press.

Anderson, Perry. 1974a. *Passages from Antiquity to Feudalism.* London: New Left Books.

———. 1974b. *Lineages of the Absolutist State.* London: New Left Books.

Andorka, Rudolf, and Tamás Farago. 1983. "Preindustrial household structure in Hungary." In Richard Wall, Jean Rodin, and Peter Laslett (eds.), *Family Forms in Historic Europe.* Cambridge: Cambridge University Press.

Angel, J. Lawrence. 1975. "Paleoecology, paleodemography, and health." In Steven Polgar (ed.), *Population, Ecology, and Social Evolution.* The Hague: Mouton.

Apter, David E. 1987. *Rethinking Development: Modernization, Dependency, and Post-Modern Politics.* Beverly Hills, Calif.: Sage.

Arizpe, Lourdes. 1977. "Women in the informal labor sector: the case of Mexico City." *Signs: Journal of Women in Culture and Society* 3:25–37.

Armstrong, W. E. 1924. "Rossel Island money: a unique monetary system." *Economic Journal* 34:423–429.

———. 1928. *Rossel Island.* Cambridge: Cambridge University Press.

Aronowitz, Stanley, and Henry A. Giroux. 1985. *Education Under Siege: The Conservative, Liberal, and Radical Debate over Schooling.* South Hadley, Mass.: Bergin and Garvey.

Arrighi, Giovanni. 1982. "A crisis of hegemony." In Samir Amin et al., *Dynamics of Global Crisis.* New York: Monthly Review Press.

Aston, T. H., and C.H.E. Philpin (eds.). 1985. *The Brenner Debate: Agrarian Class Structure and Economic Development in Pre-Industrial Europe.* Cambridge: Cambridge University Press.

Atkinson, A. B. 1983. *The Economics of Inequality.* Second edition. Oxford: Oxford University Press.

Axthelm, Pete, Gerald C. Lubenow, Michael Reese, Linda Walters, and Sylvester Monroe. 1978. "The emperor Jones." *Newsweek,* December 4, pp. 54–60.

Baran, Paul, and E. J. Hobsbawm. 1973. "The stages of economic growth: a review." In Charles K. Wilber (ed.), *The Political Economy of Development and Underdevelopment.* New York: Random House.

Barash, David P. 1977. *Sociobiology and Behavior.* New York: Elsevier.

Barnet, Richard J., and Ronald E. Müller. 1974. *Global Reach: The Power of the Multinational Corporations.* New York: Simon & Schuster (Touchstone).

Barrett, Richard E., and Martin King Whyte. 1982. "Dependency theory and Taiwan: analysis of a deviant case." *American Journal of Sociology* 87:1064–1089.

Barth, Fredrik. 1961. *Nomads of South Persia.* New York: Humanities Press.

Beals, Ralph L., and Harry Hoijer. 1971. *An Introduction to Anthropology.* Fourth edition. New York: Macmillan.

Beard, Charles. 1962. *An Economic Interpretation of the Constitution of the United States.* New York: Macmillan. (Originally published 1913.)

Beaud, Michel. 1983. *A History of Capitalism, 1500–1980.* New York: Monthly Review Press.

Becker, George. 1984. "Pietism and science: a critique of Robert K. Merton's hypothesis." *American Journal of Sociology* 89:1065–1090.

Becker, Howard S. 1963. *Outsiders: Studies in the Sociology of Deviance.* New York: Free Press.

Bell, Daniel. 1973. *The Coming of Post-Industrial Society.* New York: Basic Books.

Bellah, Robert N. 1964. "Religious evolution." *American Sociological Review* 29:358–374.

———. 1967. "Civil religion in America." *Daedalus* 96:1–21.

———. 1970. *Beyond Belief: Essays on Religion in a Post-Traditional World.* New York: Harper & Row.

Bellah, Robert N., Richard Madsen, William M. Sullivan, Ann Swidler, and Steven M. Tipton. 1985. *Habits of the Heart: Individualism and Commitment in American Life.* Berkeley: University of California Press.

Ben-David, Joseph. 1965. "The scientific role: the conditions of its establishment in Europe." *Minerva* 4:15–54.

———. 1971. *The Scientist's Role in Society.* Englewood Cliffs, N.J.: Prentice-Hall.

Benedict, Ruth. 1934. *Patterns of Culture.* Boston: Houghton Mifflin.

Bennett, H. S. 1937. *Life on the English Manor: A Study of Peasant Conditions, 1150–1400.* Cambridge: Cambridge University Press.

Berg, Ivar. 1971. *Education and Jobs: The Great Training Robbery.* Boston: Beacon Press.

Berger, Brigitte, and Peter L. Berger. 1983. *The War over the Family: Capturing the Middle Ground.* Garden City, N.Y.: Doubleday (Anchor Books).

Berger, Peter L. 1986. *The Capitalist Revolution.* New York: Basic Books.

Berger, Peter L., and Thomas Luckmann. 1966. *The Social Construction of Reality.* Garden City, N.Y.: Doubleday (Anchor Books).

Berger, Stephen D. 1974. Review of Daniel Bell, *The Coming of Post-Industrial Society. Contemporary Sociology* 3:101–105.

Berkner, Lutz K. 1972. "The stem family and the developmental cycle of the peasant household: an eighteenth-century Austrian example." *American Historical Review* 77:398–418.

Berkner, Lutz K., and John W. Shaffer. 1978. "The joint family in the Nivernais." *Journal of Family History* 3:150–162.

Bernal, J. D. 1971. *Science in History.* 4 volumes. Cambridge, Mass.: MIT Press.

Berreman, Gerald D. (ed.). 1981. *Social Inequality: Comparative and Developmental Approaches.* New York: Academic Press.

Betzig, Laura L. 1986. *Despotism and Differential Reproduction.* Hawthrone, N.Y.: Aldine de Gruyter.

Bienefeld, Manfred. 1981. "Dependency and the newly industrialising countries (NICs): towards a reappraisal." In Dudley Seers (ed.), *Dependency Theory: A Critical Assessment.* London: Frances Pinter.

Billingsley, Andrew. 1968. *Black Families in White America.* Englewood Cliffs, N.J.: Prentice-Hall.

Binford, Lewis R. 1968. "Post-Pleistocene adaptations." In S. R. Binford and L. R. Binford (eds.), *New Perspectives in Archaeology.* Chicago: Aldine.

Biraben, J. N. 1970. "Document." *Annales de démographie historique,* 441–462.

Bischof, Norbert. 1975. "Comparative ethology of incest avoidance." In Robin Fox (ed.), *Biosocial Anthropology.* London: Malaby Press.

Blalock, Hubert M., Jr. 1967. *Toward a Theory of Minority-Group Relations.* New York: Capricorn Books.

Blau, Peter, and Otis Dudley Duncan. 1967. *The American Occupational Structure.* New York: Free Press.

Blauner, Robert. 1964. *Alienation and Freedom.* Chicago: University of Chicago Press.

———. 1972. *Racial Oppression in America.* New York: Harper & Row.

Blomstrom, Magnus, and Bjorn Hettne. 1984. *Development Theory in Transition.* London: Zed Books.

Blumberg, Rae Lesser. 1976. "Kibbutz women: from the fields of revolution to the laundries of discontent." In Lynne Iglitzin and Ruth Ross (eds.), *Women in the World: A Comparative Study.* Santa Barbara, Calif.: American Bibliographic Center–Clio Press.

———. 1978. *Stratification: Socioeconomic and Sexual Inequality.* Dubuque, Iowa: Brown.

———. 1984. "A general theory of gender stratification." In Randall Collins (ed.), *Sociological Theory 1984.* San Francisco: Jossey-Bass.

Blumberg, Rae Lesser, and Maria-Pilar Garcia. 1977. "The political economy of the mother-child household." In Robert F. Winch, *Familial Organization.* New York: Free Press.

Blumberg, Rae Lesser, and Robert F. Winch. 1977. "The curvilinear relation between societal complexity and familial complexity." In Robert F. Winch, *Familial Organization.* New York: Free Press.

Blumer, Herbert. 1969. *Symbolic Interactionism.* Englewood Cliffs, N.J.: Prentice-Hall.

Bohannan, Paul, and George Dalton (eds.). 1962. *Markets in Africa.* Evanston, Ill.: Northwestern University Press.

Boli, John, Francisco O. Ramirez, and John W. Meyer. 1985. "Explaining the origins and expansion of mass education." *Comparative Education Review* 29:145–170.

Bollen, Kenneth. 1983. "World system position, dependency, and democracy: the cross-national evidence." *American Sociological Review* 48: 468–479.

Bonacich, Edna. 1972. "A theory of ethnic antagonism: the split labor market." *American Sociological Review* 37:547–559.

———. 1973. "A theory of middleman minorities." *American Sociological Review* 38:583–594.

———. 1979. "The past, present, and future of split labor market theory." In Cora B. Marrett and Cheryl Leggon (eds.), *Research in Race and Eth-*

nic Relations. Volume 1. Greenwich, Conn.: JAI Press.

———. 1980. "Class approaches to ethnicity and race." *Insurgent Sociologist* 10(2):9–23.

———. 1981. "Capitalism and race relations in South Africa: a split labor market analysis." In Maurice Zeitlin (ed.), *Political Power and Social Theory.* Volume 2. Greenwich, Conn.: JAI Press.

Bornschier, Volker, and Christopher Chase-Dunn. 1985. *Transnational Corporations and Underdevelopment*. New York: Praeger.

Bornschier, Volker, Christopher Chase-Dunn, and Richard Rubinson. 1978. "Cross-national evidence of the effects of foreign investment and aid on economic growth and inequality: a survey of findings and a reanalysis." *American Journal of Sociology* 84:651–683.

Boserup, Ester. 1965. *The Conditions of Agricultural Growth*. Chicago: Aldine.

———. 1981. *Population and Technological Change*. Chicago: University of Chicago Press.

Boswell, Terry E. 1986. "A split labor market analysis of discrimination against Chinese immigrants, 1850–1882." *American Sociological Review* 51: 352–371.

Bourdieu, Pierre, and Jean-Claude Passeron. 1977. *Reproduction: In Education, Society and Culture*. Beverly Hills, Calif.: Sage.

Bowles, Samuel, and Herbert Gintis. 1976. *Schooling in Capitalist America*. New York: Basic Books.

Brace, C. Loring. 1979. *The Stages of Human Evolution*. Second edition. Englewood Cliffs, N.J.: Prentice-Hall.

Braudel, Fernand. 1981. *The Structures of Everyday Life*. (Volume 1 of *Civilization and Capitalism, 15th–18th Century.*) New York: Harper & Row.

———. 1982. *The Wheels of Commerce*. (Volume 2 of *Civilization and Capitalism, 15th–18th Century.*) New York: Harper & Row.

———. 1984. *The Perspective of the World*. (Volume 3 of *Civilization and Capitalism, 15th–18th Century.*) New York: Harper & Row.

Braverman, Harry. 1974. *Labor and Monopoly Capital: The Degradation of Work in the Twentieth Century.* New York: Monthly Review Press.

Brenner, Robert. 1976. "Agrarian class structure and economic development in pre-industrial Europe." *Past and Present* 70:30–75.

———. 1977. "The origins of capitalist development: a critique of neo-Smithian Marxism." *New Left Review* 104:25–92.

Breuilly, John. 1985. *Nationalism and the State*. Chicago: University of Chicago Press.

Bronson, Bennet. 1972. "Farm labor and the evolution of food production." In Brian Spooner (ed.), *Population Growth: Anthropological Implications*. Cambridge, Mass.: MIT Press.

Brown, Judith K. 1975. "Iroquois women: an ethnohistoric note." In Rayna R. Reiter (ed.), *Toward an Anthropology of Women*. New York: Monthly Review Press.

Brown, Theodore M. 1970. "The College of Physicians and the acceptance of iatromechanism in England, 1665–1695." *Bulletin of the History of Medicine* 44:12–30.

Burkitt, Denis P. 1978. "Some diseases characteristic of modern Western civilization." In Michael H. Logan and Edward E. Hunt, Jr. (eds.), *Health and the Human Condition*. North Scituate, Mass.: Duxbury Press.

Burns, Edward McNall. 1973. *Western Civilizations*. Volume II. Eighth edition. New York: Norton.

Calhoun, Craig. 1982. *The Question of Class Struggle*. Chicago: University of Chicago Press.

Cameron, Kenneth Neill. 1973. *Humanity and Society: A World History.* New York: Monthly Review Press.

Cammack, Paul. 1986. "Resurgent democracy: threat and promise." *New Left Review* 157:121–128.

Campbell, Donald T. 1965. "Variation and selective retention in socio-cultural evolution." In Herbert R. Barringer, George I. Blanksten, and Raymond W. Mack (eds.), *Social Change in Developing Areas: A Reinterpretation of Evolutionary Theory.* Cambridge, Mass.: Schenkman.

Cardoso, Fernando Henrique. 1982. "Dependency and development in Latin America." In Hamza Alavi and Teodor Shanin (eds.), *Introduction to the Sociology of "Developing Societies."* London: Macmillan Press.

———. 1986. "Democracy in Latin America." *Politics and Society* 15:23–41.

Cardoso, Fernando Henrique, and Enzo Faletto. 1979. *Dependency and Development in Latin America*. Berkeley: University of California Press.

Carneiro, Robert L. 1968. "Slash-and-burn cultivation among the Kuikuru and its implications for cultural development in the Amazon Basin." In Yehudi A. Cohen (ed.), *Man in Adaptation: The Cultural Present*. Chicago: Aldine.

———. 1970. "A theory of the origin of the state." *Science* 169:733–738.

———. 1972. "The devolution of evolution." *Social Biology* 19:248–258.

———. 1973. "The four faces of evolution." In J. J. Honigmann (ed.), *Handbook of Social and Cultural Anthropology*. Chicago: Rand McNally.

———. 1978. "Political expansion as an expression of the principle of competitive exclusion." In Ronald Cohen and Elman R. Service (eds.), *Origins of the State*. Philadelphia: Institute for the Study of Human Issues.

———. 1981. "The chiefdom: precursor of the state." In Grant D. Jones and Robert R. Kautz (ed.), *The Transition to Statehood in the New World*. New York: Cambridge University Press.

———. 1985. "The role of natural selection in the evolution of culture." Unpublished manuscript. New York: American Museum of Natural History.

———. 1987. "Further reflections on resource concentration and its role in the rise of the state." In Linda Manzanilla (ed.), *Studies in the Neolithic and Urban Revolutions*. Oxford: British Archaeological Reports, International Series, No. 349.

———. 1988. "The circumscription theory: challenge and response." *American Behavioral Scientist* 31:497–511.

Carnoy, Martin. 1984. *The State and Political Theory*. Princeton: Princeton University Press.

Cashdan, Elizabeth A. 1985. "Coping with risk: reciprocity among the Basarwa of northern Botswana." *Man* 20:454–474.

———. 1989. "Hunters and gatherers: economic behavior in bands." In Stuart Plattner (ed.), *Economic Anthropology*. Stanford, Calif., Stanford University Press.

Castles, Francis G. 1978. *The Social Democratic Image of Society*. London: Routledge and Kegan Paul.

Cavalli-Sforza, L. L., and M. W. Feldman. 1981. *Cultural Transmission and Evolution*. Princeton: Princeton University Press.

Chafetz, Janet Saltzman. 1984. *Sex and Advantage: A Comparative, Macro-Structural Theory of Sex Stratification*. Totowa, N.J: Rowman and Allanheld.

Chagnon, Napoleon. 1983. *Yanomamo: The Fierce People*. Third edition. New York: Holt, Rinehart and Winston.

Chambliss, William J., and Thomas E. Ryther. 1975. *Sociology: The Discipline and Its Direction*. New York: McGraw-Hill.

Chase-Dunn, Christopher. 1975. "The effects of international economic dependence on development and inequality: a cross-national study." *American Sociological Review* 40:720–738.

———. 1982. "Socialist states in the capitalist world-economy." In Christopher Chase-Dunn (ed.), *Socialist States in the World-System*. Beverly Hills, Calif.: Sage.

———. 1989a. *Global Formation: Structures of the World-Economy*. Oxford: Blackwell.

———. 1989b. "Is a world state necessary?" Paper presented at the joint meetings of the British and American International Studies Associations, London, March 24.

Chase-Dunn, Christopher, and Kenneth O'Reilly. 1989. "Core wars of the future." In Robert K. Schaeffer (ed.), *War in the World-System*. Westport, Conn.: Greenwood Press.

Chase-Dunn, Christopher (ed.). 1982. *Socialist States in the World-System*. Beverly Hills, Calif.: Sage.

Cherlin, Andrew J. 1981. *Marriage, Divorce, Remarriage*. Cambridge, Mass.: Harvard University Press.

Childe, V. Gordon. 1936. *Man Makes Himself*. London: Watts & Co.

Chinchilla, Norma S. 1977. "Industrialization, monopoly capitalism, and women's work in Guatemala." *Signs: Journal of Women in Culture and Society* 3:38–56.

Chirot, Daniel. 1977. *Social Change in the Twentieth Century*. New York: Harcourt Brace Jovanovich.

———. 1985. "The rise of the West." *American Sociological Review* 50:181–195.

———. 1986. *Social Change in the Modern Era*. San Diego: Harcourt Brace Jovanovich.

Clarke, William C. 1966. "From extensive to intensive shifting cultivation: a succession from New Guinea." *Ethnology* 5:347–359.

Cohen, G. A. 1978. *Karl Marx's Theory of History: A Defence.* Princeton: Princeton University Press.

Cohen, Jere. 1980. "Rational capitalism in Renaissance Italy." *American Journal of Sociology* 85:1340–1355.

Cohen, Mark N. 1977. *The Food Crisis in Prehistory.* New Haven: Yale University Press.

———. 1984. "An introduction to the symposium." In Mark N. Cohen and George J. Armelagos (eds.), *Paleopathology at the Origins of Agriculture.* New York: Academic Press.

———. 1989. *Health and the Rise of Civilization.* New Haven: Yale University Press.

Cohen, Mark N., and George J. Armelagos. 1984. "Paleopathology at the origins of agriculture: editors' summation." In Mark N. Cohen and George J. Armelagos (eds.), *Paleopathology at the Origins of Agriculture.* New York: Academic Press.

Cohen, Mark N., Roy S. Malpass, and Harold G. Klein (eds.). 1980. *Biosocial Mechanisms of Population Regulation.* New Haven: Yale University Press.

Cohen, Percy. 1968. *Modern Social Theory.* New York: Basic Books.

Cohen, Ronald, and Elman R. Service (eds.). 1978. *Origins of the State.* Philadelphia: Institute for the Study of Human Issues.

Cohn, Norman. 1970. *The Pursuit of the Millennium: Revolutionary Millenarians and Mystical Anarchists of the Middle Ages.* Revised edition. New York: Oxford University Press.

Coleman, James S. 1986. "Social theory, social research, and a theory of action." *American Journal of Sociology* 91:1309–1335.

———. 1987. "Microfoundations and macrosocial behavior." In Jeffrey C. Alexander, Bernhard Giesen, Richard Munch, and Neil J. Smelser (eds.), *The Micro-Macro Link.* Berkeley: University of California Press.

Collins, Harry M. 1981. "Son of seven sexes: the social destruction of a physical phenomenon." *Social Studies of Science* 11:33–62.

Collins, Harry M., and T. J. Pinch. 1978. "The construction of the paranormal: nothing unscientific is happening." In R. Wallis (ed.), *Rejected Knowledge: Sociological Review Monograph.* Keele, England: University of Keele.

Collins, Randall. 1975. *Conflict Sociology: Toward an Explanatory Science.* New York: Academic Press.

———. 1977. "Some comparative principles of educational stratification." *Harvard Educational Review* 47:1–27.

———. 1979. *The Credential Society: An Historical Sociology of Education and Stratification.* New York: Academic Press.

———. 1980. "Weber's last theory of capitalism: a systematization." *American Sociological Review* 45:925–942.

———. 1981a. "On the microfoundations of macrosociology." *American Journal of Sociology* 86:984–1014.

———. 1981b. "Micro-translation as a theory-building strategy." In Karin Knorr and Aaron V. Cicourel (eds.), *Advances in Social Theory and Methodology.* London: Routledge & Kegan Paul.

———. 1985a. *Three Sociological Traditions.* New York: Oxford University Press.

———. 1985b. *Sociology of Marriage and the Family: Gender, Love, and Property.* Chicago: Nelson-Hall.

———. 1986. "Is 1980s sociology in the doldrums?" *American Journal of Sociology* 91:1336–1355.

———. 1988a. *Theoretical Sociology.* San Diego: Harcourt Brace Jovanovich.

———. 1988b. *Sociology of Marriage and the Family: Gender, Love, and Property.* Second edition. Chicago: Nelson-Hall.

Collins, Randall, and Sal Restivo. 1983. "Development, diversity, and conflict in the sociology of science." *Sociological Quarterly* 24:185–200.

Cook, Scott. 1966. "The obsolete 'anti-market' mentality: a critique of the substantive approach to economic anthropology." *American Anthropologist* 68:323–345.

Cott, Nancy F. 1978. "Passionlessness: an interpretation of Victorian sexual ideology, 1790–1850." *Signs: Journal of Women in Culture and Society* 4:219–236.

Cowgill, George L. 1975. "On causes and consequences of ancient and modern population changes." *American Anthropologist* 77:505–525.

Cox, Oliver C. 1948. *Caste, Class, and Race.* New York: Monthly Review Press.

Crane, George T. 1982. "The Taiwanese ascent: system, state, and movement in the world-economy." In Edward Friedman (ed.), *Ascent and Decline in the World-System.* Beverly Hills, Calif.: Sage.

Crippen, Timothy. 1988. "Old and new gods in the modern world: toward a theory of religious transformation." *Social Forces* 67:316–336.

Cumings, Bruce. 1984. "The origins and development of the Northeast Asian political economy: industrial sectors, production cycles, and political consequences." *International Organization* 38:1–40.

———. 1989. "The abortive abertura: South Korea in the light of Latin American experience." *New Left Review* 173:5–32.

Czap, Peter. 1983. "A large family: the peasants' greatest wealth; serf households in Mishino, Russia, 1814–1858." In Richard Wall, Jean Rodin, and Peter Laslett (eds.), *Family Forms in Historic Europe.* Cambridge: Cambridge University Press.

Dahl, Robert. 1961. *Who Governs? Democracy and Power in an American City.* New Haven: Yale University Press.

Dahlberg, Frances. 1981. *Woman the Gatherer.* New Haven: Yale University Press.

Dahrendorf, Ralf. 1958. "Out of utopia: toward a reorientation of sociological analysis." *American Journal of Sociology* 64:115–127.

Dalton, George. 1967. "Primitive money." In George Dalton (ed.), *Tribal and Peasant Economies.* Austin: University of Texas Press.

———. 1972. "Peasantries in anthropology and history." *Current Anthropology* 13:385–416.

———. 1974. "How exactly are peasants exploited?" *American Anthropologist* 76:553–561.

Daly, Martin, and Margo Wilson. 1978. *Sex, Evolution and Behavior.* North Scituate, Mass.: Duxbury Press.

Danhieux, Luc. 1983. "The evolving household: the case of Lampernisse, West Flanders." In Richard Wall, Jean Rodin, and Peter Laslett (eds.), *Family Forms in Historic Europe.* Cambridge: Cambridge University Press.

Davis, Howard, and Richard Scase. 1985. *Western Capitalism and State Socialism: An Introduction.* Oxford: Blackwell.

Davis, Kingsley, and Wilbert E. Moore. 1945. "Some principles of stratification." *American Sociological Review* 10:242–249.

Dawkins, Richard. 1976. *The Selfish Gene.* New York: Oxford University Press.

de Ste. Croix, G.E.M. 1981. *The Class Struggle in the Ancient Greek World.* Ithaca, N.Y.: Cornell University Press.

Degler, Carl N. 1972. "Slavery and the genesis of American race prejudice." In Donald L. Noel (ed.), *The Origins of American Slavery and Racism.* Columbus, Ohio: Merrill.

Delacroix, Jacques, and Charles C. Ragin. 1981. "Structural blockage: a cross-national study of economic dependency, state efficacy, and underdevelopment." *American Journal of Sociology* 86:1311–1347.

Diamond, Stanley. 1974. *In Search of the Primitive: A Critique of Civilization.* New Brunswick, N.J.: Transaction Books.

Divale, William Tulio, and Marvin Harris. 1976. "Population, warfare, and the male supremacist complex." *American Anthropologist* 78:521–538.

Djilas, Milovan. 1957. *The New Class.* New York: Praeger.

Dobb, Maurice. 1963. *Studies in the Development of Capitalism.* Revised edition. New York: International Publishers.

Dobzhansky, Theodosius. 1962. *Mankind Evolving.* New Haven: Yale University Press.

Domhoff, G. William. 1970. *The Higher Circles.* New York: Random House.

———. 1978. *The Powers That Be: Processes of Ruling Class Domination.* New York: Random House (Vintage Books).

———. 1983. *Who Rules America Now? A View for the '80s.* New York: Simon and Schuster (Touchstone).

Dore, Ronald. 1976. *The Diploma Disease: Education, Qualification, and Development.* Berkeley: University of California Press.

Dos Santos, Theotonio. 1970. "The structure of dependence." *American Economic Review* 60:231–236.

Douglass, William A. 1980. "The south Italian family: a critique." *Journal of Family History* 5:338–359.

Dowling, John H. 1979. "The goodfellows vs. the

Dalton gang: the assumptions of economic anthropology" *Journal of Anthropological Research* 35:292–307.

Durkheim, Emile. 1965. *The Elementary Forms of the Religious Life*. New York: Free Press. (Originally published 1912.)

Eckstein, Susan. 1986. "The impact of the Cuban Revolution: a comparative perspective." *Comparative Studies in Society and History* 28: 502–534.

Eisenstein, Zillah R. 1979. "Developing a theory of capitalist patriarchy and socialist feminism." In Zillah R. Eisenstein (ed.), *Capitalist Patriarchy and the Case for Socialist Feminism*. New York: Monthly Review Press.

Ekholm, Kajsa. 1981. "On the structure and dynamics of global systems." In J. S. Kahn and J. R. Llobera (eds.), *The Anthropology of Precapitalist Societies*. London: Macmillan Press.

Ekholm, Kajsa, and Jonathan Friedman. 1982. "'Capital' imperialism and exploitation in ancient world-systems." *Review* 4:87–109.

Eldredge, Niles, and Stephen Jay Gould. 1972. "Punctuated equilibria: an alternative to phyletic gradualism." In Thomas J. M. Schopf (ed.), *Models in Paleobiology*. San Francisco: Freeman, Cooper.

Elkins, Stanley. 1959. *Slavery: A Problem in American Institutional and Intellectual Life*. Chicago: University of Chicago Press.

Elster, Jon. 1985. *Making Sense of Marx*. Cambridge: Cambridge University Press.

Ember, Carol R. 1983. "The relative decline in women's contribution to agriculture with intensification." *American Anthropologist* 85:285–304.

Ember, Melvin, and Carol Ember. 1971. "The conditions favoring matrilocal versus patrilocal residence." *American Anthropologist* 73: 571–594.

Engels, Frederick. 1940. "The part played by labour in the transition from ape to man." In Frederick Engels, *Dialectics of Nature*. New York: International Publishers. (Originally published 1876.)

———. 1963. "Speech at the graveside of Karl Marx." In Howard Selsam and Harry Martel (eds.), *Reader in Marxist Philosophy*. New York: International Publishers. (Originally given 1883.)

———. 1970. *The Origin of the Family, Private Property, and the State*. Edited by Eleanor Burke Leacock. New York: International Publishers. (Originally published 1884.)

———. 1973. *The Condition of the Working-Class in England*. Moscow: Progress Publishers. (Originally published 1845.)

———. 1978. "The peasant war in Germany." In Karl Marx and Frederick Engels, *Collected Works*. Volume 10. New York: International Publishers. (Originally published 1850.)

Erikson, Robert, John H. Goldthorpe, and Lucienne Portocarero. 1982. "Social fluidity in industrial nations: England, France and Sweden." *British Journal of Sociology* 33:1–34.

Evans, Peter B. 1979. *Dependent Development: The Alliance of Multinational, State, and Local Capital in Brazil*. Princeton: Princeton University Press.

———. 1987. "Class, state, and dependence in East Asia: lessons for Latin Americanists." In Frederic C. Deyo (ed.), *The Political Economy of the New Asian Industrialism*. Ithaca, N.Y.: Cornell University Press.

Evans, Peter B., Dietrich Rueschemeyer, and Theda Skocpol (eds.). 1985. *Bringing the State Back In*. New York: Cambridge University Press.

Farb, Peter. 1978. *Man's Rise to Civilization*. Revised edition. New York: Bantam Books.

Farley, Reynolds. 1984. *Blacks and Whites: Narrowing the Gap?* Cambridge, Mass.: Harvard University Press.

Feyerabend, Paul. 1975. *Against Method: Outline of an Anarchistic Theory of Knowledge*. London: New Left Books.

Fiala, Robert, and Audri Gordon Lanford. 1987. "Educational ideology and the world educational revolution, 1950–1970." *Comparative Education Review* 31:315–332.

Firestone, Shulamith. 1970. *The Dialectic of Sex: The Case for Feminist Revolution*. New York: Morrow.

Flandrin, Jean-Louis. 1979. *Families in Former Times: Kinship, Household, and Sexuality in Early Modern France*. Cambridge: Cambridge University Press.

Flannery, Kent V. 1973. "The origins of agriculture." *Annual Review of Anthropology* 2:271–310.

Fluehr-Lobban, Carolyn. 1986. "Frederick Engels and Leslie White: the symbol versus the role of labor in the origin of humanity." *Dialectical Anthropology* 11:119–126.

Fogel, Robert William, and Stanley L. Engerman. 1974. *Time on the Cross: The Economics of American Negro Slavery.* Boston: Little, Brown.

Folger, J. K., and C. B. Nam. 1964. "Trends in education in relation to the occupational structure." *Sociology of Education* 38:19–33.

Foner, Philip S. 1975. *A History of Black Americans.* Westport, Conn.: Greenwood Press.

Fox, Robin. 1967. *Kinship and Marriage.* Baltimore: Penguin Books.

Frank, Andre Gunder. 1966. "The development of underdevelopment." *Monthly Review* 18(4): 17–31.

———. 1967. "Sociology of development and underdevelopment of sociology." *Catalyst* 3:20–73.

———. 1969. *Capitalism and Underdevelopment in Latin America.* New York: Monthly Review Press.

———. 1979. *Dependent Accumulation and Underdevelopment.* New York: Monthly Review Press.

———. 1980. *Crisis: In the World Economy.* New York: Holmes & Meier.

———. 1981. *Crisis: In the Third World.* New York: Holmes & Meier.

Fredrickson, George M. 1971. "Toward a social interpretation of the development of American racism." In Nathan I. Huggins, Martin Kilson, and Daniel M. Fox (eds.), *Key Issues in the Afro-American Experience.* New York: Harcourt Brace Jovanovich.

———. 1981. *White Supremacy: A Comparative Study in American and South African History.* New York: Oxford University Press.

Freeman, Richard B. 1976. *The Overeducated American.* New York: Academic Press.

Fried, Morton H. 1957. "The classification of corporate unilineal descent groups." *Journal of the Royal Anthropological Institute* 87:1–29.

———. 1967. *The Evolution of Political Society.* New York: Random House.

———. 1978. "The state, the chicken, and the egg: or, what came first?" In Ronald Cohen and Elman R. Service (eds.), *Origins of the State.* Philadelphia: Institute for the Study of Human Issues.

Friedan, Betty. 1963. *The Feminine Mystique.* New York: Dell.

Friedl, Ernestine. 1975. *Women and Men: An Anthropologist's View.* New York: Holt, Rinehart and Winston.

Friedman, Debra, and Michael Hechter. 1988. "The contribution of rational choice theory to macrosociological research." *Sociological Theory* 6:201–218.

Fröbel, Folker, Jürgen Heinrichs, and Otto Kreye. 1980. *The New International Division of Labour.* Cambridge: Cambridge University Press.

Fryer, Peter. 1984. *Staying Power: The History of Black People in Britain.* London: Pluto Press.

Furstenburg, Frank F., Jr. 1966. "Industrialization and the American family: a look backward." *American Sociological Review* 31:326–337.

Futuyma, Douglas J. 1986. *Evolutionary Biology.* Second edition. Sunderland, Mass.: Sinauer.

Galbraith, John Kenneth. 1952. *American Capitalism: The Concept of Countervailing Power.* Boston: Houghton Mifflin.

Galtung, Johan, Tore Heiestad, and Erik Rudeng. 1980. "On the decline and fall of empires: the Roman Empire and Western imperialism compared." *Review* 4:91–153.

Gardner, R. A., and B. T. Gardner. 1969. "Teaching sign language to a chimpanzee." *Science* 165: 664–672.

Garfinkel, Harold. 1967. *Studies in Ethnomethodology.* Englewood Cliffs, N.J.: Prentice-Hall.

Geertz, Clifford. 1963. *Agricultural Involution: The Processes of Ecological Change in Indonesia.* Berkeley: University of California Press.

Gellner, Ernest. 1983. *Nations and Nationalism.* Oxford: Blackwell.

Gendron, Bernard. 1977. *Technology and the Human Condition.* New York: St. Martin's Press.

Genovese, Eugene D. 1965. *The Political Economy of Slavery.* New York: Random House (Vintage Books).

———. 1969. *The World the Slaveholders Made.* New York: Random House (Vintage Books).

———. 1974. *Roll, Jordan, Roll: The World the Slaves Made.* New York: Random House (Vintage Books).

Gershenkron, Alexander. 1962. *Economic Backwardness in Historical Perspective.* Cambridge, Mass.: Harvard University Press.

Geschwender, James A. 1978. *Racial Stratification in America.* Dubuque, Iowa: Brown.

Gholson, Barry, and Peter Barker. 1985. "Kuhn,

Lakatos, and Laudan: applications in the history of physics and psychology." *American Psychologist* 40:755–769.

Gibbs, James L., Jr. 1965. "The Kpelle of Liberia." In James L. Gibbs, Jr. (ed.), *Peoples of Africa*. New York: Holt, Rinehart and Winston.

Giddens, Anthony. 1973. *The Class Structure of the Advanced Societies*. New York: Harper & Row.

———. 1980. *The Class Structure of the Advanced Societies*. Second edition. London: Hutchinson.

———. 1981. *A Contemporary Critique of Historical Materialism*. Berkeley: University of California Press.

———. 1985. *The Nation-State and Violence*. Berkeley: University of California Press.

Giddens, Anthony, and David Held (eds.). 1982. *Classes, Power, and Conflict: Classical and Contemporary Debates*. Berkeley: University of California Press.

Giele, Janet Zollinger. 1977. "Introduction: comparative perspectives on women." In Janet Zollinger Giele and Audrey Chapman Smock (eds.), *Women: Roles and Status in Eight Countries*. New York: Wiley.

Glock, Charles Y., and Robert N. Bellah (eds.). 1976. *The New Religious Consciousness*. Berkeley: University of California Press.

Glock, Charles Y., and Rodney Stark. 1965. *Religion and Society in Tension*. Chicago: Rand McNally.

Goldfarb, Jeffrey C. 1989. *Beyond Glasnost: The Post-Totalitarian Mind*. Chicago: University of Chicago Press.

Goldstein, Joshua S. 1988. *Long Cycles: Prosperity and War in the Modern Age*. New Haven: Yale University Press.

Goldthorpe, John H. 1966. "Social stratification in industrial society." In Reinhard Bendix and Seymour Martin Lipset (eds.), *Class, Status, and Power: Social Stratification in Comparative Perspective*. Second edition. New York: Free Press.

———. 1980. *Social Mobility and Class Structure in Modern Britain*. Oxford: Clarendon Press.

Goode, William J. 1970. *World Revolution and Family Patterns*. New York: Free Press.

Goodenough, Ward. 1969. "Frontiers of cultural anthropology: social organization." *Proceedings of the American Philosophical Society* 113:329–335.

Goody, Jack. 1976. *Production and Reproduction: A Comparative Study of the Domestic Domain*. Cambridge: Cambridge University Press.

Gorbachev, Mikhail. 1987. *Perestroika: New Thinking for Our Country and the World*. New York: Harper & Row.

Gorin, Zeev. 1985. "Socialist societies and world system theory: a critical survey." *Science and Society* 49:332–366.

Gould, Stephen Jay, and Niles Eldredge. 1977. "Punctuated equilibria: the tempo and mode of evolution reconsidered." *Paleobiology* 3:115–151.

Graber, Robert B., and Paul B. Roscoe. 1988. "Introduction: circumscription and the evolution of society." *American Behavioral Scientist* 31:405–415.

Granovetter, Mark. 1979. "The idea of 'advancement' in theories of social evolution and development." *American Journal of Sociology* 85:489–515.

Greaves, Richard L. 1969. "Puritanism and science: the anatomy of a controversy." *Journal of the History of Ideas* 30:345–368.

Greenfield, Sidney M. 1961. "Industrialization and the family in sociological theory." *American Journal of Sociology* 67:312–322.

Gruchy, Allan G. 1966. *Comparative Economic Systems*. Boston: Houghton Mifflin.

Gutman, Herbert G. 1976. *The Black Family in Slavery and Freedom, 1750–1925*. New York: Pantheon.

Haas, Jonathan. 1982. *The Evolution of the Prehistoric State*. New York: Columbia University Press.

Hadden, Jeffrey K. 1987. "Toward desacralizing secularization theory." *Social Forces* 65:587–611.

Hall, John A. 1985. *Powers and Liberties: The Causes and Consequences of the Rise of the West*. Berkeley: University of California Press.

Halliday, Jon. 1975. *A Political History of Japanese Capitalism*. New York: Monthly Review Press.

Hallpike, C. R. 1986. *The Principles of Social Evolution*. Oxford: Clarendon Press.

Halsey, A. H., A. F. Heath, and J. M. Ridge. 1980. *Origins and Destinations: Family, Class, and Education in Modern Britain*. Oxford: Clarendon Press.

Hamilton, Roberta. 1978. *The Liberation of Women: A Study of Patriarchy and Capitalism*. London: Allen and Unwin.

Hamilton, William D. 1964. "The genetical evolution of social behavior, parts 1 and 2." *Journal of Theoretical Biology* 7:1–51.

Handwerker, W. Penn. 1986. "The modern demographic transition: an analysis of subsistence choices and reproductive consequences." *American Anthropologist* 88:400–417.

Hardin, Garrett. 1968. "The tragedy of the commons." *Science* 162:1243–1248.

Harner, Michael J. 1970. "Population pressure and the social evolution of agriculturalists." *Southwestern Journal of Anthropology* 26:67–86.

———. 1975. "Scarcity, the factors of production, and social evolution." In Steven Polgar (ed.), *Population, Ecology, and Social Evolution.* The Hague: Mouton.

Harris, Marvin. 1964. *Patterns of Race in the Americas.* New York: Norton.

———. 1968. *The Rise of Anthropological Theory.* New York: Crowell.

———. 1971. *Culture, Man, and Nature: An Introduction to General Anthropology.* New York: Crowell.

———. 1974. *Cows, Pigs, Wars, and Witches: The Riddles of Culture.* New York: Random House.

———. 1975. *Culture, People, Nature: An Introduction to General Anthropology.* Second edition. New York: Crowell.

———. 1977. *Cannibals and Kings: The Origins of Cultures.* New York: Random House.

———. 1979. *Cultural Materialism: The Struggle for a Science of Culture.* New York: Random House.

———. 1980. *Culture, People, Nature: An Introduction to General Anthropology.* Third edition. New York: Harper & Row.

———. 1981. *America Now: The Anthropology of a Changing Culture.* New York: Simon and Schuster.

———. 1985a. *Good to Eat: Riddles of Food and Culture* New York: Simon and Schuster.

———. 1985b. *Culture, People, Nature: An Introduction to General Anthropology.* Fourth edition. New York: Harper & Row.

Harris, Marvin, and Eric B. Ross. 1978. "How beef became king." *Psychology Today* 12(5):88–94.

———. 1987. *Death, Sex, and Fertility: Population Regulation in Preindustrial and Developing Societies.* New York: Columbia University Press.

Hartmann, Heidi. 1979. "Capitalism, patriarchy, and job segregation by sex." In Zillah R. Eisenstein (ed.), *Capitalist Patriarchy and the Case for Socialist Feminism.* New York: Monthly Review Press.

Hartung, John. 1982. "Polygyny and inheritance of wealth." *Current Anthropology* 23:1–12.

Harvey, David. 1989. *The Condition of Postmodernity.* Oxford: Blackwell.

Hatch, Elvin. 1983. *Culture and Morality: The Relativity of Values in Anthropology.* New York: Columbia University Press.

Hechter, Michael. 1975. *Internal Colonialism: The Celtic Fringe in British National Development, 1536–1966.* Berkeley: University of California Press.

———. 1976. "Ethnicity and industrialization: on the proliferation of the cultural division of labor." *Ethnicity* 3:214–224.

Hechter, Michael (ed.). 1983. *The Microfoundations of Macrosociology.* Philadelphia: Temple University Press.

Hechter, Michael, and William Brustein. 1980. "Regional modes of production and patterns of state formation in western Europe." *American Journal of Sociology* 85:1061–1094.

Heilbroner, Robert L. 1963. *The Great Ascent: The Struggle for Economic Development in Our Time.* New York: Harper & Row.

———. 1972. *The Making of Economic Society.* Fourth edition. Englewood Cliffs, N.J.: Prentice-Hall.

———. 1980. *An Inquiry into the Human Prospect.* New York: Norton.

———. 1985. *The Making of Economic Society.* Seventh edition. Englewood Cliffs, N.J.: Prentice-Hall.

Hendrix, Lewellyn, and Zakir Hossain. 1988. "Women's status and mode of production: a cross-cultural test." *Signs: Journal of Women in Culture and Society* 13:437–453.

Herman, Edward, and James Petras. 1985. "Resurgent democracy: rhetoric and reality." *New Left Review* 154:83–98.

Herzog, Elizabeth. 1969. "Is there a 'breakdown' of the Negro family?" In J. Ross Eshleman (ed.), *Perspectives in Marriage and the Family: Text and Readings.* Boston: Allyn and Bacon.

Hill, Christopher. 1953. "The transition from feudalism to capitalism." *Science and Society* 17:348–351.

Hill, J. H. 1978. "Apes and language." *Annual Review of Anthropology* 7:89–112.

Hill, Kim, Hillard Kaplan, Kristen Hawkes, and Ana Magdelena Hurtado. 1985. "Men's time allocation to subsistence work among the Ache of eastern Paraguay." *Human Ecology* 13:29–47.

Hilton, Rodney (ed.). 1976. *The Transition from Feudalism to Capitalism.* London: New Left Books.

Hobsbawm, Eric J. 1968. *Industry and Empire.* New York: Pantheon.

Hockett, Charles F., and Robert Ascher. 1964. "The human revolution." *Current Anthropology* 5:135–168.

Hodges, Richard. 1988. *Primitive and Peasant Markets.* Oxford: Blackwell.

Hogbin, H. Ian. 1964. *A Guadalcanal Society: The Kaoka Speakers.* New York: Holt, Rinehart and Winston.

Holton, Robert J. 1985. *The Transition from Feudalism to Capitalism.* New York: St. Martin's Press.

Homans, George C. 1961. *Social Behavior: Its Elementary Forms.* New York: Harcourt, Brace, and World.

———. 1984. *Coming to My Senses: The Autobiography of a Sociologist.* New Brunswick, N.J.: Transaction Books.

Hoogvelt, Ankie M. M. 1982. *The Third World in Global Development.* London: Macmillan Press.

Hoselitz, Bert F. 1960. *Sociological Aspects of Economic Growth.* New York: Free Press.

Hraba, Joseph. 1979. *American Ethnicity.* Itasca, Ill.: F. E. Peacock.

Huaco, George A. 1963. "A logical analysis of the Davis-Moore theory of stratification." *American Sociological Review* 28:801–804.

———. 1986. "Ideology and general theory: the case of sociological functionalism." *Comparative Studies in Society and History* 28:34–54.

Hull, David L. 1988. *Science as a Process: An Evolutionary Account of the Social and Conceptual Development of Science.* Chicago: University of Chicago Press.

Huxley, Julian. 1942. *Evolution: The Modern Synthesis.* New York: Harper & Brothers.

Ingold, Tim. 1986. *Evolution and Social Life.* Cambridge: Cambridge University Press.

Israel, Joachim. 1971. *Alienation: From Marx to Modern Sociology.* Boston: Allyn and Bacon.

Johanson, D. C., and T. D. White. 1979. "A systematic assessment of early African hominids." *Science* 203:321–330.

Johnson, Allen W., and Timothy Earle. 1987. *The Evolution of Human Societies: From Foraging Group to Agrarian State.* Stanford Calif.: Stanford University Press.

Jolly, Alison. 1972. *The Evolution of Primate Behavior.* New York: Macmillan.

Jordan, Winthrop D. 1974. *The White Man's Burden.* New York: Oxford University Press.

Kaneda, Tatsuo. 1988. "Gorbachev's economic reforms." In P. Juviler and H. Kimura (eds.), *Gorbachev's Reforms.* Hawthorne, N.Y.: Aldine de Gruyter.

Karabel, Jerome, and A. H. Halsey. 1977. *Power and Ideology in Education.* New York: Oxford University Press.

Keesing, Roger M. 1975. *Kin Groups and Social Structure.* New York: Holt, Rinehart and Winston.

Kennedy, Paul. 1987. *The Rise and Fall of the Great Powers.* New York: Random House (Vintage Books).

Kerckhoff, Alan C., Richard T. Campbell, and Idee Winfield-Laird. 1985. "Social mobility in Great Britain and the United States." *American Journal of Sociology* 91:281–308.

Kiernan, V. G. 1965. "State and nation in Western Europe." *Past and Present* 31:20–38.

———. 1980. *State and Society in Europe, 1550–1650.* New York: St. Martin's Press.

Kirch, Patrick Vinton. 1984. *The Evolution of the Polynesian Chiefdoms.* New York: Cambridge University Press.

———. 1988. "Circumscription theory and sociopolitical evolution in Polynesia." *American Behavioral Scientist* 31:416–427.

Kohlberg, Lawrence. 1971. "From is to ought: how to commit the naturalistic fallacy and get away with it in the study of moral development." In Theodore Mischel (ed.), *Cognitive Development and Epistemology.* New York: Academic Press.

Kolko, Gabriel. 1962. *Wealth and Power in America.* New York: Praeger.

Kondratieff, Nikolai. 1984. *The Long Wave Cycle.* New York: Richardson and Snyder. (Originally published 1928.)

Kontorovich, Vladimir. 1987. "Labor problems and the prospects for accelerated economic growth."

In Maurice Friedberg and Heyward Isham (eds.), *Soviet Society Under Gorbachev.* Armonk, N.Y.: Sharpe.

Koo, Hagen. 1987. "The interplay of state, social class, and world system in East Asian development: the cases of South Korea and Taiwan." In Frederic C. Deyo (ed.), *The Political Economy of the New Asian Industrialism.* Ithaca, N.Y.: Cornell University Press.

Kottak, Conrad Phillip. 1978. *Anthropology: The Exploration of Human Diversity.* Second edition. New York: Random House.

Krantz, Grover S. 1980. "Sapienization and speech." *Current Anthropology* 21:773–792.

Kriedte, Peter. 1983. *Peasants, Landlords and Merchant Capitalists: Europe and the World Economy, 1500–1800.* Cambridge: Cambridge University Press.

Kuhn, Annette, and AnnMarie Wolpe (eds.). 1978. *Feminism and Materialism: Women and Modes of Production.* London: Routledge and Kegan Paul.

Kuhn, Thomas S. 1970. *The Structure of Scientific Revolutions.* Second edition. Chicago: University of Chicago Press.

Kumagai, Fumie. 1986. "Modernization and the family in Japan." *Journal of Family History* 11: 371–382.

Kushnirsky, F. I. 1988. "Soviet economic reform: an analysis and a model." In S. Linz and W. Moskoff (eds.), *Reorganization and Reform in the Soviet Economy.* Armonk, N.Y.: Sharpe.

Landes, David S. 1969. *The Unbound Prometheus: Technological Change and Industrial Development in Western Europe from 1750 to the Present.* New York: Cambridge University Press.

Lane, David. 1971. *The End of Inequality? Stratification Under State Socialism.* London: Penguin Books.

———. 1982. *The End of Social Inequality? Class, Status, and Power Under State Socialism.* London: Allen and Unwin.

———. 1985. *Soviet Economy and Society.* Oxford: Blackwell.

———. 1987. *Soviet Labour and the Ethic of Communism.* Boulder, Colo.: Westview Press.

Langton, John. 1979. "Darwinism and the behavioral theory of sociocultural evolution: an analysis." *American Journal of Sociology* 85:288–309.

Lanternari, Vittorio. 1963. *The Religions of the Oppressed.* New York: Knopf.

Lapidus, Gail Warshofsky. 1983. "Social trends." In Robert F. Byrnes (ed.), *After Breshnev: Sources of Soviet Conduct in the 1980s.* Bloomington: Indiana University Press.

———. 1988. "Gorbachev's agenda: domestic reforms and foreign policy reassessments." In P. Juviler and H. Kimura (eds.), *Gorbachev's Reforms.* Hawthorne, N.Y.: Aldine de Gruyter.

Lasch, Christopher. 1977. *Haven in a Heartless World: The Family Besieged.* New York: Basic Books.

———. 1979. *The Culture of Narcissism.* New York: Warner Books.

———. 1984. *The Minimal Self.* New York: Norton.

Laslett, Peter. 1977. *Family Life and Illicit Love in Earlier Generations.* Cambridge: Cambridge University Press.

———. 1983. "Family and household as work group and as kin group: areas of traditional Europe compared." In Richard Wall, Jean Rodin, and Peter Laslett (eds.), *Family Forms in Historic Europe.* Cambridge: Cambridge University Press.

Laslett, Peter, and Richard Wall. 1972. *Household and Family in Past Time.* Cambridge: Cambridge University Press.

Laudan, Larry. 1977. *Progress and Its Problems: Towards a Theory of Scientific Growth.* Berkeley: University of California Press.

———. 1982. "A note on Collins's blend of relativism and empiricism." *Social Studies of Science* 12:131–132.

———. 1984. *Science and Values: The Aims of Science and Their Role in Scientific Debate.* Berkeley: University of California Press.

Layton-Henry, Zig. 1984. *The Politics of Race in Britain.* London: Allen and Unwin.

Leach, E. R. 1954. *Political Systems of Highland Burma.* Boston: Beacon Press.

Leacock, Eleanor B. 1978. "Women's status in egalitarian society: implications for social evolution." *Current Anthropology* 19:247–275.

Leacock, Eleanor B., and Richard B. Lee (eds.). 1982. *Politics and History in Band Societies.* New York: Cambridge University Press.

Leacock, Eleanor B., and Helen I. Safa (eds.). 1986. *Women's Work: Development and the Division of Labor by Gender.* South Hadley, Mass.: Bergin and Garvey.

LeClair, Edward E., Jr., and Harold K. Schneider (eds.). 1968. *Economic Anthropology: Readings in Theory and Analysis.* New York: Holt, Rinehart and Winston.

Lee, Richard B. 1968. "What hunters do for a living, or, how to make out on scarce resources." In Richard B. Lee and Irven DeVore (eds.), *Man the Hunter.* Chicago: Aldine.

———. 1972. "The !Kung bushmen of Botswana." In M. G. Bicchieri (ed.), *Hunters and Gatherers Today.* New York: Holt, Rinehart and Winston.

———. 1978. "Politics, sexual and nonsexual, in an egalitarian society." *Social Science Information* 17:871–895.

———. 1979. *The !Kung San: Men, Women, and Work in a Foraging Society.* New York: Cambridge University Press.

———. 1984. *The Dobe !Kung.* New York: Holt, Rinehart and Winston.

Lee, Richard B., and Irven DeVore (eds.). 1968. *Man the Hunter.* Chicago: Aldine.

Leggett, Robert E. 1988. "Gorbachev's reform program: 'radical' or more of the same?" In S. Linz and W. Moskoff (eds.), *Reorganization and Reform in the Soviet Economy.* Armonk, N.Y.: Sharpe.

Lenski, Gerhard E. 1966. *Power and Privilege: A Theory of Social Stratification.* New York: McGraw-Hill.

———. 1970. *Human Societies: A Macrolevel Introduction to Sociology.* New York: McGraw-Hill.

Lenski, Gerhard E., and Jean Lenski. 1978. *Human Societies: An Introduction to Macrosociology.* Third edition. New York: McGraw-Hill.

———. 1987. *Human Societies: An Introduction to Macrosociology.* Fifth edition. New York: McGraw-Hill.

Lenski, Gerhard, and Patrick Nolan. 1984. "Trajectories of development: a test of ecological-evolutionary theory." *Social Forces* 63:1–23.

Le Roy Ladurie, Emmanuel. 1974. *The Peasants of Languedoc.* Champaign: University of Illinois Press.

Lévi-Strauss, Claude. 1963. *Structural Anthropology.* New York: Doubleday.

———. 1969. *The Elementary Structures of Kinship.* Boston: Beacon Press. (Originally published 1949.)

Leys, Colin. 1982. "African economic development in theory and practice." *Daedalus* 111(2):99–124.

Lijphart, Arend. 1977. *Democracy in Plural Societies.* New Haven: Yale University Press.

Lions, P., and M. Lachiver. 1967. "Dénombrement de la population de Brueil-en-Vexin en 1625." *Annales de démographie historique,* 521–537.

Livingstone, Frank B. 1969. "Genetics, ecology and the origins of incest and exogamy." *Current Anthropology* 10:45–61.

Lopreato, Joseph. 1984. *Human Nature and Biocultural Evolution.* Winchester, Mass.: Allen and Unwin.

Lortz, Joseph. 1972. "Why did the Reformation happen?" In Lewis W. Spitz (ed.), *The Reformation: Basic Interpretations.* Lexington, Mass.: Heath.

Lukes, Steven. 1972. *Emile Durkheim: His Life and Work.* New York: Harper & Row.

McCabe, Justine. 1983. "FBD marriage: further support for the Westermarck hypothesis of the incest taboo?" *American Anthropologist* 85:50–69.

McCord, William, and Arline McCord. 1977. *Power and Equity: An Introduction to Social Stratification.* New York: Praeger.

McNeill, William H. 1976. *Plagues and Peoples.* Garden City, N.Y.: Doubleday (Anchor Books).

———. 1982. *The Pursuit of Power: Technology, Armed Force, and Society Since A.D. 1000.* Chicago: University of Chicago Press.

Magubane, Bernard Makhosezwe. 1979. *The Political Economy of Race and Class in South Africa.* New York: Monthly Review Press.

Mair, Lucy. 1964. *Primitive Government.* Baltimore: Penguin Books.

Malefijt, Annemarie de Waal. 1968. *Religion and Culture: An Introduction to Anthropology of Religion.* New York: Macmillan.

Malinowski, Bronislaw. 1927. *Sex and Repression in Savage Society.* London: Kegan Paul.

Mandel, Ernest. 1989. *Beyond Perestroika: The Future of Gorbachev's USSR.* Translated by Gus Fagan. London: Verso.

Mandelbaum, David G. 1988. *Women's Seclusion and Men's Honor: Sex Roles in North India, Bangladesh, and Pakistan.* Tucson: University of Arizona Press.

Mandle, Joan D. 1979. *Women and Social Change in America.* Princeton: N.J.: Princeton Books.

Mann, Michael. 1986. *The Sources of Social Power. Volume 1: A History of Power from the Beginning to A.D. 1760.* Cambridge: Cambridge University Press.

———. 1988. *States, War and Capitalism.* Oxford: Blackwell.

Martin, M. Kay, and Barbara Voorhies. 1975. *Female of the Species.* New York: Columbia University Press.

Marx, Gary T. 1967. "Religion: opiate or inspiration of civil rights militancy among Negroes?" *American Sociological Review* 32:64–72.

Marx, Karl. 1963. *Karl Marx: Early Writings.* Edited by Tom Bottomore. New York: McGraw-Hill. (Originally written 1843–1844.)

———. 1967 *Capital.* Three volumes. New York: International Publishers. (Originally published 1867.)

———. 1978. "The eighteenth brumaire of Louis Bonaparte." In Robert C. Tucker (ed.), *The Marx-Engels Reader.* Second edition. New York: Norton. (Originally published 1852.)

———. 1979. "Letter to Engels." In Saul K. Padover (ed.), *The Letters of Karl Marx.* Englewood Cliffs, N.J.: Prentice-Hall. (Originally written June 18, 1862.)

Marx, Karl, and Frederick Engels. 1970. *The German Ideology.* Edited by C. J. Arthur. New York: International Publishers. (Originally written 1846.)

Matthews, Mervyn. 1978. *Privilege in the Soviet Union.* London: Allen and Unwin.

Maxwell, Nicholas. 1974a. "The rationality of scientific discovery, part I: the traditional rationality problem." *Philosophy of Science* 41:123–153.

———. 1974b. "The rationality of scientific discovery, part II: an aim oriented theory of scientific discovery." *Philosophy of Science* 41:247–295.

Mencher, Joan P. 1974. "The caste system upside down: or the not-so-mysterious East." *Current Anthropology* 15:469–494.

———. 1980. "On being an untouchable in India: a materialist perspective." In Eric B. Ross (ed.), *Beyond the Myths of Culture: Essays in Cultural Materialism.* New York: Academic Press.

Merton, Robert K. 1957. *Social Theory and Social Structure.* New York: Free Press.

———. 1961. "Bureaucratic structure and personality." In Amitai Etzioni (ed.), *Complex Organizations: A Sociological Reader.* New York: Holt, Rinehart and Winston.

———. 1970. *Science, Technology, and Society in Seventeenth Century England.* New York: Howard Fertig. (Originally published 1938.)

———. 1973. "The normative structure of science." In Robert K. Merton, *The Sociology of Science: Theoretical and Empirical Investigations.* Chicago: University of Chicago Press. (Originally published 1942.)

Meyer, John W., Francisco O. Ramirez, Richard Rubinson, and John Boli-Bennett. 1977. "The world educational revolution, 1950–1970." *Sociology of Education* 50:242–258.

Meyer, John W., David Tyack, Joane Nagel, and Audri Gordon. 1979. "Public education as nation-building in America: enrollments and bureaucratization in the American states, 1870–1930." *American Journal of Sociology* 85:591–613.

Miliband, Ralph. 1977. *Marxism and Politics.* Oxford: Oxford University Press.

Mills, C. Wright. 1956. *The Power Elite.* New York: Oxford University Press.

Minge-Klevana, Wanda. 1980. "Does labor time decrease with industrialization? a survey of time-allocation studies." *Current Anthropology* 21:279–298.

Mintz, Beth. 1975. "The President's cabinet." *The Insurgent Sociologist* 5:131–148.

Mitroff, Ian. 1974 "Norms and counter-norms in a select group of the Apollo moon scientists: a case study of the ambivalence of scientists." *American Sociological Review* 39:579–595.

Molyneux, Maxine. 1982. "Socialist societies old and new: progress toward women's emancipation?" *Monthly Review* 34(3):56–100.

Money, John, and A. A. Ehrhardt. 1972. *Man and Woman, Boy and Girl.* Baltimore: Johns Hopkins University Press.

Moore, Barrington, Jr. 1966. *Social Origins of Dictatorship and Democracy.* Boston: Beacon Press.

Morton, Peggy. 1971. "A woman's work is never done." In Edith Hoshino Altbach (ed.), *From Feminism to Liberation.* Cambridge, Mass.: Schenkman.

Moseley, K. P., and Immanuel Wallerstein. 1978. "Precapitalist social structures." *Annual Review of Sociology* 4:259–290.

Moulder, Frances V. 1977. *Japan, China and the*

Modern World Economy. New York: Cambridge University Press.

Moynihan, Daniel P. 1965. *The Negro Family: The Case for National Action.* Washington, D.C.: U.S. Government Printing Office.

Mulkay, Michael. 1976. "Norms and ideology in science." *Social Science Information.* 15:637–656.

———. 1979. *Science and the Sociology of Knowledge.* London: Allen and Unwin.

Mulligan, Lotte. 1973. "Civil War politics, religion and the royal society." *Past and Present* 59:92–116.

Murdock, George Peter. 1959. *Africa: Its Peoples and Their Culture History.* New York: McGraw-Hill.

———. 1967. *Ethnographic Atlas.* Pittsburgh: University of Pittsburgh Press.

Murdock, George Peter, and Caterina Provost. 1973. "Factors in the division of labor by sex." *Ethnology* 12:203–225.

Murphy, Raymond. 1988. *Social Closure: The Theory of Monopolization and Exclusion.* Oxford: Clarendon Press.

Mutel, Jacques. 1988. "The modernization of Japan: why has Japan succeeded in its modernization?" In Jean Baechler, John A. Hall, and Michael Mann (eds.), *Europe and the Rise of Capitalism.* Oxford: Blackwell.

Natrass, Jill. 1981. *The South African Economy: Its Growth and Change.* Cape Town: Oxford University Press.

Ndabezitha, Siyabonga W., and Stephen K. Sanderson. 1988. "Racial antagonism and the origins of apartheid in the South African gold mining industry, 1886–1924: a split labor market analysis." In Cora Bagley Marrett and Cheryl Leggon (eds.), *Research in Race and Ethnic Relations.* Volume 5. Greenwich, Conn.: JAI Press.

Needham, Joseph. 1974. "Science and society in East and West." In Sal P. Restivo and Christopher K. Vanderpool (eds.), *Comparative Studies in Science and Society.* Columbus, Ohio: Merrill.

Nef, John U. 1964. *The Conquest of the Material World.* Chicago: University of Chicago Press.

Nelson, Harry, and Robert Jurmain. 1985. *Introduction to Physical Anthropology.* Third edition. St. Paul, Minn.: West.

Noel, Donald L. 1972a. "Slavery and the rise of racism." In Donald L. Noel (ed.), *The Origins of American Slavery and Racism.* Columbus, Ohio: Merrill.

Noel, Donald L. (ed.). 1972b. *The Origins of American Slavery and Racism.* Columbus, Ohio: Merrill.

North, Doglass C., and Robert Paul Thomas. 1973. *The Rise of the Western World: A New Economic History.* New York: Cambridge University Press.

Nove, Alec. 1989. *Glasnost in Action: Cultural Renaissance in Russia.* London: Unwin Hyman.

O'Connor, James, 1973. *The Fiscal Crisis of the State.* New York: St. Martin's Press.

Office of Management and the Budget. 1973. *Social Indicators, 1973.* Washington, D.C.: U.S. Government Printing Office.

Oliver, Douglas. 1955. *A Solomon Island Society: Kinship and Leadership Among the Siuai of Bougainville.* Cambridge, Mass.: Harvard University Press.

Orloff, Ann Shola, and Theda Skocpol. 1984. "Why not equal protection? Explaining the politics of public social spending in Britain, 1900–1911, and the United States, 1880s–1920." *American Sociological Review* 49:726–750.

Ortner, Sherry. 1974. "Is female to male as nature is to culture?" In Michelle Zimbalist Rosaldo and Louise Lamphere (eds.), *Woman, Culture, and Society.* Stanford, Calif.: Stanford University Press.

Paige, Karen Ericksen, and Jeffery M. Paige. 1981. *The Politics of Reproductive Ritual.* Berkeley: University of California Press.

Palli, Heldur. 1974. "Perede strukturist ja selle uurimiset." *Proceedings of the Soviet Academy of Estonia* 23:64–76.

Parker, Seymour. 1976. "The precultural basis of the incest taboo." *American Anthropologist* 78:285–305.

Parker, Seymour, and Hilda Parker. 1979. "The myth of male superiority: rise and demise." *American Anthropologist* 81:289–309.

Parkin, Frank. 1971. *Class Inequality and Political Order: Social Stratification in Capitalist and Communist Societies.* New York: Holt, Rinehart and Winston.

———. 1979. *Marxism and Class Theory: A Bourgeois Critique.* New York: Columbia University Press.

———. 1987. *The Mind and Body Shop.* New York: Atheneum.

Parsons, Talcott. 1937. *The Structure of Social Action.* New York: McGraw-Hill.

———. 1954. "The incest taboo in relation to social structure and the socialization of the child." *British Journal of Sociology* 5:101–117.

———. 1966. *Societies: Evolutionary and Comparative Perspectives.* Englewood Cliffs, N.J.: Prentice-Hall.

———. 1971. *The System of Modern Societies.* Englewood Cliffs, N.J.: Prentice-Hall.

———. 1977. *The Evolution of Societies.* Edited by Jackson Toby. Englewood Cliffs, N.J.: Prentice-Hall.

Patterson, Orlando. 1977. *Ethnic Chauvinism: The Reactionary Impulse.* New York: Stein and Day.

———. 1982. *Slavery and Social Death: A Comparative Study.* Cambridge, Mass.: Harvard University Press.

Petras, James. 1987. "The anatomy of state terror: Chile, El Salvador and Brazil." *Science and Society* 51:314–338.

Pickering, Andrew. 1981. "Constraints on controversy: the case of the magnetic monopole." *Social Studies of Science* 11:63–93.

Piddocke, Stuart. 1965. "The potlatch system of the southern Kwakiutl: a new perspective." *Southwestern Journal of Anthropology* 21:244–264.

Pinkney, Alphonso. 1984. *The Myth of Black Progress.* New York: Cambridge University Press.

Pines, Maya. 1978. "Is sociobiology all wet?" *Psychology Today* 11(12):23–24.

Piven, Frances Fox, and Richard A. Cloward. 1971. *Regulating the Poor: The Functions of Public Welfare.* New York: Random House (Vintage Books).

Plakans, Andrejs. 1982. "Ties of kinship and kinship roles in an historic eastern European peasant community: a synchronic analysis." *Journal of Family History* 7:52–75.

Plattner, Stuart (ed.). 1989. *Economic Anthropology.* Stanford, Calif.: Stanford University Press.

Polanyi, Karl. 1957. "The economy as instituted process." In Karl Polanyi, Conrad M. Arensberg, and Harry W. Pearson (eds.), *Trade and Market in the Early Empires.* Glencoe, Ill.: Free Press.

Popenoe, David. 1988. *Disturbing the Nest: Family Change and Decline in Modern Societies.* Hawthorne, N.Y.: Aldine de Gruyter.

Popkin, Samuel L. 1979. *The Rational Peasant.* Berkeley: University of California Press.

Popper, Karl. 1959. *The Logic of Scientific Discovery.* New York: Basic Books.

Population Reference Bureau. 1989. *World Population Data Sheet.* Washington, D.C.: The Bureau.

Postan, Michael M. 1972. *The Medieval Economy and Society.* Berkeley: University of California Press.

Postman, Neil. 1979. *Teaching as a Conserving Activity.* New York: Delacorte Press.

Premack, David. 1970. "A functional analysis of language." *Journal of the Experimental Analysis of Behavior* 14:107–125.

Price, Derek de Solla. 1963. *Little Science, Big Science.* New York: Columbia University Press.

Price, T. Douglas, and James A. Brown (eds.). 1985. *Prehistoric Hunter-Gatherers.* San Diego: Academic Press.

Rabb, Theodore K. 1962. "Puritanism and the rise of experimental science in England." *Journal of World History* 7:46–67.

———. 1965. "Religion and the rise of modern science." *Past and Present* 31:111–126.

Reich, Michael. 1977. "The economics of racism." In David M. Gordon (ed.), *Problems in Political Economy.* Second edition. Lexington, Mass.: Heath.

Reiter, Rayna R. (ed.). 1975. *Toward an Anthropology of Women.* New York: Monthly Review Press.

Rex, John, and David Mason (eds.). 1986. *Theories of Race and Ethnic Relations.* Cambridge: Cambridge University Press.

Reynolds, Vernon, Vincent Falger, and Ian Vine (eds.). 1986. *The Sociobiology of Ethnocentrism.* Athens: University of Georgia Press.

Riesman, David. 1950. *The Lonely Crowd.* With the assistance of Reuel Denney and Nathan Glazer. New Haven: Yale University Press.

Ritzer, George. 1988. *Sociological Theory.* Second edition. New York: Knopf.

Robertson, H. M. 1959. "A criticism of Max Weber and his school." In Robert W. Green (ed.), *Protestantism and Capitalism: The Weber Thesis and Its Critics.* Boston: Heath.

Robertson, Roland. 1970. *The Sociological Interpretation of Religion.* New York: Schocken Books.

Rodman, Hyman. 1971. *Lower-Class Families: The*

Culture of Poverty in Negro Trinidad. New York: Oxford University Press.

Roemer, John E. 1982a. "New directions in the Marxian theory of exploitation and class." *Politics and Society* 11:253–287.

———. 1982b. *A General Theory of Exploitation and Class.* Cambridge, Mass.: Harvard University Press.

Rosaldo, Michelle, and Louise Lamphere (ed.). 1974. *Women, Culture, and Society.* Stanford, Calif.: Stanford University Press.

Rose, Hilary, and Steven Rose. 1976. "The incorporation of science." In Hilary and Steven Rose (eds.), *The Political Economy of Science.* London: Macmillan Press.

Rosenthal, Bernice Glatzer. 1975. "The role and status of women in the Soviet Union: 1917 to the present." In Ruby Rohrlich-Leavitt (ed.), *Women Cross-Culturally.* The Hague: Mouton.

Rossi, Alice S. 1984. "Gender and parenthood." *American Sociological Review* 49:1–19.

Rossides, Daniel. 1976. *The American Class System: An Introduction to Social Stratification.* Boston: Houghton Mifflin.

———. 1990. *Social Stratification: The American Class System in Comparative Perspective.* Englewood Cliffs, N.J.: Prentice Hall.

Rostow, W. W. 1960. *The Stages of Economic Growth: A Non-Communist Manifesto.* New York: Cambridge University Press.

Roxborough, Ian. 1979. *Theories of Underdevelopment.* London: Macmillan Press.

Rubin, Lillian. 1976. *Worlds of Pain: Life in the Working-Class Family.* New York: Basic Books.

Rubinson, Richard. 1986. "Class formation, politics, and institutions: schooling in the United States." *American Journal of Sociology* 92:519–548.

Rubinson, Richard, and Deborah Holtzman. 1981. "Comparative dependence and economic development." *International Journal of Comparative Sociology* 22:86–101.

Ruyle, Eugene E. 1973. "Slavery, surplus, and stratification on the Northwest Coast: the ethnoenergetics of an incipient stratification system." *Current Anthropology* 14:603–631.

Sacks, Karen. 1975. "Engels revisited: women, the organization of production, and private property." In Rayna R. Reiter (ed.), *Toward an Anthropology of Women.* New York: Monthly Review Press.

———. 1979. *Sisters and Wives: The Past and Future of Sexual Equality.* Westport, Conn.: Greenwood Press.

Safa, Helen I. 1981. "Runaway shops and female employment: the search for cheap labor." *Signs: Journal of Women in Culture and Society* 7:418–433.

Sagan, Carl. 1980. *Cosmos.* New York: Random House.

Sahlins, Marshall. 1958. *Social Stratification in Polynesia.* Seattle: University of Washington Press.

———. 1960. "Evolution: specific and general." In Marshall Sahlins and Elman Service (eds.), *Evolution and Culture.* Ann Arbor: University of Michigan Press.

———. 1963. "Poor man, rich man, big man, chief: political types in Melanesia and Polynesia." *Comparative Studies in Society and History* 5:285–303.

———. 1968. *Tribesmen.* Englewood Cliffs, N.J.: Prentice-Hall.

———. 1972. *Stone Age Economics.* Chicago: Aldine.

———. 1976a. *Culture and Practical Reason.* Chicago: University of Chicago Press.

———. 1976b. *The Use and Abuse of Biology: An Anthropological Critique of Sociobiology.* Ann Arbor: University of Michigan Press.

Samuelsson, Kurt. 1957. *Religion and Economic Action.* New York: Harper & Row.

Sanders, William T. 1972. "Population, agricultural history, and societal evolution in Mesoamerica." In Brian Spooner (ed.), *Population Growth: Anthropological Implications.* Cambridge, Mass.: MIT Press.

Sanderson, Stephen K. 1973. "Religion, politics, and morality: a study of religious and political belief systems and their relation through Kohlberg's cognitive-developmental theory of moral judgment." Unpublished Ph.D. dissertation. Lincoln: University of Nebraska.

———. 1985. "The provincialism of introductory sociology." *Teaching Sociology* 12:397–410.

———. 1987. "Eclecticism and its alternatives." In John Wilson (ed.), *Current Perspectives in Social Theory.* Volume 8. Greenwich, Conn.: JAI Press.

———. 1990. *Social Evolutionism: A Critical History.* Oxford: Blackwell.
———. In press. "The evolution of societies and world-systems." In Christopher Chase-Dunn and Thomas D. Hall (eds.), *Core/Periphery Relations in the Precapitalist Worlds.* Boulder, Colo.: Westview Press.
Sayers, Sean. 1988. "The need to work: a perspective from philosophy." In R. E. Pahl (ed.), *On Work: Historical, Comparative, and Theoretical Approaches.* Oxford: Blackwell.
Schacht, Robert M. 1988. "Circumscription theory: a critical review." *American Behavioral Scientist* 31:438–448.
Schaff, Adam. 1965. *Marxismus und das menschliche Individuum.* Vienna: Europa Verlag. (Available in English as *Marxism and the Human Individual.* New York: McGraw-Hill, 1970.)
Schlegel, Alice, and Rohn Eloul. 1988. "Marriage transactions: labor, property, and status." *American Anthropologist* 90:291–309.
Schneider, David M. 1961. "The distinctive features of matrilineal descent groups." In David M. Schneider and Kathleen Gough (eds.), *Matrilineal Kinship.* Berkeley: University of California Press.
———. 1968. *American Kinship: A Cultural Account.* Englewood Cliffs, N.J.: Prentice-Hall.
Schneider, David M., and Kathleen Gough (eds.). 1961. *Matrilineal Kinship.* Berkeley: University of California Press.
Schneider, Jane. 1977. "Was there a pre-capitalist world-system?" *Peasant Studies* 6:20–29.
Schrire, Carmel (ed.). 1984. *Past and Present in Hunter Gatherer Studies.* San Diego: Academic Press.
Scott, James C. 1976. *The Moral Economy of the Peasant.* New Haven: Yale University Press.
See, Katherine O'Sullivan, and William J. Wilson. 1988. "Race and ethnicity." In Neil J. Smelser (ed.), *Handbook of Sociology.* Beverly Hills, Calif.: Sage.
Sennett, Richard. 1976. *The Fall of Public Man.* New York: Random House (Vintage Books).
Service, Elman R. 1963. *Profiles in Ethnology.* New York: Harper & Row.
———. 1966. *The Hunters.* Englewood Cliffs, N.J.: Prentice-Hall.
———. 1971a. *Cultural Evolutionism: Theory in Practice.* New York: Holt, Rinehart and Winston.
———. 1971b. *Primitive Social Organization: An Evolutionary Perspective.* Second edition. New York: Random House.
———. 1975. *Origins of the State and Civilization.* New York: Norton.
———. 1978. "Classical and modern theories of the origins of government." In Ronald Cohen and Elman R. Service (eds.), *Origins of the State.* Philadelphia: Institute for the Study of Human Issues.
Shannon, Thomas Richard. 1989. *An Introduction to the World-System Perspective.* Boulder, Colo.: Westview Press.
Shepher, Joseph. 1971. "Mate selection among second generation kibbutz adolescents and adults." *Archives of Sexual Behavior* 1:293–307.
———. 1983. *Incest: A Biosocial View.* New York: Academic Press.
Shorter, Edward. 1975. *The Making of the Modern Family.* New York: Basic Books.
———. 1976. "Women's work: what difference did capitalism make?" *Theory and Society* 3:513–527.
Simon, Herbert A. 1976. *Administrative Behavior.* Third edition. New York: Free Press.
Simon, Julian. 1981. *The Ultimate Resource.* Princeton, N.J.: Princeton University Press.
Simpson, George Gaylord. 1949. *The Meaning of Evolution.* New Haven: Yale University Press.
———. 1953. *The Major Features of Evolution.* New York: Columbia University Press.
Sjoberg, Gideon. 1960. *The Preindustrial City.* New York: Free Press.
Skidmore, Thomas E., and Peter H. Smith. 1989. *Modern Latin America.* Second edition. New York: Oxford University Press.
Skocpol, Theda. 1977. "Wallerstein's world capitalist system: a theoretical and historical critique." *American Journal of Sociology* 82:1075–1090.
———. 1979. *States and Social Revolutions.* New York: Cambridge University Press.
———. 1980. "Political response to capitalist crisis: neo-Marxist theories of the state and the case of the New Deal." *Politics and Society* 10:155–201.
Skocpol, Theda, and John Ikenberry. 1983. "The

political formation of the American welfare state in historical and comparative perspective." *Comparative Social Research* 6:87–148.

Smith, Anthony D. 1973. *The Concept of Social Change*. London: Routledge and Kegan Paul.

———. 1981. *The Ethnic Revival*. Cambridge: Cambridge University Press.

———. 1986. *The Ethnic Origins of Nations*. Oxford: Blackwell.

Smith, Daniel Scott. 1974. "Family limitation, sexual control, and domestic feminism in Victorian America." In Mary Hartman and Lois Banner (eds.), *Clio's Consciousness Raised*. New York: Harper & Row.

Sober, Elliott. 1984. *The Nature of Selection: Evolutionary Theory in Philosophical Focus*. Cambridge, Mass.: MIT Press.

Sokoloff, Natalie J. 1980. *Between Money and Love: The Dialectics of Women's Home and Market Work*. New York: Praeger.

Spiro, Melford. 1979. *Gender and Culture: Kibbutz Women Revisited*. Durham, N.C.: Duke University Press.

Spitz, Lewis W. 1985. *The Protestant Reformation, 1517–1559*. New York: Harper & Row.

Stampp, Kenneth M. 1956. *The Peculiar Institution: Slavery in the Ante-Bellum South*. New York: Random House (Vintage Books).

Stark, Rodney, and William Sims Bainbridge. 1985. *The Future of Religion*. Berkeley: University of California Press.

Starr, Paul. 1982. *The Social Transformation of American Medicine*. New York: Basic Books.

Statesman's Year-Book 1984–85. 1984. New York: St. Martin's Press.

Stavrianos, L. S. 1975. *The World Since 1500: A Global History*. Third edition. Englewood Cliffs, N.J.: Prentice-Hall.

Stebbins, G. Ledyard. 1969. *The Basis of Progressive Evolution*. Chapel Hill: University of North Carolina Press.

———. 1974. "Adaptive shifts and evolutionary novelty: a compositionist approach." In Francisco José Ayala and Theodosius Dobzhansky (eds.), *Studies in the Philosophy of Biology*. Berkeley: University of California Press.

Stebbins, G. Ledyard, and Francisco J. Ayala. 1981. "Is a new evolutionary synthesis necessary?" *Science* 213:967–971.

Steele, Richard, Tony Fuller, and Timothy Nater. 1978. "Life in Jonestown." *Newsweek*, December 4, pp. 62, 65–66.

Steinmo, Sven. 1988. "Social democracy vs. socialism: goal adaptation in social democratic Sweden." *Politics and Society* 16:403–446.

Stephens, Evelyne Huber. 1989. "Capitalist development and democracy in South America." *Politics and Society* 17:281–352.

Stephens, John D. 1980. *The Transition from Capitalism to Socialism*. Atlantic Highlands, N.J.: Humanities Press.

Stephens, William N. 1963. *The Family in Cross-Cultural Perspective*. New York: Holt, Rinehart and Winston.

Stevenson, Paul. 1974. "Monopoly capital and inequalities in Swedish society." *The Insurgent Sociologist* 5(1):41–58.

———. 1982. "Capitalism and inequality: the negative consequences for humanity." *Contemporary Crises* 6:333–372.

Stone, Lawrence. 1979. *The Family, Sex and Marriage in England 1500–1800*. Abridged edition. New York: Harper & Row.

Sussman, Marvin B., and Lee Burchinal. 1962. "Kin family network: unheralded structure in current conceptualizations of family functioning." *Marriage and Family Living* 24:231–240.

Swanson, Guy. 1960. *The Birth of the Gods*. Ann Arbor: University of Michigan Press.

———. 1967. *Religion and Regime: A Sociological Account of the Reformation*. Ann Arbor: University of Michigan Press.

Sweezy, Paul. 1942. *The Theory of Capitalist Development*. New York: Monthly Review Press.

———. 1976. "A critique." In Rodney Hilton (ed.), *The Transition from Feudalism to Capitalism*. London: New Left Books.

———. 1980. *Post-Revolutionary Society*. New York: Monthly Review Press.

Szymanski, Albert. 1976. "Racial discrimination and white gain." *American Sociological Review* 41:403–413.

———. 1978. *The Capitalist State and the Politics of Class*. Cambridge, Mass.: Winthrop.

———. 1982. "The socialist world-system." In Christopher K. Chase-Dunn (ed.), *Socialist States in the World-System*. Beverly Hills, Calif.: Sage.

———. 1983. *Class Structure: A Critical Perspective.* New York: Praeger.

Teich, Albert H. (ed.). 1986. *Technology and the Future.* Fourth edition. New York: St. Martin's Press.

Thomas, Janet. 1988. "Women and capitalism: oppression or emancipation?" *Comparative Studies in Society and History* 30:534–549.

Thomas, Keith. 1964. "Work and leisure in pre-industrial society." *Past and Present* 29:50–66.

———. 1971. *Religion and the Decline of Magic.* New York: Scribners.

Thompson, E. P. 1963. *The Making of the English Working Class.* New York: Random House (Vintage Books).

Thompson, Paul. 1983. *The Nature of Work: An Introduction to Debates on the Labor Process.* London: Macmillan Press.

Thorne, Barrie, and Marilyn Yalom (eds.). 1982. *Rethinking the Family.* New York: Longman.

Thornton, Russell. 1981. "Demographic antecedents of a revitalization movement: population change, population size, and the 1890 Ghost Dance." *American Sociological Review* 46:88–96.

Tiger, Lionel, and Robin Fox. 1971. *The Imperial Animal.* New York: Holt, Rinehart and Winston.

Tiger, Lionel, and Joseph Shepher. 1975. *Women in the Kibbutz.* New York: Harcourt Brace Jovanovich.

Tilly, Charles. 1984. "The old new social history and the new old social history." *Review* 7:363–406.

Tilly, Charles (ed.). 1975. *The Formation of National States in Western Europe.* Princeton: Princeton University Press.

Tilly, Louise A. 1978. "The family and change." *Theory and Society* 5:421–434.

Tilly, Louise A., and Joan W. Scott. 1978. *Women, Work, and Family.* New York: Holt, Rinehart and Winston.

Toulmin, Stephen. 1972. *Human Understanding.* Princeton: Princeton University Press.

Troeltsch, Ernst. 1931. *The Social Teaching of the Christian Churches.* 2 volumes. New York: Macmillan.

Tucker, Robert C. (ed.). 1978. *The Marx-Engels Reader.* Second edition. New York: Norton.

Tumin, Melvin M. 1953. "Some principles of stratification: a critical analysis." *American Sociological Review* 18:387–393.

Turnbull, Colin. 1972. *The Mountain People.* New York: Simon & Schuster (Touchstone).

Turner, Bryan S. 1983. *Religion and Social Theory: A Materialist Perspective.* London: Heinemann.

Turner, Jonathan H., and Edna Bonacich. 1980. "Toward a composite theory of middleman minorities." *Ethnicity* 7:144–158.

Underhill, Ralph. 1975. "Economic and political antecedents of monotheism: a cross-cultural study." *American Journal of Sociology* 80:841–861.

United Nations Statistical Office. 1983. *Statistical Yearbook 1981.* New York: United Nations.

———. 1988. *1985/1986 Statistical Yearbook.* New York: United Nations.

UNESCO. 1983. *Statistical Yearbook.* Paris: UNESCO.

U.S. Bureau of the Census. 1982. *Statistical Abstract of the United States.* Washington, D.C.: U.S. Government Printing Office.

———. 1984. *Current Population Reports, Series P-60, No. 142. Money Income of Households, Families and Persons in the United States: 1982.* Washington, D.C.: U.S. Government Printing Office.

———. 1985. *Statistical Abstract of the United States.* Washington, D.C.: U.S. Government Printing Office.

———. 1988. *Statistical Abstract of the United States.* Washington, D.C.: U.S. Government Printing Office.

U.S. Department of Commerce. 1975. *Historical Statistics of the United States.* Washington, D.C.: U.S. Government Printing Office.

Useem, Michael. 1984. *The Inner Circle: Large Corporations and the Rise of Business Political Activity in the U.S. and U.K..* New York: Oxford University Press.

van den Berghe, Pierre L. 1967. *Race and Racism: A Comparative Perspective.* New York: Wiley.

———. 1973. *Age and Sex in Human Societies: A Biosocial Perspective.* Belmont, Calif.: Wadsworth.

———. 1978. *Man in Society: A Biosocial View.* Second edition. New York: Elsevier.

———. 1979. *Human Family Systems: An Evolutionary View.* New York: Elsevier.

———. 1980. "Incest and exogamy: a sociobiological

reconsideration." *Ethology and Sociobiology* 1:151–162.

———. 1981. *The Ethnic Phenomenon.* New York: Elsevier.

van den Berghe, Pierre L., and Gene M. Mesher. 1980. "Royal incest and inclusive fitness." *American Ethnologist* 7:300–317.

Vanfossen, Beth. 1979. *The Structure of Social Inequality.* Boston: Little, Brown.

Veblen, Thorstein. 1965. *The Higher Learning in America.* New York: Augustus M. Kelly. (Originally published 1918.)

Vogel, Lise. 1983. *Marxism and the Oppression of Women: Toward a Unitary Theory.* New Brunswick, N.J.: Rutgers University Press.

Wagley, Charles, and Marvin Harris. 1958. *Minorities in the New World.* New York: Columbia University Press.

Walker, P. C. Gordon. 1972. "Capitalism and the Reformation." In Lewis W. Spitz (ed.), *The Reformation: Basic Interpretations.* Lexington, Mass.: Heath.

Wallace, Anthony F. C. 1966. *Religion: An Anthropological View.* New York: Random House.

Wallerstein, Immanuel. 1974a. *The Modern World-System: Capitalist Agriculture and the Origins of the European World-Economy in the Sixteenth Century.* New York: Academic Press.

———. 1974b. "The rise and future demise of the world capitalist system: concepts for comparative analysis." *Comparative Studies in Society and History* 16:387–415.

———. 1979a. "American slavery and the capitalist world-economy." In Immanuel Wallerstein, *The Capitalist World-Economy.* New York: Cambridge University Press.

———. 1979b. "Dependence in an interdependent world: the limited possibilities of transformation within the capitalist world-economy." In Immanuel Wallerstein, *The Capitalist World-Economy.* New York: Cambridge University Press.

———. 1980. *The Modern World-System II: Mercantilism and the Consolidation of the European World-Economy, 1600–1750.* New York: Academic Press.

———. 1982. "Crisis as transition." In Samir Amin et al., *Dynamics of Global Crisis.* New York: Monthly Review Press.

———. 1983. *Historical Capitalism.* London: Verso.

———. 1984a. "Marx and history: fruitful and unfruitful emphases." *Contemporary Marxism* 9:35–43.

———. 1984b. "The quality of life in different social systems: the model and the reality." In Immanuel Wallerstein, *The Politics of the World-Economy.* New York: Cambridge University Press.

———. 1984c. "Long waves as capitalist process." *Review* 7:559–575.

———. 1984d. "Patterns and prospectives of the capitalist world-economy." In Immanuel Wallerstein, *The Politics of the World-Economy.* New York: Cambridge University Press.

———. 1989. *The Modern World-System III: The Second Era of Great Expansion of the Capitalist World-Economy, 1730–1840s.* San Diego: Academic Press.

Ward, Kathryn B. 1985. "The social consequences of the world economic system: the economic status of women and fertility." *Review* 8:561–593.

Weber, Max. 1927. *General Economic History.* With an introduction by Ira J. Cohen. New Brunswick, N.J.: Transaction Books.

———. 1958. *The Protestant Ethic and the Spirit of Capitalism.* New York: Charles Scribner's Sons. (Originally published 1905.)

———. 1978. *Economy and Society.* 2 volumes. Edited by Guenther Roth and Claus Wittich. Berkeley: University of California Press. (Originally published 1923.)

Weissner Polly. 1982. "Risk, reciprocity, and social influence on !Kung San economies." In Eleanor Leacock and Richard B. Lee (eds.), *Politics and History in Band Societies.* Cambridge: Cambridge University Press.

Wenke, Robert J. 1984. *Patterns in Prehistory: Mankind's First Three Million Years.* Second edition. New York: Oxford University Press.

Westergaard, John, and Henrietta Resler. 1975. *Class in a Capitalist Society: A Study of Contemporary Britain.* New York: Basic Books.

Westermarck, Edward. 1891. *The History of Human Marriage.* London: Macmillan Press.

White, Benjamin. 1976. "Population, involution and employment in rural Java." *Development and Change* 7:267–290.

———. 1982. "Child labour and population growth in rural Asia." *Development and Change* 13: 587–610.

White, Douglas R., and Michael L. Burton. 1988. "Causes of polygyny: ecology, economy, kinship, and warfare." *American Anthropologist* 90:871–887.

White, Leslie. 1945. "History, evolutionism, and functionalism." *Southwestern Journal of Anthropology* 1:221–248.

———. 1949. *The Science of Culture*. New York: Grove Press.

———. 1959. *The Evolution of Culture*. New York: McGraw-Hill.

Whiting, Beatrice. 1950. *Paiute Sorcery*. New York: Viking Fund Publications in Anthropology, No. 15.

Wilber, Charles K. (ed.). 1973. *The Political Economy of Development and Underdevelopment*. New York: Random House.

Wilkinson, Richard G. 1973. *Poverty and Progress: An Ecological Perspective on Economic Development*. New York: Praeger.

Williams, Eric. 1966. *Capitalism and Slavery*. New York: G. P. Putnam's Sons. (Originally published 1944.)

Wilson, Bryan. 1982. *Religion in Sociological Perspective*. New York: Oxford University Press.

Wilson, Edward O. 1975. *Sociobiology: The New Synthesis*. Cambridge, Mass.: Harvard University Press.

———. 1977. "Foreword." In David P. Barash, *Sociobiology and Behavior*. New York: Elsevier.

Wilson, William J. 1973. *Power, Racism, and Privilege*. New York: Free Press.

———. 1978. *The Declining Significance of Race*. Chicago: University of Chicago Press.

———. 1987. *The Truly Disadvantaged: The Inner City, the Underclass, and Public Policy*. Chicago: University of Chicago Press.

Winch, Robert F. 1977 *Familial Organization*. New York: Free Press.

Winch, Robert F., and Gay C. Kitson. 1977. "Types of American families: an unsatisfactory classification." In Robert F. Winch, *Familial Organization*. New York: Free Press.

Winterhalder, Bruce, and Eric Alden Smith (eds.). 1981. *Hunter-Gatherer Foraging Strategies: Ethnographic and Archaeological Analyses*. Chicago: University of Chicago Press.

Wittfogel, Karl. 1957. *Oriental Despotism*. New Haven: Yale University Press.

Wolf, Arthur P. 1970. "Childhood association and sexual attraction: a further test of the Westermarck hypothesis." *American Anthropologist* 72:503–515.

Wolf, Eric. 1966. *Peasants*. Englewood Cliffs, N.J.: Prentice-Hall.

———. 1982. *Europe and the People Without History*. Berkeley: University of California Press.

Woodburn, James. 1968. "An introduction to Hadza ecology." In Richard B. Lee and Irven DeVore (eds.), *Man the Hunter*. Chicago: Aldine.

Woolfson, Charles. 1982. *The Labour Theory of Culture*. London: Routledge & Kegan Paul.

World Bank. 1984. *World Development Report 1984*. New York: Oxford University Press.

———. 1986. *World Development Report 1986*. New York: Oxford University Press.

———. 1988. *World Development Report 1988*. New York: Oxford University Press.

Worsley, Peter. 1968. *The Trumpet Shall Sound: A Study of "Cargo" Cults in Melanesia*. New York: Schocken Books.

Wright, Erik Olin. 1978. *Class, Crisis and the State*. London: New Left Books.

———. 1979. *Class Structure and Income Determination*. New York: Academic Press.

———. 1983. "Giddens's critique of Marxism." *New Left Review* 138:11–35.

———. 1985. *Classes*. London: Verso.

Wright, Erik Olin, David Hachen, Cynthia Costello, and Joey Sprague. 1982. "The American class structure." *American Sociological Review* 47: 709–726.

Wuthnow, Robert, 1976. *The Consciousness Reformation*. Berkeley: University of California Press.

———. 1980a. "The world-economy and the institutionalization of science in seventeenth-century Europe." In Albert Bergesen (ed.), *Studies of the Modern World-System*. New York: Academic Press.

———. 1980b. "World order and religious movements." In Albert Bergesen (ed.), *Studies of the Modern World-System*. New York: Academic Press.

———. 1989. *Communities of Discourse: Ideology and Social Structure in the Reformation, the Enlightenment, and European Socialism*. Cambridge, Mass.: Harvard University Press.

Yanowitch, Murray. 1977. *Social and Economic In-*

equality in the Soviet Union. White Plains, N.Y.: Sharpe.

Yearley, Steven. 1988. *Science, Technology, and Social Change*. London: Unwin Hyman.

Yellen, J. E. 1977. *Archaeological Approaches to the Present: Models for Reconstructing the Past*. New York: Academic Press.

Yinger, J. Milton. 1970. *The Scientific Study of Religion*. New York: Macmillan.

Zaretsky, Eli. 1976. *Capitalism, the Family, and Personal Life*. New York: Harper & Row.

Zeitlin, Irving. 1973. *Rethinking Sociology: A Critique of Contemporary Theory*. Englewood Cliffs, N.J.: Prentice-Hall.

———. 1984. *The Social Condition of Humanity*. Second edition. New York: Oxford University Press.

Zelditch, Morris Jr. 1964. "Cross-cultural analyses of family structure." In H. T. Christensen (ed.), *Handbook of Marriage and the Family*. Chicago: Rand McNally.

Zelizer, Viviana A. 1985. *Pricing the Priceless Child: The Changing Social Value of Children*. New York: Basic Books.

Zinn, Maxine Baca, and D. Stanley Eitzen. 1987. *Diversity in American Families*. New York: Harper & Row.

Zemtsov, Ilya, and John Farrar. 1989. *Gorbachev: The Man and the System*. New Brunswick, N.J.: Transaction Books.

Zipf, George Kingsley. 1965. *Human Behavior and the Principle of Least Effort*. New York: Hafner. (Originally published 1949.)

Zolberg, Aristide R. 1981. "Origins of the modern world system: a missing link." *World Politics* 33:253–281.

Text and Illustration Credits

TEXT CREDITS

The author is indebted to the following for permission to reprint copyrighted material:

Academic Press and Mark N. Cohen for permission to reprint quoted material from "Paleopathology at the origins of agriculture: editors' summation," by Mark Cohen and George Armelagos, in *Paleopathology at the Origins of Agriculture*, edited by M. Cohen and G. Armelagos, copyright © 1984.

Academic Press and Randall Collins for permission to reprint quoted material and Table 1.1 from *The Credential Society* by Randall Collins, copyright © 1979.

Academic Press and Joan P. Mencher for permission to reprint quoted material from "Being an untouchable in India: a materialist perspective," by Joan P. Mencher, in *Beyond the Myths of Culture*, edited by E. Ross, copyright © 1980.

Academic Press and Robert Wuthnow for permission to reproduce Figure 3.1 from "The world-economy and the institutionalization of science in seventeenth century Europe," by Robert Wuthnow, in *Studies of the Modern World-System*, edited by A. Bergesen, copyright © 1980.

Academic Press and Robert Wuthnow for permission to reprint quoted material from "World order and religious movements," by Robert Wuthnow, in *Studies of the Modern World-System*, edited by A. Bergesen, copyright © 1980.

Aldine de Gruyter for permission to reprint quoted material from "Gorbachev's economic reforms," by Tatsuo Kaneda, in *Gorbachev's Reforms: U.S. and Japanese Assessments*, edited by P. Juviler and H. Kimura (New York: Aldine de Gruyter), copyright © 1988.

American Anthropological Association for permission to reprint quoted material from "The obsolete 'anti-market' mentality," by Scott Cook, in *American Anthropologist* 68:2, part 1, pages 323–45, copyright © 1966.

American Sociological Association and Randall Collins for permission to reprint selected quotations from "Weber's last theory of capitalism," by Randall Collins, in *American Sociological Review*, volume 45, pages 925–942, copyright © 1980.

American Sociological Association and John W. Meyer for permission to reprint Table 1 from "The world educational revolution, 1950–1970," by John Meyer et al., in *Sociology of Education*, volume 50, pages 242–258, copyright © 1977.

Association for Comparative Economic Studies for permission to reprint quoted material from "Gorbachev's reform program: 'Radical' or more of the same?" by Robert E. Leggett, in *Comparative Economic Studies*, volume 29, number 4, pages 29–53, copyright © 1987.

Basic Books, Inc., for permission to reprint quoted material from *The Making of the Modern Family* by Edward Shorter, copyright © 1975.

R. P. Dore for permission to reprint quoted material from *The Diploma Disease* by Ronald P. Dore, copyright © 1976.

Harper & Row for permission to reprint quoted material from *The Great Ascent* by Robert Heilbroner, copyright © 1963.

Harvard Educational Review for permission to reprint quoted material from "Some comparative principles of educational stratification," by Randall Collins, in *Harvard Educational Review*, 47:1, pages 1–27, copyright © 1977 by the President and Fellows of Harvard College. All rights reserved.

Harvard University Press for permission to reproduce Figure 1-4 from *Marriage, Divorce, Remarriage* by Andrew Cherlin, copyright © 1981.

Holt, Rinehart and Winston for permission to reprint quoted material from "The Kpelle of Liberia," by James Gibbs, in *Peoples of Africa*, edited by James Gibbs, copyright © 1965.

The Insurgent Sociologist for permission to reprint quoted material from "Monopoly capital and inequalities in Swedish society," by Paul Stevenson, in *The Insurgent Sociologist*, volume 5(1), pages 41–58, copyright © 1974.

International Publishers for permission to reprint quoted material from *Studies in the Development of Capitalism* by Maurice Debb, copyright © 1963.

Journal of Anthropological Research for permission to reprint quoted material from "The potlatch system of the southern Kwakiutl: a new perspective," by Stuart Piddocke, in *Southwestern Journal of Anthropology*, volume 21, pages 244–264, copyright © 1965.

Macmillan Publishing Company for permission to reprint quoted material and to reproduce figure, pages 31 and 32, from *Race and Racism* by Pierre van den Berghe, copyright © 1967.

McGraw-Hill Publishing Company for permission to reprint quoted material from *The Evolution of Political Society* by Morton Fried, copyright © 1967.

Monthly Review Foundation for permission to reprint quoted material from *A History of Capitalism, 1500–1980* by Michel Beaud, copyright © 1981 by Editions du Seuil.

Monthly Review Foundation for permission to reprint quoted material from *Accumulation on a World Scale* by Samir Amin, copyright © 1974 by Monthly Review, Inc.

Mouton de Gruyter, a Division of Walter De Gruyter & Co., for permission to reprint selected quotations from "The role and status of women in the Soviet Union: 1917 to the present," by Bernice Rosenthal, in *Women Cross-Culturally* by Ruby Rohrlich-Leavitt, copyright © 1975 by Mouton & Co., Publishers.

New Left Review for permission to reprint quoted material from "The abortive abertura: South Korea in the light of Latin American experience," by Bruce Cumings, in *New Left Review* 173, January–February 1989, pages 5–32.

W. W. Norton & Company, Inc., for permission to reprint quoted material from *An Inquiry into the Human Prospect* (updated edition) by Robert L. Heilbroner, copyright © 1980, 1975, 1974.

Oxford University Press, Inc., for permission to reprint data from Table 1.2 from "Income inequality: some dimensions of the problem," by Montek Ahluwalia, in *Redistribution with Growth*, edited by Hollish Chenery, copyright © 1974.

Oxford University Press, Inc., for permission to reprint selected data from *World Development Report 1988* by the World Bank, copyright © 1988 by the International Bank for Reconstruction and Development/The World Bank.

The Past and Present Society for permission to reprint quoted material from "Work and leisure in pre-industrial society," by Keith Thomas, in *Past and Present*, number 29 (December 1964), pages 50–62 (at pages 51–53), copyright © 1964.

Population Reference Bureau for permission to reprint selected data from World Population Data Sheet, copyright © 1989.

Random House for permission to reprint quoted material from *Cannibals and Kings* by Marvin Harris, copyright © 1977.

Random House for permission to reprint quoted material from *Cultural Materialism* by Marvin Harris, copyright © 1979.

Sage Publications and Richard B. Lee for permission to reprint quoted material from "Politics, sexual and non-sexual, in an egalitarian society," by Richard B. Lee, in *Social Science Information*, volume 17, pages 871–895, copyright © 1978.

University of Chicago Press for permission to reprint quoted material from "Cross-national evidence of the effects of foreign investment and aid on economic growth and inequality: a survey of findings and a reanalysis, by Volker Bornschier et al., in *American Journal of Sociology* 84:651–683, copyright © 1978.

University of Chicago Press for permission to reprint quoted material from "Economic and political antecedents of monotheism: a cross-cultural study," by Ralph Underhill, in *American Journal of Sociology* 80: 841–861, copyright © 1975.

University of Chicago Press for permission to reprint quoted material from "Regional modes of production and patterns of state formation in western Europe," by Michael Hechter and William Brustein, in *American Journal of Sociology* 85:1061–1094, copyright © 1980.

University of Chicago Press for permission to reprint quoted material from "Peasantries in anthropology and history," by George Dalton, in *Current Anthropology* 13:385–416, copyright © 1972.

University of Chicago Press for permission to reprint quoted material from "The caste system upside down: or the not-so-mysterious East," by Joan P. Mencher, in *Current Anthropology*, 15:469–494, copyright © 1974.

University of Chicago Press for permission to reprint quoted material from "Public education as nation-building in America: enrollments and bureaucratization in the American states, 1870–1930," by John W. Meyer, David Tyack, Joane Nagel, and Audri Gordon, in *American Journal of Sociology*, 85:591–613, copyright © 1979.

Pierre L. van den Berghe for permission to reprint Table 11 from *Human Family Systems* by Pierre L. van den Berghe, copyright © 1979.

Verse/New Left Books for permission to reproduce figure on page 63 from *Class, Crisis and the State* by Erik Olin Wright, copyright © 1978.

Yale University Press for permission to reprint Table 11.2 from *Long Cycles: Prosperity and War in the Modern Age* by Joshua S. Goldstein, copyright © 1988.

ILLUSTRATION CREDITS

Chapter 1 pp. 6, 10, 12: Culver.

Chapter 2 pp. 22, 24, 29: The American Museum of Natural History; p. 33: Wrangham, Anthro-Photo; p. 37: reproduced by permission of Punch; p. 38: P. van den Berghe.

Chapter 3 p. 53: Bettmann Archive; p. 57: Susan Harris; p. 63: Goodman, Monkmeyer.
Chapter 4 p. 68: © 1985 Newspaper Enterprises Association, Inc.; p. 71: DeVore, Anthro-Photo; p. 75: Chagnon, Anthro-Photo; p. 77: Bettmann Archive; p. 79: Granger; p. 81: Franken, Stock, Boston.
Chapter 5 p. 95: Washburn, Anthro-Photo; p. 99: © Bernheim, 1980, Woodfin Camp; p. 105: Alinari, Art Resource; p. 106: Culver Pictures.
Chapter 6 p. 119: © 1984, Eugene Gordon; p. 121: The American Museum of Natural History; p. 125: Bettmann Archive; p. 132: Monkmeyer.
Chapter 7 p. 136: Bettmann Archive; p. 139: Institut Royal du Patrimoine Artistique; p. 141: I. Wallerstein; p. 144: Culver Pictures; p. 152: Granger.
Chapter 8 p. 160: Granger; p. 165: S. K. Sanderson; p. 172: Conklin, Monkmeyer; p. 174: Goldstein, Stock, Boston; p. 182: UPI/Bettmann Newsphotos.
Chapter 9 p. 190: Maines, Stock, Boston; p. 195: Carrey, The Picture Cube; p. 206: © Holland, Stock, Boston; p. 212: © Ellis, Photo Researchers; p. 216: © Hasegawa, Taurus.
Chapter 10 p. 222: © Schrut, 1983, Taurus; p. 224: UPI/Bettmann Newsphotos; p. 226: © Spratt, The Image Works; p. 230: Sidney, Monkmeyer; p. 240: S. K. Sanderson.
Chapter 11 p. 252: Pitt Rivers Museum, Oxford; p. 255: Bernheim, Woodfin Camp; pp. 259, 266: Culver Pictures; p. 262: Barbara Bode.
Chapter 12 p. 271: Granger; p. 278: UPI/Bettmann Newsphotos; p. 281: Habans, Sygma; p. 283: AP/Wide World; p. 286: Thompson, Taurus; p. 287: Novosti, Sygma; p. 292: Hibo, Sygma.
Chapter 13 pp. 301, 303: Culver Pictures; p. 307: Bettmann Archive; p. 309: UPI/Bettmann Newsphotos; p. 311: © Reininger, 1984, Woodfin Camp; p. 313: E. Bonacich; p. 315: Granger; p. 322: Bettmann Archive; p. 328: W. J. Wilson.
Chapter 14 p. 335: Lee, Anthro-Photo; p. 338: © Wood, 1984, Taurus; p. 340: Harrison, Stock, Boston; p. 342, Bellerose, Stock, Boston; p. 345: © Berry, Magnum; p. 348: R. L. Blumberg; p. 350: Chagnon, Anthro-Photo.
Chapter 15 p. 366: Bloss, Anthro-Photo; p. 367: AP/Wide World; p. 369: Bernheim, Woodfin Camp; p. 375: © Azzi, 1982, Woodfin Camp; p. 377: © Hartley, 1979, Photo Researchers.
Chapter 16 p. 389: Granger; p. 392 (*top*): © Putnam, 1983, The Picture Cube; p. 392 (*bottom*): Forsyth, Monkmeyer; p. 395 (*top*): Gardner, The Image Works; p. 395 (*bottom*): © Grant, The Picture Cube; p. 398: © Cassidy, TSW-Click/Chicago.
Chapter 17 p. 407: S. K. Sanderson; p. 414: R. Collins; p. 418: © Crews, The Image Works; p. 420: Kalvar, Magnum; p. 422: Forsyth, Monkmeyer.
Chapter 18 p. 435: © 1984, Menzel, Stock, Boston; p. 442: © Mezey, Taurus; p. 447: Naythons/Gamma Liaison; p. 449: Culver Pictures; p. 453: Beckwith Studios; p. 456: © Myers, Stock, Boston; p. 458: Atlan, Sygma.
Chapter 19 p. 464: Culver Pictures; p. 465, 466: Granger; p. 467: © 1987, Menzel, Stock, Boston; p. 475: NASA.
Chapter 20 p. 483: S. K. Sanderson; p. 493: Conklin, Monkmeyer; p. 497: Charlon/Gamma Liaison; p. 498: United Nations.

Name Index

Note: Page numbers followed by *n* indicate material in footnotes or source notes.

Subject Index

Note: Page numbers followed by *n* indicate material in footnotes or source notes.